John Macmurray
A Biography

John E Costello

John Macmurray
A Biography

For Pat
True companion
on the way,
With gratitude & great affection,
Jock

Floris Books

First published in 2002 by Floris Books

The publishers acknowledge subsidy from
the Scottish Arts Council towards the
publication of this volume

British Library CIP Data available

ISBN 0-86315-361-5

Printed in Great Britain
by J W Arrowsmith, Bristol

Contents

Acknowledgments

Work on this book began officially with a conversation I had with John Macmurray's nephew Duncan Campbell in the coffee room of Friends House on Euston Road, London, in October 1986. It ended with a copy of the manuscript being sent to Duncan Campbell and his wife Jocelyn thirteen years later. In the intervening years, while I was president of Regis College in Toronto and able to do very little concentrated work on the project, I visited the Campbells five different times and was treated almost as one of the family each time. Duncan and Jocelyn gave me an 'access' to John Macmurray and his wife Betty that no written documents could provide; and it is they who provided me with the documents without which this book would have been very thin gruel indeed. I thank them first and best. Along with them, only one step behind, I include Duncan's late brother Alastair, Morag Miller, John Macmurray's niece, and her husband David who were trusting and disclosing with me beyond my hopes or expectation.

Along the way there have been meetings and conversations with a great number of people who knew John Macmurray as a friend or colleague. In addition to helping me immensely, some became my friends and among them I include Kenneth Barnes, Reg Sayers, ARC (Sandy) Duncan, Tess Simpson, Esther Muirhead, Errol and June Bedford, and Don Grant. Among the people who knew Macmurray personally and who joyfully helped this project along I must mention Sylvia Brown, Kay Witz (who had her 100th birthday shortly before our interview about "Darling John"), Wendy Grant, George Davie, Thomas Torrance, James Torrance, Douglas and Margaret Falconer, Douglas McClelland, Joe and Marjorie Reid, Philip Mooney and Diana Hurman, Macmurray's niece. This book depended on the generosity of many others, and among them I must thank Jeanne Warren, Eleanor Barnes, Robert Calder, Michael Fielding, Philip Hunt, Mike Tyldesley, Kenneth Rankin, Peter Heath, Howard Horsburgh and Margie Mendell. I am also grateful for the encouragement and help of Chris Boles SJ, and my Macmurray colleagues Frank Kirkpatrick, Harry Carson, Cuthbert Mann, Walter Jeffko and Tom Ewens.

When I think of people closer to home who helped me "get the job done," I am grateful especially to Moira Hughes for hours of work deciphering Macmurray's handwriting and preparing typescripts of his unpublished essays; Adrienne Pereira who joined in that work; my friends and associates at Massey College during the writing, particularly John Fraser, Ursula Franklin and Anna Luengo; and two fellow-travellers, John English SJ and John Mausert-Mooney, whose encouragement was strong and constant. To Joe Godfrey SJ: "Thank you for introducing me to Macmurray's thought." Mabel Sayers and Kay McCurran were deeply encouraging from the start. Don Loney and Brian Metcalfe, with great generosity of time and spirit, helped me be convinced, after I finished writing, that there really was a book here. To Mary Jo Leddy, fellow doctoral student who was "there" when I began reading Macmurray in earnest in 1973, and a dear friend and colleague over the years, I offer the gratitude that is owed to one who believed almost fiercely in this book over the many dry years when seeds were being planted but scarce signs of growth could be seen.

Introduction

In 1974, two years before he died, John Macmurray (1891–1976) was approached by two American students of his thought interested in doing a biography of him. Although he had slowed down considerably by then, Macmurray moved quickly to advise the young men to abandon their proposed biography. He told them: if there is anything worthy of interest about me it is to be found in my writings, not in my life; my life has been extraordinarily ordinary. Out of respect, they deferred to his wishes.

With that exchange in mind, this book could be seen as an act of betrayal. I hope for the opposite judgment of it. I am trusting that the rapid increase of interest in the very contemporary issues that Macmurray addressed decades ago will allow this biography to be seen more as an act of faithfulness than betrayal. It remains curious and puzzling for someone familiar with Macmurray's work that the current interest in many of his intellectual projects reveals little or no acquaintance with Macmurray's writings. His questions have proved to be "spot on"; but the work of the pioneer explorer remains unrecognized.

Seventy years ago Macmurray was thinking passionately, and coherently, about issues we now think of as fresh and contemporary. He wrote forcefully about the need:

(1) to include feeling and action — along with thinking — in our notion of human reason;

(2) to integrate private and public ethics;

(3) to provide the conceptual foundations for a positive conversation between science, art and religion;

(4) to go beyond the severe limitations on social theory imposed by the primacy of the individual in order to provide a sound intellectual basis for thinking about genuine world community.

In taking these directions, Macmurray asserted himself in the early 1930s as a post-modern thinker. That is, he moved incisively beyond the modern tradition begun on the continent by the idealism of Descartes, Spinoza, Leibniz and others, and in Britain by the empiricist tradition through Hobbes, Locke, Berkeley and Hume. Macmurray spanned the unbridgeable chasm struck by these Moderns between the objective and subjective, thought and feeling, the individual and the communal, public and private, and science and religion by proposing a unity in human action and relationship that was prior to theory and which theory must acknowledge and serve. It was a healing project. And he began it in the early 1930s. However, one searches almost in vain for references in contemporary writings in sociology, politics and philosophy to his profound reflection on these vital questions. It is mainly in theology that one finds his work on "the personal life" slowly being acknowledged.

The silence concerning the thought of John Macmurray in Britain and the rest of the English-speaking world is deafening. In his review of *A Hundred Years of Philosophy* leading up to the 1950s, John Passmore gave a mere footnote to Macmurray's *The Boundaries of Science* in a chapter significantly entitled "Recalcitrant Metaphysicians" — though in fairness to Passmore, his book came out in the same year Macmurray began publishing his two-volume Gifford Lectures, the fullest and best presentation of his fresh approach to philosophy. Ten years ago, when Noel Annan published his book *Our Age: English Intellectuals between the World Wars — A Group Portrait*, Macmurray was not mentioned once.

More recently and probably better known, when the British Labour Party leader Tony Blair came to power in the mid-1990s he gave an interview in which he stated: if people want to know what I am talking about when I use the word "community" they will have to read a philosopher called John Macmurray. Only a few journalists showed any curiosity in checking out Macmurray's ideas in response to that remark and, for the most part, misrepresented Macmurray's position when they reported on it. Since then, there have been a few publications, conferences and group efforts aimed at awakening an interest in Macmurray's thought but the curtain of silence remains firmly in place, though less so in North America than in Britain. The situation recalls what Dr Ursula Franklin referred to as "the strange eclipse of some geniuses," one notable example being Johann Sebastian Bach who remained essentially unknown in Europe until Mendelssohn "discovered" him in the early 1800s.

John Macmurray was a philosopher, and he said what he did to those two young men because he knew the lives of even good philosophers (perhaps especially of *good* philosophers) do not tend to be as interesting as their thought. It was the thought that made the philosopher worthy of note. But what then of the thinker's life? Macmurray addressed this question of life-context for thinking and returned to it frequently when he concerned himself with the great thinkers of western civilization. He knew it was important, even crucial, to know where a thinker was "coming from." He even, on occasion, mentioned his own life-experience in a public lecture when he felt it cast light on what he was saying. But beyond knowing context is knowing the person, and on this subject Macmurray had something powerful to say in his first lecture on Ancient Philosophy to a group of first-year undergraduates at Manchester in 1919:

> To know a man is more than to know about him: it is a question of living with him, and loving him — an achievement of mental

artistry in the execution of which the mould of your mind receives him — he *lives* in you. It must be done first hand as far as possible.[1]

That statement may represent the main apologia for this biography. Macmurray's thinking was tightly bonded to his living and that, to put it simply, is why his life is worthy of being known.

In the same lecture notes on Greek philosophy in which he made this statement, Macmurray reflected as well, by way of example, on the eternal difficulty of getting at the "real" Socrates, and he had this to say about the portrait given of Socrates by his student Plato: "All biography is a construction, and Plato is a supreme artist. This is a help not a hindrance."[2] I find this conclusion encouraging despite the limitations I bring to the task. I did not know Macmurray personally and I inevitably have my own viewpoint on his meaning, two reasons why this book must be seen very much as a construction. Unfortunately, I cannot hope to serve Macmurray anywhere near as well as we generally believe Plato served Socrates.

When he proposed to offer a thumbnail sketch of his own philosophy Macmurray summed up his project of several decades in one sentence: "The simplest expression that I can find for the thesis I have tried to maintain is this: All meaningful knowledge is for the sake of action, and all meaningful action for the sake of friendship."[3] What he did not say, but could have said, was that he had come to these conclusions through an engagement with his life — his family, the war, his wife and his friendships — as well as through an engagement with philosophy and European culture.

This biography witnesses to the effort of a contemporary man and philosopher to wrestle *in a profoundly personal way* with the issues of western civilization and the world itself in the twentieth century. A word here about how he came to address these as life and death issues will serve to signal the thrust of this book. He explored them in their most intimate as well as most historical meaning. Having survived (with a face full of shrapnel) almost three years in the trenches in the First World War, Macmurray had concluded that the war was the result of a deep sickness in the western soul, a sickness closely related to European rationalism, individualism and the western fixation on nationalism and competitiveness. He concluded that the churches too had sold out to nationalistic interests and could not be counted on to be a voice for international justice or for the kind of human relationships that would create and ensure world peace. It was in 1919, while he was still recovering from his war wounds and finishing his philosophical studies at Oxford, that Macmurray chose to dedicate his life work — whatever it might prove to be — to the cause of world peace. And despite having a deep Christian faith, he also felt forced, by way of protest and to preserve his freedom as a thinker, to dissociate himself from any of the Christian churches since the churches had so patently betrayed their original mandate to care for the world. He kept to that decision until his retirement from university life forty years later.

It is certainly because of his upbringing and his life journey, before and during the war, that Macmurray became a philosopher for whom the world matters. But there is more: his thinking was not only instructed by the past, it aimed at the future; towards a more just and more human future for all people. His private life, university teaching and public service reveal an integrated effort to live in a way that realizes the kind of personal life in community he was writing and talking about. This makes a biography of him a form of fidelity to his effort to live according to his best insights and convictions.

Macmurray spent his life as a philosopher thinking through the meaning of what he called the "personal life," a life in which the roles of, for example, consumer, citizen, worker and lover in each person are expressed in an individual freedom that is embedded in social responsibility and related to life in community in its many modes of expression and celebration.

Macmurray had a comprehensive view of the world that grounded his understanding of those human realities and relationships. Challenging René Descartes and John Locke and their successors in the early Modern tradition (1600–1750), he was convinced the universe is not a fully determined order of individual things put in motion like a clock and run by merely physical forces (a *mechanical* view of the world). Nor is it, contrary to the views of the Romantic and Darwinian traditions (1750–1918), essentially an evolutionary process of unfolding interconnected life energies (an *organic* view of the world). These dimensions of existence clearly exist, but neither viewpoint offers what, in their heyday and still to this day, was claimed for them: a comprehensive and adequate explanation of how the universe "works." Macmurray was convinced that we live and move and have our being in a *personal* universe — that is, a universe, with obvious physical and organic dimensions, that is brought into being, sustained in its existence, and drawn forward to its completion by knowledge and a *personal* love.

We live, as he put it, not in a world of mere forces or processes but in a world in which material forces and organic processes are dimensions of a personal action. In his view all human actions in the world, great and small, have their full and true meaning by being united in this personal loving action which informs the universe. However, he concluded, we have not yet found a way to think and act in terms of "the personal." We continue, at our own peril, to use mechanical and organic categories to think about human beings and their relationships to one another and to nature. We thereby make ourselves enemies of our own deepest humanity. And that, he felt, was what went radically wrong with western civilization. We have not accepted and acted on the knowledge that we enhance our relationships as human beings not through force, or by fulfilling natural needs alone, but through love.

Love can be a very cheap word, and Macmurray was terribly aware of that. As Macmurray used the term, love is not a fluffy pink sort of sentiment — what Scot could ever be charged with holding such a view! Love, as he understood it, is an affection and care for "the other" appropriate to the other's own nature and being, not according to some other (lesser or greater) mode of being or according to my own needs in terms of the other. Love, is not first of all a feeling that I have *inside* myself but rather the positive and fitting felt relationship I have *with* someone or something other than myself. I don't love *because* it makes me feel good. I love because love is what the other evokes in me and deserves from me.

In this way, Macmurray presents a view of love as both passionate and disciplining. Passionate, because I am called by the very being of the other to give nothing less than myself. Disciplining, because love is truly love only when it respects the full nature and uniqueness of the other. In this way, Macmurray bursts the bonds of modern philosophy's slavery to the primacy of subjectivity and proposes philosophically the primacy of personal relationship.

When love describes a way of relating even more than a way of feeling (which it is, too!), firm boundaries between the public and the private disappear. Love has a body, Macmurray said, and the name of love's body is justice. As a body needs a spine so love needs justice in order to give it form and firmness. Love is deep affection for the other but it is also deep respect, even reverence, for the other. Love is "true" to the degree it yearns for and works for the realization of *the other's* freedom, equality and full mutuality in relationship. It is true when it does not cling possessively but supports the other's openness to receiving the love of others and to loving all others.

We tend to read such a statement as a psychological kind of wisdom, a "spirituality" directed only to our close and intimate relations. Macmurray held that it was imperative to apply the same canons of love to public, economic and political relationships, in corporations and among nations dealing with one another. The whole world, public as well as private, runs by the same essential human laws: that life is most enhanced and peace most ensured when human beings act out of genuinely heterocentric care, affection and respect. This, for Macmurray, was not a soft ideal but an empirically testable conviction. What Macmurray offers in such a viewpoint are terms for massively critiquing the fear and greed-based individualism of Hobbes' view of humans (the one that still rules in multi-national capitalism — to the peril of nature as well as civilization) as well as the naturalistic and collectivist social philosophies of Jean-Jacques Rousseau, Karl Marx, Fascism and some forms of environmentalism. He makes plausible, in philosophical terms, a universe grounded in positive other-centred care for all, despite the fact and constant presence of fear and the immense evils, deceptions and brutalities human beings inflict on one another. He does not say love has won out; he merely asserts that love describes the truest "tilt" of the universe, our human nature and our deepest destiny. It is as evident to him as to the greatest cynic that the victory of love has not yet been realized in human affairs. Even with that in mind, he asserts just as strongly that it cannot be realized as long as we think of human relationships and social institutions and their activities in merely mechanical and organic terms. Fear and need are not our deepest truth. Gravity, power, lust and genetics do not fully determine us. Personal love, he claims, includes them all and can situate and transform them. In trying to explain how this is so he said simply: "Love is the core of rationality."

It should come as no surprise that Macmurray the philosopher held that it was most reasonable, out of a deep knowledge of this world through our science, art and personal relationships, to conclude to the existence of God. For Macmurray, God is the *Personal* Other who creates and sustains the universe as a place made for community and destined (despite our clear capacity to freely resist our nature) to live in justice and love. If the world is "personal" (and not merely mechanical or organic in its basic, operating intelligibility), then the denial of God leads, he claims, to incoherence and an irrational view of the world. It was in this conviction that Macmurray (sounding perhaps like one of Passmore's recalcitrant metaphysicians!) grounded the philosophical position he distilled into the simple statement: "all meaningful knowledge is for the sake of action, and all meaningful action for the sake of friendship." For Macmurray, friendship is the fullest and truest expression of the human and the divine. It is, by that fact, the ground and goal of all genuine religion.

Macmurray was convinced that the specific philosophical project given to the twentieth century was to "conceptualize the form of the personal" — even as earlier generations had conceptualized the form of mechanical thought and then the form of the organic.[4] This project had two dimensions to it: first, the recovery of a recognition of the fully personal from the reductionism imposed by mechanical and organic categories of thinking on human persons and social institutions. Though we are physical and organic, human beings are not just physical units or organisms. And, second, to achieve a coherent and consistent articulation of the unique logic of personal existence. Gabriel Marcel, the French existentialist whom

Macmurray knew, chose to deal with the same personal realities and with the relationship of human beings with God in a deliberately unsystematic fashion, believing that only in this refusal of systematization could we hope to avoid reducing persons to "systems." Martin Buber, whom Macmurray knew even more personally, considered himself to be the poet of this project; and he saw Macmurray as its metaphysician, and told him so. It was left to Macmurray, the commonsense Scot, to attempt *both* the reverential work of retrieval and the hard-headed work of making *coherent* sense of how the personal "works." He claimed only to have begun the job. His own work, as he said, was merely pioneering; clearing away the tangled thickets of modern egocentric and dualistic premises (within himself, as well, since he too was a child of the modern world) and pointing the way to the true mountain, not scaling its heights.[5] Few in his own generation or since, as I have noted, saw the import of his breakthroughs or followed him on his solitary path.

In fact, this philosophical enterprise was light years apart from the interests of the vast majority of Macmurray's fellow-philosophers in Britain. Dorothy Emmet, British philosopher and former student of Macmurray, called her former Balliol professor a "maverick" thinker. To her, he seemed to have withdrawn himself from colleagueship in his particular work even though he had many happy and respected academic associations. The same view of him as a loner might apply to his distance from the ecclesiastical establishment despite his very warm working relationships with Archbishop William Temple, J.H. Oldham, Walter Moberley, Canon Charles Raven, and many other churchmen. In the early to mid-1930s Macmurray condemned what he called the "false" Christianity of the institutional churches. He proposed that "true" Christianity was based in Judaism and Jesus. He rejected the Greek and Roman heritage in Christianity as negative accretions that weighed the church down and deflected it from its mandate to transform the world. He wrote and spoke, when he addressed Christian groups, on behalf of a future-oriented view of the Christian mission, one that acknowledged that to promote justice and love in the world was essentially to be working in companionship with God's Spirit in the world. His version of Christianity could be seen as an early twentieth century effort (shared by many socially-oriented church people, such as Temple and Oldham) at re-thinking the church's role in the world that anticipates the liberation theologies formulated in the final third of the century. For Macmurray, as well as for many Latin-American theologians of the 1960s and 1970s, the effort was not unrelated to his definite, though strictly limited, sympathy for Marx's thought during the 1930s. However, his focus on personal intimacy as well as on large, historical perspectives gave him a deeper and more inclusive view of what "counts" in a society that could be considered a sign of God's Kingdom in the world.

Consequently, for a variety of reasons Macmurray proved to be a puzzle for many colleagues and associates. He alienated many university colleagues throughout his career by understanding religion to be a serious philosophical issue. As I've indicated he saw genuine religion not only as a construct to make the world an intelligible whole but even more as a way of living, as the very form of positive personal action shaping our relationships in the world and with one another. He proposed a relational view of religion and understood the genuinely personal to be essentially identical with the genuinely religious. In this way, God was taken out of the sky and put into historical and intimate relationships in a way that made many people raised on a belief in the separation of God and the world quite bewildered — even frightened. He saw human beings as primarily social, thereby undercutting the individualistic focus that most modern philosophy assumed. From that inclusive perspective, he condemned capitalism for canonizing competition and self-interest and for making economic values primary and independent of any social and institutional accountability. Economic values, in his positive view of them, must be situated within and subordinate to the fuller human values of cooperation and community, both with nature and in society.

Macmurray also appeared to many academics as a rebel who trivialized their high calling. He lowered himself in the eyes of many academics by going on the public airwaves in 1930 and talking philosophy to the "masses." In the end, it was said (by no less prominent a scholar than Gilbert Ryle) that he wrote and spoke too simply. Consequently, although many were convinced they understood him, few were convinced that he had anything profound to say since his views as he expressed them appeared uncomplicated, even obvious. Late in his life, Macmurray told Daniel Wako, a university acquaintance in Kenya, that he had come to regret this simplified expression he had laboured to achieve, precisely because of this appearance that his philosophy was simple to understand.

Consequently, despite his appeal to those undergraduates in North America who still study his thought, to the BBC listeners in the early 1930's in Britain who were so taken by the quiet voice of the wise professor, and to the thousands of students who flocked to his classes in Oxford (1922–28), London (1928–44) and Edinburgh (1944–58) and who even in their greying years still speak of him with reverence, Macmurray has remained the best kept secret of British philosophy in the twentieth century.

This biography is an attempt to present, in both a positive and sometimes critical light, the intimate entanglement of Macmurray's life with his thought. As the chapter headings outline, the journey runs from his earliest years shaped by the Presbyterian and evangelical culture in late nineteenth and early twentieth century Scotland, through his university years in Glasgow (that were so formative for both the man and philosopher), his war years, and his university teaching career spanning four decades, with all the social and public involvements those years included. Right into his retirement years and even in the ending of his life there is no way to separate his love of nature and hiking, his companionship with his wife and friends, his teaching, and his journeys across the seas on behalf of university education throughout the Commonwealth, from his philosophy of freedom in community. There is, in fact, no separating his reflections on genuine intimacy from his yearning for a genuine world society.

The attractiveness of his thought for a younger reader might arise from his capacity to bring together what modern philosophy and our cultural wisdom insist on treating as opposites: thinking and acting, emotion and reason, freedom and responsibility, love and scientific knowledge, the religious and the fully human, the intimate and the historical, the secular and the sacred, even the empirical and the mystical. It could be said that Macmurray's life as much as his thought was at once pre-modern and post-modern in his refusal to accept these separations. He was, as well, inevitably modern; and that may be part of the reason a biography of him makes sense to us when it didn't to him — he did not necessarily realize the tight relationship between the narrative of his life and the narrative of his work. In the end, his thought is inseparable from his life, though hardly determined by merely his own experience.

In his effort to be open to full human experience and yet move towards a comprehensive viewpoint, Macmurray gives room for both the secular reader and the religious believer to feel respected. In that context, a word to the secular reader is in order. The early life of Macmurray is marked profoundly by religion. His vocabulary and style of thinking in his early years (see Chapters 1 and 2) are unswervingly religious because that is the culture in which he was raised. The intensity of his youthful journal (Chapters 3 and 4) may come across as excessively fervid, disconcertingly so, to non-believers, and even to contemporary Christians. The language of such experience becomes more bearable if we understand his religious transformation as an attempt to engage a profoundly held faith with his own humanity, moving from an unreal to a more real image of God. That the young man scrutinizes his developing emotions, relationships and view of the world from the perspective of an intimate faith in Christ is something we must respectfully accept in him. This is simply the person he is.

For readers not trained in philosophy, I offer both an early-warning system and a word of encouragement. There are occasional sorties into philosophically related matters in Chapters 3 to 6. Chapter 7, entitled "Discovering the Personal," is perhaps the most relentlessly philosophical in the book. Here, along with parts of Chapters 11, 12, 13 and 15, is where the development in Macmurray's philosophical thinking is most amply traced. For students of philosophy, I plead only this: the book is biography, not philosophy, and not even an introduction to Macmurray's philosophy. For a full, true and fair access to his thinking, only a reading of his own writings will suffice.

The most serious encouragement I can offer to readers at both ends of this spectrum and those in between is this: although only slightly recognized in the twentieth century, John Macmurray is surely a philosophical voice for the twenty-first century. *His* issues — concerning the personal life, community, world society, the ordering of our various human activities into a promising form of integration, respect for nature as well as for human rights and friendship, a living relationship between justice and love (e.g. the use of the language of "forgiveness" in discussing how to deal with world debt) — are issues increasingly being recognized at *this* time. Since the bombing of the World Trade Centre in New York on September 11, 2001, Macmurray's questions are being raised anew and explored with wide attentiveness by very diverse audiences. Whether the question is terrorism, global warming, the pain and injustice created by a relentlessly demanding and unaccountable global economic system, the migration of peoples, gender equality, religion, or the grounds for genuine intimacy, some help for ploughing through these thickets can be found in this systematic, integrating, compassionate, and immensely hopeful thinker.

George MacLeod, the founder of the new community of Iona and friend of John Macmurray once remarked: "We haven't made much of Macmurray because we haven't yet caught up with him."[6] That may have been a sound observation fifty years ago. It may not be as true anymore.

Chapter 1

A Protestant Childhood

Kirkcudbrightshire, Kintyre & Aberdeen (1891–1909)

The early years (1891–1900)

In 1896, five-year-old John Macmurray crossed the threshold of the elementary school in Maxwellton, Kirkcudbrightshire, for the first time and within minutes was being looked on as something of a prodigy. Of the various books present in the school it was clear he could read even those being used in the highest grades. When the astonished teacher asked him what he wanted to be when he grew up, the lad looked up and said solemnly: "a man of knowledge."[1]

One might be tempted to credit this skill and wisdom, to say nothing of composure, to a rare, personal quality. After all, it was obvious the boy was gifted. However, his precocious performance and extraordinary maturity of purpose came to flower — as did the gifts of many renowned Scottish academics, scholars and writers — in the very ordinary, even dull, circumstances of life that reigned during the eighteenth and nineteenth centuries in the small towns and countryside of the west of Scotland. The love of learning so characteristic at all social levels in Scotland was due to the country's centuries-old democratic attitude to education which had been strengthened institutionally in its early years by the powerful influence of the church reformer John Knox. Schooling was for everyone because everyone was a child of God. Consequently, education in Scotland was promised and offered to all children, with special care given to the poor, and this was a heritage that was still alive throughout Scotland when Macmurray was a child.

However, John Macmurray found particular support for this tradition in his own home, in the person of James, his father whom he described years later as having the Scottish "reverence for learning."[2] This conviction in James was not because of any higher education he had received since, as a member of a working class family, university studies had lain well beyond the possibilities of his family to provide.

James Macmurray, John's father, was born in 1858 in Alexandria, a

modest town snuggled into the foot of Loch Lomond in
Dumbartonshire, just north of Glasgow. His own father had worked in
a dye factory in Alexandria and family lore has him associated with the
invention of a red dye that became significant well beyond its hometown. If that was true, there is no indication that it helped to improve
the modest economic conditions of the family. James was raised in the
strong Presbyterian traditions that marked Scottish society at the time,
and it is clear he embraced them fully. So much so that, while still in
his twenties and with the blessing of his parents, he was preparing to go
to China to fulfil his chosen vocation as a missionary. His departure for
China was delayed by the social turmoil being caused by the Boxer
Rebellion, but the dream ended entirely when his father died suddenly.
He remained in Scotland and served as the sole support for his mother and
an ailing sister.

On October 20, 1889, in the District of Troqueer near Dumfries,
James Macmurray married Mary Anna Grierson who lived in Troqueer
with her family. And what a family it was! Mary Anna was the second
of the eleven children that Lilias Halliday Grierson bore to her husband
Joseph after their marriage in 1864. The Griersons had been long-time
residents of Kirkcudbrightshire. One of their claims to fame as a family was their relationship by marriage to Thomas Carlyle, the famous
Scottish essayist and historian. Even in her old age, John's mother
remembered the time when, as a child, she was swinging leisurely on
the fence-gate at their house in Racks in Dumfriesshire on a hot summer's day, and spied her Uncle Thomas coming up the path to pay the
family a visit.

Mary Anna was a strong-willed young woman when she married the
thirty-five year-old James Macmurray in her hometown. Because of
James' work, the couple moved to Maxweltown near Dumfries, the
main commercial centre of the agricultural area of Kirkcudbrightshire.
They set up their first home at 1 Ryedale Terrace and were living there
when their first child, John, was born on February 16, 1891. A daughter, Helen, followed in September 1892 and a third child, Lilias, named
after Mrs Macmurray's mother, in November 1894.

James Macmurray, although reduced from his missionary ambitions
to a career in the civil service, was a man of strong religious ideals and
his wife shared his convictions with an equal determination and rigour.
Consequently, the Presbyterian faith in which both parents had been
formed was far more significant in the influence they wielded in their
children's lives than their formal education. This was hardly surprising.
Presbyterianism was both a faith and a social institution, and it touched
every aspect of life in the villages and towns of the west of Scotland

where both of Macmurray's parents grew up. On Sundays it dominated entirely. The requirement to "rest" on Sunday held true even for children, and the Macmurray children recalled vividly that on Sundays their spontaneous outbursts of joy and laughter were firmly censured by their father. Habits of churchgoing included morning service and some form of Sunday school or a Bible class. The sabbath day often ended with evening prayers or another public service. For some, the practice of their faith included regular prayers together as a family. This was the custom in the Macmurray family where parents and children offered daily prayers on their knees in the parlour. It was a practice that the children would never have thought of questioning, though they did it often with little of the freedom or joy that the Scriptures proclaimed to be the inheritance of the children of God.

This Calvinist culture that shaped a firm, even militant, way of life in Scottish society clearly formed the character of its children, including the young John Macmurray. In addition to providing even the simplest child with a significant knowledge of biblical texts, it formed strict moral principles and helped to give to each a high level of social identity. In addition, for a child so inclined, and this was true of John, it provided the atmosphere for cultivating reflectiveness, and served the development of a personality paradoxically rich in both a spirit of independence and a sense of discipleship.

Somewhat unusually for the time, Mrs Macmurray taught all her children, John as well as the girls, to help with the housework. As a result, John became completely comfortable doing domestic things and throughout his married life did much of the housecleaning, though little of the cooking, which never became his strength. He also turned his hand to furniture-making, house painting and, his most beloved activity of all, gardening. There was no doubt in his mind that it was his mother's influence that made these sorties into the practical feel natural and desirable. As his philosophy developed, and he realized how "intellectual" a person he tended to be by nature, they also became matters of conviction.

In late 1896 or early in 1897, the family moved to Campbeltown, Kintyre, in Argyllshire when Mr Macmurray continues his work as internal excise officer. There was a daily boat to and from Glasgow, and most of the excitement, especially for a young boy, was around the harbour. It was there that John was all but drowned one day by his little sister Lilias. John was sitting, fishing from the harbour steps. Lilias couldn't resist the temptation to give him a little push and he fell in. He was rescued by a fisherman who jumped into the water fully clothed. Lilias meanwhile ran home in a panic and shouted to her mother:

"John's in the water! John's in the water!" Shaking her, her mother said: "But is he *out* of the water?" "Yes," she replied. The victory of cool, common sense was complete.

Early in 1899, Mrs Macmurray gave birth to Mary, their fourth child. In her early childhood it became apparent that Mary had a some- what undefined emotional illness that affected her personality. She was an intelligent and witty girl who even showed sparks of genius, but she had a strange, emotional instability. It expressed itself in sudden bouts of fierce anger, severe depression and forms of religious anxiety and fanaticism. Because of this illness, Mary's growing years and early adulthood marked the family life with a certain sadness, and also a special silence. Both before her death at the relatively young age of thirty-five and afterwards, there seems almost to have been a family agreement, perhaps never openly expressed, not to speak of Mary's "problem." This attitude seemed even to preclude talking with one another freely and naturally about her as a mem- ber of their family.

In her childhood and youth, Mary was an integral part of life in family but her parents were at a loss about how to help her as she needed. Despite the affection and care she received, particularly from her father who had a great compassion for her, she had to be placed in a home in Dumfries in her last years. She died there on June 14, 1934, almost a year to the day after her father had passed away at the family home in Peebles in 1933 at the age of seventy-nine. She was buried next to him in the family plot of the cemetery in Glasgow. Neither before nor after her passing does any of the family correspondence still in existence make mention of her.

By contrast, a special bond of affection grew during those early years between John and his sister Helen (always known as Ella) who was only eighteen months younger. As they grew in friendship it was clear their interests and temperaments varied considerably but a kinship in spirit developed between them and became the emotional centre of their childhood. During those years, John and his sister Helen spent their summer holidays with their maternal grandmother in Racks whose only street petered out directly on the Solway Firth. Both children loved the countryside. Their grandfather Grierson worked for the railroad and tried to eke out a better living for his large family by keeping a few sheep in a nearby field where the children spent their days exploring and catching frogs in the stream. The tracks of the Glasgow-Carlisle line ran along the bottom of that field and John recalled the two of them running through the sheep to the edge of the field where they would cheer the trains as they passed. It was at Racks, too, that John learned to tell the time from the grandfather clock, an eighteenth century heir- loom that was the pride of the family.

A few months after Mary's birth in 1899, the family pulled up stakes and left their tiny town in the west of Scotland for Aberdeen. In 1965, John Macmurray gave a talk in which he offered his listeners one of the rare autobiographical asides to find a place in his public lectures. With a simplicity equal to that of the child of five on his first day of school but with the wisdom and gratitude of a lifetime behind him, he recapped how his own journey as "a man of knowledge" had been made possible.

> The old Scottish faith in education was still alive in the last decade of the nineteenth century and my father shared it in full measure. I was his eldest child; and when I was eight years old he had himself and his family moved — he held a post in the civil service — from Campbelltown [*sic*] in the far south-west of Argyllshire, at his own charges, to Aberdeen, for the sake of his children's education. [3]

James Macmurray chose Aberdeen because it was a city with an ancient and proven tradition in education where the excellence of his children's academic formation could be assured. There is no doubt that his eldest son was foremost in his mind at that time.

School Days (1899–1909)

The Aberdeen that eight-year-old John Macmurray discovered would have brought a significant expansion of his horizons. Although its role was that of a regional centre — in that respect, not unlike Maxweltown and Dumfries — Aberdeen was much larger. Aberdeen had the added dimensions that come with being a cultural centre and a university town, and in 1899 might have had something of the air of a rather out-sized market town. (When Robert Burns passed through it in 1787 he called it a "lazy town!")

The family moved into No. 90 Duthie Terrace, an undistinguished house on a small, undistinguished street on the west side of the city centre. John's only memory of that first house was that a flock of birds would occupy a parapet of the wall across the way every morning, except on Sundays. On July 26, 1901, Joseph, the last of the five children, was born. Perhaps because of this new addition, the family moved within a year or so to a larger house at 60 Whitehall Road, closer to the centre of town, where they lived for the next four years.

A family portrait [see photo section] taken early in 1903 shows everyone looking directly into the camera. As was the custom of the time, no one was smiling. It is a portrait of order and respectability. The images we have of the Macmurray parents, apart from family pictures and a few anecdotes, include a couple of highly interpretive ones from John's future wife, Betty Campbell. She described Mrs Macmurray as "having brown eyes filled with repressed energy, searching one's face as if enticing one but yet seemed coldly aloof." There are some in the family who felt it wasn't entirely irrelevant in Mrs Macmurray's character that as well as being the niece of the acerbic Thomas Carlyle she was related to Grierson of Lar, a persecutor of the Covenanters.[4] Mr Macmurray made a different kind of impression on Betty when she was still a young girl visiting her friend Helen at the Macmurray home in Aberdeen. As she recalled years later in her memoir notes, he was a man with a fairly long body but very short legs:

> ... the neatest, prettiest man, plump and pink, I had ever seen. John got his gentle side from him. He was always formally dressed. He took cold baths every day even when there was hot water! John's father ordered barrels of apples from Canada, when they could be grown in Britain. He would order through Civil Service stores in London when, in Moffat or Peebles [where they lived in later years], he could get it around the corner!

She remembered him as also being "terribly didactic and rational." One night when they were all out looking up at the stars, he clearly enjoyed teaching her that what she had called the Plough was *really* Ursa Major. And during prayers, for which she joined them once, "the parents would direct, direct, direct." They had a living faith, to be sure, but it was terribly important to them that it be celebrated in a proper manner.

The Presbyterian culture held sway in the Macmurray household, with two major differences that John Macmurray could discern and which he later judged to be critical elements in his development. First, his religion was not restricted to worship and discipline. As he told his Swarthmore Lecture listeners in 1965, "My religious training made me familiar with theology from an early age and encouraged the systematic study of scripture." He found there was a significant role for intelligence encouraged in the learning of his religion. Second, despite "the distrust and suppression of emotion in favour of the revealed truth" that ruled in the prevailing Calvinism, an element of fervour in addition to conviction entered the religious sensibility in his family. He recounts how that happened:

Shortly after their marriage, my father and mother were both greatly affected by the mission of the American evangelists, Moody and Sankey. This influence did not displace the earlier religious attitude, but it added something that made it more alive, more personal, more forward-looking. It brought a warmth of feeling to the over-intellectual formality of the old Presbyterianism. The family religion became actively concerned with spreading the gospel and critical of the state of the Church religion round about. It took on a missionary quality.[5]

In Aberdeen, James joined one of the Baptist churches near their home. Then, as John described it decades later:

... on discovering some irregularity in its financial accounts, he left it, and joined a meeting of the Plymouth Brethren. Thereafter we attended their meetings for worship on Sunday morning and an independent evangelistic mission-hall in the evening.[6]

This combination of worship, the Plymouth Brethren style, still rather straight-laced, and the evangelical, more rich in feeling and expression, became the form of religious practice for the family for the next several years. The changes initiated by his father in the family's religious practice and the motives behind his moves from one church to another revealed values that were clearly being absorbed by young John for his later life: a need for religion to be honest, outward looking, energetic, celebrated with feeling, and meaningful in a personal way. In addition to these positive marks, there was his father's requirement to criticize religion when it failed institutionally to meet these standards. In all of this, the son proved to be an extremely apt student.

The main influences on Macmurray from within his family were profound but humble; and, because of their fixation on religion, rather limited. In later years, his mother looked with cool suspicion rather than pride on her son's intellectual vocation. She felt his thinking was a threat to his faith. In fact she expressed the view on one occasion that she would have been just as happy if he had become a carpenter. In that, she was a "plain woman" as the Scots use this term. But she was clearly more than that. Mrs Macmurray was, and remained to the end, a formidable woman until her death at the great age of 105. She ruled her own home until her husband died; and in her old age, when living with her daughter Lilias, was judged to be the "one in charge" of that household as well. Her granddaughter Morag, after spending considerable time in her presence over the years, believed the view of her grandmother as a dominating person was exaggerated, perhaps even wrong. She felt it was truer to say Mrs Macmurray was dominant rather than domineer-ing; she was clear on who she was and what she wanted her children to be. That did not mean they had to be imitators of her way of living but, rather, principled Christians who lived their faith with integrity. In prac-tice, however, it may have been very hard for any of her children, including John, to feel the difference in this subtle distinction. In those early years, John was given a caring and extremely principled upbring-ing, but it also seems that, mainly because of this tone, the home was not a particularly warm or relaxed one. Even into his own old age John loved his mother and cared for her, but always with a reverence and solicitude that was not unrelated to the biblical "fear of the Lord."

Macmurray's nephew Alastair — known in the family as Asty — who lived with John and Betty Macmurray during his university years, felt John's family background, particularly the influence of his mother, may have marked him with a certain emotional constraint. Macmurray certainly felt an emotional constriction in himself and strove valiantly to loosen the dominance of intellect in his character. However, even though the atmosphere in his family may have ensured that a sense of responsibility rather than emotional spontaneity dominated in all the children, in John it never overshadowed the affability, gentleness and generosity of spirit that formed his character. In later life his wife Betty was to acknowledge that he had a fierce temper, but it showed itself rarely. He was usually filled with good humour and loved jokes, often jokes he told at his own expense. He had been trained in the religion of his home not to think of himself first or even to think of himself as of any particular value at all. All the children of James and Mary Anna learned the lesson well, and John may have actually become the freest of them all in both seeing the truth in this conviction and in overcom-ing its stern limitations.

Having noted the shadow side of this upbringing it is crucial to add that, due to this same formation, throughout his own 85 years of life John Macmurray was never left in doubt about what constituted the Gospel's "pearl of great price" — that for which one would be ready to give everything. Bertrand Russell observed about Immanuel Kant that in his exploration of knowledge he was a sceptic, but in his moral the-ory he remained at his mother's knee. It could be said that John Macmurray did not move all that far from his mother's knee when, as a philosopher and public figure, he calmly taught that "love is the core of rationality."[7] He had come to know that truth through his parents' faith and practices. And despite all the limitations in the way they were taught, these were great riches and they stayed with him for a lifetime.

John's health in his childhood and right through his university years was not strong. Just before coming to Aberdeen he had undergone a tuberculosis-related operation on a gland in his neck. It was done by a country doctor and was performed when John was on holidays at his grandparents' farm at Racks where his mother's older sister Jeannie was firmly in charge. When the bandages were removed, the doctor, along with family members, was appalled by the ugly scar that stood out on the left side of John's neck. Stunned by the disfigurement, the doctor enquired in solicitous confusion: "What is he to be?" Aunt Jeannie, knowing the family hopes and airing her own ambitions for him replied: "A missionary." The doctor's face lit up with relief: "Oh, then it won't matter." In his adulthood, Macmurray was, in fact, a handsome man. For most of his adult life, he wore a beard that covered over this neck scar. The beard also served to soften the line of a slight indentation in his cheek near his nose which resulted from a wound he suffered in the Great War.

Because of his son's fragile health, John's father chose to send him to Aberdeen Grammar School thinking that the studies there would be less onerous on him than at the more high-powered rival institution, Robert Gordon's College. John seemed to enjoy life at the Grammar School. It was the school where graduates were expected to proceed to studies in the classics and where all the boys held to the opinion that Robert Gordon's prepared lads to become mere artisans! It was also the school of Lord Byron, a fact they were never allowed to forget. However, in 1905, after spending two years there, John won a scholarship to Robert Gordon's. Going to Gordon's meant a longer walk from 31 Mile End Avenue where the family had moved that year, but this seemed no great burden, and the academic benefits proved worthwhile.

Despite the advantages of Gordon's, the move from the Grammar School may have caused some emotional wrenching for the young lad. There is only one place where one might find reason to surmise it. In 1921 Macmurray gave a talk on Scottish education to the Caledonian Society in Johannesburg, South Africa, in which he spent some time describing the democratic nature of the Scottish universities, so different from those in England at the time. He invited his listeners into the fiercely competitive spirit of the Bursary Competition in the Scottish schools in the North during the tense weeks leading up to the final examinations as a symbol of the democratic spirit of Scottish educational culture in action. His graphic and playful account of it comes after brilliantly setting the stage:

> ... While I was a pupil of the Aberdeen Grammar school, a body
> of half a dozen highlanders from Skye, all of them over 30, some

of them quite grey-haired, descended upon the city in quest of
education. They betook themselves to the rival institution,
Robert Gordon's College, to prepare for the Bursary
Competition and the University. But before they had been there
more than a week, they took umbrage at some remark of the
Headmaster's that seemed to imply a slight to the Hiela'
[Highland] character: so they shook the dust of the College off
their feet and transferred themselves and their allegiance to the
Grammar. I shall never forget the scene when they stalked into
the great hall for morning prayers for the first time with set
determined faces and took their places among us. The whole
school rose to its feet and cheered itself hoarse, and it was fully
a quarter of an hour before the hubbub could be quelled and the
routine of the day begun.

Over the years, Robert Gordon's College had grown in numbers and
prestige, and among its claims to fame was that it was the school of G.
Croom Robertson, the first Professor at the University of London.
Within a year or so of John's arrival there, it became apparent to at least
some of the teachers that they might have among their students another
quiet but rising star.

   Macmurray attended Robert Gordon's from 1905 until 1909. He took
the usual course of studies which included Latin, Greek, French, English
and Mathematics. He asked for and received permission to take chemistry as an extra course. It was not a choice enthusiastically supported in
the college partly because science was still looked down on as a merely
functional subject but mainly because the added course might interfere
with his Bursary competition preparation in the spring, not a matter of
indifference to the headmaster or his teachers. By the time this chemistry
course was completed Macmurray's interest in science had deepened
and he had gained a beginner's appreciation of the genius at work in the
scientific method. But we have to wait until his autobiographical reflections in 1965 to know how deeply science had captivated his imagination at this age and even earlier. While he was still in elementary school
he developed what, at the age of seventy-four, he called:

   an early and continuing interest in science. It began, before I had
   reached my teens, with astronomy. Ball's *Starland* was my
   textbook, and it came to me as a revelation. It was followed by a
   strong interest in biology, so that during my schooldays I read
   every book that I could find on the plant and animal life of the
   world ... If I had my own way I should have become a scientist.[8]

The added workload brought on by the chemistry course apparently didn't slow him down in his other studies. In April 1909, he was congratulated in the student publication, *The Gordonian*, for his second place finish in the Bursary competition. The resulting funds supported his costs at the University of Glasgow where he enrolled just a few months later.

During his last two years at Gordon's, John made one good friend named Duncan Davidson Campbell whom he enjoyed being with, at least partly because Duncan, too, came from a devout evangelical family. To visit Duncan at home, John had to take the train from Aberdeen up the Dee Valley to Inchmarlo where Duncan's father worked as farm manager on the manor there. It was a trip that introduced him to some of the most beautiful country in Aberdeenshire. Apart from this, he seems to have had no special friends and to have engaged in few extracurricular activities at school, reflecting, perhaps, his character as a serious, hardworking and religiously minded young man.

John's last year at Robert Gordon's College happened to coincide with the fiftieth anniversary of the evangelical Revival that had started in 1859 and moved across Scotland. That enthusiasm was to be repeated in Queen Victoria's Jubilee year of 1909 with the missions of Torrie and Alexander, and Macmurray attests that he and his family were by no means untouched by the power of that mission.[9] The success of the revival throughout Scotland was at least partly due to the willingness of its preachers to travel through the countryside with tents to preach and pray where the people lived. As the Revival movement spread, these tent-gatherings became known as the "clout kirk" or "clouty kirk" (cloth church) because of the huge, billowy tents in which the people met. It was not usual for a clout kirk to be pitched in the city, but Aberdeen had one. It was located in the Castlegate on Justice Street between the Fish Market on the quay and the police headquarters, a good enough place — as Betty Macmurray later recalled — to catch the sailor home from the sea and to attract the town lads and lassies "roamin' in the gloamin'." It was called the Gordon Evangelical Mission.

The Macmurray family came to the Gordon Mission for worship most Sunday evenings. John had met Joseph A. Smith and John G. Smith, the two men who conducted the evangelical mission in Aberdeenshire, and Joseph immediately spied in the fervent and biblically knowledgeable young Macmurray a potential addition to their preaching team. He invited John to assist with the Sunday evening services and all services during school holidays, including the summer travelling mission through Aberdeenshire. So John began his career as an

evangelical "witness" at the age of seventeen by welcoming worship-
pers at the door and doing what was needed to help things run smoothly.
This involvement would undoubtedly have pleased his parents. The
same could not be said for all the influences that were about to touch
their son's life as he and his family prepared to leave Aberdeen for
Glasgow where James would serve as Principal Officer of the Inland
Revenue Department, and John would enrol in the university so marked
in those early years of the twentieth century by the heritage of Edward
Caird and A.A. Bowman, and the continuing presence of Henry Jones.[10]

Chapter 2

Transformed by Science and Love

Aberdeen and Glasgow (1909–12)

Religion meets Science

On December 26, 1908, halfway through his last year at Robert Gordon's College and two months shy of his eighteenth birthday John Macmurray decided to start a personal journal. Until May 5, 1913, just one month before the end of his undergraduate life at the University of Glasgow, he continued to write in it filling 172 pages of a 6 x 8-inch notebook with personal reflections and original poems. Uniting the entire journal are his reflections on the profound changes in his personal life that result from all his experiences and discoveries. He strives not just to know himself but to respond generously and faithfully through this new self-knowledge to the purpose he finds in the world. The changes that mark him in these five years reflect not only a spiritual journey, though that would have been enough. They reflect radical transformation of a soul. Beyond that, they form a template that shapes profoundly both the man and the philosopher he is about to become. To read this journal is to find oneself on the intellectual, emotional and vocational ground out of which Macmurray's philosophy, even in its latest and most mature expression, grew and flowered. But let us begin at the beginning!

Immediately before making his first entry the young Macmurray outlines a daily timetable that included religious exercises frequent enough to challenge any monk. His schedule for Sundays confirms the traditional practices mentioned earlier; but it is his weekdays that are surprising. He got up at 6:00 am, put in half an hour on devotions followed by half an hour for mathematics and then allowed himself ten minutes for breakfast. This already monastic debut to the day was followed by thirty minutes of family worship, then he was off to school by 8:30. When he returned home at 4:30 pm he read for half an hour till tea-time, then there was family worship again at 5:30. At 6:00 he studied Latin, Bible Study at 7:00, and Greek at 8:00. He took some outdoor exercise for a mere fifteen minutes at 8:45! His day ended with the study of English at 9:00, French at 9:45 and bed at 10:30. There is no mention of any bedtime snack for a growing youth! This is a rigorous regimen,

and deliberately so, as his first contributions reveal. He begins his journal with a self-conscious poem on the importance of using time well, and
his first reflection is a truly evangelical commentary on his poem:

> Life is too serious to be taken haphazard. We are born for a
> purpose; we are saved for a purpose; we are predestinated unto
> good works which God hath before ordained that we should walk
> in them. And looking forward on the life that lies ahead, catching a
> gleam of the light of eternity amidst the brilliant darkness of this
> world's night, I realize the need there is of consecrating every
> moment to the master's use, of use every hour for his service. This
> book is intended as a personal record of daily life and conduct, ever
> to keep before me the object of life, the goal of the race, "that I
> might know Him." On bended knee, I spread it before thee, O
> Master.

At the end of this consecration of himself to God he fixes his signature,
and at this time he was still spelling his name "MacMurray." The following Sunday the family attended the evening service at the Gordon
Evangelical Mission and when he returned home John wrote:

> Enjoyed the day's services very much. The Lord was manifestly
> present among us. I believe some souls found Jesus tonight ... O for
> a band of sincere young men to stand for God and God's truth in
> this day of declension and worldliness ... O that God would enable
> me to speak out for Him there, to seek to woo and win some
> precious soul to Jesus' bleeding feet ... O God, how far I have been
> from walking before thee and being perfect.

This is strong stuff and to contemporary eyes it appears inflated, even
excessive. But a sympathetic reader can discern in the young man's early
perfectionism the contours of a generous and serving character. However,
as much as he wants to give himself over to Christ he records in only
slightly veiled language that his sexual urges sometimes overwhelm him
causing him to tumble from the ideals he set for himself. This failure to
live chastely drags him to depths of despondency:

> I am insincere. Such is the expression of my character. I profess
> myself a Christian, I live a selfish life. I proclaim my holiness to
> others and in secret I harbour thoughts and perform deeds which
> ought to send the blush to my cheek, and which move me, in
> reality, not at all. In short, I am a hypocrite and see no help for
> it. By nature, I am shallow, characterless, without any conscience

for sin. I know it, I admit it, and it moves me not. I have no desire to be anything else, I have no power to form a purpose and to stay by it. I cannot trust myself, I cannot even despise myself. Such I am, and such I will be to the end and so will pass into the presence of Him I have wronged and misrepresented. I have tried to honour him and failed at the outset every time. It seems useless to try again.

And yet within four days he has been restored from this self-loathing to a tranquil sense of God's presence. He is able to see his life and its meaning intimately bonded to a fuller dimension of being:

I find that the soul of beauty is truth, and all that is not true is deformity. Further, eternal beauty must be founded on eternal truth; only as the truth of God shines in upon our souls can they unfold their noble forms and glowing colours and soar from the darkness of death into living, captivating beauty. I have longed for beauty, for the charm which wins the [sic] admiration and affection; I find that its secret lies in sincerity, in simple truth. For divine truth is ever truly simple and at the command of every man. I seize upon it as the only gleam that can brighten my heavenward path. I will be truly simple and simply true. I will seek to please God and my own better knowledge. In my Father's strength, I WILL.

These two entries, written so close together, give the contours of the struggle between weakness and will that was especially acute for a spiritually generous young man like Macmurray. The conclusion to this entry, with its suggestion of a level of resolution, is by no means the end of this conflict for him as further entries reveal right up to the last weeks of this journal four and a half years later. The flight into abstraction, so evident in these entries, often characterizes young intellectuals who are filled with deep convictions. And there is no doubting the dominance of the intellectual in Macmurray's personality, very strong in his early life and still present but much softened and complemented by warmth in his later years. It formed a barrier to the flow of simple feeling in him which revealed itself in his early friendships.[1] Later in life, he came to believe that intellectualism of this idealistic sort is rooted in a lack of emotional spontaneity, a charge he often laid against himself.

In the spring of 1909, John's father was moved by the Inland Revenue Department to Glasgow. The family readied itself to leave Aberdeen just as John was finishing at Robert Gordon's College. His leaving certificate shows good standing in all his main subjects but no mention is made of his beloved chemistry which he was taking as an extra subject. That autumn, after he and his family had settled into their new home at 59 Cadder Street, John enrolled at the University of Glasgow in Honours Classics. It was a very reluctant choice. Due to the strong persuasion of the headmaster at Gordon's (who wanted another scholarship student to pin on his lapel) and his new director of studies at Glasgow, he signed up for Classics even though he would have far preferred to take science. Much later, in a 1949 talk, he summed up his education in this way: "Ever since 1919 I have felt that I was educated for a world in which I have never lived; and have had to live in a world for which I was never educated."[2] By 1919 he had come to appreciate that the preference for the Classics held by his academic advisors in 1909 was based more on nostalgia and élitism than on reality. This post-war insight never left him. It helped him to effect a turn away from his culture's constant backward glance in search of the good life towards a more empirically based and future-oriented vision for education and action in the world.

Despite the limited enthusiasm he had for his programme of studies he threw himself into university life with a flourish. In his first year he took Ordinary Latin and Greek. He did well but his performance was not exceptional. Although he won no distinctions in Latin that year, Gilbert Davies awarded him a second prize in Greek prose. He also studied Logic with Robert Latta and was awarded a first-class certificate of merit by this rigorous professor. In his third year he was allowed to take some optional courses which included English Language and Literature with William Macneile-Dixon. It was a course where, as he confided in an end-of-term letter to his sister Helen, "I am out of all countenance with 70% and a dozen gentlemen ahead of me." But there was compensation for his wounded pride. That same year he was able to enrol in Professor John Gregory's Geology course where he was "the only arts student in a large class of pure and applied scientists and mining engineers" and managed to carry off the gold medal.[3]

On arriving at the university, he had immediately joined the Student Christian Movement which was an immensely vital group throughout Great Britain at that time. Since he still accepted that the mission in China was his destiny John also joined the Student Volunteer Missionary Union where he established a reputation for militant, evangelical fervour. In addition he accepted responsibility for a bible class for students his own age at the Glasgow Mission Hall where he attended services. It was in preparing for that class that he began applying the scientific method he was learning to a reading of the biblical texts, and the results were explosive. When he applied scientific canons of evidence and verification to Paul's Letter to the Romans he found many of his inherited Christian doctrines collapsed around him, almost as they did for the young Martin Luther four hundred years earlier. The destruction of these traditional teachings did not destroy his faith, nor his belief in the need for sound theology. He was led to question not his faith but the dogma that had been handed down to him. His faith in Christ, as he testified years later, was unshaken, its truth grounded in the love and faith of his parents not in the dogmas they and churchmen had, in good faith but ignorance, handed on to him. However, even as faith in Christ remained the pole star in his firmament, it became clear to him that the *formulations* of that faith, like the formulations of every kind of human knowing, are not static and timeless; they can and must develop as they rub up against new historical realities. From that point in 1910, and over the next two years, he studied the Gospels and the other letters of St Paul through the lens of this fresh methodology.

On the basis of this work he was driven to affirm a necessary unity between science and religion since they were both genuine human activities and functioned in one world. It was a view of both human knowing and the world that he held to throughout his life. Religious doctrine, he wrote some twenty years later, must learn to grow up if it is to be embraced by intelligent adults in an adult way. It must submit to the essential rules of human knowing and not try to escape them. Religion that accepts adulthood manifests this maturity in several ways in its formulation of its truth:

> it gives up any pretension to absolute, timeless formulations.
> it displays a humble attentiveness to its proper evidence an chooses always to be open to new evidence.
> it remains open to constant revision in its propositions as new data and related understandings require such revision.
> it fosters genuine collaboration with persons of diverse views and viewpoints so that the effects of bias and ideology might be minimized.
> it puts into practice the conviction that religious doctrines, like scientific formulations, are, in some sense, testable and verifiable in experience; they are not true simply because some human authority or tradition proclaims them so.

On this last point he later concluded that *religious truths are verifiable only in living by them within community*; just as scientific truths are tested in acting upon them. This was a position he stated clearly in the early thirties, but it had not yet dawned for him in 1910 and 1911.

As early as March 1911, John wrote in his journal that he felt his life was becoming deeper and more full of meaning. A major conversion came suddenly in an experience and insight that freed him profoundly at the depths of his spirit. It freed him from anguish over sexual matters since it definitively challenged the idealistic perfectionism he had been trying to live by. He tells his story: He had been required to preach on a day when he was still morose over recent failures in sexual purity. Much to his surprise his preaching had been powerful and effective. In an instant he saw for himself what Luther had seen so deeply about his own relationship as a sinner to God:

> Had great liberty at the Bridge of Weir in preaching the gospel. How foolish of me it was to think that the gospel of the grace of God could be commended by nobility of character or set off by any resolution of mine. My thoughts have been running this week in another channel. I am to seek to form no character of my own but to allow the strength of God my Father to infuse itself in that spiritual nature which is in its origin the life of God — thus setting aside all that is naturally mine and seeking to realize that it is "not I but Christ who liveth in me." Another thought: Ideals are not rainbows — distant and unapproachable — but atmospheres to permeate all the *little things*.

This move beyond moralistic self-absorption, beyond living by fear and constant self-measurement in relation to ideal standards, was a transformation that would stay with him throughout his life. So too would his transforming insight that ideals are real to the degree they can be and are incarnate in human actions. A month later on June 6, as his school year was coming to an end, this spiritual insight deepens and simplifies in him:

> I have a thought which I wish to express as a mark of this day of my life. It is the answer which most satisfies my heart to the question: "What mean I by 'the presence of Christ in my life'?" Is it not just this: that God has twined into one my life and Christ's — the life that He recognizes in me? And that He makes the duties of each day's earthly existence part of His own eternal work. The joys are Christ's joys, the sorrows are Christ's sorrows, the triumphs are His triumphs. What of the failures? These are mine, but even these He hews into stepping-stones on which to rise ...

It may take a bit of knowledge of the Christian mystical tradition to appreciate how profound this insight is at the level of personal liberation. Macmurray is becoming aware that St Paul's famous Zen-like pronouncement about Christ living in him is much more than a pious phrase. It means something like this: I have not lost one bit of *my* identity; in fact I have for the first time actually grown into it. But it happens only when I let another enter into the very centre of my life. I am not "me" because of the complex of my fears, my strivings and ambitions or my little ego. These do not define the true me. And this goes for my virtues and vices, as well — they mark me, but they don't define me. I am grounded in my selfhood by being grounded in a loving other whose presence penetrates my whole being. I am already, in my deepest identity, *who I am* by the love of this God who is at once my intimate companion yet also the one who has power to command my life; and when I follow his command, then only am I truly free. This is the kind of insight that is being consciously appropriated by him.

But his conviction that his action is part of God's action in the world, and God is part of his action is equally "mind-blowing" for the young man. As he is beginning to appreciate, his life and God's life are part of *one* mystery. Human nature is not evil, or apart from God; it is good, and in God. He begins to see his work, *everything* he does and is, not just his preaching, as potentially sharing in the work of releasing light in the world. His own actions are, therefore, of nothing less than "eternal" importance, and they are so because of this *relationship* which is at the very heart of things. This profound insight into the relationship that grounds and forms personal existence lies at the heart of the Hebrew and Christian revelation, and it can be said that Macmurray's philosophy of relationship literally begins to be formed with this entry in his journal. But if that relationship makes "all being holy," it also results in the "secularization of God" because it takes God from the sky, sees God alive in all being, and makes God as real and present in him as his own breathing. There is no separation between God and (his) reality. The opposition between this *relational* viewpoint exploding in his mind and the modern, ego-centred view of human nature that arose in the age of science and the Enlightenment will become a foundational point of dialectical engagement in Macmurray's future philosophical reflections.

This understanding of how *relationship forms our very being* represents the beginning of a revolution in his image of Christianity and of himself as a Christian and a person. It will also provide the foundations for his philosophical (in contrast to faith-based) understanding of human nature when he comes to formulate it a few years later. The roots of his mature philosophical attitude and viewpoint lie here in Glasgow, even though he does not yet see any of these implications. In fact he still struggles, in some puzzlement, with this new congeniality he finds between God's work and his own human work as part of the destiny of the world. It is, after all, a fresh and even scary consideration to raise from within his evangelical tradition. This intuition, that the "secular" is the bearer of the sacred, is revolutionary for him — and profoundly attractive. The sense that the world is *one* and that religion and science are distinct but related expressions of one reality parallels in him the beginning of his appreciation of the intimate relation between the divine and the genuinely human. This entry in his journal could be seen as implicitly the launching of his life-long struggle against dualism in religion, and in philosophy, as well.

His religion is being totally reshaped. His view of Christ is being transformed and the effects of that change will resonate in his view of the world in his later philosophy. Christ becomes for Macmurray a dynamic personal being alive in the world and working for the world's completion in love. The young Macmurray, without having the language to express it, has intimations of a Christ who is at once universal and completely intimate to each individual. In this Christ, he now appreciates, *all* true knowledge and *all* good action, no matter how diverse they may be in type or form (e.g., science, art and religion), come into a unity. This sense of an ultimate, living unity of all diverse forms of knowing begins intuitively to set the terms for his future philosophical view of the unity of the mechanical and organic dimensions of being *within* the comprehensive scope of the personal. But here it is just beginning to take form, not as philosophy but as a reflection arising out of his personal experience and his science-influenced re-interpretation of his faith.

Transformed by Love

In the summer of 1911, John Macmurray returned to the summer campaign with Mr Smith's travelling mission in Aberdeenshire on the basis of a promise he made the summer before. He had wanted to preach the Good News but it was also a way for him to earn a little money during vacation to help pay for his education. What he could not foresee in October 1910 when he made that commitment was that less than a year later he would have these new understandings and new feelings that came from his "scientific" reading of the Scriptures. They were destined to create huge resistance in him to the mission's version of "being saved" and to the rhetorical way it delivered its message. This conflict was seriously accelerated by another momentous event in his life. During that summer, although he never breathed a word of it to anyone but his sister Helen, he fell totally in love with Elizabeth Hyde Campbell, the young woman who was eventually to become his wife.

Betty Campbell had not just appeared out of thin air in 1911. She was the younger sister of John's school friend, Duncan Campbell, and during the time the boys were getting to know each other, she was becoming friends with John's sister Ella (Helen) at Central School where the two girls were in the same class. Sometime in 1907, Duncan had told his sister about the brilliant John Macmurray whom he called a genius and expected one day might even become Prime Minister. He also told her about John's evangelical faith which so resembled the religion of the Campbell household. So, even though she confessed to being nervous at the prospect of seeing her brother's friend, Betty had accompanied Duncan to the Gordon Mission tent one Sunday evening where, as she recounted years later, she saw "a grave and serious young man, above medium height, with dark hair neatly brushed back from his high forehead ... standing at the entrance to the tent handing out hymn books and unself-consciously singing in a very loud voice." His mind was clearly on higher things. She doesn't say if he even noticed her.

A few weeks later, Ella invited Betty to visit her at 31 Mile End Avenue, the final residence of the Macmurray family during their time in Aberdeen. Betty accepted the invitation with fear and trembling since this would be her first actual meeting with John. Betty was playing the piano when John arrived home and after greeting him she graciously left the stool and invited him to play. With self-assurance he accepted the invitation since, as she noted later, "he wasn't outwardly a modest young man." He had been teaching himself the piano and was confident of what he had learned. He sat down, and proceeded to play the Moonlight Sonata labouriously and excruciatingly. She recalled that he especially massacred the third movement. There is no report on whether John was aware that he was not exactly overwhelming his new audience.

Betty and Duncan Campbell belonged to a far from uninteresting family. Their father, George Campbell had been a young farmer from Banchory widely known for his love of the violin and his skill in playing it. But he was also one of those few Christians who actually took to heart the injunction to love God above all things. So when Lord Aberdeen selected George and requested him to go to the Gordon Memorial Mission station in South Africa, George decided to accept the call. He picked up his precious violin and shattered it over his knee as a sign that he was definitively breaking from his old way of life. In fact, he never played the fiddle again. The mission was in Umsinga, Natal, in Zulu territory north of the Tugela river. George Campbell and his young wife laboured there for only a short time before the Zulu uprising took place. The missionaries were immediately ordered out of the area by the government and shipped back home. George's wife died on the return trip and was buried at sea.

Bereft, and without a clear future, he returned to the Banchory area. He soon met a young woman who was beginning to make a name for herself as a writer of evangelical tracts and they married. Because he had a reputation for dependability and good work, George was hired to be the farm manager by Mr Duncan Davidson, the laird of the manor at Inchmarlo near Banchory in the Dee Valley. The lady of the manor, Mrs Angela Davidson, was a fervent evangelical and was delighted to know that the young Mrs Campbell was none other than the writer of the tracts that were burning their way into the hearts of so many revivalists. The young couple moved into "The Home Farm," a small property and house situated a half-mile up the hill looking down on the manor house below.

The Campbell's first child was a boy, and he was named after the laird who agreed to be his godfather. How well he served in that role is another issue. About two years later, on December 23, 1891, the Campbells had a daughter who they named after Lady Hyde Clarke, a wealthy woman who took to her bed when she was widowed and remained there for forty years! Lady Hyde Clarke had been comforted by Mrs Campbell's religious writings at the time of her husband's death, and they corresponded thereafter. She requested that she be the child's godmother and that the girl take the name of Hyde. Mrs Campbell, as she told her children later, thought that some good might come of this if she managed the relationship in the interests of her new daughter. So the baby was christened Elizabeth Hyde Campbell. She was called Betty in her family and by their friends but the nickname "Hydie" followed her as well. It was the name that John Macmurray knew her by when he met her and the name that filled his poetry as he grew to love her.

Betty Campbell's family, in her early years, was awash with the evangelical language and sentiment that filled her mother's writings. Her mother, as she recalled, "was always nagging at me to be converted." Eventually she *was* converted and grew to have a great intimacy with Jesus. Later, as she looked back on that period of her life with the perspective of decades, she was convinced her religion at the time was genuine. It was love. As she, a born romantic, put it in her memoir notes, "Jesus was my first lover."

In 1908, the lady of the manor became ill and died. By some kind of preternatural coincidence, Betty's father died on the same day. The family, required to leave the farm within a month, moved into Aberdeen and took a house at 54 Forest Avenue. The laird had promised to give Mrs Campbell a pension of fifty pounds a year but he made this payment only once. The result was a life of simplicity always verging on poverty for them. Betty managed to cover her school fees with a small gift from her godmother. This annuity, with added help from the relatively new Carnegie Trust Grant (instituted to cover normal fees for all students of Scottish descent), was used to finance her degree in English Literature and Anglo-Saxon which she completed in 1915 at the University of Aberdeen.

During that year of great transition for the Campbells, John and Betty met each other more or less by chance when John went to the Campbell home to spend time with Duncan or when Betty came to see Ella at the Macmurrays. In both families the boys were less than two years older than their sisters. The relationship among the four of them became so comfortable that, after the Macmurray family moved to Glasgow in 1909, Ella and John stayed over at the Campbells' house whenever they came to Aberdeen.

When Macmurray left Glasgow after term ended in mid-June, 1911, his summer work on the mission began almost at once. The first mission was held in Whitehouse, Aberdeenshire where he preached but apparently with little positive effect even after a month. By July 18, he reflects on the sheer ordinariness of each day's experience:

> I wonder if it is worth the while to seek after the deep experiences rather than to jog along in contented mediocrity. Does it pay to seek for visions and passions of love and the heroics of service? Certainly that path is hedged with difficulties and set thick with temptations.

He had spent the weekend before this in Aberdeen at the Campbells. He says he stayed overnight "with Duncan," but it is clear that it is now not only Duncan who draws him there:

> On Saturday, Hyde, Duncan and I played golf on the links; spending a forenoon whose pure pleasure will not soon be forgotten. To these two I am knit by a love that is eternal: no distance, no cross-purpose, no emotion, no busy toil or heavy burden of life shall ever avail to blunt the keenness of its edge or overcome its pure, tender passion. 'Love never faileth.' Only I would that I might weed out all the tangles of selfishness from the garden of my love, that its fragrance be untainted and its beauty unimpaired.

A reader of this rather florid and overwrought reflection might be forgiven for suspecting that it is not in his relationship with his schoolfriend Duncan that he is so exercised about weeding out "all the tangles of self-ishness from the garden of my love." There is indeed something else going on here, forming quickly but as yet undeclared even to himself. Soon afterwards, having written his first poem without a religious theme, one that secretly expressed his budding love for Betty, he reflects openly:

> These days are memorable. Duncan is very kind, and develops powers of mind quite unnoticed before. With Hyde, — if there was any doubt of it before, there is none now — I have fallen in love, but dare not tell her so. I am not worthy to blacken her shoes. I fear to visit them too much lest I should take advantage of her sweet simplicity of friendship. I would not for an empire win her by

anything but pure nobility — and God knows how much I am
lacking right there!

The noble idealism in this first testament to Eros matches that of his earlier religious outpourings.

However other personal developments are at work in him, as well. A
long reflection on August 12 from the mission in Craigievar acknowledges
that he is beginning to appreciate his own power with people. We see the
first signs that the wine of his personal growth is no longer able to mature
in the old wineskins of the evangelical mission:

> Meetings here are promising. I preached last night and held the
> meeting from beginning to end without a break. I did not think
> before that I had any gift of this kind; yet I feel that every time I
> preach my power with men grows marvellously. We have got the
> ear of the young people.
>
> I begin to grow very weary of this life. There is not nearly
> enough to do. Mr Smith spends most of the day cycling here and
> there to visit well-known friends of his. These continual tea-
> drinking expeditions are a great bore to me and I care very little to
> discuss village politics and ministers and vegetables with farmers'
> wives and daughters or even the farmers themselves. I want to
> work and can find no time for work because there is too much play
> to be got through. Even the meetings get wearisome, since I know
> almost all the addresses off by heart now.

He ends this entry with his first sortie into social analysis. For all its
apparently prosaic observations, it contains an edge that will deepen and
mature rapidly, especially when it is applied to the institutional
churches:

> The country is too prosperous just now to be godly. Everywhere
> there are signs of Fortune's smile: but the men on whom God
> showers his best gifts are enjoying them too much to say thank-
> you. The root of the difficulty is the indifference and selfishness of
> the professing Christians. God help the sinners when the saints get
> indifferent!

Family news, both good and bad, had also affected him over these summer months. His July 18 journal entry records his happiness that Ella, his
favourite sister, had come second in the whole of Britain in the Civil
Service Examination.

> Another sweet incident of these days was dear Ella's magnificent
> success ... I was scarcely surprised but my delight and pride knew
> no bounds. I believe that I have often underrated Ella: simply
> because of the way in which she obscures and sacrifices herself.

To this day, Helen's achievement is remembered by the members of even
the next generation as an event that gave the family great pride. Perhaps it
remained the only accomplishment in the public arena by another member
of the family that could stand alongside the successes that came to John
over his professional life.

Later, while the mission was at Craigievar, word came in a letter that
Betty's mother, a psychically fragile person, had been taken to the hospital of the Royal Asylum at the doctor's advice. The shock was immense
for John, as his journal records some weeks after the event:

> I was still dazed when I wrote to Duncan and sought to comfort
> him, very incoherently, I fear, yet with real deep sympathy. Soon
> the bewilderment melted and left me with a heavy pain at my heart,
> sharper even than when Mr Campbell died. I was younger then.
> The next day I wrote to Hydie, a letter which was the beginning of
> a great change in me.

He goes on to say he wrote to her partly because he felt his response to
Duncan was partial, and in this letter to Betty he was completing it. He
was convinced at the time he was writing simply in "sympathy." In fact, it
was a declaration of his love to which she responded positively and in
kind. He notes that the positive response he received to his letter declaring
his love for Betty has "widened the breach between the old life and the
new. A wider range of reading helped to bring to me a larger interest in life
outside my narrow sphere." What he meant was that in early September,
after the mission moved over the hill into the valley of the Dee and pitched
their tent at Torphins, alongside his customary hours of biblical study and
analysis, Elizabeth Barrett Browning's sonnets had became "his one passion."

At this point Macmurray's journal bursts with poems like crocuses out
of the warming soil in spring. In one sonnet he compares the image of a
hard-working farmer preparing a field with the kind of mature and responsible love he wishes to offer Hydie, whom he addresses in his poems at
this time under the code-name of Agnes. The beauty of natural flowers,
which he admits to freely, is contrasted to that of cultivated crops in the
sextet that ends the poem and his preference between the wild and the cultivated is clearly stated:

I loved thee, Agnes, even in that young spring
When daisies and shy violets peeped beneath
the marbly foxgloves. But for love's harvesting,
The clustered corn-spike in its golden sheath
Fruit of the furrow, is a nobler thing
Than the untamed blossoms on the natural heath.

Orderliness in love was John's choice, and it was true to his character. As we shall see, this was hardly the way Betty felt love should be.

The summer mission ended strongly on September 28 in Torphins and was followed by a week of relaxation in Aberdeen. He went to be with Duncan and Betty, of course, and the three of them spent their evenings together. But Duncan worked during the day, and this gave John and Betty full afternoons to wander in the fields and simply be together and enjoy their newly declared love for one another. He read poetry to her from both Robert and Elizabeth Barrett Browning and felt their love was being very ennobled in the process. In her own memoirs years later Betty, who was always much less fixed on "nobility" as a feature of love, confesses that the two of them were wandering in "a broth of delicious sentiment" at that time. She remembers mainly that John was rather formal in his manner on those walks and that she found the Browning poetry both unintelligible and boring.

John returned to the family home in Glasgow ("very empty now that Ella and Lily are in London" — where they had taken up their new jobs) to prepare for his third year of university. On October 9, he begins in his journal a long reflection on his past six weeks that puts much greater texture on his appreciation of that important time. At the heart of this review was the firm sense that he had changed for the better over those weeks in the summer. There was new strength, as his preaching revealed, but there was as well a new vulnerability opened up in him in falling in love and it formed a piece with the feeling of strength. In this spirit, he enters his third year. In fact, the autumn was filled with activities including more initiatives with the Student Volunteer Mission Union, the recommencement of his bible class ("with a phenomenal attendance of twenty-four") and his first geological excursions. Because he was so involved with his Christian groups or because of his solemn and militant manner of doing so, even into this third year at university he felt himself to be on the outside of ordinary university life. As he wrote to Helen a couple of months later when she wished him well:

Your wish for success I am less confident about ... that I am not a favourite either with professors or students is perfectly plain; as also that I do not win gold medals. But I do not grieve: perhaps the success will be all the greater when it comes, and better worth.

His sexual energy continues to throw him into the anguish of self-contradiction but the signs of growth in him are revealed in his larger and deeper view of his constantly changing life and his attraction to a modern way of seeing things:

> I feel the restraint of that miserable weakness, and reserve that arises, I doubt not from consciousness that my life is hardly square with my profession, and my profession is somewhat out of line with my belief. I begin to feel as never before the strength and trend of the current of modern thought. Almost against my will, my dogmas and beliefs are being shaken and modified, the viewpoint is shifting ...

At Christmastime, Ella and Lily came home to Glasgow, and Betty also came for the holidays. John felt those days were beautiful beyond description.

> For in those glorious days I won my Hydie for myself, and our two lives, whose spirit-currents for the last two years have flowed so close together, burst the barrier between them and were mingled in a flood of love.

As though this degree of rapture were not enough, he undertakes "to chronicle the steps by which I climbed the stair to the palace of love." Essentially, his firm intention to maintain "friendship" until he was more worthy of "love" came crashing down around his head under the force of his reawakened feeling for her. The situation for expressing it came in an unexpected moment of solitude for the two of them. He held her hand gently, then drew her to him and then kissed her. Her response was total:

> So it was that the last barrier was broken for ever between us — and not a word spoken. We knew then that our God had made us one in heart and spirit, and that whatever the future might hold for us, no power on earth could break that bond. I spoke not of love to Hyde, only said 'Goodnight' and ran and flung myself down upon my knees to pour out my thanksgiving to God ...

Some days later, they were able to find time alone again and each expressed in words the same feelings of love for the other. At the piano, they sang songs together, but now with new meaning:

The last song we sang was "The Lord Will Provide," and as the last words died away, I knelt at her side as she sat, with hands clasped around her, and told of the dawning and the deepening of my love for her and how my whole being lay as an offering at her feet. Even now I can feel the thrill of the joy that possessed me when from her lips I heard that her love had been as long and as deep as mine and that henceforth she and I were to be lovers.

Her departure left him in acute loneliness but, as he reflected in an entry on February16 which was his birthday, he was left with:

[my] face looking to the future glad with hope. My strength is new, my purpose is new, my life itself moves in a higher sphere with larger meaning. The first part of my life ended in its triumph when I won Hyde for myself — now a new life begins in which I must win myself for Hyde. The fight will be stern, not without noise and dust, weariness and blood — but it will be a victory. The past is proof of this.

Chapter 3

Opening Up to the World (1912–1913)

"That fateful summer of 1912"

After the Christmas holidays of 1911, James Macmurray accompanied his
two daughters to London when they returned to their jobs. His purpose in
going was to explore the possibility of moving the family there. His own
poor health made him determined to take early retirement, even within a
matter of months. Furthermore, with only one year left in John's time at
university, and with both Helen and Lilias already settled in London there
seemed to be little reason for remaining in Glasgow and some good reasons
to make London the family base. The decision was made, and by the end
of May 1912, the rest of the family except for John had moved to London.

Although his interior life was turning upside down at every level,
Macmurray had a huge success that spring which he records simply: "At
the end of March I finished up my Geology class, winning the medal and
the Cowie Prize and passing the degree examination." Even with that he
can't resist a small burst of self-deprecation, combined with vanity: "I
hardly think that the medal should have gone to me, for there was one man
my superior in the subject, I feel sure." At Easter break in April, he went
to London for the first time in his life and was astounded by the city.

> I count it amongst the great experiences of my life. It has brought
> home to me how much bigger the world is than I had thought, and
> how much work there is to do in it. London is wonderful,
> bewildering, fascinating. It seems to go on for ever, one great
> being, and yet always different: loving and hating, toiling and
> playing, serving God and the devil, breaking hearts, sealing loves,
> buying and selling merchandise and the souls of men; sinning,
> sinning, sinning, and yet all the while unconsciously winning
> nearer to the end of sin. Ah, London, London, devourer of the
> people, yet nurse of mighty men, thou mighty paradox, gateway at
> once to heaven and hell, I have eaten of thy lotus-buds, and I love
> thee to the forgetting of my homeland.

While he was there, he had an interview with the acting secretary of the
China Inland Mission. The man appears to have responded with sympathy

to Macmurray but also with a keen and wise intuition. He advised John to continue at college for another year and prepare himself for educational work in China. But a spectre hovered over that prospect. Macmurray had actually not been well for a long time and on May 5 he complained of this constant sickness:

> Ill-health attends me like a shadow. All day yesterday I lay in bed, heavy with pain and weariness. I could wish with all my heart for a few months of buoyant vigorous health. The result would be startling, I think.

He went for the medical examination required by the Mission Society. While he waited back in Glasgow for the doctor's report he confessed: "... I am a little afraid that the result will not be favourable to my foreign missionary projects." He hastened to add, perhaps even too quickly: "Of this I am certain, that it cannot be prejudicial to the Master's projects for me." John continued unwell throughout the whole of that spring and at the end of the summer the doctors agreed that his health was not good enough for him to consider the foreign missions. The decision not to go to China was taken not only with peace but with relief since the form of his religion and his attitude to public religion were now moving in a direction that, as he put it later, "quite unfitted me for a missionary's life." The changes he experienced within himself during what he refers to as "that fateful summer of 1912" can be felt already in this journal entry from May 1:

> Spiritual life has become a hard conflict. Sometimes I can scarcely believe in anything! Meanwhile the unrealities and unconscious hypocrisies of Christians have got swollen out in my mind into cant and humbug, and I am ready to cast them all to the four winds, and to bury myself in the pleasures of folly. Where it will all end I know not. But it has its good as well as its distracting side. It drives me to be honest and true with myself and with God above all.

This is a sharper turn than we have seen thus far in his view of religious practice. It is one thing to be bored with tea and chit-chat on home visits in rural Aberdeenshire, but quite another to be finding hypocrisy, cant and humbug in the way Christians, in general, are living their religion. Even to speak of "Christians" in this disparaging manner puts a distance between something new and something old in himself, and this is a jolting experience for him. Nor have we ever before seen him, even in jest, so cavalier about the attractiveness of tipping the tables of moral propriety and giving himself over to some reckless, irresponsible behaviour. Neither "pleasure" nor "folly" have ever before been granted a positive place in his discourse.

Something is definitely loosening up in him. And his critique does not end there:

> I am revolted to find how much trumpery mouthing there has been in my religion; and I suppose, in everything else equally if only I took the trouble to hunt it out. Strange that creatures such as we can put on airs and practise oratory in the very sanctuary of the Highest. From this, at least, I am determined to be free. Better to be an infidel than avow a religion which I do not believe.

So, he now lays the knife of judgment directly to his own neck. He charges himself with "putting on airs" in his preaching, and presenting with certitude and confidence doctrines he is no longer sure he believes in. He vows to avoid this phoneyness. But again, even as the turmoil grows, his faith in God is not compromised, only deepened; God remains his "one, true foundation." In fact God not only survives the onslaught but provides — along with science, falling in love, and his growing sense of his own personal energy and purpose — the power-base for an attack on a form of religion that begins to feel profoundly unreal to him. His is not a faith crisis; it is a sociological one. His intellectual and emotional growth are now no longer reconcilable with the evangelical version of doctrine and modes of believing and preaching he has been practising up to this point in his life. He speaks of "a certain undefinable shrinking from 'piousness' and established forms," but he is not at all sure what it all means or what he can hope might take its place. But the breakdown of the older patterns and the building up of a startling synthesis of the human and the divine were both picking up speed with every passing week.

In June he had moved, at least for the summer, to the family's new house at 70 Crouch Hill Avenue in North London. Very quickly, as he got his bearings, he began seeing the move to London from Glasgow as a symbol, as well as a further cause, of the massive upheaval taking place in him.

> I wonder whether I am still the same. Something is unchanged I feel, yet perhaps less than I would have believed ... Yes, it is strange to be in London; but at least one knows that one is there. It is stranger still to be in a world which allows neither of latitude or longitude, pole or equator, nor can tell day from night or up from down, in a world where every component particle seems to have slipped its connection with all else and gone blindly wandering on in search of it knows not what — in fact, not to know where one is in spirit, while still tantalised with the conviction that one is somewhere. I just feel like that. The great truths on which my

childhood and youth were grounded are slipping away from me one
after another; not that I no longer believe them; then I should know
where I was, but I cannot tell, think as I will, whether I believe
them or not.

Then, he pinpoints the issue he faces with regard to whatever truth he
holds at present or will come to hold in the future:

> Everything has hitherto been believed on the authority of others
> and of their experience. Now I refuse, and must refuse, to build my
> hopes for all that is highest and best upon an untested authority —
> however high — or to wrestle through the struggle we call life in
> contest for the truth of another's experience.

On the basis of just such liberating convictions, it is fair to say that his
true religious homeland is not so much destroyed as transformed, not
so much lost as perhaps discovered consciously for the first time, In a
long reflection from within this painful transformation he writes
poignantly:

> I am convinced that no man can do a man's work unless he have a
> man's conviction in his heart about the central things. And a
> conviction is born of experience, not without pangs and travail.
> Would I be a man if I could set my life to defend the dogmas a
> man has created? But where is God? Why has he hidden himself?"

Anguishing, he prays from deep in his heart using phrases (perhaps from
a written prayer) that could have been plucked directly from St Ignatius of
Loyola — whose writings Macmurray never knew:

> Ah, Lord God, pity my feeble faith in thy Almightiness; the groping
> of my blind hands in the blaze of Thy Light of light. Give me eyes
> that I may see Thee. A heart that I may know Thee, a will that I may
> follow Thee. I am sore stricken, unless thou succour me ...

Yet, just two weeks later, with much more clarity and peace, he concludes
firmly:

> If God lives at all, if our life is not — as it is not — the creation of
> an "idiot power," the God who created needs, hungers, cries, in the
> human heart must needs fill them. To fear that faith cannot be
> found would be a denial of God. The cry for God, the blind
> groping for Him, is it not conclusive that a knowledge of God is

within our reach. So thus far I know and believe. The noblest lives are linked with the highest beliefs. Faith is the social glue. When we cease to believe, we cease to live — either to man or God. Unbelief is spiritual death and intellectual death. It abolishes Love and enthrones suspicion, — paralyses governments, religions, friendships, all societies of men. 'We must believe or die'.

We can go a step farther. If faith be necessary to life, then agnosticism is a denial of God's wisdom as well as of His power. It says in effect: 'God has created a life that needs faith: He has created no means to supply the life with faith.'

Thus faith is possible or life is impossible. It is my duty to find the faith which satisfies the need. To fail in the quest is to perish utterly: and can only arise from insincerity or lack of earnestness in the searching.

What an amazing statement from a twenty-one year-old: "It is my duty to find the faith which satisfies the need." Despite his own alarm, as well as that of his parents, he sees the changes as God's work in him, and not a sign that God is lost to him. He feels he is being prepared by God for something else. He ends this powerful reflection with a prayer that resembles the "Lead Kindly Light" of John Henry Newman some seventy years earlier, ending with the words: "... Reveal Thyself, Thyself, — that I may know Thee and thy Life. This is my prayer. In my measure I would live as Thou and love as Thou."

Revolutionary times

The young Macmurray has gone through huge changes — his falling in love which changed his understanding of the foundational place of love in the world, his appropriation of the scientific method and his use of it in his reading of Scripture, and his shift away from seeing himself as a missionary in a religious organization towards dedicating himself to the world in a more inclusive but far less "churchy" form of service.Although his sense of being a "missionary" survives and even flourishes, its focus has shifted significantly. As he observes: "... the time has come when I must begin to recognize my own life as under my own power, to be spent of my own free will upon others."

In the midst of this deep interior change he drank deeply of the newness of London. He also took time to do translations of poems by Victor Hugo and to write more poetry himself. In a stunningly comprehensive reflection, he notes what his wanderings in the streets of London have contributed to his own inner life:

> Not only through my own measured life in thought and experience
> does questioning come. I begin to feel that other lives are round
> me, all important, essential to the scheme of things, yet many
> crushed and bruised and battered into insensibility by wrong and
> injustice, many frozen into insensibility by ease and plenty. I
> wonder which is worst — poverty or riches.
>
> ... I must have a faith that can face these things and their
> fellows ... I must find a faith that claims all that is awful as God's
> necessity, and triumphs in hope of His glory through it all. Is it
> possible? Oh! It must be, must be ... Above all I must find a faith
> that will work, for the test of worth in a man's thought is the
> measure of that which his hands have accomplished.

A reader needs to step back and take a breath after cracking open so many
nuggets in so short a space. The young man contemplates in order: the
deep social nature of human beings, the destructive power of riches as well
as poverty, the question of evil and God — in the startling claim that faith
must see "all that is awful as God's necessity" — and finally a faith that
is effective, a faith that situates the truthfulness of the head and heart in
the fruitfulness of the hands — a clear option for the primacy of the practical even, and especially, in religion. These ideas and convictions, completely new to Macmurray that summer, would become so deeply sown in
the furrows of his soul that they would bear fruit in his philosophical work
over the course of six decades.

By the end of July, these changes happening in John are simply too
much for his parents to bear:

> Father and mother have spoken what I felt all along they have been
> thinking. They see the change in me, and are alarmed. They believe
> that it is all wrong, all sin, and the penalty for neglecting the Word
> of God and prayer ... that my difficulties and struggles are nothing
> else than a darkness which I have brought upon myself.

His parents want him to quit school and take exams for a position in the
Civil Service since they have no more money to train him for a career in
teaching. They are clearly hoping to rescue some goods from the sinking
ship as they see their son's recognizable Christianity slipping slowly
beneath the waves. His response to their fear and anger is a masterpiece of
moderation and maturity for one so young and in such vulnerable straits:

> There is much true in all this, and I am entirely glad that they have
> spoken so reasonably and so plainly. Certainly I have not read the
> Bible much lately ... Yet all is not true. Much of the longing and

desire in me, the tumult of big thoughts, is good. The questions I
have raised need to be answered. Father and Mother have never had
occasion to face modern thought — it has never met them as a
barrier in their road, and so they fail partly to understand. In the
main, however, they are right. In grappling with these problems —
all the problems of modern existence — I ought to seek God first ...

As for practical difficulties, I do not see my way through. Yet I
think that another year at College is essential and that God has
provided for it. I have powers of mind still untried. I might be able
to make money by writing and by private teaching. The thought of
clerking labour fills me with horror, yet it may be necessary. Do
thou, O Christ, be my guide!

With that, he prepared on September 5 to leave London for a month-long
visit to Aberdeen before returning to Glasgow for his final year of university. He wrote:

I have not the least doubt in asserting that it has been the most
revolutionary period in my life, and that what has happened in it
will have a larger result in my life than the events of any similar
period.

This prediction will prove to be exactly true. In reviewing the influences
that galvanized his change, he takes note of "the preachers whom I have
heard — Mr Brown and Dr Weeks: whose thought is much broader, more
sympathetic, more fundamental than any which I have been accustomed
to." And he cites his ever-deepening affection for Betty as the greatest
cause of his inner transformation. It is clear that he rejoiced in the man he
was becoming, and this flowed over in his visit with Betty. Referring to
the time with her, he wrote:

The only way I can express it is by saying that I was absolutely
happy ... Early in our stay together we became definitely engaged
to one another. We undertook definitely our responsibilities — I to
provide for her in the days to come, when she will be my wife: she
to undertake all the responsibilities and duties of a wife when the
time shall have come for us to enter into the closer relationship.
Meanwhile, in spirit we are already man and wife. This is the most
inexpressible happiness which has ever entered into my life.[1]

The confirmation of their love released him for even greater dedication in
his studies and his determination to "prepare myself through my studies to
exert the largest influence in the world on behalf of Christ which it is

possible for me to do." He decided to work for the Snell Exhibition, a prestigious scholarship to Balliol College, Oxford, awarded each year to a Scottish university student. To win it was to be assured of freedom from financial worries for a period of four years. He knew it was his only hope of being able to manage further studies at that time in his life. Throughout the autumn, poetry continued to flow from his pen, mainly sonnets and lyrics, and included among it, since it said so much to his feelings, a transcription of Robert Burns' "Ma heart's as lichsome as a bird."

His energy had never before been so much from within himself or so focused. Sometime in November 1912 (four months sooner than he had expected them taking place!) Macmurray sat the examinations for the Snell Exhibition and won it, partly, he said, because the questions fell right in the areas which he had studied most and partly because his keenest challenger decided not to take the exam. In fact, only three candidates sat the exam. Professor Phillmore, who chaired the Examiners Committee made up of Professors Davies, Macneile-Dixon and himself, had a slightly different take on the matter. In a letter to the Master of Balliol informing him of the recommendation of John Macmurray, he noted that "the field was smaller than usual but the selected candidate is fully up to the level of our last few ... he has excellent abilities and is very industrious and very teachable."

At the end of December, during his Christmas holidays in London, John met Reverend Richard Roberts, the pastor at Crouch Hill Presbyterian Church just down the street from his parents' new home, and "learned from him about the foundation and purpose of the Swanwick Free Church Fellowship" which attracted him deeply. Its goals, as he recorded them, are:

> ... to rise in a positive faith, to cast off the burden of a negative religiousness and theology, to face the facts in fearless trust, to rediscover the will of God in our generation, above all to learn the secrets of [word effaced] experience and let them teach us the meaning of dogma.

This would have suited him perfectly. As a result of his religion becoming more united with his experience, Macmurray is able to see more clearly the strains and contradictions in the world around him. He is led to critique society's entrapment in what he calls the "prejudices and bonds of useless tradition." Society, he finds, is as hooked on inadequate certainties as he had been. On January 11, 1913, given that the start of the war is slightly more than a year away, he observes almost prophetically:

> Our whole civilization is overstrained and may smash up suddenly. The strain is apparent everywhere, and the attempts to repair

matters are absurdly inadequate. What we need is a new life springing up from the very germs and bursting with its own vitality the dead seed-cloak of our old, effete, semi-pagan civilization. We are like square pins in round holes. The irksomeness of the forms which do not answer our needs, and the restraint of meaningless traditions make the very truth of the past distasteful ... I have continually to tear the fundamental morality of our society to pieces, even at the expense of wrecking my own prospects. It is just possible that the Swanwick fellowship may hold the first germs of the coming thing. For something is coming without a doubt.

A new sense of mission

In the final pages of the notebook and halfway through 1913, it is as though the young man grasped both the meaning of life in its eternal dimensions and the full temper of the times in which he was living. He accurately intuits the historical cataclysm about to engulf Europe because of what he observed to be the decadence, loss of direction, and moral chaos into which the European nations had by 1913 irretrievably fallen.

He ends his reflections on this period of huge and almost seismic transformation in himself saying: "Why should I complain, who have Hydie's arms and breast for consolation?" On February 16, his twenty-second birthday, he continues this reflection: "My darling has made me anew, for God and man and herself ... This year has been the seedbed of my first true religious experience." He acknowledges that during the year earthly love almost supplanted his religious life, so deep and passionate did it become. By year-end, things have changed, but so too has his perspective on Betty and the place in his spirit where he has come ashore:

There seems to be no distinction left between winning her and winning heaven. Nor is this a mere sick lover's exaggeration: it is a spiritual insight which has come of knowing that for a man to have learned to love fully and perfectly the woman of his choice is to have attained to the fulness of the measure of the stature of Christ. My love has grown to mean this by small degrees, and will spread out in greener, stronger life in the year ahead ... I have not attained. Rather, I have caught an amazing view of the immensity of the height to be attained.

He acknowledges his passion is still tainted with selfishness, but asks for:

... not less but more passion, only let it be under a still finer
restraint ... Give me also a scorn of all insincerity and a manliness
that accepts its own responsibility: to temper all, a tenderness of
sympathy which will take me out of myself. Why may I not be one
who enters into the lives of others?

In reflecting on his most recent visit with Betty, he notes:

... these days, like all other days with Hydie, leave me with a gulf
between the present and the past. There is no power on earth for
change equal to love ...

And well he might say that. During that year alone, starting with the "fateful summer of 1912" and up to the summer of 1913, Macmurray wrote
over thirty poems, some but not all of which were love poems. There is
among them a particularly poignant but deeply veiled sonnet written on
April 25, 1913 entitled *Then shall we know,* a clear reference to St Paul's
famous paean to love in 1 Corinthians 13. It is dedicated: 'To M.W.' and
begins "There is no answer, sister. Ask no more." It ends:

Who knows what mean those bursts of splendid song
Whose echoes reach us from the outer air?
'Tis a full wondrous room wherein thus long
We wait the guardian of the golden stair.
And when he calls us shortly from the throng,
We will not ask. There is no question there.

The poem is almost surely dedicated to his sister Mary. If this conjecture is
correct, the poem contains the first trace of any reference to Mary by John,
and in it we feel it may be the only response he is able to offer to her. He
has no answer; but he believes firmly an answer, personal and loving, will
be revealed, and before which "We will not ask. There is no question there."
    In his next to last entry in this journal, the only journal he ever kept in
his life, he seems to sing out and celebrate, rather than merely state, the
richness of his new discoveries:

My knowledge has increased in large measure: especially my
knowledge of life. Gaps have been filled up, the whole more closely
assimilated, the borders widened. The unity of all knowledge and the
higher unity of all life have revealed themselves; so that goodness
and truth and beauty have each claimed and been granted an
essential place in every scheme of things. Poetry, patriotism,
philosophy, human affection, music, art and many other things; all
the range of human knowledge, indeed, has been admitted to

association with the spiritual ideal. I long for the spiritual to
penetrate all these and make them part of a single life, with its face
towards, God, and the coming of His Kingdom in its view.

It is a rare thing to find simultaneously such an embrace of modern thought
along with such a conviction about God and the unity of knowledge lying
beyond science. The twenty-two year-old's personal development at the
levels of thought, feeling and his sense of public vocation is expressed in
this remarkable credo, one might even say manifesto, where, at once, true
distinctions are respected and formerly unbridgeable divisions melt away.
It is impossible not to pause almost reverently before this paragraph, as
though before the defining canvas of a brilliant artist's first period in which
most of his unique contributions yet to come are being radiantly
telegraphed. One marvels at the degree to which this paragraph in his
youthful journal expresses in magnificent compactness the landscape of the
entire philosophical project of the mature thinker. It is as though everything
from this point on is a search mainly for the means of expression, for the
appropriate categories and language for that expression, not for the essential goal, direction or substance of his conviction.

His thoughts on May 5, 1913, the last entry in his journal, are a firm but
passionate expression of faith in light of everything he sees and anticipates:

The future is more intense than ever before. I am not afraid. Let
God decide what it shall be. My Hydie is with me ... [and] out of
the pressure and vicissitude of life ... there rises one fact, the
eternal fact of *Christ.*

The entries of this journal taken together reflect a profound personal transformation over four and a half years. It was even more significant because
Macmurray was conscious and articulate about both his changes and the
power within them for the good of the world. All parts of him — intellect,
emotions, and religious faith — had been touched, transformed, and released
for new living. He knew he had changed definitively. What he could not
know at the time is that the change was so radical and so sound that in subsequent years it was never seriously challenged, let alone overturned.

After completing his Classics degree at Glasgow with First Class
Honours in September 1913, Macmurray went immediately to Oxford and
enrolled in the Classics degree course known as Greats. He had noted
months earlier in a January 13 letter to Mr Bailey, the academic administrator at Balliol, that "both philosophy and history have been largely overlooked in my course of study until now, and are subjects which really
interest me." He chose philosophy.

Chapter 4

Oxford and the War Years (1913-1919)

The spirit of Balliol

In the last third of the nineteenth century and on into the early years of the twentieth, Balliol College, Oxford, had gained the reputation of being the centre of liberal theology and democratic socialist thinking in Britain. The great classical translator and Christian scholar Benjamin Jowett did much to create that focus during his time as Master from 1870 to 1893, and the tradition was only strengthened when he was followed in the position by the Scottish idealist, Edward Caird. Brilliant men joined them, including Thomas Green (who died early in Jowett's tenure), R.L. Nettleship, Henry Scott Holland and Charles Gore (destined to be Archbishop of Canterbury), the founders of the Christian Social Union, and finally, Arnold Toynbee and A.D. Lindsay. All of them exercised great influence at Balliol as the founding fathers or later exponents of a British Idealism that blended Hegel and Kant with Christian faith to create a philosophical vindication of religious experience.

All members of this Balliol movement believed in progress. Their "social idealism" asserted the spiritual unity of the human person and held for an active participation of human beings in the unfolding of God's "absolute Spirit" in history, this view of humanity's cooperation with God receiving its major thrust from Thomas Green in the mid-nineteenth century. It created a philosophical optimism in the Idealists' position that led to a rather confident and heady version of Christianity's active role in making history. They were convinced that moral effort would bring about continuing development not only in a given society, but for humanity at large. The spirit of Balliol was grounded in liberal Christian conviction which linked human care for the world with the Gospel mandate to serve the Kingdom of God.

Jowett was succeeded as Master by Caird (1893–1907) who made the torch of social democracy burn even more brightly. Like Jowett, he affirmed the university's "vocation" in the world and bravely applied it to the students themselves by encouraging the undergraduates to see their years at Balliol in terms of two priorities: their first duty was to self-culture, their own education in mind and sensibility. Their second was to prepare themselves to go out from the college and discover why, in such a

rich country, so many were poor.[1] This was pretty heady stuff for an institution that, during the early nineteenth century, had presented itself
proudly as Oxford's bastion of conservative élitism.

In fact, several of Balliol's alumni, such as Henry Asquith (under
Jowett), and Lord Beveridge, R.H. Tawney and William Temple (all
undergraduates together under Caird) went on to live out Caird's social
challenge with great effect. At the end of the nineteenth century, it is likely
that the ethos of the college was as Scottish as at any time in its history.
Balliol's Christian socialism, aiming at a universal sharing of the world's
goods in a community life based on values lodged in common humanity,
was a long-standing aspect of Scottish Christianity. It is almost surely
because of its strong Protestant Christianity that Balliol's philosophical
idealism found the necessary passion to turn into graduates into fervent
socialists with both a mission and practical goals for transforming society.
Balliol in 1913 was still a philosophical environment in which John
Macmurray would feel very much at home.

However, some retrenchment had been attempted. When Macmurray
arrived on the scene the master was James Leigh Strachan Davidson
(1907–16), a gentle man who was voted in at least partly to cool down the
ardour for Caird's vision of the university as an engine for changing society. He did not disappoint. He was a conservative man as well as a gentle
one who accepted the mandate to serve the ancient and venerable tradition
of the College rather than seeking adventuresome ways of advancing it
even further in its worldly claims. Even with this more restrained
approach, the spirit of earlier days continued to be supported both inside
and outside the College.

Despite his parents' incapacity to help him financially with his year at
Oxford, the Snell Exhibition plus a loan offered to him by Reverend Richard
Roberts, his former pastor, set Macmurray up adequately for the first year.
His tutor was A.D. Lindsay, a socially-active young don in his seventh year
at Balliol. As part of the Balliol socialist tradition, Lindsay certainly helped
to strengthen Macmurray's interest in seeing studies as a preparation for a
life of action and public service. His political allegiances were clearly left-
of-centre, and Macmurray would have found his sense of a democracy
rooted in the people rather congenial, given the directions of his own recent
thinking on decadence in society and stultifying structures in both politics
and the church. Arnold Toynbee had become a Fellow in 1912, but there are
no indications that Macmurray did any formal study with him in 1913–14.

In that year before the war, despite having many acquaintances,
Macmurray seems to have entered into only two friendships that were significant for him. The relaxing one was with Arthur Howard, an Australian
who enjoyed punting and travel and aroused Macmurray's attraction to
both. The other, much more intense, was with a brilliant South African

named Jan Hofmeyr with whom he shared constant conversation, as well as his Christian faith. Hofmeyr was a child prodigy from whose journey through his somewhat sad and relatively short life (he died at fifty-four) became the subject of a major biography by Alan Paton, author of *Cry the Beloved Country*. In 1909, at the age of fifteen, he graduated with first-class honours, and was awarded a Rhodes Scholarship. It was decided to "halt the boy in his headlong course," so he did not go to Oxford until 1913. In anticipation of Hofmeyr's arrival, A.L. Smith, a Senior Fellow who was to succeed Strachan Davidson as Master in 1916, had told senior undergraduates that a very important person was coming from South Africa and that he might one day be prime minister there. What he eventually thought of England might depend on them!

Sometime that autumn, Macmurray and Hofmeyr met on the stairs on their way to a meeting of the Student Christian Movement (SCM). In addition to being non-Anglicans, John and "Hoffie" soon found they had much else in common including their Presbyterian backgrounds and a conviction that their Christian faith should make a difference in shaping the world. Both of them found the students who came from the British public schools a real trial, so the maverick attitude they formed towards the dominant culture at Oxford was firmly in place very early in the year. Macmurray loved talking ideas with Hofmeyr and it was a common thing to see them walking arm in arm in the quadrangle in intense discussion with one another. They would talk, as John recalled, in the "most fundamental terms." Nevertheless, as John confessed to Betty, he found it difficult to be intimate with Hofmeyr. Conversation at a personal and emotional level did not flower between the two young men despite their shared religious and intellectual interests.

Despite these limitations, together they hatched a plan to revitalize the SCM, and because of their style of thinking, both were soon looked on as heretics. Walter Paton, an assistant secretary for SCM of Great Britain and Ireland, had visited the Oxford SCM that autumn and buttonholed Hofmeyr and Macmurray for some significant talks once he heard how prominent they were choosing to be in shaping SCM directions at Oxford. In a January 9, 1914 letter to his friend and colleague, Reverend Roberts, Paton wrote in part:

> I saw a good deal of Macmurray and Hofmeyr. Macmurray is an awfully sound chap, he has obviously developed very greatly since his earlier days at Glasgow when his Plymouth Brother [*sic*] proclivities used to cause difficulties at the Bible circles.

The Paton letter to Roberts is enlightening for another reason. In a postscript Paton writes: "I've been thinking a lot about you leaving

Crouch Hill [Presbyterian Church]," and he goes on to express the hope that Roberts will not stop being a member of a church-related group with which he has served as a key member. From other sources we know that Roberts was deeply associated with the Free Church Fellowship at that time; in fact, he had introduced Macmurray to it. Roberts was a courageous man in presenting his ideas and convictions. After war began in 1914 and his German-speaking parishioners suddenly stopped coming to church, Roberts gave a sermon at Crouch Hill Presbyterian recommending that the congregation embrace a radical Christian pacifism. For his pains, his furious congregation encouraged him to seek perfection elsewhere than in their pulpit. So as 1914 wound down, Roberts, without a church appointment, was planning for the kind of ministry he felt was needed at the time. He was helping to lay the foundations for the Fellowship of Reconciliation (FOR) during those months, and early in 1915 he became the secretary for the new organization.

Macmurray had been studying German on his own, and was planning throughout the spring of 1914 to go to Germany that summer with his Australian friend Arthur Howard. As Betty reports in her memoir notes, "John was at Littlehampton when the review of our fleet at Portsmouth was just over. He saw the British fleet leaving Portsmouth to take up a battle position in the event of war." These events, as well as acceding to a request from his father that he tutor a young man who needed academic help, made John put off going to Germany. His friend Arthur Howard made the trip regardless and ended up being interned in Germany for the length of the war.

During the year, John continued to write poetry. There is one love sonnet, written in London in September 1914, where he shows hints of the modern sensibility that is taking shape in him, and shows signs of the attention he had given to Robert Browning's poetry over the three or four previous years. It begins:

> It was your beauty netted my desire
> In our love's soft first dawn among the pines.
> How my eyes yearned along the tender lines
> That framed your face against a wild white briar!
> Your motion played upon me. Hidden mines
> Of hunger in me, stirred to strange designs
> Burst at your touches into flaming fire.

The marks of the past are clearly there, but so too are signs of greater suppleness of line and a certain immediacy of feeling. However, he seems to lose the new gains almost entirely as he moves into his closing sextet:

> O Love, I paid my life for your embrace,
> And I revelled in the princely prize,
> Softly unveiling higher, holier grace
> You hushed me to a wonderful surmise.
> Till now, before the inmost altar-place
> I wait and pray with unuplifted eyes.

Ironically, it was precisely this treatment of Betty as a holy object and himself as unworthy slave that had so irritated Betty during their summer of courting in 1911. She recalled with understanding but also with fatigue, how he would simply touch her hand or give her the most discreet of embraces and feel as though their relationship had been consummated by the touch. She apparently had no such confusions. Although not prepared, or perhaps even able at this time, to challenge him in such a delicate area of feeling, she, far more than he, began intuiting from these situations the differences in their natures, differences that would become much more pronounced for her as time went on.

However, there is one poem, the last poem of that period in his life, written on September 24, 1914, in which Macmurray breaks loose from the idyllic vise and allows himself to feel something of his immense sadness and the potential ultimacy in his leaving her and going to war. It is filled with a sense of the unmentioned crisis of history that has enveloped Betty and him, and their hoped for life together. It is among the most emotionally honest of his early poems. It remains utterly disciplined despite the profound feeling that imbues it. The choice of luxuriant language seems deliberate in order to heighten the starkness revealed in the final verse. And yet the feeling is in no way veiled by the language; rather, it is even more revealed because of the tension he creates:

> Wilt thou forget me? Why should'st thou remember
> Old faded feelings which young life has torn,
> Old garments of the soul, road-stained and worn,
> The dawny kisses of one dear December;
>
> The days when waking Love, one sweet September,
> Lifted her lashes among the fresh-mown corn;
> The sun-flushed breaking of our bridal morn,
> The altar-fire, the incense and the ember.
>
> Or wilt thou rather, when my face has faded
> Beneath a misty past's engulfing sea,
> These soft blue eyes by drooping lashes shaded
> Lean glad towards some dearer lover's pleas,

> And through shy lips with purest passion laded
> Whisper "Dear heart, I never loved but thee."

It is a poem that forcefully reveals the young man as something other than a mere shepherd-boy in his emotional self-awareness. He felt deeply, and here he allows himself to push to the cruel and bitter end an image of not only loss, but the most gentle and cool betrayal of what to him feels so sacred, fixed and eternal. To have a sacred love ended by a bullet was one thing. To visualize it ending as a victim of a calculated denial of the love that had been posing as naive innocence, that was much harder to consider. Only rarely, it seems, did Macmurray voluntarily allow himself to go down to this raw place where ambivalent emotions play in the soul. And even more rarely did he choose to express it openly.

When war was declared John went to see his pastor and advisor, Richard Roberts, and asked him if he should enlist. Roberts was against it. John heard Roberts through, including Roberts' reasons for his own pacifism, then left. His doctor too thought he should postpone any decision. Macmurray didn't consult his parents. His father always considered him not very strong so John couldn't expect them to favour his joining the army. There is no record of correspondence between John and Betty on this particular point, or on any of the traumatic events which were about to take place, since, by agreement, they destroyed all the correspondence they received during those years before they boarded the ship for South Africa in January, 1921. He went back to Oxford and stayed with the Master of Balliol, Strachan Davidson, hoping to find some war work in Oxford. Nothing was forthcoming so he returned to London and joined the Royal Army Medical Corps (RAMC) because, although still unsettled in his mind about pacifism, he was not yet prepared to join a fighting unit. If his health was still not good, it remains a puzzle how he was accepted into any part of the active war effort, even the Medical Corps.

Training for combat

Britain sent an Expeditionary Force to France immediately. The British Army just as immediately began occupying many locations in the south east of England for training thousands of new recruits and preparing them for quick despatch to the Continent. John was assigned to the 40th Field Ambulance Unit and was sent to Salisbury Plain which remained his headquarters until he was shipped to the front midway through 1915. The only letter we have from his early days in training was written to Richard Roberts on October 2, 1914 from Tidworth Park Camp:

I have had neither time nor facilities for writing until now. I was
sent to Aldershot first and then a few days later to Tidworth. The
whole time seems to have been employed in a steady fight of wits
and force to appropriate a fair share of rather scanty and ill-
organised provisions. We are in tents, sleeping on the ground, and
since yesterday have three blankets each. Previously we had one,
then two. The first night was awful, a night to be remembered.
Fancy 200 men in a lecture room, just large enough to give them all
laying space on the floor. The room had been smoked in viciously
for two hours and a half before bedtime. A large proportion of the
men looked as if they had never washed since the day they were
born. The language was lurid. Some of the scum could swear in six
colours. It ended in a dozen of us leaving together and sleeping (as
far as we could through our shiver-fits) in a cow shed with one side
open, on top of some planks, with one blanket apiece. That was
miserable. But our condition has steadily improved.

   Drilling and marching and field lectures in frost [word illegible]
are the order of the day. We rise at 5:30 or 6, crawl naked under a
pump and then get a jam-jar of tea: after which we parade and go
for a morning run before breakfast in column over the hills. Two
parades after breakfast: one for drill, one for a lecture: in the
afternoon we go for a route march of 4 or 5 miles.

   It is a healthy hard life. A touch of frost means an uncomfortable
night: there is no time for thinking or reading — no tables or
chairs: food which is not in the best French style served in
makeshift dishes &c. But I am enjoying it. We have a good tent:
three are R.C.s, of the rest two are intending to be clergy. (One of
the remarkable things about camp is the prevalence of the religious
element amongst the better class of recruits.) We have prayers
every night. I take them for Protestants: another fellow for the
R.C.s.

   From all that I can gather we will take the field next spring: and
military opinion seems to be that the armies will rest for the winter.
They say that the war will certainly not be over before we get to
the front. As for the ethics of the thing; the idealism and even the
progress of events — it is lost to sight here in the dust of
preparation.

   Kindest regards to Mrs Roberts and the children,
                     Ever yours,
                     John Macmurray

The letter is cram-packed with nuggets, not all of them shiny. It contains
an unusually graphic description of the daily routine of the recruits. It also

gives us a glimpse into the cultural jolt Macmurray received in being thrust among these men. His own family was not high class, but it did have a strong sense of proprieties and manners. The word "scum" is not one we would expect to come from his pen in a description of how he sees and feels about other people, no matter what their smells or language. So the pump at dawn was clearly not the only cold bath he was subjected to in these first days in the army. However, equally amazing is his openness and suppleness, of body, mind and spirit. He is already enjoying the rigour of training (where is his poor health now?). He sees the goodness of people and the quality of their spirits. Professor Phillmore was right; Macmurray was indeed teachable.

The toughest part of the letter to read many years later is, of course, its last paragraph. "Military opinion" was already showing itself dead wrong in its estimation of how this war would be fought. There was no winter "rest" (as in days of yore); and there was indeed a continuance of fighting beyond the spring, as predicted. As for the ethics of the thing, as time went by there was only a progressive dehumanization of the perspectives, methods and values by which the war was waged and in the ways that the British civilian population responded to Germany.

That winter, the recruits among whom Macmurray found himself were billeted in Paignton, South Devon. He stayed with a Mrs Harper at 6 Croft Terrace from where he wrote on December 22 to Roberts. He says he is getting ready for his first six-day leave and will be going to Aberdeen, with a possible stopover in London on the way back during which he hopes to be in touch with Roberts. He tells Roberts that he finds the British public and the press behaving in a very troubling manner:

> What a queer anomaly of a Christmas this will be, with
> Christendom out to kill. I can do no thinking under these
> conditions: only week after week I just feel a steadier pressure of
> the hopelessness of expecting this war to end war or do anything
> but weaken the whole moral resistance of Europe. The Press has
> been shameful, and the people have been only too ready to learn to
> slander and hate and boast blatantly. It makes one feel that the
> country is hardly worth fighting for. Though that, of course, is a
> Pagan calculation.

The perception he offers here remains with him: that people who call themselves Christians have become not the opponents of boasting, slander and hatred but their propagators, and they somehow feel strengthened in loyalty to the country by cultivating this darkness of spirit. This anomaly will come up again and again for him over the coming four years, and on one occasion it will prove to be critical in his personal

development. He is already thinking that the war will produce some serious reflection and writing for him even though he knows it is not yet
time for that. He continues to express the view as he did earlier in his
journal that this society and the church in this society have lost their
moral bearings.

John did get to Aberdeen where he visited Betty and her mother as well
as Duncan and Duncan's new wife Mary. Mary was a Kincardineshire girl,
a good bit older than Duncan. She had been a kind of companion-helper
in the Campbell home, and that's where Duncan had come to know her. At
this time they were all living in a small house called Carmount Cottage on
a quiet street in Stonehaven, fifteen miles south of Aberdeen. In a
February 1915 letter to Helen, Duncan Campbell inquires about her health
and then asks "How is your witty sister, Mary?"; the sole reference to
Mary in anyone's saved correspondence. John's visit "at the New Year"
was mentioned, then Duncan complains about having to ask her for all the
news because "John isn't very good at giving family history."

Later that spring, Helen came to visit John in Paignton where they
spent what John called wonderful time together. It was, as he recalled for
her in a letter many months later, "a holiday memorable to me no less than
to you; one of the happiest, freest times of my life." Perhaps this holiday
brought back to him the glorious summer days they had spent together as
children at Racks, exploring nature and wordlessly forming the bond of
love that would last between them for a lifetime.

By the early summer of 1915, the drilling and forced marches diminished and gave way to training in more specialized and useful skills.
Macmurray had been transferred to the 58th Field Ambulance, 'A' Section,
and was now located in No. 1 Camp, Sling, near Salisbury. In addition to
his training as an orderly, Macmurray reports in a May 27 letter to Helen
that he has become proficient in Morse and Semaphore — with flags,
lamp and heliograph — and is still working to improve his receiving
skills. He has also been:

> ... reading up principles of tactics, strategy and administration. All
> this in preparation for my new sphere of service. For it is pretty
> certain now that I am to get a commission shortly. The only
> obstacle — the permission of the C.O. here — I passed
> successfully this morning, and Sandy Lindsay wrote to say that if I
> could get this, he could easily get me a commission. Don't mention
> it to Father or Mother or indeed to anybody. It is just possible that
> there may be a hitch somewhere yet.

The letter goes on to explain that because of a recent decision, out of the
two thousand men in the five field ambulances at Salisbury two hundred

are to be transferred to Infantry. The decision, he surmises, is due to the relatively small number of casualties amongst the RAMC at the front, which has left the army with a larger medical service than it requires. They were cutting the medical corps down partly to get more fighting soldiers and because of the difficulty in procuring officers for fighting units. In fact, John's commission did not come through because he withdrew his application. He was convinced that once the second army arrived in France the war would end in a month or two and felt he could serve the army as well where he was in the ambulance corps.

In this letter John commiserates with Helen. The man she loved, a young German named Hermann who had come to England to work and study and whom she was planning to marry, had been forced by the war to leave England and become part of the German fighting forces. Soon after her holiday with John in Paignton, Helen was informed that Hermann had been killed in action. It devastated the shy girl and the pain threw her even more deeply into her natural introversion, a depression from which, it could be said, she never fully recovered. At the end of this same letter John asks Helen to send a postcard to Betty who will be taking her final exams for her degree in a short time, just to cheer her up. He then tells his sister:

> Sandy [Lindsay] sent me a book of Toynbee's on Nationality and the war — an attempt to reconstruct the map of Europe in a practical fashion on the supposition that the Allies win and agree to treat Germany with consideration and kindliness. I shall send you the book when I have read it, just to glance at. It is pretty good in some ways, but rather laughable. His attempts at being practical are so thoroughly Utopian.

Macmurray wants to start thinking about these things but in this instance the idealism of Toynbee is not believable to him when it runs into the vengeful attitudes he sees taking shape in British society. What he believes must give way is the utopianism. This mild attack on Toynbee represents only the beginning of a steady demythologizing of the idealism that was the regular philosophical air he breathed at Balliol just a short time before. He can sense already that the war will demolish it entirely.

Close to the front

In August 1915, the 58th Field Ambulance of RAMC had joined the 19th Division of the British Expeditionary Force in France near Merville where John was immediately put in charge of a small, four-bed hospital for officers. He wrote to his sister from this camp on August 9 asking her to send him two things: a bit more money so he can buy some food to supplement the poor army rations, and the first volume of Thomas Carlyle's *Frederick the Great*. He tells her to try for a cheap copy and even directs her to Charing Cross Road in London where secondhand bookstores would probably have it. The rest of the letter, he acknowledges, must sound as if it is coming from a holiday resort since life in France to that time had been rather gentle on Macmurray and his RAMC mates. They had been spending an inordinate amount of time just swimming, but he predicts this idyllic existence is on the verge of coming to an end. He also reports to her on his first sighting, well in the distance, of an air battle between squadrons of planes. The copy of Carlyle came in short order, followed soon by the other two volumes of the work, and over the weeks of late autumn going into winter John would escape during his off-time to a small upstairs room which he used as a study. He had put large maps on the walls and there he gave himself to the study of Frederick the Great. This hideaway was discovered by an officer in charge who removed John's small heater, making it impossible for him to continue using the room.

His letter to Helen on September 12 for her birthday thanks her for the three books. The letter itself is entirely given to consoling her in her pain over Hermann's death and expressing the belief that her suffering will, in the end, form a strength in her that will make deep love even more possible. It is painful to read this letter knowing that some years later Helen did move into another relationship which failed to compare with her first one. She married a man who was seen by other family members as sad and ineffectual, and who, knowing that his wife was far more endowed and refined than he, spent much of their married life diminishing her.

In connection with John's growing sense of being surrounded by death, there is a story about having a vision that he told over the years only to his family and very few close friends. There are minor discrepancies in the accounts that relate the story, but the jist of it went like this: He was in a tent filled with men, smelly and half-drunk, when out of the darkness a shadowy figure approached him and said: "You will not be killed in this war. You will return to help remake the world." As his wife Betty noted in her own diaries years later, this remained the most treasured prophecy of his life — "to remake the world;" so like the Hebrew phrase: *tikkun olam*, to mend or heal the world. In Professor David Cairns' account years later, the remaking referred specifically to creating a philosophy.

His October 6, 1915 letter to Helen contains the only testimony outside his journals of the feeling he had for how his own weakness and God's strength were intertwined in him during his painful journey through his university years. He shares that part of his life with his beloved sister because she believes his strength is simply natural to him — a strength from which she has benefited so much. He writes frankly and with great vulnerability — as a gift to her — to let her know how much suffering and effort went into whatever is seen in him as "strength." The letter ends with news of many things:

> ... last night old Burrows was over from the 59th who had all the luck. Four of their men were severely wounded, and two have been recommended for the DCM [Distinguished Combat Medal] by Bramhall. Twice they were shelled out of their dressing station, and hair-breadth escapes came to everybody. They did marvels, I believe: the fighting Colonel in the trenches wanted to mention them all, and old Bramhall could hardly contain his joy. Seventy-two hours at a stretch they did, with no sleep. Heroes all! Perhaps we shall get our chance soon — in the second phase of the great battle, sounds of which are beginning to rise about us. If it succeeds it should mean a wholesale German retirement on the length of the front.

He goes on to give her his view of the battleline which is divided in two at Loos with on one side the British moving up to the Belgian coast and, on the other, the French heading towards Champagne in an intended double-flanking movement. In a subsequent letter he sends her good wishes for her upcoming holiday and wishes her some joyful music in place of the current "low sad music of humanity," scribbling out for her four bars of song in 6/8 time that he knew she would recognize.

Sometime in the autumn John Macmurray, No. 40540, was promoted to the rank of Lance Corporal and was sent with the 58th Field Ambulance to Loos. His assignment there, in simple terms, was to check whether the wounded needed the doctor's attention or could be seen by orderlies. But the more complex element in his job was the introduction of the evaluation procedure known as "triage." Slightly wounded men were cared for with some ease, usually by orderlies. But priority in treatment of seriously wounded men was determined not only on the basis of their chances for survival but also on their likelihood of being restored to fighting form. Restoring men to health so that they could return to the front was declared the top priority in giving treatment. It was in this setting of acute moral opportunism that Macmurray came to review his choice to be in the ambulance corps rather than in a fighting unit. If he was healing men only to fight again then his work was not "humanitarian" but simply one more aspect of the British fighting effort.

Early in December he became sick with what seems to have been a serious attack of influenza. His next letter to Helen came on December 10 from the Overflow Ward of No. 13 General Hospital in Boulogne. In the upper left-hand corner of the first page and swinging down to mid-page, he drew in excellent detail the fluttering flags of the five major nations of Europe involved in the conflict. He confesses that he has been depressed as well as ill, but has enjoyed the solitude, the first in fourteen months, that the war has afforded him. He gives her a vivid description of the muddy conditions and of a soldier who stepped into a huge shell hole and almost drowned in liquid mud. With regard to his commission which she must have been inquiring about he tells her "I still think I can serve the army better where I am," so he says he is not prepared to renew the application that he withdrew some months earlier:

> ... and I won't lick anybody's boots for promotion; and it pretty nearly comes to that. As for being killed or wounded, I should be rather glad of either. It would be a release. I don't count my life as of such great value to anybody that it should be spared. Indeed if anything would drive me to seek a transfer it would be the desire for a more dangerous post. I have enjoyed one night in France thoroughly, and that was the night I was under fire.

This is certainly a point where he deserves a little relief, or laughter, from someone who loves him. The signs of depression are clear in the self-centredness of his perspective here, to say nothing of the downright silliness, verging on offensiveness, of saying to this dear sister that his life is not "of such great value to anybody." He swings into a full paragraph on his readiness for death, and one must grant that there are signs in it of a deep spiritual freedom as well as depression. There is much to admire in the letter, including the focus he takes at the end:

> ... Only I do want to do work; heavy, hard work that uses up all one's best energy and counts in this fight for peace and liberty and cleanness of life. This is what I see worth while, and only this, — with the big stern Love that is the heart of it. Yet I should have no regrets if I found that service only here and death for England's honour at the end of it; nor should I wish you to have pain either.

Although he was on the mend at the time, he was still not back in action by Christmas Day when Helen's next letter arrived at his bed in "I" Company's No. 1 Convalescent Depot in Boulogne. He answers her immediately, rushing to share with her a poem that he read recently, written by H.C. Harwood, an acquaintance of his at Balliol. "There is no need to tell you that it is powerful ... and there is scarcely a line of it that I have not dreamed myself; though there is a note of bitterness and antagonism that I never read into my thoughts." He makes a point of noting — with her dear Hermann in mind — that the title "From the youth of all nations" includes German youth.

He quotes the poem in full, so moved is he by its insight, honesty, and bite. It begins:

> Think not, my elders, to rejoice
> when from the nations' wreck we rise
> With a new thunder in our voice
> And a new lightning in our eyes.
>
> You called with patriotic sneers
> And drums and sentimental songs.
> We came from out the vernal years
> Thus bloodily to right your wrongs.
>
> The sins of many centuries
> Sealed by your ignorance and fright
> Have earned us these our agonies:
> the thunderous appalling night,
>
> When from the lurid darkness came
> the pains of poison and of shell
> The broken heart, the world's ill-fame
> The lonely arrogance of hell.

The poem goes on for ten more stanzas with equal punch, and ends fiercely:

> And on the brooding weary brows
> Of stronger sons, close enemies,
> Is writ the ruin of your house
> and swift usurping dynasties.

John underlines words and phrases in the poem — in stanzas not quoted here — that struck him sharply, and refers to them as he tries to explain why he finds the poem so true:

> I can recall the very day when I 'passed the Styx' as he puts it. I have seen Kitchener's army growing 'bitter with the truth.' That phrase is tragically right. The songs are gone. The old army — what is left of it — still cheers itself with its obscenity. Kitchener's has simply grown silent and grim, and little by little it is growing

bitter. What can you expect? I wonder whether it is fair to put it in its
bare ghastliness? Only to you ... But men grow to love one another
with a strange intensity out here. And then a man has to sweep up
the remains of his friend with a brush and shovel — and it won't half
fill an empty sand-bag. That's IT! Can you wonder that they curse
under their breath when some fool tries to sing "Tipperary", or that
the bitterness comes into their souls? What will it be [like] if there
are another twelve months, or more even, to be endured?

O Ella! I think I can sympathize with the great souls who would
leave Germany to wreak her will and only trust in God ... Surely the
man, the nation to whom power has been given, is the minister of
God to execute judgment for the oppressed and fatherless. If I change,
it is that I wish I were in the full horror of it, to share the worst ...

Helen has sent him a short quotation from Francis Thompson which he
receives as a Christmas gift and calls "a draught of clear water (Do you
know that I have not had one in five months?)." He signs off saying he
"must write to Hydie."

To the Cameron Highlanders

By March, it is clear Macmurray had left Loos and had spent many weeks
at the front where he did taste the full brunt of things. He decided to
reawaken his application for a commission. In his letters at the time — as
we just saw — he says he is drawn to join a fighting unit in order "to share
the worst." Much later in life and thinking of the triage norms that ruled
in the ambulance tents, he said with typical understatement that he had
simply concluded that he "was as much a part of a fighting organization
as if he had been in the firing line," so he felt he might as well be in combat. He had written to Sandy Lindsay asking him once again, as his Balliol
tutor, to recommend him for a commission and a change to a fighting unit.
In it we sense the reasons why he is compelled to act now.

In spite of the weather, the work at the line was what I enjoyed
best. You feel you are in things there. You are among the guns and
going to and from the trenches, getting potted at by unseen
Germans, and dodging shrapnel and Jack Johnson. The luck of the
Ambulance has become almost proverbial ... Only last week a shell
burst actually in the dispensary at one of our dressing stations, a
room about ten feet square, where there were several men at work,
and not one was injured and only one suffered from concussion.
Everybody marvels at our fortune.

With regard to the renewal of his request for endorsement he confesses somewhat sheepishly to Lindsay:

> And still the war lingers on. I thought in my foolishness last summer, that when the new armies got out, the war would be over in a month or two. And now, though the end seems to be coming out of the dimness, nobody seriously feels sure that it can end this year.

The March 14, 1916 letter (misdated March 14, 1914!) was only one of several that passed between the two men as they discussed with hope, and scepticism, the actual possibilities for "the furtherance and maintenance of the organization for peace." He reflects on an issue that has already concerned the two of them some months earlier over the Toynbee book:

> There seems to be a good deal in Snowden's contention in the House that the utter defeat of German arms might not be such a guarantee of future peace as a settlement ... I have a fear of the results of a German debacle because of the bitterness of the French especially. Will the British sense of justice be a sufficient counterfoil?

This prophetic apprehension he feels ('prophetic' because it so closely anticipates the spirit that was finally in play at Versailles) will remain with him throughout the rest of the war. He, on the other hand, is not approving any kind of cheap conciliation, any resolution that overlooks or denies the realities of spirit and justice at the heart of the struggle:

> Peace can be bought too dear: even the future peace of the world can be bought too dear if we are to mortgage our spiritual possessions for it. There must be no suggestion of yielding for a moment to wrong and injustice; and with the strong duty to punish. I have admired the way in which the governments have stood their ground against much hostile criticism on one side and another: refusing to yield to the military power for power's sake partly in the question of the blockade and on the other question of conscription. They have really done their utmost to prevent the ideal which was the starting point of the war for us from slipping away in the longing to get this business over and done with. I like the way they have steadily refused to exact reprisals according to the law of Moses, an eye for an eye, a tooth for a tooth.

Perhaps out of fatigue over the current intractability of the situation he allows his spirit to dream somewhat lyrically in the presence of his friend and tutor:

> It is comforting anyhow to remember that it will end somehow, even if it does issue in a troubled period of evil life. No doubt we shall have to let the softness of life go, and all the beauties that belong to twilight-time. Austerity will have to take the place of delicacy: strength will have to replace tenderness; courage will be instead of sentiment. But we shall have the morning glory; the frank, cool air and the lark's song, with man going forth to his labours in the great fields, the beginning rather than the aging of an epoch. And with God's help we shall have strength to do our work.

Macmurray closes the letter with an interesting political confession, the main features of which will remain a developing issue for him for years, especially during the 1930s when he encountered the thought of Karl Marx, supported the Russian experiment, and confronted the rise of Fascism:

> By-the-bye, my experience with men out here has undermined my faith in Socialism as a practical creed. You get to know men here in a way that you can't at home, even in Coll. And though it tends to kindliness and sympathy, at the same time it makes you doubt whether it is at all safe to trust them to deal with large intricate problems, or even to pass judgment on the results of others' dealing. Am I turning Conservative or what? It seems to me that all these men that I know and thoroughly like, are quite incapable of passing judgment on any subject that is not entirely within the range of their own experience and training. Especially my attempts to get working men amongst them to subordinate their class idea to the idea of a state that includes it, has often been met by the statement that to do so seems honestly to them to be playing the traitor to their fellow workers. Doesn't that cut at the roots of all democratic government?
>
> I had better stop or I shall go on yarning all night, and I have to get up and see that nobody gets too much of the tea rations. *Sic itur ad astra* [Such is our journey to the stars].
> > Yours ever sincerely,
> > > John Macmurray
> > > (40540) L/Cpl. RAMC
> > > 58th F. A.

Although no paper trail is available for what transpired during the next few months, it is clear that Lindsay supported Macmurray's application. John was sent to cadet school for training before being granted his commission. The exhaustive listing of the alumni of the Aberdeen Grammar School includes John Macmurray's name, and records that he received his commission as a Second Lieutenant on June 1, 1916 and was transferred to the Queen's Own Cameron Highlanders. He was assigned to the Seventh Battalion, and went immediately to the Somme to join the men he would be leading. His own quiet words in the Swarthmore Lecture almost fifty years after the event capture that moment starkly:

> After I was commissioned I went alone to join my platoon on the Somme. I found the men I was to command in a reserve trench, well behind the front line. It was a quiet evening, and I had walked over a mile of open ground to reach them. They were having tea; and I joined them in an angle of the trench. I sat with one of them on one side of the corner, a second was sitting at the corner itself, jesting with a third who was just round the corner so that I could hear but not see him. A few minutes after I had sat down we heard the whine of a shell coming towards us. It landed in our trench, just around the corner, and exploded. When the smoke cleared my neighbour and I rushed to the corner to see what had happened. We found the man round the corner dead — almost cut in two by a flying shard. The man at the corner was bleeding profusely. We shouted for stretcher-bearers, and they took him away, but it seemed unlikely that he could live. Of the four or us who had been talking together a moment before, two were left. As my introduction to the life of a fighting man in the trenches, it was, of course, a shock. But very soon that sort of thing was commonplace — part of the routine of daily life.

Macmurray was citing this story in the context of telling his audience what he had shared with his sister Helen in his letter to her six months before: that he was becoming familiar with death and was losing his fear of it. As he noted simply to his audience in 1964: "For the combatant soldier it [death] is not an idea; it is a stark, ever-present, unavoidable fact." The effect of this experience was to shape his attitude to life, of course, but more specifically to shape his religious development. He recalls this religious transformation, and articulates the nature of his change in this way:

> In the field of theory, of belief, nothing happened. It was as though such questions had been put into cold storage 'for the duration.'

> Religion, however, and therefore religious development is not
> primarily a matter of beliefs. The beliefs, so far as they are real, are
> derivative. The real religion from which they are derived, lies in the
> depths of one's own being; its development is a development of
> one's personality itself. Through the experience of war I moved a
> long way towards my own reality.

In later years, as a philosopher, Macmurray proposed that there are only
two fundamental motives in human beings: love and fear. As he saw it,
fear is ideally and appropriately subordinate to love as an intentional
dimension in human action. In retrospect, there can be no doubt that he
was helped by his daily life in the trenches in achieving his understanding
of their proper relationship.

Apparently, the awareness of death didn't colour everything, or it got
put into the background sometimes by more immediate interests. Long
after the war, Macmurray laughingly told his friend Kenneth Barnes of an
incident when one of the British soldiers shot down a duck that was flying
over the trenches and it fell in no-man's-land. Macmurray decided to fetch
the potential dinner. He crawled out, retrieved the duck, and was just about
to crawl over his parapet when a German machine gun opened fire. As he
came over the edge he could feel the bullets ripping through his kilt. He
also, on occasion, took walks at night in no-man's-land with a sergeant
who loved talking about philosophy. One night they were hailed in
German from a very short distance away, and they discovered to their
shock that, in the darkness, they had come right to the edge of the German
trenches. They threw themselves flat on the ground by the German sand-
bags just as the German guard, no more than a few yards from them, shot
a flare into the sky. The German soldier must have used the flare to check
the full breadth of no man's land. In looking out over the full field of
vision, he missed the two Brits lying at his head-level, just a few feet away,
apparently too close to be seen.

The sheer closeness of the opposing forces revealed in this story created at times an understanding and even sympathy between them as well.
Macmurray tried to explain this fellow-feeling to his Swarthmore audience almost sixty years later:

> I remember one night in the frontline, where we had been
> enjoying a quiet time, with a Saxon regiment opposite. We had
> been carrying on our war on the principle, "Don't bother us and
> we won't bother you." On this night a Saxon soldier on patrol
> slipped over to our trench and dropped a card on us. It read — in
> English — "Watch out! The Prussians are taking over
> tomorrow."[2]

Marriage in wartime

Sometime during that summer John and Betty hatched the idea of getting married very soon rather than waiting for the war to be over. John made his request to Command, specifying that it was in order to get married. He was granted leave in early October for three days only, including travel, since the fighting at the Somme was raging and he was needed there. When he arrived in London they quickly bought a wedding ring. It was too big for Betty's finger and needed to be adjusted later. In fact it never quite fitted and she unfortunately lost the ring while playing in the leaves with her nephew in France some twenty years later.

The tiny wedding party, with John's sister Lilias as the main witness, kept its October 9 morning appointment with the Justice of the Peace, but the marriage was almost derailed by John's integrity. The office was in Westminster and was validated only for weddings of persons living within that area. When the information was taken on the couple, John was asked for his address and he gave it as 70 Crouch Hill, the family home, which was in North London. The official thundered: "That's not in Westminster!" Childlike, John responded: "But that's where I live." The impatient functionary turned on him with irritation: "Do you want to get married or not?" A Westminster address was quickly found and the marriage took place. To her last days, Betty preferred to refer to it as their "elopement" — and in one sense that's what it was. Their only wedding gift was a dozen silver fish knives and forks given by a friend of Betty's. They had pork pie as their marriage lunch, and tried to have pork pie on each anniversary thereafter. They spent their honeymoon night at the Randolph in Oxford. Curiously, the marriage certificate contains John's proper address, but lists his age as twenty-six. On October 9, 1916 he was still twenty-five.

John rushed back to France the next day to rejoin his men in the bitter fighting taking place on the Somme battlefield. After only a short time back in France, he suffered a severely sprained ankle (later diagnosed as an injury that probably included a broken bone). He was returned to England and spent three weeks in hospital after which he was released on sick-leave. Since Betty had taken a teaching position in a private girls' school in the south of England and was thoroughly busy, he went to convalesce in Stonehaven where he joined Duncan's wife Mary with her new son Duncan Ian at the home of Mary's mother and her second husband, Mr Pyper.

There, at Carmount Cottage, while his foot was still healing, he was granted a period of peace and tranquillity which he thoroughly enjoyed, and which allowed him to put some focus on his life. There was work for his hands, but there was also, for the first time in months, the chance to do some serious writing. On January 24, 1917 he tells Helen:

I have apprenticed myself to Mr Pyper here as a carpenter. It is a
trade with a glorious roll of honour from Noah downwards. He
makes cartwheels while I make photo frames, but we use the same
tools.

My other work — of writing — proceeds rather slowly. I have
finished an article on 'Trench religion,' and intend to proceed with
one called 'The old men and the young men,' which will be
concerned chiefly with the new 'spiritualism' which we used to
trace [?] before the war, and the effects which the war is likely to
have upon it. I have plenty of others in the corners of my brain, and
I dub this lot 'Leaves from a trench philosophy.' When I get several
completed I shall offer them to some of the more serious
magazines, and have them rejected as unmarketable, but never
mind! You will read them, anyhow, and I imagine you will find
them interesting, if only because you are disproportionately fond of
your brother.

This letter reveals that Duncan finally did enlist in 1916, and John gives
Helen Duncan's address in France where he is with the First London
Scottish Regiment. Duncan Ian, the first child of Duncan and Mary, was
filling the house with new life:

Baby is delightful, and quite fond of his Uncle John. The
appellation makes me feel old. It sounded quite startling at first. He
makes me want one of my own so much! Mary is well and very
charming. Beyond these two I have no acquaintances and don't feel
like knowing anyone.

He ends his letter commenting on a burst of heaviness about the state of
things that Helen must have shared with him. It shows some of the new
sharp edge that Macmurray's judgment is developing even though his
spirit remains profoundly positive:

Don't worry about the world. It is too catastrophic for any big
disaster to add appreciably to its 'tragedy,' and too full of an
increasing purpose to be wrong at heart. All that a mighty outburst
of destruction can do is to show it [to] us for what it is, and for that
let us thank it. We do not wish to found our life on any fallacy. We
have to learn faith in spite of fatality, and love in spite of subtle
enmities. Else these would lose their point, and death regain its
sting. Don't let's forget either that *we* invented gunpowder and took
it to our bosoms. We are hoist with our own petard this time. The
Chinese don't get blown sky-high in hundreds.

He wishes her joy in her walk to Brighton, then closes: "And beware of the village Inns. They look well, but they charge damnably!" Then signs off:

Yours in transcendent affection
John Macmurray

The article called "Trench Religion" he refers to here is Macmurray's first identifiable piece of published writing. He sent it to a review but had heard nothing from them about it. It saw the light of day only in 1919, not as a named article but as an anonymous few pages in a book entitled *The Army and Religion: An Enquiry and its Bearing upon the Religious Life of the Nation*. The book, put together under YMCA auspices and edited by a hugely prestigious committee, was a collection of soldiers' responses to questions concerning the effects of war on their religion. There followed a courageous and incisive conclusion written by the principal editor Professor David S. Cairns, on the severe challenge extended to the churches by these testimonies. In a nutshell, it was really another take, only this time from a religious perspective, on "the hypocrisy of the elders and their social institutions" as expressed by Siegfried Sassoon, Robert Graves, Robert Nichols, Edmund Blunden and Wilfred Owens in many of their poems, and by Macmurray's Balliol acquaintance, H.C. Harwood, quoted earlier. Without dealing with the questions in turn, since he had already thought deeply about them on his own and written about them, Macmurray simply sent the committee his already written article and left it to them to use his material as they saw fit. Macmurray's approach in his short piece was grim:

> The comradeship with Death is the most potent but not the only
> circumstance of the battlefield which alters the spiritual balance.
> The limbo of the soldier's vaguer feeling is intensely coloured by a
> sense of unspeakable impotence in the face of gigantic forces of
> destruction. Nowhere, as in a great army, does a man's littleness and
> unimportance stare on him so startlingly. Nowhere, as on a
> battlefield, is there such evidence of the powerlessness of the
> mightiest human organization to protect his own small individuality.
> A millimetre's deflection in the laying of a gun is the difference
> between life and death to him. He knows how a shell will burst
> between two men, blowing one to pieces, yet leaving the other
> unhurt and amazed. He has crouched in holes in the earth, with
> earthy smells in his nostrils, and listened to the hum of a thousand
> unseen menaces under the placid stars. What eats his soul is the
> knowledge that all this violence is blind. Chance rules as an autocrat

in the metropolis of our most perfect mechanism. Is it strange that
the child of these conditions should be a thorough fatalist?[3]

He completes his statement with two compact reflections: one on the
direct relationship between freedom and responsibility in a soldier in
which he concludes: Diminish the first, and you necessarily diminish the
second; face up to it. The second addresses the image of God that "works"
in a battlefield setting:

> The soldier's God is once more the God of Battles, who clothes
> Himself with the storm. He is not the judge of righteousness and
> wrong, not the friend of the fatherless and the widow's protector,
> not holy, or just, or good, but simply the controller of all the
> forces of Nature which burst from the little grasp of man; the
> Lord of Fate and the Master of Life and Death ... What a man
> needs beyond his own power to command he seeks from
> Providence, and the soldier's prayer is for protection, for strength,
> for perennial spring of inspiration to courage. His God is one who
> can supply all these.[4]

Confronting the dark spirits

Such feeling, easily understood at the front and totally shocking in the
streets of London, points to the huge and growing differences between the
soldiers and the civilians at home. The difference will rise up dramatically
for Macmurray in a slightly different form just a few weeks after he wrote
this letter.

It is probably not accurate to describe this paragraph as the "completion" of Macmurray's statement. A careful reading of the book reveals
minimally half a dozen other excerpts attributed to "an officer in a Scottish
Regiment" that sound very much like Macmurray. It is reasonable to
assume that his longer article was cut up into fragments and made to fit
into the publication under the different thematic headings chosen by the
editors.

The most powerful story retained of his war years is arguably his own
account of a sermon he gave in early 1917 "in a church in North London"
— perhaps at Crouch Hill Presbyterian Church itself. The build-up within
himself to the sermon came from two sources: first, his growing conviction,
along with Lindsay and many others, that genuine peace must be based on
a genuine desire for reconciliation in Europe with just terms of surrender
being offered to the defeated party. Second, from what he had felt during
his first leave as a major change for the worse in public attitude and

sentiment in Britain. Perhaps the most vivid symbol of this on city streets was the arbitrary pinning — often by young women — of a white feather (the symbol of cowardice) on to the lapels of unsuspecting young men in civilian clothes as they walked by. It was a huge personal insult perpetrated out of a massive blindness to personal rights and decency, brought on by a darkness that the populace at large seemed bent on embracing. As he recalled almost fifty years later in his Swarthmore Lecture:

> I was shocked by the change in their attitude of mind. I felt as though an evil spirit had entered them, a spirit of malice and hatred. Before twenty-four hours had passed I wanted to get back to the trenches, where for all the misery and destruction, the spiritual atmosphere was relatively clean. It was, I think, the ignorant and superstitious hatred of the Germans, and the equally ignorant and unreal glorification of us, in the trenches, as heroes that had this effect. In France we were not heroes, nor expected to be; and we did not hate Germans, at least not the Germans in the trenches opposite. We understood them, and they understood us. We were sharing the same spurious and obscene life, no doubt with the same feelings ... A gulf had been fixed, it seemed, between ourselves and our friends and acquaintances in civilian life. We had ceased to understand each other. I can remember feeling, as I returned from this leave ... that now most of the pacifists were in the trenches.[5]

In the sermon he urged the congregation to distance themselves from a spirit of vengeance towards the Germans and to prepare themselves for the genuinely Christian work of reconciliation. As he told his Swarthmore Lecture listeners: "the congregation took it badly; I could feel a cold hostility menacing me; and no one spoke to me after the service was over."[6] This was an insult very few preachers ever had to endure. Moved deeply by this experience, which he perceived not as a rejection of him personally but a rejection of the Gospel in favour of self-righteous patriotism, Macmurray turned decisively away from any institutional affiliation for expressing his Christian faith. He went on to say in his Swarthmore account of the event:

> I was not, however, tempted to abandon religion. I justified my refusal to join a religious organization to myself — I had no desire to parade it — as a personal Christian protest against a spurious Christianity. I spoke and wrote thereafter in defence of religion and Christianity; but I thought of the churches as the various national religions of Europe.[7]

Much later in life when asked by his friend, Kenneth Barnes, about the reasons for his choice, he added other strategic dimensions to his primary vision and conviction: I did it, he said, to ensure that I would have complete freedom to think my own thoughts and express my own views without being compromised and without having to worry about embarrassing any colleagues. He held to this choice to follow Christ apart from membership in a church until 1959 when, the year after his retirement from the University of Edinburgh, he and his wife Betty joined the Quakers in Jordans where they had returned to live. In this decision we see in John Macmurray a willingness, perhaps even a preference, to choose his own path and even to walk alone, a choice that more than one colleague later on characterized as his "maverick" way of doing philosophy as well as living his life.

Macmurray returned to active service at the beginning of March but wasn't sent back to France directly. He went on army business to Invergordon, then Tillicoultry and finally to Stirling where he stayed for several weeks training boys under nineteen years of age. It was a very pleasant change from usual army work, he says to Richard Roberts on June 4, "because of the youthful keenness and ingenuousness of the boys. What a relief that is after growing accustomed to the evasions and correct incivility of the seasoned 'old soldier'." His friend Roberts had moved to the United States and was a pastor in Brooklyn, New York. Macmurray comments on the USA's entry into the war, wondering if it will shorten or prolong the war. He tells Roberts of the article he has written, and of the interest of the YMCA committee in the ideas he has expressed:

> I don't feel that I have much to tell them except the one portentous
> fact which burned itself into me — while some parts of trench life
> almost invariably produce an intense religious emotion, the men
> who experience that emotion seem rarely to have the slightest idea
> that the state of their minds has any conceivable connection with
> Christianity. I don't think that is too strong a statement and I think
> also that one can see reasons why it should be so. As to finding a
> remedy; it is beyond my powers. I don't think that people are very
> anxious for a remedy. The war is producing a reaction to comfort
> and somnolence. 'Let us alone' say they; 'we have had enough of
> fighting and disturbance for a life-time.' Is it very surprising? At
> the same time there will surely be individuals who will come out of
> the fight with a fiery determination not to let things rest until the
> disease which threw us into the indescribable futility of battle is
> diagnosed, and treated and cured, if that may be.

The paragraph reveals Macmurray's own appreciation of elements he believes must be faced if Europe is to find a way forward after the war. He is clearly comfortable already with identifying under the rubric of "religion" personal experiences that are quite unrelated to membership in a church. Apart from the huge contrast this distinction offers to the fervent evangelical he was just six years earlier, it is the first articulation we have of a perception that has been developing in him since that fateful year of 1912–13: namely that the genuinely religious is at one with the genuinely human. He does hope that the Christian churches might teach this as a basic truth of Christianity, but he notes that they have failed completely to accept this view or to convey it to their members. Religion for the typical Christian, as he finds confirmed at the front, is essentially to "do and say religious things." The result is a constant split in life: some experiences are called "religious" and others are not. There is no understanding, he complains, that *all* personal experience is open to a religious interpretation and expression. This analysis is the first phase of what flowers into his 1930s distinction between "true" and "false" Christianity.

His intuition that people preferred a respite and a time of comfort rather than facing the real challenges that confronted them was confirmed by much that would take place in the 1920s throughout Europe and America. He was aware, as we saw earlier, that a spirit of vengeance might dominate in formulating the terms for armistice, and he knew this would make justice and reconciliation impossible to achieve in Europe. During this prolonged stay in Britain, he was not given reason to be any less apprehensive on this score.

Arras: his final battle

There is no record of exactly when Macmurray returned to France, but when he got there in the summer of 1917 it seems evident that news of his teaching skills came with him and he was assigned to work in a school at the front for much of the next few months. The schoolwork, whatever it was he did there, was a consuming business that took his whole day from early morning till late at night. It included meeting people from every part of the front, Americans included, and a chance to form new friendships.

That spring, the Cameron Highlanders were among the many regiments (Camerons, Suffolks, Gordons, Seaforths, and so on), helping to hold the lines at Arras along the Arras-Cambrai road. On March 20, 1918, with a major German attack expected, he was returned to the trenches and was given command of B Company which was situated in the front lines. He was delighted to be back in the trenches where, as he put it, he had far more time to himself.

John wrote to Helen that day saying "things are fairly quiet in spite of all rumours about the famous German offensive." In fact, those "rumours" were based on firm information and expectations. In October 1917, the Bolsheviks had seized power in Petrograd and that had ended the fighting in the east due to the arrangement General Erich Ludendorff had made with Vladimir Lenin. In April 1917, Ludendorff had helped to shuttle Lenin from Switzerland to Finland, and at Brest-Litovsk in December he demanded his payment: control over Finland, the Baltic states, the Ukraine, and Crimea as far as the Caspian Sea. These demands were effectively in place by March of 1918. Ludendorff was now free to look westward for a final decision, and the Allies knew that. Ludendorff selected the Arras-St Quentin sector towards the Somme and Amiens as the point of primary attack for the so-called Michael offensive, viewing this section as the point of least resistance.[8]

That massive offensive and the fight that followed, known to military history as the Battle of Arras, was, in fact, to start the very next day. In that light, it is something between ironic and painful to read John's report to his sister of the upbeat spirit among the British troops, a report heightened by his own very positive feelings at the time he was writing:

> We are all in the best of spirits, and the men treat the German threat as a huge joke. In fact, we are so prepared morally as well as in defensive measures that there isn't the ghost of a chance for old Hindenburg and Ludendorff. I don't think they would manage to take our first line of trenches — and that is only the beginning!
>
> So cheer up and keep smiling. It may not be this year yet that we beat the Bosch but beat him we will, and thoroughly ... Would you believe that the morale of the British army is at least as good as it has ever been? That is no exaggeration. And its efficiency is, if anything, higher. There seems to be a tendency to pessimism at home. Well! You can take it from me that there is none out here.

He tells her that lately he has pondered a lot on Browning's lines about Dante and has felt the meaning of them:

> Dante, who loved well because he hated,
> Hated wickedness which hinders loving ...

> Sometimes I grow eager for a fight, face to face and bayonet to bayonet when I think of the months and months of love the makers of this war have robbed me of. And somehow I do not feel that it is a selfish, foolish hatred. There is a universality in it. And I don't forget, even though we should have been enemies on the field, that they robbed you too of your lover who was my friend. Poor little sister! I know that you don't forget; and I don't either.

In place of the customary long, deep assault lines that went over the top, Ludendorff deployed new infantry tactics featuring small groups of automatic riflemen, gas and smoke shells, and mobile artillery fire. The attack began with furious and unrelenting shelling at 2:00 am. 'B' Company came in for a good deal of the bombardment prior to the infantry attack and also much of the gas sent over in the dark hours before dawn. In a long letter to Helen a full month later — a letter accompanied by excellent sketches of the terrain and the lines that were under attack with a listing of the regiments, divisions and companies involved in the defence — John gives an extremely detailed description of the events that transpired between March 21 and 28. For the 28th, the day he was severely wounded, he gives an almost minute-by-minute account of his movements right down to the modified retreat manoeuvre he attempted with 'B' Company in order to get another shot at the Germans advancing to their left along the ridge, and to save 'B' Company from complete annihilation by being outflanked. It was a move he unfortunately was prevented from completing:

> Well! We got near where I wanted to be. I remember just starting to halt the men. I shouted the 'HALT' once only I think, and then something hit me on the side of the head — it felt like the side of a house; and I have only a confused memory of staggering along the remainder of the way in rear of the men, and ultimately walking into the trench where the Gordons were. They directed me to their aid-post after tying up my head, and I wandered off again for another half mile through another barrage until I found it. I can remember dashing across the corner of the road beside the aid-post after lying for some minutes in a ditch on the side of it, and scrambling up the bank on the other [side], while [sic] a big shell burst in the middle of the road about five yards behind me and pretty well blew me into the arms of a dear little American doctor, as cool as a cucumber. Then I collapsed and made a fool of myself, I think.

In all, three companies of the battalion were wiped out, including his own. But the mighty defensive effort had saved Arras, and it foiled Ludendorff's plan to drive the British against the Channel coast. Ludendorff had to seek his cherished breakthrough elsewhere, at Lys, and again between Soissons and Reims. It was a breakthrough the Allies never granted him. After see-saw attacks and ripostes throughout the spring and summer, the August 8 Allied attack, in which the British tanks, underestimated by Ludendorff, dealt the blow that was the beginning of the end for the German army and the exhausted German nation.

But for John Macmurray, as of March 28 the war was over. He had taken several pieces of shrapnel in his body and face, and surgery was required. A piece of steel hit him under the right cheek bone moved up his face, lodging finally between his eyes within a few millimetres of his optic nerve. As his wife remembered, some of the shrapnel was never removed because of the delicacy of attempting to do so. The doctors apparently weren't so delicate in presenting their case: "We could only remove it by taking his nose to pieces," she reports them saying.

Macmurray was carried to Arras, treated as well as possible, then shipped back to Britain for the first stage of his convalescence in Yorkshire. He was in No. 3 Northern General Hospital near Aberdeen a couple of weeks later when he wrote to Helen, on April 21, the letter that detailed so minutely the defence of Arras and his company's role in the battle. By this time he knew he was the only one of 'B' Company to survive and he confessed to Helen that he felt guilty for surviving since, as leader, he should have been the first to suffer what befell his men. This is not how Command saw it, however. Macmurray's presence of mind, his clever strategic intention, his solicitous leadership of his men and his bravery under fire were recognized. For his gallant effort he won the Military Cross. And he observed ruefully thereafter that he was the only soldier he knew who was decorated for running away.

After spending a short time in another Aberdeen hospital closer to Stonehaven, Macmurray was sent to a military hospital at Banavie on the Caledonian Canal near Inverlochy for prolonged rest and recovery. Betty came to be near him. She moved into a small room at a hostel in Corpach, a short distance south of the hospital on Loch Eil. They would visit every day, and when John's strength returned they were able to take long walks. On clear days they could admire the peak of Ben Nevis to the East, and once they even hiked up it. They loved boating and would be gone for hours on the water. Betty recalls they would allow the rowboat to drift out of Loch Eil at ebb-tide, head south to the more open waters of Loch Linnhe and return to the dock with the help of the full-tide some hours later. On these boating trips they talked and read and sometimes just lay back and breathed the sea air. They also fished, and when they caught one, usually plaice, they would cook and eat it on the stony beach.

John and Betty shared a strange and wild experience from one of these boating expeditions, a story that they held to for the full length of their days. They were well down Loch Linnhe on this particular day and apparently had made a mistake about the tide times. They only woke up to that fact late in the afternoon when they realized the tide was against them just as they wanted to head back. The return trip was slow and difficult even though there was no wind and no waves. As darkness began falling they were in sight of their harbour but still well out from it. Suddenly, in the gathering gloom, some kind of large beast with a long neck and a small head, shaped like an upside-down rubber boot, rose up out of the water not far from their boat then sank back down, only to rise up again. It did this three times. John let out a shout and made for the nearest land. When they reached it, they pulled up the boat and ran for their lives. They immediately told some fishermen about the incident but the next day, when the fishermen went down to the shore to check things out, there was nothing to see but a few friendly seals bobbing in the morning sunlight.

John was quite reluctant to let the story out widely since it seemed so farfetched. He checked discreetly with Aldous Huxley, who began at Balliol the same day Macmurray did, to see if people of science had any information that might cast light on the event. Nothing surfaced. Over the years, John actually enjoyed telling the story at parties and he would sit up and give sound effects when he got to the section where the beast appeared and roared at them. But as Betty remembered and recounted the event, it was not the beast but John who had roared!

Balliol and the turn to philosophy

The end of the war came for them a week before it arrived for the rest of the world. One evening, someone from the scattered community that lived there at the end of the Caledonian Canal reported they had heard that armistice had been declared. A great party was immediately thrown together. It was only the next morning that they discovered that it was a false alarm. One week later, the war actually ended. Much later, in conversations about the war with his friend Kenneth Barnes, John once said that as far as he knew he went right through the war without killing or maiming anyone.[9]

Soon after New Year 1919, when the cadet trainees had been cleared out of Balliol, Macmurray returned to Oxford. He was granted the John Locke scholarship, and enrolled in the shortened course in Greats which would see him finishing by September. It meant he could not end with a *summa cum laude* or a *cum laude* but he could graduate "with distinction" — which he proceeded to do.

He was still in uniform for this "invalided year," as were the majority of the students at Balliol in the Hilary and Trinity terms in 1919. During that spring, he was invited to Buckingham Palace where, in full regalia, he was awarded the Military Cross by King George V. Helen accompanied him, and there is a photo of the clean-shaven but moustached young man standing at his full height — an inch or so under six feet — in front of the palace staring fiercely out, a cigarette in hand and his delighted sister at his side. On the back of the picture, years later when she was preparing her memoirs, Betty wrote plaintively: "Why didn't I go?"

R.H. Tawney had become a fellow at Balliol in 1918 and Macmurray undoubtedly met him and talked with him during the seven months they were there together. Both men, following different paths, had concluded that much of official religion was formed and even defined by social forces. Their interests and paths would cross more than once in the turbulent thirties.

With little time to spare for any outside activity, Macmurray dove into his philosophy with energy. After an unfortunate incident at a university public lecture, he found himself with a particular focus for much of his study during that shortened year. Professor Lindemann had been invited to lecture on Einstein's recent discoveries, especially his theory of relativity. He did so, and apparently during the question-period, two Oxford philosophers, Professor Joseph and Professor J.A. Smith of Balliol, stood up and used logic and ideas — with no reference to actual data or experiments — to prove Einstein's theory false. Their performance disgusted Macmurray, and he was confirmed then and there to look on Idealism with a baleful eye. It was a decision that had been gathering to a head in him through, among other things, his recent experiences of institutional religion and civic patriotism during the war.

But there was another side to the coin he found intriguing. His empiricist-minded colleagues, generally called Realists at the time, had recently presented their manifesto in which they were making equally apodictic claims, only this time from a materialist rather than an idealist perspective. There had been enough unresolved head-butting between the two sides for Macmurray to observe that the opposing positions were not only irreconcilable, but their proponents were not even able to be fruitfully engaged in the same conversation unless some different set of premises could be found to give a fresh hold on the problems. In the face of these puzzling philosophical squabbles among his colleagues, he decided to read alternately the continental Rationalists and the British Empiricists.[10] In this exercise he discovered a significant feature that guided his reading of different philosophies in the future. Both camps, he noted, had diametrically opposed perceptions of reality and about how judgments of "reality" were constituted. Yet both employed a common underlying set of assumptions about the nature of reality; in this case, it was an acceptance that the universe and all the beings in it were able to be represented only in atomistic terms. Identity, in other words, was defined in terms of an isolated, clear and distinct individuality, definable within its own internal terms, and this held true whether that was an idea in the mind (Rationalists) or a perception made by the senses (Empiricists). Both the Rationalists and the Empiricists shared one foundation, he concluded; they were both locked into the same "mechanical" mode of representing reality. Both held to an identical metaphysical premise: the primacy and irreducibility of the discrete, individual entity. Once this similarity was discovered, he was able to locate further hidden, and shared, premises that both sides simply took for granted in their propositions and positions and which went unquestioned in their arguments.

Religion, yes — the churches, no!

We have already seen how during the war Macmurray, along with his youthful contemporaries, developed a deep disenchantment with his society, its institutions and its leadership. From the example just discussed, the same disenchantment rose up for him concerning philosophical activity as it was being pursued in the universities. Both politics and philosophy, as he saw it, were working out of bankrupt categories. Bad religion, however, remained for Macmurray the ground-zero of the social decay because it shaped the most foundational of the cultural and moral supports for any civilization's way of acting. In the section of his Swarthmore Lecture dealing with the post-war period he comes right to the point about why the young felt so betrayed and on what grounds he believed the betrayal rested:

> When I asked myself, as I did, why I had given up the churches, and why so many of my contemporaries had given up religion by identifying it with the churches, the answer I found for myself and for them was that we could no longer believe in their *bona fides;* that they did not mean what they said; so that what they said, even if it were true, had become irrelevant. I still consider that this is what stands between the world and the church — this question of bad faith — and not intellectual difficulties about out-dated myths or cosmologies. The difficulties are no longer intellectual or theoretical at all. They are *moral* ...[11]

Many of his contemporaries had, as he said, identified religion with the churches and so given up on religion entirely. He himself did not do so and he tells us why:

> The difference in my case was that the process was carried through within an unquestionable conviction that whatever might be true about the traditional Christianity in which I had been trained, religion itself is not merely valid, but central in human life. Consequently my personal development resulted in a deep scepticism of all the traditional expressions of religion, and so

brought me down to the bedrock of a belief in the reality of
religious experience; indeed in the validity of Christianity,
whatever Christianity might really be. It left everything else
doubtful.[12]

But he went even further. If religion is so fundamental to human life and
society, then in his mind it was not only Christianity that "had to be rediscovered and recreated," it was the whole of society and the very civilization on which it rested. With the perspective of almost fifty more years of
life, he summarized for his Swarthmore Lecture audience the full scope of
his convictions as they had taken shape at that time in his life:

When I left the army and my university studies in 1919, it was
without any religious attachment, with a suspicion about the validity
of theology, and as a confirmed realist. I had shed the idealism of
my pre-war outlook. I had gained a purpose in life; for when I said
'Never again!' I meant it as a dedication to the elimination of war
from human life. Whatever sphere of activity I might find myself
involved in — and my hope then was that it might be on the staff of
the new 'League of Nations' — I intended to use it to this end.
When it appeared that I was to spend my life teaching philosophy,
this became the underlying purpose of all my philosophizing. To
this task I brought a mind that had become deeply sceptical of the
principles underlying the European civilization in which I had been
brought up and which had issued in the savage destruction and
stupid waste in which I had played my part ...[13]

In 1919, he was still left with the question thrust upon him by the "savage
destruction and stupid waste created in his own generation" —: What was the
sickness in European civilization that had permitted the war to happen, and
with such brutalizing ferocity? He did not know, but he was able to locate
himself, both in method and conviction, as he launched himself forward:

Convinced that the source of error must be deeply hidden, I
decided, as a rule to guide my search for it, to distrust and question
especially those principles of whose truth I found my elders most
unshakably convinced.

    So far as concerned religion I was still a convinced Christian
with no doubt that the religious issue was the most central and
most important of all issues. But I had given up all the churches;
I had turned from the past and was looking to the future,
believing that Christianity had to be rediscovered and
recreated.[14]

In this slightest of sketches he notes some of the features of the journey he was setting out on, a journey that could no longer find its course along the paths defined by either the modern continental or British philosophical traditions. In September 1919, after completing his examinations with distinction for the Honours MA in *Litterae Humaniores* and three months after leaving the army, Macmurray accepted a position as Lecturer in Philosophy at Manchester University at the invitation of Professor Samuel Alexander. He was ready to set out on his pilgrimage.

Chapter 5

Serving the Good of Society:

Manchester and Witwatersrand (1919–22)

When John Macmurray arrived at the University of Manchester in September 1919, Samuel Alexander, the professor who hired him, had just finished preparing his 1915 Gifford Lectures for publication. The book came out in 1920 under the title *Space, Time and Deity*. It was a work that Macmurray read with interest, though hardly with full agreement, as later notes between the two men reveal. Alexander, too, had given up on the idealist ethics dominant in late nineteenth century Oxford. After studying biology and psychology he developed a philosophy that was more closely related to the empirical sciences and which made a place for feeling within knowing, an approach that would have been of some interest to Macmurray. However, it was more likely a recommendation by A.D. Lindsay at Balliol rather than shared interests that moved Alexander to choose Macmurray for a lectureship at Manchester.

There are few traces left of Macmurray's sixteen-month sojourn as a Lecturer in Political Philosophy at Manchester.[1] The only outside report on his performance comes from a one-sentence statement in an article written about him in Johannesburg a couple of years later:

> Prior to coming to Johannesburg, Mr Macmurray was lecturer in ethics and political science at the Manchester University. His lectures were always followed with keen interest and — the test of a real teacher — caused lively discussions in corridors and common rooms.[2]

The only surviving letter he wrote that refers to his Manchester time was written seven years later, and does so only in passing. Yet even that little conveys an impression, like the momentary flash of a face in the window of a fast-moving train:

> My dear Irene,
> (If I may still be so bold as to use the name that keeps you as I used to know you — it seems so long ago). It was very delightful to have such a long letter from you, and to be recalled to memories

of Manchester and all the young enthusiasms that haunted it. Of course I haven't forgotten them or your place in them: that would be sheer ingratitude to you and life and the Father of life ...[3]

The letter was to Irene Grant, a bright and politically attuned young woman who had written to Macmurray from New Zealand asking him for the titles of books and article on a question she knew concerned him. Macmurray and Irene had been associated in Student Christian Movement (SCM) work on the Manchester campus during the 1919–20 school year where they had shared in discussions and projects relating to the effort to achieve world justice. This renewal of contact, building on an approach to John made by her husband Donald a year earlier, was the beginning of a long and warm relationship for John and Betty Macmurray with Irene and Donald Grant. Donald Grant had served as Travelling Secretary for SCM during World War I, and in the closing months of the war he had been jailed at Dartmoor prison as a conscientious objector. His interests in international relations were motivated by a religious vision of what would be required for world peace to be a realistic goal. This orientation made Grant and Macmurray congenial friends, and fellow-workers when rare occasion provided for it, throughout their active lives.

More than forty years after this time, Macmurray recalled that it was while preparing a talk on faith to students at Manchester that he came to realize that 'faith' as presented by Jesus in the New Testament does not refer primarily to an act of the mind in response to a body of doctrine.[4] It is first a conversion to an attitude of trust in the face of everything life brings, even in its most challenging and difficult features. It is based, he discovered, on the knowledge that comes from a personal encounter; for a Christian, an encounter in one's spirit and relationships with Christ as a living presence. Responding to revelation is not, he concluded, an assent to doctrine as much as a surrender in trust to a love which sustains one despite everything. Doctrine, as the product of conceptualization, was to be seen as entirely secondary. This articulation of the meaning of faith helped him realize that the Gospel terms "repentance" and "conversion" referred to this "change of heart," and produced a change in the essential stance of a person in face of all that life brings, a change from anxiety to trust, from self-concern to a self-forgetting care for others. The spiritual change was primary; any intellectual aspect was a subordinate dimension imbedded in this profound, existential shift to radical trust. This insight gained at Manchester was an instance of the beginning philosopher putting a name on the transformations he had undergone as a youth at university and as a soldier with his companions during the war. What was true of genuine religion in this matter of trust was, he believed, true of genuine human relationship, as well.

Learning with Socrates

Although the signposts marking this sixteen-month journey at Manchester are few and far between, something does remain from Macmurray's academic work — a set of lecture-notes for a course that he offered on "The History of Greek Philosophy: From Thales to Socrates."[5] Among other things, they offer a first snapshot of Macmurray the teacher, the activity during his life for which he was most revered and remembered.

It is in his approach to the students that we find already in 1919 the features that made him a spellbinding lecturer. His opening statement on the scope and purpose of a history of philosophy is in fact a question, and it hits his youthful, post-war audience right where they live: "What is the use of history?" In 1919 it was perhaps a question they felt they could raise with a touch of despair or cynicism with one another in the quadrangle or over lunch, but not in an emotionally honest way with a professor in the formal setting of a class. He launches in:

> We collect grains of fact. We rake among the ashes of the past. We grub in the rubbish heaps of time. Why all this labour over systems, kingdoms, sorrows and triumphs that are dead and done with?
>
> Is it merely a matter of interest? A vague impulse to know for knowing's sake? Does it rank with golf, or the latest novel by H.G. Wells or the latest effusion of E.W. Wilcox [a writer of light romances]? ...
>
> 'Knowledge for knowledge's sake' or 'art for art's sake' are claims that hide a grain of truth in a bushel of error. All human activity is for life's sake — Lengthen your cords & strengthen your stakes — life more abundant, copious, spreading out, clutching at the very gate-ways to the stars.
>
> This is the meaning of History to us ...

With that opening, we can imagine the students, even the ones who dreaded the thought of a whole year of ancient Greek thought, were pretty well awake — and only three minutes into the course.

But what could be suspected as a mere pitch for relevance by a fast talker with a quiver full of metaphors reveals itself as an enticing entry into a work of serious, painstaking excavation that uncovers for the students bit by bit the power of the past within the present, and the power of the philosopher, the power of the "Idea," at the heart of history — and the present. Before ten minutes have passed, he has given a convincing case for believing firmly that the Greek thinkers live now, within our own thinking and in the shape of our society. But knowing how esoteric and detached the philosopher can appear, he plays the "existential" card that he carries not from his reading but from his own life-journey:

> This leads to another point: The philosopher is the philosophy. He is the focus of the whole thought of his generation and its history. In him it reveals its scheme, its essential nature, what it unconsciously meant. But his philosophy is more — it is what he made of all that, as we say — His is the mould into which it was run, and it bears his image & superscription. That is why it is a Unique thing with an Individuality of its own — and why it baffles an expositor. To understand the philosophy fully you have to understand the circumstances, the forces of history, the society that in him became a man and in the man became a thought, a system of Ideas.

Then comes the even more intimate element in this existential focus on the power of Ideas:

> To know a man is more than to know about him: it is a question of living with him, and loving him — an achievement of mental artistry in the execution of which the mould of your mind receives him — he *lives* in you. It must be done at first hand as far as possible.
>   This is what I mean by a History of Philosophy, and the point of view I want you to take with me.

One could hardly blame a student who decided then and there to stick with the course on the grounds that, in his own way, "this man speaks with authority unlike the scribes and pharisees." And that is what comes through. In just the short span of his course introduction Macmurray has presented himself, without ever speaking about himself. Everything he says about "knowing a man" first-hand he has learned in the trenches and in his blessed friendship with his sister Helen. Everything about the kind of knowing that comes only with loving he has learned passionately and gently in his love for Hydie, and in the intimacy of comradeship in life and death at the front. And everything he says about the philosopher carrying his era within himself could, although he would never have said so, be taken as a description of himself at that moment in his life. And the ease and confidence contained in the closing statement :"This is ... the point of view that I want you to take with me" is at once free and committed. It is Macmurray trusting his transformed vocation as a "missionary." It is really an invitation to the class to walk with him as apprentices and companions.

The course content is not that unusual, since it is only an introduction.

But the professor radiates throughout the course the special knowledge
that has come from his classical training. What characterizes the course as
a history of philosophy is how Macmurray is true to his word in drawing
the students into the very heart of the questions that were exercising each
of the early Greek philosophers — and how their social setting and the
thinking of their predecessors helped to generate their questions. The pressures of history and politics, trade and economics, the incursions of
Egyptian mensuration and Babylonian astrology leading to Greek abstraction and generalization, Orphic mysticism, and revivals in religion with
the Pythagoreans, are called on to show how the philosophers' questions
fed on new events and knowledge. These in turn generated fresh questions
that deepened and advanced first in cosmology and then — with the
Sophists and Socrates — in the human issues of truth and ethical conduct.
Running through it all from the time of Heraclitus and Parmenides
onwards, we find the development of thought itself through dialectic and
the refinement of the questions through its methods. And the aim of it
all is:

> ... to know these men, and to know them as moments in a history,
> an evolution which has now reached us — to see them as elements
> now in our own thinking ... We shall see how it [the stream of
> thought] is held together by a single dominant question which in
> the very act of being answered transforms itself into some subtler,
> more elusive and more urgent shape.

It is when the course comes to the Sophists and Plato that Macmurray
opens up his background in classics full bore. He demonstrates dialectic
at work in the present for his students by presenting them with the Taylor-
Burnett controversy on how, in the three sources of Aristophanes, Plato
and Xenophon, one might hope to arrive at the closest possible knowledge
of the "real" Socrates.

By good fortune, in having this set of notes we have access to what is
almost surely the first time Macmurray drew up his understanding of the
triadic development of major movements in thought. At the outset we
have the School of Miletus represented first by Thales — the first philosopher — followed by Anaximander and then Anaximenes. Late in the
course he identifies a new triad in Socrates, Plato, and Aristotle. Finally,
he notes a parallel triad in Jesus, the author of the Gospel of John, and St
Paul. The form of the relationship he proposes is first that of the Master
(or Founder) who presents the vision and reveals the method of living in
his own life; followed by the Artist, who grasps the spirit of the Master
and sketches out the vision systematically in its largest dimensions; and
finally comes the Scientist, the empirical thinker who refines and corrects

the system with an eye to detail and the relationship of particulars within the whole.

He states explicitly that the initial outburst of discovery is intrinsically a *religious* discovery. The second is a work in *art* and the third, a work of *science*. One might suspect that he would have done the same for Aeschylus, Sophocles and Euripides respectively. He does apply the schema to Western civilization some ten years later when he holds that the roots of our civilization are Hebrew, Greek and Roman influences in that order; with Christianity, as the spiritual shaper of subsequent Western civilization, being the synthetic bearer of the best, and worst, of these three influences.

There is much that is provocative, even attractive, in this schema since it seems to offer rich possibilities for maintaining a unity while allowing for important distinctions. It also encourages a sense of cumulative development and finally reflects an integrating synthesis that is compelling and, on many counts, credible. There may be a certain seductiveness in thinking in binary or triadic terms once one has an insight that points that way, a bit like painting the planet in one's favourite colour. In fact, at least one point of hesitation arises with one of Macmurray's triads by his location of St Paul in the third spot in his Christian triad. Although Paul's writings do provide for him being considered the "scientist" — the detail person and the articulator of doctrine — over against the Johannine Gospel's author expressing an "artistic" theology of Christ's "glorification," the fact is Paul's letters were written anywhere between forty to sixty years before John's Gospel. So the question arises: How does Macmurray deal with the scientist coming before the artist in this case, and without any dependence by the scientist on the articulations of the artist? Either the artist comes prior to the scientist by way of natural, evolutionary necessity, or there is something in the Christian triad as he proposes it here that doesn't seem to fit the schema. It seems to be a clear example of a significant idea that still needs work.

Macmurray ends his parenthetical remarks on his triad of Master, Artist and Scientist with the remark: "This is worthwhile comparing to the theological doctrine of the Trinity." One can only surmise at what level he found the schema illumining for Trinitarian theology; or the Trinity, perhaps, as an analogical support for the schema. Because of this triadic notion of development and the predominance of his subsequent notion of community as a unity of distinct persons, one might expect Macmurray to have had Trinitarian interests throughout his philosophical development. On the contrary, this is, to all appearances, one of only two instances in his writing where, in addressing the philosophical understanding of personal relationships, he refers to the Trinity.

The course ends with Macmurray considering the life and thought of Socrates, the philosopher in the course he admired most. He notes how humbled, yet moved, Socrates was to hear that, in answer to the question: "Who is the wisest of all people?" the wise woman Diotima had declared there was no one wiser than Socrates. Only by intense reflection did he find the meaning of the answer, namely that the vast majority of people thought they knew things even though they were quite ignorant. He at least knew that he knew nothing. Macmurray takes off from this point:

> At this time Socrates was not yet 40. But he had found his mission. He felt himself called by god to prepare the way of true knowledge by convincing his fellow-citizens of their profound ignorance on all questions that matter for life. And in doing so he turned away from science and "thinking in the air" [a proposal made by Anaximenes that he had taken seriously]. To bring his questions nearer home to practical life. He gave up everything for this — and he called it his "Service of God" and himself the "fellow-slave" of Apollo's swans. He was intensely in earnest about this faith.

He ends — as he began — with a passionate statement of the nature and worthiness, even the necessity, of doing philosophy as a profound service to the world. And his words about Socrates are as true about himself. In this first laboratory of his life-vocation, he shows "he was intensely in earnest about this faith."

Move to South Africa

It was probably late in 1920 while he was in his second year at Manchester that John received a letter from Jan Hofmeyr, his Balliol friend now back in South Africa, offering him the Chair of Philosophy at the University of Witwatersrand in Johannesburg. Both John and Betty were immediately excited by the prospect of going to South Africa. For him, it was a major appointment early in his career, and an opportunity to see some of the world outside Britain and the trenches of France. For Betty it was like a dream come true to go to the land where her father had been a missionary and, as she felt, retrieve a part of her own heritage in doing so. It was also for John the promise of a renewal of his friendship with one of his dearest friends.

Hofmeyr's rise had been nothing less than amazing. He had returned to South Africa in 1916 and the next year, at the age of twenty-two, had become Professor of Classics at Witwatersrand University. Two years later, at the ripe age of twenty-four, he was offered the Principalship of the University. In writing to John, Hoffie said he might be going into politics and hinted that John might think of doing so, too: "The professorship might be a stepping-stone to politics."

Within weeks, arrangements had been made to leave Manchester. As Betty Macmurray recalls in notes for her memoirs, on leaving she and John destroyed a trunkful of letters — all the correspondence they had received over the years, including his letters to her from the front and from Oxford. They repeated this sad act of destruction at least four times over the years, always at the point when they were making a major move and had no room for storage. Much later, Betty considered those acts of destroying their history a "crime" (and a biographer would be tempted to agree with her!). But in 1921, with their future lying ahead of them, John encouraged it, wanting nothing relating to the war left around their home.

They sailed from Britain at the end of January 1921. When they arrived in Johannesburg, John and Betty were guests of the Hofmeyrs for their first week or two in the country while they sought accommodation. Jan Hofmeyr lived with his mother, and it took Betty Macmurray no time at all to see that Mrs Hofmeyr was something of a moral tyrant in the life of her son. It was *her* values that ran his life and *her* judgment to which he submitted, minimally every evening at the dinner table. It was a relief for the Macmurrays when they found a bungalow of their own.

Their overwhelming impression during those first weeks was of dust and heat. Nothing they had experienced before could have prepared them for it, except perhaps John's experience of endless acres of mud at the front. Soon after they arrived, there was a plague of locusts that devastated everything. The locusts were so numerous that when they took off in flight after ravaging one field and heading for the next, they darkened the sun. It was not a particularly propitious beginning, and for two biblically-educated people the similarity of this event to one of the plagues that accosted Pharaoh would not have escaped their notice, especially since both of them suffered attacks of dysentery and influenza, as well.

After a month or so, things became more normal. They had a servant named Kubugwane who slowly revealed himself as a true personality. He managed to give Betty the feeling that there was a constant competition between him and her as to who was really head of the Macmurray household. Slowly, she came to understand this aura of independence as deeply related to maintaining his dignity in the presence of his white "boss lady," and learned to accommodate it. As a welcome gift from someone, Betty had been given a friendly white terrier they called Jessica who clearly loved them both and remained with them the full twenty-two months they were in Johannesburg.

Challenging Realism and Idealism

John moved immediately into his life at the university and was immediately overwhelmed. He found himself with sixteen lectures a week, in addition to his administrative burdens. He shared his first impressions with Samuel Alexander:

> ... it is certainly freer and opener — with opportunities for valuable work and study — though on the other hand it lacks the maturity and depth that only a long tradition can impart to a social life.[6]

He finds the standards are clearly inferior to those in Britain and proposes this is not all due to being a "young" country. In his analysis, one can, with hindsight, feel the roots that gave rise to the apartheid policy that would become law twenty-five years later. He told Alexander:

> ... at bottom I think it is owing to the Native population which makes the white population an aristocracy. As a result, the students are so crammed with self-conceit that there is no room in their heads for any knowledge. One spends one's time trying to convince them of ignorance, and the effect is practically nil. If they can't understand a thing the first time they hear it, they are apt to jump to the conclusion that it is the lecturer's fault. There is no atmosphere, no background.

But he had arrived just as the bill had gone through Parliament making Witwatersrand an independent university, and he expected the new identity would be the occasion for starting a deeper standard of academic life. "Personally, I like it, and I find that my own thinking is getting on fairly rapidly: and the first free opportunity will find me ready to put something down on paper."

He tells Alexander that he has been trying to digest his *Space, Time and Deity,* the best systematic statement to date of the new Realism, but confesses gently to his former boss: "I'm not quite satisfied yet with the pure Realist position — on the point of personality." It seems to remove the need for 'soul' on the one hand, and then replace it with an activity of selecting objects and organizing them. But, Macmurray observes:

> ... I am not satisfied that the selection of independent objects organized by attention is not itself a new independent entity in space-time, with properties peculiar to itself.

In his view, the unity of the self in knowing has been taken only part of the way by Realism. This letter reveals for the first time, Macmurray's focus on personality as the central question for contemporary philosophy. In fact, it was hardly a new topic with him. "The persistent theme of 'personality,' human and divine, figured large among liberal Christians at the turn of the century," and it certainly figured large in the conversations around "socialist" Balliol.[7]

The question of how personality is understood now begins to become the explicit backdrop for his reading and lecturing. We still have from this period Macmurray's lecture notes on Bernard Bosanquet's *Philosophical Theory of the State* and his reading notes on Gürke's *Medieval Forms*. Macmurray praises the work of Bosanquet, the late nineteenth century British Idealist, as being:

> English Hegelianism at its best: marked by a strenuous effort at concreteness of an ideal kind. But (a) not really in touch with the essence of the modern political movement and (b) strangled by the attempt to represent the concrete state's life as the synthesis of Law and Conscience in terms of the Hegelian metaphysics.
>
> It is at its best in the criticism, which is very acute and subtle, of the modern historical development of pure philosophical theory of the state: (a) in its attack on the 'theories of the first look' — Bentham & Mill, Spencer, Marx & the modern Sociologists (Durkheim, Tarde, Le Bon), though it succeeds by taking all of these as *systems* and showing their inadequacy as systems; (b) in its constructive criticism of Rousseau and his influence on Kant, Fichte and Hegel.

He finds the book's constructive value "is great at resisting the tendency to partial views and in its insistence on the fundamentally psychical nature of social life," even though Bosanquet carries the analogy too far. Regarding this claim, he is able to insist "that society is not a mere repetition of individuals (cf. Tarde's *Imitation*) but an organization of them." Macmurray applauds this affirmation and believes it shows that Bosanquet has a "grip on the full spiritual nature of social life and on its unity as an organized whole."

His criticism hits at several points, most of which are related to the Hegelian foundations of the position. In Macmurray's judgment, Bosanquet's need to have the Ideal and the Actual realized in a concrete state leaves him fixed onto nationalism as the pivot for the state. He also finds that:

> the metaphysical pressure to identify the actual State with what it is trying to be leads to a constant misuse of language ... There is a constant indefiniteness in concepts, e.g. of 'Self,' and a confusion

of the distinction between abstract and concrete with the distinction between Real and Apparent.

The result is an optimistic fatalism through the tacit assumption that the Ideal and the Actual must coincide in the State. This is denied in words, but it is implicit in the theory.

Further there is a distinct limitation of sympathy to one type of state: the independent Unitary State — a single and absolute authority for each individual.

The book provides a focus for Macmurray to re-enter the essentially biological metaphor that functions in Hegelian thought and that underlies Rousseau's view of the "Real will" — which is always more than the "actual will" of any individual or group of individuals. The State is modelled on a biological species, and the individual on a biological organism viewed as "part" of the species-whole. Transferred to the political order it is evident that "It" (the State as whole) is more real than "we" (individuals or group as parts) are. And any expression of my freedom depends on my conformity to the realization of the True or Real will. The centre of gravity is thrown outside the individual and placed in the collective, as is evident, for example, in Plato's *Republic*. The individual is lost by being conceived of as only a part serving the whole. This, Macmurray finds to be very unsatisfactory.

It was in political theories of the Middle Ages that Macmurray found principles different from those admitted into the modern discourse on politics. He leaned on Gürcke, and proposed a bibliography containing Aquinas, Dante and Wycliffe as well as contemporary commentators on the papacy, the divine right of kings, the politics of the Middle Ages in general and the Council of Constance in particular. He noted that the struggle between mediaeval ideas and the newer antique-modern ideas focused precisely on the status of the individual or group within the state. He concluded that "political thought, when it is genuinely Mediaeval, starts from the Whole but ascribes an intrinsic value to every partial whole down to and including the Individual." This principle arose, he concluded, from the Christian understanding of each individual as being a creation in the image and likeness of God. Or, as St Paul put it, an individual called to live in "the freedom of the children of God."

Macmurray is thinking through the implications of both materialist and organic views of the person and society within the new modern traditions in which these forms of thinking arose. From his letter to Professor Alexander we know that he is doing it by asking whether or not the full reality of personality is being acknowledged in the mechanical and organic theories of state and society being offered. He finds Bosanquet inadequate because Bosanquet remains locked into organic presuppositions that make it impossible for a free individual self to appear without reverting to a materialist view of society. Macmurray is discovering in this reading the ground for the development of his own thinking on the matter by settling with greater precision on where and why both materialist (Hobbes) and organic (Rousseau) models for thinking of human beings and human society are inadequate. For a *human* unity to be accounted for, some category beyond these two, but one that includes the best of each, is needed. What he wants included is a respect for free individuality within a free society; but as yet he has no adequate contemporary language to describe it. With the benefit of hindsight, we can see in these lecture notes the seeds for his notion of 'the personal' as a distinct and unique category slowly being prepared for planting. We can also see him continuing to distance himself from the dominant idealist tradition at Balliol.

Walking with the people

But not all of Macmurray's time was spent on school and scholarship. In Johannesburg, there was a plan to establish a committee of whites and educated blacks to discuss problems which the Africans wished to bring forward. John was invited to be a founding member since he had already become involved in social issues, especially with those concerned with workers and with native blacks and their housing problems.

As a member of the new committee he became involved with a protest against the Transvaal government's decision to impose a poll tax of two pounds on each person throughout the whole province. The tax was far too heavy for the blacks, many of whom had no work. Under pressure from the protest, the government reduced the tax on blacks to one pound, but even this amount seemed outrageous to the committee. After discussion they decided to consult a leading lawyer. He reported that the reduction of the tax in respect of the natives was a breach of the law since the law forbade the imposition of differential taxation between blacks and whites. The committee decided to make a test case and asked the central government to restrain the provincial government from collecting the tax until the case could be heard. The government refused, and the tax collections went ahead. The case, however, was heard and won. The collection of the tax had to be stopped.

In one public speech on the matter, when feelings among his fellow-protesters were running high, Macmurray began his talk with rhetorical flourishes that roused the crowd to new heights of feeling. Suddenly he stopped speaking. Silence fell. And he said: "You see, any fool can do that!" And he continued his speech in a quiet and measured tone, concentrating on facts rather than emotions.

In contrast to this gentle delivery which characterized his professional style throughout his life, there is a delicious example of him deliberately giving in to rhetorical excess in an after-dinner speech about the excellence of Scottish education and Scottish universities to his fellow Scots at the Caledonian Society of Johannesburg. The speech, already mentioned in connection with the Bursary competition in Scottish schools, sparkles with the wit, humour and the command of language for which Macmurray became well-known. But for all its fun, the speech is a *tour de force* on the genius and democratic prescience manifested in the six hundred years of Scottish education since the founding of St Andrew's University, and a statement of its spiritual core. In Scottish education, Macmurray told his audience, there is no separating religion from metaphysics, no separating metaphysics from education and, finally, no separating education from the people. So, the roots of education are as deep and wide as the roots of the people in all of their convictions and aspirations. Consequently:

> ... its essence is its tradition, its solidarity with the life of the town
> and country where it lives and works: and its greatness is
> determined by the depth to which its roots penetrate into the heart
> and history of its land.

He praises John Knox as the greatest of Scotsmen for the monumental feat of setting up the foundations of Scottish education as every Scot knows it to this day. He reminds his audience:

> It included provision for the establishment of a school in
> connection with every kirk or parish, in which all children should
> taught the ordinary branches of elementary education including
> Latin; the provision of secondary schools in all important towns,
> and University education for all, rich or poor, who showed aptness
> to profit by it. The rich were compelled to educate their children at
> their own expense. The poor who could not pay were to be
> supported by the Church, so that rich and poor alike, if they were
> 'of good engine' as he [Knox] quaintly puts it, should continue at
> the secondary schools 'until the commonwealth have profit of
> them' and should then proceed to the University, or be sent to 'a
> handicraft or other profitable exercise.'

And he repeats for emphasis: "Note the phrase 'until the commonwealth have profit of them'." The essential need for the university to serve the good of society is at the heart of this vision, he exclaims. But perhaps equally so is the:

... obliteration of all respect for wealth and rank, and even for the superficial qualities of social polish or what the Englishmen would call good breeding, and value above most other things. There is an essential roughness about it, a veritable contempt for gentility of any sort. At heart the Scot is not a gentleman — he almost takes it as an insult if you call him one; he has a shrewd suspicion you are pulling his leg.

At this point in his speech Macmurray offers a touch of autobiography to demonstrate his point, a lovely interlude in this sortie into the history of the Scottish national identity that brings us back to an earlier moment in his life:

I remember well the impression that my first visit to London made on me (it was during a vacation while I was a student at Glasgow), a feeling of consternation lest my hat shouldn't be straight on my head, that my tie was getting out of position, and that my boots were far too square at the toe. I remember with what diffidence I forced myself into the shops because of the elegant dress and highly cultured speech of the shop girls. Of course I knew that it was all on the surface — and that the most elegant Englishman was more or less of a whited sepulchre — but that knowledge was painfully impotent to chase away the bogey of boorishness from my feelings about myself. I felt much as so many grown ups do in the presence of small children — hopelessly inferior and out of place. Perhaps that is the secret of the hidden distaste for things English that abides until the end in the Scottish heart. He feels that he is being cheated by outward show into an unreal inferiority. At bottom it is a fine, even a great quality — it grows from that essential democracy that fears and detests humbug and cant and shadow of reason, obscuring the real human value of a man and thwarting the possibilities of true human achievement. It is a mad world, my masters, where the rich fool is respected and the poor wise man is of little account.

Equally memorable in the speech is Macmurray's description of why the humanities are the core of the curriculum of the Scottish university: in fact, this vision of democratic education and the place of the humanities in it was at the very heart of Macmurray's vision and vocation in education — the main work of his life. The speech was a good one. But for the discerning listener, what was being offered that night was not only a lesson in Scottish history but also a glimpse into the soul and the future purposes of an extraordinary philosopher and practitioner of education.

To lighten up their lives, John and Betty took dancing lessons. John loved them but Betty hated them due to what she called a deep-seated shyness that invaded her as soon as she took to the dance floor. They both played the piano but John's playing continued to leave something to be desired. As Betty complained in her diaries, he never learned to stop pounding the keys. Apparently, as much as he wished to master the instrument, he was never able to stop thinking through his moves from one note to the next when he played. Later, in the 1930s, Betty paid Trevor Fisher, an Australian pianist friend of theirs in London, to give John lessons. John took the lessons gladly. Trevor's observation was that John tried to bully the notes out of the keys. So, to the end, John was, in Betty's eyes, and ears, not a pianist but a philosopher playing at the piano. Nonetheless, she did admit he had a great understanding of music and a deep emotional appreciation of it. So much so that his sensitivity to music, which outstripped her own, made Betty — who felt herself to be the emotional and artistic one — puzzled and sometimes jealous. In the end, she consoled herself with the reluctant conclusion that music simply wasn't her forte.

Unlike all their neighbours in Johannesburg, the Macmurrays didn't have a guard dog at their house and Betty often wondered why the house escaped being robbed since this was a fairly common occurrence in their area. One cold morning she looked out the window of their bungalow and saw a man on the open seat watching cattle. She sent Kuby her servant out with a cup of coffee. The man returned the cup and gave Betty the royal salute of a chief. It transpired that he had been of high rank, and because of what he knew of John's work for the blacks had instructed the boys never to burgle their house.

John continued to work in the Johannesburg community through the Workers' Education Association (WEA) and his involvement with the social justice committee. He also gave lectures in the city and entranced people with his clarity and depth of thought. His speech "On the Working of the League of Nations" was a quiet but impassioned appeal for loyal support for the League.[8] Another lecture entitled "The True Policy of Labour" was a courageous exercise in political and social philosophy as well as in social commitment. He proposed that labour had two major goals: the improvement of wages and conditions for workers in the immediate future and, second, the abolition of the capitalist system and the achievement of a different and more just social order. He recognized that these two goals demanded different policies and that the weakness of labour was from the clashing of the two policies.[9]

His talks present a socialist position that should have given Sandy Lindsay assurance that John, despite his disavowal in his letter from the front, had not given up on socialism. His case, even as reported in the

Johannesburg Star, was put clearly, as usual: Referring to the two goals he envisages for labour, he asserts that the new world order is the more fundamental goal and it requires the democratization of industry. For this, three assumptions have to be made.

> every man has a right to freedom in the great essential things of human life. No man should be in a position to dictate the conditions of his freedom to another. This rules out all autocracies.
> the control of masses of capital under modern conditions means the control of the conditions of a decent human life for millions of our fellow men. As a result they become less and less democratic because more and more departments become dependent on finance, and finance is still controlled autocratically.
> the only possible control of industry that will increase democracy is an international one.

From this he concluded that the League of Nations was the germ of whatever democracy the future held, and so support of it should hold first place in any labour policy. Such a policy should make its appeal to all men of good will with no distinctions of class or wealth. To do that it must start with the individual trade union and aim not at enhancing its bargaining power so much as at making it a centre of broad human interests. From there a real unity of trade unions can be attempted as well as collaboration with every institution — political, social and religious — which could be inspired with its own ideals.

As the *Star* reports, Macmurray concluded this talk:

> by pointing out that the crucial test of the meaning of the Labour movement in South Africa was its attitude to the native and to the League of Nations, and by appealing for the suppression of sectionalism and the initiation of a policy that would take long, broad views and work patiently and quickly for a distant goal.

The clarity of Macmurray's thinking shines through in this talk. The doubts he declared in his letter to Lindsay about the working class's understanding and power for wide vision underwent a major transformation while he was in South Africa. Meeting with workers and working with them to achieve social justice had decisively moved him to trust and respect them. The talk also reveals a socialist foundation for political and economic relations. And for all his ideals he was nothing if not particular and concrete in his specific proposals. One letter to the editor of the *Star,* after his talk on the League of Nations, said it all:

... from what I have deduced from this and other public lectures of
his he seems to be the only one of several professional
philosophers I have known in South Africa who is getting away
from the comfortable academic groove and who is dedicating his
subject and his brains to a definite and precious ideal.

Heading home: the end of a friendship

Early in the autumn of 1922, John received an invitation to become a
Fellow and Tutor at Balliol. If he accepted, the appointment would be
made in November and the duties would begin at the start of the new year.
Both John and Betty were ready to go. The appointment meant a return to
Oxford and to his own college, a place where he was sure he would be able
to work to his maximum on the philosophical ideas that were taking
greater shape in him with every passing day.

Before John and Betty left Witwatersrand University, a distressing
event occurred which ended his friendship with Jan Hofmeyr and left him
with a feeling of deep bitterness verging on despair. The quarrel was not a
personal one. It involved the whole university. Principal Hofmeyr had
been informed of an improper liaison between Professor Stibbe, head of
Anatomy in the Department of Medicine, and one of the college typists.
Mrs Hofmeyr had already given ample evidence that when her son became
Principal she had set herself up to judge the conduct and morals of the university staff. In this case, her influence passed through her son to the
University Council which, although the full membership was not present,
voted with the Principal to sever Dr Stibbe's connection with the university. Those members who had not been present at the meeting demurred.
Hofmeyr raised the stakes by declaring that the Council must choose
between him and the accused. The Council decided to do two things: first,
to try to persuade the doctor to resign, implying, but not stating, that otherwise he would be dismissed and that would be a black mark against his
name for any future employment possibility. Second, to destroy the
Minutes of the first meeting, with its record of the doctor's dismissal. The
doctor agreed to resign, not knowing that, with the Minutes destroyed, he
was no longer "dismissed."

Because the Senate had not been consulted, proper procedures for dismissal of a faculty member had clearly not been followed. Word of this
breach of due process got to members of the Senate and other faculty
members. John Macmurray was approached by Senate representatives and
asked if he would lead the effort to reinstate the professor. The injustice
done to the professor was patent. So, despite his personal feelings
for Hofmeyr, Macmurray could not refuse the invitation to head the

campaign. Though it was not yet public knowledge, he also knew by this time that he was going to Oxford within weeks, and this, in his judgment, made him the faculty member with the least to lose in the delicate situation.

Macmurray and his colleagues, with little effort, were able to expose both the breach of procedures and the untoward behaviour of the principal and the council. The doctor was reinstated, the Principal was humiliated, and Macmurray was overwhelmed with chagrin and bitterness. He was chagrined because he knew Hoffie's mother was behind the whole thing and he also knew — with her out of it — the whole matter could have been handled at the outset over a cup of tea. He was embittered and distressed because the Principal turned his back forever on Macmurray, his old and dearest friend. Hofmeyr had made a huge political and moral blunder from which he never fully recovered at the university. He stayed on as Principal and Professor of Classics until the end of the 1924 academic year, then left to become Administrator of Transvaal Province. Although he served as Vice-Chancellor of the university from 1926 to 1930, Hofmeyr's career for the twenty or so years remaining to him were spent in politics — as he had intimated in his 1921 letter to Macmurray. He served successively as Minister of the Interior, Public Health and Education, Mines and finally of Finance. His involvement in public life in South Africa was considerable, but his self-confidence had been damaged and some commentators felt that his influence was persistently shadowed by the event at the university. He served as Acting Prime Minister seven times but did not live to fulfil the prediction of A.L. Smith that he might reach the top position. Jan Hofmeyr died at the age of fifty-four, a somewhat pathetic figure, predeceasing his manipulative and perhaps even more pathetic mother.[10]

With regard to the long-term effect of this rupture in friendship on John, Betty noted simply that this event "was the first big nail in the coffin of his idealism. Even the war, shattering as its implications were, hadn't bruised his spirit so badly ... John was never the same ... buoyant person he had been."

Macmurray was formally appointed to Balliol on November 23, 1922 . The College Minutes show that he was named to a "War Memorial Fellowship and Tutorship in the Classics."[11] He was also appointed Jowett Lecturer in Philosophy, a title held by his tutor A.D. Lindsay from 1910 to 1922.[12] Macmurray resigned from his position at Witwatersrand and announced his departure from Johannesburg to the groups with whom he had been working in the city. His colleagues at the university put on a farewell dinner for him. The Workers' Education Association had a gathering to thank him for his service to them. In the course of it "a surprise presentation was made to Professor Macmurray, and it was obvious that the gift was an expression of sincere admiration." The farewell story that appeared about him in the *Rand Daily Mail* was to the point:

... his departure from the University of Witwatersrand for Balliol College, Oxford, will be severely felt both in the University and in the town. Quiet, modest, restrained, he is yet a strong personality with remarkable qualities of leadership. His lectures ... both to students and the general public, have been distinguished by originality and great force.

... It is quite safe to predict that his voice and pen will soon be powerful in and out of Oxford. Great things are anticipated of him as a philosophical writer and thinker.

On November 27, 1922, the Macmurrays took a train to Cape Town where a few days later they boarded the *Briton* for their voyage home. They had left their much loved terrier Jessica in Johannesburg to make a new home with some friends. As the train pulled out of the station Jes, who had somehow got loose, appeared on the platform and began running alongside the moving train looking up all the while at her mistress. Betty pressed her face against the window and looked back at her, waving and waving. She stopped only well after the dog was out of sight.

Chapter 6

The Balliol Don (1922–28)

The pall that hung over their departure from South Africa due to the Hofmeyr affair was somewhat lifted for John and Betty once they arrived in England. The *Briton* pulled into port just a few days before Christmas 1922 and the excitement of being home for the first time in twenty-three months as well as the anticipation of family visits took some of the edge off John's depressed feelings. If that wasn't enough, the winter weather, so different from the sultry conditions they had just left, shocked them into having to deal with their immediate situation.

After visiting family in Scotland over the holidays, John and Betty arrived in Oxford in early January only to discover that the new house being built for them at 5 Mansfield Road was not quite finished. John, as a don, was still expected to live in college. However since women were not permitted to live in the college, temporary digs were found for Betty in the High Street, in an upstairs flat over the Bullingdon Club. That became the place where they had their meals and lived as normally as they could until the house was completed. Normality for those few weeks included trying to ignore, as much as they could, the boisterous noise from the club below that often went on well into the night. Their new house on Mansfield Road was well situated, a ten minute walk away from Balliol, perfect for a bit of exercise at the beginning and end of each day.

It was probably within hours of crossing the threshold at Balliol that Macmurray met Charles Richard Morris, a bright twenty-three year old who had been appointed Fellow and Tutor the year before. Both men were vibrant additions to the college staff and it took no time at all for them to make their mark with the students. Sylvia Brown, one of Macmurray's students, attended his lectures mainly as a personal support for her best friend Dorothy Emmet who had found herself the only woman in the class. Over seventy years later she was able to write: "I can still picture the wild-looking, prophet-like figure who inspired us in Balliol Hall ..."[1] Her friend Dorothy, who became the Professor of Philosophy at Manchester, confirmed that initial impression of Macmurray as "wild, insightful, and at times entertaining as a lecturer."[2]

In fact, both Macmurray and Morris may have, at times, gone a bit over the edge in their performances in the lecture hall. Student jokes arose around Oxford that in their classes you were likely to hear not what Kant or Plato actually said but what these professors felt they ought to have said! Somewhat in this same spirit, Macmurray laughed at himself when, on one occasion, he held an audience spellbound for an hour on Leibniz only to confide to a friend afterwards that he had based his whole lecture on one sentence: "The monad does not have windows." Even if there is a touch of truth in his statement, one can believe there was some self-deprecating modesty as well since, in the summer of 1923, just a few months after arriving at Balliol, Macmurray gave his first set of Jowett Lectures which included significant attention to Leibniz.

The Jowett lectures

The Jowett Lectures of 1923, entitled "The Historical Approach to Modern Idealism," were given in Trinity term. In them, Macmurray presented the usual suspects: Descartes, Spinoza and Leibniz from the continental tradition, and Locke, Berkeley and Hume from the British side. What is distinctive about the course is the effort to present the decisive shape of the problematic that focuses not only the work of each thinker but the assumptions embraced by these early modern thinkers taken together.

As he introduces Descartes, Macmurray tells his listeners:

> ... you will never understand a great thinker if you start where he starts — in this case the Cogito. Instead you want to know first the assumptions, usually unconscious, with which he starts ... by his assumptions I mean the floating atmosphere of outlook and feeling which is the current 'opinion' of his time. There is a 'public opinion' in science as well as in politics. The philosophic discoverer has found an important flaw in it ...

Here, Macmurray is intent on giving his students some appreciation of what Johann Gottfried Herder called the *Schwerpunkt,* the intellectual and emotional "centre of gravity" of a society. It is something Macmurray has already concluded is a pivot for philosophical as well as sociological analysis of an era, in this case the early Modern Period in Europe. Thirty years later, in his Gifford Lectures, Macmurray had settled on referring to this unity-pattern shaping the thought and feeling of a person, a culture, or a civilization as its "mode of apperception."[3]

Following his own lead, Macmurray locates the revolutionary quality of René Descartes, not first of all in his *Cogito ergo sum* but in the deeper shift underlying it, namely: "the vindication, in the whole sphere of thought, of the triumph of the individual mind over the claims of authority ... [which included] the questions of the Protestant Reformation ... and the new mathematical methods which were touching the foundations of modern science." He notes the intimate connection between Descartes and Martin Luther who came one hundred years earlier. According to Macmurray, Luther had been driven to assert something like this: "I trust God in myself. I don't need any outside authority to tell me who God is, or if God is pleased or displeased with me. I can handle that by myself." After that, Christianity in the west could never be the same. Luther had shifted to a completely fresh viewpoint on faith: the freedom of the individual to live in God without a "parent's" guidance, approbation or constraint, and the freedom to know and decide individually about God's truth. Luther couldn't realize then he was proposing a fresh standpoint not only for religious faith but for the whole of living. This perspective, Macmurray stated, is the pure originality of the era we now know as "modernity." His observation on the meaning of that first move on the part of any initiating genius in philosophy (in this case, Descartes) is illuminating and instructive, since it anticipates his attitude to his own "pioneering" effort to shift the standpoint in philosophy.

> ... It is his honour to have substituted the truth, or a nearer approach
> to the truth in that particular. But one life is too short to trace out
> even the more important ramifications of a fundamental substitution
> of this kind. That will take generations — perhaps many generations,
> as in the case of Descartes. For the discoverer — even the greatest —
> it is sufficient glory to have put his finger upon the weak spot and to
> have indicated, however vaguely, the lines of necessary change.
> Along with this there will necessarily be found [in his thought] a
> mass of acceptances from the older system which he has undermined,
> and which historians, easily wise after the event, can see to be
> inconsistent with the change that has been made in the substructure.

Precisely what constitutes this "certainty of inner experience," and what that implies for our knowledge of self as well as our knowledge of the world, necessarily became the central problematic and project of the philosophers of the modern era.[4] Macmurray encourages his students not only to study the thought of each of the six philosophers in detail, but also *to see the thinking of each one as a connecting link in an historical movement of thinking* — the thorny issue of how to understand and justify this assumption of the "certainty of inner experience."

In fact, Macmurray is doing something much more in the Jowett lectures; he is sharpening his own analysis of the *logic* of the mechanical mode of apperception. He is deepening his grasp of the pervasive effect on human attitudes, relationships and institutions that resulted from the instrumental, technical viewpoint gradually becoming the almost unquestioned "atmosphere of feeling and outlook which is the 'common opinion' of the time."

This predominance of the mechanical viewpoint was hardly news for Macmurray. He knew the dislocating social changes caused by the Industrial Revolution and the views that drove it. Even more, he knew the effects of this mechanical logic from the First World War. He had seen howitzers and machine-guns anonymously translate living men into cannon fodder. He had seen the generals treat thousands of men simply as fighting "units," sending them to certain death in battle strategies defined exclusively for a "show of force" rather than as a necessary action for ending the war. He had seen the application of the principles of triage in the ambulance tents, and knew that this method of valuation revealed the perfect and pure reduction of human beings to fighting machines. So, he knew first-hand how the application of this violently reductionist mode of apperception to all levels of human affairs was deeply related to the sickness and insanity in the heart of Europe. This course of lectures was just one stage in his long effort, as a philosopher, to understand it thoroughly — before he challenged it thoroughly.

The Jowett lectures were completed by the end of June, and for two weeks in July, John and Betty, along with their friend May Anderson, took a vigorous walking holiday in the Swiss Alps. Both Macmurrays were terrific walkers and they were glad to escape Oxford for the open spaces. They had ideal weather, and fresh adventures each day in climbing in the mountains or trudging through the valleys. It was a glorious vacation.

Balliol and A.D. Lindsay

Back at Oxford John prepared for his autumn lectures. On September 14, 1923, in the leisure afforded him before the students returned, he began a Commonplace Book which opens with the first journal-like reflection on record from him, apart from his letters, since his youthful diary ended ten years earlier:

> One discovers that the rift between the old and the young which the
> war produced is lasting: The younger men are lost — don't know
> what they want nor which way to turn. The older men have never
> been lost, and that's the mischief: for they look on our wildness and
> woolliness as a degeneracy. They consider that a nervous reaction
> from war-strain has disordered our emotional outlook: we are merely
> restive. This assumption is that the old ways and the old standards
> stand; and that we are to be pitied because we are unable owing to

'nerves' or something as abnormal, to settle down i.e., to accept the pre-war standards of value and conditions of social existence.

But we know that it is they who are blind. True, we don't know where to turn or how to move: we drift. Some of us satisfy ourself [*sic*] with the 'eat and drink, for tomorrow we die' of a blasé disillusionment. Some of us want to substitute the spirit of the war-comradeship for the petty conventions of social morality. Others of us just look on, keep silent, and fret, knowing our impuissance. But we have this in common, that we know that there is no going back to what was before the war. That is a bankrupt system. Mussolini and fascism are the first genuine production of this new need [?]. Something similar is likely to follow everywhere. It is the death of Democracy considered as a system of government founded upon the Rousseau tradition of liberty.

This was probably a reflection on life inside Balliol as well as in the nation and beyond. The current Master of Balliol, Arthur Lionel Smith, was a much more energetic, outward-looking and creative man than Strachan Davidson had been. To the horror of some of his older colleagues, he was also much more democratic in his convictions. He had strong interests in the Workers' Education Association (WEA) and had started the WEA Summer School at Oxford in 1910 which spread quickly to other universities across England. The sight of workers wandering through the courtyard each summer, as though they belonged there, was more than many of the old-guard among the Balliol Fellows could endure. When Smith died in early 1924, they were clearly hoping to get their ship, which they saw leaning dangerously to the left, back on to an even keel. They looked to their elder colleagues Cyril Bailey, Harold Hartley or A.W. Pickard-Cambridge as ideal candidates for the captain's chair.

Resistance to this desire for retrenchment arose primarily among the younger Fellows who believed that the only way into the future was, as Macmurray suggested, "beyond the dead past." Although they were not alone, Duncan Campbell Macgregor, Charles Morris and John Macmurray were the main voices in the forward-looking party. Macmurray took a decisive role in proposing his old mentor A.D. Lindsay to succeed as Master. Lindsay had done well as a Fellow of Balliol from 1906 until 1922 when he accepted the Chair of Moral Philosophy at Glasgow. Lindsay had personal friends among the older Fellows, but that did not mean they would like Balliol to be led by him. The Labour Party had, for the first time in history, formed a national government just the year before. Lindsay was known to be a member of the Independent Labour Party which often represented views even more left than those of the government. To further stimulate apprehension it was well known that, in Glasgow, Lindsay was teaching the thought of Karl Marx and had published a book on Marx's *Das Kapital.* His old Balliol friends liked him — but they did not want him as Master. Besides, Sandy Lindsay was only forty-five years old; too young, they felt, for the leadership position.

Macmurray visited Lindsay in Glasgow for the sake of offering a thorough perspective on the feelings and rationale of the younger Fellows. He later wrote to Lindsay on behalf of the group who looked favourably on him coming to Balliol. In the letter Macmurray observed: "It is wonderful how Balliol does somehow at crises like this rise to the occasion and do the big thing, in spite of doubts and fears."[5] Despite his great reluctance to leave Glasgow after having spent only two years there and in the midst of many unfinished projects, Lindsay finally agreed to make himself available for the Balliol position. In a close vote, he was elected Master and took over the helm in the autumn of 1924.

Lindsay held the position for twenty-five years and, as occurs in any career marked by large undertakings, he managed to create both allies and enemies. Given his felicitous efforts at matchmaking, John Macmurray might have been found unambiguously in the former group. But surprisingly, after Lindsay had been there a while it seems that Macmurray did not fall into the allied camp, the reasons for this being unclear since many of their personal and professional convictions overlapped. In her biography of Lindsay, his daughter Lady Drusilla Scott briefly addresses the post-honeymoon period of her father's early years as Master of Balliol. Her silence in relation to Macmurray is thundering:

> Charles Morris, of the younger Fellows who had wanted Lindsay
> back, was the most consistent ally of his policies, and John Fulton,
> who came as a Fellow shortly afterwards, became another; they
> both belonged firmly to the A.L. Smith tradition and shared
> Lindsay's interests in the W.E.A. and his concern with the changing
> world outside the College; both went on to important Vice-
> Chancellorships, but for the most of the long span of Lindsay's
> Mastership they were there with him.[6]

Certainly, Morris was "there" with Lindsay in the literal sense of being a Fellow of Balliol until the early 1940s, leaving Balliol just a few years before Lindsay himself. But that is not the only kind of "being there" she suggests. Conspicuously absent from her list of young supporters after 1924 is Macmurray; conspicuously, because he is cited by Lady Scott just a few paragraphs earlier as the leader and representative of the group that wanted Lindsay to come to Balliol. Equally surprising is the implication that the unmentioned former supporters, Macmurray and Macgregor, may *not* have been in the A.L. Smith tradition or did not back Lindsay's WEA initiatives, or were not open to the university's interest in the "changing world." In fact, there is much to indicate that a care for education in its widest forms made up a substantial dimension of Macmurray's career. He was also hugely concerned about the political and economic implications of philosophical ideas, and addressed these questions both academically and in public presentations, especially during the thirties and early forties. And he did so from a socialist viewpoint, even, in the early Thirties, one deeply influenced by Marx. The explanation for a falling out between these men whose views of the world had such affinities, if there was one, must be found elsewhere.

Lindsay and his wife Erica socialized on many occasions with John and Betty Macmurray. As Betty recalled, John and Erica genuinely enjoyed one another's company and were able to converse and read poetry with one another with great ease on these outings. On the other hand, Betty found that Lindsay, although affable, could also be rude in a teasing and condescending way with John. He seemed to delight in finding ways to embarrass him and even poke fun "at John's philosophical ideas and humanitarian attitudes," but she was never sure why he took such a super-cilious attitude to her husband.

In her delightful little article for the Balliol alumni magazine entitled "Memories of a Balliol Stepdaughter" Professor Dorothy Emmet classifies Macmurray as a "maverick philosopher" along with R.G. Collingwood. She then recounts a memory that might suggest there was something other than bias or paranoia in Betty Macmurray's account of how Lindsay viewed John Macmurray:

> I remember once reading an essay to Lindsay in which I produced
> some view as from the *Critique of Pure Reason*; he asked me
> "Where did you get hold of that idea?" and when I said "From Mr
> Macmurray's lecture," he laughed and said "That explains it." I
> found that there was a story in Balliol that John had never read
> beyond the Preface to the Second Edition of the *Critique*. And his
> lectures were a great construction of what Kant really meant on the
> basis of this.[7]

For Betty, not surprisingly, the fault was Sandy's, not John's. For her, it came down to the difference between John being emotionally a more sim-ple and direct man, and Sandy having amply adopted "the Oxford attitude." By this she meant an élitist self-complacency that she found diminishing and exhausting. She said this holier-than-thou scepticism mixed with cer-tainty regularly reminded her of the saying: "Cambridge produced the

Reformers, and Oxford burned them." She felt Lindsay's *principles* were democratic but once the talk ended he was temperamentally a snob and an aristocrat who lacked the common touch; adding mordantly: "like so many other intellectuals who fight for freedom" [for the poor].

This view of Lindsay was, in fact, not unique to her. Drusilla Scott quoted in her biography a statement in which he was pilloried on this point much earlier in his career at Balliol:

> The writer of the *Isis* article years before had seen the duality [in Lindsay]. 'By nature a lotus eater, a reactionary and a believer in aristocracy, he has deluded himself and his friends into regarding him as an idealist, a radical, a collectivist.'[8]

A larger perspective might be suggested. Differences between Macmurray and Lindsay may simply have grown deeper since their earlier acquaintance. Each of them, as Professor Emmet's anecdote suggests, had developed distinctive philosophical thoughts as well as a distinctive manner.[9] It may have taken working together as colleagues, not as tutor and student, for these differences to come forward and be felt. The only indication we have from Macmurray himself that he might, after the first year of the Master's new tenure, have become disappointed with Lindsay is a very indirect one. In his Commonplace Book, he writes a reflection that focuses on the larger social situation in Britain but could suggest a more local application, as well:

> Outward changes are very slow: we are where we were, more or less. The majority are enjoying what there is to enjoy. The thinkers aren't much farther on: the politicians are peculiarly sterile, even for politicians. The Labour movement lost enthusiasm with the fiasco of the Labour government. The vast conservative reaction is just as unsatisfactory to everybody. It has made no difference — and doesn't propose to make any. It really stands for a refusal — nation-wide — to look facts in the face and raise important questions. Never have I found it harder to think, or work, or face issues. Institutions are continuing to exist not because people are satisfied with them; but because they have agreed to let things alone to take their course, to forget enthusiasms, and live from hand to mouth. This mood will last a long time, I expect. The old ideas seem to have got a grip again: but it is a spurious appearance. We are making them do, in default of any others, and in default of the energy to try experiments and to think hard. There is a very prevalent, a sort of galvanic sense of duty; coupled with an attempt to make

pleasure the important business. 'Do your duty, and *live* the rest
of the time.' This can't really last, because it isn't alive: Reason
and imagination have different objects. For the time, we live by
what we are familiar with, and conceal from ourselves as far as
we can, that we don't believe it. (July 3, 1925)

Even if this statement is not aimed at Balliol, it is probable that life at
Balliol is not entirely excluded from it. Lindsay was indeed outward-looking with his democratic convictions, but it was not evident even to his
daughter-biographer that any of these principles were being applied to the
college itself. Lady Scott observed that her father made such a point of
caring for the sensibilities of the old guard that, during his first years, it
can be shown that, in referring to past masters, he quoted the conservative
Strachan Davidson more than he did the liberal A.L. Smith, even though
Smith was far more his model. The dualism noted by the *Isis* writer may
also have struck Macmurray when he reviewed Lindsay's practical strategies for inside Balliol. There were certainly no signs of an "education for
democracy" applied to the structures in the college!

There is no evidence that the differences between the two men were
ever openly expressed. They seem to have remained professionally amicable until Lindsay's death. Apart from the Professor Emmet story, the
closest thing we have to a view of John Macmurray from Lindsay came in
1928, after Macmurray's own philosophy was taking definite shape, and
he had just left Balliol for his new position in London. That summer,
Lindsay observed to young David Cairns who had been tutored by
Macmurray for his last two years:

I'm worried about John. He is beginning to talk as if religion had
only to do with the relations of finite persons, and God seems to
have faded out. When he was here, the rest of us could tell him he
was talking nonsense. Now he is away, there is no one to check him!

That could, of course, be the solicitude of friendship rather than paternal-
ism talking. But there is slight indication in the remark of the kind of sympathetic understanding one might have looked for in someone talking to a
student about a friend. The issue must remain in shadows.

The don and his students

In his teaching and tutoring, Macmurray gave himself generously to his students. There is ample testimony that he was a tutor who was encouraging,
critical, provocative and very forthcoming with the new ideas that were

filling his own mind during those energetic years. During those years he taught David Cairns who became Professor of Practical Theology at Aberdeen, John Findlay who became a Professor of philosophy himself, Hugh Gaitskell who was to become a faculty member in Political Science at University College, London, in the 1930s and eventually head of the Labour Party, and Sir Richard Acland, Labour politician and educator who founded the short-lived Commonwealth Movement along with J.B. Priestley. Eugene Forsey, the Canadian constitutional expert, and Donald Creighton, the eminent Canadian historian, were just two of many students from abroad who were also influenced by him. Professor David Cairns captured the feeling of gratitude of many, though the faith element he mentions here may not have figured in the relationship many others had with Macmurray:

> John Macmurray was my tutor for Greats when I was at Balliol in 1924–28, and I owed him an immense debt for the careful and considerate way he went with me, a young man of 22 in 1926, fascinated by the problems of philosophy, yet practically drowning in confusion, and holding out my hands to clutch any straw. He gave me much more than that, and I was reassured by the fact that he and Charles Morris, the philosophy tutors, and Sandy Lindsay, the Master, were all professedly Christian.[10]

In later years, many of his students remembered Macmurray fondly and stayed in touch with him throughout their professional years, mainly because they found him kind and solicitous for their welfare. For Sir William Stuart Murie, Macmurray was an "extremely sympathetic" tutor who would critique his ideas but never in a cruel or superior way. "One felt one had come into contact with Socrates," Murie observed, using an image repeated by many of Macmurray's students throughout his years of teaching.[11] He stimulated a feeling of reverence in a great number of his students, as well. Dame Alex (Kilroy) Meynell, in her book entitled *Public Servant, Private Woman,* attested to his influence on her basic moral outlook. She confessed that her attitude to public service and her convictions about forming a society that made room for everyone were formed, in large part, by having John Macmurray as her tutor.

When he came to Balliol from Canada as a Rhodes Scholar, the constitutional expert and senator Eugene Forsey had been recommended to Macmurray by his old friend Richard Roberts who had, by the mid-1920s, left the United States and moved to Toronto. Forsey was at sea in philosophy even more than Cairns. He found Macmurray patient with him but honest enough not to propose that he make a career in philosophy. Interestingly, Forsey remembered his tutor Macmurray as an out-and-out Kantian.[12] Kant, despite the great respect Macmurray had for him, was hardly the only focus of his philosophical concerns at the time.

Macmurray was remembered by many of his students as being quite strongly anti-Idealist at the time, although this did not automatically mean he had fallen into the Realist arms of John Cook Wilson and his followers. Macmurray found his outlook was very different from people like W.D. Ross, whose ethics made much of "what the ordinary man would say," and H.A. Prichard, Professor of Moral Philosophy at Oxford, whose naturalistic view of perception placed him very close to Cook Wilson. Cairns reports: "I remember him telling me a story, perhaps a bit unkind, about the mental distress Prichard got into about purely abstract issues." Although Pritchard's reaction was almost surely a discomfort with Idealism, another sort of abstract attitude only deepened at Balliol as the new linguistic philosophy took root and effectively reduced the scope of much British philosophy. Macmurray's philosophical perspectives were more mainstream than that, and much more far-reaching in their theoretical and practical concern.

There is a story about a book planned by Macmurray and Charles Morris that continues to be a bit of a puzzle even to this day. Around the time the two men met, Morris was beginning a book with his wife Mary entitled *A History of Political Ideas*. It was published in 1924. Soon after that Morris and Macmurray began planning a book they would write together. On December 5, 1924, they formally contracted with Macmillan to do the book which would be called *Modern Philosophy Since the Time of Hegel*. The manuscript was to be delivered to the publishers within three years of the signing date, as the Memorandum of Agreement stipulates. It also notes that fifty pounds would be delivered to each of the authors at the time of signing: "... on account of the royalties arranged to be paid under Clauses 4 and 5 of this Memorandum of Agreement." If the conditions were not fulfilled, the advance each received was to be returned to the publishers. The book never saw the light of day, and it is not clear why not. Certainly one obstacle may have been Morris' absence during the 1926–27 year when he went to the USA as professor of philosophy at the University of Michigan. A rumour began that the advance money had not been returned to the publisher and, although the rumour was never widely diffused, neither was it fully dispelled. It is more than interesting that when this rumour was recalled in the mid-1990s by Professor George Davie who knew Macmurray, the tale ended: "But no one for an instant believed he was capable of behaving like that."[13]

Social life at Oxford

Beyond the college, there was time at Oxford for lighter things, as well. Both John and Betty joined the Bach Choir. During auditions, John faked being a tenor because they needed tenors. They were accepted and were delighted with being part of that year's singing of the St Matthew Passion. On one occasion, Betty went to choir practice, even though she had laryngitis, thinking she could just mouth the words and still learn something more of the music. As she reports, Sir Hugh Allen stopped the singing and said to her: "You, there! Why are you sitting there like a tame slug not singing?" She was deeply hurt, partly by the public criticism — and partly because she hated slugs. But it was just one more incident that confirmed for her that rudeness was not a vice at Oxford, and she expected, and got, no apology. It was while they were in the choir that she came to the realization that she would never be good at music. She came to the conclusion: John understands music; I only enjoy it. Quietly assessing that this was another ground on which she could not flourish on the same footing as he, she began to take painting lessons.

However, the experience in the choir added to her growing discomfort at Oxford. Her relief came from John's quiet understanding of the deeper cause of her feeling. He confessed that Oxford had a way of making you feel you didn't belong if you weren't educated there. Her major complaint when depression set in was clear to her only years later: "I was play acting all the time." She did not add what those who knew her were able to add: Some of the time, Betty very much enjoyed play acting.

On the bright side, she enjoyed being the wife of a don, and was more than able to make her way in most social settings despite her negative view of most social life at Oxford. She was often in demand as a chaperone — an Oxford rule — probably because she was more than willing to be understanding of young people. One of her happiest memories of Oxford was simply the sound of the young men laughing; laughter breaking out in groups in conversation along the Broad, laughter floating over the water from punts. It felt full of light to her, and it raised strongly contrasting images of her own youth which was marked by such religious intensity and domestic seriousness. Only when she heard the great bursts of healthy, free youthful laughter did she realize how heavy and often solemn that upbringing had been.

Of all the *faux pas* she committed during their five and a half years at Balliol, the one that Betty laughed about most easily was the time she and John were putting on a dinner and they decided to invite John's colleague, the lecturer and author, C.E.M. Joad and his wife as guests. Professor Joad was married three times over the years, and when Betty wrote to Mrs Joad asking her to dinner she got the reply: "I'd love to! But I'm not the current Mrs Joad."

The house on Mansfield Road was big compared to what they had been used to, but there was an advantage for the college in building it so large. Balliol faculty with space to spare in their homes were invited to offer accommodation to international students as part of the college's good relations with influential families abroad. In their first time round in this programme, the Macmurrays took in a pleasant and quiet young Parsee named Cowaje, son of the head of the Parsees, Sir Jamsetsee. Because his Zoroastrian religion would not permit him to extinguish fire, either John or Betty regularly had to tramp up the stairs to his room, especially during the winter months, to turn off the gas fire for him. Betty recalled with perverse delight an incident that occurred when John was invited to go punting on the river by one of the Indian students. Dressed to the nines, he accompanied the young man to the launch area. John was in the process of alerting the young man to the delicacy of balance required in a punt when the student, already comfortably seated and anxious to head out, suddenly pushed the boat away from the dock with his paddle. John was left with all his weight leaning on the pole while the boat slowly moved away from under him. The end was inevitable. He tumbled headlong into the water, drenching his finest linen suit and soaking his good shoes. He had to walk all the way home through Oxford in that condition, and arrived at the house as cross as a wet cat.

But, the most memorable social event in their time at Balliol was their invitation to lunch with William Lord Asquith, the Liberal ex-prime minister. Joining them were his wife Margot, Tony, their son, Lady Bonham-Carter with her baby, Mark, and Princess Bibisco, Margot's daughter. The reason for the invitation was a talk Asquith wanted to have with John who was Tony's tutor. Asquith was concerned that Tony, who was maintaining strong upper Second Class marks at Oxford, was not really holding up his end in light of the academic performance of his Uncle Henry and other members of the family over the years. Could some changes be made, he was wondering, to ensure that Tony would come down from Oxford with a First. Macmurray was confident Tony was performing at his level and spoke encouragingly about his work. This was not the response Asquith was hoping for. He allowed that Tony was working, but turned his attention with irritation on how the college had slipped since that radical Lindsay had taken over. He was effectively saying that Tony's grades were lower than they should be, and this was because Balliol and its new Master were not pulling *their* weight. John disagreed with that view, and said so. Lord Asquith then took occasion to dump on the programme of Modern Greats — a programme that Lindsay had been instrumental in getting started when he was a don at Balliol years before. He railed against the cheap pursuit of "relevance" and stated categorically that the college should insist that students start at the start, namely, with the Greeks. Macmurray, quite angry at this point, countered: "No, it is far better to start now, then work back to the start; and besides, the Greeks weren't the start at all." At that, the infuriated Asquith left the conversation and the room. Later, John reflected that Asquith was the crustiest conservative he had ever met. The meeting did no harm whatever to his relationship with Tony.

The writer Joyce Cary was one Oxford friend they both dearly loved and who, in Betty's estimation, was definitely not "Oxford" in the pejorative sense. Cary had an El Greco face, and was the gentlest man she had met to that point. He would come for tea each Sunday, and each time, as Betty reports, he would "open doors" for her through his sensitivity to nature and to art. It was through him that she learned this was the kind of person she so much enjoyed being with: a feeling person, an artist. John and Joyce would go on long walks during which they would discuss art and poetry, with especially memorable conversations on Le Corbusier and functionalism. When the Macmurrays got a car, the three of them would drive out to the country on Sundays. It was a warm relationship that endured until Joyce Cary's death some thirty years later.

It was while they were at Oxford that Betty became very aware that her faith no longer had any focus. She and John talked about their youthful, evangelical years, and John insisted that he had never really been converted to that form of religion. It would probably be more accurate to say that he had never been truly himself in it but it is interesting that this is not how he saw it. Betty, on the other hand, felt she had been genuinely converted, that she had known Jesus with love, and he had known her; but ten years later that seemed to have disappeared. They went occasionally to a Presbyterian church at Oxford, but John's decision not to be committed to any denomination left them unanchored in terms of a tradition or a community. John seemed satisfied with this arrangement considering he was exploring his faith along exciting but more intellectual lines at the time; but the absence of rituals and faith friendships left Betty bereft and disoriented. In her growing love for artistic expression, she found herself drawn to the "cold formality" of the Anglican service. Much later, she discovered how powerfully attractive she found the rituals of the Roman Catholic Church. As she said, the sacraments made it feel like the body was a positive thing and mattered in religion. Meanwhile, her discontent deepened. She knew she was longing for more intimate relationships and more emotional expression than Oxford society seemed able to provide. Both John and Betty wanted children but, despite their fondest hopes, Betty sadly did not get pregnant during these years.[14] It was at Oxford that, for the first time, as though searching for something new and different — or ending something — she cut off the long hair she had had since childhood.

During this time, John was working at a feverish pace on his courses and on his first publications. He was also preparing his sections for the book he and Morris had undertaken. At the heart of his work, however, was the personal philosophical purpose he had proposed for himself some five years earlier when he went to his first job at Manchester. As his lecture notes and publications show, all of his work was directed by his own guiding questions. He read Aristotle and Stoicism, Kant and the German Romantics, and did work across the history of western philosophy on the Theory of the State. Lecture notes in various courses in ethics show that he was giving the students the advantages not only of the classical authors in the field but of his own developing thinking on how those thinkers intersected, or didn't, with contemporary problematics.

He had stayed in touch with his friend Richard Roberts who had moved to Toronto from New York. He continued to use Roberts as a sounding board for personal questions, and also wrote him letters that remain a unique source for glimpsing his personal feelings about the genesis of his own philosophy and how it was being received.[15] On October 22, 1925, he wrote Roberts to ask for his advice on an invitation Macmurray was told might be coming from Princeton asking him to take a professorship there.

> What I want is not so much ordinary information: but the kind of understanding of the situation which would enable me to form some fairly rational estimates of the scope that I should have of the difficulties and possibilities. It is the intellectual and spiritual side of the situation that I feel quite unable to form an judgment upon. Oxford gives one all the stimulus to create work in philosophy but denies the time to do it; and does tend to make one a hack-teacher in fact. Princeton would reverse this, would it? Or would it not?

There is no record of anything coming of this offer. Clearly he stayed at Balliol. However, slightly more than two years later, Macmurray was offered a position at a university in Canada, evidently at the suggestion of Roberts, and he wrote to convey his gratitude to Roberts, and tell him why he was about to refuse it.

> I think I should decline the Canadian Professorship, on the ground that my work is clear to me now, and that I can do it best in this country — though there is much about Canada that tempts me. The work would be very easy for me and leave a lot of free time: and that is a main consideration. But for thinking out the philosophy of Personality, which is my main job, it is better to be in the older civilization than in

the new one. Even here I am finding myself too much pressed by
outside demands and forcing myself to refuse them.[16]

He certainly was allowing himself to be pressed from all sides. Apart from
his philosophical society activities and publications, he had renewed his
connection with the Student Christian Movement and responded to their
request for two articles on the topic of "Economic Laws and Social
Progress" in *The Student Movement*.

He contributed to various publications, but responded most frequently
to the requests of the *British Weekly*. In his January 1927 review of J.C.
Smuts' book *Holism and Evolution* in the *British Weekly,* John praised the
work as a solid identification of the central problem of philosophy in
terms of concrete personality; however, he charges Smuts with applying
organic thinking to questions of personality. He noted that Smuts was
hardly alone in this category error since "mathematicians like Professor
Whitehead are trying to reinterpet the classical physics in terms of an
organic concept of nature." John charged this position with being another
form of naturalism, a viewpoint that is invalid, as Idealism showed, since
it "ignores the reflexive character of personal consciousness. Personality
is at once a continuation of the development of Nature and a reflection
upon it." The review was clearly an occasion to flag the direction of his
own thinking at the time.

But his writing was not all so serious, or pointed towards his own philosophical agenda. In a September 1927 *British Weekly* book review of
Ernest Barker's *National Character,* Macmurray notes that his review has
little bite because the book has little bite. After summarizing the contents,
he humorously but somewhat mordantly, observes, "In the result, we have
to thank Dr Barker for ... a book full of living interest and ripe wisdom. If
it leaves us with the impression that its author has sifted all that is known
of national character, but that nobody knows very much, that is probably
the simple truth."

Sometime during their last years in Oxford, Betty told John that she had
become involved sexually with another man. John was devastated. He
knew Betty had been unhappy with Oxford, as well as unhappy and dislocated in herself much of the time, but he also had felt there was little he
could do to change things for her. After making her announcement, Betty
rushed to tell him that she had not lost her love for him in the slightest —
in fact her love for him was secure and even growing. It was simply that
with the young man she had met, she felt a physical passion that she had
never felt before. She confessed to John that she felt she was coming alive
sensually for the first time. Using a language with which they were both
very familiar, she felt she was being reborn; but carnally. It had to do with
feeling alive, and this had to do with becoming more alive as a whole

person. It had by no means replaced her love for John, nor was it anywhere near as deep; it was just different from her love for John, and somehow necessary for her. She asked for his acceptance of the relationship.

Recollecting that time many years afterwards, Betty wrote: "No longer was I confused about my fundamental need ... The 'sunbeam for Jesus' was out. Mother's little kid was dead. What was I now?" She only knew that she was quite open and anxious to discover the answer. As for John, she felt this change in her was the second great shock to his life — displacing in importance the disillusionment and pain he felt at the way his friendship with Hofmeyr had been ended.

As she wrote in her memoirs years later, "John and I held hands and wept." When words came for Betty, they were words meant to console but perhaps also to challenge her husband. The ones she had available and that meant everything to her were the words expressing his philosophy that she heard coming from her husband's mouth at parties and with guests over their own dinner table. She reminded him of the need for personal freedom in *every* aspect of life that he taught so passionately. She reminded him of his own view that children become mature individuals by "resisting" their given circumstances, by risking expressing their own desire in action. She was obviously not a child, but in this she felt she was somehow like a child, one who had not yet discovered or expressed this part of herself that was now welling up in her. And she recalled for him the central place he gave to trust in any genuine, free relationship. She was asking him for that trust. She made it clear that no one could ever replace him in her life and she did not in the least want to leave their marriage; but that she needed this other dimension in her living, as well. She wondered aloud with him if her actions and her request for his approval to continue in the relationship was not the first real test of his faith in his own philosophy. At some point, then or sometime later, she said she understood that the freedom to have other sexual partners she was asking of him was something she must equally grant to him.

In the end, they came to a shared decision. Each of them began by affirming that their friendship and their marriage was the absolute relationship in their lives and that no other relationship would be allowed to threaten it. They pledged that to one another. They promised with regard to other sexual partners to be open with one another, and to foster in their marriage whatever would promise to deepen their own love and friendship. They both probably knew, without ever mentioning it at the time, that their childlessness had something to do with this turn of events in their life. This would come clear for each of them only later.

There is no evidence that John acted on this new understanding in the short term, but he clearly admits to doing so, on occasion, during their subsequent years in London. Betty continued in her relationship with her friend, whose name was Jack Barry. He came to the house, and John met him. On occasion, they all socialized together.

John carried this new reality in a place of silence in him but he also reflected deeply on its meaning. Overwhelming as it was, he took seriously Betty's statement that she might be living out the philosophy of human development that he was making his own, and that this was a test for him. In an early letter to his sister whose marriage was not going well, John had responded to Helen's self-destructive feelings and scolded her for concealing them from him. "Please share your troubles with me," he wrote. "Let me carry them. Hiding them from me is the greatest of pains for me." He went on:

> I believe in love. I've learned to trust love — in all its forms from
> the lowest to the highest, on the physical plane and on the spiritual.
> That is a tremendous risk, but it's worth it.

Then he added, perhaps wryly and laughing a bit at himself: "St Paul and Socrates got it right about what we know — not much."[17]

Meanwhile at 5 Mansfield Road, John and Betty entertained, and in their socializing, tried in a way that never got beyond straining, to enjoy life at Oxford. Betty, and John too in his own way, found Oxford society élitist, self-enclosed and extremely judgmental. But for her, it was also condescending and suffocating in its narrowness. Betty was not an intellectual. She was a feeler, a budding artist and, as she saw it, there was simply no place for her kind of person in that kind of society. When, in the summer of 1928, John was invited to accept the Grote Professorship in Mind and Logic at University College, London, vacated by the retirement of Professor G. Dawes-Hicks, she couldn't wait to leave.

1. *John Macmurray (stand-ing) with his sister, Helen (1895).*

2. *A couple of years after moving to Aberdeen the Macmurray family posed for a formal portrait. John stands behind his mother, Mary Anna, who holds Joseph, the youngest child. Beside John is Helen and then Lilias. Mary sits beside her father, James (1903).*

3. John Macmurray sits for his official Balliol portrait as Snell Exhibitioner, shortly after coming to Oxford (October, 1913).

4. After supper, Macmurray (standing, right) with other enlisted men near Salisbury at the outset of military training. Macmurray joined the Royal Army Medical Corps as a way of expressing the anti-violence convictions which he held at the time (October 1914).

5. *John Macmurray and Elizabeth Hyde (Betty) Campbell, three months after they were married. John was back in Scotland recovering from a broken foot he sustained during the Battle of the Somme (spring 1917).*

6. *John Macmurray leaving Buckingham Palace with his sister, Helen, after receiving the Military Cross for gallantry in war (around 1918).*

7. John Macmurray looking like D.H. Lawrence at the time when Lawrence's writing about the goodness of sensuality was impressing him deeply (c. 1935).

8. Macmurray in the Laurentians north of Montreal, just before giving the workshop in Belleville, Ontario, which made him a mentor for many "social Gospel" Protestants and SCMers in Canada (June, 1936).

9. John Macmurray (left) in a reflective chat with John Middleton Murry at the Adelphi Centre (summer 1937).

10. The dashing & dapper Macmurray, possibly at University College, London (around 1937).

11. After giving a summer course in Siljanskolan, Sweden, Macmurray prepares a talk for Swedish Radio which he delivered just days before the outbreak of the Second World War (September 1939).

12. Relaxing after giving "an inspiring interview" in Aberystwyth, Wales, where University College was evacuated due to the wartime blitz that destroyed great sections of the University of London, including Macmurray's office (February 17, 1940).

15 (Opposite). Portrait of John Macmurray taken in New York to advertise his Danforth Lectures. He spoke at thirty colleges and universities across the USA during this 99-day tour (autumn 1958).

13. Betty at 10 Bright's Crescent in Edinburgh with their deaf cat Jeremy, whose exploits fascinated T.S. Eliot when he visited and heard of them (1944).

14. On a public occasion during his tenure as Dean of Arts and Sciences at the University of Edinburgh: from left to right, John Macmurray and the Head of the Social Sciences Department pose with Clement Attlee, and Sir Edward Appleton, Principal of the University (around 1956?).

16. John Macmurray in his study at Hatherly Brake, their home in Jordans, Buckinghamshire, where he and Betty lived for twelve years after retiring from the University of Edinburgh in 1958.

17. John Macmurray back in Edinburgh (early 1970s).

18. John and Betty at Mansionhouse Road, their last home where they lived with Duncan and Jocelyn Campbell and their children (1975).

All photos available with the permission of the John Macmurray Trust.

Chapter 7

Discovering the Personal (1925–28)

During his time at Oxford, Macmurray spent long hours in his study at home, working on the many projects he had accepted in his first two years at Balliol. Most prominent among these, until the project fell through, was the book he was writing with Charles Morris. He had also been elected a member of the Aristotelian Society in 1924, and had committed himself to giving a presentation entitled "Is Art a Form of Apprehension or Expression?" on July 26, 1925, for a Society symposium chaired by Samuel Alexander, his old boss at Manchester, and including Macmurray's colleague C.E.M. Joad as a contributor. Starting in 1925 and stretching over his remaining three years at Oxford, the man who had yet to publish anything under his own name produced at least two and sometimes three or more articles each year in both academic and popular journals.

What is transparent from his publications and the numerous sets of reading and lecture notes from these years is the clear focus in his philosophical purpose. He was pursuing issues that related directly to the convictions about the "unity of knowledge" he had expressed at the end of his journal in 1913. He had not "grown beyond" these fervent convictions, despite the dislocated and sceptical temper of the times and despite his own conclusion, along with many at Oxford, that Idealism did not provide the terms for a genuine unity. With his commitment made in 1919 to explore the means to achieve genuine justice and peace in the world as backdrop, he was studying the foundations of western civilization, looking for the fault-lines in its dominant views of morality, polity, knowledge and religion. He was, of course, searching in that history for positive philosophical avenues that might help find a way to heal the massive contradictions in western society and the European soul. His reading and lecture notes reveal that he studied the Greeks and Roman Stoicism, touched on the Hebrew and early Christian (pre-Constantinian) heritage, but concentrated most on later developments in Modern philosophy, especially the German Romantics who contended so strongly with Kant.

His inquiries focused on the Modern period because he was convinced that, for all their great contributions, modern categories of thinking were responsible for many of the deepest problems that beset western society. The first and classical phase of Modern history (c.1600–1750) had developed and become dominated by a mechanical conception of unity arising out of the dominance of experimental physics (the science of inanimate matter) as providing the normative way of achieving knowledge. The Romantic second phase (c.1750–1917) driven by the science of living things and their relations (biology), articulated an organic paradigm for knowing based not on mathematically identical units but on diversity, development through differentiation, a harmony of functions and an inbuilt finality as each being strove towards its self-realization in the midst of dialectical relationships at every level. Again, this conception of unity was commonplace.

Macmurray's interest, as he began his own search, was not to focus on these two conceptions of unity, but to note that once they became the paradigms for viewing the world they were habitually applied to human beings, their institutions and their societies. In the nineteenth century, they contended fiercely with one another in a contest for dominance that in western society continues in our own day. As his 1921 letter to Samuel Alexander indicates, he was already convinced that mechanical and organic conceptions of unity were inadequate for understanding human beings and describing their behaviour and relationships. However, he needed to explore both conceptions with respect since he was equally sure that what was true of each must somehow be incorporated into the fuller conception of unity that he believed was needed in order to do justice to what is distinctively human. How could this higher integration be expressed? At this point, he simply knew it must involve a fuller notion of reason than had been thus far achieved in modern philosophy, and that became his goal: to articulate the form of a logic that did justice to the supra-organic mode of being called "the personal." So, almost as soon as he arrived in Oxford, he turned his attention to an intensive study of the rise of the organic mode of apperception with one purpose in mind: to locate, in its advances and limitations, the footholds and pitfalls on his way to a contemporary, reconstructed view of reason that would be adequate to human beings in their individual and their social existence.

Exploring the German Romantics

Macmurray had already read Rousseau who was the first to present a full-blown organic view of persons and society. However, it was to the eighteenth and nineteenth century Romantic thinkers in Germany that Macmurray turned in his search for a fuller view of reason since they had forged their views in response to Kant, and it was in wrestling with Kant, not in bypassing him, that he believed the breakthrough must be sought.

A sketch of this German Romantic view of truth is needed to understand Macmurray's philosophical journey at this point in his career. In

1759, after a profound religious conversion, Johann Georg Hamann (1730–88), a close friend in Koenigsberg of Immanuel Kant, proclaimed a faith in "the universal presence of God in the world speaking to human beings through everything in their nature and history." Hamann denied the capacity of abstracting scientific reason to relate to these deep truths and realities. He also rejected his friend Kant's unwillingness to accept the view that knowledge could be gained beyond the limits imposed by science. Offering an alternate vision of knowing, Hamann proposed faith, and his younger friend Johann Gottfried Herder along with Lessing and Jacobi proposed aesthetic intuition and creative imagination as the purest and fullest form of knowing. When reality is "revealed" in this mode of knowing the essential unity of truth and beauty is also revealed for there is a "harmony" in truth that is grasped only through feeling.

In this Romantic challenge to positivism, emotion is not the enemy of truth-seeking but a necessary ground for it. On this view, feeling is more faithful to the fullness of knowing than intellect, discovery is as much a work of intuition as of sense observation, and true knowing is more an artistic judgment than a scientific one since artistic imagination (and, for Hamann at least, religious faith and commitment) is the medium par excellence by which truth is not only discovered but created. The human being is not an observer of reality from outside it, but a participant who comes to knowledge only from within that which makes him who he is. Only with such a view of human knowing, asserted the German Romantics, could the unity and fullness of being be respected and enhanced.

This vision of the interconnectedness of all things, and of judgment as a creative act based in faith and feeling, inevitably transforms the meaning of history, as well. The individual is a child of nature but cannot be understood as existing prior to or in isolation from society. Every individual is a part of both nature and society, and his or her very individuality is formed only in and through both. Because the human being is social by nature, culture with all its artifacts, rituals and symbolic meanings is what gives meaning and substance to personal existence, not some disincarnate law of science that suggests "one size fits all," a rule that reduces individuals to identical units. Romantic thought overthrew the inanimate object as the metaphor and template for understanding reality and adopted the model of living beings in their full interconnectivity.

While exploring this tradition Macmurray read J.G. Fichte, Schelling, Schopenhauer and Schleiermacher in addition to Hamann, Herder and Jacobi. He did extensive note-taking and commentary on Schopenhauer and Schleiermacher for his class lectures, and wrote a carefully analytic essay on Johann Friedrich Herbart (1776–1841), almost surely prepared for a public lecture. He shows in his progress through the German

Romantics that he is at once receptive to and critical of the transformation
of knowing introduced by the primacy they gave to aesthetic intuition over
an exclusively intellectual activity. In this particular shift they made, he
recognizes a place for feeling in the functioning of reason that casts light
for him on his own personal transformation ten years earlier when he fell
in love with Betty. The conviction that feeling is already a form of knowing, one that actually provides the foundation and full ambiance for
"facts," appeals to him as a distinct advance over an exclusively intellectual notion of reason. It is an insight that will prove to be foundational for
his own creative work in the coming years.[1]

Macmurray was also refining his understanding of the different "log-
ics" at work in the different conceptions of unity. The mechanical viewpoint, defined by mathematics, required a logic that was merely formal.
The organic conception, on the other hand, produced the need for a *dialectical* logic, the expression of which reached its greatest refinement in
Hegel's thought. It forced him to acknowledge that whatever way an
advance might be made towards a philosophy of the distinctively human,
it would necessarily have to be a logic that included, in some manner, the
gains made by the two earlier modes of thought.

It was always the social and political applications of the organic conception of being that most struck Macmurray, and here he came to understand more fully the implications of the concept of finality that lay at the
heart of Romantic thought. In this teleological view, within each being and
specific to its nature there is a mature form to which it strives. Each being
ideally progresses to its own self-realization. Each organic entity, under
positive conditions, develops through natural stages towards its own ideal
fulfilment (for example, an acorn is "programmed" to grow into an oak).
And — to extend the image logically — to the degree that all things are
interconnected each is part of a dynamic, shared unfolding of the universe
which must have its own finality, as well, in terms of which we are all only
"parts".

The effect of this notion of an in-built, historical finality on the imagination of western Europe in the nineteenth century cannot be exaggerated. It proposed that individuals, institutions, sciences, religions, nations
and states — all things great and small — are dynamic parts of a progressively unfolding universe. All are progressing, in a dialectical fashion (that
is, by way of competitive struggle and conflict as well as mutual cooperation) towards a mature completion. We, and the universe of which, on this
model, we are functional parts, are now, therefore, only potentially what
we can and should become. History and every human action necessarily
participate in this cosmic development and are servants of it. Just as
the world evolves to its fullness, so each participating member, while
serving its function in the universe, is aspiring to and striving for its own

self-realization. Here is the philosophical heart of the western notion of evolution and progress. In the early 1920s it was the dominant conception of unity, a commonplace notion for educated people, and the point here is not to present it as though it were a new discovery for Macmurray at that time. He was impressed not by the theory, which was well-known, but by its sometimes blatant, sometimes subtle application to human life and social institutions. Vast implications came to light when he appreciated how much an organic model, along with the mechanical one, was effectively ruling the thinking, practices and policies of the Europe of the Industrial Revolution, leading into and through the First World War. He was struck by the absence of public recognition of this fact after the war.

It was while reading the German Romantics that Macmurray was forcefully struck by nineteenth century Europe's captivity by this apparently exalted image of human existence. Admittedly, it was an advance over a mechanical notion of human beings and their relationships and institutions. But it still provided a diminishing image of human beings. Human beings were, despite the invitation to both compete and cooperate in the development of the world, victims and/or beneficiaries of a finality over which they had no control. On the organic model of thinking of human action they were not free in any true sense but only in the sense of being able to choose Necessity. Their high purposes were only subordinate aspects of a finality that was beyond consciousness and therefore beyond knowledge and free action. Was this image of human existence a genuine reason for exaltation? He was convinced it was both wrong and very dangerous as a model for human action and society, especially since it encouraged a nature-based politics (identity in social relations based on blood, ethnicity, nationalism, the State, and so on) that was put forward by some political and social movements as the truest form of self-transcendence.

As Macmurray noted in his second 1923 journal reflection quoted earlier, an organic view of society is the ideological heart of the ominous, collectivist version of democracy inherited from Rousseau. It is inadequate to human beings, he had noted in his 1921 reading of Bosanquet, but now he sees how it is positively dangerous when it forms the declared identity and purpose of the nation-based State. As early as 1923, with the recent rise to power of Mussolini and the rumbling right-wing discontent in Weimar Germany, Macmurray was made apprehensive by the organically defined polities he saw taking shape in Europe.

But back to his search for an adequate philosophical conception of human knowledge, freedom and action! The Romantic view of knowledge and politics (that knowing was essentially an aesthetic intuition and the body politic and its actions were defined in terms of a "General Will") confirmed his apprehensiveness since it had no disciplined and publicly

accountable method of verification except for the strength of the feeling or
will that grounded it. This position, he concluded, was immensely open to
relativism in knowledge and totalitarianism in social and political life.
How could any objectivity be achieved in moral judgments? The
Romantics, within the terms of knowing they explored, could not manage
it. How could freedom be credible in a world that was effectively determined by innate finalities? Macmurray was forced to conclude that the
Romantic position had certainly allowed for art, morality, culture and religion to enter into legitimate human discourse and, therefore, had achieved
more inclusiveness than mechanical reductionism allowed, but at the cost
of adequately accounting for human knowing, individuality and freedom
since Romanticism, at root, remained essentially a form of naturalism.

Kant had proposed a more discriminating view of knowing, one that
distinguished carefully the areas of science, art and morality. In the Third
Critique, for example, he distinguished, over against the Romantics, judgments of truth from judgments of beauty. He also refused the fuzzy notion
of teleology any role in judgments of truth. But to maintain an objective
place for art, morality and religion, he had been forced to distinguish
between the world as experienced (phenomena) and the world as it truly
exists in itself (noumena), between one kind of knowledge for science and
another — more like a "not knowing" — for morality, art and religion.
Macmurray asked: could Kant's important distinctions be maintained, but
without requiring this radical dualism between Understanding and
Reason? Could the lamb of freedom ever lie down amicably, as part of the
same family, with the lion of determinism? Kant himself was unable to
provide that pasture.

Macmurray could see that Kant was trying to preserve the legitimacy
of the scientific view of knowledge while still acknowledging an objective
basis for art, morality and religion. The Romantics, on the other hand,
seemed content to throw out the baby of scientific method with the bath-
water of rationalism. Macmurray discovered elements of truth on both
sides. The dilemma was fundamental, and it is broached here at such
length only because it was so central for Macmurray himself as he tried to
find his way beyond what he considered two partial and inadequate conceptions of unity in the personal order.

In his effort to pick his way through the minefield of this debate,
Macmurray prepared a detailed set of notes, about sixty pages in all, entitled
"Kantians and Anti-Kantians" in which he sketches the positions taken by the
main philosophers engaged in the fray. A distilled version of Macmurray's
take on the debate can be found in his chapter called "Kant and the
Romantics" in The Self as Agent, the first volume of his Gifford lectures.

So, what, we may ask, was the result for Macmurray of giving so much
attention to this philosophical struggle? Two major advances for him have

already been mentioned. From the Romantics, despite their tendency to characterize the aesthetic (faith and feeling) and the scientific (reason) as opposite modes of knowledge, Macmurray sharpened considerably his understanding that reason must include feeling as well as intellect as a constitutive element in its full exercise. From it, he developed an expanded and fuller notion of knowing, one that he would eventually propose to associate with a fuller and integrating notion of reason. He also learned much about the dangers of applying the organic model of unity to human affairs, knowledge that would stand him in good service when he read Marx in the early 1930s and when, soon afterwards, he came to state his case against Fascism — taking the view that both Communism and Fascism were grounded in organic images of human beings and society.

Kant, on the other hand, taught Macmurray to cherish the need for all forms of knowing to respect some form of "rational" method. The Romantics proposed a foundational place for feeling in knowing but had no adequate explanation of how one is able to discern an *appropriate* ordering and verifying of knowledge. If, to use Kant's expression, the Positivists had failed "to deny knowledge in order to make room for faith," it seemed to Kant that the Romantics had equivalently failed to deny the looseness of their faith/feeling in order to make room for the disciplined verification, and falsification, required by knowledge. The Romantics had gained in comprehension, but they had lost in discrimination. Macmurray was left, from his study of this contest, convinced that he must seek out the best of both inspirations: the fullest *scope* of reason, on the one hand and, on the other, the need for a disciplined, appropriate and varied exercise of reason. He knew beyond doubt that although science, art, morality and religion are not identical, they can come together in the same person, and therefore, ideally, can and must come together in theory and in society. They must be both accessible and made accountable to reason in the fullness in which he was now beginning to contemplate it.

It was at this point in the battle that Macmurray came to one of his most significant philosophical conclusions: that action, not thinking, is the primary and most inclusive domain of human reason in its expression. His approach to this problematic came from his reading of Kant. The notion of Reason developed by Kant in the Second and Third Critiques was primarily practical, not theoretical. This was a radical shift from the primacy put on the theoretical in the first Critique, and it created a radical incoherence in Kant's efforts to relate the theoretical and the practical. However, Kant's shift of viewpoint, in order to save and ground morality and religion, gave Macmurray a powerful insight: *action is conceptually prior to thinking*. Theory arises from action and receives its verification in action. All western philosophy, starting with the Greeks, that made contemplation conceptually more foundational than action had proven unable to present a coherent view of how action relates to theory. However, if action is taken as primary, theory might be coherently understood as a constitutive dimension of action. Radical dualism would disappear. Equivalently, mechanical and organic elements in behaviour would be seen as constitutive dimensions of free, intentional and deliberate action. Material bodies and organic impulses would not be the starting point for trying to then understand free action; they would be known, by abstraction, as constitutive aspects of action. Action would be the full and immediate reality which, when examined, would reveal the dimensions of "object" and "impulse" as constitutive elements within it.[2]

The development in his thinking towards more refined ways of characterizing distinctively human behaviour is occurring rapidly. He finds that within free action he can locate both the organic (impulse) and the material (the world of the materially given) as constitutive but subordinate dimensions. "Action" is now the characteristic of the mode of unity constituting personality. In his acceptance of the prior status of the practical, Macmurray has translated his insights from Kant and the Romantics into a systematic exploration of human action that shows promise of achieving coherence and adequacy at once. Both qualities, he suggests, might find a promising common pivot in the same reality: free, human agency carried out in relation to and with fellow free agents. From this point forward, it can be said he truly walks in his own shoes.

He had no illusions about how difficult it would be to effect what he would later call this Third Revolution in scientific philosophy and social thinking based on the primacy of human action. He had found Schopenhauer a particularly sympathetic fellow-traveller around the thorny struggle between the claims of the artistic and the scientific tempers in philosophy. Macmurray's final reflection on Schopenhauer's struggle with this major dilemma and his essential pessimism around it was both lucid and somewhat prophetic in terms of future events and the philosophical directions he himself was about to take:

> The deliberate achievement of rational purposes in the face of the opposition of organic impulses must remain an enigma until the organic view is transcended, and it can only be transcended when it has been worked out through its application in a spirit of the hardest realism to all the problems of thought and practical organization, in science and philosophy, in art and invention, in the organization of economic and political life, and in the spheres of morality and religion. The Realism of the nineteenth century is the empirical phase of the philosophy of the organism, and it must work itself out into scepticism through experiment.[3]

Despite his premonitions about Mussolini and the failing Rousseau tradition in democracy, little could he imagine in 1925, the cost for Europe, its Jews, and the rest of the world that "working itself out into scepticism" would take.

One further spark struck his imagination in his reading of the Romantic thinker Friedrich Heinrich Jacobi (1743–1814), which led him to make the following observation. "In the certainty of existence, the 'I' and the 'Thou' are so immediately one that the onesideness of Idealism or Realism is out of the question." Macmurray goes on: "Jacobi is interested in the facts of consciousness. He is a modern. His standpoint is well called that of superior personality. The Absolute justification of moral individuality." And then he notes: "This would be perfect if it could escape subjectivism by accepting an objective revelation of God in a human personality." In this note — which he marked in the margin with a large "NB!!" — we catch a glimpse of Macmurray's more and more conscious use of the term "personality" for characterizing what he believed to be the distinctive and necessary focal point for philosophy in the post-modern period.[4]

Faith and verification

How Macmurray got stimulated to pursue this line of thinking is not irrelevant since, although the essential conviction around it was there since his own youthful transformation, the thinking did not all arise simply from within himself. As early as March, 1924, John had been drawn by Canon Burnett Streeter of Queen's College, Cambridge, into a series of weekend meetings on the relationship of faith and science. Streeter began with only discussions as his objective, but by October 1925 the flow of ideas and agreement was so promising, he developed the intention of publishing as a book the essays that had been presented for discussion. He saw the volume as a significant advance beyond his own effort to correlate science and religion in his recent, but not yet published, book called *Reality*.

Knowing something of these meetings casts light, as well, on the kind of "outside involvements" Macmurray was permitting himself during this extremely intense period in the development of his own thought. Streeter was an Anglican priest who had found his niche as a Christian intellectual in bringing together groups of Christian professors at Oxford to explore significant faith issues in the light of contemporary advances in knowledge in all areas: psychology, philosophy, art, biblical research, prayer, economics, politics, and, in this instance, science. He would serve as editor of the book containing the essays that were produced as a result of this particular set of discussions. From beginning to end, Streeter made each of these books a genuinely collaborative effort with all participants having their say about the final product.

The whole concept was able to be realized through the generous offer by Miss Lily Dougall of her Cumnor house near Oxford, as the gathering place for the conversations. Miss Dougall herself had participated in Streeter's first four 'shared' books entitled *The Spirit, Immortality, Concerning Prayer* and *Foundations,* each of which had brought together scholars and churchmen such as Cyril Emmet, Seth Pringle-Pattison, A. Clutton-Brock, J.A. Hatfield, Harold Anson, R.G. Collingwood, Rufus Jones, W.H. Moberley, R.G. Parsons, William Temple and others. The books answered a genuine need and went through several printings. However, the old 'Cumnor Group' was shattered by the deaths, within six months of one another, of Emmet, Clutton-Brock, and Miss Dougall herself.

Streeter — who had declared to friends that he probably would have renounced his Orders in despair of the Church except for the hope he had received from the small community that gathered for these projects — looked outward, and drew in Chilcott, a Tutor in Classics at Lady Margaret Hall, Russell, a University Lecturer in Inorganic Chemistry, and Macmurray, as a philosopher, for the discussions he had in mind. The book that came out of the meetings would be called *Adventure: The Faith of Science and the Science of Faith.* These occasional weekend conversations which stretched over some eighteen months involved, at different times, about ten participants including J.A. Hatfield, the only remaining member of the original group, Professor Julian Huxley of New College, and Professor. H.J. Paton who had recently left Queen's College for a position at the University of Glasgow.

On July 22, 1925, during the course of these occasional meetings, Macmurray wrote to his friend Richard Roberts, now living in Canada, giving him a profile of the direction his new thinking was taking. It previews material that he will feature in his two contributions to *Adventure*:

My philosophy — apart from the revelation of God in Christ,
which is my faith — would be frankly pessimistic and sceptical.
Put as against Absolute Idealism — Hegel and Bradley — I
maintain that the world is not self-explanatory and that life is not
self-sufficing: that this can be proved ... Philosophically, rational
knowledge at its best can only assume its principles hypothetically,
and cannot even suggest their probability. Hume has never been
answered, and can't be. Kant accepted his conclusions, and rightly.
I have undertaken to show by cold logic that the idea of God (apart
from revelation) i.e, apart from a recognition by faith of the
Divinity of the Man Christ Jesus, is entirely empty and negative. At
most, God is for thought a necessary hypothesis — and I should
state it thus "that *if* the world is to be comprehended, it must be in

terms of personality." But that is a purely sceptical conclusion in itself: for the comprehension of the world in terms of personality demands the positive comprehension of a particular personality, and the personality of God can only be defined negatively, in terms of infinites, i.e., as radically different in kind from any personality known to us. If there is to be knowledge of God, it must be positive knowledge of character. Now we can only know persons by acquaintance or, if you like, by friendship, sympathy, love. And my conclusion is therefore that until we can be acquainted with a particular person, and say of him that his personality is the revelation of God's personality: positing necessarily a relation of identity between the two, then we can have *no* knowledge of God, and therefore no knowledge at all which is well grounded. Logically we relapse into scepticism of reason. For this reason, I insist ... as an antidote to what is the prevalent view, that Faith is a matter of Will — not the will to believe, but the will to Be — to feel, to act and know. And as a matter of fact your suggestion for a complementary text "Stand fast in the liberty wherewith Christ has made you free," is exactly what I am trying to insist on.

Macmurray prepared two essays for *Adventure*. The first, entitled "Beyond Knowledge," challenges at its roots the split Kant bequeathed to subsequent philosophy between science (the domain of sure knowledge) and religion along with morality (a domain "beyond knowledge"). He did this by proposing that "faith" in the human sense of the word, applies in science as well as religion. Further, he concluded that the faith at work in science — a faith in the intelligibility of the universe and the power of the human mind to overcome error — reveals the essentially Christian roots and enduring context of science.

His second article in the book, "Objectivity in Religion," builds on the conclusions of the first one. In it, Macmurray self-consciously proposes to accept as a religious hypothesis the incarnation of the divine in Jesus of Nazareth. He then proceeds to explore the "scientific" criteria for validating the reasonableness of such a hypothesis. This article places front and centre a theme that will remain central in Macmurray's philosophy throughout his life: the need for objective validity in the domain of religion if religion is to have genuine meaning at all. At this stage of his thinking and publishing he is quite content to refer to the genuine (as opposed to the false) intellectual tradition in Christianity as "scientific."[5]

A glance at Macmurray's essay "Beyond Knowledge" reveals ideas that, in their freshness, still have the power to startle. With the Kantian heritage firmly in mind, he begins his essay distinguishing firmly between faith and knowledge:

The roots of our life strike deep into mystery, and religion demands
that we should live our lives, and order our conduct, with constant
reference to a mystery that passes our comprehension. If our
purposes are to be determined by clear knowledge, they must
perforce be narrow and ignoble purposes. It is the unseen things
that are eternal, the incomprehensible things that claim our deepest
loyalty. When we lift up our heads to face a human destiny, we find
that we are beyond knowledge and must walk in faith.[6]

The aim of the essay is to define the antithesis between faith and knowledge appropriately — over against misconstruals of it in western philosophy and theology — so that he can show a deep integration in knowledge
is possible between science and religion. He claims that faith is not a form
of knowledge but a practical attitude of the will that is needed to do science as much as to embrace religion.

Macmurray shows the affinities between science and religion by going
to the heart of human knowing and examining what goes on when we seek
and find knowledge. Science, he notes, rests upon the conviction that there
is no certain knowledge. It assumes correctly that all knowledge is more
or less well-grounded belief; and all beliefs, without exception, must be
tested in experiment before they can be accepted. Experiment, however,
and here is the twist, is only possible on the basis of the belief which it
tests and helps to reshape. Science cannot be done if the scientist is fundamentally agnostic. Even when questioning or doubting, the scientist
proceeds out of a confident faith in the intelligibility of the universe, and
that a truer belief will take the place of a less adequate one. Science, therefore, starts not from facts but from beliefs, and lives by continuous and
deliberate testing and remodelling of beliefs that are found to be faulty. It
is a practical activity for the removal of ignorance.

Macmurray then makes the surprising claim that genuine Christian
faith operates out of the same attitude. Faith is primarily not knowledge
about doctrines, but an attitude of trust in the goodness of God and, therefore, in the goodness and meaningfulness of the world. In a course he presented on "The Theory of the State" while this essay was being prepared,
Macmurray proposed the unusual view that Christianity — at its best, the
faith of Jesus — is thoroughly empirical, and in no way idealist. In making this claim, he rushed in to distinguish the faith lived and taught by
Jesus from the focus on doctrine and dogma ("the faith") and controlling
power taken by the Christian churches over the centuries. He based his
case on the clear dependency of Jesus on personal encounter in freedom,
not ideas or social influence, for evoking in others the faith in God as a
personal, loving Father. At the heart of the Gospel, Macmurray claimed in
those lectures, lie the empirical principles "Come and see," "by their fruits

you shall know them," and "wherever there is love, there is God." The decision to "trust" is verified by the abundance of life and power that flow not just from Jesus but from all who live in this trust and express it in genuine care for others. He suggests to his students that "By their fruits you shall know them" is a "scientific" category of verification in action. All claims to being in touch with the truth (God) are tested by whether or not they lead to hope in and service of greater freedom, justice, faith, hope and love in oneself and in others.

On this basis, Macmurray makes the startling assertion in "Beyond Knowledge" that in the intellectual field, the terms "scientific" and "Christian," properly understood, are synonymous. In both science and Christianity, what lies beyond knowledge is action, and both ground true knowledge in terms of action. Both, he concludes, insist upon an action that is rational because it is governed not by instinct or intuition (mystical or otherwise) but by deliberate convictions and ideals.

At the end of this article, he reveals, in summary, another angle on the point to which he has come at this time in his philosophical explorations. Religion, he states, is wider than science. It includes art and morality as well, and unites the three in the idea of Personality, of which all are functions. In his synopsis of the article, he concludes:

> The failure of the modern world is a failure to be scientific and Christian except in the narrow field of science in the strict sense. We need a moral life of faith, an artistic life of faith, and a religious life of faith in addition to the intellectual life of faith which science has created through its unconscious appreciation of the teaching of Christ. The failure to realize spontaneity and creative adventure in the more spiritual aspects of life has meant the destruction of the unity of personality, and the building of a vast machinery of material power without the creation of spiritual resources adequate to its control. This can only be remedied if we spread the spirit of science over the whole of life, and in the unity of personality thus achieved realize a truly Christian religion, as a complete life of adventurous spontaneity and creative experiment.[7]

It is a sweeping thesis. This synopsis of it is bristling with simplified assertions and potential areas of misinterpretation. Macmurray can look like a very loose thinker with equally loose, though very firm, conclusions. His call for the spread of the spirit of science over the whole of life, for example, could look like an affirmation of positivism if one read "methods of the physical sciences" in place of "spirit of science." His positive description of religion as needing to be grounded scientifically would puzzle many, especially in the light of the opening paragraph of his essay quoted earlier.

Objectivity in religion

In "Objectivity in Religion" he tries to develop this case. Here, he shows his first efforts at naming the "logic" that is at work in personal action. It is a matter of great interest to him because personality offers two avenues of great promise: the one mentioned earlier, namely the potential for achieving a unitary understanding of the impersonal within the fuller domain of the personal, and second, a category in which the being of God can most appropriately be addressed. As he will say: if there is a God, God must be at least personal.[8] Both issues are implicated in this essay as Macmurray tries to unpack the meaning he invests in personality. He notes in his synopsis of the article that neither the mechanical nor the organic "conceptions of individuality can be applied to God, since in both cases the individual is such through limitation, and in both cases particularity and universality are mutually exclusive."[9] He goes on to give a lengthy but nonetheless marvellously succinct statement of the distinctive "logic" or modality of being at play in personality:

> Persons, however, cannot be described in terms of either the mathematical or organic type of unit. In personality the individual and the universal, so far from excluding one another, are essentially reciprocal. An individual is a person through self-transcendence, or objectivity. This conception, although unfamiliar to analytical thought, is really a commonplace of human experience, and can be exemplified in every sphere of human activity. Self-transcendence is easily recognized if we examine the idea of responsibility which is inseparable from personal individuality. A person is responsible precisely because his individuality consists in his power to act for and live in and through other individuals. There are degrees of self-transcendence. Genius depends upon a high degree of self-transcendence in one sphere or another. The higher the degree of self-transcendence, the more unique the individuality of the genius. In cases of extreme powers of self-transcendence, we talk of universality, as when we say that Shakespeare is universal. Absolute personality would therefore involve absolute universality in all aspects and spheres of activity, and this absolute universality would imply an absolute uniqueness or individuality. There is therefore no ground for hesitation in applying the idea of personality to God, since an absolutely universal personality must be an absolutely unique individual. The immanence and the transcendence of God are not mutually exclusive characteristics, but simply the absolute

expression, in their necessary reciprocity, of the fundamental
nature of all personality.[10]

Macmurray's interest in the essay is to locate the "scientific" terms for the
possibility of claiming objectivity in religion. In postulating Jesus as the
incarnation of the divine, he is attempting to present an historical, flesh
and blood foothold in particularity for testing Christ as, at once, the historically particular and the universal presence of God. The hypothesis, he
attempts to show, can be submitted to criteria of reasonableness which
relate to the promotion of holiness and goodness in the human order. If
Jesus the Christ fulfils the conditions, what is verified is not the hypothesis but its reasonableness.

Regardless of what one thinks of Macmurray's hypothesis, his purpose
is clear: to assert the existence of objectivity in religion by placing it
methodologically within a spectrum of faith and reasonableness *along with*
all other human ways of knowing and acting. He knows intuitively that the
meaning of "scientific" and "method" in relation to personal life and religion must be vastly more complex than it is in physics and the life sciences.
He is simply saying that there must be some essential continuity, as well,
since all are instances of knowledge in action. What the differences are and
how they can be accurately expressed philosophically is not something he
is yet able to answer. His proposal, however, is a profound challenge to the
complete dualism of the Modern tradition with regard to science and religion in both its thinking and practice. Against that tradition, he asserts:

> ... religion cannot give up on its claims to objective truth, and there
> can be only one truth. Religion must either include science and art
> and morality, unifying these in a complete conception of
> personality, or find no place at all.[11]

This use of the term "scientific" in relation to Christianity gave
Macmurray lots of trouble with various audiences. In the July 1925 letter
to Richard Roberts, he included a copy of a sermon he had recently given
that contained some of these ideas.[12] He told Roberts he was roundly
accused of being a pantheist by several members of the congregation.
Others, taking the reverse tack but arriving at the same point, felt his scientific attitude simply reduced his views to "humanism" or to a "glorious
optimism." Few apparently could appreciate his view that religion is and
must be objective, that is, grounded in reality, God's reality and the
world's. A merely subjective religion, he suggested, is a religion in which
one could conclude, feel and do what one wants, with no necessary connection to objective reality; with no criteria, therefore, for discerning and
determining the true and solid thing from the illusory and nutty.

Just before writing that letter to Roberts, and while he was preparing sketches for the essays in *Adventure*, Macmurray went to Swanwick, the home of the free, religious fellowship that interested him and Roberts ten years earlier, where he talked to the Science and Theology students on the question of science and Christian doctrine. He told Roberts:

> I tried to show that if you really apply the scientific attitude to Christian experience, all ground of opposition between science and theology disappears without in the least throwing any doubt upon the doctrines of Christianity, however much it may involve modifications of formulation.

He went on to suggest to the students that if "revelation" is revelation of a *person* then this occurs in personal encounter, and no formula representing this encounter can ever be fixed once for all. As personal relations are on the move, he said, so too are our inadequate formulations of them. The issue is the nature of God, and God can't be captured in a formula. God, and the things of God, including our efforts to formulate God's ways, are on the move. Every formulation is tentative and needs revision if it is to be faithful to the living truth. We have no record of how the students received those proposals but, in 1925, they were almost surely unlike anything they expected to hear from a Christian professor of philosophy.

In 1926, Macmurray published two articles, one entitled "Christianity: Pagan or Scientific?", and the other "The Function of Experiment in Knowledge." The first presents an initial take on his view of history: namely that Greek, Roman and Hebrew influences are the key ones in shaping western civilization. The second sketches his epistemology. Both can also be read as efforts to present, from different angles, his case for objectivity in religion and for seeing a natural affinity between the manner in which knowledge grows and develops in science and the similar way he believed it should grow and develop in theological formulations.

John received a six-month academic leave starting in March 1926. He and Betty spent most of it in Scotland where they visited family and he had the leisure to continue his reading and writing. Towards the end of their stay, he did a meticulous reading of Rudolph Hermann Lotze's *Microcosmus*, a vast work whose major thesis was a rejection of the view that all mental and physical phenomena can be explained in scientific terms. The issues were seminal. Macmurray took sixty-three pages of careful notes which reveal his growing understanding of his own issues as he goes through the book. During this reading, he worked out his own negative position with regard to vitalism ("It covers our ignorance instead of lessening it.") and any sense of a consciousness within the life-process. It was from Lotze that he met a theory of consciousness that does not fuse the elements which it unifies but maintains their distinctiveness, and from Lotze — along with the nineteenth century Romantics he was reading — that he became convinced that feeling contains the principle of Reason, which demands the conformity of the actual to forms which it values: a *Reason appreciative of Worth*.[13] Lotze also characterized the distinctively human element in mental processes, and their manifestations even at the lowest levels of experience, as "Objectivity," a concept that will stay with Macmurray and become refined by him. But at the heart of Lotze's theory of society and the state Macmurray finds "the fatal weakness of the organic idea. What is demanded of us is the willing self-subordination of the individual to helping on what is a material, organic process." It is a demand he will recognize in historical flesh in Nazism less than ten years later. And yet Lotze rejects entirely Hegel's universal Idea of humanity which negates the value of individuals and their struggles. In the end, Macmurray receives not so much direction but intellectual clarification of his own thoughts from Lotze's *tour de force*. And even his final distancing of himself from Lotze's organic thinking will serve to sharpen his own articulation of the distinctiveness of the personal.

On his return to Oxford, he was asked by the *British Weekly* on its fortieth anniversary to provide its readers with a popular article on philosophy over that period of time. "The Influence of British Philosophy during these Forty Years" presents hints of Macmurray's own directions for the first time to a broader public. In it, he notes the contributions of the British Idealists T.H. Green, Bernard Bosanquet, Edward Caird, F.H. Bradley, J.E.M. McTaggart, James Ward, J.B. Baillie and Henry Jones. He comments on the Realist reaction to Idealism in John Cook Wilson, Bertrand Russell, G.E. Moore and A.N. Whitehead, and praises Samuel Alexander's great work. He concludes on a note with which we are already familiar: that Hegelianism, in defeating the mechanical conception of mind, succumbed in turn to an organic model of categorizing being, a move to dialectical logic that was clearly more complex and truer to life than formal logic, and yet a logic incapable of representing persons in their spiritual distinctiveness, that is, in their constitution as persons through relationship with other persons. He ends the article with a summary of his conviction concerning the need for twentieth-century philosophy to focus on the problem of "personality" as the critical requirement of philosophy in our time and to recognize that the new evolutionary empiricism is not fit to handle it. A new, integrating philosophy is needed.

Adventure was finally published in 1927. Macmurray wrote to Richard Roberts saying: "It has had a good reception over here and has puzzled a

lot of people in the right way. The reviews take entirely opposite attitudes
— which is a good sign, I think."[14]

Generating puzzlement, misunderstanding and even anger was going to
become a major problem for Macmurray a few years down the road when
he gave talks on the BBC in which he used the adjectives "real" and
"unreal" to distinguish kinds of thinking, feeling, and even people. This
was not usual terminology for most listeners. It is worth recalling that
even A.D. Lindsay, a sophisticated Christian intellectual, after hearing
Macmurray express his developing ideas in various contexts, wondered
aloud to young David Cairns about whether God had just been quietly
folded into human personality in Macmurray's thinking — and disappeared there.

That conversation would have taken place only a month or so before
the publication of "What I Live By," an article for students in which
John repeated his view that science is, in fact, a manifestation of God's
spirit in the world. But, by now, he is feeling his failure to communicate this message: "I cannot understand why this should seem to be a
paradox, and yet it does. Men talk of science almost as if it were the
antithesis of Christianity instead of its manifestation."[15] But in that
same article, Macmurray stated plainly for the students ideas that he
had broached in 1925 to Roberts, ideas that could only have given
Lindsay reassurance:

> Philosophically, a belief in God is necessary, since the character of
> the world's unity can only be personal. Only an absolute personality
> can be the ground of the existence of finite persons ... A knowledge
> of God, however simple, as distinct from the bare belief that God
> exists, can only come to us from our experience of human persons
> and our estimation of their worth ... I am convinced that if we are
> to have any knowledge of God which is real knowledge and not
> beautiful nonsense, it can only be through knowing a human person
> who is himself the image of the divine personality and who reveals
> God to us by revealing himself. How should we know him if we
> should find him walking our world and talking one of its babel of
> tongues? By his power to subdue all things unto himself, to focus
> and unify in his own personality the variety of human effort and
> achievement, to make life one, to make all mankind one family, to
> establish the Kingdom of Heaven in our world.
>   Either Christ is the man whom the knowledge of God demands,
> or there is none.[16]

After this article, John stopped using the term "scientific" about religion
and began exploring an expanded use of the term "rational." It was not a

great advance with regard to dispelling the fog for those labouring under modern definitions of terms. But it was truer to his own project which necessarily included a deepening and widening of the meaning and application of "reason" as a term which would, as the defining meaning of what was unique in human existence, include *everything* in personal action that contributes to a true and appropriate relationship to God, and to the world in its unity and its diverse constituents. In fact, in 1932, after the popular set of BBC lectures in which he presented many of his developing ideas, he would be driven by interested but puzzled listeners to address many questions that arose around what he meant by, among other things, the rationality of religion.[17]

John slowly came to acknowledge that the work that lay before him, philosophically and pedagogically, was massive and at a very basic level. He knew he was trying to do many things at once: he was expanding the extension of the term "objective" to the full scope of "the real" — including the personal — while refusing to allow that to be determined only by mechanical and organic categories. He was suggesting implicitly that the *method*s for determining objectivity in art and in religion respectively had yet to be found philosophically, and yet it must be possible to do so. He was also, as we have just seen, trying to do with the term "reason" (and the adjective "rational") what he was doing to the term "objective" — extend its meaning to include all the powers in the human person that allow us to relate as fully as possible to "the real." Developing, in even a rudimentary way, the meaning of his basic position on the primacy of personality proved to be the work of the next few years; and, in fact, the essential work of his professional lifetime.

It was in the autumn of 1925, and at the request of his friend Donald Grant who edited the student publication *Vox Studentium,* that Macmurray made his first effort, in an article entitled "Personality," to articulate at some length what he meant by that term and everything he understood to constitute it. It included all the descriptives touched on in the past few pages. Personality is, he suggested, essentially mysterious, free, imaginative, disciplined and disciplining, deliberating and determining, creative, purposive, experimenting, open to transformation, democratic, the centre of both common humanity and individual genius, the integrating home of the impersonal in the human being within the personal, the form and substance of love in all human relationships — intimate, social and political. This was much more than a taxonomy of properties. He touched on the intrinsic interconnectedness of these expressions of personality and proposed them as diverse but united dimensions of a self-transcending relationship of the person with the world outside himself or herself.

He told the students that both the individualism and the socialism of the west were still sub-human — conceived respectively in mere mechanical and organic terms, and therefore being acted out in the world as distortions of the ideal of genuine individuality and genuine social life. To "personalize" all things human was precisely the shared vocation he wanted them to recognize in themselves, and the shared purpose they should embrace as Christians. The article stands as an extraordinary first effort since the substance of his subsequent developments in his philosophy of the personal can be seen embedded in the profile presented here.

That first article on the nature of personality highlights what was becoming increasingly apparent in Macmurray's reflections when he was speaking to fellow-Christians: a growing identification between what he meant by *making the world more personal* and what he meant by the specific vocation of Christianity in the world.

An unusually graphic and provocative expression of this growing conviction occurs in a letter he sent — at their request — to a group conference planning the March 1928 meeting of the International Missionary Council in Jerusalem. After acknowledging the enlightened tone of the three papers on world religions sent for him to preview, Macmurray draws attention to what appears to be a shift in missionary policy: "No longer must we condemn the other religions as false: we must see in them imperfect lights, or gropings in the dark after the truth as it is in Christ." He says to his colleagues: "this may be the right line of missionary policy in the present situation; it is certainly more sensible and right-minded than the old one." If this is so, other considerations arise and he proposes to present his doubts and hesitations, even though they "are radical, and perhaps one-sided and cranky."

He then offers the planning group some very pointed reflections, of which only four paragraphs remain. Their significance outweighs their apparent offensiveness, but for this to be seen he must be allowed to speak for himself:

> There is first a general danger in comparing Christianity with other religions and picking out for emphasis what they have in common. That is all right in a university class-room, or in merely historical study. As a basis of policy it seems to me to be gratuitously weak. The essential question is to discover what Christianity has to give to the world that no other religion can give — in any degree. The difference has to be one of Kind. Unless Christianity is essentially and radically different from other religions; unless there is some sense in which it is just right and they are just wrong; then there isn't much to be said for the missionary drive.
>
> One of the profoundest remarks which I have come across about religion is Collingwood's *Speculum Mentis*. He says that

religion reached its climax in Christ; and in doing so it ceased to be religion. Using religion in this sense — and it is the only sense in which it can be used when one studies comparative religion — he seems to me to be just right. Much that belongs to religion in this sense permeates what we call Christianity — both in doctrine, spiritual outlook and organization. And I have a conviction that the points which the various world religions have in common with Christianity are in large measure the points which are not specifically Christian, but merely religious.

Is there, then, something unique to Christianity? He says there is. He proposes that it is "the spirit of Christ" that launched the revolution impelling human beings to seek openness in truth, freedom in action, equality in relationships and full community *for all people*. For Macmurray *this* movement to universality in the search for freedom and equality in community expresses the uniqueness of what he calls "true" Christianity. It is unique, as he will say later in his life, because it is self-conscious about this *intention* towards universal community. In other words, he implies to his colleagues, the *true* Christian spirit is not bound necessarily to *any* church or world religion. *Any* action or movement that advances this openness, freedom, equality and participation for all is thereby truly in and of the Christian revolution — even though the actors or the movement may firmly refuse that label. Conversely, wherever religion, customs, politics or economics serve as an obstacle to this movement to freedom, equality and inclusiveness they will be overcome by this spirit for life. On this understanding Macmurray offers the view that "the spirit of Christ," as force for the *personalization* of the world, serves to end foundational status to religions, in the sense in which this word is commonly used.

He then makes an even more startling claim: that this spirit of openness which he calls "Christianity at its best" is being expressed most fully not in the churches but in modern science, modern commerce and democracy. "These are the things that the East wants from us: and on the whole it does *not* want our Christianity." And yet this desire, he says, constitutes a great social and religious challenge to the East even as it did, and continues to do, in the West. Just as science, democracy and commerce — as specific forms of the urge to full personalization in community — "smashed," for example, the forms of religion, politics, economics and cultures of Christian mediaeval society in the west, they can be expected to effect a similarly forceful revolution in the religions and social forms of the non-Christian East.

He urges his Christian colleagues not to cling to religious traditions — whether in the East or the West — that may prevent rather than enhance the growth of freedom, equality and community for all peoples and

individuals. He effectively asserts: what is of Life in the religions of East
or the West will surely survive, though in a vastly transformed way. What
is not of service to greater life for all will pass. His hope is that the
Christian missionary vision will have the faith and courage to let it pass.
He clearly does not expect the Christian churches or the non-Christian
religions — or even his colleagues — to support this view of "true"
Christianity. "The religions are on the whole quiescences," he writes.
"They seek to make men at home and comfortable in his [*sic*] world." This
is clearly not his view of what genuine religion should be doing in the
world.

He concludes his letter with a claim that, though baldly stated, nevertheless follows from his view that the release of the spirit of openness in the
world is, as a movement, the spirit of what he calls "Christianity at its best:"

> But the destructive forces — science, democracy, even commerce
> — are inseparable from their Christian milieu. They demand a
> Christian society to make them possible; and there are imbedded in
> them the radical elements of the Christian outlook. After all, it was
> Christianity which produced these great creative and destructive
> forces: and they are its evidence and its triumph. And the non-
> Christian world is crying out for them. Is not this the missionary
> opportunity? Unfortunately our own Christian organization either
> disregards or actually disowns these children of its own
> regenerative work.

In this letter, Macmurray reveals he was aware that he expected to be misunderstood. He knew he was being politically incorrect but he wasn't
intending either to offend or to avoid doing so. A careful reading helps one
avoid dismissing it out-of-hand as the letter of a religious imperialist.
Macmurray is not asserting the superiority of his religious "club" over
against the others. In fact, to the degree Christianity is itself a "club" it is
simply one religion among others and fails, in his judgment, to be genuinely following the way of Jesus.

The destruction in the forms of religion he talks about arises not as a
result of an aggressive or hostile act on the part of Christian missionaries;
he has already in this letter joined in rejecting that kind of aggressive
model of Christian mission. Inevitably, he suggests, it was from among the
Christianized peoples that the responsibility and privilege of recognizing
the rights to free action of each person and *all* persons expressed themselves first in the human family.

Macmurray is talking here mainly about what he calls the spirit of
Christ and its inner imperatives. From that perspective he identifies activity for liberation for all as the heart of genuine Christianity — and vice

versa. This is the sensitive issue, but it states plainly where he stands. His final remark about the religions as quiescences will get far more attention from him in the 1930s. It refers to their spiritualising of their view of themselves, on the one hand, and their political self-promotion on the other. He will excoriate the false silence of religions (in the face of human rights denied by governments and powers) as well as their humiliating submissiveness to secular powers when it serves their own status in society.

Questions arise in the face of the high certainties that form the substance of this letter. It could be asked whether Macmurray believed the other world religions had anything substantial to contribute to human progress. If this liberating power at the heart of Christianity is bigger and even other than the Christian churches, is there any room for holding the view that this power might be more advanced in some aspects of the other world religions? And if this is so, might that mean these other religions, to say nothing of irreligious movements for good, could actually have a role in, to use his language, "Christianizing" Christianity? As we will see, in just a few years he will be affirming this position quite openly.

In connection with what he suggests science, democracy and commerce will do to the non-Christian religions, some seventy-five years after this letter was written we can now ask with some fervour: what happens to science, democracy and commerce in the west when they separate themselves, as they have done, from their Christian roots? Are not the commercialization of science, the hollowing out of democracy, and the self-interested globalization of commerce not signs that these allegedly liberating activities have lost much of their power for liberation? Have they gone, or at least are they going — because of a loss of sound motives and direction — demonic themselves? If so, where is the spirit for true liberation that Macmurray describes to be found? And given the west's almost total separation from its Christian roots, who holds the gyroscope that can track its movement in history? This will, it might be added now, in less than two decades become both his question and his pain.

The near coincidence Macmurray claims to discover in the two ventures of acting on the primacy of personality in the world and carrying out the Christian mission provides ample temptation for one to think he is actually presenting the Gospel when he claims to be professing philosophy. He was certainly charged, on occasion, with identifying those roles. He tried to distinguish carefully between when he is speaking as a philosopher and when he speaks as a Christian. He disciplined himself to do his philosophical thinking within the boundaries of rational thought and discourse. He did not, for example, employ Christian categories or texts in his arguments, or discuss Christian faith from the perspective of a believer, in his courses or in his exclusively philosophical publications. In fact, he managed this so well during his years as a professor that there were many students and colleagues who were surprised when they discovered inadvertently that Professor Macmurray was a committed Christian.

Nevertheless, Macmurray is not simply a philosopher of religion; he is essentially a religious philosopher. *Every* thinker, he would insist, works from a standpoint. His own standpoint is not primarily mechanical or organic; it is personal. And for him, as he stated to the students in "What I Live By," the personal, when it is accepted in its fullness, simply *is* religious, at least in his broad and nuanced use of the term. The critical distinction he insists on is that although his subject matter is often religious in nature, he examines it within the constraints of philosophical methodology. The fact that he developed much of his thinking in dialogue with Christian scholars who were also analysing the nature of Christianity does not discount the strenuously rational and non-confessional mode of his explorations in the professional lectures, essays and publications where he is "doing philosophy."

The intellectual, emotional and perhaps even religious, struggles going on in Macmurray at this time in his life are highlighted in an August 1928 letter he wrote to David S. Cairns, the father of young David, Macmurray's student who had just graduated with a first from Balliol. This letter is written within days of the publication of "What I Live By" in which Macmurray gave a strong, even confessional statement about God and Christ. After speaking at length about David's merits and prospects, John thanks Professor Cairns for promising to send a copy of his book on "Faith." He then confesses in a remarkably open way:

> I'm not at all satisfied with my own position. It is too dogmatic and
> *a priori.* Indeed for the last year or two I've just got deeper and
> deeper into scepticism — and I haven't yet struck bottom. That is
> where my stress on 'experiment' comes from. I have been drawn to
> conclude that what philosophy needs is a Humean scepticism on
> the side of *practical* philosophy as a preparation for a
> reconstruction of the whole philosophical field. And I often find
> myself thinking that so far I've been myself doing what I criticise
> others for doing — seeking short-cuts to certainty. It seems to me
> that most ethical, social and religious teaching is vitiated —
> philosophically, and I can't but feel that in the long run that means
> practically also — by assumptions of the form that "whatever is, is
> 'best'" — by subtle suggestions that the business of thought in the
> practical sphere is to maintain the current and entrenched
> convictions of the cultured.[18]

The scepticism Macmurray is talking about here could be read as reflecting struggles in his religious faith as well as his convictions about the inadequacy of current philosophy to handle the serious issues of the times. But there are no indications of that, and there are reasons to believe it is essentially a philosophical problem not a religious one. The letter is worthy of note for another reason: this is the first time since the war that he has pointed his ire against organized religion, and against the mainline culture the churches spend so much of their energy supporting and consoling.

The letter to the Missionary Council was written in January, a few months before John was invited to accept the Grote Professorship in Mind and Logic at University College, London. The letter to Professor Cairns was written in August, just three weeks before John and Betty moved to London. Looking back on both letters from the perspective of all that would take place in the coming sixteen years at the University of London, one can find here the seeds of many of the perspectives, convictions and issues that found their voice in him in London during the turbulent thirties and the disjointed years of the Second World War.

Chapter 8

Seeking the Logic of Friendship (1928–30)

John and Betty decided to make their move from Oxford to London over the course of two days in early September 1928. Three days before the move, with everything already packed and ready, Betty was stricken with recurring abdominal pains and had to stay in bed. John convinced her to go to Aberdeen and see the doctors who knew her best while he managed the final stages of the move and clean-up. That Saturday, while he was organizing things in their new flat in Bolton Studios, he received a telegram saying that Betty's doctors had decided an operation was required. On Monday, the earliest he could get away, John threw his luggage into their bull-nose Morris and drove north arriving in Aberdeen the next morning. The operation took place the next day. The doctors discovered a tumour on or near her ovary but decided to leave it. They believed it would not be a danger; while removing it would upset her system badly and probably destroy any chances of having children. They told John she could possibly have a child but, with this condition, there would be a high chance of a miscarriage if she became pregnant.[1]

Betty recovered well and, as John reported to Richard Roberts on February 19, 1929, she experienced six months of very good health. Just two weeks after that letter was sent she once again suffered acute pains and was rushed to the hospital where she was diagnosed with acute peritonitis. Her life hung by a thread for two days. An operation on March 23 discovered the problem area and resulted in the removal of her appendix and an infected ovary and fallopian tube. A month later, when another infection raged up unexpectedly, the doctors were forced to operate again. They discovered Betty had actually suffered an ectopic pregnancy which had burst her remaining fallopian tube and was causing continuous haemorrhaging. The internal bleeding was stopped and the burst tube and blood clots removed after which she slowly began to recover her strength. After describing all this to his sister Helen, John reflected sadly:

> It's awfully hard luck on her, isn't it? And she has been so eager to have her baby — and now to be cheated of it twice ... She's been marvellously cheerful throughout — just full of courage. I admire her more than ever!

That ended their chances for children. In many ways, as they admitted late in life, the absence of children and of even the possibility of having a child shaped their lives considerably, especially during the 1930s which lay just ahead of them.

It was Jack Barry who had located the flat in London, in Bolton Studios, Redcliffe Street, to which John and Betty moved when they left Balliol.[2] Barry moved there, as well, and lived for a while in his own flat in the Studios, which were constructed to provide accommodation and meals for writers and artists. A dozen studios for writers lay on the south side of the building, and another dozen for painters were on the north side, with a kitchen and dining room in between. The Macmurrays were given No. 23 on the second floor on the writers' side. The painters, as Betty complained with envy, also had their own baths! A bubble-covered corridor on the first level and a tunnel in the basement linked the two sections together.

The studios themselves were lovely. In the Macmurrays', there was an open living area with walls of dark oak and parquet floors, and a small staircase with carved banisters leading to the half-floor above where there were two bedrooms. From the upper level, one could look down on the main living area with its orange curtains, Indian rugs and baby grand piano. There was no kitchen since the meals were served in the central dining area. And those meals, in the judgment of everyone there, were abominable. But John and Betty were delighted with their place, as were most others, so complaints even about the food were minimal. As John told his friend Roberts in that same letter:

> We both like London much better than Oxford. The climate for one
> thing — the life and freedom of the big city for another. And I'm
> getting some — though not too much — time to read and write. It's
> difficult turning down all the people who want one to help them,
> but I do my best.

The University of London that John joined was a fairly young institution in Britain.[3] Its first college, University College, London (UCL) — which was Macmurray's — had come into existence in 1826 only through a major struggle against the élitist powers of the time. A very forthright account by the late Dr G. Carey Foster of the context of that struggle appeared in the UCL calendars from Macmurray's time at the University. Foster pulls no punches:

> The foundation of University College resulted from an attempt to
> establish a great University in London. Soon after 1820 the
> importance of such a University seems to have become widely

recognised among educational reformers and the friends of political
and intellectual progress. The range of studies that were effectively
cultivated at Oxford and Cambridge at this time was narrow: little
provision was made for the study of the languages or literatures of
modern Europe, or of natural or experimental science; the
organization and traditions encouraged an expensive mode of life
among the students; the whole constitution and atmosphere of both
Universities were strongly pervaded with clericalism: at Oxford,
subscription to the Thirty-nine Articles of Religion was required as
a condition of admission into the University, and at Cambridge a
declaration of *bona fide* membership of the Church of England was
required on taking the Bachelor's Degree. It is not easy to ascertain
to whom the idea first occurred of founding a London University as
a remedy for this state of things.

By the time it celebrated its hundredth anniversary, just a few years after
Macmurray's arrival there, the university had grown to include thirty-six
federated colleges of many shapes and sizes including — along with
University and King's Colleges — Birkbeck, Bedford, the London
School of Medicine for Women, Imperial College of Science and
Technology as well as the still young London School of Economics
(LSE). It had been the first university to admit women to degrees. By that
time, there were just over 1330 teachers for 13,000 full-time and 4,000
part-time students.[4]

Macmurray would not have had any difficulty with Dr Carey Foster's
description of the open and experimental spirit that grounded the university. In fact, he loved it. Within a few months he became known among
his colleagues on the UCL campus as someone who might drop by the
science labs just "to see what was going on." When time allowed, he also
popped into the art studios on campus. On these visits, he enjoyed hearing of the kinds of questions being raised and the new directions being
taken in both fields. Beyond the sheer pleasure of these visits, his hope
was to grow in his understanding of what was happening in contemporary
science and contemporary art for the sake of his own philosophical development.

The Philosophy faculty at UCL in 1928 was small, made up of
Macmurray as department head and S.V. Keeling as lecturer. During that
first year, Macmurray taught courses in Theory of Knowledge, Moral and
Political Philosophy, Ethical and Social Philosophy, Advanced Ethics with
special reference to Kant, Greek Ethics with special reference to Plato, a
General Course of Greek Philosophy with special reference to Plato, the
Philosophy of Kant, and the Philosophy of Romanticism from Kant to
Hegel. The last two advanced courses met only once a week, but all the

others met at least twice. It was, to say the least, a demanding amount of work. It is hardly surprising that in his first "Report of the Work of the Grote Professor" to the college secretary a few years after his arrival at UCL, Macmurray began by recalling that heavy load of lectures:

> On taking up my duties ... in 1928 I decided to re-organize the work of the Department in the following way:
>
> To cut down the number of lectures given considerably in order to allow for an extension of individual work both on the part of the teaching staff and of the students concerned, and to develop, as opportunity offered, a number of seminar classes for discussion and a number of extra-curricular classes to extend the interest in Philosophy amongst students who were unable to take any of the regular classes offered by the Department. *My aim has been throughout to make the teaching of philosophy less a matter of specialized and technical work than one of cultural and educational importance, while maintaining as high a level of technical excellence amongst the necessarily small number of students who wish to devote themselves to Philosophy as their exclusive interest.* [italics mine] The justification for this course is that under prevailing conditions very few students, even of those who have a real interest in Philosophy, can afford to devote themselves to the exclusive study of a subject which provides no immediate prospect of a career.

In addition to revealing Macmurray's approach to philosophy this practical strategy reflected the democratic spirit of the university. It also bore fruit immediately in the increased number of students from other departments who felt less intimidated about taking a course in philosophy, and those numbers rose steadily over the next few years. Macmurray was also able in those first few years to convince the heads of philosophy in the other University of London colleges — especially King's College and the London School of Economics (LSE) — to integrate their work for the Honours Degree students on an intercollegiate basis. This would offer exposure to more professors and therefore to even more specialized options for the advanced students. Years later when Macmurray was leaving his position for the Moral Chair in Edinburgh, he was congratulated in the Minutes for these creative, even ecumenical, initiatives.

The demands of this first academic year, including the anxieties and deep sadness generated by Betty's acute health crises, would normally be considered more than enough to fill up those months. In fact, his philosophical thinking exploded and reached the public in many articles and public presentations. During that year he presented his inaugural lecture and gave a ground-breaking paper at an Aristotelian Society symposium. He delivered the major address and gave two seminar presentations at the Student Christian Movement Quadrennial conference, wrote a lengthy "memorandum" for Archbishop Temple's clergy training programme, and preached a sermon in the College Chapel at Balliol — all of which caused a stir. But this is not a profile of mere busyness. All these writings taken together constitute a steady and unified advance in his self-imposed project of conceptualizing the logical form of of the personal.

On November 19, 1928, Macmurray gave the inaugural address recognizing his appointment as Grote Professor at University College. He chose as his subject "The Unity of Modern Problems," a give-away sign that he was about to question the inadequate mode of apperception that grounded the many problematic areas of modern life. To strike the philosophical focus he wants the audience to grasp, he notes the curious fact that when we speak of patriotism, it is commonplace to believe in "space-patriots" (people who are faithful to their geographical place, nation and flag) but most uncommon in our culture to think of "time-patriots" (those who are faithful to the problems and promises of their time or era). He sees genuine philosophers as time-patriots even to the extent sometimes, as in the case of Socrates, of being martyred for their witness to the fresh forms of the eternal within a particular era. He then proceeds to explore what he believes are the philosophical contours of the major problematic greeting their own generation at the end of the 1920s.

The first half of the address is given over to noting the unity-patterns that mark the mechanical and organic periods of Modern history described earlier. But there are fresh twists here. He emphasizes that the logical schema or unity-pattern that dominated the early modern period gave way only when fresh experiences drove inquirers outside the schema thereby revealing the schema's inadequacy for handling the new historically generated questions and needs. The birth of the organic phase of thinking came when it was no longer plausible to believe that the Self could be understood on the model of "substance" and must be conceived through a richer and more complex schema, that of a *living* thing. So, the new schema arose necessarily as a response by those late eighteenth and early nineteenth century thinkers and artists who, as he emphasized, were faithful to the problematic of their time. Both epochs explore the timeless issue of Selfhood but the organic schema does so by filling in for the inadequacies of the mechanical — until its inadequacies, in turn, were laid bare in their own generation.

This organic model of political thinking, he states, was a root cause for why that war took place. It led European countries to conceive of themselves as dynamic organisms whose constant expansion required more and more colonial resources in order to achieve their maturity. This self-centred perspective on national identity drove them to seek those resources in Africa, Asia and the Americas (the "environment" off which they lived), all the while competing viciously with one another (on the biological model of the survival of the fittest) for markets to feed their own development. In a way that he had never explored so thoroughly before Macmurray identifies the limitations of this organic self-definition imposed on human societies as a foundational flaw in the self-image and activities of European nations that led directly to the 1914–18 war. It was precisely because the European imagination, fixated in the organic schema as the only way to think of national identity, was not prepared to conceive of European cooperation as more basic and sound — and needed by their times — than nationalistic competition. War was the inevitable outcome of that organic perspective in feeling, imagination and public action colliding with situations demanding intelligent compromise and cooperation. Macmurray suggests that now, in the late 1920s (and this was exactly one year before the Great Crash), Europeans may be ready to recognize that neither mechanical nor organic unity-patterns are adequate to understand or guide the relationships of persons, either in their most intimate forms or in their social and political institutions. He indicates that the discovery of a method for European countries to learn to behave as members of a community is both necessary and urgent.

He moves into his positive proposals by reminding his audience that persons are not identical with their functions; they transcend them. A person is not a mere function of his or her work, allegiances, nation, etc.; rather, these are functions of persons. That is, the state is not an end in itself which the person serves but rather the state is a servant of the persons who put it in place and who make up its citizenry. No institution, Macmurray concludes, is worth the sacrifice of the meanest person. From this reversal of conventional values, there follows inevitably the collapse of the romanticized, heroic "duty" or "service" basis for morality. Macmurray suggests that duty, as a moral concept, arises from within an organic self-understanding. It has its place in human affairs but only as a subordinate dimension in genuine love and affection. It is Stoicism, not Christianity, that canonizes Duty as the ultimate form of morality.

In this opposition he finds between duty and love, Macmurray turns from public to intimate relations and addresses the human meaning of sexuality. He shows that sex, thrust into a merely organic perspective in the nineteenth century, began by being outrageously sentimentalized and ended, with Freud, by being effectively brutalized. Women were glorified by nineteenth century Europe, first in an erotic miasma and then in the mysticism of motherhood; but in both cases women were enslaved within an organic perspective defined by men for whom they "functioned." They were defined exclusively by their roles, Macmurray asserts, and not allowed to be persons, who are more than able to define themselves. As if this were not shocking enough to hear in a philosophical lecture he gets more pointed with his listeners:

> The truth is that our young men and women are busy repudiating the organic conception of the Self. They will not any longer allow the relations of the sexes to be dominated by sex. They despise, and rightly, the idea that they are essentially organisms. They are beginning, experimentally, and with many failures, no doubt, to feel their way to a higher conception of Self, upon which to base the deliberate organization of their lives — a conception in which they are persons, and in which the personal relationships dominate, control, and subordinate all organic functions — a conception whose key-word, perhaps, is friendship.[5]

He finds in this new attitude of post-war students one of several reasons for suggesting tentatively ("I may well be wrong," he asserts) that the Great War closed the Romantic Era. But what is most significant here is the large and inclusive perspective from which he defines what he believes to be the philosophical burden of his time:

> ... the unity of modern problems is the problem of discovering or constructing (in this connection the terms are synonymous) a new schema of the Self, which shall transcend both the mechanical and the organic schema; and which will enable us to construct, consciously and deliberately, a civilization whose mechanical and organic structures will be at the service of a personal life, whose meaning and essence is friendship.[6]

It is, he asserts, "a philosophical problem demanding for its solution a philosophical insight into the concrete variety of contemporary life: ..." Then, with a tinge of humour, but with utter seriousness, he concludes: "and you will have come to the conclusion that for me philosophy is essentially logic."[7]

There are many surprising features in this grand canvas. We have heard some of it before in his essay "Personality," written for students three years earlier. But in that essay he presented descriptively many dimensions of the life of personality. Here we find cultural and structural analysis that manages to introduce, at once, the most exalted elements of content along with efforts at discerning logical form. He lands tentatively on the term "friendship" to describe the full content of personal living. He knew "friendship" could easily be seen as a soft and woolly category, one that modern canons of objectivity, so distant from

Aristotle's, would not even allow into philosophical discourse. But, Macmurray insists he is addressing a real mode of "being," and requires of himself that friendship be explored within the context of *a logical* inquiry into the structure of personal life, not on the basis of some kind of "feel good" experience. "Friendship" is proposed as the most adequate term he can find at the time to represent the reality he wants to highlight. It is proposed as a logical category designating a mode of being: a fully positive personal relationship. In that sense, his inaugural address at UCL launches a search for a logic adequate to represent philosophically the personal life.

His disciplined exposure of the inadequacies of the logic of the mechanical and organic schemas for describing personal relationship provides us with Macmurray's first attempt to characterize friendship as the normative form of the personal life. He ends the talk fully aware that, philosophically speaking, he has disembarked on the shores of a new world: the place where the most exalted of human relationships must be pressed to reveal what the philosopher, tied to the rules of his *métier,* might legitimately but humbly demand of it: access to its inner logic. And he must undertake his exploration through the jungle of modernist assumptions which, before he takes a step, holds that his "El Dorado" is, practically viewed, an impossible dream, and theoretically viewed, lacking in truth value.

Within six weeks, Macmurray was given the opportunity to advance his thinking on the personal, but here he is given a more pastoral than professional setting. Since its inceptions in 1896, the Student Christian Movement (SCM) had met in a grand five-day conference every four years. Because of the unstinting enthusiasm and hard work over those years on the part of its general secretary, Canon Tissington Tatlow, the Quadrennial had grown into a massive gathering of over two thousand of the brightest and the best students from universities in Britain and the former colonies. For its speakers, it also drew on the brightest and best Christian voices from the universities, the missions, and the Anglican and Protestant churches in Britain. The 1929 Quadrennial took place in Liverpool, January 2 to 7, and was built around the theme "The Purpose of God in the Life of the World." It featured presenters such as Canon Charles Raven of Ely Cathedral and Fellow of Christ's College, Cambridge, who was to become a well-known pacifist during the 1930s, Dr W.R. Maltby, A.D. Lindsay, Master of Balliol, Archbishop William Temple of York, J.H. Oldham, the great leader of dialogue and action for a creative and respecting approach to missionary theology and ministry, and many other church-related luminaries. Among them was John Macmurray who was asked to give the keynote address on the first full day of the conference, and to lead two seminars on the two following days.

Macmurray's address called "Ye Are my Friends" was delivered in his typically gentle and somewhat musical voice with his distinct but mild Scottish accent. Despite this unassuming medium, he managed to set off a few explosives in the imaginations of his listeners as he made his way through a talk which, as he told Richard Roberts later, was most difficult for him to prepare. It is a talk that arose at once out of the pain and joys of his own deepest experiences with Betty, and out of his meditation on the Jesus he met in the Scriptures and his experience. The first explosive was lobbed about two minutes into the talk, almost without notice, and its unsettling effects were felt for the rest of his presentation:

> The purpose of God in the life of the world is a web of purposes which has a single centre, from which all the threads go out and to which they all return. Only from the centre can we begin to trace the plan of it. From any other point it will seem a meaningless tangle.
>
> Copernicus made a revolution in human knowledge merely by shifting the centre of the solar system from the earth to the sun. The world-revolution of the Christians came when Jesus discovered the true centre of human life.
>
> "Not servants but friends" is the proclamation of the revolution. The key-word of the Christian Gospel is not service but friendship. Of late, I believe, we have been thinking too much in terms of service — service of God and the world.
>
> There is nothing distinctively Christian about that ...
>
> "But surely," you will say, "we are called as Christians to serve Christ and to serve the world." No, we are called to be the friends of Christ and the friends of men. That is not at all the same thing.[8]

In making his case for friendship — a term he now seems to have embraced not tentatively but with firm conviction — Macmurray appealed first and last to the students' own experience to discern the distinction between friendship and service. When he focused on Jesus, he noted that Jesus came to bring life, that he was not anxious to leave this life; that he suffered and died not that we might do the same but that we might live. And that his one and only command was that we love one another. Jesus commended us, paradoxically, to a command in which perfect obedience to it was to live in perfect freedom. To live in friendship and to live in freedom are not opposites but the two sides of the same coin. In true friendship, the flourishing of genuine togetherness *effects* the flourishing of genuine individuality — and vice versa. In philosophical or theological language, we might say that the message of Jesus implies that the movement to self-transcendence through love for the other achieves the deepening of self-immanence. To give myself over, is to become myself truly. So, Macmurray continued, when Jesus speaks of persons being "saved" he means living in this friendship/freedom that marks the best of personal relationships. Neither knowledge, nor beauty, nor goodness can "save" a single soul; only friendship in the sense Jesus used the term can do that. "Friendship," he concludes, "is the supreme value in life and the source of all other values." But, as in his inaugural address, he is more than aware of how soft, clichéd and banal this statement might sound so he anticipates that perception head on and leads the students carefully down a path they would hardly have expected:

> Do you think that this is too simple and easy? Simple, it is, perhaps, but not easy. There is nothing we fear more than friendship, nothing that strikes more terror into us than freedom. If this seems a strange saying, it must be because you are confusing friendship with friendliness. Friendliness is not to be despised, but it is only the imitation of a friendship and a poor substitute for the real thing. It is really a refined form of service, and often rather a superficial one. But friendship knows no reservations, it gives not sympathy or comfort, or advice to help, but rather itself.
>
> To be a friend is to be yourself for another person. It means committing yourself completely and revealing yourself completely without reserve. It means putting all your cards on the table and taking the consequences. It means stark reality between persons without pretence or sentimentality. How many of us could bear to be found out completely for what we are by someone else? Most of us shrink from finding ourselves out. Even with our intimates we wear a mask and insist upon their wearing one. We have tastes and decencies and dignities that we must defend, and all of them are defences against friendship. They are the lifebelts that keep us on the surface of that sea of intimate relations, and we cling to them in terror of drowning in the limitlessness depths of personality.
>
> So pretence creeps in and sentimentality, the grossest sin of all against friendship. Honest hatred is better than the pretence of love. There are amongst us those who are willing to spend time and thought and strength and money in the service of others in order to retain the isolation of our own personality, to conceal as it were the fraud we are guilty of in refusing to give ourselves. All that service is of no avail. What men need from is us love, not moving acts: friendship, not friendly services ... Friendship means losing ourselves, and that is apt to be a terrifying experience.[9]

As Tissington Tatlow testified in his summary of the conference for the *Student Movement* a month or so later, Macmurray's talk was the most provocative of the conference. It seemed to be received by the students along one of three lines: for one part of the audience it was the finest and most prophetic talk they had ever heard. For a second group it was just the Gospel of John rehashed: what's the big deal? And for the third there was a sense of puzzlement about the message but a feeling that something very important was being said in it.

If one were to say that this talk is mainly a sermon, someone else could equally make the case that it is much more than that. Even in this context of Christian community, it represents the continuance of Macmurray's search for the logic of the personal. That the social context was not primarily philosophical does not invalidate the philosophical truths being articulated here.[10] In his effort to advance his thought, Macmurray was referring to the best source book on his subject that he knew and to the best proof-base he could find, personal experience — his and theirs. In the SCM context he is indeed stating deep Christian truths to fellow Christians but what he is finding in the Gospel is a presentation of the terms by which the logic of friendship is revealed. In the Gospel texts, Macmurray found clues, not proofs, for the logic of how personality acts. In recognizing that friendship and freedom are presented as *necessary* correlatives in personal relationship he finds himself discovering the dynamics of a logic that seems to accomplish two apparently opposing goals at once: it preserves and enhances both individuality (as the organic logic failed to do) and relationship (as the mechanical logic failed to do). Love creates togetherness, and the exercise of freedom in love reveals and enhances individuality — both at once. When love is given over to the risks of freedom and when freedom is given over to the vulnerability of loving both seem to defy their very natures. And yet both not only flourish at once but do so through a necessary mutual interdependence. This is the reality for which he is seeking the logic!

The gospels express this relationship in paradoxical words: "the one who wishes to find himself must lose himself." Only the one who has actually done it knows it is true. As Macmurray wrote in *Adventure*, the deepest immanence is achieved in the deepest act of freely given self-transcendence. He is attempting to make the case that this is not a conclusion based in religious revelation but in the empirical base of personal experience. Personal life exceeds mechanical (formal) logic in one way and organic (dialectical) logic in another but it indicates the need for a fuller logic that includes both of these within it. Macmurray is just beginning, in a very tentative way, to integrate his new philosophical thinking with his experience. Every step is new territory for him but he is becoming convinced he is cutting a true path.

He sent a copy of his presentation to Roberts and received positive support from his old friend. He wrote back to Roberts:

> I am glad that you found my Liverpool effort to your liking:
> because I was a bit depressed about it — my first effort really to
> put my philosophical conclusions into every-day dress. And it was
> the outcome of pretty hard experience. When you get that into
> words for everybody, it looks bold and empty. Even so, it is rather
> negative: and I'm stuck there. But if you find it worthwhile, do use
> it in any way you please.[11]

The pretty hard experience he is noting here is, we can assume, at least partly related to how he himself has come to freedom with Betty confessing that she was sexually involved with another man despite her deep love for John and her commitment to their marriage. On the day this letter to Roberts was written John and Betty were just a few weeks away from the medical crisis described earlier. The fact that it concluded in her no longer being able to become pregnant and the two of them not able to be parents together would have been more "hard experience" that John had to draw into his love for her.

Probably as a result of hearing his talk at the SCM conference and noting the impression he made on the young people there, Archbishop William Temple of York asked Macmurray to prepare a "memorandum" — a text stating a position that would serve as a basis for discussion — for a Conference on the Preparation of the Ministry being held in early April. He wanted John to explore what he felt might be a genuine basis from which a Christian apologetic for the modern world might be launched, and to state frankly what obstacles to that he saw in the Church. From his talks with Macmurray, Temple was aware of John's position on the massive failure of the churches to defend the values of humanity and the Gospel against the idolatries of patriotism and materialism leading up to and during the Great War. It was clearly in the light of that knowledge that Temple took the risk and made his request.

William Temple's comfort with Macmurray was at least partly because he himself was no church mouse. Temple had an expansive attitude to Christianity and its mission in the world. He believed firmly in the capacity of mind to apprehend reality. He believed in an active and intimately present God in history, and therefore had no time for those who regarded human evolution as a product of blind chance. For Temple, the spiritual situated the technical, not vice versa; but this did not make him hostile to technology or science. As he put it in one of his talks, "unless all existence is a medium of Revelation, no particular Revelation is possible." In fact, the later writings and talks of Temple sound some of Macmurray's favoured themes and one might conjecture about the lines of influence in, for example, Temple's conviction that the supreme characteristic of life was its personal nature and the gathering of persons in community. He also held that religious experience was really the whole experience of the religious person, that God chooses the world as his way of being known, and that Christianity was the most material of the religions.[12] In these convictions, regardless of their provenance, he was at least carrying the same goods in his pack and going in the same direction as Macmurray. In fact, in their day-to-day activities they were walking on different paths and Temple held, for example, a much more benign view of the State and the Churches than Macmurray.

The memorandum for Temple was not easy for Macmurray to write. He complained to Roberts:

> I'm a bit obsessed now with the fear that I am sheltering under the wing of a Christianity that I don't really believe in — or at least being interpreted in terms of a Christianity which is poles asunder from my central meaning. I feel inclined to write a pamphlet on the question "Was Christ a Christian?" with a thoroughly negative answer. What Christianity there is seems to me sometimes so completely bound up with a civilization that is, in my opinion, pretty fundamentally incompatible with the attitude of Christ. I'm rather stumped in my efforts to write a memorandum for Temple's conference on the problems facing the church.[13]

Nevertheless Macmurray got the job done within the month. It is a twenty-page *tour de force* of cultural analysis from a Christian perspective, highlighting the multiple hypocrisies and gross materialism of pre-war British society. Cultural blindness he found to be true of the churches as much as of secular society. The churches were fully complicit with maintaining the myth of constant progress. They accepted without murmur the dog-eat-dog competitiveness that underlay European economic practice, and supported the "Britain first" attitude at home. Except for a few brave prophets, they left unquestioned the total materialization of values in society such that the spiritual yearnings of people ended up, along with social manners, as the petty servants of the material goals of society at large. He tells the churchmen bluntly that many young people he has met at the university are finding the church so lacking in credibility that they have turned away from association with it in order to save their own spiritual integrity.

In this document, he takes up his analysis of the peculiar sickness in the spiritual life of Europe that he described in his inaugural and at Liverpool as "sentimentality." Sentimentality, in Macmurray's vocabulary and at this point in his social analysis, is the continuing choice to reverence God, morality, religion, love, family, women, sexuality, etc. in words and ideas only. They have no effective power in most people's individual lives and none in the life of society. The war exposed, for all to see, that "the spiritual life of England was on the whole and in this sense sentimental." To put it simply, it was "not *real.*" He cites the systematic, state-sponsored cultivation of hatred for Germans and the "use" of young women by their elders in the white feather campaign of humiliation against young British men not in the military as examples, during the war, of the obscene abuse of the human spirit and community values for nationalistic ends. He suggests that any thoroughgoing effort to re-establish the Church as the spiritual centre of modern life must begin with the transformation of its own action in the world, so that its own behaviour provides the grounds for clearing it of the charge and the suspicion of sentimentality. He tells them: "the task involves convincing the world at large not that the Church is *right,* but that the Church is *real* ...," that it actually believes what it *says* it believes, and tries sincerely to live by it. This for Macmurray is genuine sentiment, as opposed to sentimentality which is false at its core.

When he turns to a therapy for this disease he has diagnosed, he turns to his new convictions about the personal life. As for a method for conversion, Macmurray proposes that the churches join with the spiritually-minded non-churchgoers in a shared "insistence upon the absolute value of human personality and the primacy of the personal life." This is a meeting place for people of good intention on all sides.

His last dart is a challenge to the churches to overcome their denominational differences and cosy separateness. If they want to be believable they have to make concrete moves towards becoming genuinely ecumenical. The secular powers, he notes, are attempting a League of Nations, something that Christians, specifically called "to be one," seem unable or unwilling to do. He insists that ecumenism in the Gospel does not require the relinquishing, let alone the suppression, of distinct cultural traditions in the churches. Genuine union is dependent not on monochromatic sameness but on a shared faith in God through Jesus for the world. Without genuine ecumenism the young will not find in the cosy compartments of the many churches a genuine spiritual power for the healing and advance of the damaged personal life of the world.

At first blush this is not a reflection on the personal life directly, and yet in it Macmurray makes significant advances in his thinking about the nature of the personal life. First, he identifies the proclamation and advance of a genuinely personal life as lying at the heart of Christian mission. Second, in this document Macmurray does an even more thorough analysis of the *distortions in values and action that led to the Great War,*

and confirms that the failure in faith and creative action in society is intimately related to the submission of persons and institutions to a dominant
organic system of operating values. Third, he locates the failure in two
betrayals of the spirit: (a) a *sentimentality* in personal and religious values
which rendered them powerless to challenge the dominant materialism
and nationalism; and (b) *the cultivation of ideological hatred and divisions* — the demonization of the "Other" — in order to hide inner contradictions and to enhance a self-image of moral righteousness. Having faced
the specific reasons for the failure, he is now more prepared to contemplate the positive dimensions of personal life.

A few days after he left York and returned to London, a small package
arrived in the mail from Archbishop Temple. When he opened it up,
Macmurray found the sooty toothbrush he used to clean his Primus stove,
and realized he must have left it in the guest bathroom at the Archbishop's
house. It was accompanied by a simple note: "You left your toothbrush
behind."

In most of his public presentations, Macmurray was not having an easy
time conveying what he meant by the personal life to his colleagues and
listeners. He felt frustrated that people, especially his Christian listeners,
could not see the contradictions that flourished everywhere. He told
Roberts in late March that he wasn't very pleased with the memorandum
he did for Temple, and used the letter to express his frustration at Christian
blindness to the problem:

> It is the inhumanity, the impersonalness of the brutal business of
> modern civilization that is getting my goat, and the easy transition
> that is made from it to Christianity — where I look for a glaring
> discordance. The subtlety with which Utilitarianism has decked
> Christ's gospel out into the peacock of Imperialism and industrial
> monopoly. Masses of people — Christian and anti-Christian —
> seem to crave to identify Christianity with Britain maintaining the
> "Freedom of the Seas" by force of battleships and for the
> enhancement of commerce and prestige. It's a shallow civilization
> we've got. People don't seem to know, Dick, what I mean when I
> talk about a *personal* life. 'What's the use of it?' is what they ask.[14]

This frustration did not put him off diving even more deeply into his subject. Two months later, on May 27, he joined Hilda Oakley in an
Aristotelian Society symposium entitled "The Principle of Personality in
Experience." It proved to be the point at which Macmurray was able to
articulate the most coherent philosophical expression to date of his
steadily developing insights into the nature and functioning of personality.
To follow the many elements of the arguments would require quoting the

entire paper. But the conclusions alone reveal the advances his thinking has made over the course of only a few months:

> Personal knowledge is a distinct type of knowledge, not a moment or an aspect within impersonal knowledge. Personal knowledge *of* someone is radically different from an impersonal knowledge *about* someone — or something.
>
> Personal knowledge is necessarily mutual. If A knows B, then B knows A. This implies also that in personal knowledge we can know a person "more intimately" without necessarily having an increase in information. In other words, personal knowledge is not just a function of facts but a function of feeling. Feeling is, then, somehow a form of knowing, even a deeper form of knowing.
>
> Following on this, if spirit is inherently personal, then 'value' is a wider term than 'understanding' and includes 'understanding' at least implicitly.
>
> Mind, therefore, is a subordinate aspect of personality, personality is not a subordinate aspect of mind. There are no individual minds, just individual persons — who think.
>
> The highest and most comprehensive mode of knowledge is the mutual knowledge of two persons. Different forms of impersonal knowledge are all normatively subordinate dimensions within personal knowledge.
>
> The full relationship between two persons in which knowledge and activity are fused inseparable aspects is best expressed by the term 'communion.'
>
> Personality, then, *is realized* in the unity of two persons in communion.
>
> If personality is the fullest bearer of value, then Absolute Reality is personal, and God is a personal Absolute. We would then have a right to speak of the completest experience of Reality as communion with God.[15]

Again, just as he did in his inaugural address, Macmurray ends by insisting that his objective has been to draw attention to a *logical* problem. Of course he has done so and it is a legitimate statement for him to make. But despite the validity of this claim and perspective one begins to wonder if he does not use this assertion about the essentially logical nature of his project to anticipate those who might be tempted, given his subject matter and his conclusions, to accuse him of merely indulging in fluffy platitudes.

The major advances seem to be in both the content of his claims and the fleshing out of the logical project. This article contains hints of a significant philosophical revolution, one that overthrows the Cartesian premises at their very foundations. Mind is here a dimension of person, not vice versa — a total rejection of Descartes' founding premise. Impersonal knowledge (science, essentially) is dethroned and situated as a subordinate dimension within the fuller scope of personal knowledge. Valuing is not radically other than knowing, it is a form of knowing that depends on facts but is fuller than facts and contains the facts within it. This immediately suggests that he accepts from the Romantics that *feeling* is a form of knowing and therefore a mode of achieving cognitive objectivity — all heresy within scientific assumptions. And finally, personal knowledge is achieved by way of mutual participation, quite the opposite of detached observation; and is most expressive in mutual *action,* thereby implying that knowledge (theory) is a dimension of action, not vice versa, as modern philosophy demands. The conversion in foundational premises is massive and total.

It is no wonder that Macmurray, driven by such reversing insights, finds few listeners who grasp his point. For him, it is philosophically new, but experientially it is as plain as the nose on his face. He shares this feeling at some length in an October 20, 1929, letter to his friend Roberts. The letter, in fact, recoups much of what he presented to his colleagues in May:

> I'm giving tomorrow the first of a series of five public lectures in University College on the Phenomenology of the Personal. It is about Personal Freedom and the problem of ethics. It may only be my own pride or blindness: but I think I am entering a field which is absolutely virgin soil for the philosophers, and calling for a construction of modern philosophy from top to bottom. It seems to me that we have never yet begun the effort to understand the Personal at all and that we don't yet have the logical apparatus to do it. We *know* persons and personal activities — nothing better: but when we try to understand them or express them we do so always by impersonal analogies — drawn from the physical or the organic world. And the logical structure of the personal is radically different from either of these. That is why you get philosophers saying that Subjective Idealism is irrefutable, although everybody *knows* that it isn't true. All modern philosophy seems to me to arrive, by a logical necessity, at a position where it denies the truth of what we all know to be true without a shadow of doubt. Even the realists don't dare to more than assert that the independent reality of things outside us is a reasonable hypothesis. And it isn't a hypothesis, but a fact that we know for certain — if we don't know that, we don't know anything at all, certainly not enough to build a philosophy on.

I think I understand how this preposterous position arises — it is just the *reductio ad absurdum* of the effort to understand the personal through a conception of structure which is inadequate to its nature. If you start in this way, you naturally are forced to the conclusion that you know nothing, but there is no knowledge for the simple reason that knowing is a personal activity. You have really assumed that knowing is impossible in assuming that you can analyse a person in impersonal terms. For, by definition, to know is to grasp a reality other than and independent of your own, and it is this that your assumption denies by assuming that knowing is a special case of causal relation or of functional adaptation.

So I want to start by recognizing the objectivity of persons as the fundamental fact of our experience; this capacity to apprehend and enjoy an independent reality: and I think I can show that such a capacity involves the mutual unity of persons, that is to say, personal communion. This is really my starting-point — that persons exist and are real in and through communion: and in my few lectures we can attempt to point this out empirically over the whole personal field. When they are finished I shall get them published, if Macmillan will like them, and I think he will.

That final remark suggests he was still on good terms with Daniel Macmillan even after the fiasco over the book he and Morris had promised that publishing house and then reneged on. The lectures Macmurray refers to here were never published and, to this day, they have not been found; or, at least, not firmly identified.[16] In addition to summarizing his focus, the letter to Roberts represents Macmurray's first use of the nominative term "the personal" — the expression he will stay with until the end of his days of writing on the subject. Up to this time he has stuck with the term "personality" — and, in fact, he continued to use it for a few more years — even though there are some signs he was getting restive with the ambiguity between the psychological meaning of the term "personality" and the philosophical category of being "personal" which was his focus and concern.

In May, just before his major presentation at the Aristotelian Society, John went back to Balliol for the first time since his farewell the summer before. There, he delivered a sermon entitled "The Kingdom of Heaven" that achieves yet another advance in his thinking. The entire sermon rests on a plea to the students to dwell in, rather than attempt to escape from, the paradoxes Jesus uses to reveal the truth. Personal truth, as opposed to impersonal truth, is such that it defies full linguistic expression, and that is what the paradoxes of Jesus respect and reveal.

He takes up the particular paradox Jesus proclaims: that the Kingdom of God is at once "within you" and "not of this world." He notes the abuses that arise when only one pole of the paradox is kept alive. An exclusive concentration on the first pole leads to a false sense that the work of building the world of progress and prosperity is actually identical to the work of the Kingdom. The Kingdom is thereby reduced and domesticated by worldly interests and complacent men of action. On the other hand, the second statement taken on its own can suggest that action in this world is not the issue, that having holy ideas and good feelings are the heart of the matter since the world, in itself, is quite unredeemable. In this pole, he effectively identifies what he meant earlier by sentimentalized, unreal values and religion. In this sermon, he comes very close to naming this version of religion as "ideal" — a term he will land on and cling to within a couple of years.

John ends the sermon by holding both poles together, and translating the term Kingdom of Heaven into Kingdom of Friendship, noting that Jesus did not separate love of God from love of neighbour. He urges his young listeners, as they prepare to leave the university for their chosen lives in society, to cherish first whatever reflects and expresses this kingdom of friendship — *at once* already within us, and yet beyond what worldly, self-interested values are able to provide. He urges them to ensure that all other claims to kingly status by worldly values be required by them to meet the relational and moral criteria found in true friendship. As in his address to the SCM a few months earlier, the sermon reveals Macmurray's amazing capacity to integrate the most professional and abstruse of his explorations of the personal with the most concrete and immediate searchings of people for fuller life. Implicit in both forms of expression, of course, are the joys and struggles and longings in his own life.

It was his twelve lectures on Reality and Freedom, transmitted on BBC Radio in the spring of 1930, that allowed Macmurray to pull together his thinking on what it meant to live the personal life as opposed to something less full than that. They led him to distinguish between "being real" as opposed to "being unreal" in our thinking and feelings, and he applied the same distinction to people — all quite fresh and different language for his listeners. He asserted with utter simplicity his position on how we become real and complete in our selfhood:

> ... the apprehended character of the self depends on the apprehended character of the not-self from which it is distinguished. I apprehend myself as body in apprehending bodies in the external world. I apprehend myself as a living creature in distinction from living creatures in the world which are not myself. Similarly, I apprehend myself as a self, that is to say, as a person, only in and through the apprehension of other persons in the world who are not myself.[17]

Having given his listeners in the first six lectures a good idea of what he meant by his expanded notion of reality, one that included feelings and relationships in it, he turned to the issue of freedom. He explored the specific form of freedom as well as the form of morality that arose from within each of the mechanical, organic and personal unity-patterns.

It was when he presented the implications of the personal form of freedom and morality that he most excited or enraged his many listeners. For the enthusiastic ones it was as though he had named their own pain and hope as well as their own deeper understanding of things. For the offended ones it seemed that he had replaced God by personal relationships among human beings, that he had thrown out all sense of law in the areas of feeling and sexuality and given the youth *carte blanche* to do whatever they felt like doing. The radio talks had a huge audience, and the correspondence, pro and con, suggested few listeners were left unengaged.

In his October 10, 1930, letter to Roberts, he mentioned the vicious reaction to the talks on the part of some, and summarized his main point about feelings. "The trouble is I am pushing Protestantism to its logical conclusions, and in the field of morality." By this he meant: the liberation to think for oneself launched by Luther must now be followed by the second phase in the liberation of the person — the liberation of feeling. He was convinced that the only way to decide among feelings is first of all to feel them. Living is not a question of trying to control feelings. Rather, it is an absolute imperative to free them up, free them to be felt, expressed and directed towards worthy actions. Only when feelings are allowed to be expressed in the clear light of day, can illusory feelings be discriminated from true ones, that is, feelings that lead to sound values, just as liberated thinking leads to discriminating unsound judgments from the sound ones that respect reality and lead to action that enhances reality. Without this freedom, we are destined to live by mechanical and organic categories which do nothing but diminish rather than realize the human. He was fully aware, and told his audience, that his proposals were full of risk and required experimentation. When fearful members of the audience contemplated this degree of openness, some accused Macmurray in the BBC's magazine, *The Listener,* of sedition and materialism.

As he said to Roberts, the reaction was honest; it meant people appreciated how huge was the revolution involved in choosing to allow freedom for others, in choosing risk and vulnerability and hope in our personal relations in place of certainty, contracts and control. It was hardly his manner to tell them that he knew by personal experience what he was talking about. But he noted the abyss that lay between relationships of duty and contract over against those based on love and trust. Merely social relations, as in an organization or in the accepted nineteenth century version of marriage in Britain, are dominated by a purpose, he noted for his friend.

This makes them "organic" and sub-personal. They are totally different from personal relationships of love or friendship:

> The bond between friends will generate common purposes — lots
> of them — but it is not constituted by them. It is a bond of personal
> fellowship. And it is essentially religious — the analogy at the
> finite level of the relationship between man and God ...

This distinction between merely "social" and "personal" morality makes no sense to his hearers, he finds. When he says "personal," they hear "individual" — and attack him for being an individualist — a position he condemned. They can only think in the "individual-society" antithesis, and have no basis in their liberal thought-patterns to grasp that he is speaking of a third category, a fuller *mode of being*, that can apply to both individuals and their social relationships.

He finds he has the same problem when he tries to indicate that true emotion, like true thinking, is essentially objective, not a mere reaction to stimulus. What he only hinted at in "The Principle of Personality in Experience" he is now prepared to say forcefully: Emotion is our avenue to apprehend true *values* just as true thinking clarifies the meaning of *facts*. He finds that this psychological arena is the real field of combat, the one where people are most challenged:

> And there comes the rub. For thought can only function if it is
> free and experimental (carrying with it the continual risk of
> mistakes and failure) and so real feeling can only function if it
> too is free and experimental, with the same risk. We have learned
> — after a long struggle — to set thought free. But in the field of
> emotion and value we are still in the general atmosphere of the
> Middle Ages: determining values by an instinct based on
> tradition. It won't do any longer. Science has put a vast power of
> achieving purposes at the disposal of mean and women, and the
> emotional forces which inevitably determine the uses to which it
> is put are mostly perverted or stunted or vulgarized. It is the
> emotional life of our world that is the danger spot: and it is
> freedom that it needs if it is to grow, and grow straight. I mean
> that we must stop dictating to people the ways in which they are
> to feel, and instead we must insist on expressing, in speech and
> action. The feelings that are really in us.
> ... Everyone seems to say at once 'But how dangerous! What is
> going to happen if you let people give a free rein to their feelings?'
> I have answered simply: 'I don't know. A revolution of some sort, I
> suppose; and a lot of mistakes in conduct that will demand

sympathy and involve suffering; and, in the end, the coming of the Kingdom of Heaven.'

He hears in the response to him "the voice of a terror of life and of a disbelief in God." He tells Roberts: They seem to feel "it means revolution and atheism and immorality."

> And they are right, in a queer crooked sense, with the sharpened wits that fear always give. Yet I cannot help feeling that I am merely repeating what I learned from the gospels, and learned to understand in experience. A belief in God is a belief in the ultimate goodness of the world he is running, and of the human nature he has made in his own likeness: and that you have got to trust it and go on trusting it.
>   ... I am prepared to bank upon the faith that the essence of nature — human and divine — is love. And to trust to that, with no other security. But I know quite well that the acceptance of such a creed would be death to the present order of society, possibly including the churches, unless they were to come out of it and be separate.

The flow of his thinking is now a torrent. His BBC lectures distilled all his thinking to date on the difference between "reality" and "unreality" in thinking, feeling and living. When he tells Roberts that he is only following up on the implications of the Protestant insight he means that no force outside the self can replace or dictate the imperatives of personal expression. That's what it means to be free. First the liberation of thinking (with science), and now the demand for the liberation of feeling. It inevitably leads — as it will — to the liberation of action.[18] His challenge to outside authority and control in the personal order is not, in his view, the elimination of any and all authority and direction in living; far from it. Rather, it is the promise of a healing and rectitude in how these are discovered and exercised. Intelligence counts. Free choice counts. Responsibility counts.

The root of all authority, he suggests, is God's nature, and ours; and that nature, he believes, is at once, love and freedom. Love, concrete and specific, is the compass for all our obedience and guidance, including in our feelings. To support this view, he appeals to St Augustine's famous dictum "Love, and do what you want" which, he noted to Roberts, was also expressed by Harry Jones (former Moral Professor at Glasgow) as: "Love God and rip!"[19] As he had already told the students at Liverpool, following the imperatives of love and of friendship is no easy thing. But the question remains: where do these imperatives come from? If God is only an idea, my wants have no true imperative shaping them.

This final step in the first, massive stage of Macmurray's unfolding of the logic of friendship came within weeks. He found himself using the word "sacrilege" to describe what occurs if one speaks of an intimate friend in impersonal terms with a third person. He knew that word was appropriate, but it was only when he actually used it that he allowed himself to see, as though for the first time, that "the personal," as he understood it, *is* the domain of the sacred. This had a powerful effect on him because it provided him with the grounds to assert what he had for so long felt: that *the personal, as an inclusive category of being, was identically the religious.*

Again, this conversion is best expressed in a letter to Roberts on November 13, 1930, barely a month later after the last one. In it, he notes his dissatisfaction with Rudolph Otto's view that the idea of the holy is a deeply internal experience. With such a completely subjective definition, Macmurray finds no basis to distinguish between real and unreal religion. His own view is that:

> ... unreal religion is religion which is mere idea, divorced from the concreteness of finite experience ... real religion must fasten itself to life, and obtain a foothold in the finite. In other words the idea of the holy must be attached to something real in experience. Only then does the question of religious error arise. This gives us a clue to the nature of falsity in religion: one could call it a misplacement of the idea of the holy. *What* a man feels to be sacred, *what* raises the sense of reverence and holiness in him, may not be in itself and in its nature sacred or holy at all. Then our question becomes: what is it in experience that is objectively sacred in its own right? Not (as the religious psychologists ask): what is it that people feel reverence for? No! What *ought* they to feel reverence for? To that my answer would be: 'The personal, or friendship or love — all these being, to my thinking, one and the same.' ... We must take our shoes from our feet when we enter the field of the personal.

Returning to the inspiration behind his 1927 essay "Objectivity in Religion," he reaffirms that there "must be an incarnation of the divine before 'Love God' means anything practical, anything more than the canonization of the structure of one's own educated or miseducated or uneducated conscience." So the question: "When is the feeling of reverence rightly directed?" is the heart of the matter.

> That seems to me the vital question. What is God, if I am to love him? If the answer is 'Jesus' then the question means: 'What is Jesus?' And my question then becomes: 'What did Jesus feel to be

holy and sacred and inviolable? Only when I answer that question does my own position emerge clearly. I shall treat personality and the relation of persons in love, as sacred and to be reverenced, and *nothing else*. Whatever is impersonal must not be reverenced or treated as sacred — on penalty of losing our soul. To do so is to be idolatrous, to worship as God what is not God. And to treat what is personal impersonally is to pollute a holy thing.

This is the conversion to objectivity that removes religion, in Macmurray's philosophy not from the domain of personal experience but from being determined by and enslaved to mere subjectivity, on the one hand, and merely external authority on the other. With this identity of the personal and the religious, Macmurray ensures a genuine place for religion in scientific discourse and in public action aimed at making people less likely to be victims of impersonal forms of behaviour. He provides a way of conceiving a credible basis for claiming objective knowledge in the field of religious action, and in theology, its reflective component.[20]

As he acknowledged later to his friend and colleague A.R.C. Duncan, he was helped considerably in making this move with such conviction by having heard Professor Schick's lectures in early 1930 on the processes of verification. Verification is not merely a function of intellectual coherence, as the rationalists hold, or feeling and aesthetic intuition, as held by the Romantics. *It is action* — especially our experience as interaction with others (containing as it does both intelligence and emotion engaging the world) — *that is the full field of verification*. Macmurray had been moving consistently in this direction for at least five years. His ethics lectures at Balliol show that he had effectively been teaching a philosophy based on the primacy of action. But Schick helped to bring the insight into explicit judgment and firm conviction. With that methodological step taken, the grounds for the possibility of objectivity in personal relationships was assured.[21]

When a full review of Macmurray's writings is done from the perspective of his specific project of conceptualizing the logic or form of the personal, a case might be made that with this letter of November 13, 1930, the essential structure has been put in place. Significant developments and advances lie ahead in both concepts and terminology; this is unquestionable. Several of them can justifiably be seen as much more than minor developments of the position he reached at the end of 1930. But do any of them constitute the kind of advance represented by the insight expressed in this letter to Roberts? Even the marvellous Gifford Lectures could be viewed as a work of genius more at the level of synthesis than seminal thinking.

The 1930s were to be important years, even crucial ones, from many points of view, but in Macmurray's own mind, as he looked back on them, they were a time when he was significantly deflected from his essential mission as a philosopher.[22] In 1944 he was to tell Provost Pye of the University of London that he was drawn to accept the offer of the Moral Chair at Edinburgh because there he might find an ambiance more suitable than bustling London for making a last attempt at articulating his own philosophy.

Chapter 9

The BBC and the Philosopher (1930-34)

It was with his twelve talks on BBC Radio in 1930 that Macmurray became something of a public figure.[1] How he got to be invited to offer the talks is a bit of a story in itself. When the British Broadcasting Corporation took over the work of the British Broadcasting Company in January 1927, its managers shared a vision of radio as a potentially great medium for education, especially adult education. John Reith, the crusty BBC director general, accepted all the recommendations presented in Sir Henry Hadow's Advisory Committee's report called *New Ventures in Broadcasting*. He immediately set up a Central Council which was responsible for educational policy in the area of adult education broadcasting at all levels. Its duties included designing programmes, choosing speakers, starting a weekly educational publication called *The Listener,* and creating Area Councils for creating and nurturing local "Listening Groups" across the country, and giving feedback to the Central Council. The Council had many prestigious members, including its first Chairman, Lord Justice Sankey. When Sankey resigned in 1929 to join Prime Minister Ramsay Macdonald's cabinet as Lord Chancellor, he was succeeded by the Archbishop of York, William Temple, who already knew Macmurray from their earlier work together earlier that year.

It was undoubtedly Temple who proposed Macmurray's name as a philosopher who could do the job for them in a series being contemplated on "some philosophical problems." Charles Siepmann, head of the Talks Department, had been named secretary to the council, in addition to his other work, a few months before he moved the Talks Department in December 1929 to its new broadcast studios in Savoy Hill. It was his duty to sound out potential speakers, and his account — in the foreword to *Freedom in the Modern World* — of his first meeting with Macmurray lacks nothing in the art of portraiture:

> ... At my request he came to see me at Savoy Hill. I remember the
> room (very official), the chair in which he sat (also grimly official),
> the interruptions of colleagues and office boys and telephone bells.
> We sat as strangers, a little on the defensive, with the wariness of
> first acquaintance. I told him of our needs and hopes and we
> discussed philosophy and the difficulty of making dry bones live.

We warmed to our subject and to one another. A few minutes later
the author of this book sat speaking at a microphone in what was
then No.6 studio; and with the dispassionate inhumanity of the
broadcasting official I remember sitting with a colleague weighing
the quality and substance of that quiet voice with the endearing
Scottish brogue which came to us through our headphones. Well, he
might do, we coldly calculated! I recall these details because they
were incidents of a first acquaintance which has since ripened to
friendship ... Nor are such personal recollections wholly irrelevant.
For the contagion of personality which then made a warmth out of
the chill of first acquaintance and sensitive reserve has since become
part of the experience of many who will be readers of this book.
Few would have expected that at the height of a beguiling summer
and at the unlikely hour of eight of the evening twelve broadcast
talks on Philosophy would have produced a miniature renaissance
among thousands of English listeners. In that sense, at least, the
talks made broadcast history. The pamphlet which introduced them
and which is here republished, became a 'best-seller.'[2]

Siepmann summarizes here, in the briefest terms, a broadcasting event
stretching from April 28 to July 14 that made a major impact in the country at the outset of the BBC's adult education programming. There are sto-
ries of housewives in villages across England, as eight o'clock on
Mondays approached, taking off their aprons and rushing, along with ordinary working men, to the house in the village that had the wireless set
where the local Listening Group gathered to hear Professor Macmurray
and then discuss his thoughts with one another.

Macmurray had written for the Listening Groups a twenty-eight-
page pamphlet entitled "Today and Tomorrow: A Philosophy of Freedom" which introduced his overall theme at some length, gave
summaries of the individual talks with questions that could be of help
in the Listening Group discussions, and ended with a book list that was
in no way condescending. The list included major works of political,
ethical and cultural relevance to the theme of freedom. Lord Acton,
Machiavelli, John Stuart Mill, Plato, Rousseau, Henry Sidgwick, Afred
Adler, Aldous Huxley, D.H. Lawrence. Wyndham Lewis and a few others were included in the selection that was at once broad and basic. The
pamphlet was simply and lucidly written. It sold out immediately and
needed to be reprinted frequently during that summer while the talks
were going on.

Two months after the series ended, the executive committee of the
Central Council met to review its overwhelming impact. They were confirmed in their feeling about the power of radio for education. They also

proposed Macmurray's pamphlet as a model for planning future pamphlets. The success was palpable. From that point, and over the coming three years, a huge expansion in programming and outreach took place in the BBC's adult education broadcasting. By the end of 1930, there were more than a thousand Listening Groups active in England, and the Central Council made it their work to provide for their growth by organizing courses, initiating summer schools for group leaders, and offering pamphlets and supporting literature to these groups who came together informally and spontaneously.

Macmurray and the BBC had made the arrangements for the Today and Tomorrow series only in February and March of 1930, and the weekly talks were to begin broadcasting at the end of April. Macmurray took a short period of time to line up what he wanted to say, decided on his titles, then wrote the famous pamphlet. On April 13, he wrote his sister Helen saying he would like to come and visit her for a day or two: "... but until I get onto the BBC talks and see how long it is going to take to put them into shape I can't reckon how rushed I am going to be."[3] That was just two weeks before the first lecture was delivered! As the series went on, John was writing each lecture just before it was to be delivered on the air. He wrote to his friend Donald Grant in Vienna on June 1 complaining about how hectic life was because of the radio talks. "I never get one written before the boy from *The Listener* is at the door waiting to take it away."[4]

Despite the extremely short time Macmurray was able to devote to each talk, it would be a mistake to think — either critically or admiringly — that the talks were created "off the top of his head" over these twelve weeks. Much of what Macmurray put into those talks was material he had researched and been thinking about for years. Much of it, especially his reflections on the Christian, Greek and Roman (Stoic) modes of morality, was already being developed in a more academic style in his proposed first book to be entitled *The Western Tradition* which he was in the process of writing at the time. But, for these talks, he had determined to avoid specialized philosophical jargon and to use ordinary, non-technical language wherever that was possible. Later he acknowledged that in following this path he came to understand many philosophical problems in a completely fresh way himself.[5] In the end, the BBC talks had a similar effect on him as his work with the unions in South Africa. He was confirmed in his trust in the intelligence and clarity of working-class people. He deepened his pedagogical skills and his philosophy of education. He also grew in his appreciation of how intimately the means and manner of communication were connected to real understanding. Certainly, for many of the people listening to him, Macmurray was the first philosopher they had heard who talked in a way they could understand, and in a manner they could trust.

The relaxed manner of his talks, he acknowledged, was partly due to the added comfort he had in having a small audience in the studio with him. Betty came to give him moral support, along with her friend Jack Barry and another friend from Bolton Studios, Marvyn Logden. They gave John the sense of contact with his audience that he needed, and it seems to have worked.

John told Donald Grant that people were appreciative of the talks; in fact:

> ... too appreciative, I think: they don't really grasp the implication. One man did write to say that all he could gather was that I am an 'anarchist preaching anarchy.' I felt that he had understood something ... The real fuss, if there is any, will come over the second last one, which is to be a wholehearted attack upon the moral ideal of social service.[6]

He was right. By the time the talks ended *The Listener* bristled with letters to the editor that were virulently judgmental of Macmurray. Douglas Jerrold wrote in the *English Review* that Professor Macmurray had travestied Christian morality "in the name of mental science," and complained that his views were "tendentious" and too "advanced." A critic at the *Observer* tore into him, as well. Father Vincent McNabb OP, in a double-barrelled attack in the *Catholic Times,* charged Macmurray with undermining society and religion, and the BBC with complicity in "the propagation of Leninism." Martin D'Arcy SJ joined the opposition by accusing Macmurray of supporting the decay of religion by his denial of law and his promotion of "freedom of feeling" as the necessary ground for a truly free religion.[7] As Macmurray noted to Richard Roberts:

> The Roman Catholic attack was quite vicious, and included an 'Open Letter to the Prime Minister' under the heading 'Is It Sedition?' The effort to prevent me from speaking on the wireless still goes on ... I have taken no notice of it, beyond a short letter in *The Listener*, the organ of the BBC, and half a column in the *Observer*."[8]

A month later, after he had received some words of consolation and support from Roberts, he wrote back thanking him for the letter:

> I was glad to have it — though I really wasn't surprised or upset by the press attacks. They are stimulating on the whole, and they do enable a man to know where he stands in the concrete and in the community.[9]

Radio as democracy in action

The BBC, as well, was not deterred by the opposition. A defence of Macmurray's right to speak his mind on the airwaves as a philosopher (he was not speaking as "a religious teacher," they asserted) was published as a leader in *The Listener*. Siepmann, along with the council members, took the controversy as a sign of life. Their confidence in Macmurray was demonstrated less than a year later when he was asked to be an editor as well as contributor to "The Changing World" Series, the BBC's most ambitious project in adult education to that point in its young history. It brought together economists, scientists, philosophers and men of letters to address six different but related themes connected with the sometimes very disconcerting experience of living in a rapidly changing world.

Macmurray was put in charge of editing the Friday presentations on "Education and Leisure." He was to write the introductory pamphlet and do six of the talks in the Autumn of 1931. He was asked to give four more talks in the Spring of 1932 in the Sunday "Modern Dilemma" Series and these, along with the first twelve on Reality and Freedom, formed the text of *Freedom in the Modern World*, which, in fact, became his first book. Macmurray was also to give the final appraisal of the series as a whole. In that review presented to *Listener* readers on April 13, 1932, after noting the imperfections and even failures they had experienced along the way, he judged the series to have been a success as an experiment in integrated learning. He included in this success the developments made in the technique of broadcasting as well as the spirit of freedom that was growing in the use of broadcasting for education. He concluded:

> 'The Changing World' programme will form a standard of
> reference for the judgment of future programmes (not in this
> country alone); already it stands as a landmark in the development
> of educational broadcasting.[10]

The editor's leader in this same issue applauds the series on two major counts: it was a massive exercise in complex social analysis put into simple language for all to understand. And, second, it supports Macmurray's insight that the experience taught us "that any subject, however controversial, can be treated in broadcast talks and treated with frankness and firmness, provided it is treated in the spirit of obvious sincerity."[11] The writer (Charles Siepmann, perhaps), in a pioneering act of solid media analysis, goes on to note the BBC has learned that:

The voice has revealed itself as the true test of an individual's
sincerity; and thereby we have discovered the real safeguard of
broadcasting. This sincerity is a quality that is only too easily
disguised in the written word, as well as on the stage and the public
platform. But it cannot be disguised at the microphone, because of
the intimacy of the associations that it creates. If speakers exercise
restraint, that is because their imagination appreciates the feelings
and opinions of those who listen to them. On the other hand, the
listener hearing the voice of the speaker, which admits of no
pretence, loses his suspicion he is being 'got at,' and can proceed to
form his own opinions without fear of being the victim of bias.
This is what Professor Macmurray calls 'the real secret of
democratic broadcasting.'

Macmurray's deliberate association of democracy and broadcasting was
not a passing observation, but a deep insight into the relationship between
human freedom and psychology and radio as a unique form of social communication. Macmurray's own talks in the autumn of 1931 had all focused
on the deep connection between democracy and authentic education for
the present and future. Under titles such as "Is Education Necessary?",
"Can We Trust the Experts?", "Coming to Grips with Democracy",
"Training the Child to Live" and "Is a Democratic Culture Possible?" he
had explored all the hard questions facing the English people at the end of
an aristocratic era in education and at the edge of a new political and social
reality in which their past traditions were not automatically helpful but,
perhaps, even handicaps in meeting the requirements of the world unfolding around them. His own sincerity had powerfully affected Siepmann,
and it had proven to be powerful with the listeners who, according to
innumerable testimonies, felt respected by him as he spoke. As a broad-
caster himself he was, in a sense, a living example of the democratic manner of expression he and the BBC officials were discovering that radio
could serve so well.

Perhaps most instructive in both the editor's reflection and
Macmurray's article is their articulation of the values constituting this
"democratic broadcasting" which they were discovering consciously,
almost week by week, as they went along. Frankness and firmness, sincerity, emotional restraint in the speaker that left room for the listener to
hear the ideas and appropriate their meaning without feeling constrained
by rhetorical persuasion, and, finally, the opportunity to discuss and act
together for people (in the Listening Groups) who live and work together.
The prospects, in the spring of 1932, seemed almost limitless for great
social advantages to come from this unique blend of the national interest,
local settings, and a care for the common good. It promised the promotion

of a genuine people-based culture, with politics as only one of its constituents and servants. As well, it offered a form of education that is in service of free understanding and shared, social action. And all this without exams!

The end of a brave experiment

Unfortunately, this taste for stimulating reflectiveness and dealing with issues of substance that flourished in the Council of the early thirties at the BBC — and still existed in the culture at large — was not to last. Ironically, in his 1930 and 1932 BBC talks, Macmurray had noted the split in the modern individual's (and modern society's) soul between truths that were still affirmed by the intellect but no longer had the power of conviction in the heart. They were beliefs, he had suggested, that we are no longer prepared to work for or make sacrifices for. Collectively and individually, we have lost our "faith," the faith grounding our very life that gave us meaning and purpose as a society. As a result, we have lost the shared, social values that are the expression of such faith.

This modern malaise, described in *Freedom in the Modern World* by Macmurray, was a disease at work in the bones of the BBC as well as in the culture at large. Questions were being raised about whether the Listening Groups were worth so much of the BBC's attention and so many of its resources. The need of these Groups for "fixed" listening times was already being challenged by the "flexibility" wanted by general listeners who were looking to radio not for education but for news, dramas, popular music, and even entertainment. Adult education, which required serious, reflective participation by the listener, was just not "sexy" enough to sustain the BBC's support given other new pressures being put on its programming and scheduling.

In 1934, as this weakening of focus and resolve was taking shape at the BBC, Macmurray was called on for two lectures in a series on "Freedom and Authority in the Modern World." With the pall of Fascism already spreading over western Europe, he spoke on the topics "Freedom Is Power" and "Democracy in the Balance." In the talks he claimed that democracy had progressively become ineffective because it had lost touch with the base of freedom in community that was deeper than merely political relationships, and that politics was meant to serve. To lose touch with the religious roots of culture was, he said, to lose a capacity to live our politics and economics in a free and appropriate manner. Without being rooted in deeper cultural values, they end up dominating cultural life rather than serving the fuller life of which they were only subordinate aspects. Political and economic authority in this distorted situation, as we see in Italy and Germany, become dominant over the lives of people and societies, with no deeper, human values limiting their extension and use. Macmurray's plea was for a socialism that, by the will of the people, would put limits on those in political and economic authority to ensure that they function as participants, not overlords, of society.

This message could have profited the BBC as well as the larger society. There is no sign that the talks had any salubrious effect, on the BBC or on the public order. At the end of 1933 the group talks on the BBC had been reduced from five to three a week. In 1934 the Central Council's commission was ended, and its mandate was not renewed. The year after, Siepmann was removed from his post as Director of Talks. As Philip Hunt observes, "the era of the Listening Groups was drawing to a close."

Macmurray's two major proposals after 1934 for a series of broadcasts were received with something between indifference and hostility by key BBC officials. In 1936, after he had made required revisions to a proposal he had submitted the previous year for talks on the sources of Christianity and western civilization, the proposal had been rejected by the director general, John Reith, himself. The Controller of Programming, in appealing to Reith for a judgment, considered Macmurray's ideas to be verging on communism. But Reith rejected them, rather, as poor Christian theology because he could not accept Macmurray's view that the promotion of equality and freedom for persons *in this world* was, in fact, the teaching of Christ. A bit more ominously, in Macmurray's views he found, as well, an over-emphasis on the positive role of the Jews in forming the identity of western civilization. In late 1936, with Oswald Mosley and his British Union of Fascists at their most obstreperous, Reith did not want the BBC to be joining Macmurray in, as he put it, "trailing the coat" for the Jews.[12]

A second major initiative fared only slightly better. Macmurray's outlines for his four 1941 talks on "Persons and Functions" were found to be woolly, abstract and banal — in some cases, just religious meanderings rather than philosophical arguments. In fact, they were very clearly expressed, but they located facts within a larger unity of values, and he spoke easily of this as a necessary connection.[13] Some BBC officials by this time felt their average listener would find this approach gratuitous and sermonizing. A declaration of objective values that was formerly very acceptable in public conversation and discourse was now felt to be private and explicitly religious in a way that was now judged no longer acceptable on the airwaves — except for Sunday mornings. And perhaps even worse, they felt the audience would be bored by the Professor's hair-splitting distinctions between the meaning of "personal" and "functional." As Hunt succinctly observed, by 1941 "the average listener in Britain had other things on his mind."[14]

They were proved right; and it can be said that Macmurray had already named the malady quite exactly in his earlier talks on their own pro-grammes. After the 1941 talks were given, the tepid response by listeners suggested the BBC naysayers had correctly grasped the disposition of many members of their audience. They had read correctly that, as the 1930s moved into the 1940s, John's measured style of speaking and his clear invitation to his listeners to reflect deeply on the most fundamental issues at stake in society, were outside the kind of radio they felt their audiences would relate to. The disciples of Socrates, it seems, were being supplanted by a new crop of listeners more than ready to turn to Sophists for the latest opinions, delivered with a certain style. In the developing new age of talk shows specializing in artificially induced contentiousness and thirty-second sound bites, Macmurray's star had sunk behind the clouds if not below the horizon entirely. In the years that followed the war, C.E.M. Joad was to be anointed as the anchor at the BBC who would pro-vide for the new era's educated set. For some observers, that choice said everything about the nature of the cultural shift that was taking place in society and had already made its mark at the BBC by the mid-1930s. Macmurray gave a few isolated talks on society and the outlook for liberal democracy on the BBC in the late 1940s, and a set of four in 1956 on the topic "What Is Religion About?" There were a few others relating to phi-losophy and culture, given in Scotland when he was professor at the University of Edinburgh, that were quite delightful, especially the one on "Common Sense in Scottish Philosophy." In 1964, after he had retired from university work, he delivered four Lenten talks entitled "To Save From Fear," and ended his BBC connections a short time later with some school talks on the nature of religion.

These presentations were not negligible. But they were isolated offer-ings, light years away from the vibrant engagement generated in the early 1930s when life was simpler and radio — still in its youth — was able to deal with serious topics in "prime time" and take on as a noble mandate the education of the ordinary people in Britain who had little access to public education apart from radio.

Chapter 10

Imagining a New Society (1928–33)

When they arrived in London John and Betty knew of the celebrated coterie of writers and artists known as the Bloomsbury Group and it seems both of them had an initial fascination for the experimental quality of the Bloomsbury approach to life, though there was no great likelihood of them being invited to penetrate that tight circle. John was looking for a way of liberating his own emotions as well as understanding feelings more deeply — a major focus of his work. But something put them off and the Bloomsbury style became far less impressive to both of them as time passed. Perhaps the Bloomsbury folk were too self-consciously flagrant in their anti-conventional lifestyle; they had, after all, announced themselves as "people who lived in squares and loved in triangles," and they loved to shock. Yet that in itself was hardly the sole reason John and Betty never accepted them as models for themselves. John's reservation was probably related to the self-absorption and narcissism they projected, the aura of being overly-impressed by their own press clippings, the apparent incapacity to care for much outside their own circle. For Betty it might have been simply her fine instinct for survival. In that group — for different but similar reasons to those that were in play at Balliol — she could have found herself once again being treated with condescension as the little outsider with no gifts to offer. That was definitely a feeling she did not need to revisit, and certainly not just as her own bud, as she saw it, was about to bloom.

One of the signs of breaking from her past was her effort to take possession of it in the novel she had begun to write. She produced a strongly autobiographical book that ends while the couple, with tensions and infidelities in their relationship newly exposed, is still at Oxford. She called her book *Out of the Earth*, a conscious nod to the Genesis account of God's creation of man and woman. In the copy she autographed and gave to John, she wrote concerning the heroine of the book: "Wouldn't Adam be disgusted if his rib produced such a female?" When she did her final typing and sent the manuscript to Gollancz in January 1933, she wrote to Irene Grant saying: "As far as I'm concerned it is past and buried, and seems to have no very personal relationship to me at all. All the same I do want it published." And it was, but only in the summer of 1935.[1] It was reviewed dismissively in the *New Statesman* as "undigested D.H. Lawrence."

After settling into their new home John and Betty began forming friendships across a spectrum of people that Oxford had not been able to provide. Betty met and associated with several people who became *her* friends rather than friends of both of them. It was a natural development given their personalities. Besides, being open to such relationships was more and more common in London at the time and it was also part of the freedom beyond conventions that Betty and John had subscribed to a couple of years earlier at the critical juncture in their own relationship. At Bolton Studios Betty gravitated towards the artists, and their friends to whom she was introduced. In the course of those gatherings she and John frequently met Kenneth Clark, Ben Nicholson and Henry Moore and his wife. She also started to explore London, and what she would call her Bohemian side began to flourish. At Bolton Studios the maids dubbed her the "Gay Duchess" because of the sense of social style and dress she was quickly developing. It may also have been that her liaison with Jack Barry could hardly be hidden in such close quarters. By this time, with her understanding with John in place, she may not have even tried to hide it.

Naming the demons

John's conviction about his need for greater emotional freedom was confirmed once he got settled in London and felt the pulse of the city around him. He felt the need in himself but he felt it for his society at large as well. These needs were, and remained for him, two sides of the same coin. As his philosophy developed John very deliberately focused on the need for a liberation of feeling as the natural and necessary sequel in Europe's development to the liberation of thought that had occurred in the successful rise of science. By the early 1930s he had concluded that the changes needed in society could not be learned from any philosophy books he had seen to date. The German Romantics had attempted their revolution of feeling but it had collapsed in Britain into sentimentalism, into social forms and rituals of feeling rather than a mature acceptance and appropriation of sexual, emotional and spiritual feeling in individuals and society. As he saw it that revolution in the area of feeling was awaiting a second shot of courage and imagination — a breakthrough he could feel coming as a result of the breakdown of Victorian values since the war.

The writings of D.H. Lawrence, including *Lady Chatterley's Lover* which had just come out in 1928, provided a literary breakthrough into the domain of feeling for him that supplemented the lessons he was learning through his wife's choices. In his October 10, 1930, letter to Richard Roberts, John tried to convey his impressions of Lawrence's work and why he felt Lawrence was so important:

I've been profoundly moved by the work of D.H. Lawrence. Have
you tried to estimate it seriously? It is having a great influence on
masses of young people here, and I expect also in America. That
put me to reading him seriously; and the more I read (after I had
got over the inevitable shock of his freedom in talking about the
body and sex in particular) the more impressed I was. Not so much
by his views, nor even by his artistry with words, but by the man
himself. I felt I was in contact with a new kind of consciousness;
with a spirit which saw things and handled things in the world to
which I was just blind, and had no means of seeing ... You might
feel quite differently about him. I feel so perhaps just because he is
the one modern writer whom I have felt that I cannot criticize; but
from whom I must just learn — because he is conscious of life in a
way in which I am not.

This intense concern for the conversion needed in his own feeling life and
in western society as a whole was matched, at this same time, by a passionate concern for another constriction of freedom: the abuse of authority that he saw in Europe in politics and religion. Earlier that year he had
confided to his sister Helen:

I'm getting more interested in Religion now than I have been for a
long time: but the more I think of it the less room can I see for
churches and organizations, with their creeds and ritual. They seem
to be incompatible with the spirit of Jesus ... Sometimes I think —
rather bitterly — that the most anti-christian thing in the world
today is Christianity! It is so dead-set against freedom and life
more abundant. 'Love people — oh! Yes, so long as they are not
criminals or immoral, or unbelievers or Bolsheviks or members of
a rival state or dirty Huns.' Which all means, so long as they do
what you want them to do, and think as you want them to think.
'They make a desert and call it peace.' To Hell with them![2]

Sandwiched between this February letter to Helen and the October one to
Roberts was one written on June 5, 1930, to Donald Grant. In it this passionate iconoclasm, surfacing in him during the very time that he was
preparing and delivering his supremely placid and disciplined BBC lectures, takes aim at his third, main target:

The real enemy of the gospel and of morality is the worship of the
state and organization. I've been trying to persuade my people [his
BBC listeners] that nationality is not an ideal but a historical
accident — a combination of political unity with cultural unity.

And the democratic ideal is to thrust the state right out of the
cultural field and keep it out. There is, it seems to me, no reason
for any particular state organization, except a utilitarian one.
Political unity is a means to an end, and the best state is the state
that works best; which means, I think, the one that secures the
maximum of justice. Where the boundaries of any state should lie
ought to depend on pure convenience from the point of view of
government. Above all, we mustn't think of the state as if it were a
cultural or a moral entity. I even go to the length of saying that the
state ought never, on any account, to base its action on moral
grounds.

He knows this view counters everything that Europeans have been taught
from the cradle. And the pressure of this Romantic theory of democracy,
as Macmurray had noted in his Commonplace book in 1923 and in certain
unpublished lectures afterwards, was to push constantly towards a mysticism of the national State as the public expression of the people themselves. As he told Grant, this worship of the state was precisely the poison
(the political "sentimentalism") that needed to be excised from Europe if
hope for peace were to be realistic.

His critique of the authoritarianism of the Church and the State was
being supplemented by his rejection of the conventional icons of duty and
service that caused so much suppression of immediate feeling. He knew
all three issues were personal ones for him. But he was equally convinced
that his thinking was not mere projection of his individual limitations onto
others. Emotional repression, faithless religion, and domination by the
state were, first of all, not *his* problems but rather the major shadows, the
areas of deepest unfreedom, in western civilization itself. He had been
shaped by that civilization; it had not been shaped by him! The search for
a better form of society was intrinsically related in his imagination to a
process of liberation that addressed all three issues at once. His own problem with feelings he was already meeting by a conscious search for liberation. He wanted more emotional freedom and felt, as he had said to
Roberts, that he had to learn it from the ground up.

Betty had recently returned from a springtime trip to the Balkans where
she went with a woman don from Somerville College, Oxford. Throughout the trip she sent letters back to John praising the countryside, noting
the rough simplicity of their accommodation ("We're brushing our teeth with
wine to avoid the water ...") and complaining of the small-mindedness of
her travelling companion from whom she parted before the trip ended.
John loved the new experience for her but envied it for himself as well. He
was very taken by the connection between freedom and the simplicity of
living conditions she talked about throughout her trip. Referring to that

trip John confesses in a letter to the Grants his desire to visit them. He acknowledges that his yearning for a change of scene is tied into deep turmoil he feels in himself and sees around him:

> Indeed I am seriously thinking of throwing up my professorship
> and scraping some sort of livelihood with my pen — so as to be
> free from responsibility to institutions: so as to be free to say what
> I think and act as I feel right. Perhaps I shall some day soon
> summon the courage to do it. Even to be a professor is to be
> something other than a simple human being. It makes me quite
> depressed at times to find myself a respected pillar of respectable
> society. Even Dean Inge respects me, and I find that hard to bear.

Back in 1917, after his powerful sermon endorsing post-war reconciliation, John had been able to leave his affiliation with the churches when this need for freedom from complicity and for freedom of expression in religion came over him. But now his problem on both counts is not just with the churches but European society and even western civilization itself. That leaves him little room to manoeuvre, except to seek somehow the reconstruction of society itself.[3] And that is how he begins viewing his primary concern as early as 1929.

In February 1931, John wrote a strange and wonderful letter to his sister Helen from his sick-bed "because there is no reason for writing it."[4] In the letter, after talking about how hard he finds it to live his own life with his own desires, he observes to her how so many people are committing suicide because they have lost their money, "when for most of them that is the first real chance they ever had of living their own lives. For money is just the power to make other people do things for you." Then he turns the charge against himself:

> What amazes me most in myself is to discover how much I *expect*
> other people to do for me, and how deeply ingrained in me the idea
> is that other people have *a right* to expect me to do things for them.
> It's all wickedness. The wickedest idea of all is the idea of duty.
> But it is perhaps inevitable when there is no religion ... Life isn't
> responsibility, surely. I prefer the text about the 'God that giveth in
> all things, richly, *to enjoy.*' Don't you?

The letter is revealing on many counts. First, there is the repeated affinity he finds between the social mores of modern society and the constrictions he finds so firmly in place in himself and others — forces that lead away from natural living, from just being, from accepting that work and responsibility are properly *subordinate* to enjoyment rather than vice versa, as was the case in British society. He has a feeling for something freer but finds himself and other people tied up in knots, not really wanting the simplicity that is true to their *real* lives. Interesting as well is his insight into how duty gets glorified in a society that has lost touch with God. God, he says, wants us to *enjoy* the goodness of life not to be slaves who displace the true and simple direction of our human desires by constant striving and self-imposed pressures.

He tells her of some of the philosophical thinking — as well as feeling — that has gone into creating his deep discomfort. Much of his insight for the Liverpool presentation to the Student Christian Movement (SCM) and his Reality and Freedom talks on the BBC came from months of research for his first book, *The Western Tradition*. He tells Helen that this proposed book is giving him lots of trouble. He is collecting opinions on whether it should be published serially, and asks for her views. The problem he finds with it was succinctly expressed a few months later in a letter to Samuel Alexander, his old boss and colleague at Manchester:

> I'm wrestling with the last chapter of my first book. It is a queer book and I'm afraid terribly unsatisfactory. Intended to be the first of a series of three, it is directed to discovering the problem of philosophy in our day: and to do that I've tried to give some account of the inner development of the European tradition; to find in that way some clue to the human situation in the world. I'm afraid it breaks with all recent philosophical tradition, and will hardly be recognized as philosophy. At the worst it may be nonsense: at the best it may suggest something by way of a beginning.[5]

In the end, despite plans being made with Macmillan to bring it out in the autumn of 1932, *The Western Tradition* was never published — probably because it was trying to do too much at the level of combining sweeping historical analysis with contemporary social diagnostic. The contents of the manuscript were revised considerably and can be traced in three of Macmurray's books: *Freedom in the Modern World* (1932), *Interpreting the Universe* (1933), and *The Clue to History* (1938). *The Clue to History* went through its own reconstruction as well since it began as a series of radio talks rejected in 1935 and again in 1936 by the BBC. Although effectively written in 1935, the book — entitled *Christianity and the Religions of Europe* at the time — was published only in 1938 by SCM because in the mid-1930s Victor Gollancz and Faber & Faber, along with the BBC, had found the manuscript too hot to handle in its highly positive view of the Hebrew contribution to western society and Christianity. The sections in *The Western Tradition* on the medieval and early modern world made their way in vastly amended form into two of John's three chapters in *Some Makers of the Modern Spirit*, a book he edited based on a series intended for the BBC in 1933.[6] A collaborator in that volume was Father Martin D'Arcy SJ, one of the critics who had responded so negatively to John's Reality and Freedom lectures.

In *The Western Tradition* John had formulated his proposal that the spiritual heritage of Europe was shaped essentially by a combination of Hebrew, Greek and Roman influences which had poured themselves into the Christian crucible in varying proportions. In his view, there had been no serious integration of them, and the Roman had effectively won out. He was convinced that the Christian ideal of life in the spirit, *the freedom of the children of God*, had never established itself in Europe as the dominant tradition. In other words, the *moral* tradition of Europe has never been a truly Christian tradition.[7] As he saw it, the dominant influence in the moral tradition of Europe — and still flourishing there in the twentieth century all around him and in his own skin — was the Stoicism of the Romans. Duty and service based on law rather than love and enjoyment based on freedom of spirit, was the main European moral ideal and imperative, despite what people said about the dominance of their Christian heritage.

Exploring a new social order

At the outset of the 1930s, along with many others in Britain — all of whom had varying reasons for their choices — Macmurray consciously rejected this Stoic tradition. He knew he was undertaking to explore the form of a new society. Aided by the startling example of his wife Betty who was making her own choices for freedom, his efforts to envision a truer view of human living had reached some philosophical expression in his view of freedom as grounded in friendship that ended his BBC talks. But the power of these two energies — freedom and friendship — had as yet little or no social expression in his life. And, apart from what had overwhelmed and pleased him in D.H. Lawrence, he saw little expression of them in society. The combination of free individuals in a free society of friends was yet to take flesh. This was the *practical* need, as he saw it. And, at the outset of the 1930s, it seemed a natural expression of his personal vocation to assist in creating — as well as in understanding — the conditions for a peace and justice-based society.

After spending three years in Bolton Studios John and Betty were ready to move on. They had both grown tired of the terrible food at the Studios — Betty described it as greasy stews and vegetables in "swimsuits" — and they wanted to cook for themselves. They also wanted to entertain without the worry of disturbing others or breaking the rules of the house, which they had done frequently enough. They moved to Kensington for a very short time and finally settled at 1 Sussex House, Glenilla Road, NW3, near Belsize Park where they would stay for the next seven years. Around that same time, John's parents had made their final move as a family from Moffat, in south-central Scotland, to the town of Peebles, about 20 miles south of Edinburgh. It was while visiting his family in the new home at 60 Eliot Park in August 1932 that John wrote to Irene Grant who had just arrived in Britain as he was leaving for Scotland. In the letter he poured out to her his first ideas about the new society she and Donald, as much as he, were interested in working towards:

> I am most anxious to have a talk with you as soon as possible. I have a scheme of social action forming in my mind the bigness of which makes me think I must be mad: ... It is the idea of forming within the existing social order, a new social order which would make itself experimentally, on some kind of communist basis, as completely self contained as possible, and within that framework develops a new type of social life in all its aspects. The governing nucleus of the society — which would be international and federal if possible — should constitute itself a cabinet and lay careful plans for taking over the government of Europe in the event of a collapse of the economic and political machinery. It would, as a matter of policy, avoid all appearance of revolutionary activity based on violence and would use-non-cooperation as its defence against positive attack. And it would make every effort to keep within the law throughout, basing its own discipline and regulation upon the free acceptance of its members of them. I have no details yet in mind that are definite.
>
> This sounds terribly preposterous, I know. Perhaps it is. But I have a feeling that a considerable number of the young people are eating their hearts out because they can find no way out into creative social action from the nightmare inaction of the present social system which sits on their chest.[8]

There is no record of the immediate response of Irene or Donald to this self-consciously vague and idyllic initiative! Most noteworthy in this letter is John's effort to channel his conviction about the need for social change into a vision that he proposes for the sake of the youth, the ones who want an alternative to the tired old ways but are not yet in a position to take the lead. How it would actually work is clearly not his main concern at this point. And his notion of a cabinet appointed by itself and poised to "take over" the government in case of disaster, with no force to defend it against challengers, certainly qualifies for his adjective: "preposterous."

In this first envisioning of a new society, he seems interested most of all in ensuring a radical break from the rotten foundations, namely, the destructive individualism, competition and nationalism that permeated the social and political values that led to the war and continued to endure in Europe three years after the Crash has overwhelmed the economies of most western nations. He is trying in his mind to first of all get the spirit and basic relationships right; knowing that the structures, whatever they may prove to be, can only be as sound as the foundations. And those foundations for the new society as he envisages them are to be communal, cooperative, international, non-violent — and federated as well in order to preserve valuable cultural differences within the new political unity.

Noticeable in the letter is his almost casual statement that the new society must be constructed "on some kind of communist basis." John had already read Karl Marx's later writings, including *Das Kapital*, but it is not clear when he did so for the first time.[9] Just before going to see his parents in August, he had contributed to a summer school held by the Society of Friends at the Woodbrooke Centre near Birmingham. It was at this conference that he first met Kenneth Barnes, a teacher at Bedales school who was interested in experimental education for youth and who ended up, along with his wife Frances, starting Wennington School in Lancashire based on educational principles Kenneth derived from Macmurray's thinking. It was the beginning of a life-long relationship between the two men. This summer school was also where John met Julius Hecker, a Russian philosopher working in the educational service of the Soviet Union, who would soon become a professor at Moscow University. It was the first time John had been exposed to a first-hand review of the progress of the revolution by a Russian. He was profoundly impressed by Hecker who was at once a supporter of the revolution, a man of deep religious sympathies, and a disciplined philosopher who was able to explain a situation without the need to proselytize his listeners. From this meeting it seems Hecker was impressed by Macmurray as well since he asked John to write a foreword to his book *Moscow Dialogues* which was due to be published in early 1933. Macmurray did so and in that short foreword reveals a great sympathy for the effort of Russia to guide its revolution by means of a comprehensive and integrating philosophy. Macmurray's impressions of the revolution, at least at the theoretical level, were clearly both strong and favourable:

> Modern Russia is the first experiment that the world has seen, in planning a complete social life. It is not merely a planned economy that Russia is after. Its economic plan is merely part of a wider

plan, and is itself dictated by a philosophical theory which covers every aspect of life. Communism stands or falls by its philosophy, and the leaders of Russia are perfectly aware of it. For them it is an elementary principle that a definite and consistent philosophical theory is the only basis on which a planned society such as they desire can be constructed.[10]

This foreword, written on January 10, 1933, is the first public expression of Macmurray's positive disposition towards the revolution in Russia and more must be said about that later. Although he is clearly addressing only the theoretical foundation of the revolution here, not its practices, Macmurray speaks with an assurance about the perspectives of the leaders in Russia that is surprising since, apart from the testimony of a few well-known British visitors to Russia, almost the only evidence to support such a major claim was their own word about it. One could wonder whether he is really addressing here the position of the leaders of the Russian revolution or expressing his own theoretical view that *any* vision for *any* new society has its best chance of being effective if there is an integrating and comprehensive philosophy grounding its actions and programmes.[11] Within a month Betty will have given him for his birthday the first volume of Trotsky's *History of the Russian Revolution* which he devoured in an effort to expand his knowledge of "the brave experiment."

Discovering Marx

In April, a few months before he met Julius Hecker, John had been invited by J.H. Oldham, an Anglican layman, to participate in a two-day conference that would include Joseph Needham, an Anglican lay member of the Oratory of the Good Shepherd as well as Professor of the History of Science at Gonville and Caius College, Cambridge, A.D. Lindsay of Balliol, John Middleton Murry the friend of D.H. Lawrence and literary expert in Blake, Shakespeare and Keats and — at that time — a communist, A.L. Rowse and several other lay thinkers as well as some religious leaders. The purpose was vague. It seemed from the reading list enclosed with the letter to be a meeting to seek a new vision for Christianity in contemporary society especially in the light of the rapid growth of Communism. This was precisely the kind of thing that was exercising John so strenuously so he accepted at once. The conference took place at the beginning of October 1932 and proved to be a turning point in Macmurray's understanding of the social, intellectual and religious "situation" in which they found themselves. On the first day, the participants were invited to discuss the question "What is Christianity?" As Macmurray described the scene years later:

> ... We did so for the whole of that day, and in the evening we came to the unanimous conclusion that we did not know. The next day we went on to ask how we could find out; and after a long discussion we concluded that before we could discover what Christianity is we should have to study two other questions. The first of these was the nature of modern Communism, the other was the problem of sex.[12]

We have no way of knowing if these were actually Macmurray's own concerns that surfaced — with some acceptance by the others — and were adopted as their agenda or whether it was an instance of great synchronicity of feeling and viewpoint among the participants. One of the members was appointed to prepare a paper on Communism and Christianity while the others were to read as widely as they could. Macmurray remembered years later that:

> It was this conference which led me to undertake a thorough study of the early writings of Karl Marx, with an eye to discovering, in particular, the historical relation between Marxism and the Christian tradition. I was astonished to find how close the relation was ... I, at least, found that I learned a great deal about Christianity by this study, and especially by coming to understand the reasons behind Marx's rejection of religion ... The basic reason was his conviction that religion was the popular, and therefore the important form of idealism ...[13]

Macmurray was overcome by the light this insight shed on his own distress with organized religion over the years since the end of the war. In the face of the struggles, needs and desires that people experience in life, Christianity seems to have abdicated any serious concern for the *material* dimensions of life–which are plainly reflected as concerns in the Gospel. In its place the church offered people "pie in the sky when you die." In other words the church gave up on the importance of *this* life in all its concreteness by asserting the prior importance of a *next* life. This continuing choice of the churches, as he now saw it, was a betrayal of the mandate of Jesus to love God *now*–manifested by feeding the hungry, clothing the naked, and working for justice in a felt, effective way for the sake of building up the community. What was left in the church in relation to the material level was what Macmurray to this point in his writing had been calling "sentimentality," resulting in a loss of credibility for the church.

Through this reading he had come to know from Marx the structural form of this kind of religion, and he had it in philosophical language with which he was very familiar. The problem with Christianity was "idealism" — affirming ideas in place of doing actions. With this intellectual key he was able to enter into a much fuller understanding of his own criticisms, and his own best aspirations as well. What he hated in organized religion was its idealism and its subsequent hypocrisy. What he loved in the religion of Jesus was its realism and sincerity; the real engagement of Jesus with people just as they are. He knew instantly that although the main attitude in the religion of the churches crumbled under the Marxist charge, the religion of Jesus and the gospels remained untouched by Marx's condemnation.

> I became convinced that idealism and religion are, in the end, incompatible with one another. Their identification by Marx is the basic error of Marxism. Idealist religion is *unreal*. Marx would have been justified in calling for the reform of religion but not for its rejection.

Having already studied the structure of the Roman Empire's influence on European civilization so much for his first book, it was not difficult to isolate the historical point at which the church systematically betrayed its master:

> When I looked for the cause of the idealizing of Christianity, I found it in the acceptance by the church of the Roman Empire ... the process which led to the creation of a hierarchical and authoritarian church parallel to and modelled to some extent upon the organization of the Roman State ... In becoming the religion of the Roman Empire the Church was logically bound to distinguish between the spiritual and material realms, and to recognize the ordering of the latter as the proper sphere of the State. The function of the Church had to become, in effect, ... a purely spiritual one.

But Macmurray went farther than that. He looked at the Marxist proposals concerning the goals of revolution and came to the following startling conclusion:

> It seemed, indeed, that modern Communism might well be that half of Christianity which had been dropped by the Church in favour of an accommodation with Rome, coming back to assert itself against the part that had been retained.
> With this I was committed to rediscover a Christianity which is non-idealist.

It was a moment of "return" for him; a moment when he could with some peace *experience* himself again as a Christian. Since 1917 he had held to a faith in Jesus but he was confused about what that meant in his work and living. In addition, it was a major advance for him. He knew now, with a clarity he did not have earlier, why he stood where he did after that fateful sermon in 1917 saying "Yes" to Jesus, and "No" to the churches. Now, his thinking joined his feeling. He could, as he had written to Helen two years earlier "become more interested in religion than I have been for a long time." He could reaffirm and deepen his Christian faith by supporting *any* effort undertaken *any*where to build up a world of justice and love with the attitude and methods of Jesus. His search for a new society, which he had always believed was a work intimately related to the gospel's notion of the Kingdom of God, was receiving fuller spiritual grounding as well as a material form from this Marx-induced re-appropriation of his Christian faith and vocation. This goes a long way towards explaining his essential sympathy throughout the thirties for the goals of the Russian experiment which, for all its mistakes and errors, strove for a socialism that seemed to him far more compatible with the social reality of the "Kingdom of God" than the West's capitalist individualism.

Vienna: the Grants and Polanyi

At the very time John was devouring the works of the early Marx which had just re-surfaced to public view, he and Betty accepted the invitation of Irene and Donald Grant to spend their Christmas vacation in Vienna where Donald had been serving as the director of the International Fellowship of Reconciliation since 1929. They arrived in Vienna shortly after Christmas and Betty immediately came down with a vicious cold that kept her in bed most of the ten days or so that they were there.

They both met the lively Esther "Tess" Simpson (*née* Sinovich), Donald's indefatigable secretary who, just weeks after the Macmurrays left Vienna, returned to Britain to work even more indefatigably for German and Jewish refugee scholars escaping the Nazis.[14] Donald and Irene also took John to visit their friends Karl and Ilona Polanyi, leftist Hungarian emigrés who had settled in Vienna after Ilona who had been a student leader in the Communist Party in Hungary was thrown out of the party in 1922 after criticizing its internal corruption. Karl had been the first president of the famous Galilei youth group that had been formed in 1908 to expose and resist the corruption of the Empire. The predominantly leftist politics that flourished in Vienna since the war were much more supportive of the views and convictions of these two Hungarian intellectuals. Karl wrote penetrating essays for the *Oesterreichische Volkswirt*

(Vienna's version of *The Economist*), using that channel for developing and expressing his distinctively inclusive political analysis of the complex forces swirling in Europe at the time. Karl had met Donald Grant in 1929 after Donald had left him a packet of some publications of the Christian-socialist student group he was leading. Polanyi had written back saying: "I like the papers you left very much. I know of no group whose ideas so closely resemble mine as do those of your group."[15] Through Donald's socialist reading of the New Testament, Polanyi was given a new way of understanding Christianity and its potential for humanizing the world. It was a perspective he, unlike Ilona who was deeply suspicious of religion, found convincing. By the time Macmurray arrived Donald had already talked about him and his ideas with "Karli," so all three were attuned to one another's way of reading history and contemporary problems. They simply had to point to the page where they would break into the music, pick up their instruments, and begin to play.

For Macmurray the meetings with Polanyi were a rare opportunity to grow in his understanding of Marx's critique of capitalism and his theory of exploitation within capitalism with the help of a man who knew Marx's thought well. Both men were synthetic thinkers with deeply spiritual sensibilities. They saw social change as requiring a spiritual base as well as a theoretical framework. Their similar readings of Marx's notion of alienation and objectification led them to similar views of what would be needed to form a society grounded in democratic and spiritual relationships. Marx, through Polanyi, taught Macmurray a more nuanced understanding of what it means for action to be prior to theory. For Marx, theory and practice were united, with theory imbedded in action. Macmurray had already come a distance along that road on his own, but without the economic and social analysis he was now getting.

Polanyi's analysis emphasized the internal contradictions in capitalism. In capitalism, the economy is disembedded from society for selfish motives. This wrenching of economic affairs from their natural place among other human needs and desires and cultural activities results in a conflict between economic interests and human interests in, for example, public order, health, education, civic participation, and cultural flourishing. Economic activity is meant to *serve* these larger human interests; however, under capitalism, commerce was no longer accountable to the broader social reality. This viewpoint turned lights on for Macmurray in his own diagnosis of European society and his dreams for a reconstructed social order.

Macmurray, in turn, taught Polanyi to think about what he described as "spiritual" in terms of "the personal." Macmurray also knew more of the detailed history of democracy in the West, and this was gladly gobbled up by Polanyi. Since both men were convinced that Christianity contained a fuller and deeper perspective on human nature and social transformation than Marx offered, they were able to critique Marx's conclusions and go beyond them. Macmurray left Vienna in early January exhilarated and enthusiastic. He had a much deeper sympathy for Marx and fresh thoughts for a new social vision. He also came away with much sharper understandings that were crucial for bringing together his notion of friendship in freedom with the goal of a just social order in his developing philosophy of the personal.

He left Vienna with something that touched him intimately, as well. The visit with Donald and Irene, whom he and Betty were growing to love so much, awakened hopes for starting a new kind of communal living. Donald had told John that the rise to power of Hitler would quickly lead to closing the International Fellowship of Reconciliation (IFOR) office in Vienna. He and Irene would be returning to Britain — but to what? John promised to try to arrange for a temporary base for Donald at UCL, for a sabbatical year during which Donald could plan for his future work. Within two days of his return to London, John wrote Donald a deeply affectionate and supportive letter. He acknowledged that Donald might feel bereft "after following the one road that seemed set for you for so many years." He noted that he had reached a point like that himself:

> ... and I remember how it made me want to fall asleep and never wake up again. I found later, to my surprise, that all that it meant was going straight on at a different level, a deeper level. Perhaps you'll find the same. I hope so. Though I have the feeling in my bones that we can only find the deeper level together, and not separately, each for himself ... I think we've got to find a positive expression and create the life we want, in ourselves and together in community, cutting out all the negatives, and discovering how to be different together. Perhaps to let the old world destroy itself in us and outside us, and start again.[16]

The experience he refers to so obliquely was almost surely his reaction, back in their Balliol years, to the news from Betty that she had a lover. But the letter reveals how he came through it and his thoughts now suggest how far he has come in wanting to situate even intimate things in a social and supportive setting. For him, at this point, finding a form of community that provides intimacy yet accepts the job of witnessing to a fresh form of society running counter to the larger society feels utterly crucial. The Grants and Macmurrays had already begun talking about setting up house together in London in order to form an experimental "social unit" that might help them to detoxify themselves from the worst of social individualism, and perhaps be a model to others for a new society. Betty was not spontaneously attracted to this community idea that seemed to please John, Donald and Irene so much. She warmed to it a bit only because of her marvellous time in Vienna where she fell in love with both Grants.[17] She knew she was an individualist and felt herself far more an artistic type than a social reformer: she simply disliked the idea of community, especially one with a theory behind it. The difference between Betty and John on this matter could hardly be more stark.

New social experiments in Britain

Back in London the desire for a fresh beginning for society had led John to become associated with various associations and individuals interested in fostering a new social experiment. The moral fall-out from the war and the continuing Depression with its staggering rates of unemployment, made many people more than ready to scuttle the old ways and try to create a new thing. That spirit was in the air.

A.R. Orage, who owned and edited the progressivist weekly journal the *New Age* from 1908 to 1922, had already stimulated that spirit.[18] He had been a genius at sniffing out themes filled with social electricity and then finding first-class writers not only willing but anxious to argue their case, for or against — and for free! In the pages of the *New Age,* George Bernard Shaw and G.K. Chesterton battled over socialism, to the delight and education of the readers. Guild Socialism had been mentioned as a potential successor to capitalism in Fabian circles for many years.[19] But it sprang into a much wider conversation in Britain once Orage invited S.G. Hobson and then the indefatigable G.D.H. Cole to present the case for it. Orage followed this promising direction with an intense yet puzzling interest in monetary reform that led him to highlight Major C.H. Douglas's theory of social credit. The *New Age*'s support helped to plant the seeds of the worldwide social credit movement. At the same time, Orage's interest in spirituality led him to explore Adlerian psychology along with mysticism and the occult access to "secret knowledge," all stimulated by Ouspensky — whom Orage knew — and his master, Gurdjieff. It was in the context of this spiritual searching that Orage met Dimitrije Mitrinovic, a Serbian emigré whose ten articles on "World Affairs" in the *New Age* in 1920–21 had exposed a vaguely mystical, apocalyptic and universalist vision of society founded in the basic fact of our common humanity. Ten years later, from autumn 1932 onwards, Mitrinovic's passionate heralding of a new Kingdom would rub up against Macmurray's own searching at the meetings of various socialist groups coming to life in London.

The groups that sprang up in the early 1930s naturally espoused visions based on the values of cooperation and community. Each one, however, had either its own reasons for "faith" in a socialist vision or its own "creed" about how these values translated into political and economic structures. By the mid-1930s anti-Fascism was an explicit part of the concerns of most of them. Along with the variety of groups, one can trace a variety of publications that sprang up like mushrooms. Most of them came into the world in a flurry of enthusiasm, then folded after a few years, or sooner, usually because of ideological or personal ruptures that led to defection from the groups or from lack of funds; often, both at once.

The Eleventh Hour Group, The New Europe Group and The New Britain Movement were loosely related gatherings of like-minded people, with partly overlapping membership. Within a matter of a year or two several other groups sprang up not only with new ideas but with practical experiments for a new society. In 1932, Macmurray began associating with a few of these groups in London out of his interest in hearing other views of how a new society might be created. He knew of Mitrinovic's community, met J.B. Priestley and heard of his efforts, continued his connections with Oldham and met John Middleton Murry and other fervent types, all looking to start the future in the present.

At this time, he also came to support the experiment sponsored by the Order of Woodcraft Chivalry taking place in the New Forest in Hampshire, a place where he and Betty went frequently to hike. The Order, which has been described as a "New Age" alternative to Boy Scouts, was begun by Ernest Westlake and his two children, Aubrey and Margaret. It was a back-to-the-earth movement that was trying to withdraw from the worst effects of their fractured society, especially unemployment and homelessness, by creating human community based on a relationship with nature and the kind of work required to sustain life simply. It aimed at developing sound competencies, and learning cooperation. It was called Grith Fyrd, Saxon for "Peace Army."[20]

Macmurray liked the idea of the project and contributed generously to it for a short time after he met Aubrey Westlake in London. Over the course of a few months in early 1933, he attained the status of a guru for Aubrey Westlake, probably because Westlake came to the New Britain meetings and heard John speaking there. Westlake brought John to a weekend conference at Welwyn Garden City where, on February 17, he gave an address to the gathered friends of the Grith Fyrd Movement. He gave a plain and simple talk that supported their goals and values, and expressed his own hopes for such experiments.[21] The talk reveals John's love for the outdoors and his belief that the natural setting and its demands for cooperation are automatically a form of education quite apart from the explicit goals of the programme.

In London, Macmurray was briefly associated with the Eleventh Hour Group where he met with Priestley and a few people he would join up with again ten years later in the short-lived Commonwealth Movement. He was most active in the New Britain Movement which was created out of the New Europe Group by those who, though they believed in a pan-European perspective, felt there was a call to be made to the British people to exercise their specific gifts and responsibilities in Britain itself at this crucial moment in history. It got launched during a meeting in November 1932, and Macmurray was made president of the corporation. He did his best over the next few months to bring some order into what was always, at best, a very moveable and uncertain feast.[22]

On January 9, the day after he wrote to Donald Grant, John wrote a letter to the editor of the *New Britain Quarterly* congratulating the staff on its very first issue. He praises their capacity to see the various problems in society in their relationship to one another, and not in isolation:

> There is only one point at which they all meet, and that is the personal lives of the individuals concerned. *New Britain* seems to me to have grasped this point in its endeavour to relate all the aspects of the modern problem to one another by seeing them all as particular expressions in different fields of the one central problem of the recreation of social personality.[23]

He could have been quoting himself; but, in fact, others clearly shared that hope. This second issue also contained a manifesto of the New Britain Group that laid out its vision and strategy for the restructuring of society. The basic goal, of course, was the increase of equality, fraternity and liberty for all. This, for the New Britain Group, meant that cooperation, not competition, must be the founding value for relationships among citizens. It also meant that economics was to be understood as only a dimension of the wider concern of politics, and politics — the good of order — was to find its true relationship as a subordinate dimension within the fullest and widest domain of culture. Culture included all aspects of society through which people lived their spiritual relationships with one another as freely and fully as possible. Many members of the New Britain Group espoused Rudolf Steiner's theory of the Threefold State which proposed three distinct functions of the State — the economic, the political and the cultural — and three Chambers in government for carrying them out. In 1934 this debt to Steiner was effectively acknowledged when the editors commissioned some articles written by Karl Polanyi on Steiner's concept.

The New Britain approach, which Macmurray shared to a significant degree, spoke to many in Britain. Subscriptions to the publication grew, and local New Britain groups sprang up spontaneously across the country to discuss and build on the basic ideas expressed in the publication. Interest was so high that a decision was made to suppress the *Quarterly* and institute a *New Britain Weekly*. The new journal came into existence on May 24, 1933. In that first issue, and for each of the next six issues, Macmurray provided an article on a topic of current, public significance that moved the reader to understand more deeply the social issues that the New Britain Movement proposed to engage.

In his first article, "An Invitation to the Young Men and Women of Britain," he notes to the youth of the day that the passage from an age of scarcity to one of plenty is upon them and yet there are no forms of social life from the old Britain for living in an age of plenty in a humane and promising way.

> There lies your urgent and immediate task. You have to create the
> social order of the age of plenty, and to do so you have to re-create
> yourselves, and your social relationships, upon a new pattern.
> Only in this way can the new forms of co-operation begin and the
> new community emerge. Already you have shown that you know
> this ...[24]

First thoughts on Fascism

In his subsequent articles Macmurray continues his teaching. He distinguishes between having a practical vision and the temptation to an "idealist" stance that does not go beyond thought into action.[25] In an article called "Fascism?" he distinguishes nationality (positive) from nationalism (negative) by noting that "Nationality is a fact. Nationalism is a policy." He goes on to show that the New Britain Movement wishes to build the elements of its case on the best virtues of British nationality while firmly rejecting nationalism, the essential basis of Fascism.

> Fascism is the last, the most fanatical, and the most irrational form
> of nationalism. It stands against all that is more real in the cultural
> impulse of modern Europe. Even so, this falseness is made possible
> only by a truth which it can distort and disfigure for its own
> nefarious purposes. That truth is the truth of nationality. The
> suppression through the development of science, industrialism, and
> general mechanization of our natural humanities — of which
> nationality is one — has, in fact, obliterated the real differences
> between nations. The more the mass-man emerges the more like
> one another do the nations become. Nationality is driven into the
> subconscious and prepares an explosion ... Suppressed nationality

is the easy prey of all the buccaneers on the seas of our industrial chaos.[26]

On this view, he charges Communism with making a huge error: attempting to suppress nationality in an effort to base a new order on the fact of class. For this reason:

> ... it necessarily provokes Fascism as its antithesis in any country which has been for long a nation. The more successful is the Communist propaganda in Britain the more certain does Fascism become. Fascism is a real possibility in this country. Communism is not. The task therefore is to make Fascism impossible, and this can be done by short-circuiting the process which generates it. We have to create a true cultural expression for nationality which will prevent the misuse of it for nationalist and imperialist purposes. We must drive a wedge between nationality and nationalism. This is the true task of the anti-Fascist, and it is the task which we unhesitatingly and uncompromisingly accept as our own.

The article reveals Macmurray's rapidly developing thinking in the light of events in Germany. In his February 20 letter to Irene Grant he had already stated that "it seems clear now that Europe has chosen the path of revolution: The accession of Hitler makes that definite." He says, almost prophetically, that the whole of Europe's future direction will be determined by its response to the German choice for "civil war" and "I don't see that is possible to turn back." Since his conversations with Karl Polanyi, just six weeks before he wrote that letter, he has evidently accepted much from Marx's dialectic. In his letter to Irene Grant and in his series in the *New Britain*, Marx's method is helping him to understand both the nature of Fascism and how to fight it. And, as he notes, the method is necessary for critiquing Marxism itself!

In February he was completely engrossed in writing three major lectures on the Philosophy of Communism which he was going to deliver at the University in a matter of weeks. He tells Irene that he expects them to shake things up a bit at UCL, but wishes he could run them by Karli "because they owe a good bit to a talk with him one day." Macmurray was referring to his new insight that state-capitalism must be Fascist in that "it involves ... the perpetuation of nationalism, and the imposition of discipline from above "for the good of the people." He is convinced that:

> the new form of social order must crystallize out of the experience of the masses; it cannot be the result of the thinking and planning of an educated class. Otherwise, it is not democracy.

His lectures were published that year as *The Philosophy of Communism.*[27] In them he unfolds his view of the origins of communist philosophy, the general principles of Marxist theory and his questions concerning the validity of the theory. Many of the basic ideas pursued in them have already been noted — especially the unity of theory and practice, and the need for a scientific theory of society in order to embark on deliberate social action under the control of human understanding. He concludes that "the Marxist holds that the real substance of society is persons in relation."[28] It is a view he accepts fully. He looks now for a planned society, if society is to be genuinely humanized, but maintains a vital distinction between democratic planning and state control in society. He is convinced that only through Marxist method, but not the acceptance of all its principles, can historical freedom be realized.

His main criticism of Marxism is metaphysical and therefore foundational. He rejects Marx's view that human reality follows organic laws. On that basis he counters everything in Marx that suggests a denial of human freedom in the movement of history. Macmurray explores what it means to direct action through knowledge and concludes: "we escape from the determination of natural laws by understanding natural law and accepting it as the rule of our own action."[29] Knowledge and freedom effect a transformation of our development as natural beings. Marx holds for this view and this renders his "materialism" and "determinism" self-contradictory. In later works he will advance his critique of Marx even further. But among the most seminal of the new thoughts he brings to his effort to construct a new society is his conviction that:

> ... the development of capitalism in the economic field has brought us to the point at which its successful working is incompatible with democracy as we know it.[30]

The necessary discipline required to make economic development serve everyone must be chosen democratically and with maturity by the people or be imposed by a fascist dictatorship. But, he says, no one — including Marx — foresaw the possibility that democracy might, with the consent of the masses, go overboard in the interests of a purely economic solution such that democracy itself might:

> ... be destroyed in the interests of a state-form which is purely economic and administrative. Yet this is precisely what has happened and is happening in the development of Fascism. Such a solution, by which politics is swallowed up in economics, was, until it actually happened in Italy, simply inconceivable to the

> European mind ... Fascism is not a new form of politics. It is the
> negation of politics. For politics is simply that field of human
> organization which exists to secure to men and women their rights
> as human beings against the impact of powers and forces which do
> not recognize their humanity.[31]

This inversion of economic and political interests is one of the chief manifestations of Fascism, apart from its other sicknesses, that challenge civilization at its roots. Macmurray developed his teaching on this view in the
New Britain.

> Capitalism and democracy are now incompatible. If capitalism is to
> be made workable, democracy must go. If democracy is to be made
> workable, capitalism must go. There is no third course open to us
> between these two. They are absolute alternatives set for us by the
> development of history.[32]

From this point on throughout the 1930s Macmurray would lend every
effort he could to the exposé of the social pretensions and perversions of
Fascism. Much of that would be done in cooperation with Karl Polanyi
who had just visited during May and June with Donald Grant to scout out
the London scene for future work.

A new social unit?

Macmurray's second to last article in his series for the *New Britain*
returned to the intimacy pole in its relation to the historical pole. He
addressed the decline of the family and asked about the new form of
"social unit" that might be imagined to replace the nuclear family as the
basis for the new society. His reflections appear not to have advanced
beyond the terms in the early correspondence with the Grants. He wants
the intimacy of family while including the self-transcendence enabled by
others in the group who are not members of the blood-based family. His
proposal is of two families "marrying one another, if I may use that analogy, so that all the resources and all the responsibilities of each are
pooled."[33] He clearly envisages a sexual sharing as a likely if not
inevitable part of this arrangement as well.

This approach was possibly confirmed for him in the very week before
he wrote his article. Donald Grant had come to London in early June to
lay plans for his future work and stayed with the Macmurrays. Donald and
Betty were drawn to each other, and they effectively co-habited with
each other during those days. John was in the position of admiring and

affirming the "new life" in the household because of the new intimacy between the two of them. On June 17, just hours after Donald left to return to Vienna, John received a telegram from his family that his father was seriously ill. He immediately took a train for his parents' home, and continued on board a letter he had begun writing to Irene. He told her of Donald's visit, noting that both Donald and Betty "blossomed and glowed together."

While John was away at his father's bedside, Betty wrote to Donald on the 18th expressing the same feeling. Betty clearly felt healed. Her move towards other lovers had been, in her own perception, a necessary move to a "pagan" part of her being that had been untouched and unrecognized by the Christianity that had so defined her and even suffocated her in her youth. In moving in that direction she had traded away the religious for the pagan — a choice she simply had to make if she was to claim for the first time a critical part of herself, her sensuality. It was an absolute and disjunctive move made out of anger, fatigue and frustrated desire, and she felt she had to say "no" to her Christianity in order to say "yes" to her feelings. Years later, as she prepared her memoirs, she reflected poignantly about that choice so long ago: "At Oxford, I traded Jesus for other lovers. It was a bad choice." But here, in these intense days with Donald, very much a sensual man and very much a Christian, a further transformation had swept through her. She tells Donald:

> I have been one with you in the ultimate places — pagan and
> Christian — for the first time in all my life. I lost my divided self,
> and I can never be the same again. It seems as if you had taken all
> the love I have given in different ways to different people (& it has
> been gigantic) — both pagan & Christian — & brought them
> together; two rivers joining together in one sea, & Jesus, the most
> viciously discarded lover, whom I have treated as a whore, is there
> again to be married — not lustfully appreciated, but the essence of
> his principles given a free channel inside me. In imagination I
> should like to kiss your feet. But in reality I know my flood of joy
> for you would embrace the whole of you.

This letter needs no commentary, except to note the evocative power Betty invested in this message by appealing to Scriptural images: the return of the prostituting wife, in Ezekiel 16, and the converted prostitute washing the feet of Jesus with her tears, and Jesus washing Peter's feet at the Last Supper in the gospels; images that resonated strongly in her heart and imagination. She acknowledges that their visit to Donald and Irene has thrown her off stride considerably because, she says, "you are a Jesus man & yet almost completely a Lawrence man which means that a reconciliation of the two might be achievable." But she looks for it not by concentrating on personality, as her husband does. "The world is reeking with personality & that's one of the things that is wrong with it. Only by losing personality can we find ourselves." She concludes that the spirit moves through us in ways that have little to do with thinking, with the conscious self. What she feels is "an urge to get at the quick of life in darkness, & be renewed in darkness. A sharp distinction, as between day & night."

That June, as her letter to Donald reveals, she felt the reconciliation of the two forces within her because of her profound sharing with him, a sexual sharing that was, most deeply, a spiritual one. Her final reflection in that letter paradoxically expresses a profound oneness with her husband in his yearning for a healing in intimacy that is also a healing for the world — a healing, that is, in the social forms of living in the world. But her language is that of the artist. In her appeal to the pagan gods within, she does sound like Lawrence — and did, on at least one occasion, call herself a female Lawrence. In her belief that these forces have no discipline, understanding or articulation in themselves she confirms her distance from her husband's view and shows herself to be a Romantic. But in appealing to that which lies beyond understanding in both disposition and response, she joins with her husband who, in his BBC Radio talks, made it clear that there comes a time in a diseased culture when it is not possible to trust one's own actions; one must wait and hope in silence for a fresh wind to blow through the soul. At that level, John could even be seen as her ally in supporting the notion of giving oneself over to a "holy darkness." He certainly expressed something of that towards the end in his youthful journal. Unfortunately, after he discovered the idealist disease at the heart of European religion, his attitude to religious mysticism of any sort was often one of suspicion. Further letters of great tenderness following this encounter reveal that Irene, after some struggle which she shared with John, has accepted the new dimension that has been created in the relationship between Donald and Betty. All four of them declare they are still open to some form of community living once the Grants return to Britain as a family but the divergence in their motives has become more evident and even more complicated.

James Macmurray died on June 18, shortly after his son John arrived at the family home. Before he died, James had been brought to Glasgow at his own request so that he could see the island of Aran for one last time. Helen came for the funeral from West Wickham in Kent where she was working with pre-school children, and Joseph, now married, came from Moffat where he worked as a city-gardener. Lilias was away at the time, serving as a missionary at St Andrew's Colonial Homes at Kalimpong in north-east India. When the cortège went by, the people by the roadside doffed their hats and bowed, a traditional country gesture that touched Helen deeply.

In a July 9 letter to Donald, John thanks him for his condolences but says nothing further about his father, his mother, his brother or sisters, or even his own feelings over losing his father. For all his desire to live more freely in his emotions, something in his feelings about his family — except for his relationship with Helen — seems to remain blocked. The feeling is there, but complicated, stuck, and apparently untouchable.

Six days before that letter from John, Betty had written to Donald with her own inimitable version of the recent events but, again, not one that reveals any pain over the loss of her father-in-law, or sympathy for John's mother.

> Father's death & mother's widowhood, from a worldly standpoint, left us a bit unprepared. Mother came South last week, but has gone to stay, for the moment, with her daughter. She looks like a scared, timid, little field mouse, scared by the harvester. Father she always regarded more as a patriarch — a male God — than as a man. And yet, or because of it, the home was ruled matriarchally as it so often is, & the man's guts die. Now she is ours to care for ... and Mary in a mental home.

This is the voice and perspective of a wife who is sure she has traced her husband's self-confessed problems with emotion to their source. In a letter to Irene Grant in July, John will confess as much. Betty's letter also anticipated by a week John's announcement to Donald that he was resigning from the presidency of the New Britain Group. In his letter John tells Donald things got worse since he was there in June. As he anticipates his summer break from the university John puts the issue briefly:

> The central group is completely incapable of any kind of order; and my effort to pull them together was a complete failure. I can't leave London for months and let them use my name for the kind of things they are likely to do. It has been an experience. I don't want any more of it. Though something may still come out of the local groups.[34]

It is not clear when John actually resigned. His departure was reported in the *New Britain* only five months later on November 15, 1933.[35] He began associating with an organization called the New Social Unit Group hoping for something more specific and perhaps less pretentious in terms of social conversion. We have only John's letter to Donald suggesting the nature of the group, a view given through the lens of his own interests:

It has thrown me back on the old question of personal relations. I
see little hope in parties and organizations. We have got to get
deeper than that. I want to move towards some kind of real
fundamental social unit — something new to take the place of the
family — but larger and able to provide the basis for the
development of individuality for women, and for intimate relations
between women and between men. Something like that is the
necessary basis of a real communism. The communism people are
talking about is pseudo. It's only the last phase of individualism.
I'll believe in the desire for communism when I find people who
want to *live* communally. I don't know that I do — very much,
when it comes to this point. But I'm sure that it is the next big step
in the evolution of human society.[36]

He ends his letter to Donald in a more muted tone on the old theme of
forming a new social unit together: "... there will be something for us all
here perhaps that will bring us and keep us together. I hope so."

The need for emotional rationality

Two weeks later, John and Betty got an old car, threw their tent and camping gear into it, and headed southwest to Cornwall for their holidays. This
was one of their favourite ways of taking a break, begun when they were
at Oxford and continued while they were in London.

On this particular holiday in the summer of 1933, they pitched their tent
near St Austell, around the middle of the bay looking out to sea, and proceeded to spend several days just sleeping, reading, swimming and — as
John told Irene in a long letter on July 27 — hardly even talking. When it
rained, they stayed in the tent reading, writing and sometimes chatting. It
was a break from work and pressures in the city that they both needed. In
her memoir notes years later, Betty recalled the joy of those days, but also
remembered the hours of unbroken silence in a questioning and sad mood,
wondering if they had been completely honest with each other when they
talked in the tent about their lovers — relationships they had promised not
to hide. This is the first reference to John having also entered into sexual
relationships outside their marriage. He had always, as Betty attests, been
deeply attractive to women, and attracted to them, but his sense of duty to
her in these matters — as well as his overwhelming and consistent conviction that Betty simply was *the* woman in his life — made him reluctant
to act on the permission they had given one another. At another level, it is
possible, even likely, that he simply did not need such liaisons in the same
way Betty acknowledges she did.

This whole experiment in liberation occasionally had its humorous side, too. Once, around that time, they went to Scotland for their summer holidays and there had been a gathering one evening with their friends Nan Shepherd and May Anderson both of whom were shy around men. In the course of the evening, talk of sexual matters arose and, with a courage engendered by the conversation and their longtime relationships with one another, May asked Betty if John could go to bed with her. She meant simply: lie with her under the covers in the same bed for a while. And her desire was equally simple: she wanted to be able to say, even to herself, that she had been in bed with a man at least once in her life. Apparently it was accomplished, with care and tenderness and good humour all round. But the situation was not without its sexual tension. John had caught the eye of all three of these women when all of them were young — and Betty had known from that time how attractive he could be to some women — especially those who were less than self-confident about their own sensuality and attractiveness.[37]

Dr Ephrosyne Sideropoulo was certainly one of those women. She was not the prettiest of the women who had shown interest in John. She was, in fact, a very plain person. She wore thick glasses and was shy and restrained in company. She met John at UCL, became entranced with his philosophy — but mainly with him — and worked long hours with utter devotion typing his books and essays for publication. She apparently took by dictation a substantial part of John's *Creative Society* and then typed out the book before and after his editing.[38] "Ephro," as she was known to everyone associated with the Macmurray household, was John's faithful secretarial assistant at UCL from the early 1930s until just before he left London for Edinburgh in 1944. She regularly came by the Macmurray home to do John's academic work and occasionally lingered to help around the house, sometimes using Betty's ear when they were alone to complain about the vicissitudes of her rather narrow life. Betty frankly found Ephro hard to take. She was around the house too much for Betty's taste, and she was fixated in a worshipful way on John. With Ephro, Betty's emotional compass usually managed to be pointed somewhere between kind, tolerant and irritated, but there are clear indications that tolerant-to-irritated was her fixed course and often it was the best she could do.[39]

But on the beach at St Austell, John's silence may not have been determined by hesitation to talk about any sexual encounter he may have had. He was completely exhausted on three counts especially: a very heavy term, the convulsions in the New Britain Group, and the family changes and responsibilities that fell on him after his father's death. He needed to rest. And yet he felt the need as well to come to grips with his enduring desire for a new society in the light of the collapse of his recent organizational involvements and the growing unlikelihood of the Macmurrays and Grants coming together in community. He was also becoming more and more shaken by the implications of the rising Fascism in Europe. So even in the sun and by the sea, and free from the burden of duties and claims on his time, he pondered on what might be a promising way for him to proceed from this point after he returned to London.

Irene had asked him about what she observed was a connection being claimed by some people between D.H. Lawrence and Fascism, despite Lawrence's declared revulsion for Fascism before his death. Why, she asked John, was Lawrence's work so susceptible to being attractive to the same people who were attracted to Fascism. John had been thinking of the same matter and offered her his best thoughts to that point on it. He noted first that Lawrence was clearly on one side only in the battle between social convention and the animal power in the blood as expressing the truth of human nature. John noted the inadequacy in this appeal to instincts *against* reason, the belly *against* the head.

> The anti-intellectualist bias of Lawrence's attitude makes people easily duped. They defend themselves against having an intellectual understanding and so any thought-out plan. So the people who *have* a plan can lead them by the nose, and do ... But the deepest part still is that anti-intellectualism is interpreted as anti-rationalism. This is where Lawrence is just wrong ... he can only run away from Fascism when his guts lead him to it; because he feels it's wrong: but he doesn't know *why* it's wrong, nor what is right that would negate it. He will equate his lower centres with primitive unconsciousness ... So he goes looking into the dim planetary past and its relics to find the consciousness he is after; and it isn't there. It is ahead of us, to be developed; and it means the *rationality* of his lower centres. That is what I have always meant by insisting that we have somehow to develop an emotional objectivity or rationality. We have to square the communal thing with individual rationality and independence. Lawrence leads to Fascism not because he is wrong in his general line, or in his criticism of us, but because there is this *rationality* missing; and it isn't intellectual rationality. It is that new consciousness of his at the rational level.

As John notes here, his own response to Lawrence — and to Fascism on this point — had already begun to take shape in his philosophy quite apart from either of them. He simply does not accept Lawrence's effort to reclaim primitive feeling as an automatic advance in the battle against the constrictions of social conventions and rule-based ethics. Getting in touch with primary visceral feeling is absolutely necessary, as he has recognized and desires to do. But feeling is not simply this primitive unconscious push of vital hunger. As he said in *Freedom in the Modern World*, and again in talks delivered since, that will appear two years later as *Reason and Emotion*, feeling has its own capacity to be discriminating, that is, to respond to the other according to the other's own nature (therefore, objectively) not just according to one's own drives and needs.[40] There is a capacity in human beings to have feelings that are *real,* that is, related to others *objectively* — as they are. Macmurray gives the name "emotional rationality" to this capacity to have feelings that are formed by the other person (or landscape, or object), as opposed to feelings being merely a function of my own needs. In other words, feelings can be objective and true — just as intellect can. Feeling is necessary to know true value and goodness, just as intellect and sense combine to provide us with true facts. As a society, he asserts, we have not recognized this capacity for feeling to be objective the way we take it for granted in the area of intellect, i.e., scientific knowing. As such, he concludes what is needed with regard to the crucial liberation of feeling in human life requires an *advance* — a free expression of emotional rationality in our relationships — not a regression in the direction of giving ourselves over to undifferentiated, instinctive attraction or repulsion under the guise of an act of mystical union and genuine self-transcendence. Lawrence retrieved something precious and necessary, Macmurray concludes; he just wasn't able to go farther and grasp the true nature of human feeling.

This consideration of Lawrence and how he is being interpreted by people is hardly an aside for John in relation to the Britain he sees around him. As he says to Irene: " ... there is no possibility of a revolutionary Communist movement in this country for a long time to come; and there is a steady drift towards a mild, constitutional Fascism." Apparently it was already clear in his mind that it wasn't just an isolated few, such as the Prince of Wales — soon to be king — or Oswald Mosley, who was soon to create the British Fascist Party, who represented such a drift in Britain. Here, in this letter to Irene Grant, he offers his final statement on what he has been hoping for when he speaks of a new society and a new social unit, and why he feels he needs to touch it and feel it for it to be meaningful:

> We have to try to create a communist life for ourselves without
> waiting for a mass-movement, and work from that basis of
> experience to the mass-movement. I'm not thinking of running
> away, and seeking something for myself and my friends in a little

enclave. It is the Communist Society of the World I am after. But to
do something to that end I feel I need the experience of communal
life as intuitional basis for intellectual expression. I want the feel
and the taste of a real material individuality in a social unit which
is not abstract but concrete — containing all the aspects of human
life in it. We've got to think good and hard — but thinking is
always the expression of immediate experience, and imagination
can't help it out very far in default of the concrete experience of
what it wants to formulate. Thinking is vicious when it is not
instrumental.

What Macmurray actually means by emotional rationality, at the intimate
as well as the historical level, is telegraphed in his final paragraph to
Irene in response to her confession of sad and confused feelings about
Donald, their sexuality, and how it relates to loving one another and letting her husband be free — a situation John has had to deal with himself.
He admits "how it can hurt and make one come very near to the wish for
death":

I can't pretend to have discovered the clue to that mystery. It lies
somewhere in a mutual integrity between people that is only to be
achieved where there is complete freedom to love and to refrain
from loving as one must. We have to find out for ourselves, and it
hurts. The discipline of the object of love is my test. Love must
make for fullness of life in the other or all the others, or there is
something wrong.

He concludes with a highly personal reflection touching each of them, and
it must have been a consoling one for her:

I don't trust myself in sex very much: I was too deeply damaged
there when I was young. I trust Betty very fully — she is naturally
sound and singularly uncomplicated. And of all the men I know I
should trust Donald most completely. He has a wonderful integrity
which is somehow physical. So you and I are saved by our lovers.[41]

The Grants arrived in Britain from Vienna late that summer. John and
Betty, together with the Grant family, spent some holiday time in the New
Forest, and John introduced them all to the Grith Fyrd community where
they stayed for a while. The enthusiasm of living in their first community
experiment caught them all up over those few days but Betty wrote Irene
from Aberdeen a few weeks later agreeing with Irene that the excitement
passed for her too almost as soon as they had left the camp. She rejoices

however in knowing that Donald and Irene and the children will be in London and will be "near to us."[42]

Thus, the desire for forming community in one household together that was generated over the first half of the year had become significantly modified by August. And by September their decision was not to pursue it. It is hard to say exactly why. An uncertain work future for Donald was a major feature in the decision of the Grants to find a place of their own. But there were probably more than practicalities involved. In the end, there may have been insufficient desire to live in community in *each* of them. Betty had been honest enough to say from the outset that she was not keen on community living. She was perhaps more confused in those feelings because of her love for both Donald and Irene, and especially after her passionate encounter with Donald. But that very encounter, and Betty's almost mystical response to it, may also have moved the Grants, individually and together — as partners and as parents — to review the wisdom of the proposal. As for John, he had revealed some rather significant feelings to Irene as far back as April 16 to which he may not have been able or willing to give the attention they deserved:

> I'm rather spent; and feel as if I had done all I could do, and that younger people must carry on now. I'm just beginning to feel a trifle Victorian in my habits. I can't get my instincts to change to keep company with my ideas. So I don't know how to live the life that I know is the right one. But that is probably temporary. At least I hope so.[43]

Well, it wasn't completely temporary. It was true to life, as his later letter to Donald revealed. At some level in himself, he wasn't all that sure of how keen *he* was on community life or, at least, how prepared he was to live it. As much as John wanted to remake his feelings to conform to what he *perceived* to be the requirements for his emotional liberation and the needs of society, he knew he could not change himself on demand. For all his intellectual resistance to idealism in any form, this deliberate "plan" to convert his feelings and construct a new form of social living reveals itself, in the passage of just a few months, as a hope tinged with a large degree of its own idealism. This is confirmed in a variety of examples throughout his life. His proposal for a new "social unit" in the *New Britain* article on that subject in June was hasty and ill-considered, one might even say irresponsible, considering he was possibly influencing thousands of readers who respected his judgment on a very tender and serious subject. His idea of "couples marrying each other" as the model of the new social unit to replace the nuclear family was an idea that was just striking him and had been given no time to mature. It did not arise from the wisdom of long experience or any careful evidence gathering from the experience of others. The final word should be the most concrete one: had John simply *listened* to Betty as she revealed her feelings throughout the spring in many ways, including words, he would have known that she simply did not want to live in community.

John was also slowly awakening to the fact that the intense striving he had brought to this search for a new form of social living was threatening a genuine peace and freedom in him, and perhaps in others. On September 14, while in Aberdeen with Betty for their holidays, he wrote Irene a letter that suggests the whole process has brought about a spiritual liberation in him, and it gave him the confidence to be quite direct with her. In just a couple of weeks back in London from Vienna, Irene had come to know of John's very positive reputation among left-leaning people there who saw him as a leader. She was solicitous for his health, given the steady stream of invitations coming at him from them. And she was also proposing some political directions they might collaborate on when he returned. In response to that proposal, he was very clear with her, and showed his spiritual freedom in its finest form:

> ... don't worry about the people who look to me for a lead. I've learned not to be hurried by them; and I shall know when the time comes, if it does. I'm just going steadily on solving my own problem; and I'm sure the only thing to do is to refuse to take responsibility for what will happen; and to concentrate on saying what reveals itself as the truth without reckoning the consequences either to oneself or others: and not to be drawn into speech or into silence by other people's urgencies.

He tells her how wonderful it was to see her; and he has no words for her yet:

> ... except that you are not to be afraid, but quite quiet in the depths of you and at peace with yourself. Out of that will come the creativeness. I distrust your sense of urgency — even about Fascism. We are not responsible for what will be; and there is no short cut to freedom. Let's be quiet and still and expectant: then things will happen, where they have to happen first — in us, and between us.
>
> That isn't an alternative to political or social action, but a condition of its value and success. We *must* rid ourselves of idealism. The form of polity or economic system or educational organization that can arise is determined by the kind of people in whom it rises.

This acknowledgment of the interior conditions required for individual and social freedom is not new in John. And he knew he himself was in need of constant conversion towards it. In his "Introductory" to *Some Makers of the Modern Spirit* which he was editing at the time he made the point that history is formed by events and circumstances, but also by the inner spirit, ideas, motives and attitudes which determine the way not only individuals but societies deal with their circumstances. But he knows it is relatively difficult for Irene to acknowledge the interior life. He knows she is, as her son later described her: "a political creature through and through,"[44] and he will get to know that even more over the next few years. So he needs to remind her that the individual freedom of revolutionaries has everything to do with the freedom to be hoped for from the social revolution they are launching. He returns to the social and political arena where she is more at home, but even here he is more challenging than comforting:

> And I don't see much hope of a revolution releasing forces which
> would crystallize into any better — and I mean myself, more
> communist — society than we have, in any Western, industrial
> nation. The advance to Socialism can happen quite simply when
> sufficient numbers of people want it. And that means when they
> really want to be more social and communal in their ways of living.
> Socialism as an ideal is only the imaginary counterweight to the
> reality of an increasing individualism. If the imagination produced
> a revolution, it would still be the reality which would create the
> social form.

Referring to the Grith Fyrd experiment in the New Forest that they visited together the month before, he praises Peter Scott and Aubrey Westlake "because they are actively seeking a new and more communal way of living for themselves." But he also has words of criticism for their experiment that reveal how far-reaching his own imagination goes when he conceives a genuinely alternative way of social life together:

> I am also quite clear that they are all in danger from their own
> idealism and individualism of conceiving their new life on the
> primitive patriarchal model ... the patriarchal business will fail,
> that's all; and they may be broken and discouraged — which would
> be dangerous perhaps. I return myself to the real problem, and pray
> for strength and courage and capacity to keep on facing the real
> situation. Create communion and community: the reality of it, not
> the form or appearance of it: discard pretence. In the attempt, we
> shall discover the conditions of the new life. But until we have
> created in ourselves and between ourselves at least the vigorous

> shoots of a new consciousness which is communal, there is no
> point in setting up the forms of a communal society.[45]

John ends by saying how much he looks forward to the journey with her
that will unfold. But, as for the kind of revolution he hopes for and
believes the world needs, he is more and more ready to assert that it is as
much a matter of method as goal, and that is a very different perspective
for her. He is more convinced than ever that it requires right relationships
at three levels: the individual, the small community and the larger society.
At this point, he has come to a quiet conviction that the conversion of the
larger society is a massive enterprise for which the West is nowhere near
ready or open. In *Some Makers of the Modern Spirit* he concluded that the
push of the modern spirit in Europe was towards concrete freedom for the
individual at all levels of existence. With the Industrial Revolution having
made a culture of plenty possible for all, the critical question was clear:
"... are we prepared to realize democracy, are we prepared to implement
the promises of equal freedom in the practical field of the economic
life?"[46] Having raised the question, he was more and more convinced that
the answer in Europe and Britain was "No." What remains? To work
towards the world revolution in two ways: by letting go of responsibility
for it but continuing to want it and asking faithfully for the dispositions
needed for it to be "given." And, second, by cultivating at the level of individual and small community living those conditions that might help the
fuller revolution take place. What might look like a political surrender to
some is, in fact, read by him as a spiritual advance. It has created the clear
attitude he will bring into the struggle against Fascism and the effort to
create a genuine Christian community — both of which face them in the
immediate future.

Chapter 11

Walking with Polanyi:

Engaging Marxism and Fascism (1933–35)

The autumn of 1933 saw Macmurray well launched into one of the busiest periods of his life, the very thing he had encouraged Irene Grant to avoid. At University College, London (UCL), he was just completing his two-year term as Dean of the Faculty of Arts during which time he had promoted the intercollegiate courses for senior students, mainly with King's College, Bedford College and the London School of Economics. He continued his informal professional encounters with colleagues in other departments, chatting often with J.C. Flugel about humanistic theories in psychology and psychiatry, and visiting, in his lab, J.B.S. Haldane, the great geneticist, who had left Cambridge that autumn for the freer atmosphere of UCL. Haldane's father, an excellent scientist, had been a Christian and an idealist, as were many in his generation. His son, perhaps following the spirit of his own generation, became more and more an outspoken materialist. Despite that difference, Haldane and Macmurray were able to share their socialist views and a public resistance to Fascism during the rest of the thirties.

UCL and the young socialists

Because of their earlier relationship at Balliol, John and Hugh Gaitskell fell into an easy though sporadic relationship again at UCL where Gaitskell was a lecturer in the Political Economy department.[1] Partly through Gaitskell, John renewed contact with Richard Crossman, Richard Acland and Evan Durbin, who had been his students at Oxford, and all of whom were pursuing political careers in the Labour Party. Gaitskell asserted himself a bit with his old master that year by writing a mildly critical review of *Freedom in the Modern World* in the UCL student magazine.

Crossman, who had finished his first degree in Classics the year Macmurray left Balliol, was teaching at Oxford and in the Workers Education Association. Acland who had come from landed gentry had graduated in 1927. His involvement in politics carried on a long family tradition of reformist public service, and when he reconnected with John his election to the House was only a year off. Associated with those social- ists was the mercurial Tom Driberg who had joined the Communist Party at the age of fifteen and had been at Balliol during Macmurray's years there, though he refused to sit any exams. Open, even flagrantly so, about his homosexuality, he almost lost himself in the shady side of life in London and had to be rescued by Edith Sitwell, and helped by Lord Beaverbrook who gave him a column in the *Daily Express*. Driberg would be loosely associated with Acland in the Commonwealth Movement in the early 1940s, but ran as an independent in 1942 and won a seat for Labour in 1945 which he held for twenty years. Driberg would occasionally stop by to see Macmurray, and it seems John played something of the role of a spiritual director in the early 1930s for the volatile young man. Evan Durbin was the outstanding hopeful among these young socialist thinkers who had come through Oxford at the same time. He was helping to shape the policy and direction of the Labour Party during the early 1930s when he and Macmurray met up again. He had become an academic economist at the London School of Economics in 1929 and was striving to put together a form of socialist planning that was infused with democratic methods and public ownership even while it concentrated on central eco- nomic strategies. In the 1930s he was resisting Marxism, and found Macmurray's focus on the personal more attractive that Marxism for the kind of socialism he envisioned. Some claim to have found influences of Macmurray's philosophy in Durbin's 1940 book *The Politics of Democratic Socialism*. Tragically, shortly after the war, at the age of forty- two, he was drowned while trying to rescue two children. There were many who felt the Labour Party had lost its next leader in his passing.[2] Because of the conversations they had at this time, Crossman, Acland and others later gave credit to Macmurray (as Durbin had earlier) for provid- ing them with the philosophical underpinnings for a democratic socialism that could be rigorous but did not need to fall into the arms of com- munism.

Despite John's many involvements beyond the university his students do not seem to have suffered. His lectures were given to packed halls and his seminars were immensely popular. Macmurray often lectured without a note, not because he was complacent but because of the preparation he had done and the command he had of his subject. He spoke in a quiet voice and rather slowly, elaborating his key point by going around it from various angles, opening it up as he went. He made a point of not over- packing his lectures with too many ideas and the result was it gave his stu- dents a chance to enter into the experience of philosophical thinking.[3] His personal power in the classroom was immense. Macmurray gave many students the visceral impression his niece Diana had from her earliest years when she observed: "When I was young, I used to listen to Uncle John because I felt everything he was saying was true — quite apart from being interesting, which it was."[4] This quality of Macmurray's teaching was reflected rather dramatically by Wilfrid Taylor in *The Scotsman* years later when he described stopping by a seminar being held by John at UCL in the early 1930s:

> ... we gatecrashed a seminar conducted by the delightful John Macmurray. It was an enchanting scene. Professor Macmurray, looking and sounding intensely Socratic, sat on a chair while all around him sprawled eager-beaver students of every colour and pigment, some of them in robes. As we listened to the professor, the embodiment of concentrated practical wisdom, penetrating the impenetrable with marvellous oracular authority, we wondered if we had strolled from Gower Street into ancient Athens. Philosophy vibrated with vitality at U.C. [University College][5]

Macmurray's humour in his lectures was not overlooked by the *University College Magazine* which advertised itself as a magazine launched "for students and for faculty who still considered themselves students" — a class into which Macmurray would have been delighted to fall. In June 1934 he was included among quotable quotes by the editor of "In and Out of the Cloisters" for his sardonic remark: "Examinations are digging up the roots to see how the flowers are growing." A short time later, the editors found memorable Macmurray's equally iconoclastic definition: "An expert is a man who doesn't know anything else."

He gave his time readily to the various student societies that called on him to chair their functions. In this role, he served the Socialist Society and a special anti-war meeting in early 1933 convoked by a mixed gathering of interested student societies, a meeting that featured, as the first speaker, John Strachey, the well-known Communist and soon-to-be editor along with Victor Gollancz and Harold Laski of the Left Book Club. Macmurray was also President of the Philosophical Society in the late thirties and gave talks at various other societies. In addition to these UCL activities, he was made a member of a University of London Council for Psychical Investigation along with Cyril Burt, J.C. Flugel, his undergraduate Balliol colleague C.E.M. Joad, and C.A. Mace — the functions of which can only be surmised.

In the months leading up to September 1933, Macmurray had maintained a crushing pace in both publishing and public lectures. *The Philosophy of Communism* had been followed quickly by *Interpreting the Universe* and *Some Makers of the Modern Spirit* which he edited and to which he contributed — all published in 1933. *Freedom in the Modern*

World, published the year before, was going through multiple reprints that occasioned many invitations to develop his views on disputed questions arising from those provocative radio talks. As a result he gave some well-crafted talks to a variety of audiences on subjects as diverse as "Education of the Emotions," "The Conservation of Personality" (a lecture on the immortality of the soul), and "The Early Discipline of Personality" (presented to the Froebel Society) which were published as chapters of his upcoming book *Reason and Emotion.*

After his book on communism came out Macmurray became known as both a supporter and critic of Marxism. This was hardly a comfortable place to stand at a time when the dominant question assaulting every educated and conscientious person was quickly becoming: "Whose side are you on?" In the company of conventional liberals and traditional Christians Macmurray tended to dwell on the essentially fresh, valid and creative aspects of Marxist theory — especially Marx's criticism of the idealism permeating institutional Christianity and his challenges to dualism.[6] In debate with convinced Marxists, he was inclined to challenge their contentment with an exclusively organic and determinist view of history and the human person which, as he noted, makes Marxism — itself a very spiritual intrusion into world history — self-contradictory. He also enjoyed pointing out that any theory based on dialectics cannot be defended with absolutist language and categories, a habit into which many passionate defenders of Marx fell. Macmurray was honing his understanding of Marx by doing a close reading, along with Karl Polanyi, of the Landshut & Meyer edition of Marx's early writings (1837–47) entitled *Der Historische Materialismus,* published in 1932. His preparation for that reading was not superficial. He had read Hegel some years before while at Balliol. His minute analysis of Lotze's *Microcosmus* around the same time had helped to give him some critical distance in relation to organic modes of thinking and this proved invaluable when he read Marx. Although deeply attracted to Marx he was already inoculated against Marx's organic foundations.

Macmurray began receiving invitations to conferences sponsored by representatives of both positions as well as by those in between who were simply looking for intelligent debate about the vital social issues of the time. The Society for Cultural Relations responded to "an urgent demand from large numbers of interested individuals that the philosophy guiding the practice of Modern Russia might be expounded in a form intelligible to the layman" by holding a conference on "Dialectical Materialism." It included the scientists H. Levy and J.D. Bernal along with Professor Carritt of Oxford, Macmurray and others.

Macmurray also wrote three long chapters in 1934 as the first section of a book called *Marxism* that was being edited by John Middleton

Murry.[7] N.A. Holdaway and G.D.H. Cole, the great proponent of Guild
Socialism, were the other contributors. In his first chapter on "The
Nature of Philosophy" he went to some pains to explain how he understood the Marxist doctrine of "the unity of thought and action" — perhaps recalling Carritt's dismissal of his views on this point in the earlier
conference.[8] In his next chapter he reinterpreted the term "materialism"
positively as a result of the healing he proposed for the false separation
of mind and matter. "The new materialist," he observes, "is a materialist not because he overthrows ideals but because he is primarily concerned with the conditions of their realization."[9] In this chapter in
Marxism Macmurray gave his best and clearest presentation to date on
the practical difference between being an idealist and being a realist —
or what he calls here, a "new materialist." He then offered as his second
point the clearest articulation he ever gave of the difference between
pragmatism (the truth is what works satisfactorily) and the philosophy
of truth represented by dialectical materialism. The failure to make this
distinction properly, he concluded, leads to confusing the relationship
of systems of belief to social activity, a failure which opens the way to
the creation and manipulative use of ideologies in society. This conclusion launched him in his third chapter into a study of the nature and
social function of ideologies. One of his preliminary conclusions on
this theme is fairly predictable but was stated with great simplicity:

> A consistent dialectical materialism must maintain stoutly that an
> ideology is effective or rational for human purposes in proportion
> to its truth, and in view of its conviction that the unity of thought
> and practice must be concerned to establish an ideology which is
> *true* ... Since social belief is social action it is impossible to believe
> the truth, or even to discover it, while living a social life that is
> incompatible with it.[10]

Christianity and the social revolution

At this stage of his thinking about Marxism, Macmurray was indirectly
working out elements in his own philosophy, and doing so essentially in
the light of his acceptance of Marx's understanding of the unity of thought
and action.

As though that kind of workload were not enough, he was preparing
these essays for *Marxism* at the same time as he was beginning work with
Karl Polanyi, Joseph Needham and others on a book that would focus on
the fresh challenges Marxism and Fascism brought to Christianity in light
of the developing situation in Europe. Polanyi had moved to London that

autumn and, partly because of his lack of any economic base, lived with John and Betty for several months before finding a place of his own, at which time his wife and daughter came from Vienna to join him. There was time to talk; and the idea for a book on this subject probably arose out of their earliest conversations.

The book being planned was actually meant to come out as soon as possible in order to serve as a riposte to a book entitled *Christianity and the Crisis* that had been published a few months earlier. *Crisis* was a 600-page collection of essays by prestigious Christian leaders built around the consoling premise that Christianity had the wherewithal to withstand the current social crisis just as it did one hundred years earlier when William Wilberforce and others accomplished in the Great Emancipation Act the liberation of both Black Slavery and White Slavery. To the horror of its more politically attuned readers the book barely acknowledged Communism, and made no mention of Fascism at all; the word didn't even appear in the index. The question that rose up urgently among left-leaning Christians was: Which crisis was that book addressing?!!

A decision was taken quickly, with Polanyi and Macmurray at the heart of it, to put out a book that actually engaged Fascism and Communism in their theoretical assumptions and practical implications. Although there would be a clear Christian set of reflections going on in its pages it would differ from *Crisis* not only in addressing the current political movements in Europe but also by allowing Communists to speak for themselves, with foreign voices included. There would be diverse premises as well as diverse viewpoints at work since that was the truth of the world in which they found themselves. It would also include a study of historical efforts over the centuries on the part of Christian groups to set up communities that reflected communist principles, all in an effort to learn from them.

In order to achieve a bridge for dialogue rather than total rupture with the authors of *Crisis*, the editors — Polanyi, Donald Kitchin and John Lewis — put together an editorial committee that included Charles Raven, the well-respected Regius Professor of Divinity in Cambridge and Canon of Ely Cathedral; Joseph Needham, Fellow of Caius College, Cambridge, who would later write an encyclopedic work on the history of technology in China; and Macmurray. By the spring of 1934 they were ready to get going. After some debate, the title of the book had been settled on: it would be called *Christianity and the Social Revolution*. Lining up authors and articles required an exercise of patience and restraint beyond the ordinary. In June, when communist sympathizers seemed over-represented, Canon Raven threatened to withdraw from the project. Proposed titles such as John Lewis' "Communism the Heir to the Christian Tradition" as well as the vigour of some of the attacks on the church were problematic for Raven. Even having a title containing the word "revolution" seemed to Raven unnecessarily inciting in the approval it could appear to grant to Marxism and the Soviet experiment. Raven's presence remained tenuous to the end; but, to their relief, he decided to remain on the editorial board and agreed to do the Introduction. Macmurray's new friend, Julius Hecker, agreed to participate and was happily involved in seeking out other Russian voices. In the end, only one Russian in addition to Hecker himself produced an essay acceptable to the editors. Archbishop Temple, Jacques Maritain, N. Berdyaeff and others were approached but demurred for various reasons. R.H. Tawney sent his regrets, but only because of time constraints. Others remained possible to the end but then failed to provide an article, or at least a satisfactory one.[11] Reinhold Niebuhr, the American Protestant theologian; John Lewis, the staunch communist lecturer in social philosophy at Cambridge; Wystan Auden; as well as Polanyi, Needham, Macmurray and several others contributed. Lewis, Needham, Gilbert Clive Binyon and Macmurray each provided two essays.

Polanyi guided the editorial team and worked closely with Joseph Needham in choosing and balancing authors and viewpoints. On June 8, he wrote to Needham saying he was just at a conference at High Leigh where John Macmurray "read several papers on Religion and Politics":

> I could not help feeling ... that he has now reached a stage in his
> thinking which designates a signal advance in our general
> philosophical position and is perhaps the beginning of a very great
> change in the method of dealing with these subjects.[12]

It is clear from the Polanyi correspondence that Macmurray is having a strong role in editorial judgments. On September 7, 1933, just days after the idea for the book had first popped up, Macmurray himself had written to Donald Kitchin concerning the purpose of the book. In that letter asking Kitchin to join the editorial team he had stated that although diversity of viewpoint must flourish, it is "essential to find a basis of unity for the book." John's own philosophical development in the subsequent weeks seems to have given Polanyi the sense that, in Macmurray's ideas, the desired point of unity was being found. According to the plan, Macmurray was preparing an essay on "The Early Development of Marx's Thought." In the end he was asked for a second one as well to serve as a something of a retrospective take on what had gone before. He titled this summary essay: "Christianity and Communism: Towards a Synthesis."

Politics and economics in community

His thesis in that epilogue is carried by his notion of "direct" (face-to-face) relations and "indirect" (not face-to-face) relations of persons to one another. Marx, he notes, deplores the indirectness created in economic relations by the complexities of the industrial world. Macmurray agreed the breakdown in direct relations in economics was a problem that was not being adequately met. But he states that this situation in the conditions of labour is not the ground of all human problems, as Marx proposes. One could have direct exchange relations with one's neighbour as a fellow-consumer but that is not yet a direct relation with him or her as a *person*. As he put it:

> ... economic relations, however direct, do not themselves suffice to establish community between human beings. To these there must be added a mutual recognition of one another as fellows in the sharing of a common life.
>
> All human community is a structure of direct relations between human beings. Community cannot be constituted by indirect relations, or defined by them.[13]

His first conclusion is that human society cannot be determined essentially by economic motives since economic relations, direct or indirect, are only one partial aspect of full human relating. To flesh out his view, Macmurray distinguishes two types of human motives, "hunger" and "love." Hunger is the expression of the need for survival, and we use things and even other persons to satisfy that purpose. Hunger is, therefore, egocentric by its very nature. Love, on the other hand, is the human desire and capacity to care for the other for the other's own sake. Human beings and their societies, he says, live necessarily by both motives. However they are not to be conceived of as parallel but totally separate urges. Love (heterocentric care and affection) ideally contains the hunger (self-caring) motive *within* itself as a necessary, constitutive but subordinate aspect of its full reality. In ideal personal living, love serves as the fuller context for hunger-expression, as can be seen frequently in good parent-love and the relationship of true friends.

Taking a larger social perspective he asserts further that "the co-operation of men for economic purposes would be impossible apart from the impulse to enter into community."[14] What is he saying here? Economic interests, in his view, are normatively embedded in communal ones. The urge to community (love) *includes* the urge to thrive individually (survival) and the urge to function cooperatively (service) as subordinate and constitutive dimensions within it. But the urge to communion, the social expression of love that includes individual or group activities within it, is the natural, normative, comprehensive *and most basic* goal towards which any expression of competition and cooperation must lead. The realization of a form of community that achieves social union *and* self-realization is, on Macmurray's view, the fullest and truest expression of human nature.

It is on the basis of that analysis, articulated from within a dialectical view of history, that Macmurray reveals a Christian social realism that he feels goes beyond Marx. He is not against "power." Courageous individual initiatives in science, technology, politics, art and religion are necessary if growth and changes for the better are to occur. They are often extremely dislocating and inevitably cause suffering in societies — as the Industrial Revolution and global outreach reveal. But Macmurray is aware that disruption and destruction in society and community most frequently arises from the initiative of individuals and groups who are not "communally" motivated. Macmurray is not denying or attempting to suppress the flourishing of the individual or groups of individuals nor is he denying the inevitable conflict that arises between individual initiatives and the current version of social life with all its natural inertia. However, he does challenge and deny that individual initiative is ethically a self-sufficient norm for human action, just as he challenges and denies the vaguely mystical — or rigidly dictated — collectivism produced by organic thinking in whatever form it takes: Rousseau's, Marx's or Hitler's. He holds that all capitalist vision and values are grounded for their very existence in the non-capitalist values of civil society (justice, peace, good order). And civic values, in turn, can only flourish if they are supported by the values of community (trust, freedom, knowledge, and love-based engagement of persons together in culture and living) which all transcend a merely political definition. Economics is accountable to civil society just as civil society is accountable to community in terms of the comprehensive good being envisaged. Macmurray was proposing a dialectical and dialogical integration of initiative (competition), participation (cooperation) and celebration (living in community). This is the ethical form of his social personalism. Against Marx, he holds that it is at once spiritual and material since, as he wrote in *Reason and Emotion,* "the spiritual is not other than the material, but inclusive of it. Spirit is not other than body but more than body."[15] He is in solidarity with Marx in his willingness to take seriously the material conditions of life. This is the way he was thinking in 1934 when he was writing this final essay for *Christianity and the Social Revolution* and producing many other works on related themes.

Having put the collectivist Marx in his place (and the individualistic Hobbes and Locke, as well) with his category of "personal action," Macmurray turns his guns on historical Christianity. He supports the

Marxist condemnation of idealism which accounts for so much traditional Christian theory and practice. Supernaturalism, which has so infected Christianity, is the idealist enemy of real religion, he claims. The true reference of religion is not some "other world," but "the field of direct human relationships, and these are as much a part of ordinary experience as any other. Indeed they are its core."[16]

Language like this about the nature of religion did not sit well with all those interested in the book that was coming to birth. Apparently, it was not only Charles Raven who had problems with the orientation of the proposed book; Macmurray's old associate A.D. Lindsay did, as well. On October 11, 1934, Polanyi had written to fellow-editor Needham saying that Macmurray, having just returned from a conference that involved an encounter with his less radical associates Archbishop Temple and J.H. Oldham, "was met by a great surprise at York. Both Temple and Oldham just agreed ... with his general attitude [on this point]. The Master of Balliol [A.D. Lindsay] fought a losing fight."[17] It seems that sometime after Temple had decided not to write an essay for the new book John had gone to York for this conference, almost surely sponsored by Temple, which the other three men attended. Either in a public talk or in a less formal setting Macmurray had presented his thesis for attempting a conceptual bridging between Marxism and Christianity in just these terms of conceiving of direct personal relationships as, at once, the proper completion of Marxism and a legitimate expression of the Christian's mission in the world. A.D. Lindsay, seems to have again, as he did in his 1928 conversation with young David Cairns, felt that Macmurray had reduced Christianity to merely human terms. Temple and Oldham don't seem to have come to the same conclusion. When the book came out Macmurray seems almost to be addressing the apprehensions of his old Master and colleague in his last paragraph of the essay, though hardly in terms that would make Lindsay more comfortable:

> But if religion rejects supernaturalism, must it not reject God and cease to be religion? Not at all. Either God is natural or religion is nonsense. The idea of Nature which excludes God is itself the product of dualism. God is no more supernatural than Matter. Both are infinites, and lie beyond all their finite manifestations. God is infinite personally; and personality dissociated from matter in idea is purely ideal — that is to say, non-existent. God is real; and therefore he is the ultimate synthesis of matter and spirit, of Nature and Man.[18]

The book was almost ready to go to press by the end of 1934. However, Polanyi had accepted an invitation by the Institute of International

Education to go to the United States and it would keep him away for four months. *Christianity and the Social Revolution* was finally published by Victor Gollancz towards the end of 1935. It was generally well received. R.H. Tawney's long review, with light-hearted turns of phrase, recognized it as a massive and disparate work built on a belief in principles (rare in our day!), but defying any unity of premises or conclusions, despite, he observed, Macmurray's fine efforts at synthesis.[19] Reinhold Niebuhr, reviewing a book to which he has contributed, found, on the other hand, that "the basic point of agreement in the book ... is that human life is a unity ...". He praises the depth and breadth of the work, historically and systematically, especially the contributions of Needham and Macmurray.[20] His own, left unmentioned in his review, was also a most worthy contribution.

A "materialist" Christianity?

But this was not the end of Macmurray's exploration of the relation of Christianity and Marxism. In 1935 Macmurray published a provocative, even swashbuckling, book called *Creative Society: A Study of the Relation of Christianity to Communism* in which the influence of Marx on Macmurray's rethinking of the meaning of Christianity became most obvious. It is likely he was producing *Creative Society* at the same that *Christianity and the Social Revolution* was being prepared.[21] It was in this book that Macmurray articulated most forcefully his view of the incarnate and anti-Idealist nature of the form of religion lived by Jesus. Real religion, he stated, is incarnate. And Jesus, along with everything else he is, is indeed a social reformer, just as *all* the prophets were. As a genuine religious prophet, he was not merely that, but he was necessarily that.

Creative Society focuses on the Kingdom that is to be heralded and struggled for in this world, not in some after-world. The tendency to look to another world, to a beyond, as the locus of Christ's message, he dubbed "false religion." Most Christian religion, he concluded, was infected by dualism; that is, by the destructive virus of other-worldly Idealism in its thinking, and by Roman stoicism and brutal materialism in its practice.

When he tried to define the authentic ground of Christianity, Macmurray leaned heavily on what he called the unitary and materialist nature of Hebrew religion. He attempted to think through the marks of "real religion" from two poles at once: the eschatological vision of the Kingdom taught by the ancient Hebrew prophets and by Jesus, and the work already being undertaken historically, on various fronts, to achieve equality and freedom in full fellowship here in this world. He believed these historical efforts, and the joyful celebration of life that went with them, were the genuine social signs that God's will was actually being done by human beings.

In *Creative Society,* despite his immense sympathy for Marx, Macmurray confirmed and even deepened his view of the limitations of Marxism that he noted at the end of his 1933 work on *The Philosophy of Communism* and his 1934 work in *Christianity and the Social Revolution.* He returns to Marx's rejection of religion and focuses his critical gaze not on Marx's dismissal of God but on *his refusal to place the self-transcending nature of personal relating in this world at the heart of his anthropology.* In Macmurray's view, Marx, by his choice of hunger over love as the essential motive in human beings, left his theory bereft and one-dimensional, no longer able to interpret the power and beauty of his own deepest insights into humanity and history; insights, shaped by desire for freedom and goodness, that were clearly more than economic and shaped by far more than just organic drives.

The book is filled with gems of profound wisdom on what it is to be fully rational and "personal," expressed in astonishingly simple and lucid language. Macmurray ended this book of his adulthood as he ended the journal of his adolescence: by critiquing the hypocrisy of organized Christianity while holding firmly to the person of Jesus and the utter worthiness of the Gospel as a guide for action. *Creative Society* is the most explicit and grand expression of his conviction that at the heart of the Christian Gospel, and its essentially Hebrew roots, lay a far truer support of personhood and community than Marxism could ever offer.[22] On the other hand, prepared in haste and in the white hot temper shared by all his associates on the Left in the mid-thirties, it is also grounded in a huge optimism about the affinities between Marxism and Christianity that he would later qualify significantly — after the horrors of these and later years in the Soviet Union were more widely known and the invasion of Hungary was there to shock the world.

Left unmentioned so far in this portrait of Macmurray's intellectual and literary journey in those few short years is the influence of Karl Polanyi on his understanding of Fascism, especially the Fascism of Hitler and the National Socialists in Germany. In "The Essence of Fascism," his long essay in *Christianity and the Social Revolution,* Polanyi traces out the reasons for defining Fascism as essentially an attack against socialism and its convictions with regard to the values of freedom, equality and democracy. Contrary to the standard middle-class view that socialism crushes personality, Polanyi holds the Fascists are the ones who are the enemies of genuine individuality. The Fascists, he proposes, realized that "[s]ocialism is the heir to Individualism. It is the economic system under which the substance of Individualism can alone be preserved in the modern world."[23] In Germany, unlike Italy and Spain, the fascists took up their cause at the most profound philosophical level and created their own rationality for their actions.

In their attacks on socialism and its alliance with democracy, Polanyi observed, they also realized that Christianity was the seed-bed in Europe of the sacredness of the individual person. To counter socialism the Fascists inevitably would have to counter Christianity. There was a direct line between democracy, socialism and Christianity, and for the German Fascists, Christianity was the source of the pro-individual, pro-universal brotherhood principles guiding all these western traditions. And if its conviction was God-given then God, too, must go; for if there is a God who creates all human beings then there is necessarily a Brotherhood of Man, a version of "human togetherness" the very opposite to what Hitler envisaged. What Polanyi saw so clearly in his 1935 analysis of the theoretical roots of Fascism was not only the necessary movement towards atheism in the movement but the need for Nazism to take on the status of religion–as the only religion.

The journey towards this radical spiritual autonomy of the titanic individual had been flagged by Nietzsche in his "Superman" and dramatically portrayed by Dostoevsky in the character of Kiriloff in *The Possessed* — with disastrous results in both cases. The choice by the Nazis to subscribe to and pursue this view of reality and apply it to the State confirmed that Christianity and Fascism must be completely incompatible. Through their court-philosophers Othmar Spann of Vienna, Ludwig Klages and Alfred Rosenberg, the Nazis instituted vitalism, totalitarianism and racism as the true ideological weapons to achieve their goal. Again, and from every angle, the thesis is confirmed: the forces for individual freedom and universal brotherhood in all their forms constitute the enemies of the Fascist state. This summary hardly does justice to Polanyi's position but it does sketch the lines shaping his thesis. The power and perspecticve of this essay, filled with historical detail and nuanced philosophical analysis, Macmurray could not have found anywhere else in Britain in 1933.

Conspicuous by its absence, however, is any reference in the essay to the Jews, either as the monotheistic community from which Christianity and the philosophy of universal brotherhood sprang, or as the most vulnerable target-community of Nazi hatred. The Nazis were already strongly anti-Semitic and Hitler knew that the personalist/universalist view of one humanity under one God, a view the Nazis despised, was introduced to the world by the Jews. Polanyi, coming from Vienna — as well as from a family with Jewish origins — was more than aware of the radically negative attitude and increasing violent behaviour of the Nazis towards Jews. Why he passed over mentioning the Jews as the primary focus of Nazi hatred (and the reasons why that was so) in such a foundational and comprehensive essay remains a mystery. We can only assume that in this essay he was talking most directly to a Christian audience and calling them to stand up and take responsibility within their *own* tradition for the current social situation in Europe. If Christians took their Christianity seriously, he seemed to be suggesting, any acceptance of Hitler was immoral and self-contradictory; open resistance was a necessary act of integrity, and neutrality was impossible. Tragically, the crucial, though partial, message of this essay, which was soon to become a fulfilled prophecy, went unheard or unrecognized. The thesis that both Polanyi and Macmurray shared was too much for Britons in the mid-1930s to hear.

In preparing this book, Macmurray was both educated about Fascism and confirmed in his own developing philosophy. His work on personality was pioneering and his association of the development of personality with Christianity, democracy, socialism and the Hebrew roots of Christianity was long-standing. But there is no doubt that Polanyi's analysis of German Fascism *in religious terms* increased Macmurray's appreciation for the evil of Fascism and the reasons why it must be countered as a profound human and religious perversion. However, his analysis of institutional Christianity had prepared him for appreciating as well the profoundly tragic abdication of the churches between 1934 and 1944 through their willful blindness to the full meaning of Fascism as a philosophy of human nature and a programme to destroy genuine individuality and democratic society. The mutual development of their philosophies from 1933 to 1935 made it both possible and attractive for Macmurray and Polanyi to collaborate with their friend, Irene Grant, in providing a united focus for the tiny Christian Left Movement that began to take shape in the summer of 1935.

Chapter 12

Life in London and the Struggle
with Pacifism (1935–39)

Despite the heavy workload John put on himself during the mid-1930s he
and Betty also found time to get to know London better and make many
new friends. Betty especially had come to know a whole different side of
city-life since she had decided to try to become a serious artist. The artist
who accepted her for lessons was Roy de Maistre, an Australian who had
come to London in 1930 and had already made his presence felt in the
artistic community. Betty had met him at his studio in 13 Eccleston Street
where she was swept away by his canvasses that were, as she reported,
"full of colour, ethereal and brilliant — bathing one in light."[1] De Maistre
was short, bald and portly but his presence "was firm and direct, and he,
as well as his pictures, seemed to radiate light, a freshness, a clarity and
cleanness of face."

Roy de Maistre, Betty acknowledged years later, was the best and most
satisfying relationship she had outside of marriage. He was homosexual
and that had the effect of freeing their friendship in a way that helped
Betty to *feel* the meaning of what John meant when he spoke of specifically personal relating. Those were the days when Betty felt she flowered.
"I was so absorbed at that time in my work, painting furiously for hours
every day, leaving the housework to my dear housekeeper Mrs Brown who
served us faithfully." It was, as she said often, the richest period of her life.

Although Betty never found John's university friends as much fun as
her own — and she claims he admitted this, too — the Macmurrays entertained frequently and generously. After one of these gatherings Richard
Crossman was overheard to complain: "There's too much wine and drink
at Macmurray parties." Later, he apologized profusely when he heard he
had been reported — or, as he said, misreported — to Betty as saying the
guests were "bathing in wine." If it had been true John would have enjoyed
the role of loosening up the serious young Crossman. John was working
on that in himself; why not Crossman, too.

Rayner Heppenstall became a friend they both enjoyed. He was an
aspiring novelist, poet and literary critic who eventually produced books
in all three areas. He was working at that time at the new Adelphi Centre,
running the community centre, even doing much of the cooking. He had

plans to get married but had barely two coins to rub together in his pocket. In his book *Four Absentees* he tells the story of his marriage at which Herbert Read and Max Plowman were the witnesses:

> The Macmurrays did a rather specially nice thing. I had run into John Macmurray two or three days before in Glenloch Road, Hampstead, where I had taken a room. It seemed he lived just round the corner. I told him I was getting married on Saturday, and he said he would like to give me a party. So what was arranged was that my wife and I should invite our friends to his flat and go round ourselves late on Saturday afternoon, when all would be ready. The Macmurrays would then go out, returning later as guests and ringing the doorbell. They laid on everything, including caviar.[2]

Around the same time, John began working with Tess Simpson in her valiant efforts through the Academic Assistance Council (AAC) to offer a *pied à terre* in British universities for the many refugee scholars who were fleeing Germany after the consolidation of Nazi power. The AAC, begun by Lord Beveridge who was then still head of the London School of Economics, had as its goal the placement of these scholars in a British university with full financial support for exactly one year. During this time they would be able to become better known in the English-speaking world and have the leisure to seek a more permanent university placement in Britain or abroad. In 1934 the AAC — renamed two years later as the Society for the Protection of Science and Learning (SPSL) — was headed by Walter Adams who had been a history professor at University College, London, and knew Macmurray. The AAC had selected certain British professors to whom they would turn for an educated opinion on the merit of these displaced academics and it seems that Walter and Tess leaned frequently on Macmurray to offer a judgment on philosophers who had come to Britain.[3]

John gladly took on this role because of his own political convictions but perhaps with greater alacrity because of his former colleagueship with Adams and his personal affection and respect for Tess. He began in the autumn of 1934 by reading the manuscripts of some of these scholars and sending his initial assessment of their work back to Tess. One of the first whose work he appraised was Theodor Adorno, one of the founders of the Frankfurt School of Critical Theory. Macmurray and Adorno met immediately after Adorno came to Britain in 1934 and it was through him that Macmurray got to know something of other German philosophers who came to Britain a little later such as Karl Popper and Alfred Sohn Rethel. It was interesting for him to discover that many of these men were thinking about the same social issues that were preoccupying him. It also seems that Macmurray played something of the role of mentor to Adorno for a short time, and some researchers have surmised that he influenced Adorno's thinking in significant ways.[4] In a conversation late in his life Macmurray apparently gave Popper credit for giving him a basic insight into the nature of Fascism.[5]

On May 27, 1935, John wrote to the Provost asking for leave from his duties at the College during the third term in 1936. If it were granted he would be free from the beginning of April until early October. He had received multiple invitations from the United States and Canada to offer lectures, conduct short summer sessions, and give occasional talks. As his letter noted he had already been able to make arrangements for the work of the department to be covered during the next summer term if he were able to be absent. On June 4 permission was granted and John and Betty began almost a year ahead to plan the trip that would take them away from Britain for almost three months and to North America for the first time. For John the year included preparing to present the Terry Lectures at Yale and the Deems Lectures at New York University, along with everything else he was doing. In addition he had to think about the outline for a ten-day summer school at Blue Ridges, North Carolina, and a week-long session at Albert College in Belleville, Ontario, with a group of socially oriented Canadian Christians with strong SCM connections.

Reason and emotion

Just a few weeks later he had the pleasure of holding in his hands the first copy of *Reason and Emotion*, a collection of essays on diverse topics but all somehow related to advancing and clarifying the idea of rationality in emotion that he had presented in his BBC Radio talks. The essays on education and ethics have already been mentioned. But the fresh material in the book included the opening three chapters on "Reason in the Emotional Life" in which he carefully expanded and explained his concept of emotional rationality. He felt his position was a creative breakthrough beyond the dualism of modern thinking that proposed intellect alone as capable of "objective" judgment while emotion was unrelievably subjective. The modern view offered no coherent theory of how thought and feeling could be integrated.

Macmurray's attempt at an integrating and comprehensive theory of reason was in some ways a return to the Greek appreciation for that which constituted the "distinctively human" in human beings. He asserted that "Whatever is a characteristic and essential expression of human nature must be an expression of reason."[6] Reason for him was the capacity to relate to the other, any other, *according to the other's own nature*. "Reason is thus our capacity for objectivity."[7] And that kind of 'objective' relating was possible, he had already concluded, not only in thinking but also in feeling and *primarily* in action — most fully in the interacting of persons with one another. Reason, on this model, is not first of all thinking truly. It is found first of all and most inclusively in acting well, with appropriate feeling and true thinking seen as necessary, constitutive and subordinate dimensions *within* good action.

The book was well received by some readers, especially young people. The chapters entitled "The Virtue of Chastity" and "The Personal Life" were honest, refreshing, hopeful and profound in their situating of human sexual relating within the context of friendship rather than patriarchally defined and controlled, gender roles. They expressed his conviction that the sexual life of human beings can be integrated consciously and deliberately into the *personal* life which is deeper, more inclusive and freer than merely organic or functional responses. Friendship, the positive form of the personal life, includes but goes beyond stimulus and response reactions of attraction or mere lust. Its centre, based in freedom and responsibility, is able to escape not the influence of, but control by, organic drives. It is also a form of relating that steadily diminishes the compulsion to engage in domination and submission games induced by fear and tradition.[8] It is within the terms of friendship alone that sexuality can become personal and, therefore, genuinely sincere and free.

It might be suggested that on this subject Macmurray was simply reflecting the post-war attitude to sexuality of the avant-garde in the early thirties. This hardly does justice to the meaning he gives to "sincerity" or "emotional truthfulness" as the grounding value in sexual relationships. It was far different from a mere licence for having serial lovers. His position, as he stated in letters to friends, made chastity harder to achieve not easier because he was proposing a passage beyond an intellectual control of feeling (Stoic morality) towards a freedom *in* feeling. If achieved, it allowed for chastity to be expressed as a spontaneity, not an imposed duty. For Macmurray, chastity seen as "emotional sincerity" was simply one more specific articulation of his conviction that human life could be fully realized only in friendship.

The chapters on science and religion in *Reason and Emotion* put science and religion back into one world. His position healed intellectual divisions and hostilities between science (hard-headed) and religion (soft-headed) that no longer made sense to many students. His identification of religious desire with *the human desire to become fully real* was fresh. His development of that view of religion to include giving oneself freely in friendship in an other-centred way, even at great cost to oneself, was not new but it fostered a new respect for religion in his young readers. And his proposal that this self-giving desire exercised a deep imperative on every person to strive for the creation of not only a "fuller self" but of a world community grounded in justice and love, this made religion concrete in a way that was compelling and for many — especially his youthful readers — convincing.

For great numbers of his students in London, Macmurray's book, and his teaching, drew the *intimate* and the *historical* aspects of life into coherence with one another. His book proposed a "seamless garment" ethic that brought all fields of human action together and overcame not the distinction of the public from the private, but their division. Inevitably, as Marjorie Reeves recalled from the packed lecture hall at University College, many students found in his philosophy a powerful invitation to help build a world community based on relationships of justice and friendship that he described. Many other people with no access to the university found *Reason and Emotion* had a similar effect on them.[9] The book remained a puzzle to some older reviewers who saw in it not intimations of a needed philosophical and social revolution but a collection of scriptural aphorisms mixed with an overly humanized view of religion along with a dreamy vision of community, and, more than anything, a dangerous permissiveness about relationships and sexuality, in particular, that avoided the kind of *realpolitik* and discipline over feelings needed for living in a broken and evil world.

Middleton Murry and the Adelphi

During the early to mid-thirties, Macmurray's lectures on education, political theory, society and religion were making him something of a wisdom figure for a wide selection of fellow explorers. One of those was John Middleton Murry. Macmurray's earlier mentioned contributions to the 1935 *Marxism* book had increased Middleton Murry's respect for him as a radical thinker, and Murry became anxious to bring Macmurray into the Adelphi Centre he was setting up. The Centre was to offer courses and programmes for people seeking a new society, and to publish its own journal also known as *The Adelphi*. Murry envisaged that the centre might become a commune under his leadership which could form the nucleus for a new society — only one of several taking shape in London at the time! It was with the hope of drawing Macmurray into his core group that Middleton Murry asked him, towards the end of 1935, to become one of the directors of the new venture. Middleton Murry had, or so he imagined, sweetened the pot for Macmurray by noting that the description for legal purposes that he was proposing as the objective of the "company" was:

> ... the education of adults and children in accordance with the
> philosophy, principle and methods set forth in the writings of John
> Middleton Murry and Professor John Macmurray.[10]

Macmurray was clearly a reluctant debutante, unwilling to be dragged out on to the floor to dance to music of Middleton Murry's choosing. His reluctance was justified. Murry was captured well when he was described as "the best-hated man of letters of his time" in Britain. Brilliant and assertive, he was also self-absorbed in a way that was at once innocent and perverse. In the course of preparing the book, Macmurray had already experienced Murry's self-serving and acerbic way of dealing with people as well as his emotional and intellectual volatility. At root, Macmurray's reluctance may have had more to do with what one of Murry's biographers described as his constant striving to make an effect and Macmurray's never needing to do so. Macmurray was not entranced by the prospect of having his name formally associated with the Adelphi Centre or his credibility tied too closely to Murry's often shifting and self-referential view of the world. For a variety of reasons, including possibly his resignation as President of the New Britain Group and the fairly recent demise of his own hopes for living in community, he wrote of his feelings to Irene Grant in the gentle language for which he was well-known: "I don't quite like it, and I feel like saying I won't join them at present."[11]

Nevertheless he did participate in some functions at the Centre. The most significant event of all was the month-long summer school that drew hundreds of people of all social and economic levels in society to listen, discuss and work together in August 1936. The summer school had been planned much earlier, but it was made more intense and pointed by the outbreak of the Spanish Civil War the month before, leading to the deeply-felt conviction on the Left that intervention on the part of Britain in defence of the legitimately elected Republican Government was required. Macmurray shared that position.

Middleton Murry attracted many prominent leftists with highly individual viewpoints to the sessions. The diversity of viewpoints can be imagined in the list of speakers who accepted his invitation: John Strachey, Karl Polanyi, Reinhold Niebuhr, George Orwell, John Hampden Jackson, Sam Higgenbottam and John Macmurray. As F.A. Lea, a biographer of Middleton Murry reports, even at this summer school Middleton Murry had managed to give the impression to some participants that he felt he was personally orchestrating history. In fact Lea saw Macmurray, not Middleton Murry, as "the dominant influence" at the summer school, even though Macmurray was there for only the second week, having arrived in England from New York at the very end of July.[12]

Macmurray was not the only colleague to have hesitations about Middleton Murry. Max Plowman, a long-standing friend and associate of Murry's, had written to Mrs Mary Marr, an associate, on February 29, 1932 concerning his doubts about working with Murry:

Something holds me up — even against my will. I feel that his
whole show is something that ought to be *included* in something
greater ... that what we *want* is a great *religious* movement & that
John is a man whose faith has failed so that he now is making a
pseudo-religious movement, really by way of compensation. I go
all the way with anyone who makes the spiritual basis *cardinal*
(like Macmurray).[13]

The reference to Macmurray was not incidental and it launches into front
stage centre the reawakening of the issue of pacifism for Macmurray as
well as many of his contemporaries. When Max Plowman — a pacifist
since he resigned from the British Army in 1918 — first met Macmurray
in 1932 he had high hopes for a close collaboration with him. By the early
1930s pacifism had effectively become Plowman's religion. Plowman,
essentially a poet and literary man with great affection for Blake, saw in
Macmurray an intellectual with a strongly religious foundation to his
socialist view of the world, and he knew pacifism needed an intellectual
articulation along with other channels for developing and communicating
its values to possible converts. He also knew that Macmurray could bridge
between Marxist ideas and what Plowman called "the intelligent bourgeoisie who are beginning to read the signs." As he wrote to Middleton
Murry two weeks earlier after hearing Macmurray give some talks, pre-
sumably the "Modern Dilemma" series John did in January and early
February on the BBC:

That's why I welcomed old Macmurray's talks. He was definitely
pioneering — harrowing the ground — preaching Communism
without using the word — undermining long-established prejudices
— enabling people to think fundamentally — getting into the
hearts & minds of people ideas which they would have scouted
[around] had he labelled them.[14]

Plowman was trying to get Murry to include Macmurray in his hopes and
plans. He gave Murry an interesting observation that helps to cast light on
Macmurray's association with the New Britain. It seems Plowman had
met Macmurray at a dinner prior to a speech John made to the New Britain
group on June 13, 1933, and from that encounter he wrote to Murry:

Don't be unduly prejudiced by his association with "New Britain."
He's not tied very tight there; as he told me of his own accord on
the way home (we travelled together to Belsize Park) but he wants
to give a leg-up to all sorts of new movements & this is merely
one, from which I think he expects to slip out quite soon ... I told

you he looked like Lawrence. He confessed to us last night that
Lawrence had meant more to him than anybody.[15]

One can wonder if this reference to Murry's recently departed friend D.H.
Lawrence was intended to influence him towards accepting Macmurray.
In fact, Macmurray at this time in his life *did* look a great deal like
Lawrence (see photo section). He had let his beard grow and it came out
thick and uniformly dark brown. It covered over the scar on the right side
of his face where his cheekbone had been broken by the shrapnel. The
wound had left his face with a slight twist to the right that was more
noticeable when he smiled, which he did often. He shaped his beard somewhat in the same style as Lawrence's had been. In profile from the left, he
could be taken for Lawrence, except that John's nose had a straighter and
more noble line. But face on, the refinement of Macmurray's features
made him clearly the more handsome of the two. And Macmurray, slightly
above medium height, cut a finer figure than Lawrence did.

Having praised Macmurray to Middleton Murry, it was, in fact,
Plowman who soon changed his views. As things worked out, his affirmation of Macmurray's message and method became seriously qualified
over the coming year. When *Interpreting the Universe* came out in 1933,
he was saddened — and perhaps with good reason — at Macmurray's
treatment of thinking as ratiocination alone. Plowman, who was a devotee
of Blake, felt Macmurray had left no room for thinking as imagination. He
complains to Middleton Murry that Macmurray's position involves:

> ... the divorce of thought from emotion which poetry shows to be
> impossible ... Imagination, as I see it, is dynamic disinterestedness.
> I think Macmurray confuses it (as Lawrence confused it) with
> spontaneity. Spontaneity is childish: imagination is adult; & I don't
> believe we shall understand the philosophy of imagination without
> a proper psychological understanding of the periods of growth.[16]

This is an interesting observation since it suggests that Macmurray is overlooking the connection between thought and emotion, a connection
Macmurray believes is at the heart of his intellectual purposes. In must be
said that Plowman does accurately represent Macmurray's views in the
second chapter of *Interpreting the Universe* where he is using science
alone as his implicit model for analysing knowing. It isn't wide enough a
view of thinking and Plowman notes that fact with alarm. However
Plowman goes even farther. He relates this kind of reduced version of
thinking to the reason for Marx's conclusions about "inevitability" in history and fears Macmurray is falling too far into Marx's embrace. It is quite
a leap for Plowman to make.

By October, he is convinced of it. *The Adelphi* is about to print a whole chapter of Macmurray's *Philosophy of Communism* in its December issue. It is a book that Plowman feels, as good as it is, has lost "the one thing needful." He tells a friend:

> Marx is to politics what Darwin is to religion — the acid solvent.
> Well, we can't live on acid solvents & the world is very hungry.
> That's all there is to be said about it. But I'm sorry Macmurray has
> been lured down that road. I suspected it from his last book & here
> it is. Well, it's a *cul de sac*. That's what J.M.M. has really
> discovered. Now Macmurray has got to do the same. He will. Bet
> cher a bob![*sic*]. [17]

It seems Plowman believed he had won his bet with himself and was given occasion to feel vindicated. On December 1,1935 — the very week John was writing to Irene Grant about not becoming associated with *The Adelphi* — Plowman wrote to his friend Jack Common on the issue of the sacredness of the individual *now*, not in some future social condition. To defend his case he quotes Macmurray who states that all rational investigation and planning "is without meaning unless it is the means to one end — the living of the personal life of community in joy & freedom. To sacrifice life to its own conditions is the ultimate insincerity & the real denial of God."[18] But the acceptance of Macmurray back into Plowman's fold was not to last. Hardly a month later Plowman was complaining to Geoffrey West about Middleton Murry's tendency to see the Centre as a place to gather together on the basis of weakness, trusting only in the power of conversation. He observes about Murry: he wants to change everything! Plowman says he feels something similar about Macmurray:

> I [have] come to mistrust the whole bag of social reformists &
> revolutionaries. They want to change everything, & will end up
> changing nothing ... now I feel we want action at a definite point,
> & that's what the war-issue gives us. It's a case of the things
> hidden from the wise & prudent being revealed to babes I believe.[19]

The pacifist debate

The firmest nail in the coffin of Macmurray's credibility for Plowman came when, in early May 1937, John refused the invitation from Plowman to become a member of the Peace Pledge Union (PPU) which would have meant rejecting both rearmament by Britain and war itself. It has been impossible to find a copy of Macmurray's first letter responding to Plowman's invitation; we have only the parts Plowman quoted back to him. In this letter to Plowman Macmurray, referring to the impending conflict in Europe, apparently spoke of it as an event that would "break up the superficial restraints & reveal a demoralization that was there all the time. In so doing, it forces the world to face the facts about itself."

Although he does not say it in so many words, Plowman clearly finds Macmurray's above-it-all attitude very strange and his analysis of what all-out war would mean trivial to the point of being scandalous. In a May 4 letter he irately challenges Macmurray for those remarks: "What I cannot really understand is how you manage to achieve so detached a view of something so personally affecting." He acknowledges the complexities involved in making a choice for pacifism then throws back at Macmurray: "But surely in any conscious person there is a point of resistance to the existing order at which he finds himself unable to cooperate in it. That point, I now suggest, is to be found in active participation in war." He accuses Macmurray of looking at the impending war on the model of a medieval therapeutic "bloodletting," apparently healthy for the sake of a state of future equanimity in the life of Europe and the world.

Plowman's final defence of pacifism in the letter — and he had recently published a small book on the subject — is a telling one. It is made in the face of the horrors of *modern* warfare, already revealed in the "wholesale massacre for the purpose of terrorism" going on in Spain. It is on the basis of the unavoidably *indiscriminate* destruction required of *all* participants in modern warfare that Plowman rests his case for pacifism at this time in history. Macmurray's return letter was immediate:

I doubt if it possible to explain to you why I feel as I do about this business. It *is* a matter of conscience. What I feel is that you are really allowing your feeling of loathing for war to overwhelm your conscience. I think that the real bitterness of the situation is that our consciences are divided. I feel passionately against war. I also feel as passionately the duty of defending the victims of war. If I engage in war I am involved in doing things that are horrible to think of. If I refrain from taking up arms in defence of people who are wantonly attacked and destroyed by the war makers I do something which is just as horrible, and I am not sure that it isn't more demoralizing.

All this talk of war-resistance is dodging the issue. I want to create the conditions in which there will be no war to resist. It's no use your saying that you would have to accept a contradictory view of me if I took up arms to fight. Of course you would. We are living in a contradictory world. All of us are in contradiction with

ourselves, and only a contradictory view of any of us can be a true
one. Of course it seems to me criminal to commit murder. But it
also seems as criminal to stand by and see murder committed. To
see injustice done without interfering to prevent it or to stop it is
profoundly immoral. If this is a contradiction it's a contradiction in
the world, not in you or me, and your don't get rid of it by
suppressing half of your conscience.

Macmurray goes on to identify precisely what he means by the new con-
tradictoriness in the world that needs to be exposed and ended, with huge
risks impending if it isn't:

What has happened is that the world has changed and war in the
traditional sense doesn't exist any more. The fact that war is no longer
declared or recognized is not merely a dodge. It is a symbol of the
truth. Germany and Italy are not at war with Spain. Italy was never at
war with Abyssinia, nor Japan with China. But German aeroplanes
have just wiped out Guernica. That has got to be stopped. And one of
the things that is preventing it being stopped is just what you people
humorously call war-resistance. That's what I feel passionately in my
conscience. To talk about the Basque boys that I met as being guilty
of making war is criminal in its absurdity. They *are* the real war-
resisters. And if they win, Europe will be a long step nearer the end of
war. If they lose because we refused to help them, because we are
determined not to be involved, then we shall be guilty of having made
a vastly greater war inevitable.

The historical prophecy at the end of that statement needs no commentary.
Macmurray is writing Plowman with the passion that is fresh in him from
a fact-finding trip to Spain just a few weeks before this exchange (a fuller
account is given in Chapter 13). His reference to the Basques was immediate and personal; he had met them. He ends his letter by recalling a point
he apparently made in his first letter to Plowman:

That was why I told you that I would refuse to acknowledge the
right of a Government to involve me in war. The new situation is
that I will fight for justice against aggression, for freedom against
tyranny, without any regard to nationality or patriotism. From the
point of view of my conscience what has become of no importance
is the side that the Government of my own country takes. You are
still thinking of how to stop war between Governments. That
question is a thing of the past. Look at Spain and you will see that.
It's worth remembering that at this moment the British government

is waging war on an independent community in Waziristan. But that isn't war either. Or is it?

What makes Macmurray's position notable here is his unambiguous rejection of national loyalties or citizenship as the basis for making moral judgments about the issue over which he and Plowman are contending. In fact, many young people from Britain, the United States, Canada and other western countries had already assumed all the elements of Macmurray's argument and acted on them when they joined the Republican forces against the Falangists in Spain.

Soon after this exchange Plowman began using the term war-renunciation rather than war-resistance to describe his objective, and we can only wonder if Macmurray's letter had anything to do with that change. In fact the letter was vintage Macmurray. His charge that the *roots* of war were not being addressed by the pacifists any more than by the aggressors was not perversity on his part. Genuine pacifism, in Macmurray's view, had to relate to *all* abuse of power — of which war is only the most clear and dramatic instance.

For some years, starting with the First World War, Macmurray had condemned *everything* in society that creates injustice and therefore undermines the grounds for true peace. The ethics of "duty," church legalism, nationalism, capitalism, structural unemployment, the inequality of the sexes, state oppression — supported by group and role-loyalties, myths and lies — all these are abuses of power that diminish persons and their societies terribly, even though they are most often exercised without the support of bullets. All of them, he had concluded, undermine peace, and he was certainly not alone in making this distinction.[20] His position was hardly "detached," as Plowman charged. It was very committed, but at a level different from the more concentrated, perhaps more fundamentalist, focus taken by the Peace Pledge Union in 1937.

What would it take to end war?

Plowman's letter clearly brought Macmurray back to the edge of an issue he had recently worked through, at least conceptually, with Polanyi at the end of 1935. That struggle and its resolution for him and Polanyi may explain why he was so ready to offer Plowman an answer on the very same day Plowman's second letter arrived. In 1935 Macmurray and Polanyi had been discussing how Christians decided where and when they could no longer cooperate with their own government. At that time, Polanyi had noted that a Christian's cooperation with a State *at anytime* must be based on a determination that the *end* that the State was serving was just and good. Polanyi's position in a nutshell went like this:

> We could cooperate with a government or society which had
> accepted the task of creating a universal society on a basis of
> common humanity as its job, and on that basis we could
> compromise on the means and the speed with which it was to be
> carried out. What we must not do is to cooperate in terms of any
> other conception of the end.[21]

On that basis, one might wonder if a Christian could cooperate with any government that has ever existed! But the issues surrounding war and pacifism had been discussed by Macmurray and Polanyi in a context that was both wider and more pointed than the one Macmurray felt was being embraced by the PPU, consequently they raised points overlooked in Plowman's more immediate focus. In a paper called "The Meaning of Peace" Polanyi had traced out further elements of the position reflected in Macmurray's two letters to Plowman, and it went as follows: To insist on a peaceful world "now" is simply to assume that we could carry on today without the institution of war. If we can carry on without war as an instrument to solve problems, then it must be abolished at all costs and no other task can claim priority over this one. Polanyi called this the "postulate of peace," and its validity depends on the truth of the premise: that we are ready to live without war. Clearly the urgent need for a final resolution in a conflict must be recognized. But, he asks, how can this be achieved practically and effectively at this time in history? Can we say that the function served by war is able to be served by another judicial and another political method — either now in place, or able to be put in place, to which nations are willing to give their allegiance? This is the only condition on which we can hope to have war become obsolete.

Polanyi proposes that pacifist policy is based on the erroneous belief that war is just an outlet for feelings and psychological needs, that it has no vital functions of a more external nature in the past (e.g., territorial disputes) and that it can, therefore, be simply abolished once enough people recognized its horrors. He calls this attitude a "fateful illusion." He holds for the credibility of viewing war as occasioned by more objectively based conflicts. If this is so then objectively based, agreed-upon structures of conflict-resolution are the only way empirically to achieve genuine reconciliation. Without such structures firmly in place he concluded that the need for armed conflict had not yet passed away. The pacifists, he says, avoid the historical, empirical elements of this analysis and jump to their conclusion because war causes suffering and destruction, and they are understandably repelled and revolted by it. But subjective horror is not enough; objective structures to achieve justice are the only adequate method for ensuring true peace. Polanyi then proposes the concrete conditions needed:

> If war is to be abolished, international order must take its place.
> But no international order is conceivable without a new
> international economic order to replace that which is passing away.

This will not be simple to attain due to the entrenched interests that keep nations from achieving the political conditions for it to happen. Thus, our world economic structures are based on and foster relationships that breed conflict while refusing the construction of peaceful and just means to resolve them. The peaceful alternatives to war, he suggests, are not yet in place

> The setting up of an international peace order cannot, therefore, be brought to fruition by a simple refusal to fight, but only by the actual achievement of the institutional basis of such an order. The first step towards the achievement of this end lies in the transformation of our capitalist nation-states into actual communities by bringing economic life under the control of the common people and abolishing thereby the property cleavage in society.

The final section of the paper on the reform of consciousness needed for such a transformation may have been written by Macmurray. It characterizes the ethics of the New Testament as both pacifist and communist. This implied a rejection by the early Church of society as a set of permanent institutions. Human consciousness itself was transformed in the Gospels "by the discovery of the personal nature of human life and the essential freedom of personality ... Neither institutions nor customs, nor laws, but community as a relationship of persons was the substance of social existence."

The conclusion of the case is clear and forceful: Although pacifism must always be active as a leaven in society struggling anarchically against the control of persons by institutions and their endemic violence, it is not yet able to become the spirit determining policy in our society. Why is that? Not because of wars, first of all, but because of the cause of wars — the fact that our societies are still in thrall to the myth of "the inescapable nature of institutional society." If and when social institutions serve persons and communities and refuse to dominate them, and if this behaviour is protected by legislation and court structures put in place by consent, then there is a basis for making pacifism not only a moral stand but a legal requirement. Until such time, it must be allowed that persons, having done all they could to achieve justice and resist injustice, might choose the final resistance of violence — direct, personal, discriminate, and of human proportions — in order to preserve life, and even, in the great mystery of things, to preserve those institutions that are most needed and helpful for achieving the eventual elimination of war from social relationships.[22] In Spain, that would have translated into a need to preserve the democratically constituted Republic and its elected government.

There is a critical point made in Plowman's letter that deserves attention and it is not addressed in Polanyi's paper nor, apparently, by Macmurray in either of his two letters. Plowman was clearly making the case that this conceptual framework fell apart under the conditions of modern, technological war-making. *Necessarily* indiscriminate killing of innocent people — resulting, for example, from the shelling or aerial bombing of towns — rendered modern war unjust and immoral. The result of this new situation, he was claiming to Macmurray, was that a stand needed to be taken for pacifism now and into any foreseeable future as long as sophisticated technology continued to define a society's life. After World War I — and especially after the bombing of cities and civilians in Spain in 1937 — there was no longer any way modern warfare could be morally justifiable. Despite Macmurray's trenchant case for resistance to injustice and oppression in his May 5 letter he avoided this question entirely, and Plowman, on this particular point, surely felt unanswered.

Plowman closed the book on Macmurray a year later in 1938 when Macmurray's *The Clue to History* was finally published to wide acclaim in some socialist circles. Stafford Cripps, a strong socialist who was to become Lord Privy Seal during the war, was so taken with it he gave a copy to the Queen Mother. *The Adelphi* ran a symposium on it featuring several reviews of the book, the best of which, Plowman admitted, was Maud Petre's, which looked favourably on it. He confessed to her his own view that:

> It works out into a failed attempt to short-circuit what I understand
> as real Christianity. It makes it both theoretic and historic, & the
> longer I live the more I become convinced that Christianity needs
> to be continually redeemed from religious history; that the
> backward-looking eye is the bane — indeed the grave — of true
> religion.[23]

Macmurray, of course, couldn't have agreed more, and once again Plowman could be charged with reading too little of Macmurray and of missing the power for the present and the future imbedded in Macmurray's appeal to the Hebrew roots of Christianity. But there seems to have been no way of saving Macmurray from the flames. A month later, Plowman says essentially the same thing, only more simply and trenchantly, in a letter to an author-friend and associate at the Adelphi Centre:

> I didn't like John Macmurray's book as you may have gathered. He is altogether too knowing for me & I mistrust the university philosopher as "activist." I prefer the order of being first & doing second.[24]

So, the heart of the matter for Plowman was Macmurray's lack of concreteness while sounding omniscient, his focus in religion on past history rather than current facts and needs, and his apparent tendency to be an intellectual "activist" rather than a person who is able simply to "be." All three charges actually come close to the bone in their judgment of Macmurray but this is not the place to deal with them. In the end, both men seem somehow to have missed each other's essential point. Macmurray seems to have missed Plowman's urgent and insightful appeal about waking up to the meaning of *modern* war-making. Plowman seems to have missed the spiritual heart and vision imbuing Macmurray's intellectual work, in general, and the reasons for his very concrete resistance to pacifist war-resistance, in particular.

Part of the sadness in this "missed" relationship was that it was such a near-miss — discounting, of course that element of personal "chemistry" required for any vibrant friendship to come alive. Plowman went on to spend the next two years, the last years of his life, editing *The Adelphi* and helping to run a farm called The Oaks, at Langham, near Colchester in Essex, which was an extension of the Adelphi Centre. The farm was to be the Centre's educational and community base, its farming experiment, and its Community Land Training Association — with all three projects aimed at preparing younger pacifists for life on the land, free of enslavement to the city and, as far as possible, from industrial technology. One irony in the organization is that despite Macmurray's lack of active partnership in it, the defining Articles of the Association still made reference to his writings "and those that might yet come from his pen," along with the writings of Middleton Murry, as the basis for the educational activities.[25] A second irony is that the Colchester community was precisely the kind of experiment Macmurray warmly supported in the Grith Fyrd project. There is no sign that Plowman ever knew how much Macmurray had hoped to live in community, though Macmurray's community would likely have been closer to the city where his work lay. Nor did Plowman know how much Macmurray shared his deep critique of the alienating pressures of modern society or of John's concrete and humble methods for attempting to escape their sway in his gardening, camping, bird-watching and piano-playing.

Both of these men were raised in the Plymouth Brethren tradition. Both threw it over in their early twenties but remained adamantly "religious" and Christian apart from the churches in a similar manner. Both joined the Royal Army Medical Corps in 1914, and both gave that up in 1916 for a commission in an active regiment. Both of them in 1918 swore themselves to a life-work for peace — each in his own way — and both were seeking community that was at once intimate and yet open in intention to the entire human family.

One is tempted to think that if Plowman and Macmurray couldn't have got together, who from that crowd of clever, insightful and yearning individuals claiming to point the way to the future could have done so? We can look back on Middleton Murry, Mitrinovic, Joad, Plowman and Macmurray, and many others in London alone, striving in the1930s for some creative and alternative way of conceiving of human society and of living it — and come to the conclusion that good opportunities were missed at least partly because of the huge independence of spirit and style of each of them. The gifts of independence and solitary initiative required in the prophetic initiator prove not to be the ones most needed for community-building. In fact, they often prove to be problematic after the communal initiative gets launched.

Perhaps we should not try to make too much of Macmurray and Plowman not coming to agreement. The simple facts of living determined much of Macmurray's and Plowman's course. There was, in fact, little natural occasion for these two men to meet. Macmurray "refused" Plowman on the Peace Pledge invitation for his own good reasons, and the way that was expressed — perhaps even more than John's actual reasons — cut Plowman to the quick. Those letters, more than any of his formal writings, had changed John's status for Plowman from ally to one who was part of the problem. Finally, Plowman was fast to make judgments, and it seems that he felt he understood Macmurray far more than he actually did.

Plowman's letter to Macmurray raised some excellent issues. His final characterization of John as a university idealist playing activist games probably said as much about Plowman's own hurt feelings (perhaps including his never having been able to attend a university) as it did about Macmurray. But it could also be a blow that came close to the mark. For example, Macmurray was extremely positive about the Jews in his writings and at this very time was helping Jewish refugee scholars get to England and find a home there. In November, 1937 he wrote a stunning letter to Rev Eric Fenn (see p.273) in which he condemned the Nazi anti-Jewish laws. Yet he seems not to have publicly addressed the plight of the Jews in hopes of galvanizing public response. Since a judgment of indifference on his part in this matter is absurd, one is moved to ask: Was action of that "activist" sort not the direction in which he saw his life directed? It certainly seemed not to be his choice. More personally, by the end of the 1930s he was clearly facing the demise of his hopes for a new kind of society even while he saw looming on the horizon the threat of an end to society even as they knew it. Both forces had their influence on him. He was being drawn, more than he had been in some years, to begin writing his philosophy of the personal. This was his life work, the thing he was meant to do "for the world." And was it not his to do in the world as it stood at the time? — just as some Jewish artists themselves, as an act of integrity and fidelity, made beautiful art on the edge of the abyss and just as Etty Hillesum wrote paeans of gratitude for the beauty of life even as she was forcibly brought to Auschwitz and to her end. These are questions that arise and hover over this period of Macmurray's life as a result of Plowman's criticisms. They are beyond judgment, perhaps, but not beyond wonder.

The Polanyi paper which reflects so much of John's own thought and language, shows where John's concerns did lie: the setting up of a democratic, international order to deal with the many issues that could never be solved by nation-states or economic corporations. But more to the point in the late Thirties, the evil he saw at the heart of Fascism made him convinced that it must not win out. This was a religious stand on his part based on the view he shared with Polanyi that Fascist ideology and practice, in its Nazi form, was radically anti-personal. On that profound basis — one which included the other horrors implicitly within it — he was clearly convinced of the need for armed resistance to Fascism.

In 1959, John Macmurray joined the Quakers and at that time declared himself "for the sake of conscience" a pacifist. However he did not on that account deny his own past convictions or reject the right and obligation of others who, equally in conscience, felt morally compelled to resist violent aggression by fighting it.[26] At the age of eighty, Macmurray confirms that had he been young enough in the Second World War he would have fought to resist Hitler and all he stood for. [27]

Macmurray comes closest to Plowman in his final recorded statement on the matter of pacifism. In a March 19, 1972 letter to Reg Sayers in Canada he acknowledges "the main point is that I am now a fully convinced pacifist." The reasons for that transformation apparently had little directly to do with events during or after the Second World War. Nuclear weapons and the Holocaust, for example, are not mentioned by him in that context. His change was occasioned by two things: a need to correct his early acceptance of Marx's dialectical view of history, and his continuing study of the life and methods of Jesus. Concerning his 1933 and 1934 views of Marx's dialectical materialism, he wrote almost forty years later:

> I should say now that the error I detected in my first study of Marx has become now much more important. I thought then that in spite of the flaw it might still prove correct in its prophecy of the coming collapse of capitalism; and I still say it might, but with a good deal less conviction. It was correct for Russia (with some failures) but

now it has definitely failed in Russia, to the extent that is obvious to everyone outside Russia, even to the Chinese. There are still some in Russia who realize the failure, though they are mostly in jail or on the way there. The great change in my attitude is that this development of dialectical materialism in Russia *and* in China has shown clearly that a violent revolution produces a violent society. Now that I am writing about "The Philosophy of Jesus,"... I am wholly convinced that he was right in refusing to use military power to achieve the social change that he sought. He did so on the recognition that if he defeated the Roman armies (as the Maccabees nearly did a century earlier) he would only have set up another Roman Empire under a new name. The alternative, which he thought out thoroughly, was to transform the Empire from within, by the Hebrew understanding of what makes a "lasting human society" — the phrase is Marx's.[28]

The letter is important for many reasons. It reveals Macmurray openly acknowledging errors in his earlier thinking, not something he did with great regularity. More pointedly, it shows him implicitly confessing to a naiveté and perhaps a certain wilful blindness with regard to the evils of the despotic regime in the Soviet Union over the years: in its genocidal policies towards the Ukrainians in the early to mid-1930s, in the show trials, in the regular purges, executions and repressions, and even in the treatment of religious believers at the very time he was studying and reporting so benignly on that dimension of life in the Soviet Union — none of which he attended to adequately or allowed to challenge or change his support for the Soviet Union as a brave "social experiment." Finally, the letter presents the grounds for his own pacifism.

Plowman died in 1940, just three years after his exchange with Macmurray over pacifism. Years later, Macmurray came to share Plowman's stand, but on the basis of a different insight from Plowman's: that war *creates* war-making people and war-making societies; the cycle inevitably continues. It must be broken.

In the end, it is the essentially relational aspect of personal existence and communal living — his own deepest philosophical insight about personhood — that shapes Macmurray's conclusion about pacifism, not the high-tech nature of the weapons, the anonymity in their functioning, or the indiscriminate destruction they cause. It is a response more than a solution. Although it is profound from a moral perspective, it may not be completely satisfying. Had Plowman stood at "the top of the mountain" waiting to greet Macmurray some thirty-five years later, he would undoubtedly have rejoiced at John's arrival, but he would have noticed that Macmurray got there by a different path.

Chapter 13

The Christian Left, Spain and America (1935–40)

In his September 14, 1933 letter to Irene Grant (see p.216f), John had gone at length into what he meant by emotional rationality and how human sexuality is a primary field where emotional rationality is needed. The advantage he foresaw was that living would be far more a living "in, with and through desire" rather than a repressed working against desire. The latter view — a suspicious, oppositional attitude to feeling which dominated in the west — fostered a negative ethic that arises inevitably when mind is seen as "higher" and desire as "lower," the former as good and the latter as not so good — or not good at all, as the Stoics asserted. John went so far as to suggest this "living in, with and through desire" that he found so hard to describe in words applied at all levels of life not just to sexuality or other physical and emotional hungers. In fact, he concludes this reflection with Irene by turning his intuition towards questions of politics and community, and he muses with her:

Perhaps this is why we have to cease to attack Fascism directly. 'Forgive them, for they know not what they do' is probably the right attitude (I don't mean morally right but psychologically right) though I admit I find it hard to feel like that. Being afraid of it will precipitate it. There is only one thing to be done, and that is to concentrate on the creation of emotional rationality, on bringing to birth in ourselves and others a new form of human consciousness which will make communism possible. We have somehow to create community as a human experience. Then we will be communists. But all the so-called communists I've met are mechanized individuals — gramophones playing one record, and that one old and scratched.

He ended the letter sharing a meditative, even vulnerable, feeling:

I've talked enough! These things are not discovered or created by talking. But talking is a relief sometimes. Personally, I feel so tired with my own struggle that I find myself wondering at times whether I haven't done my share of pioneering, and haven't earned the right to throw it on other shoulders now, and take a rest; work out the philosophy of it quietly and without haste. But I don't suppose I shall be able to do that. The point I've reached is not a resting-place: it's more like a beginning.[1]

The vision of the Christian Left

In fact it *was* more like a beginning, as the previous two chapters show. But it was also a kind of beginning in terms of his relationship with Irene Grant as she — against John's sage advice to go slowly — plunged into a new life in London connected with the Auxiliary Movement (the "Aux") of the Student Christian Movement (SCM). The Aux was the section of the SCM made up of its alumni, people who were no longer students but wished, in their adulthood, for the same Christian challenges and community that characterized their lives when they were in university.

Throughout 1934–35, Donald and Irene Grant became significant players in the SCM Auxiliary in London. At the same time, Donald began his new career as a journeying commentator on international affairs. This work frequently took him to the United States where he would lecture for two or three months at a time before returning home. Left in London with the children, Irene gave free rein to her political interests, concentrating mainly on cultivating the growing, small group of Auxiliary members who were becoming more convinced with each passing day that their Christianity demanded political action for the healing of society. Specifically, they concluded that it required them to support two political goals: a socialist economic order based in the working class and functioning according to democratic principles; and a full resistance to Fascism — which had capitalism as its economic engine. The religious vision underlying and guiding this political thrust was to transform society in the direction of becoming a fully democratic community for all.

Their conviction that the Judeo-Christian notion of the Kingdom of God necessarily had a political dimension to it did not sit easily with some leaders and members of the Aux. Nevertheless, at the March 7–8, 1936, meeting of the General Committee, the socially oriented members received formal approval to continue their political explorations within the Auxiliary. The new group, with John Macmurray and Karl Polanyi as their court philosophers, provisionally called themselves the Auxiliary Christian Left.

The members of the Christian Left (CL) were mainly young people from London, with a few coming from Oxford, and even Manchester and Leeds, as was the case for Kenneth Muir and his wife Mary. The transition from being ten to twenty people having occasional meetings at the Grants' home at 25 Pyecombe Corner to gaining a group identity had happened in the summer of 1935 when, with Donald Grant's leadership, they held a

week-long conference that they called a Q Camp; "Q" because it would be
a place where all questions could be raised. It took place at a lovely spot
called Sandy Balls in the New Forest, Hampshire. John Macmurray, with
his Grith Fyrd connections and his long familiarity with the New Forest
hiking trails, undoubtedly had a hand in lining up the venue.

The Q Camp was a live-in experience. Everyone, under the direction of
David Cass-Beggs, participated in the work and the fun and each one was
free to speak at the meetings which were led in the most informal manner
by Donald Grant. In addition to the urgent historical realities that filled
their agenda, the gathering was consciously structured on the acceptance
of a primary place for nature in human community — so campfires, hiking and singing featured strongly, along with the self-consciously liberating act of swimming together in the nude.

John Macmurray and Karl Polanyi were there for the week. The guiding philosophy for the event, as an exercise *in* community and as an education *for* community, was Macmurray's. It rested on the conviction that
the way to a positive future required the development of an integrated personality within the individual and an integration of economic and political
activities as dimensions within full personal relationships in community.
And this view of community was inclusive; it pointed to society, to a
world community of equals, the opposite of the Aryan domination proposed by the Nazis. The wholeness of the vision, united with immediate
practice, captivated the participants. Many, like Barbara Cass-Beggs, a
founding member of the Christian Left, felt they had for the first time
come to know what their Christianity, grounded in the mystery of the
Incarnation, meant concretely and why it must be communal and socialist
in its expression if it was to take flesh in the world.[2]

Macmurray's most significant contribution to the Christian Left, from
its beginnings in 1935 to its quiet ending in 1941, was his effort to draw it
to a primarily *religious* rather than political or economic standpoint in
defining its identity and work for society. What Macmurray meant by that
was explored frequently — by him and others — in the pages of the *News
Sheet of the Auxiliary Christian Left* which was born in July 1936. In a
January 18, 1936 exploratory meeting, he had been asked to lay out his
view of the Christian Left's essential purpose. He began historically, by
noting that thus far both the Left and the traditionalists in the Aux think of
politics and religion separately. For the Right, politics was completely distinct from religion. For the Left, it was more of a layer-cake: a Christian
basis is located, then the correct political implication is drawn, and a politically defined action is planned; from that point on, the win/lose, competitive methods and motives of politics, not the integrating and reconciling
methods and motives of the Gospel, held sway as they pursued their goals.
In that sense, both the Right and the Left were dualist and fragmentary.

Contrary to both these views, Macmurray proposed that there is *one* problem in Europe they had to face, and it is a religious problem. It has political and economic dimensions, of course, but these are dimensions within a larger cultural issue. What is needed, he stated, is a *religious* revolution in attitude and relationship, and this personal transformation — in individuals and groups — must inevitably include the political and economic elements of the full transformation they envisaged. What he meant by that puzzling statement came clearer when they grasped that Macmurray was proposing firmly what they already believed vaguely themselves, that religion is not first of all about doctrines, creeds and rituals. As a deep and universal human expression, *religion is about community*. Religion is the expression of the radical human need and desire for full fellowship. In its fullest form it is the celebration of the community already given, and achieved. The religious was the personal, and vice versa.

From this perspective, the *one* problem that required a cure was the failure of the nations of Europe to live communally, or even to want to do so. To do so would have meant living in a way that enhances the freedom and equality of each one and an openness to having all others share in this relating. Forming community in this sense of the term is the truest and most inclusive objective of human nature. Politics and economics are dimensions within the fundamental issue of life in community and that issue is: how can we be released from fear in order to cultivate mutual trust so that our relationships can be more free, and therefore, more real, more just and more loving? As Macmurray proposed: to live all aspects of our personal relationships with one another in mutual trust, justice and affection is what it means for religion to take flesh and be real. He urged the members of the Christian Left to take this essentially religious perspective in their advocacy of socialism, in their resistance to Fascism, and in creating the forms of their own community with one another.

This theory, imbuing the practice of the Q Camp, proved convincing. When the members came to articulate their position as Christian socialists for their fellow Aux members, Macmurray's ideas clearly dominate in the CL's first formulation of their view of the world and themselves — a document called "The Christian Task":

> There are no problems of human life which are not religious
> problems, which are not problems of the relationship of persons
> and therefore of their relation to God. We believe, as Christians,
> that the way we behave in our relations to one another is the focus
> of all the problems of our common humanity. The particular
> questions of our political and economic life are also in every case
> problems of the relationships of persons to one another.[3]

Both Macmurray and Polanyi played central roles in the CL's self-education. The weekend meetings at the Grants' house were times when Macmurray or Polanyi — or Kenneth Ingram who had joined the group and quickly became a popularizer of Macmurray's ideas — might be present to give further developments in their analysis of Christianity or world affairs. Polanyi provided the backbone of this social analysis, and he was there more often than John. But as both Kenneth Muir and William Gibson, a Canadian studying at Oxford, remember, Macmurray was most impressive as a voice of quiet reason in the midst of a society bloated with rhetoric and ranting. He was convincing and persuasive because his analysis seemed sound, he was not argumentative, and he respected each member's freedom. Both men found Macmurray one of the most brilliant, committed, and yet unpretentious intellectuals they ever met.[4] Besides, Muir added, "Macmurray's heresies confirmed my own!"

This religious orientation Macmurray proposed for the CL had to be regularly reiterated, and its spiritual meaning explored. In a short essay in the CL's *News Sheet* in 1937, called "A Provisional Basis for the Christian Left," Macmurray restated his position: *The nature of our motives, convictions, methods of advocacy and forms of community must be primarily religious, not primarily political.* This attitude, he said, was their only guarantee of freedom in even the most mundane of their actions — including their methods of challenging or resisting persons or groups. It wasn't an issue of being denominational. It was a concern to be foundational. The emphasis was needed. In the mid to late 1930s exclusively political and economic analysis was standard fare. For the communists, the resistance to Fascism was seen politically: Fascism must not be allowed to derail their basic mission to overthrow capitalism. The same was true of groups of the centre and the right — their own political purposes were their primary interest.

Macmurray's viewpoint was strange territory, and it is not certain that, with the social atmosphere so polluted with the ideology of absolutely needing to pull the world in one direction or another, all of the CL members were able to understand it. He had to work on the "spirituality" as well as the concept of his foundational approach. We are not required to focus on success, he told them, we are only required to be faithful in doing the right thing. Many of them really didn't understand the implications of him saying that it was God's world and God was faithful — and powerful. That was fine for evangelical fundamentalists, some must have felt, but was this the Macmurray who wanted a "communist" society to be the result of all these efforts? The righteous outrage expressed by some CL members to political and economic evils moved him to remind them that: "It is the will of God that things should sometimes not happen according to the will of God."[5] That was hard to grasp and harder to accept, given the liberal values of progress, rationalism and functional achievements embedded in their psyches. But many did see what he meant when he spoke of a free and specifically Christian *attitude* in social struggles.

Irene Grant needed the regular reminder as much as any of them. She was a feisty person whose instincts in public engagements were basically political. She was mainly responsible for any confrontational tone taken by the CL with Zoe Fairfield and the other "unconverted" traditionalists on the Auxiliary's General Committee. Although she may not have said it outright in the Aux meetings, Irene wanted the General Committee to affirm the CL position and make it official Auxiliary policy. Macmurray spent much time showing her how this was a suppression of the Committee members' freedom to hold their own views.

He, as much as Irene Grant, was a proponent of the need to transform society. Few were more forceful or clear about the nature and evil of Fascism or more encouraging about finding ways to achieve what he called "a *genuine* communist way of life." But he never seemed to lose sight of the kind of transformation that was required; the kind that leads to free, equal and mutual relations among persons rather than simply creating new forms of political or economic organization that left basic injustices in place. His was an interpretation of what it means to be "radical" for which there was only occasional recognition and meagre gratitude. Among his professional colleagues and occasional associates on the Left such as Professor Haldane, Harold Laski, John Middleton Murry, John Strachey and others, Macmurray's reluctance to embrace Marxism unreservedly on the grounds of his critique of its foundations were sometimes seen as outdated and pedantic, though he always commanded their respect. On the other hand, some administrators at the BBC, Max Plowman of the Peace Pledge Union — as we have seen — and some of his Anglican associates found his sympathy for Marx and for an eventual synthesis of the best of communism and Christianity, altogether too sanguine and uncritical, even rash and dangerous.

John's relationship with Irene was complex because in addition to being a philosophical guide for her CL enterprise he had a close and affectionate relationship with her and her husband Donald. His affection for her, for a short period of time, seems to have become physically intimate. In mid-March, when the CL was finally accepted as a group within the Auxiliary, John and Betty were making preparations to leave for their four months in the U.S. and Canada, and for him that required a lot of time on the many lectures he would be delivering in America. He was totally exhausted and felt himself pulled in various directions — and this included pulled by his feelings about not seeing Irene for so long. After one particularly consoling evening with her he wrote:

> Bright and lovely,
>
> You got in first! ... [a reference to a letter from her arriving before he could write to her] ...
>
> It was to tell you just what you told me that I meant to write: and I find that you know all about it already. That when I do get alone with you I feel an atmosphere that is home and health and water to swim in and sunshine to glow with. That is all — and isn't it enough, my dear, for any little human rabbit? It is so good and comfortable and makes me draw long breaths to gulp it down and store it up. I'm so under pressure to get things done and give things — and I have really so little to give. I've just kept plodding along like the tortoise for a long time up one long lane, and it turns out by chance that a lot of people suddenly want to know what's at the end of it. Well! Well! ...
>
> I wish I *wasn't* going to America. It is so far away and so strange. And I should so like to be here for this occasion so that I could be free to see you a little more. That one evening meant so much, and made something whole ...

Just before John and Betty left for Southampton where they were taking the *Bremen* to New York, a letter came to him from Irene in which she tells him that a dashing, young New Zealander, a doctor named Doug Jolly, had come into her life. He was a man whom John had met at different times, including at one or two of the Christian Left meetings. After spending the first few days on board ship just sleeping and resting from his exhausting months, John wrote her a letter that seems to come from a place of restored quiet and strength in him. He mentions that the days of resting have now made him glad to be on this trip, glad for this chance to break away from the pressures and demands and be able to experience something new. Only briefly at the end of this letter does he address her news. And his response is that of a dear, wise, and emotionally free friend. He refers first to the account in her letter of a vision she had in which, sitting by her father, she saw "all of us being in love together," and he assures her of its essential truthfulness:

> ... it is the heart of our only reality. It was good of you to tell me about it: and about Doug. You will mean a great deal to him, I know: and he to you, I hope. I like him a lot. Find the centre of peace between you and keep it, my dear.
>
> My warm love to you. I hold you close and dear, body and spirit, knowing both.

Earlier in that same letter, John continues to encourage her to do what she can within the limits of integrity to keep the CL inside the Auxiliary. He says he has written to Zoe Fairfield, one of Irene's conservative opponents in the administration of the SCM, asking her, too, to work for their unity. He says he put it to Zoe that the Auxiliary and its CL section are on the very cusp of the essential crisis of Protestantism over the centuries: how, in the face of creative progress, to keep new movements *within* the community and not force them out, to become yet one more sect. Over the course of the summer he wrote Irene two more letters on the subject. He is firm with her in keeping the essential goal in mind, and yet creative in his proposals for a way of proceeding with the Aux to avoid unnecessary conflict. John wrote to Irene on June 2:

> We must resolutely refuse to be drawn into political or social action on a *non-religious* basis. We must resist the temptation to *use* religion for political or social ends. And we mustn't yield to the subtle impulse to be a minority movement for the sake of protest and to relieve our emotions. God is doing the job, not us: and he is 100% efficient.

He goes on, giving a vision of the CL's purpose that is extraordinary in its image of the possibilities of this little enterprise:

> We have to let the Christian Left create itself, shape itself into an instrument that can lead the workers movement in England as the CP [Communist Party] can't. And its power will reside in its *religious* drive. It won't do to identify the Socialist movement with Christianity — for then there is no point in Christianity, and the CP is right.[6]

It is amazing that he would think of the tiny Christian Left group having any such potential role in the nation. It is even more amazing that he would believe a group of completely middle-class people, who had perhaps never been in a factory or on a farm a day in their lives, could achieve a leadership place among the workers. But his basic meaning is clear: *whoever* comes to play the role of genuine leadership must act from this personal and community-based perspective — or their leadership won't last. The letter ends with a caring comment on a job-offer that was made to Irene from the Auxiliary. His response is full of concern for Donald and her, and his affection for them both is transparent and genuine.

A taste of North America

Meanwhile, John and Betty were in America, and England was behind them! New York gave Betty an immediate impression of speed and motion, and in the public relationships in the hotel and restaurants she was struck by the lack of class differences and the greater equality of the sexes. When John went to be photographed for the public relations materials she went to a beauty parlour and was struck by the ad: "It's smart to be beautiful." It said everything she was feeling about the attitude to life in this boisterous, new country.

They went to Yale first where John was delivering the Terry Lectures. These were lectures sponsored by a foundation created by Dwight H. Terry in 1924 to promote not new investigations in science, but:

> ... the assimilation and interpretation of that which has been or shall be hereafter discovered, and its application to human welfare, especially by the building of the truths of science and philosophy into the structure of a broadened and purified religion.[7]

John's three lectures followed the directives of the lectureship in detail. He opened up for his audience his thinking on the essential role of empirical — as opposed to dogmatic or traditional — thinking in the progressive movement of humanity. He distinguished empirical thinking in science from that required in art and also in religion, holding for its legitimacy in all three fields. Having set up the terms of his focus, he presented his position on empirical thinking in religion and located its proper domain in the practical field of personal relationships. The Terry lectures were published that year by Yale University Press under the title *The Structure of Religious Experience*. The book received many good reviews. The major exception was that of Martin D'Arcy SJ, his arch-critic from the BBC talks, who classified Macmurray as a communist and then pilloried his views of dualism, religion and God as utter nonsense.

After a one-day stop at Smith College, the Macmurrays launched into the Canadian portion of their trip. John was to be the feature speaker at a Student Christian Movement (SCM) gathering at a camp sixty miles north of Montreal in the Laurentians (which Betty mistakenly called the Alleghenies) where they stayed in a small cabin. This first exposure to Canada was in fact quite an exposure. The temperature on the first night went down to an unusual minus eight degrees. In a letter to his mother, John complained about the cold by night ("the water froze that night in the flower vases; and in Montreal they had snow!") and the mosquitoes by day. Betty enjoyed the whole thing. She found the young Canadian men charming, more simple and less sophisticated than English students but gentle, and with a forthrightness combined with shyness in their manner that she liked.

The Macmurrays enjoyed as much as they could the roughness of the bush setting, and noted the ease of the young Canadians in it. They conveyed a different feeling than English people showed in what they called "the forest." He knew, he told his mother, he would be glad to be home.

When they returned to Montreal, they were the guests of John's former student Eugene Forsey for a couple of days before going on a ten-day holiday in the hills of Vermont overlooking Lake Champlain. His "next assignment," as he told his mother, was the commencement address and a students' conference at a girls' school at Northfield, Minnesota, founded by D.L. Moody. He knew his mother, whose religious worship was so shaped by the Moody and Sankey evangelical missionary tours of Scotland in the late 1800s, would be glad to know that.

They returned to New York where, in the course of some of the hottest days of that summer, Macmurray delivered the Deems Lectures on "The Philosophy of Psychology" at New York University. In the lectures he compared the analysis of human motives in modern psychology with the treatment of human motivation in Christianity. But when it came to preparing the lectures for publication, he omitted the reference to religious psychology and concentrated on scientific psychology, but with a fresh twist: he attempted a comprehensive articulation of the difference between "motive" as explored by science (organic) and "intention" — a motive imbued with knowledge (personal) — as studied in philosophy. The completely revised lectures were published after a three-year delay as *The Boundaries of Science,* and they provided the basis for his future treatment of motive and intention in his philosophy of human action in *The Self as Agent.*

Betty didn't attend these lectures. She paid attention to her heart condition and stayed at the hotel, trying to resist the heat which was totally different than anything they had experienced in England. Her solicitude for herself was not to be shared. She went to the hairdresser's and after settling into the chair complained slightly — more to make conversation — about the effect of the heat on her heart. The hairdresser chimed up in a loud voice and with a minimum of sympathy: "Forget your heart, dearie, and think about God." It may have been good advice, but she wasn't prepared to act on it just yet.

On June 20, after visiting Niagara Falls, the Macmurrays arrived in Toronto to spend a few days with John's old friend Richard Roberts and his wife — where he gave a sermon at Sherbourne United, Roberts' church. John also gave a talk to a special group Roberts had lined up for the occasion. Roberts had just finished a term as Moderator of the new United Church of Canada and it was a group of his close associates he gathered that evening to hear John. When he wrote to his daughter Gwen on June 25, Roberts' enthusiasm about John and the visit was unbounded. "He is in great form — and I am pretty sure he is the man in the Providence of God who is marking out the pattern of the next phase of Christianity."[8]

John's last major engagement in Canada was a week-long conference with SCM leaders and other church-related people at Albert College in Belleville, 100 miles east of Toronto, which began on June 25. This was a special gathering of about forty people, most of whom had strong associations with the Fellowship for a Christian Social Order, a group of Canadian Protestants who were doing serious and sophisticated Christian analysis of the relationship of Christianity to society. They were just that year publishing a collection of essays called *Towards the Christian Revolution* that took a similar attitude as that taken by the editors of *Christianity and the Social Revolution* which had just come out in Britain. So Macmurray's audience was already primed for his viewpoint. However, as Reverend Ernest Thomas testified in a summary of the conference he wrote, except perhaps for Eugene Forsey and those who had heard John speak a few weeks earlier in the Laurentians, they were not prepared for the immense power of the person as well as the words.[9]

It was a conference on "Religion in the Modern World" and only a twenty-five-page set of notes taken by Eugene Forsey's wife, Harriet, and one short article remain as a record of Macmurray's presentations on his major themes of religion, the church, Jesus, the central issues of our time, class structure, idealism, the equality of the sexes, education, dualism, etc. Much of the freshness of his view of Jesus here will appear in published form two years later in *The Clue to History* — an already finished book looking for a brave publisher. In Belleville, Macmurray developed his theme of Christianity as essentially a spiritual historical force arising from Jesus. The reign of God includes the injection of social energies such as the Renaissance, the Enlightenment and Marxism which were resisted by the churches and yet contain elements essential for humanization and for the spreading of God's kingdom. At times in its history, the church has been able to be the ally of creative breakthroughs of the spirit, but usually, Macmurray concluded, it has been reactive, defensive and resistant to them.

The power in Macmurray's expression as well as his analysis radiates in his opening statement on class differences and how those in power, out of personal discomfort, refuse even to recognize these social differences:

> The Communist is not talking about ideas, but facts. Rich and poor don't belong to the same community at all. The emotional and moral attitudes of security and insecurity are different. The moral values of secure people are wrong. That's what's wrong with us.

The difference between the moral codes is not in the propositions but in the emotional emphasis, the *feeling* of what is most wrong. The bourgeois feel shocked, terribly shocked, by the idea of violence, the unemployed man does not. Moral wrong depends on the community: if the community doesn't provide food, it has broken a contract. In these circumstances stealing may be legally, but not morally, wrong for the unemployed. To secure people, violence or revolution is awful! If you must starve, you *must* starve quietly. The working class can't feel that way. The working man is nearer feeling in accordance with the facts. Ultimately there arise two forms of consciousness, two different ways of thinking and feeling, which cannot get along together.

... *It is now impossible to frame any economic policy in the interests of both classes.* To talk of a nice compromise is just hot air. Neither policy is in the interests of society as a whole because there isn't any society as a whole. There are two societies, and the pathetic thing is not that they struggle against each other but that they go on struggling to work together! [10]

Despite the intensity generated by such elements in Macmurray's talks, the conference was a relaxed event, with a talk by John in the morning, discussion groups in the afternoon, and a prayer and question period in the evening — both led by Macmurray himself. The effects of this week penetrated the discussions and decisions of SCM bodies in Ontario and Montreal for the three years leading up to the war, and for some, even beyond. And John himself wrote to Richard Roberts a few months later saying: "The Seminar at Belleville was the high spot of the tour, and was one of the most remarkable experiences of my life. Something happened then — and I hadn't much to do with it."[11]

The last leg of their journey took them to Blue Ridge, North Carolina, where John conducted a week-long course. It was a powerful experience for the participants, and it resulted in the provost and dean of UCL receiving letters in the autumn from the president of the University of North Carolina asking if John might be released for a term in order to teach on their campus at Chapel Hill. John was open to it, but permission was not granted by the UCL administration. Jeffrey Campbell, the only black student on the summer course, was deeply impressed with John and asked if he could come to England and study further with him. He came two years later and lingered so long in the summer of 1939 that he missed his passage home; hostilities began and he had to stay on in Britain. He was there during the entire war and, due to his lack of resources, spent much of that time as a guest of the Macmurrays.

On July 24, John and Betty boarded the *Europa* for home. Within a week of arriving, John went to the Adelphi Centre's Summer School in Colchester mentioned earlier, bringing to it some of the ardour that was generated in Belleville. Free at last, he and Betty motored north and spent the last two weeks of August with family in Scotland. With all that accomplished, and with school beginning in October, John collapsed with fatigue. It was a sickness that lasted for three months during which, as told Richard Roberts in a December letter, he had to "cut everything down to a minimum; do no writing and no lecturing outside of necessary work and generally keep out of things. I'm hoping that with the New Year I shall be able to start on some serious writing."[12]

Love as universal law

While he was still laid up with his sickness, he had to miss an important meeting of the Christian Left which was considering a break from the SCM Auxiliary. By this point, John himself had concluded that the Christian Left might realistically leave the Auxiliary. Nevertheless, he had positive reasons for that view, and he felt driven to write to Irene Grant: "the substance of what I would want to have said" at the meeting. It sounds like a repetition of his standard message to her but there is a difference in tone that suggests a deepening of his appropriation of the ideas he has come to embrace:

> The function of the Christian Left is to rediscover and recreate Christianity as a determining force in the contemporary world. This is its unique task. *You must affirm this and reaffirm it and never forget it.* We have to work at a level which is above the political and social, though inclusive of it; and no political theory or sociological analysis can help us in this. If we identify our task with the political one, if political reformation is our conscious objective, then we should cut religion out entirely, and join in the direct political effort in an effective political fashion.[13]

Macmurray is remarkably directive here. One wonders if the strength of his statement is due to a deepening conviction in himself. There are reasons for thinking that way. Since the summer — perhaps since the seminar in Belleville — Macmurray seems to have become even more clear about the view of Jesus that shapes the thesis of his not-yet-published book, *The Clue to History*. He wrote about this point in his December letter to Roberts and he did so with a sense of "breakthrough" that is matched only by his earlier letters on discovering the primary and inclusive place of "personality" as the focus for contemporary philosophy:

The core of it is very simple. It is the assertion that Jesus made
the critical discovery in human history and that it is *true* in the
ordinary common-sense meaning of the term. It was a discovery
that human life *is* personal, not organic or 'natural.' Which
means, as Jesus saw, that if you try to form human community
on any organic basis (like family, nationality, race — in fact
'blood and soil') it will necessarily collapse. You are trying to
do something that is, in the nature of the case, impossible.
Since that discovery was made, human history has been
different; and we *can't* go back on it. Because it is *true*. You
can reject it, but it is exactly like rejecting the law of gravitation.
You can't escape from it. Because it is the truth about your own
nature; not the truth about what we ought to be but the truth
about what we are.

This kind of language reveals in simpler terms what Macmurray has
been saying for almost ten years about what he means by emotional and
religious objectivity. He means that emotion and religion can be true
(convictions and practices that are based on *the way the world is*), and
when they *do* relate to the way things are, they are as objective as scientific facts. Here, John is sharing with his friend some of the implications for one's view of history when this view of reality is taken
seriously:

There is, you see, a peculiarity about discovering the truth about
human nature. It is the truth about yourself — and all men.
Hence it stands as knowledge in a unique position. It is self-
realization. It involves certainty. And since it is universal truth, it
defines the objective of human development, the end of human
history. The end is inevitable — a universal society on the basis
of common humanity whose structure is defined by freedom and
equality. But this inevitability is not external to us. It is
immanent in us. In other words, for a man to discover the truth
about human nature is itself to transform his own motives. For he
has discovered what he himself (and everyone else) *really* wants.
It was this knowledge ... which enabled Jesus to ... send out that
band of simple folk, at the height of the greatness of Rome — to
create in the world the kingdom of Heaven; and to tell them that
they would be persecuted, jailed and killed — and that they
couldn't possibly fail. But he was right and he knew it with
scientific precision; not as a 'life' or 'faith' in our watered down
sense of the term, but as a prophecy better grounded in
knowledge than a scientist's prediction of an eclipse.[14]

This view of Jesus, however, does not apply to the church, as far as John can see:

> ... Oh Dick! The churches. They don't believe this; it isn't in the least what they are after. In every great crisis of history they have fought in these wars on the anti-Christian side. This is plain history. Yet the driving force of history is Christianity — the thing that Jesus did to humanity by his discovery.[15]

This period of 1936 — starting with the seminar in Belleville and ending with this December letter — marks the first time Macmurray has linked three things so closely: his own insight about "the personal" as the radical, comprehensive and ultimate law of nature, his conviction that Jesus was the one who discovered that fact, taught it, and acted on it — and therefore introduced it into the conscious workings of human history — and finally the fact that, in the light of Marxist dialectical development, the time in history for the recognition of "the personal" as what Jesus was all about, is now.

It is this threefold conviction of Macmurray's that perhaps provides the template for understanding his positive view not only of the Russian Revolution during the 1930s, but also of every revolution that has achieved a genuine advance in the process of personalization. Explicitly Christian or not, each advance of the genuine spirit of humanity has, according to Macmurray, expressed a moment in the unfolding of the true Christian mission: to serve as the centre of theory and practice for the transformation of human relationships to greater freedom, equality and mutuality in full fellowship for the human race.

On the one hand, this can appear as a thoroughly inclusive view of Christianity. One the other, it can seem arrogant and gratuitous to give Christianity such an exclusive (and inclusive) role in world history. Macmurray had had to face that in his 1928 letter to the Jerusalem conference of the Missionary Council — and he did not pull back from his claim (see p.148). He clearly means for his view of Christianity to be seen as an open and expansive view that makes room for the action of the non-Christian believer, the non-believer, and the atheist to be on the side of the cooperative effort to bring this process of personalization into our active and conscious history. It also allows, conversely, that a Christian or even a Christian church might be an enemy — or an ally — of this development.

Life, he asserts, is essentially action. This does not mean that consciousness and good theory are irrelevant in action, he notes in a later letter to Irene Grant.[16] But he proposes a dialectical synthesizing of all historical actions for genuine liberation by seeing good action as not totally vitiated by limited or even inadequate theory — as he found in the living faith but bad theology of his parents. In a very different but still related context, he was casting light on this view when he reflected that "the empiricism of science is a partial realization of the empiricism of the gospels."[17] From 1936 onwards, Macmurray is moved in a more concentrated way by the understanding that the kind of community and social witness he has been striving for entails a "rediscovery of Christianity" — the term he used in his October letter to Irene Grant and again in more than one lecture he gave over subsequent years.[18]

In this context of God's immanence in *all* of history, Roberts has asked John where his thought stands in relation to the thinking of the great Protestant theologian Karl Barth. The answer is swift and incisive:

> ... I don't think you can combine Barth and me. It is like trying to combine capitalism and democracy — indeed it is the religious form of that effort. The emphasis on the transcendence of God is itself a denial of the transcendence of God. For the transcendence of God *is* his immanence; and his immanence is his transcendence. God in action is the history of the world — his immanence in fact — not a function of his transcendence. Barth's *effect* is to push God farther into the sky, whatever he may *say.* He releases Christians, by his emotional effect, from their own immanent responsibility. They cannot understand history — so why try? This is Barthianism. Whereas Jesus' teaching is the declaration of the meaning of history as the basis for understanding and prophecy.[19]

For Macmurray, three things are needed for integrated and free social action: first, grasping what constitutes the directing energy in history (God's truth and love); second, appreciating to the degree we can what God *is doing and intends to do* in history; and third, believing God will not fail in this goal. This is precisely what allows a person to be at once anchored in God *and* the world, and infused by both the love of God *and* the need and desire of the world. It allows for a faith-based *and* intelligent engagement with others in history.

Macmurray believes dualisms are defeated by this approach. Although he has held this position throughout his adult life, it reaches a mature expression in the mid-thirties and allows him to look with hope on the Christian Left as a possible expression of what he called the "rediscovery of Christianity" that is so much needed in all countries of Europe at the time. The smallness and slowness of spirit of Jesus' own troupe of companions helps to keep John from being discouraged when he looks at the small and struggling numbers in the Christian Left.

Religious freedom and the Spanish civil war

The outbreak of civil war in Spain in July 1936 was a wake-up call for many democratically minded people who were still hoping, despite the rise of Fascism and Italy's invasion of Abyssinia, that the countries of Europe would conduct their business according to the rule of law. Spain was the most dramatic demonstration that democracy itself was under major threat in Europe. Intervention by Britain was widely discussed throughout the nation, and was rejected by the government despite general support in Britain for the legitimately elected Republican Government in Spain. Developments in Spain changed by the week as both the Republicans and Franco's Falangists drew international support. Doug Jolly, for many months a member of the Christian Left, left for Spain to serve as a doctor among the Republican forces. He also worked with civilians caught in the conflict and those suffering the horror of indiscriminate aerial bombing of Republican-held towns and cities.

In Britain, throughout the winter and into the spring of 1937, charges of Republican brutality against the Spanish Catholic Church countered charges of Falangist atrocities against Republican supporters. Macmurray was asked to join a religious delegation being sent at the invitation of the Spanish Republican government to monitor freedom of religion and investigate the charges against the government of religious persecution. It was an ecumenical group made up of Dr Hewlett Johnson, Dean of Canterbury Cathedral, and Father E.O. Iredell, Vicar of St Clement's, Monica Whately and M. Beer as Roman Catholic members, Kenneth Ingram, Olga Levertoff and Hannah Laurie as Anglican members, and D.R. Davies together with Macmurray being listed as representatives of the "Protestant Free Churches." After being delayed by the British Foreign Office which at first refused to grant them visas, the delegation left London on March 29 for Paris where they met with the Spanish ambassador and a Basque delegation. The Basques surprised the British when they presented their defence of the Republic and its programme of reorganization "as the explicit application of Christian principles of social justice."[20]

The delegation, despite some minor setbacks, was allowed to visit Barcelona, Valencia, Madrid, Bilbao, Santander and other areas where the Falangist accusations of persecution were directed. In Bilbao, they mixed in freely with political prisoners and heard their version of events and their condition in prison. The delegation reported that "the promise of the Spanish Government to provide facilities for a free enquiry were amply fulfilled." Their strongest impression was of "the normality of life and the complete order which prevails in all the towns and cities which we visited." The delegates were especially impressed with their visit to the Basque country. They also witnessed the bombing of the little town of Durango by six Falangist planes. Two of their members actually visited the front lines near Durango and witnessed the long lines of fleeing refugees walking the forty-two kilometres from Durango to Bilbao.

The thirty-two-page report was written immediately on their return to Britain and was supported by all the delegates. It noted that churches in Spain were open, liturgies were being celebrated and attendance was high. They emphasized the role of religion as a social force among the Basques, and noted the strong efforts of the rebels to portray the government as anti-religious. The report was detailed and nuanced. With regard to attacks by the government forces against churches, priests and nuns, it stated that although some attacks had happened, they were motivated not by a an attack on religion but on rebel politics. The attacks were against *political* allegiances and actions of individuals and groups involved in using religion and the churches to attack the Republican government. Where churches were serving the needs of people without undermining their allegiance to the Republican government, they were left untouched. It was a unanimous report from a diverse group of delegates on a touchy situation. Whatever effect it had on the British public, it certainly influenced John Macmurray. The trip to the Basque country especially helped to confirm his view of how religious motives can direct and imbue social and political actions. He and Kenneth Ingram both brought this message back to the many groups they spoke to in England after that, as well as to the Christian Left. The feeling that remained from this trip played a strong role, as we saw, in Macmurray's response to Max Plowman on the problematic elements in British pacifism (see p.242).

On his return home, Macmurray believed the Republic's strength would result in an imminent victory. On May 19, he wrote to Irene Grant who was in the United States:

> I wasn't long enough there [Spain] really to know. But it does
> make a difference and I feel quieter about it now — because I've
> seen the rebirth of a nation; and somehow the immediate questions
> of loss and gain, even the horrors of the bombardment of Guernica,
> left me less visibly disturbed. Because something is happening that
> is pure gain, and that cannot be undone. Actually I believe that the
> government is winning ...[21]

He went on to describe the losses suffered by Franco as critical, and says he expects the last phase of the war to be launched with a government offensive in the very near future, since Italy and Germany are effectively out of the picture now. As an appraisal of future directions, it proved to be disastrously wrong. It was a fond hope that was totally dashed in the ensuing months.

Refusing to meet with the Nazis

Within months of this trip, and almost surely because of his educational work in Britain after it, John was invited by Reverend Eric Fenn, the former assistant to Archbishop Temple, to join a delegation to Berlin to talk with representatives of the Nazi government. His answer to Father Fenn concerning the intentions of the Nazis redeemed completely any lack of clairvoyance he may have displayed in his letter to Irene Grant about the future in Spain. Only here he was on firmer ground: passing judgment on what was *in fact* happening in Germany and on the values the Nazis actually showed they stood for. No crystal ball was needed in this case.[22]

He began by refusing the invitation outright: "It can do nothing but harm, in my opinion, and I am quite opposed to it. I do not see how it is possible to admit to Nazi leaders that there is any basis for discussion, or even partial agreement, without compromising both Christian and democratic principles." The Nazis had apparently required an agreement that nothing shared in the talks could be used for propaganda, and Macmurray dissects in a few, fine strokes the duplicity reflected in that demand. Then he turns to the soft-mindedness of the Christians who are willing to go and talk to the Nazis:

> I wish that good people in this country could manage to escape from the fog of liberal attitudes. It is a kind of moral blindness. I know what you feel about it. "Such a visit shows a readiness to be friendly. Does not Christ teach us to love our enemies?" Precisely: but that is the very reason why this visit is compromising to Christianity. For what it says is: "You and we are not enemies. We are really friends." Or do you propose to say to the Nazi leaders, "You and we are enemies. Yet, as Christians, we love you in spite of that. Until you set free your pacifists and stop your anti-Jew activities, and repeal the laws under which they suffer, there can be no peace between us, but only a sword?" Of course you do not intend to say that. On those terms the discussion would come to an end before it started ... How can you plead the cause of truth with people who are convinced that truth should be suppressed if it is in the interests of the German regime?

He then cites the two reasons why he has written in this forceful way:

The first is that I believe your parties in Berlin are compromising
Christianity and making it harder for the Evangelical Christian in
Germany to stand firm in his faith. I know you don't think so ...
But Karl Barth [who was forced to leave Germany by the Nazis]
took the opportunity, when he was over here last, to plead with
Christians to understand this before it was too late. The second
reason for my letter is that your invitation to me to join you,
knowing what my views are, is an invitation to me to compromise
them and myself. I know you don't mean that or realize it. But I
think you ought to. If I did not say to the Germans what I believe
about their behaviour, I should be deceiving them. If I did, I should
make your conference impossible. You can't want me to do the
latter.

Macmurray puts the situation at this historical junction plainly to Fenn:
the Nazis would rather go to war than create just laws that would, in freedom, allow Germany to go communist. They prefer war to communism.
They have made their choice against freedom, and it is an evil choice. In
the language of John's Gospel, he says, they see the light and have chosen
darkness, so they are condemned. Macmurray, at this point, ends his letter
with the most incisive cut of all against the British individuals planning
the trip:

But you are still in the romantic liberal attitude which thinks that
this cannot be the condemnation: that it is a matter of people
wanting the good but not understanding things properly. Believe
me, the Nazis, and particularly their chosen leader, understand
things better than your people do. What we did to them after the
war — our acts which spoke louder than our words — revealed it
to them. And what they believe is that, whatever you may say, in
the long run you will mean in action what they mean — that
anything is better than a Communist regime. They don't pay
attention to our *words* any more. They believe that whatever we
say, when it comes to the point of deciding whether to allow
England to go Communist, we shall join them — not the
Russians. Because when it comes to war, there can only be two
sides.

It goes without saying that the edgy alliance between Russia and the western allies after 1941 left the question of a fundamental choice between
Fascism and Communism profoundly ambiguous during the war years; it
does not deny the truth of Macmurray's final statement. Macmurray ended
his letter to Reverend Fenn with a postscript: "I should like the reasons for

my refusal to join the party to be known to all its members." It is not clear whether after this devastating letter that particular party actually went to Germany. But we do know from their BBC exchanges in 1941 that relations between Macmurray and Fenn remained amicable.

The Christian Left: apogee and decline

The Christian Left reached its highest and its most turbulent point in 1937–38. During the late spring and summer of 1937, Irene Grant was in the USA lecturing. Much planning and activity was carried on without her leadership — including planning for the summer conference at Sandy Balls which was attended by Macmurray, Ingram, Polanyi, and Gregory Vlastos who joined them while on sabbatical leave. In early 1937, it also launched its training weekends in which Macmurray and Polanyi played major roles.

In the May Day parade for the unemployed, the CL contingent carried a banner featuring the design of a cross superimposed on a hammer and sickle. It was becoming a popular image for many groups of Christian socialists, not just the Christian Left, and had already been used on the dust-jacket of Macmurray's *Creative Society* the year before. Outrage over the use of this design reached the floor of the House of Commons, and a memorial registering the protest of many members of the House of Commons against the use of the image was submitted and recorded. A similar protest containing the signatures of a great number of peers, clerics, military officers and members of the professions was also submitted along with it. The CL reacted with a letter to the editor of the *Times* where the kerfuffle in Parliament was reported and the design was referred to in a disparaging manner. It was the most public notice that the Christian Left ever received — and there is no sign that their name even appeared in the protest or the reporting.

During that summer, grand plans were made to replace the *News Sheet* with a new monthly magazine called the *Christian Left*, with Kenneth Ingram taking editorial responsibility and Macmurray, Polanyi, Fanny Street and Kenneth Muir on the board with him. The first issue was due in October.

The magazine never made it beyond the drawing board. Serious differences had arisen within the Christian Left about who, among its members and associates, had the right to participate in decisions about its functioning and its future directions. Some context is helpful here. By 1937, the CL membership was expanding. Groups had sprung up in Scotland, Northampton, Manchester and Bath, alongside the Oxford group and others south of London, and the numbers of mainly young people subscribing to the News Sheet and wishing to be associated with CL goals were growing. Three layers of association seemed to be taking shape: those founding members who lived the CL as a community experience and a religious base, those who were associate members by being in other groups outside London — many of whom had mainly political motives for their association, and those who subscribed to the *News Sheet* and had only a loose though sympathetic association.

The question arose: shall major decisions be made by everyone who participated at any level? Or only by those throughout the country who were actively involved in meetings in a CL group? Or exclusively by the small, founding community in London, along with the few, such as the Cass-Beggs and their friends from Oxford and a very few others who participated fully? The crisis was substantial. To include the first two groups just named was to dilute the experiential base which was essential to the reality of the CL and made them a community rather than a political party. But to assert an exclusive or dominant role for the founding group was to offend democratic principles and to create a hierarchy along lines that the CL was trying to combat in society at large.

The struggle opened up such conflict, that Kenneth Ingram, who supported the more inclusive view of the CL as the way for the future, resigned from the editorial board. Despite an article in the October *News Sheet* recommending the more open model, Macmurray and Polanyi along with others opted for the necessity of making a commitment to CL principles in order to ensure the CL remained a community. It was an affirmation of the religious identity of the group, in opposition to the political one that had been playing an increased role. The "religious" position won out at the general meeting in November.

The Christian Left was asked by the Auxiliary to undertake preparations for a major conference on the Christian Answer to Fascism, proposed earlier by Christian Left members of the Aux, to be held in August 1938 at St Asaph, Wales. As they began their planning early in 1938, Irene Grant was preparing to depart for a second lecture trip to the United States. Before leaving in February, she wrote to John and sent him a copy of a letter she had sent to the *Magazine* in which she had stated "our *sole* concern is with the birth and future of the working-class movement." Macmurray wrote her back quickly:

> ... That makes me wonder. I'm quite sure it never could be *my* sole
> concern, or even my chief concern. I couldn't find my sole concern
> in any 'movement,' however proper and urgent I thought it. And,
> my dear, I don't think it *is* your sole concern either ... You forget
> that Russia and the Working-Class Movement and all these terms
> you use are abstractions.[23]

The letter ends with Macmurray saying "But never mind! It isn't of much importance; since it is only theory revolving in its own cage ..." This is his affection taking the edge off his reflection — a break from the incisive judgment that he was able to offer Eric Fenn earlier. But more may be happening here. By this time, Macmurray must have realized that, for all her positive energy, Irene "just wasn't getting it." He wasn't worried by that. As he concluded with her: "the dialectical process works — in the CL and in you and in me, whatever we say." Macmurray consistently showed this peace and freedom in situations where important differences among people of good will could not be resolved. But it must have made him wonder about Irene, and ponder about the difficulty of, as Gandhi was saying at this time, living in the truth and thinking clearly about it.

The St Asaph conference that August attracted one hundred people and was a significant educational experience for the participants. Macmurray gave talks on the nature of religion, the nature of Christianity, and Fascism and Christianity. Polanyi spoke once, on the Philosophy of Fascism. The other speakers ranged over various aspects of Fascism, and Gregory Vlastos spoke directly on the Christian Answer to Fascism. The participants concluded that a reconstructed Christianity expressed in socialism was the only positive response to Fascism. It was hardly a surprising outcome given who the speakers were, and the Christian Left organization and agenda.[24]

The St Asaph conference was the high point of the Christian Left. Starting that September, funds were desperately low and the *News Sheet* became simply a typed copy rather than a printed document. The committee elected at the end of 1938 was energetic, but the creeping and apparently unstoppable energies of war that were gathering put a sombre note on all efforts to challenge Fascism, prevent war and create a new society.

John Macmurray remained associated with the Christian Left to the end. By the summer of 1940, with war already well underway and the Nazis having made huge and sudden gains in Europe, the attention of Britons was diverted entirely towards Europe and their own self-defence. The *News Sheet* was discontinued, but Christian Left voices and ideas, including Macmurray's, continued to be heard in the regularly monthly feature "From the Christian Left," in the *Left News*. The list of contributors to that journal expanded during the war to include what David Ormrod called "a widening circle of radical Christian socialists."[25] But the little group that began at 25 Pyecombe Corner in 1935 and continued together for five tumultuous years were driven by the war in different directions.

The contributions of Macmurray to the exploration of the nature of Christianity and its effective role in human revolutions remain a powerful advance in both social analysis and the philosophical foundations for Christian ecclesiology. Those themes and dynamics were explored again, thirty years later, by Liberation Theology and base communities in the churches of Latin America, the Philippines and Africa as well as in much of the work of the World Council of Churches. Macmurray's belief in a "religious" base as the necessary foundation for political and economic action for socialism, both critical and constructive, has been only partially pursued. Much of the theory that he, along with Polanyi, proposed through the Christian Left in the 1930s, apart from a few exceptions, remains dormant, perhaps awaiting resuscitation by faith-based groups in a creative form across national borders and at the heart of market-driven societies as the new millennium begins.

Chapter 14

Living in the Shadows:

Jordans, Aberystwyth and London (1939–44)

In the autumn of 1937 the Macmurrays moved to 49 Cadogan Street in Chelsea. It was right across from a Roman Catholic convent and church that, as Betty noticed, provided the statue of Our Lady for the May procession each year. During the two years they stayed there, John's early training in domesticity didn't desert him and, apart from his many jobs around the house, he continued his dress-making for Betty and his piano lessons with Trevor Fisher.

At the university, in addition to his visits to labs and art studios, Macmurray began giving more attention to psychology. In his 1936 Deems lectures in New York, published as *The Boundaries of Science,* he had explored an appropriate methodology for philosophical inquiry in psychology, but realized more work needed to be done in his effort to understand the organic within the personal in the domain of human action.[1]

That same year, Dr Ian Suttie published a book entitled *The Origins of Love and Hate* in which he proposed that Freud's notion of libido was too narrow to describe human motivation, and should be replaced by the broader and deeper notion of a "need for companionship." Love, not sexual desire, is the primary factor in the infant's relationship with its mother. Love, he asserted, is a larger and truer explanatory category for human behaviour than lust. As one reviewer put it: in Suttie's view company is more important than copulation. Suttie also accused Freud of anti-feminism in his fixation on patriarchal power and concluded that anxiety and hate do not spring from fear of father, as Freud proposed, but are generated by frustrations of the love and sociability we are all born to give and receive — women as well as men, infants as well as adults.

Suttie's theories confirmed and expanded Macmurray's own convictions concerning the primacy of personal relationship and love as the most foundational human motive. From that point on, he drew substantially on Suttie's work in order to express more concretely his own view of motivation in personal action. By 1938, his talks on what he meant by the personal life leaned heavily on psychology and education, and had stirred up attention among professionals in various fields. He was invited to give a paper to the Medical Society of Individual Psychology in 1938 which he called "A Philosopher Looks at Psychotherapy." In it he proposed to the doctors a "personal" as opposed to an "organic" focus for doing medicine, especially in diagnosis and therapy. Treat persons, not diseases, was his suggestion, since the disease can be better known and treated when one attends to the whole person. He advanced his philosophical reflections on psychology, especially around the relationship of love and fear to the development of freedom and rationality, connections he had already addressed in *Reason and Emotion, Creative Society* and *The Clue to History* which was finally published in 1938.

At UCL, Macmurray concentrated on improving the breadth of courses for general students and the teaching of sound methodology for those specializing in philosophy.[2] He hired Alastair (Sandy) Duncan for the faculty after the young man had completed his work at Edinburgh. A.E. Taylor, the Moral Professor at Edinburgh — the man John would eventually succeed in the Moral Chair there — told young Duncan as he was leaving for London: "Don't let Macmurray lead you too far astray." It sounds like Taylor shared A.D. Lindsay's perception of John as something of a renegade. But it also showed that members of the academe kept track of one another's work and Macmurray's — especially in the 1930s — was quite different from Taylor's own meticulous work on Plato and Aristotle and the philosophy of God.

In August 1937, just before they moved to Cadogan Street, John and Betty received a message that Duncan Davidson Campbell, Betty's brother and John's best friend as a youth, had been found dead at the foot of a sea-cliff near Stonehaven in Scotland. It had been one of his favourite places to visit, and he did so often, enjoying the view and the birdlife. John and Betty rushed north to be with Duncan's wife, Mary, and their two boys, Duncan Ian and Alastair, now young men. Mary, Betty and John made arrangements that reflected that in many ways John and Betty were already second parents for the boys. The Campbells had been left in dire financial straits, so as Mary moved in to live with and care for her mother, Alastair moved to London to live with the Macmurrays and begin his university studies at UCL. Duncan Ian, who had just finished his degree with a First Class degree in Classics, left that autumn for China where he worked in Shanghai for the Jardine Matheson Company. The distance between them was great, but the sense of being one family with the Macmurrays became more and more a simple fact that would mark their lives for their remaining years.

On September 29, 1938, just after the big Christian Left conference at St Asaph ended and right before Duncan Ian left for China, the Munich conference began and Macmurray along with the rest of the world witnessed in Prime Minister Chamberlain precisely the kind of blind liberal attitude that John had warned Eric Fenn about. From that point on, despite his continuing efforts with the Christian Left and other organizations, Macmurray was convinced that war would be unavoidable.

Jordans: living in a Quaker village

Sometime in April, 1939, Macmurray was invited to speak at a conference being held in the Quaker Meeting House at Jordans, a village in Buckinghamshire, about thirty minutes by car northwest of London. He drove there with Betty and at the conference met Dr Bevan Brown, a New Zealand psychoanalyst, who lived in Jordans but had decided to return home before the inevitable hostilities with Germany broke out. He was looking to sell his house, and when Macmurray expressed an interest, Bevan Brown, who was something of a fan of John's philosophy, told him it was his for the asking. John sprang the idea on Betty who had been entranced by the village. She knew nothing of Jordans other than that the famous Quaker William Penn, his wife, and nine of their sixteen children were buried in the tiny graveyard right next to the Quaker meeting house She was captivated by the thought of moving to the village and still being so close to London. Within two days, they took the train back and paid a visit to the Bevan-Browns to inspect the house. Betty wore a shocking pink dress John had made for her from material she had bought on sale, and the impression it made on the more homespun village folk who saw her was instantaneous and not to be shaken. They loved the house, closed the deal, and returned to London to prepare their move. They would miss their landlady Miss Fielding who had been kind to them at Cadogan, but they had less trouble moving out of the shadow of the church across the street. A few weeks earlier, John had gone to the parish priest to ask if refuge might be possible in the church basement if the Germans began bombing London. Apparently, he had been told that it would not since, unlike Miss Fielding, they were not Catholics. In fact, Cadogan Street was bombed to ruins in the Battle of Britain exactly one year later.

Though they both loved the idea of living in Jordans, leaving London was more painful for Betty than for John. Her life centred on painting and the relationships she had developed along with it. John, on the other hand, was ready to take a long break from the constant pressure put on him by political urgencies over the previous ten years. To be in Jordans would give him a chance to make more discriminating choices about his involvements. It was only many years later that Betty discovered with utter surprise from John how much their years in London, so filled with relevance and vitality for her, had, in the end, felt to him like a series of distractions from his main life work.

Months earlier John had committed himself to lead a two-week conference in Siljanskolan, Sweden, from July 25 to August 10. Despite the
threat of war he went to Sweden and while he was there gave a talk on
Swedish radio entitled "Creative Morality." In it, he spoke of the need:

> ... [at] this time of change and distress ... for a new and creative
> spirit in the moral life of the world ... This world needs to be
> transformed even if we escape war ... We are part of the first world-
> revolution out of which must come the first world-civilization. No
> nation can escape it. If we overcome our fear, we shall discover in
> ourselves the power and the laws of a creative morality.[3]

This would be a theme that would work its way into several talks John
gave during the war years. His viewpoint was simple and incisive: it is a
historical time; the time to move from a primarily nation-based view of
history to a global view. Along with it, we must move from acting out of
fear (induced by the major shift into the unknown and the loss of familiar
power-bases) to acting in faith and courage since the next step will require
a shift not only in economic and political structures but more significantly
in the centre of gravity of our relationships as we begin caring for one
another as members of one human family. *This* was the creative morality
he knew was needed.

For the most part, that summer of 1939 was actually a very enjoyable
time for them. While John was in Sweden, the ever-faithful Ephro stayed
with Betty in Jordans where they sewed cushions and made drapes for the
new house. Jeff Campbell, the black student from the United States, came
for the weekend and when he missed his boat home stayed on for the war
years, living at least part of the time with the Macmurrays. Their nephew
Alastair, one year into his university life, was also there much of the time.
Then the refugees and evacuee children began coming, and the
Macmurrays — like many others — opened their home to them. The
Friedlanders were a couple from the Rhineland, and they were offered a
sitting room, bedroom and a kitchenette. Two half-Chinese girls were sent
from London. When John and Betty heard these girls saying their prayers
at night, they wished Duncan Ian were there to help translate for them. A
short time later, they found out that the children were talking not Chinese
but Welsh! Their mother apparently was Welsh.

After the girls left, they got two boys, Alan and Denis, whose father
worked in London. They were wild children who had never had any order
in their lives, and while they were in Jordans they would do what they could
to provoke John into anger. One day Betty saw John chasing one of them in
the backyard yelling at him: "If you can kick, I can kick harder." Their parents would visit on weekends and, without a word being exchanged, expect

to be fed by the Macmurrays. When the boys returned home some weeks later, the parents wrote a note back saying: "You must certainly be missing the boys." Nowhere in the postcard could a "Thank you" be found.

After their Viennese housekeeper left — perhaps partly because of all the domestic chaos — they had an English housekeeper who came to Betty one day to complain about Jeff sunbathing in the yard without his shirt. The woman said: "I will do anything for you and the professor, but not for him!" It was a clear case of racial prejudice so Betty dismissed her immediately. Altogether, it was an interesting beginning to their time in this Quaker village of peace.

Sometime in the mid-1930s, connected with John's Adelphi work, they had been introduced to Herbert Read. They came to know him quite well since Herbert and his wife Ludo moved from London to Seer Green, the adjoining village to Jordans, around the same time that John and Betty left London. That put them only twenty minutes or so on foot from each other's front doors.

It was through Herbert and Ludo Read that the Macmurrays came to meet T.S. Eliot that summer. Betty found Eliot pleasant enough — very handsome, too — but generally he struck her as constrained and distant, as though he were concealing himself. Herbert Read confided to them that he thought Eliot's conversion to Anglicanism had done serious damage to his poetry. Eliot relaxed most with them on the occasion he met their white cat Jeremy for the first time. Jeremy, in his later years, was quite deaf. Whenever he was out of sorts because of something Betty had done to him — or not done for him — he would go to the basement and make his white coat dirty in the coalbin, then come up to the living room and saunter along the length of the mantlepiece, leaving a trail of black on the white walls. Eliot was so entranced by this behaviour that he wished out loud that he had known Jeremy before he wrote his McAvity poems. It was also reported that after reading a statement of John's on Christianity, Eliot called John the Anti-Christ. John apparently was pleased. From Eliot, that was a clear sign of being taken seriously.

It was at Ben Nicholson's art studio in London that they met Edwin Muir, the poet and prolific reviewer of fiction for *The Listener* in the mid-1930s, and his wife Willa. It was the beginning of a long and close friendship — especially between the two men. So, there was no lack of social life at Jordan's. There were the village people of longstanding, as well, including the Cooper women, Mireille and her two beautiful daughters Jocelyn and Allison whom Betty would regularly see walking arm in arm around the village on those August afternoons. Jocelyn would, some years later, marry Duncan Ian Campbell, Betty and John's nephew, after he returned from three and a half years in one of the infamous Japanese prisoner-of-war camps in Burma.

Evacuation to Aberystwyth

The University of London had begun as early as February 1939 to make "displacement" plans in the event of war (they preferred not to use the word "evacuation" in those early months because of its potentially demoralizing effects). The decision was taken in May that the plans, if needed, would be ready for implementation with the autumn term in 1939.[4] There were seven different centres outside London where the University colleges and faculties would be housed and would carry on their programmes as normally as possible. Consequently, after war was declared on September 3, several departments of University College, including Philosophy, were moved to Aberystwyth, Wales, and some went to Bangor, relatively nearby. Other colleges and faculties went to Cambridge, the medical sciences to Leatherhead, and the rest to the other designated centres.

John and Alastair both went to Aberystwyth for the beginning of term while Betty stayed on in Jordans with their refugees and evacuees. There were many other families in Jordans receiving refugees from Germany and evacuees from London, so the sounds of the children playing on the Green, often a mixture of English and German, were filled with sad regret as well as delight. John's sister Ella, her husband Arthur and their daughter Diana came up from the south-east when war was declared to avoid the expected bombing of their region of the country, and stayed for some months. In "Aber," Alastair went into the students' residence and John stayed with Professor Aaron for the first while, then moved to a small place of his own at 64 Marine Terrace. Sandy Duncan had left the faculty for the army but that caused no crisis because many students had done so as well and fewer classes were needed. Keeling and John divided up the classes and soldiered on in their diminished circumstances. John only had to teach five hours a week. It was an ideal time to get working on his own projects, but it was not to be.

On November 3 he wrote to Kenneth Barnes that he was "trying to get a start on the statement of my philosophy. But it doesn't go very well. I could do it better in a dug out at the front."[5] He goes on in that letter to give an extensive reflection on the "phoniness" of the war. His prognostications here, as much as those about Spain almost three years earlier (concerning the bombing of towns), were not to be confirmed by events. He concludes with the view about the war that will be his conviction throughout its duration: that the underlying *cultural* breakup was more significant than the political and military destruction:

> ... I have no real interest in the war and the war-politics. The
> destruction of human relationships goes on, and of the basis of

human culture. The breaking up of homes — children running
wild, the breakdown of education: the pathetic failure of the
religious organizations to find anything to say that is not being said
better by the politicians — all these things weigh on me more than
the war. And I feel helpless, and without great confidence in the
capacity of any of us to do anything about it.

This mood deepened throughout the grey days of November and
December. Writing to Barnes again on November 25, he confirmed his
feeling that "politics is not the centre of the crisis" and there is little a
minority like us can do.

... Socialism is going to be produced by the pressure of events
without our help — probably catastrophically ... and it may be a
thoroughly nasty world that comes with it, where everybody has
forgotten what it means to be human, and love is a matter of
disturbances in glandular secretions ...

He says he is glad at the impending death of capitalism.[6] This letter
reveals the objective elements at play in a depression that will be a main,
though well-covered, feature of his life for the next few years. In May, he
wrote in the same spirit to Irene Grant, asking her:

... what it feels like to be in the break-up we talked about and
prophesied, and never quite believed in ... I just want to weep
quietly over the rubble heaps of French and Belgian towns. And it's
no consolation to have foreseen and foretold it; rather the opposite:
it underlines one's helplessness. We have to sit and watch Germany
commit suicide and drag the whole of Europe with her into the
senseless massacre.
    Ah well! We've got to go through this to reach the other side.
Perhaps we forgot the death and resurrection symbol a little ...[7]

This last statement is quite an admission and is worth some attention since
Macmurray had taken such a firmly religious view of history. Despite his
frequent affirmation at the Christian Left of God's presence in the world,
the Christian Left did not seek out or find any way of simply *celebrating*
together this faith and hope. They did not pray together. The Christian Left
believed in love but did not manage to find a way to celebrate, with the
central Christian mysteries of the crucifixion and resurrection of Jesus, the
source and continuity of that love in their community. In this passing statement to Irene some two years later, Macmurray seems to recognize the
implications of this absence in the life of the CL community.

The need Macmurray had for a sympathetic community of support during his time in Aberystwyth makes it surprising that he never joined the
Moot, the Christian-inspired discussion group that J.H. Oldham began in
1938. Oldham's vision was of a group "loyal to one another and to the pursuits of the mind, with no thought of publication or joint public statements ...,"[8] made up of intellectuals of all stripes who were willing to view
the intellectual and historical crises of their times through a wide variety of
perspectives. The regular members of the Moot actually formed something
of a community. There was a simple form of worship connected with the
meetings, as well. It was the breadth of personal gifts and intellectual perspectives that drew Karl Mannheim, the great sociologist, to the group
early on. The same can be said for Michael Polanyi, the scientist turned
philosopher and younger brother of Karl, who remained a regular member
until the group ended in 1948.

Why would Macmurray not have become a part of such a group which
concerned itself with the issues that were his food and drink and did so
from a very similar perspective? In addition, its character as a community
of the heart as well as an exchange of the head was precisely what he
believed in — and needed — during these early years of the war. It is hard
to believe he was not invited. It is equally difficult to believe he would
have refused the invitation. It just never happened. There are no indications of any falling out between Macmurray and Oldham, apart from
John's sympathies for Marxist dialectics with which Oldham was never
comfortable.[9] One can't help feeling that the Moot would have been good
for Macmurray at this time in his life. Among other things, it would have
brought him into conversation with Michael Polanyi. Despite their significantly different approaches to politics and social analysis, one can only
wonder if their respective sets of Gifford Lectures, both delivered in the
early 1950s with such similar themes and sensitivities, would have been
any different had they met and talked about their work, which apparently
never happened.

The personal depression that had already set in for John was not
determined primarily by the physical conditions in Aberystwyth or the
decline in the number of students, though these aspects added to it. It
had come upon him earlier, as he noted in his May 1940 letter to Irene
Grant:

> ... it would be so comforting to be near you and to talk to you now
> and then, and hold your hand a little. I've felt very lonely these last
> two years — and pressed back into the solitariness I had hoped to
> escape from. That can be borne if there is urgent work to do: but
> that has failed more and more. It hasn't seemed possible to write or
> worthwhile to teach.

But his next sentence to her was: "I didn't mean to talk about myself like this — only to say 'Hello!' to you and say: 'Cheer up! We're not dead yet! ...'" He tells her to visit them in Jordans that summer, where he expects to "be free until October; or until the government wants me." The government, as we shall see, didn't want him, and he deeply missed not being called to a role in defending democracy against Fascism. It left him bereft and feeling deeply unworthy.

The summer of 1940, despite the fierce Battle of Britain that began towards the end of August, was the most magical time of their five years in — and out of — Jordans. Mary, Alastair and Duncan's mother whom John and Betty loved a great deal, came down from Scotland to spend the summer with them, and there was immediately more laughter and joy in the house. The summer was hot, and because of petrol-rationing, bikes replaced cars everywhere, slowing life down deliciously for Betty and John. There was a solidarity among everyone in the village and in the villages and towns around Jordans, due to their sharing in the war effort. Betty bought some hens from a Quaker gentleman, each of which she named. And she swore that when she called out to Penelope, Belinda, Maggie and the others, they recognized their names and came to her. When she and John would return from a day in London, the hens would see them approaching and come clucking wildly down the road to greet them. The hens gave them fine eggs, as well as the pleasure of their company, at a difficult time.

John loved the feel of the village though its details often escaped him. He acknowledged to Betty that he did not have a strong visual imagination. One day, he returned home on his bike from a shopping trip in Beaconsfield, three to four miles away, wrapped in smiles and a feeling of well-being. He told Betty that when he was coming out of a store, a woman well up the street and across the way, had spied him and given a great wave of greeting. Surprised but delighted, he waved back warmly. "Silly goose," said Betty, "that was me!" He laughed uproariously at himself. For her, that simplicity and purity of heart was one of the most endearing things about him.

Macmurray was put in charge of the village firefighters. At least twice a week he would marshal his troops on the village green and run them through their paces. He took this seriously, partly because of his experience in war already, and partly because he knew the houses in Jordans, some with extremely flammable roofs, could go up in flames if his team were not sharp and effective. Many would come out to the green to witness the drills and fire-practices. They knew it was not make believe. Each night in the later weeks of that summer — and sometimes even by day — German planes would fly over Jordans on their way home after hitting London. John cared for the lawn and planted a vegetable garden. Betty kept the roses and chrysanthemums which that summer were large and abundant. And every evening, Betty remembered later, when they sat out in the warm air and darkness fell gently on the village, the perfume of the flowers along with the song of the crickets would surround them, the glow-worms glowed, and the fireflies — despite the strict blackout rules — would flagrantly flash their bottoms at the German bombers returning to their bases.

That summer, before the Battle of Britain began, University College returned from Aberystwyth to Gower Street. Ironically, the return took place hardly a week before the massive attack began. The college was bombed unmercifully in September 1940, and among the areas "smashed to smithereens," as John put it to Tess Simpson, was John's office with all his books and papers. He later tried to lessen the impact of this destruction on his personal work by joking that most of the books were review copies anyway. But it is possible that the absence of most lecture notes from his UCL years and the disappearance of the text for many of the talks he gave — including his five 1929 talks at UCL on "The Phenomenology of the Personal" — can be attributed to the bombing.[10]

The London Blitz continued unabated until May 1941. In November 1940, just days before the Germans bombed Coventry, UCL was back at Aberystwyth and did not return to London until the summer of 1944. With the the university's sojourn in Wales prolonged, Betty felt she and John should be together. So after Christmas she sadly rented out Home Base to a local girls' school that needed to house nine of its students. John, Betty and Alastair were to return to Jordans only during the summer holidays that year, when the students themselves were away.

In Aberystwyth, John and Betty took a sea-front flat that had been arranged for them, and Betty's reaction the day they arrived was vintage Elizabeth Hyde Campbell: "What a dump! I shall never forget the first sight of it, and the misery I felt. The wind was howling and waves roaring and splashing as we arrived. I thought the sea at any moment might cross the promenade and invade our house!" There was coal dust on the floor "that rose in clouds like locusts" when one tried to clean. The water in the taps was "cold only." And the shared bath upstairs Betty promptly declared out-of-bounds for herself because there was a child with impetigo who used it. Once their pipes burst because of the cold. And the final indignity: they had a double bed with a vinyl-covered mattress that somehow rose up in the middle, so that regularly one of them would turn over and suddenly end up on the floor. Jeremy, their cat, used to sit on the parapet overlooking the sea, and Betty would fear for his safety since, being deaf, he might not notice when the tide came crashing in. And she noticed with quiet admiration how the man upstairs woke at four each morning to go to work and then came home to care for his sick daughter.

It was real life; and she saw it in that light. Every Sunday, Alastair would come for lunch, often with another student, usually Jeff Campbell. Around this time John cut off his beard and left himself only a moustache, giving a face to the world that it had not seen since the late 1920s. Perhaps it was done to help him feel differently about himself; as though something fresh were still possible in what, for him personally, felt like a terribly stagnant time.

In early 1940, John had begun to study Russian along with his nephew. Alastair took courses but John preferred to use books. He finally ended up with some long-playing records for pronunciation help. Some progress was made. John learned to read it adequately enough to help translate a chemistry paper for Alastair. His speaking knowledge was at least a few notches lower. Once, they were visited by a very large Russian woman, and John, in a burst of enthusiasm and theatrics, threw his arms out and delivered a grand welcome to her in Russian — something he had obviously memorized from one of his records. She was so overcome with delight she swallowed him up in a bear hug. When she released him, she let go with a stream of Russian. Later, John ruefully confessed to Betty that he hadn't understood a word she said.

Exploring the meaning of freedom

On their return to Aberystwyth, the Philosophy department course enrolment was reduced by almost seventy-five percent as more and more students joined the armed services and those who remained in university turned to more technical or practical areas of interest. There were some outside calls on Macmurray's time and knowledge, and he gladly accepted these "missions" to serve others since they represented lifelines thrown to him, as well.

One of these was a late 1940 request from Francis Williams for a text from him on religion and democracy. It was for a series called "The Democratic Order," dedicated to a thoughtful consideration of the directions for increasing British democracy even as the war was still being fought. Earlier numbers had been written by Tom Wintringham (a politician who would be part of the Common Wealth Movement which was just coming to birth), Herbert Read, Richie Calder, Professor W.M. Macmillan, Douglas Jay and others.

His sixty-three-page booklet, entitled *Challenge to the Churches,* pulled together in a fresh and direct way key Macmurray themes: the situating of politics within the larger scope of culture (religion), the identification of democracy as, first of all, religious in spirit for it is a seeking for personal freedom and equality, and therefore a way of testifying that "all political authority is limited" even though politics is the way in which democratic goals are realized. He states that religion — essentially a relationship with God — is therefore essentially a way of understanding and living in society, especially focused on how society becomes true community. Building on Suttie, he brings in the relationship of love and fear as the two founding motives in human beings, notes the value of fear in human affairs and indicates the misuse and abuse of fear in totalitarianism. Finally, he shows the true vocation of religion is to be creative, not conservative; it is an expression of faith in freedom and equality. He exposes Nazism as false religion, and outlines what he considers to be the mission of Christianity: to proclaim and serve the development of *universal* community. He cites the failure of the churches and concludes that looking to the ways of the past will automatically close down any credibility for either the church or politics at this juncture in history. The conditions of democracy, he concludes, require a vehicle for unity and only Christianity can provide it: "It must function as the religion of the new community which is struggling to be born."[11]

What is most evident in this small book is the mellowing of Macmurray's thinking. Marx is nowhere to be seen. He is not mentioned, nor is any of his terminology called on despite the fact that the democracy Macmurray indicates as "a brotherhood of common men," is undoubtedly socialist. This book appeals to the best of the democratic tradition in the west and the best of Christian tradition and practice over the centuries. Nor, despite its title, is there any dramatic condemnation of the churches though the analysis of their past failures is not softened. Now, however, he is much more conciliatory in terms of who can be an agent of the new community. Despite all past failures, transformation has always been possible, he writes, even in the churches. It is a remarkable shift, not in analysis but in tone, and in the direction he takes to find trustworthy and credible sources for his readers.

Macmurray's second "call to mission" was in March 1941 when he was asked to join the celebrations at Bangor in honour of the foundation of University College and to give the Foundation Address. He was delighted to do so, and took "The New Community" as his theme. He did so partly because the departments at Bangor had been striving valiantly to grow as a community even while in exile. But, it was mainly because it was an occasion for him to share with the students some of the thoughts he had put into Challenge to the Churches — his deepest convictions about the kind of moral and spiritual community their tradition called them to be. It included the university and was at least a community that would not be defeated by Fascism — as Dunkirk and the Battle of Britain had just proved. He assured them that they were part of a struggle that a creative and positive future depended on; that is, a struggle to maintain a faith in justice, in freedom, in truth and love. If this faith can be saved, the new community can flourish more strongly than ever. If it cannot, "the history of our culture is at an end, and we are for the dark."

> I do not think for a moment that the issue is in doubt. Truth is stronger than falsehood, however cunning; hope will always triumph over despair, however heavily armed; love, with its readiness for self-sacrifice, is a match for hatred, which for all its threatening visage has fear and cowardice at its heart. We can assert this with utter confidence, because the negative is only possible through the positive, and depends on it. How can death overcome life, when it is the mere negative of life? How can evil be other than parasitic upon good?
>
> You may think, perhaps, that this is idealism, or merely wishful thinking. To me it seems to be sober realism. Over and over again in history it has been vindicated. It has been proved already in this war ...[12]

The talk was classic Macmurray. It was a restating of his essential faith that soared above the depression he was feeling at the time. It tied in his finest reflections on Christianity along with the humanistic tradition in education that carried the Christian thrust. It was this spiritual and intellectual power in John that sometimes mesmerized people. It sometimes had the opposite effect, as well. His nephew Alastair, fifty years later, commented with some sympathy on some reasons for the minority viewpoint:

> He certainly had a way of sounding dogmatic, as though no other position was possible. But, after knowing him, you came to see that this was not an act of dominating others — he was, in fact, the gentlest of men. It was an expression of a faith that was fixed within him, and often it overwhelmed people who had never felt faith like that in their lives. But it made it hard to ask him questions; and made it hard for him to entertain and explore questions openly and easily.[13]

Quite apart from John's personal style, the course of history at the time could legitimately cause one to pause a bit before the fervour and conviction in this speech, so much like the radio talk he gave in Sweden. After the Holocaust and the bombing of Hiroshima and Nagasaki, a certain silence, bewilderment and scepticism understandably occupied the western soul about the spiritual possibilities for human beings that John proclaims here with such strength. It is not that Macmurray's words — in this talk or any of his talks — ring false or hollow. Rather, it is that they sound bugles that seem encouraging only in more human-sized battles. After 1945, even more than after 1918, these phrases can seem to come from a distant green planet, a garden, a place we no longer have the power to reach. This historical curtailment of heroic vision, even and perhaps especially the heroics of faith, did not leave Macmurray untouched after the war ended, though his own faith did not fail. He regretfully realized there were far fewer people who drank from its wells, breathed its air, or spoke its language. And that left him, in a deep part of himself — and despite his fabulously good humour and generosity of spirit — locked in a certain unrelievable loneliness. He was banished by historical circumstances from his natural milieu, a fish out of water, an artist without a culture, a believer with no community.

His last major involvement in 1941 was preparing the series of four talks for the BBC mentioned much earlier. At the BBC, his friendly contact was none other than Reverend Eric Fenn who had become the director of Religious Broadcasting. The series was to be called "Persons and Functions," probably a title offered by John himself. It was not a prepossessing title, and that was perhaps an ominous sign of the growing distance between Macmurray and the contemporary communications media of radio and, eventually, of television: John was unable, and probably unwilling, to "tart up" his titles, his language and his style of vocal presentation in order to draw in his audience. He was a plain realist from an earlier time who could not walk easily on the glistening webs just beginning to be woven by the image industries to attract and keep their listeners.

What is worthy of note is the main thesis of these talks. Macmurray presents his view of what he calls the "functional" dimension of human action and, in contrast to it, the fuller "personal" form of human action of which the functional is a part. He stated his position in this way: "the personal is always *through* the functional life; the functional life is always *for* the personal life." It was a way for him to get beyond body-soul dualism in practical issues while insisting on the "moreness" of personal life in all its expressions. It represents a development of concreteness in his thinking — begun in *Creative Society* — that would feature significantly in his final major work, the Gifford Lectures.

Macmurray began to be more attentive to the concrete and social aspects of his philosophy when he started reading Marx. He intensified that focus on the concrete with his reading of Suttie, and it gets further development in *Challenge to the Churches* and his reflections on employment, society and community in his BBC series on Persons and Functions. But the pivotal reflection for these more recent directions was the chapter he did for Ruth Nanda Anshen's book *Freedom: Its Meaning* in 1940 which was published in Britain only in 1942. His essay, entitled "Freedom in the Personal Nexus," challenges abstract views of the problem of freedom. There is no freedom apart from particular circumstances and, if that is so, the essential question is not "Are we free?" but "How free are we?" Real freedom, Macmurray says, depends upon the character of the nexus of the personal relations in which we are involved. Freedom is always a conditioned freedom, and it is always relational: I am only as free as you allow me to be, and you are only as free as I allow you to be.

Macmurray wants to build on this concrete fact. The conditions which either increase or decrease our freedom are lodged not in the stars but in our personal relationships, intimate and societal. And any limitation of freedom, beyond the order of physical nature, must have its source in us and, consequently, can be remedied only by altering our relationships as persons. Freedom as a problem arises not simply in a lack of power, but in a lack of power relative to a real desire. Having said that, he indicates that a society can actually diminish freedom even while increasing power through new technology because false desires and false freedoms are insinuated by means of propaganda into the nexus of personal relations in society. People end up "having" more things and "being" less free, because the nexus is defined by the unreal expectation that more or better things automatically bring more or better personal freedom. Equivalently, modern dictatorships — economic or political — can have much more power than the old dictators to control persons. It is a mechanical nexus not a personal one that ends up defining persons in such a culture, and freedom is thereby diminished. To become more free, the *nexus,* the character of the relationship, must itself become more personal rather than impersonal.

Focused perhaps by the war which was still in its early months at the time, Macmurray emphasizes the need to define "society" (political organization and cooperation) as a subordinate but essential dimension of the fuller reality of "community" (personal, cultural union). Without this distinction, freedom can be seen as a merely political issue to be resolved by the state. This can only lead to a totalitarian state because it assumes that the interests of the state are sovereign in relation to those of the individual. He emphasizes the need to maintain the primacy of the personal nexus of community over the functional nexus of organized society if freedom is to be achieved. There can be no "technique" for achieving freedom, but only the imperfect effort to maintain and enhance the equality of persons in all relationships, including those they share in society.[14]

It is this kind of reflection that broke the grip, in Macmurray's imagination, of the dominance of a dialectical interpretation of the dynamics of society. It was stimulated by the success of the Nazis to put their own version of rational control on their society. With the Nazis, Europe saw that social planning on a massive level could be done. It was just the totally wrong kind of society that resulted from their methods.[15] For the rest of the 1940s — and beyond — Macmurray shows much greater attentiveness to the concrete conditions of freedom. His incidental popular writings and two more BBC talks reflect, as well, a deeper conviction that genuine social planning is a necessity if a universal community is to be not only desirable but possible in the contemporary world.

These perspectives can also be seen in *Constructive Democracy*, two lectures on negative and positive democracy he delivered at UCL in December 1942, and again in *Conditions of Freedom*, lectures he gave at Queen's University in Canada in January 1949. In both cases, Macmurray attempted what he called a "social philosophy," challenging, as he did so, the long-standing liberal trust in the primacy of negative democracy in the British tradition, a traditional view that was championed by Isaiah Berlin in his inaugural address ten years later on "Two Concepts of Liberty." For all their potential fruitfulness, John did not pursue those questions with the single-mindedness he knew they deserved at that time, a period when Britain was most sympathetic to and most in need of deep reflection on the foundations for a socialist reconstruction of society.[16]

A year earlier, he had been looking for some way to help in the war effort, but the provost, Alan Mauer, asked him to stay on at the college because of his importance as a senior professor respected for his wisdom and guidance. However, early in 1942, with student enrolment down even lower, all candidates for Honours Philosophy gone from Aberystwyth, and now with the permission of the Provost, John had two private meetings with Sir Stafford Cripps. Cripps was the Lord Privy Seal in Churchill's government which had come to power in May 1940, one week before the evacuation of Dunkirk. They discussed a possible war job for John. As John reported to the secretary of University College, "during these talks he Cripps expressed the opinion that I could probably serve the country best by continuing my own work as a philosopher."[17]

The winter of 1941–42 were months of deeper depression than Macmurray had known at any other time in his life. Betty had stayed on at Jordans with Ephro in the autumn of 1941 since the school girls had left, and by then Sir Frederick Ogilvie, who had rented Home Base for a few months, had departed as well. John did not even have the occasional company of Alastair in Aberystwyth since he had graduated — and, at this very time, was recovering from a broken vertebra in his back from a motorcycle accident. Added to that concern, Alastair's brother Duncan, who had become an officer with the Gordons, was missing in the Far East and the steady reports of Japanese atrocities in early 1942 were chilling every member of the family as they waited anxiously for word of him.

It was a time when John was overwhelmed with disappointment with himself and filled with self-recrimination. He complained to Betty about his worthlessness — and also about the two of them growing out of touch. It was an occasion for some very frank exchanges between them. She tried to get him to snap out of his misery. " If you go on being so introspective, my dear, life with you will be boring for yourself as well as for me! You don't mean half of what you say ..." But she did respond to his remark about their being "out of touch" more head on:

> I do know what you mean, but I don't know how it can be changed. You see I don't act your way at all ... and the less I formulate things in words, the better for my painting. I don't think it is your fault at all, mostly mine, as I am not so sensitive as you are, but more normal, and commoner and I find it difficult to be agitated about my spiritual welfare, because I haven't any! ...
>
> Perhaps I don't confide in you enough. Not as I used to. But why bother you with my conscience. You'd have all the worry and reaction then! And I'd be ready to repeat my sins. I think I'm really a-moral. But there is one thing; I'm alway sincere with you, I never pretend to feel nicer or worse to you than I do ... But I don't tell you everything I feel or do with others, because you have often said it is better not to.

She is very direct with him about what she feels is the meaning behind their mutual assurance that they belong with one another. And yet they feel sometimes so distant from each other. She again tells him how different they are, but through all the differences she finds a strong thread between them, and from him to her, that she cherishes deeply:

> As for loving, I could scarcely have been able to stand more! Perhaps our love-making didn't quite succeed — there needed to be children perhaps, our being so frantically different in other ways, but we have this steady friendship which can still be broken and marred by our beastly temperaments.
>
> I have learned a lot about myself. I have learned to be quiet, ... to form my own judgments ... and I hope we can share our likes, we can allow each other to have them gratified. I'm not sure about sex. I like my freedom and take it, but I definitely don't want you to have the same freedom! I can't understand why. I am ashamed that is how I feel. Is this going to make you introspective? I do love you and to be near you is often a benediction, and that is the best in relationships.
>
> I'm going to bed now, with my cat, my candle, and my padded jacket.

Love to you, dear John. Think better of yourself and let us
applaud you. XXXX, dear husband.
                    Yours, Betty

The intimacy of that exchange is matched by its honesty. It reveals a deep
truthfulness in her — and between them — that allows for celebrating the
friendship bond that they both always felt was God-given. It also allowed
them, most of the time, to live graciously with what Betty often called
their "chalk and cheese" differences of sensibility and temperament.

Spring came, and word came that Duncan was alive and had been in
hospital. They still did not know more than that. Having heard from him,
Betty immediately sent him a cable with love from both of them. It was,
in fact, shortly before his capture by the Japanese in the fall of Singapore.
Only after the war ended would they come to know the story.

That summer, the provost of UCL, Alan Mauer died suddenly, leaving
the college secretary temporarily in charge. Macmurray wrote to him from
Jordans in September, asking to stay in London. The case he made to him
was simple: the vastly reduced student body in philosophy at Aberystwyth
left Mr Keeling more than able to handle the required classes. He was not
pushy in his request. In fact, he gave three well-developed reasons why it
may not be wise for him to be permitted to stay away from Aberystwyth!
On the other hand, he felt he could do more good in London, and he stated
that frankly.

His volunteer services, as he told the secretary, had been called on from
another direction. Because of a connection John had made with the Anglo-
Soviet Public Relations Committee (ASPRC), he had been asked in 1941
to head its commission to research and report on freedom of religion in the
Soviet Union:

> ... with a view to helping to remove difficulties in Anglo-Soviet
> co-operation. This has involved a considerable amount of research
> and study, including learning Russian, and I am most anxious to
> complete the work. I have collected most of the necessary material
> and am at the beginning of writing the report. None of it can be
> done so conveniently as in or near London, and some of it can only
> be done at the British Museum.

He ended the request noting that he had been appointed to a governing
committee of the ASPRC, and believed it would be not only convenient
but necessary to be in London for those duties to be fulfilled. But he was
more than willing to leave the service of the college temporarily and seek
paid employment elsewhere. So, despite his "openness" to going back to
Aber, he managed to get himself well painted into a London-based corner!

What was the poor secretary to do? He consulted with various deans, and the solution offered by UCL was to keep him officially in the service of the college and allow him to be free for other work, especially his volunteer work with ASPRC. John moved out of Aberystwyth and came back to Home Base permanently.

It was shortly before that very satisfying decision was reached that John had come up with the idea of running lunchtime lectures at Gower Street featuring significant speakers on significant topics. The lectures would be free and open to the public without reserve. In his October 2 letter, the Secretary encouraged John to initiate those public lectures.[18] He did so, giving three lectures himself, and calling on several prominent faculty members to join him. The lectures were a huge success. When J.B. Priestley gave his talk — a rather poorly prepared one — a member of the audience stood up in the middle of it, started walking towards the exit, then collapsed with a crash onto the floor. Everything stopped, and as the man was helped out of the hall, Priestley was heard to mutter: "I knew my talk was bad, but I didn't think it was that bad." After the talk, John and Betty took Priestley to lunch and Betty was disappointed at how Priestley glowed when he was recognized in the restaurant. She reflected philosophically in her diary on that incident: "Sometimes, in the most fleeting moment, the full character of a man can be revealed."

At the same time as he was making his autumn arrangements with UCL, John wrote to his mother repeating to her his earlier complaints to Kenneth Barnes and Irene Grant: "I've developed such a distaste for writing that I can hardly bring myself to use a pen." This will become a recurrent theme over the coming years. It is a turmoil and humiliation that will afflict him even when he approaches the writing of letters to close and dear friends, and will last till the very end of his life.

He also told his mother he was doing some political work with Richard Acland and Priestley, "but I'm not particularly happy about it. The uncertainty about the war makes all public work questionable and unsatisfactory ..."[19] This political work refers to his collaboration with the fledgling Common Wealth Movement (CW). Much could be said about this socialist-oriented political party, but it actually formed a very short and small part of Macmurray's active involvements. The same could be said for its role in Britain during the war, especially after Labour came into power in 1945 with 393 seats and proceeded to dominate not only all left-wing politics but the whole political scene in Britain.

It is doubtful that Macmurray's departure from Common Wealth associations in 1943 was either quixotic or of huge significance relationally. As the 1942 letter to his mother stated, he was not altogether happy about it. But, apart from particular reasons, time and again he had testified that he was not primarily a political animal. He could be associated in such a venture for a short time with like-minded people, especially the CW people like Richard Acland, Tom Wintringham, J.B. Priestley, Tom Driberg and Richie Calder, to all of whom he was bound by loyalty and affection. But the essentially political form of the endeavour put him on a playing-field other than the one of his nature and choice. The separation was totally amicable, and as late as 1947 he was in friendly though rare correspondence with Acland.

Looking beyond the war

The Anglo-Soviet Public Relations Committee (ASPRC) work was more congenial. John, as a philosopher and educator, was primarily interested in the conversion of minds and hearts and imaginations. By that avenue he could serve the effort to convert societies into communities. His work in education also had a primarily spiritual interest. The ASPRC was founded at a meeting on September 3 to allow those gifts to flourish. In its brief statement of aims, it undertook: (a) to improve means of intercourse between Great Britain and the USSR, and to increase knowledge of each country in the other; (b) to take any action desirable to remove possible misunderstanding in Anglo-Soviet relations; (c) to call the attention of responsible authorities to specific needs or difficulties; (d) to study specific problems by means of sub-committees, and to prepare and circulate reports; and (e) to arrange public functions or meetings that advance the purposes of the committee.

The membership of the ASPRC was extensive, and it drew together many people with whom Macmurray had worked before such as John Middleton Murry, Harold Laski, Victor Gollancz, Richie Calder, C.E.M. Joad, J.M. Keynes, J.B.Priestley, John Strachey, Kenneth Ingram, Beatrice Webb, Leonard Woolf, as well as several highly placed and influential citizens. New members could be proposed to the executive committee by regular members, and the nominations in that first month by Mrs Rawdon-Smith were noteworthy. Her first was the Right Honourable Lord Rothschild. In December, however, she proposed the names of five others including Captain Anthony Blunt and Guy Burgess — of subsequent notoriety as agents of Soviet Russian espionage.

Macmurray was still based in Aberystwyth at the time the group was begun. Despite that, he was requested to head the committee to study the condition of religion in the Soviet Union. Immediately, he proposed to his committee a way of proceeding for preparing the report and offered a suggested outline for the report asking for the committee members' comments. He then cast his net widely asking associates to provide the names of needed experts. Among those who responded were his old SCM acquaintance Walter Paton, J.H. Oldham, now publishing the *Christian News-Letter*, Rabbi Israel Mattuck, Carl Heath (who recommended being in touch with Julius Hecker!), Sir Francis Freemantle and many others. The response Macmurray generated was generous and stretched over months. The correspondence and communication — with fervent pleas to see Macmurray when he is next in London — give solid backing to his claim to the UCL Secretary that leaving Aberystwyth and having a London base would be far preferable for the extensive work that had fallen on his shoulders.

Early in 1942, the committee called for a major conference to be held that April on the theme of "Britain and Russia in the New World Order." Macmurray was asked to speak along with Evgheny Lampert on the religious question. His approach to the question was, as usual, broad and foundational and his conclusions were clear and practical: cooperation between Britain and the Soviet Union is a good goal. To foster understanding we must grasp some key differences between West and East: Russia has never experienced the kind of democratic freedom achieved in the west around religious issues. Also there has never been in Russia a separation of church and state or as wide a distinction between the spiritual and temporal as is true in the West. The role of the Orthodox Church in supporting the Tsarist regime has been long and extensive, so the resulting resentment of official religion in Russia is essentially political, not religious. We must let the church and state in Russia find their way to a new relationship and not immediately insist that they have one like ours. Knowing the historical background is critical for understanding the Russian government's official atheism, and the violence against religion. Knowing the differences is central to generating understanding and also to offering challenges; and it is essential for realistic cooperation. Citing recent changes by the Russian government, Macmurray, though critical of the curtailment of the freedom to educate and proselytize religiously, finds reasons to hope for an increasing religious tolerance in Soviet Russia, which is all that westerners should legitimately hope for. In 1942, despite his critical view of the government's repressive policy against free religious expression, he recalls the efforts at equality in Russia and reminds his listeners that "... no structure the world has yet known has come nearer to embodying the social principles of Christianity."[20] One could be forgiven for wondering with surprise if he knew anything of that government's actions during the 1930s.

Macmurray left two thick files, one of ASPRC documents and correspondence, and the other of newspaper clippings, articles and extensive notes taken on books he read on religion in Russia. But there is no sign in

his papers of the completed report that the religion committee was to prepare. It is as though the project and the committee itself simply melted away.
After the summer of 1943, Macmurray wrote just a few items relating to this
research. In the mid-1940s, as much as a favour as by conviction, he wrote
very short, somewhat embarrassingly positive Forewords for three books in
a series on life in Russia. And in 1947, he gave a lecture published as *A
Crisis of Culture: the USSR and the West*. Effectively, after the summer of
1943, Macmurray's attention was drawn in other directions.

In September of 1943 he wrote his mother a birthday letter bragging
about the gardening prizes he got at the Jordans fair for his onions (a second), tomatoes (a first) and his French beans (a second), and also praising
some excellent portraits that Betty had recently painted. He tells her: "I've
started on a new book, too, that is long overdue," and then says no more
about it, leaving one to conjecture what that project might have been since
his next book was actually *The Conditions of Freedom,* a set of lectures
given in Canada six years later. There are no papers from 1943 that suggest material for a book.

A possible indication of work he hoped might become a book can be
found in the Upton Lectures which he gave at Manchester College,
Oxford, in May 1944. Macmurray accepted the rather large assignment of
six lectures offering a systematic exploration of "The Problem of Evil."
He uses the lectures to explore the implications of the structure of the
motives of love and fear, the difference between event and intention, the
nature of intention within action, and the constitutive context of a community of interacting persons — with its implicit distinction between egocentric and heterocentric action. In these lectures, he attempted to offer a
coherent treatment of them as ethically interrelated elements. It was a
massive undertaking.

Even a cursory reading of the lectures reveals that Macmurray, in the
early 1940s, is working out in significant detail, the ideas which make up
the essential structure and content of his Gifford Lectures which were
written and delivered ten years later. To read the Uptons beside the
Giffords is to see the difference between first exploration and mature
expression. The arguments in the Uptons are complex, but they are often
complicated, loose and even meandering in places, stating conclusions for
which the reasons and reasoning are straining and not quite in focus. That
is rarely if ever the case in the Giffords.

But textual analysis is not the point here. It does seem possible, that
despite all the political and socially engaged activities that had consumed
Macmurray in his years in London, he was able to advance his project on
a philosophy of the personal at least to some degree. He did so directly in
the 1938 essay "What Is Action?", but mainly indirectly in his other books
and essays on social, political and religious themes. The new book he

mentions so briefly to his mother — and to no one else in any correspondence at that time — was perhaps being fashioned in this first major step away from the "social" issues that so occupied him throughout the 1930s, and back into the deep-running current of his essential philosophical purpose, which, by its very nature, was unrelievably social.

In January 1944, in a letter to his mother, John gives reflections on the war that reveal as much about how his mind works as how the world went. He begins by saying he expects 1944 to be the last year of the war in Europe, despite the British and American warnings of great losses. The final big battle, he suggests, is being fought now in Russia where he expects the whole southern German army to be broken to pieces in the next few weeks. As for Europe:

> We may invade soon; but I hardly think before Easter. I've always been sure — even before the Nazis invaded Russia, that the real war was between the Soviet Union and Germany, and that Russia was certain to win it. I said so in public during the Russian attack on Finland, while she was supposed to be in alliance with Germany. I've thought a lot about the consequence; and the more I think of that, the more glad I am of it. The greatest danger to future peace is America; and we are going to have to support America because of the position of Canada, Australia and New Zealand. I think the Continent of Europe will turn against us and look to Russia to save them from us. That may not seem fair to us, and may not *be* fair; but for all that it is quite natural; and it will be good I think. For Russia represents the future; and in many ways it represents one of the triumphs of Christianity. That may sound a queer thing to say; but I am sure it is so.

He goes on to say that he is partly positive about Russia because of its spiritual energy, in contrast to western churches which:

> are worn out ... and must be radically changed before we see a new outburst of creative spiritual energy. That may come, too, from Russia; and perhaps from China. I'm afraid it is we who need the missionaries now. But it is coming; ...

He closes by saying he is convinced this is part of the way God is bringing the world into its oneness and completion; not in your time, he tells her, or in mine — but it will be accomplished.

It is hard to know, in the light of such conjectures, how to judge Macmurray's essential brilliance alongside his major misses in his particular judgments. Put crudely, he is crystal-balling here, and here as well as in other predictions about particular events, he was proved quite wrong. But predictions are not all that's going on here. Macmurray has a vivid general image of what the world would look like if it were to progress towards being the community of justice and love it is "meant" to be. He was given to visualizing certain particular events in his own time in relation to the "coming of the Kingdom" he believed God was bringing about. He believed that every historical event was part of this broken-lined, mysterious movement of the world toward's God's dominion of justice and love for all. He looked constantly, and with expectation and intelligence, for signs of it. As in the case of his enthusiasm for Marx, it led him to anticipate what the next general step in history might be for that to be realized (for instance, articulating the need to create some kind of global legislative and judicial bodies in order to hold global capitalism to account for its many fierce delinquencies).

Sometimes, he was very astute in his judgments. That was always when he judged the *nature* of a reality, individual or social, that was present and taking place — such as Fascism. He was very good, as well, at judging what one might expect when this or that nature *developed and expressed itself.* However he was apparently no more able than anyone else, to judge the moment when major developments actually would take place. Two years earlier, in the foothills of the Chilterns, he had stood with Kenneth Barnes watching the German "doodle-bugs" lighting up the night sky in the distance as they fell on London, and he pronounced solemnly: "Kenneth, we are witnessing the death of capitalism." As we noted, he acknowledged sometime later this huge miss in judgment, which he attributed to his enthusiasm for Marx's dialectical view of history.

On April 26, 1944 John informed Provost Pye of UCL that he was being sent a formal letter offering him the Chair of Moral Philosophy at Edinburgh. As he tells the provost:

To be asked to succeed Taylor is a great honour, and a Chair in Philosophy in Scotland offers very much greater scope that it ever can in England outside of Oxford. I should have much less hesitation in refusing an Oxford Professorship than a Scottish one.[21]

After presenting some further considerations, Macmurray ends the letter noting that the terms of his appointment state that he must declare before April 30 in any year if he wishes to give notice of intention to retire from his UCL post. He asks the provost for slightly more time before he makes a firm decision on the matter. The letter of invitation arrived on April 29, and the first two weeks of May were a time of discernment, a time to prepare to go to Oxford for the Upton Lectures, and a time to hand over to someone else the public lecture series he had started two years earlier. On

May 15 he announced to the Provost of UCL that he had decided to accept the offer from Edinburgh. His letter is gracious, noting that his fifteen years at UCL were marked by "nothing but kindness and consideration from all my colleagues. To part from them and the college is hard." He continues:

> The main reason for my decision is this: For many years now there has been forming in my mind a philosophical outlook which is, in large part, the result of an attempt to understand the change that is coming over our civilization. Until quite recently it seemed that even if there was something in it, it would be long before it could be generally understood. But indications have been coming one after another in recent months, from many directions, that other people are moving rapidly in the same direction, though not at the philosophical level. It seems to me that I ought to make a serious attempt in the next few years to get this philosophy stated in strict form; and Edinburgh offers an almost ideal set of conditions for doing this. In London, I could do it, if at all, only with great difficulty and with a divided attention. The idea I have may turn out to be of little value; and I may prove incompetent to work it out. But one has to the chance of these things; and I feel bound to make the attempt.[22]

There is no doubt that John was feeling that time was not limitless for this great project he had envisioned. By 1944 he had allowed his beard to grow again, and it had come back more white than brown. The offer from Edinburgh was an invitation to leave behind the almost frantically excited era that had characterized their whole time in London and to move, gently and with determination, towards quieter years and, for him, the disciplined execution of his philosophical task.

After the Upton Lectures were delivered, John and Betty spent the better part of the summer selling up and preparing for their move. They disliked leaving Jordans. But the prospect of living in Scotland, close to their families for the first time in their married life, was deeply attractive to both of them. Despite deeply mixed feelings about leaving London, especially on Betty's part, they both felt the move was right. In the middle of September, they said their final goodbyes and left. They were going home.

Chapter 15

Fighting for the Humanities (1944–58)

Their last summer in London and Jordans was so busy that John and Betty had found no time to go to Edinburgh to look for a house. When they moved at the end of the summer they went into temporary residence at 180 Dalkeith Road and only a few weeks later did they buy the house at 10 Bright's Crescent that remained their home during the fourteen years John occupied the Moral Philosophy Chair in Edinburgh. The reason for not having a more leisurely house-hunting was clear: in addition to the Upton Lectures given in May, John delivered on June 7 the Essex Hall Lecture on "Idealism in Religion." That lecture was a cultural analysis of the sorry state of religion in 1944 not only in the churches (one of his regular themes) but in the majority of people in western civilization. People in the west, Macmurray had concluded, no longer looked at either their individual or social life from a religious perspective.

For him, this was not a matter of something like leaving behind one's affiliation with a political party. It was losing the biblical vision of the human which grounded the feeling for democracy as a way of life. As he told his audience, without a social perspective that acknowledges energetically what makes for a fully human and personal life in community, postwar reconstruction — in both its vision and practice — was likely to be based on merely political and technical considerations. He judged that the form of Christianity current in the west was no longer "real" enough to move people to consider issues deeper than efficiency and cooperation as they planned for the future.

As he saw it, if Christianity was to have anything to contribute to future social planning, it had to get beyond its idealist fixations on a "next" world and express plainly what it had to contribute to *this* world. It had to encourage people to form their vision of a new society through a common ideal of the good life. For an individualistic society, he had noted the year before in his review of Sir Richard Livingstone's *Education for a World Adrift,* this required nothing less than the creation of a new culture — one that only the common people could create. He had concluded then: "To serve this process we need above all to recover an unflinching faith in common humanity."[1] He now asked: Can Christianity aid and abet such a unitary vision? Real Christianity, he told his Essex Hall listeners, would encourage people to take spiritual responsibility for their society from this perspective of the common good. Just as his talk challenged Christians to rid themselves of their other-worldliness, it was implicitly a challenge to secularists, as well, to go beyond a complacent materialism in their attitudes and premises, and serve the development of full, personal life in community in post-war societies.

The lecture was not a yearning for the past when formal religion dominated life. It It was a call to a deeper engagement with the present, with an eye to the practical needs of the future. Macmurray proposed a vision of the kind of post-nationalist, global society that the future would absolutely require if world peace and justice were ever to be achievable. This lecture was based on what had become a characteristic position held by Macmurray: that genuine Christianity expresses genuine humanity, and offers the foundations for creating and developing a positive social life. This was the vision he brought with him to his new work at the University of Edinburgh — though, within the secular context of university life, his focus was not the Gospel but the Humanities.

The University of Edinburgh had been functioning during the war, of course, but along with every other university in Britain it had been put somewhat on hold while most young people were dedicating themselves to the war effort. This slowdown was especially true in philosophy since A. E. Taylor, Macmurray's predecessor as Professor of Moral Philosophy, had fallen ill several months before his eventual retirement in 1943, leaving Professor Norman Kemp Smith to carry the burdens of both departments of philosophy in 1943–44. By 1944, the aging Kemp Smith was delighted to see Macmurray arrive, if for no other reason than to return to a manageable workload himself during this last year before his own retirement. The two men, so different in their approach to philosophy, held each other in high respect and became good friends.

Macmurray's appointment took effect on October 1, 1944, and he gave his inaugural lecture in Pollock Hall on Nicholson Street that same month. The lecture, entitled "The Contemporary Function of Moral Philosophy," unfurled his colours for all to see. He rejected a certain traditional view that moral philosophy was simply a theoretical affirmation of the eternally valid principles of morality. In some contrast to the style and stance of Taylor, Macmurray presented his belief: "that it is the business of the moralist not merely to answer the perennial questions of moral theory — but to answer them in a way that is relevant, and clearly relevant to the form in which they arise for men and women in the pattern of contemporary life."[2] The lecture articulated Macmurray's own philosophical project. First, he proposed the need for a philosophy of action to ground moral philosophy. Having located the terms for this philosophy of action in Reason, he ended by describing a view of reason and of the proper work of moral philosophy that had been forming in him for more than twenty years:

Reason itself is not a private but a mutual possession; and our personality is not in us but between us. The principles of morality are the laws of personal relationship: they are not merely norms of behaviour, but the constituent principles of those human relationships by which we live. For a relation of persons which denies them is not merely unsatisfactory; it is not a personal relationship, as a friendship for ulterior motives is not a friendship at all, but a pretence. These constitutive principles of human relationships do not change with the changes in the political and economic nexus of external society. They are eternal; and they provide the standard and the centre of reference for all values. It is here that the eternal truths of morality are to be discovered and understood. Yet these principles can operate only in the changing circumstances of history, and can be sustained only through a perennial adaptation to the flux of the external world. Indeed, the moral problem of humanity — on which moral philosophy labours to shed a growing illumination — is to maintain the subordination of the changing conditions of life and the values they embody, to the unchanging and absolute values of the personal life of mankind, the life of human fellowship.[3]

The curators of the university who elected and appointed Macmurray on May 23 to his new position had informally declared their interest in a somewhat more "prophetic" presence in the Moral Chair after the nineteen-year tenure of the prestigious and steady Taylor. After this lecture, they may have felt confirmed they were getting the goods they had ordered — a professor who was, at once, steeped in the tradition and yet thoroughly forward-looking.

The Analytic philosophers move in

However, Macmurray's first duty at Edinburgh was not to make public speeches but to build up his Moral Philosophy department, an undertaking he began in earnest in 1945. He did this in colleagueship with Arthur David Ritchie, the biologist-turned-philosopher who that year succeeded Kemp Smith in the Chair of Logic and Metaphysics. A.R.C. Duncan (Macmurray's assistant at UCL before the war) and Errol Bedford came on as lecturers. The assistants who arrived over the next few years included Peter Heath, Frederick Broadie — both of whom later became lecturers — R.J.K. (King) Murray, Kenneth Rankin, Axel Stern, Ernest Gellner and Howard Horsburgh, along with others. In addition to staff, Macmurray had to increase the number of courses as the university geared up to receive returning veterans. Aesthetics and then Social Philosophy along with a Second Ordinary class in Moral Philosophy, were soon added to the course offerings.

On coming to Edinburgh, Macmurray had resolved to cut back on the frequent public talks and activities that had marked his life in London in order to give time to his writing.[4] It was an objective he only partially achieved. In 1939 he had joined the editorial board of *Philosophy,* the journal of the British Institute of Philosophy, and continued to serve on it for almost twenty years. He also maintained his membership in the Aristotelian Society. But many of the fresh commitments he took on were embraced at least partly because of his perception that the profound cultural crisis in the west, confirmed by the war and how it was fought, was now revealing itself swiftly in the field of education.

The first meeting Dr George Davie, the great historian of the Scottish intellectual tradition, ever had with Macmurray was in late 1946. In a quiet moment at that conference, Macmurray declared to Davie who had left Edinburgh for Belfast a short time earlier : "Davie, the humanities are fighting for their life at Edinburgh, and they're losing the battle." The remedy in a nutshell, as Macmurray formulated it a short time later, was not to look backwards with nostalgia but "to conceive and teach each subject in terms of its place and function in the unitary life of contemporary civilization."[5] For him, the advance was related to, but not identical with, a kind of return to the orientation that had marked the Scottish tradition in education for so long. However, as the 1950s unfolded, he came to believe there was no will for a remedy because there was little perception or feeling that there was a problem. The technological, functional and, finally, relativist viewpoint in the culture at large was, in his view, getting an irreversible stranglehold on the aims and methods of higher education, as well.

And this held true not only, or even especially, at Edinburgh. Analytic philosophy, well dug in at Oxford and Cambridge, was now sweeping across England. It crossed over into Scotland without having to pass through any customs officers with a knowledge of or care for the Scottish tradition in higher education and the prominent place of philosophy within that tradition. By the mid-1950s the new barbarians, as Macmurray might have called them, had effectively won. Macmurray's humanistic approach to philosophy was, in the eyes of many of the new, English-trained Rylean members of the philosophy department, quaint and outmoded.

This seismic shift that relegated Macmurray's kind of philosophizing to the periphery was apparent in the process by which A.J. Ayer, John's successor to the Grote Professorship at University College, London, was chosen. In June, 1945, Provost Pye sent Macmurray a list of names of people who might be considered as candidates for the position. He asked for

Macmurray's response to each one. Macmurray gave a positive response to Braithwaite, Dorothy Emmet, Hodges, Robinson and Hardie. He had significant reservations about four others. Next to Austin, he noted simply: "I do not know anything about him." When it came to Ayer, he wrote: "Narrowly logical — though a leading light of the new logical school. I should think most unsuitable for you." Then he offered Pye three names that had not appeared on the UCL list for his consideration: W.H.F. Barnes, George Davie and D.D. Raphael — with long paragraphs on the virtues of each. Pye wrote back, profuse in his thanks, saying he would distribute Macmurray's notes as a confidential paper to the search committee. In November, Pye wrote for further advice on Davie. Davie, as luck would have it, had just recently accepted the position in Belfast so he was out of the running. Macmurray took the opportunity to mention Sinclair who was at Edinburgh under Ritchie as another possibility. In the end, none of his views seemed to matter in the least. The committee chose Ayer, and Pye wrote to Ayer saying how personally delighted he was with the committee's choice. When Ayer gave his inaugural lecture at UCL he didn't even mention Macmurray, an omission that was not only noted but considered a disgrace. The new breed in British academic philosophy had clearly arrived.[6]

The "largest classes in the country"

At Edinburgh, Macmurray's philosophy was much appreciated by the Ordinary Class students who were not yet attuned to the changing philosophical times. His Ordinary classes in Old College's Minto House on Chambers Street were regularly packed — in the early years with a mix of war veterans and the youth fresh from school. However, right to the end of his teaching years in 1958, he regularly attracted over 400 students to his Introductory Class which, as Peter Heath observes, "must have easily been the largest in the whole country." Students had a choice for their beginning philosophy between Macmurray and A.D. Ritchie, but Ritchie, despite his vast knowledge and pleasant manner, had a lecturing style that was unredeemably dull, and that may have been one reason among others why the vast majority of beginning students flocked to Macmurray. From a sheerly technical point of view, it must be said that Macmurray's own lecture style was somewhat unprepossessing:

He talked into his beard, in a gentle, mellifluous tenor which could hardly be heard beyond the third row. But students hung on his words, and crammed into his classroom well before the hour began, to get within earshot, ar at least to get a decent view of one who looked so absolutely the archetype of everything a philosopher is popularly imaged to be. The neat, silvery-white hair and beard, the rosy complexion, the clear blue eyes and puckish twinkle all gave him an air of benevolence and wisdom that tended to overpower the critical sense of his listeners, at least while they were still beginners. The more mature students — among them John Hick, the eminent theologian-to-be, and others of great ability — were much more sceptical, and found him vague, elusive and difficult to pin down in argument.[7]

This description, in capturing the aura as well as the limitations of Macmurray as a teacher, reflects the views of many of Macmurray's former students and colleagues. However, as significant as they were, appearance and style of oral delivery were hardly the sole basis of his appeal. Macmurray was perceived by most students as having a view of the world and of the purposes of human life in the world that made sense. It responded to their own questions about life and its meaning. In addition to that he was, as was mentioned, compelling in the quiet and utterly sure manner in which he articulated his philosophy.[8] When he was at Balliol, and for most of his time at UCL, he stood to lecture, and moved around with some animation while doing so. When he came to Edinburgh he sat to give his lectures. He lectured with notes on the table before him but, in fact, rarely referred to them; presenting his ideas in an unbroken flow of clear and coherent discourse almost as if the lecture were memorized. The magnetic immediacy of his communication was undoubtedly enhanced by his ideas "being largely of his own making" and addressed to life; they were not a mediation, from an exclusively historical perspective, of the thoughts of other thinkers.[9] It was enough to earn him a standing ovation at the end of one of his lecture courses, an extremely rare demonstration of enthusiasm by students for a professor's performance.

His influence over those fourteen years on the students, and through them on the country, was immeasurable. Time and again former students began their testimony about him by saying: "That man changed my life!" Peter Heath, a member of Macmurray's department for all but John's first two years, knew the students who went through Macmurray's courses and mused much later:

By moving up from London ... he still had a 'bully pulpit' with his hordes of students, many of whom went on to become school teachers and ministers and opinion-makers all over Scotland. John Mackintosh, Alan Thompson and Ron King Murray were well-known Labour MPs (the latter a High Court judge). Tom Nairn a left wing intellectual journalist. Michael Gill the producer of Kenneth Clark's world famous *Civilization* series on TV, to say nothing of the numerous Edinburgh philosophers who wound up in English or Scottish philosophy departments or, like Terry

Penelhum, Fraser Crowley, Roderick McGill and others, followed Sandy
Duncan's example and emigrated to Canada ... there is not much doubt
that Macmurray provided the impetus to most of these careers, much as
Kemp Smith had done in the previous generation when the balance of
power and numbers between the two departments had tilted the other
way.[10]

George Davie completes this picture when he noted that there were a lot
of students interested in Macmurray's ideas at Edinburgh even in the sixties after he had gone, but none of them were majoring in philosophy.

Macmurray was a particularly gentle person, encouraging to students
who came to him, and evoking deep affection in those individuals who had
been recipients of his solicitude. Respect and affection flowed from colleagues, as well. As Errol Bedford recalled, he had a quirky sense of humour
to go along with his puckish and slightly twisted smile. He enjoyed paradoxes and jokes that were subtle and reversals of expectations. He liked to
offer leading remarks that startled or puzzled, in order to get an interesting
conversation going. But he could also, on occasion, be quite sharp. Once,
during his Ordinary class, a student asked a question in the middle of
Macmurray's presentation, interrupting the master's flow. Macmurray
looked directly at the student and said quietly and incisively: "Young man,
I am giving an academic lecture, not leading a public meeting."[11]

A certain unwillingness to engage students in philosophical argument
led to Macmurray receiving more mixed reviews from his Honours students. Although they along with everyone else found him unremittingly
gracious and pleasant with them as individuals, some of these advanced
students found his use of terms irritatingly loose, and they felt he kept it
that way in order to serve his case. They also chafed under his unwillingness to engage in debate over his ideas or the neologisms, such as "con-
tinuant" or "negative" and "positive" personal relations, that he invented
to communicate them. When queried or challenged, Macmurray would
usually just restate his view; he would not be pinned down. This feature of
his seminar style added a slightly cynical dimension to the impression of
him being more of a religious prophet proclaiming eternal truth than a university teacher for whom the truth was something to be worked out col-
laboratively and by approximations. This latter way of proceeding was,
ironically, his official view about how truth is achieved. But the dialectic
he subscribed to in theory seemed, to some of them at least, sadly missing
from his personal practice in these seminars. Ironically, he also lacked the
kind of personal knowledge of them that he proposed as such a value in
his philosophy. In his seminars, it sometimes happened that he would not
be able to put a face to a student's name even after meeting with him twice
a week over the course of a full year.[12]

The combination of personal and philosophical elements that helped to give Macmurray a sense of distance seems to have resulted in even those who were his professional colleagues not knowing him philosophically. When Peter Heath observed that "Macmurray seemed to have no clear-cut philosophical ancestry, and no obvious allegiances in the subject," he was expressing a view held by many. In his Edinburgh years, Macmurray left the lecturing on the "set books" in the First Ordinary Class to Bedford and Heath. Heath, who became a lecturer after Duncan left for Canada in 1949, had the impression that Macmurray was no great scholar of the history of philosophy. Bedford, on the other hand, had few doubts about his Professor's capacities in that area. Between 1939–41 at UCL, Bedford had studied Kant's *Critique* with Macmurray and had gone to his lectures on Political Philosophy from Hobbes to Rousseau. He found them some of the best he had ever listened to. He also heard of the success of Macmurray's lectures on German Romantic Philosophy. Neither Bedford nor Heath would have had reason to know of the attention Macmurray gave to the history of philosophy during his own student years, and when he was lecturing on set books himself at Manchester, Witwatersrand and Balliol.

George Davie offers another view on this lack of acknowledging historical influences among the nineteenth and twentieth century Scottish thinkers (academics and divines) who made their mark in philosophy and theology — among whom he includes Macmurray:

> All these philosophers came out of the same tradition. They were
> not, for the most part, interested in viewing themselves historically,
> so they did not give footnotes to their own thought and did not ask
> for any to theirs. They never thought of themselves as part of a
> 'school of thought'; the very concept would probably have been
> repugnant to them. They all liked to think of themselves as free
> thinkers dealing in ideas, understanding and shaping the world ...
> Most of these Scots of the Scottish realist tendency were
> individualists — even though they often had a communitarian
> viewpoint! ...[13]

Davie, as an historian, acknowledged that Macmurray did not have a primary interest in historical issues as such; he was interested in systematic ones, and in history only to the degree it was necessary for thinking creatively. Macmurray knew Kant and Hegel well, Davie observed, "but did not overdepend on them." Formed by that tradition, Davie also knew that the diversity of views in these Scottish thinkers arose, in fact, from within a deeply shared, common culture:

When I studied here [Edinburgh], those in Honours were treated to
Norman Kemp Smith doing a spirited and brilliant defense of
Determinism in one seminar, then going on to Taylor defending
freedom right after, in another. The conclusion: Taylor had got the
better of the argument but Smith had won on conviction!

Norman Kemp Smith used to give almost inaccessible lectures in his
Ordinary classes, and tell them: "This is probably quite beyond you, but
sometime 10 years from now, it might happen that you will be hit by one
of these ideas and see what it means then." He had spent a lot of time in
Germany and believed in that old German conviction that professors
should not waste their time or reputations by trying to be too understandable.[14]

It seems Macmurray learned something from his older colleague; but, in
the finest Scottish tradition, he gave it his own fit in his dealings with colleagues. He was tolerant of the differences of philosophical viewpoint
expressed by the young men thirty years his junior, despite his philosophical divergence from them. Conversely, he never pressured the assistants
in his department to accept *his* views. He also didn't worry too much
about making himself understandable or acceptable to his colleagues,
especially after the shift in philosophical viewpoint had taken firm hold.
On February 17, 1952 he wrote to Sandy Duncan at Queens:

We jog along. The Department is active and harmonious. Both
Peter and Errol are blossoming exceedingly well. I begin now to
fear losing them. And numbers are dropping a bit ...

But any lack of communication philosophically between Macmurray and
his faculty was not because he did not know their basic position. In 1950,
Macmurray published a paper called "Some Reflections on the Analysis
of Language." Around the same time he presented two others entitled
"Language as Communication" and "The Abuse of Language in Logic."
They represented his critical encounter with the premises of Analytic philosophy from his perspective: the dialogical nature of personal existence
and the primacy of relationship — ideally heterocentric relationship — in
all personal communication. Language was not primarily expression, as
the Analysts would have it, but communication. Expression for him was a
subordinate dimension within the intention to communicate. He confirmed this viewpoint in another paper called "Logic and Psychology" in
which he proposed that there is no possibility of definitively separating
logic from pyschology, a separation that mainstream modern thought
assumed and insisted on. Feeling and thinking, he held, were integrated

elements that could be distinguished but never separated in interpersonal communication. There is no evidence these essays ever became part of Macmurray's professional communications (dialectical or otherwise!) with his departmental colleagues.

Despite the conceptual barriers and the moments missed, Macmurray's open attitude was formative for his lecturers and several of his assistants. Sandy Duncan, whose aunt was May Anderson and who had known Macmurray since he was a boy, remained a life-long friend and acknowledged Macmurray's influence on his own thinking. He wrote a small book called *The Nature of Persons* in which he distilled marvellously the essential points of Macmurray's philosophy. Macmurray found Sandy's manuscript lucid and sound, but wished that his protégé might have been more critical. Ernest Gellner, who spent years at the London School of Economics, cherished his short time in Edinburgh, and seems to have admired Macmurray more in later years — after he had been buffeted by the philosophical world a bit — than when he was on faculty there. In *Words and Things,* Gellner published a scathing denunciation of the Wittgensteinian orthodoxy that prevailed in Britain in the 1950s and 1960s. Had Gellner seen the just-mentioned essays of Macmurray's, he might have modified at least slightly his view that the old Scottish tradition, and Macmurray as its main representative in Edinburgh, was "insufficiently rigorous."[15] Broadie, a kind but eccentric man, probably knew Macmurray's thought better than any of the department members in the 1950s, and he was positive about it. Howard Horsburgh held Macmurray in high respect — even though he felt Macmurray might have given more attention to the future prospects of his assistants. Kenneth Rankin, who had studied with Macmurray as well as worked under him, did not follow the Macmurray line in his own work but was so impressed with him that, years later, he dedicated his book *The Recovery of Soul: An Aristotelian Essay* to his Edinburgh professor and boss.

By the early 1950s, the split between the older and newer approaches in British philosophy was becoming large — and unbridgeable in a way that all could see. One of the reasons Macmurray insisted on reading all 400 examination papers in his Ordinary Moral class at the end of each year (a decision which drove his wife to distraction because of the fatigue this conscientiousness brought on him) was that he could no longer trust his assistants would review the student answers on the questions covering his lectures in the spirit in which he had presented those lectures. Part of the fatigue Betty noticed in him was depression, due in part to the poor state of educational preparation evident in the beginning students. As he declared to her on one occasion: "If I followed my conscience I would have to fail over half of the first year students."

For him it was not just an old dog bemoaning the loss of his old tricks by the younger ones — who had gone and learned new tricks of their own. Macmurray was never a worshipper of the past. What he saw in the primarily functional and economic motives for attending university of many new students was a sign of the decline of western culture. The fact that analytical philosophy, both in form and content, was entirely avoiding that massive social shift was hugely dismaying to him. It reinforced his conviction that exclusive concentration on linguistic analysis was a philosophical betrayal of the whole of reality for one corner of it. For him, it was tantamount to philosophers saying: for philosophy, the world in its entirety and its concreteness does not matter. By the end of his time at Edinburgh, this gloomy view of the state of higher education had become an unbroken conviction. In his final years at the university, Macmurray seems to have found himself more at home intellectually at New College among the theologians than with most of the younger members of the philosophy department.[16]

The vision of democratic world community

The dangerous direction of Cold War militarism, the steady loss of any unifying culture in the West, the decline of religious faith, and the capsizing of higher education to the demands of the marketplace — all these taken together contributed to his occasional periods of morbidity during those years. These were well-hidden from most people and shared, for the most part, only with Betty, though he seems not to have held back from commenting with a few close friends on the enduring loneliness he had felt during much of his life after the Second World War was declared.

He also railed once with his friend Kenneth Barnes against what he called the "incubus" of Presbyterianism that still clung to him in his later years.[17] It appeared as a sense of duty and rigidity that, although it no longer owned his thoughts, still exercised a major, constraining influence in his emotional and spiritual life. He had a grand vision of what free living in feeling and spirit would be like, as he showed in his 1933 correspondence with Irene Grant, and he knew it was a sound and true vision. But, despite his best efforts, he often felt he had been unable to appropriate that vision in a spontaneous and effective way in his living. The freedom in thinking he had achieved, had come too late in life, he felt, to penetrate and convert the quality of his feelings, especially his feelings about himself. In fact, the clinging of this "incubus"may have affected his thinking more than he knew. It appears, for example, in his rather harsh view of self-love ("... for myself it is other people who matter. I matter little or nothing except for their sake."). It can be seen again in his deeply suspicious view of religious contemplation as opposed to contemplation in art which he considered both necessary and good.[18]

Perhaps it was all of this awareness taken together that moved him to do what he could to counter the cultural shift to a dominantly technological attitude to life and to propose an alternate course, at least in the area of education where he had chosen to give his professional life. Macmurray's last ten years or more of public service can be seen as an almost Quixotic tilting against the windmills of the dehumanizing instrumentalism in culture and education. The image of Don Quixote is perhaps overblown, but not without much truth. The cultural "resistance" that imbued many of Macmurray's "constructive" efforts was a conscious feature in them. He worked for success in his endeavours but learned, like Quixote, not to depend on it — an attitude he had encouraged in the members of the Christian Left. "Witnessing" to the good made sense even when succeeding in having it catch on in the way one hoped for was beyond expectation. As he said consolingly to the members of one of his Ordinary Classes at the end of the year after the prizes had been awarded to the scholarly few: "If you can't all be clever, you can at least be good."

But witnessing to what, precisely, at this point? To a deeper and truly contemporary humanism, a way of living locally with one another that was moved by a desire for a common life and committed to bringing more justice and freedom to all. He imagined the creation of democratic community — locally and globally — in economic, political and cultural relationships. In his view, it was a goal that could unite people across religions, races and nationalities. The projects that took up most of his time, and took him away from the writing of his own philosophy that he knew he should be doing, were ones that focused on personal formation in local community based on the best in sociology, psychology, science, art and religion, within this vision of a world society. It was to this positive vision — so much a part of his life since his youthful conversion to it in London in 1912 — that he dedicated the final years of his work in all the educational arenas he entered. None was too small, none too large, to capture his imagination and be worthy of his time and energy.[19]

This passionate interest led him to take an active role as Edinburgh's representative in the Inter-University Council for Higher Education in the Colonies. His service on the Council included study and lecture-visits — in 1948 to the new University of the Gold Coast and in December 1950 to Nigeria. He also visited and lectured in Kenya. He ended this aspect of his outreach only in 1957, at which time he was replaced by his former Balliol colleague C.R. Morris. In 1961, well after his retirement, he showed his genuine interest in the universities springing up in the former colonies when he spent a full semester teaching in Jamaica. On each of his international sojourns Macmurray's large and integrated vision of an education aiming at the formation of persons in and for community struck a hugely responsive chord in audiences as well as in his associates in the new universities who were trying to find their own directions, grounded in their own culture, as the era of colonization was coming to an end.

Closer to home, Macmurray was a friend of George MacLeod, founder of the new Iona Community which was guided by a vision of how the religious past might provide seeds, in a contemporary form of community living, for a creative future for western society. MacLeod had shaped that vision, at least in part, in conversations with John Macmurray. Macmurray supported MacLeod's efforts by becoming a director and fundraiser for the Iona community, especially in its early years. MacLeod, as they heard from others, seems to have rewarded John by quoting him all over the United States as saying that religion is the greatest enemy of Christianity. In their later years, Betty's diary records John's dismay, verging on disdain, when he saw that his friend George, after making the Honours List, was beginning to sign his name "MacLeod of Fuinary."

It was in this same spirit of exploring fresh visions that Macmurray accepted an invitation in 1946 from the College of Preceptors in London, the chartered body of the teaching profession, to deliver the Payne Lectures on "The Principles of Personal Culture," a title he had selected himself. The three lectures were entitled: "The Integrity of the Personal", "Culture and Function," and "Freedom in Community." In the first, he articulated his seamless garment view of "the personal" as the ideal mode of human living, as individuals and as society. In presenting his case, he challenged his listeners to see that there was not a different ethic for private and public forums, but a continuous one that noted we were persons only in relation and we were responsible to and for one another even in our solitude. It was a highly un-British case to make!

In "Culture and Function," he built on this first talk by distinguishing the notion of "society" (a cooperative enterprise maintained by justice and a harmony of functions) from "community" (the full expression of their togetherness by members of a society — in personal communion through culture). Community is not other than society, it is more than society since communion contains cooperation within its expression but in itself is more than cooperation. Education, he claimed, must aim to serve both realities at once but with a vision that situates the functional, social goal (learning skills and aptitudes) as a subordinate dimension within the cultural one (personal formation and development in community). These are not two separate kinds of education but two aspects of the *same* education process, he insisted. It is impossible to teach any technical growth whatever without producing some cultural effect. Equally, it is impossible to enhance cultural expression without stimulating growth in technical competence.

But the latter should be integrated within the former and directed to its service. In other words, every growth in technical know-how should be taught in a context of responsibility — to people and to our culture; taught so as to open the student to live a fully personal life and to serve such values in the present and towards the future. If this subordinate relationship is lost (usually because the humanistic questions concerning the nature of our civilization are no longer entertained), even the most refined cultural pursuits deflate into functional or merely trivial ones.

Macmurray was convinced the development of personality depends not on skills-training but on formation as an interplay within personal relationship. It is a formation in patterns of motivation, not technical skills. This is done by the interaction of the student with the teacher and the students with one another under the teacher's guidance. It is at once a formation in individuality and in community, both requiring freedom for their realization. In his third lecture, Macmurray traced out the meaning and development of freedom in the social sphere, that is, education as a formation *in* community and *for* community. It focused on the necessary link between freedom and responsibility.

It was a distilled but comprehensive journey through his philosophy of education. Leaning on the work of the psychologist, Dr Ian Suttie, the Payne Lectures developed at some length the development of the infant as a person from the very outset of life, effected primarily through the child's relationship with its mother. The personhood of the infant was a crucial point on which Macmurray insisted. Along with the distinction between society and community, it would receive a chapter of its own in his second set of Gifford Lectures called *Persons in Relation*.

We can also see indications in the Payne Lectures of Macmurray's growing sensitivity to how much our *actual* freedom (as opposed to persons seen as *absolute* "centres" of freedom) is conditioned by our relationships with others and our society. Unavoidably, we either enhance or limit one another's freedom, and we must take responsibility for that fact. In these lectures, he grows in his articulation of the social nature of freedom — that we become free only in personal relationship (community), and only in community can we express our freedom. These explorations set the table for the Dunning Lectures which he delivered at Queen's University, Ontario, in January 1949 and published as *The Conditions of Freedom*. It was in those lectures that he developed further the difference between conditional freedom ("If you don't grant me my freedom, I can't be free") and absolute freedom ("We are all born free"). In a 1951 letter to a sympathetic inquirer, he commented that these lectures were "the first expression of my social thinking."[20] They were, in his mind, his first real effort to articulate principles for a social philosophy that took into account the limitations of the human, what Kant referred to as "the crooked timber of humanity." The basic insights guiding his thinking in *The Conditions of Freedom* were anticipated in the Payne Lectures.

By 1947, in addition to his international work, Macmurray had become involved in adult education at Edinburgh through the extramural work of the University. He soon became a member, and then the Chair, of the University Extra-mural Committee. His views on adult education, which he shared with adult educators at their Dunblane Conference in 1947, had two prongs to it: adult education must be allowed to be experimental, and research must be done to discover the methods by which adults learn best. He was convinced the university lecture system was not ideal, but was equally convinced fresh and effective methods could be found for adult workers who returned later in life to formal education.

Newbattle Abbey: an educational dream

Newbattle Abbey College (NAC), established in a stately building bequeathed by Lord Lothian in 1937 to Scottish adult education, along with its furniture and library, was situated near Dalkeith in Midlothian, about ten miles from Edinburgh. It was intended to be a residential college for working class students to undertake or advance their education in the sciences and humanities. Workers were expected to get a year's leave from their jobs in order to undertake the studies. Macmurray was named to the Executive Committee of NAC as the representative of the university. In that role, and on the basis of long friendship, he recommended the poet Edwin Muir for the position of warden at the college. Muir was an extremely sensitive man who had shown great gifts in the area of poetry and literary criticism. He was, however, despite his service as a member of the British Council in Prague and then in Florence, not experienced as an administrator or as a fund-raiser, nor was he endowed with a gift for public relations.

The college began with a humanistic philosophy of education in place — an approach strongly influenced by Macmurray — but with very little assurance of how it would be financed. The executive committee, which included Ernest Greenhill of WEA fame as Chair, Lady Margaret Kerr — a member of Lord Lothian's family, W.D. Ritchie, an educator from the Borders, and John Macmurray, the only university-based representative, had no idea who would cover the deficit if the college were unable to pay its way. In fact, it took very little time for them to fall into severe doubts about whether the kind of college they had set up would ever be able to pay its way. Macmurray himself admitted much later in a letter to Edwin Muir's widow that he had not thought through how financing the institution would be ensured; he had just hoped its success would draw the support it needed. Along with the rest of the committee members he soon discovered, to his astonishment, that there was very little enthusiasm in Scotland for the kind of college they had set up. Even worse, it became clear that the unions and the workers themselves began feeling that the programme was not fulfilling its goals. It did not return the workers to their jobs or improve the character of the unions. It turned the worker-students into new bourgeoisie who, after their year of education, sought other ways of living and working in society. This particular turn of events exposed the social and cultural naiveté of the founders — and this included Macmurray and Muir, as well. They had applied a leisure class model of education to a working class group of adults with little or no reference to the "world" they came from and to which they were intended to return. The fish were taken out of water and equipped with wings. Why, when they could fly, would they prefer to return exclusively to the sea? Macmurray confirmed this much later, honestly and bluntly:

> The Trade Unions were dead against us. The kind of College we were trying to create and for which Edwin was an ideal head, would simply imbue their members, if they went to it, with a desire to climb into a higher class and they would be lost to Trade Unionism. They are probably right ... This was a very difficult situation, and I, as the major believer in this kind of University-type, poor man's College, had to bear the brunt.[21]

By 1954, the financial problems had increased and so did problems between administration, staff, and finally on the committee itself. Some wanted the school to change over from a residential model to week-long and weekend courses which suited workers much more. Muir was unable to handle the conflict, let alone see it as a creative challenge. The committee could no longer support the status quo and Muir lost hope that he could exercise any constructive role at the college. When, almost miraculously, an invitation came for him to be the Charles Eliot Norton Visiting Professor at Harvard for 1955–56, he snapped at the chance, submitted his resignation, and left Newbattle Abbey immediately, a wounded but wiser man. Soon after Edwin and Willa departed, Macmurray retired from the committee. Apart from appearances that were mere formalities, he had no further connection with the bold experiment[22].

For Macmurray, Newbattle Abbey was probably the most idealistic but ill-advised venture he supported in his missionary effort to keep a humanistic and integrated education alive in Scotland. He seems to have averted his eyes from reality at several points — none of which needs review. On the other hand, it was a valiant effort to cut through élitism in terms of wanting to share the best of the tradition with those who, to that point, had not had the opportunity to be exposed to it in a reflective manner. The energy and vision behind the endeavour were thoroughly democratic and altruistic.

Newbattle Abbey was perhaps the most significant confirmation for Macmurray that the failure of desire for the humanities tradition that he found in the university had penetrated every corner of the wider society in Scotland, as well. The spirit of technology was advancing like a glacier, taking the humanities before it. Culturally speaking, it felt to him like the beginning of a new ice age.

Almost twenty years later, Macmurray gathered into book form his Payne Lectures along with other lectures he had given on educational themes over his years at Edinburgh. When he submitted the manuscript to Faber — the Press that had already published nine of his books — Faber sent him their regrets. That refusal to publish his work was the first he had been forced to endure and it hurt him considerably.[23] It was, for him, indisputable evidence that his views on education were no longer relevant. To put it bluntly, by 1971 they simply wouldn't "sell."

Family and friends

But there was family life as counterpoint to all these work activities and projects. Duncan, their nephew, once released from the army in 1945, had come to live with them while he studied education at the university. He soon met Jocelyn Cooper whom the Macmurrays knew as a young girl in Jordans, and they were married in 1947 in the Jordans Meeting House.

During their time in Edinburgh the Macmurrays continued to provide financially for the needs of his mother who was living with his sister Lilias and her husband, Robert Burnside, and finally with Lilias alone after Robert died. Betty and John would visit them in Fortingall where they lived during part of the 1950s but it was more of a duty than a delight, something Betty admitted freely and John rarely if ever acknowledged. On these visits, Mrs Macmurray would never fail to exert her maternal rights in conversation with John. She continued her inquisitorial role regarding his faith which she felt was disappearing entirely. After he appeared on the television show called the Brains Trust in January, 1957 his mother wrote him a letter with a postscript from the Book of Proverbs: "Trust in the Lord with all thy strength, and lean not on thine own understanding." In fact, John's mother had refused to see the show since she had heard Julian Huxley, an atheist, was also going to be on it — and then it was broadcast on a Sunday! On another occasion some years later when they were visiting her right after he had given his four BBC Radio talks on "To Save from Fear," Betty overheard Mrs Macmurray complaining bitterly to John: "But where is God in all this, John? Where is God in all this?" The charge that God had tumbled like a falling star from his philosophical galaxy continued to plague him. It was as though A.D. Lindsay, A.E. Taylor and his mother were unwittingly conspiring, not as the Three Sisters but more as the ghost of Banquo, to remind him of a murder he had committed but chose to ignore. In fact, his mother's views on his religion mattered to him deeply. And Betty, pushed into the supporting role of Lady Macbeth in this scenario, often felt in those later years that John came away from these visits with his mother depressed and "less a man" than when he arrived.

Betty and John managed with remarkable harmony, according to their different and sometimes opposing gifts, to make their house a home. Betty managed, in a way that mystified David Miller, her artist-nephew by marriage, to have one wall of their dining room painted such that the colour at floor-level began as mauve and ever-so-gradually turned into a subtle pink by the time it reached the ceiling. John's contribution was the ceiling. On the day he painted it white, his assistant Peter Heath arrived to find him standing on the covered table dressed in nothing but his bathing suit, with the paint-brush in one hand and an umbrella in the other to protect himself from dripping paint. He greeted Heath at the door without a hint of self-consciousness, commenting matter-of-factly that it was the only practical way to do that kind of job.

John would keep meticulous records of their spending but neither of them would let that in any way affect their spending habits. And these were sometimes quirky. They would buy unattractive paintings and hang them, only to throw them out when they tired of them — sometimes very soon after they were bought. The same went for furniture, including several overstuffed chairs during those years. Betty was always a lavish entertainer at her dinner parties and John was the meticulous host. He sometimes polished the silver two even three times before the guests arrived. At one memorable dinner, he took out a tape measure and appealed to complex mathematical formulas to prepare a melon for cutting so that all five diners would be assured of a portion that was exactly the same size as the others. On more than one of these occasions, and in front of her guests, Betty expressed her impatience with their Danish cook who always seemed to overdo the vegetables. Perhaps it reminded her of the invariably sodden meals she had detested so much at the Bolton Studios in London twenty years before.

John and Betty had a huge circle of friends and led a very active social life during those years. Among their closest friends from the university were Professors Jackson, Orr, Kemmer, Drever, Ritchie and their wives, Reverend Lindall and Richie Calder, and also Sir William (Bill) Calder, the Principal of the university. Errol and June Bedford, John and Margery Pilley, the Renwicks and the Munroes and others

were frequent guests. John loved the company of women and he listened to them when they spoke in a way most men don't. Women appreciated that in him.[24]

Both of them were enthusiastically active in the Scottish art scene.
They frequently went to lectures and art exhibitions, and were close
friends of Sir William MacTaggart, Anne Redpath, Robert Lyon,
Principal of the Art College, Eric Schilsky and Mary Sturrock — all
well-known Scottish artists. John's friendship with Professor Drever
and Dr Winifred Rushforth, as well as with other psychologists and analysts kept his interests in that field very much alive.

It was at Bright's Crescent that Macmurray often met with his scientific colleague, Max Born.[25] It was also where he had his conversations
with Gabriel Marcel when Marcel came to Edinburgh to give his two
sets of Gifford Lectures in 1948–49. There was a huge similarity in the
philosophical themes pursued by the two men (though not in their
philosophical method!), but there are no records of correspondence
between them — partly because John and Betty persisted in their distressing habit of burning all their correspondence before each of their
major moves. It was also in their living room that John met for three
hours with Martin Buber — a thinker whose insight into the "I-Thou"
relationship resonated deeply with the views of Macmurray and Marcel
on personal relationships. After their long conversation Buber is quoted
as saying: "I see no difference between us. It is simply that you are the
metaphysician and I am the poet."[26] One snippet of a letter from Buber
to John remains, but only as transcribed by Betty into her journal before
the letter itself went the way of all the others they received. It was written on December 6, 1957, after Buber heard from John that he and
Betty would soon be retiring and leaving Edinburgh. The letter ends:

> May I take this opportunity to tell you that without being in touch
> with you I felt all these years the silent communication going on
> between you and me.
>   With kindest regards,
>   Martin Buber[27]

At Bright's Crescent John took up gardening with a vengeance and did it
with a methodical intent that challenged the famed punctuality of
Immanuel Kant. Every spring he used a tape measure to plan out the spac-
ing between plants for his rose garden. In the same spirit he used hand
clippers to cut the errant blades of grass that had escaped his mower. He
weeded daisies with an ethical, even missionary zeal; to the point that
Betty once exploded: "Why can't we have a messy garden for a change?!!
I like a messy garden!" But to no avail.

John kept lists on his hobby areas of geology and birding. He saved vast amounts of string in neat rolls and, to Betty's great dismay, took up the piano again but with no greater success than earlier; the "thumping," as she described it, of years past was entirely recognizable. In his efforts to become a practical as well as a theoretically gifted person, John had begun some years earlier making dresses for his wife, and he carried out this chosen project with an exactness that drove the more easygoing Betty to distraction. She was required on some occasions to stand on the dining room table while he adjusted the height of a hem currently under construction by walking around it with a ruler measuring its exact distance from the tabletop. The dresses turned out beautifully, and Betty was happy to wear them.

About ten years after they arrived in Edinburgh, John and Betty decided to buy a car, the first since before the war. It greatly extended their activities. They took trips into the hills where they walked for hours, and to the seashore for bird-watching and more walking. They both loved having the freedom of movement the car gave them, and it provided the opportunity for them to visit old haunts and head to the west for tours around the countryside where John had spent his earliest years.

The Gifford lectures: a life work achieved

During the 1950s, Macmurray gave a great number of public lectures, some of which were written out to the last word. They dealt with issues of "pure" philosophy such as the ones mentioned earlier on the philosophy of language and one, on the primacy of action over thought that he incisively titled "Cogito Ergo Non Sum." Far more were philosophical reflections on social issues. He spoke on subjects as diverse as the philosophy of government, the contemporary task of religion, mental health and personal relationship, and the conditions of marriage today — in which essay his convictions on the equality of men and women are clear for all to see. And, of course, there were the most important lectures of all — the two sets of Gifford Lectures which were delivered at Glasgow University in 1953 and 1954.[28] On June 16, soon after he completed the 1954 set of lectures, he received an honorary L.L.D. from Glasgow, his undergraduate university.

It was in his Giffords, published as *The Self as Agent* and *Persons in Relation*, that Macmurray brought to fullest articulation his philosophical reflections on what he called "the form of the personal." In these lectures he clearly advances his thought. He also refines his language and categories into greater coherence and clarity. Granting that, it can also be claimed that the kernel of his position in the Giffords can be traced back to the formative experiences of his youth recorded in his early journal, and begins to take its shape with his earliest writings in the 1920s. Macmurray's Giffords contain both the origins and the stages along the way of the intellectual, emotional and spiritual journey of their author.

In his book on the Gifford Lectures over their first one hundred years, Neil Spurway observed that even considering the hugely significant Gifford offerings of other memorable lecturers (Samuel Alexander, Alfred North Whitehead, John Dewey, Gabriel Marcel, Reinhold Niebuhr and Michael Polanyi among them) the series by John Macmurray was "arguably one of the most systematic Natural Theologies the benefaction has yet elicited."[29] It is interesting to note that as "systematic" as he wished to be in his thinking, Macmurray himself never confused being systematic with being "complete." He always chose to refer to his efforts "to conceive the logic and form of the personal" as a pioneering work and in no way a finished project.

Those lectures, as lucid and perceptive as they are, were produced not in the peace "at the top of the mountain" but with great struggle and often in turmoil. John was overcome in the early 1950s by an almost habitual revulsion to writing. At the beginning of 1952, precisely at the time he had to begin writing the ten talks for each of the two sets of lectures he decided, for reasons known only to himself, to try to give up smoking. It was an imprudent decision, and Betty as well as he suffered for it. Betty had to hound him back to his desk regularly for the lectures to finally get written. He was deflecting himself into many other things, including helping Sandy Duncan get a publisher for his book on Kant, which, of course, John had taken the time to read and comment on. On September 19, 1952 he told Duncan:

> We start again in a fortnight, with two new assistants. I'm just
> finished the visit examination [a visit to examine another British
> university]. So I'm in the worst of tempers; especially as the
> Gifford Lectures are not nearly so far advanced as they should be
> and I seem to have got bogged down. And I haven't seen anybody
> for a long time.

Just six weeks later, on November 1, he tells Duncan: "I start my Giffords in January and am quite desperate about them. All I have written seems useless; and there is little time to remake it. Well, well!"

His life got more complicated early in the new year by his appointment to the University Court, an important post that he could not refuse. He also developed a pain or "stitch" in his side that stayed with him throughout the spring that he was travelling to Glasgow to deliver his first set of Giffords and on into the summer. In fact, it was only in the course of presenting that first series of lectures that the later ones in the series were completed.[30] In the end, the coaxing and prodding he required from his wife to produce his *magnum opus* — and then to revise the books for publication — should have earned Betty a best supporting actress award for her share in his success. Once it was all over she records:

John felt the lectures were on a very high level indeed. He felt also that they might appear so simplified and clear that nobody will recognize their revolutionary and original quality. He is prepared that they be ignored. "But," he says, "so was Hume's, the greatest of treatises. If they are not appreciated now I know they will be when today's day is over."

The lectures were, in fact, his fullest and most coherent formulation of the philosophy he felt was his lifework. They presented the essential insights into "the personal" that had begun to find expression for him starting with his 1921 letter to Samuel Alexander. What distinguishes the Giffords is not to be found in changes made in his founding intuitions — there are none — but in the advances he has made in conceptualizing the form of the personal, as he put it. That involved his effort to identify and articulate the logic of the personal as it expresses itself in all aspects of human relating and in the structure of the universe itself. In the next to last paragraph of his four-page "Introductory" to *The Self as Agent* he gave the shortest and best summary of his claims in undertaking this foundational task. The statement also articulated the scope of each of the two volumes:

The simplest expression that I can find for the thesis I have tried to maintain is this: All meaningful knowledge is for the sake of action, and all meaningful action for the sake of friendship.[31]

The Self as Agent presented his case for claiming the primacy of action over thinking in human knowing, a case he began making with his Jowett Lectures in 1923. "Action" is now described as knowledge-imbued activity; it is activity directed by an intention. In his attempt to specify the relation of thinking as a dimension within acting, Macmurray comes up with language that he applies to many other examples of personal logic at work in the concrete: thinking is necessary, constitutive, but subordinate in human action. This rather terse formula is fleshed out in his chapter on "Agent and Subject" in four claims, which must be taken together in order to express the full structure of personal logic:

1. The Self is agent and exists only as agent.
2. The Self is subject but cannot exist as subject. It can be subject only because it is agent.
3. The Self is subject in and for the Self as agent.
4. The Self can be agent only by being also subject.[32]

On this model, Macmurray reaffirms his case for why it is impossible for human beings to be understood exclusively in terms of mechanical "events" or organic "processes." Physical events happen, and processes take place under certain organic conditions. But in human existence these dimensions of our reality are transformed by knowledge, freedom, hope, love, etc. and self-consciousness. Consequently, they are better understood not as full determiners of human action but as subordinate dimensions of human action.

This choice of language expresses Macmurray's effort to articulate the relationship between action and the reflection which is a constitutive dimension of it. As a form of logic, it is more complex than the formal logic adequate for mechanical thinking or the dialectical logic needed in organic thinking. He proposes what seems to be a "dialectical-dialogical" logic since the opposites of thinking and acting do not destroy each other in their transformation but, in fact, feed each other's distinctness.

To describe this relationship, he introduced new language he had been working on since the early Forties, and spoke of thinking as a "negative" which helped to constitute action as its "positive."[33] Macmurray concluded this first set of lectures by attending to what light this offered to a philosophical view of the universe as a whole. He extended his claim for the primacy of action to a larger claim: that the World can be coherently understood not as a mechanical event or an organic process but only as a personal action. Such a claim, he knows, begs the question: "Whose action?", and it is at this point that he has gone as far as he can go within the viewpoint of the Self considered from the perspective of "individuality."

Contrary to the early tradition of modern philosophy, in Macmurray's thinking the "individual" is already a second-order concept since, as he will assert in his second series of lectures published as *Persons in Relation*, the Self is a "person" and persons only develop *as persons* in relation to other persons. We come to be who we are as personal *individuals* only in personal *relationship*. The positive form of that relationship which goes by many names: love, friendship, fellowship, communion and community, to offer the ones that Macmurray used at different times, and sometimes interchangeably. Because the meaning of the word "love" had become so distorted in western societies, Macmurray frequently chose, in these lectures, to speak of "positive" personal relations in contrast to negative ones, that is, those based on fear and/or hatred.

It was in this second set of lectures that Macmurray developed — on both the intimate level of mother and child as well as the much wider level of politics and society — the implications of his longstanding claim that the fulfilment of all meaningful action is in friendship, that is, in our capacity to love others for their own sake. His view of the nature of human beings countered head-on Hobbes' view that human beings can be defined by a fear of the other (nature and our fellow human beings) and therefore by a primary need for self-preservation. For Macmurray, fear, although always one basic dimension in human motivation, is not *the* basic truth in human motives. An "urge to communion," not the urge to self-mainte-nance and self-protection, is the truest expression of personal motivation. The urge to communion, he had concluded after his reading of Suttie in 1936, is the basic and primary urge in human beings. Fear is a necessary, constitutive but subordinate aspect of motivation in ideal human action. The human person, though always imbued with some aspect of fear and self-care in his actions, is capable of caring for others, even caring for oth-ers first. Acting from the motive of care for others leads paradoxically to genuine self-realization.

In this second set of his Gifford Lectures Macmurray makes his claim about friendship being "our true nature" a universal goal. Put simply: If positive personal relations are normative for genuine human living then the goal of this desire is the achievement of a community of *all* human beings in positive personal relations. Nothing else could fulfil us. Nothing else could ethically constitute a truer human goal. The unity of all human beings in relationships that realize freedom, equality and full mutuality is the inevitable and *necessary* goal of this urge to communion. This "natu-ral" goal of human beings is not to be achieved easily, as he knew too well, since in our freedom we are more than capable of not following our best natures.

As a philosopher, Macmurray's purpose here was to state and elucidate in its normative implications this law "written into" our human nature, so different from Hobbes' version of that law. Macmurray's view of human nature makes the meaning of self-realization radically social, not individ-ualistic. It also proposes that the building of positive relations requires that there be essentially *one* ethic for all human interaction — not one for pri-vate life (altruistic care for the other), and a totally contradictory one for public life (cutthroat competition). Public relationships are subject to the same ethical imperatives as the ethics of individual or family relation-ships: they must aim for full community in freedom and equality, and be open to the participation in that community by others. This was not the dominant view of human beings at work in western society during the modern era.

This issue of "the dominant philosophical view of human beings" at work in western society exercised Macmurray greatly in this second set of Giffords as well as in many earlier unpublished essays. He was very con-scious that he was challenging the liberal tradition at its foundations. The primacy placed on individuality, and therefore self-interest, creates an inevitable primacy for competition over cooperation, to say nothing of communal trust and affection, in public relationships. This self-centred attitude renders "irrational" any effort to think and act in terms of the good of the other, let alone the good of all. Macmurray understood these prevalent modern convictions as deviations from our true nature that lead inevitably to the frustration of our truest good. He concluded that despite the many benefits of the modern era, self-interest, competition and property-holding as the legitimized, even canonized, grounds for public relationships, play a substantial part in creating the social sickness of the west.

In these lectures, then, he confirms the judgments he made when he was reading Bosanquet's *Theory of the State* in 1921–22: that the mechanical and organic views of personal relationships in democratic states are not only bankrupt but self-contradictory. The essential distinctiveness of the unique human person and of community could not be conceptually expressed in these views. There has been no coherent effort at a fuller view of human beings and their life in society offered thus far in the west.

Macmurray offered his "personal" viewpoint as a challenge to and an advance beyond the depersonalization of the individual and society resulting from a politics and economics that assume mechanical-organic principles in human affairs. Corporate capitalism, Fascism and Communism, as he proposed in his 1954 lectures, all reveal not just the accidental but the *necessary* failings that arise from institutions and social action based on this truncated view of human beings. For Macmurray, neither competition (Hobbes) nor cooperation (Rousseau) alone express what is contained in that basic urge to communion with other persons. Only care for both the individual person in his or her individuality and for the gathering of free persons in a shared life of meanings and values can create the form of society that Macmurray refers to as "community." It entails a group living not only in shared order, but in consciously shared values and affection. For Macmurray, love is not aery-fairy; it has a body and the name of love's body is justice. Justice, as the cooperative structure of order, participation and the provision and distributions of goods for all, is the necessary ground in society for a goal that lies beyond mere justice, the goal of an untrammelled engagement in living fully, in celebrating life, in all its joys, sorrows, promise and limitations. It will only be achievable, he concluded — recalling the devastations of both the First and Second World Wars — when the pursuit of justice arises from the deeper motive of love. Action that leads to genuine community for all is a normative way of acting, Macmurray concluded, simply because this is the kind of beings we are, by nature, and by destiny.

With this view of the goal of all individual expression and cooperation in place, Macmurray was able to express the ethical imperative required for a society to reach for its own fruition and that of others, the fruition he called "community." From the perspective of this thirty-year-old theme in his thinking, he suggested the following normative dynamic for action and relationships: *All competition is for the sake of cooperation, and all cooperation is for the sake of communion*. Macmurray conceded that it might be very difficult to discern when such an appropriate form of relationship or action might actually be taking place — especially on a large, historical scale. Nonetheless, he suggests, complexity in discernment does not vitiate the validity of the norm. The norm of genuine community for all, if it were challenged, would have to be challenged on other terms.

As Macmurray ended his first set of Giffords with a chapter on "The World as One Action," he ended his second and final series with a parallel chapter on "The Personal Universe." His claim — one that had marked his thinking from his earliest years — was that the world is intelligible only if it is imagined as one action (not one event or one process). Here, he concludes that this one action is love; not gravity or genetic adaptation, etc. alone. And love is only possible if the universe is viewed as "personal," not merely an organism subject to processes, or a mechanism subject to physical forces — though these are dimensions *within* loving.

Consequently, he concludes by claiming that his philosophy demands, for its coherence and reasonableness, the affirmation of the existence of a personal God who is at once creator, sustainer, animator and final goal of the universe in all its striving for self-realization and communion. The urge to communion as the deepest expression of human desire and action is objectively able to be fulfilled in union with this personal God and with all others in the universe; no lesser view could make any sense of persons *as persons*. It is not in the least surprising, he suggests, that the movement to atheism in the history of western philosophy is intimately related to the desire to interpret the world (and therefore human persons, as well) in exclusively mechanical or organic terms. To maintain such claims, he notes, (a) is gratuitous. It is itself an unprovable act of "faith" in a reductionist viewpoint. And it (b) leaves the world incoherent; that is, with no terms adequate to explain the distinctively personal experiences of knowledge, love, forgiveness, self-sacrifice and what the non-Christian Vaclav Havel, following Macmurray and many others, calls the human urge to "the transcendent."

Macmurray began his work critiquing modern philosophy for the *theoretical* (putting thinking first) and *egocentric* (putting self-interest first) character of its starting point. He proposed a replacement of those premises with the primacy of action and of personal relationship in which genuine care for the other for the other's own sake is a genuine possibility for human beings. He completed the circle of his critique and construction with this final lecture on "The Personal Universe." In making this affirmation of the reasonableness of the existence of God, he knew the pitfalls of medieval theocracy and religious authoritarianism — to which he himself might be described as neuralgically sensitive — but he did not fear a return to them. This was partly because of the influence of science that contrasted in the mid-twentieth century to the clear weakness of institutional religion throughout the west. But it was also because he was well acquainted with the secular, reductionist dogmas of scientism and the indiscriminate trust in technology and mere use-value that were the natural offspring of modern philosophy. He felt these "idolatries" to be much more immediate threats to a civilized life and the achievement of world community. As he asserted mordantly at the end of his final talk:

We began by noting that modern philosophy had been driven by its own logic in the direction of atheism. We may end by recognizing that the nearer it draws to this conclusion the nearer it comes to its own extinction. The opposition of science and religion has compelled philosophy to distinguish itself more and more from religion and to model itself upon science. Once philosophy was the handmaid of theology; now it knocks at the door of science and asks for employment as a general cleaner-up. But science has really no need of such assistance. It prefers to tidy up for itself.[34]

Despite his humble assertions concerning the merely pioneering character of his life-work in philosophy, the two sets of lectures, taken together, represent a profoundly coherent philosophic effort of symphonic proportions. Although a few contemporaries have launched equally incisive or even more extensive constructions of modern thought, none has risked such a massive or coherent effort at creative construction. In Macmurray's Giffords, the best orientations of Greek and medieval philosophy had been combined with elements of modern philosophy and psychology in a work that pointed the way to a positive, post-modern synthesis, an integration that attended at once to the most intimate and the most extensive dimensions of human life and the universe itself. If the universe is truly described as "personal," this situates at once the essential terms for understanding personal relationships, society, ecology and the use of the planet's resources. Macmurray's perspective certainly qualifies as "religious" in the total scope he gives to philosophy to make judgments concerning what is "real" and "unreal." Macmurray never attempted to deny this impression. Philosophy, as he concluded, "is theology which has abandoned dogmatism, and has become in a newer and wider sense a Natural Theology."[35] This was not language likely to attract a quick and large philosophical audience in Europe or America in the 1950s and afterwards. But it clearly confirms the observation stated earlier that Macmurray was essentially a religious philosopher, not simply a philosopher of religion.

Unfortunately *The Self as Agent (SA),* the volume of Macmurray's first set of lectures, was published only in 1957. And *Persons in Relation (PR)* followed it a full four years later in 1961, seven years after those lectures were given. This is perhaps testimony to the amount of coaxing and cajoling Betty reports she had to apply to John to get the revisions for publication completed. This lapse in time influenced the critical reviews for *SA* since both volumes could not be judged as the integrated whole they were intended to be. Although it was unanimous that Macmurray was "onto something important" in *SA*, there was substantial agreement among D.D. Raphael, Dorothy Emmet and some others that the work seemed "elusive," They felt it was insufficiently specific and, while advancing its case, failed to engage other contemporary trends in philosophy. John Hick, under the guise of claiming not to know what Macmurray was "on about," gave a clipped, almost caricaturing exposition of Macmurray's thesis while deliberately offering no judgment on the work at all. From a former student — granted one who did not seem, by reports, to have appreciated Macmurray's style or viewpoint — it was dismissive to the point of insult. The Frederick Copleston and A.R.C. Duncan reviews remained expository for the most part, but were positive about the promise contained in Macmurray's opening onto "the personal." Raphael and Emmet found Macmurray's use of "negative" and "positive" as descriptors of relationships as well as dimensions of being quite unsatisfactory in their vagueness. Loose thinking in loose language was their most trenchant judgment.

When *PR* came out in 1961, D.D. Raphael became a convert, finding much in it that responded to the unfinished business he had found in *SA*. He especially appreciated the much fuller treatment given by Macmurray to "the negative being a necessary, constitutive but subordinate dimension of the positive." Dorothy Emmet, Errol Harris (who published two rather different reviews), and Margaret Chaterjee in India, to cite only a few, found much to praise in Macmurray's exploration of personal relations but were left unsatisfied by the unfinished development of one or several of the essential notions supporting his position. Taken together, they cited as examples of this unfinishedness, his development of his concepts of mutuality, religion, freedom and God. Emmet also cited the lack of development and nuance in his view of the connection between personal and impersonal relations among human beings. Harris noted especially the same absence in his view of the relations between human beings and the world of nature. One admirer of Whitehead felt that Nature and the panoply of impersonal constituents that are required in order for "fully positive, personal relations" even to be possible were not adequately incorporated into Macmurray's grand scheme as entities with their own distinctive status and dignity. In other words, although there was a clear place in his categories for ecological thinking, so hell-bent was he on staking out a place for the personal that he remained a pre-ecological thinker in terms of acknowledging with energy the critical value of nature. Ironically, Macmurray was also charged by one critic with leaving "personal relations" looking like an "idealist" construct, precisely the kind of thing he had most wished to avoid. However, for all the reviewers of *PR* there was a clear recognition that something fresh, integrating and significant had been accomplished in these volumes on "The Form of the Personal."

Macmurray would have agreed with many of the judgments about his position requiring much more work. His defence appears in his regular claim, in both his formal publications and his later correspondence, that his was only a "pioneering" effort. He never claimed for it the status of a finished philosophy, and in fact explicitly denied that status for his thinking on several occasions. On the other hand, he could have challenged many of these judgments. The nature of some of the criticisms indicate that his meaning was simply misunderstood, possibly for the same reasons he himself found it so hard to articulate the new viewpoint: because his mind and theirs had been shaped so completely by a viewpoint that took for granted the primacy of the "thinking self" and the plethora of dualisms that arose inevitably from that starting point. They brought that viewpoint to their study of his action-based, relational thinking, and missed what might be called the vital intuition behind what he was doing.

On the other hand, it might be conjectured that had he engaged earlier and more publicly the perceptions of such worthy and sympathetic reviewers as Emmet, Raphael and Harris, he might have developed his concepts and refined his language in a way that might have disarmed some of these criticisms. One is left wondering: What more might have been accomplished in his "pioneering" work had he — as Dorothy Emmet wished — entrusted his early articulations of these views to a dialectical engagement with colleagues, as he had done in his Aristotelean Society symposia. Then again, it may have precisely been in such engagements, as well as in his BBC work, that he came to conclude that the gulf between him and most other British philosophers existed at a level that could not be resolved by "discussion" alone. Gilbert Ryle had harshly remarked that "Macmurray's first volume should have been entitled: *The Self as a Gent!*" For Ryle and many of his analytic colleagues, their worst suspicions about Macmurray proved true in the Giffords, and there was probably no way Macmurray could have prevented or mitigated their reaction. To analytic ears, Macmurray's work was tonal music written in a fiercely atonal era and played on cumbersome early, even foreign, instruments. They simply walked out of the hall scornfully or — and this applies to most of them — on the basis of negative reviews by their friends, never even went inside to hear the music for themselves.

Macmurray's later correspondence shows that he was very aware that his thinking required development and criticism, despite the paradox of having apparently resisted dealing with questions or criticism in his graduate seminars in the 1950s. His resistance to doing the further thinking himself — let alone doing it in the public forum — probably had many causes, some of which have been touched on earlier. To all of them we can almost certainly, by the end of the Sixties, add aging. But no effort to praise adequately Macmurray's accomplishment in his Giffords needs to avoid the element of truth in Dorothy Emmet's judgment that Macmurray left many loose ends.[36]

The charge of having left loose ends in his two-volume major work did not surprise Macmurray's nephew, Alastair Campbell, who observed that: "John did a lot of things, yes, but he was not a disciplined man." The Giffords may reflect to some degree that aspect of his character. However, given that his work was on entirely new terrain, the two volumes testify just as much to what he *could* do when he submitted himself, even though reluctantly, to serious discipline. A final word might be said in Macmurray's defence even though it can appear as an unworthy and niggardly *ad hominem* response to his critics. There is nothing in the work of any of his critics or their British or American peers at that time that can touch the grandness of synthetic vision, future-looking imagination, relevance to the contemporary situation of the world, and lucidity of expression transparent on every page of Macmurray's Gifford Lectures. The "honorary" doctorate he received from Glasgow University at the end of his second series of talks was a worthy recognition but as an honorary award it may have been misnamed: the degree was, in fact, well "earned" — earned over the course of a lifetime.

The end of a culture

Betty's diaries note the passing joys and sorrows of their final years on Bright's Crescent. In the mid-1950s she reports a homely yet significant conversation she and John had as they ended their dinner one evening:

> We were talking about Jesus and Christianity, and John said he
> deliberately never joined any church 'in order that he could quite
> fearlessly say what his beliefs are ... and that a great deal of Church
> Christianity is phoney.' I responded: 'I now think that a discipline
> of avowed Christianity in connection with some recognized
> institution might have helped me to live a better life.' He said:
> 'Why not now?' I said: 'It's too late now.' He said: 'Then it was
> always too late!' Then he got fearfully glum and depressed. He said
> he has spent all his life trying to understand Jesus and God and the
> Universe and he finds he knows nothing. 'Do you not like being

alive, ' I asked. 'NO! I sometimes wish I were dead!' This makes
me furious and I reply that that is a wicked statement. 'Don't you
ever feel like that,' he asks. 'No! Never that I were dead! I hate the
thought of it. When do you feel like that?' 'Mostly at night,' he
replies, looking a veritable martyr. I think it's partly physical. 'But
it's quite a common experience! The psychologists know all about
it.!' 'Oh, you and your psychologists — you're all too clever for
me,' I reply. 'Don't keep saying: "You're too clever." It's not true;
you're just defending yourself.' 'Against what?!! ...' Then we went
and washed up our supper dishes.

Betty's continuing surprise at his declarations of profound loneliness is
understandable — despite the fact that she has been hearing it, on and off
again, since 1941. It contrasted so sharply with his other happily social
self which she saw most often and deeply appreciated, and of which she
was, at times, even jealous. She notes: "It is wonderful how J keeps going.
He has great resources of energy and doesn't waste it nervously." She
observed once after they had thrown a party when some stayed later and
John was tired: "How kind and tolerant he is with everybody. Never embittered if people encroach on his time and patience." One entry towards the
end of their time in Edinburgh confirms this quality in him as she recalls
with chagrin the arrival of Frederick Broadie, one of John's lecturers, at
the front door early on the morning of New Year's Day 1956 with the finished index he was preparing for John's book, *The Self as Agent.* She frets
at John's gentle incapacity, even after some hours on this special day, to
see Broadie out the door. This gentleness featured in the Macmurray so
many recognized. Betty continued significantly: "If only I could write his
biography up to date. I have asked his old mother to write about her early
days but she just laughs. She would have given such a lot of simple anecdotes in detail."

Her 1950s diary, patchy as it is, tells of events in their lives and offers
some intimate yet publicly significant observations. More than once in its
pages, she bewails the lack of recognition given to John's philosophy in
academic circles. She notes that he himself never complains of it, but she
feels sure he is deeply disappointed by the public silence.[37] In one entry,
she recalls with huge warmth, the arrival at the door, on his eightieth birthday, of Professor Norman Kemp Smith, former colleague and dear friend
who, with a great smile, shyly announced: "Today I've become an
octogeranium." Well before this birthday, Kemp Smith, a happily married
man, had confessed to them in a conversation that he regretted never having had a passionate love relationship during his life. It was an acknowledgment that drew him closer to their hearts. On John's own birthday that
year, Betty bought a beautiful hearth rug in old gold to surprise him.

Also a coffee pot. And she adds with humour and self-knowledge: "I wonder what else I can think of will please both of us." They went to see Jacques Tati in *Mr Hulot's Holiday* and John laughed till the tears came. Apart from gardening, hiking and the occasional movie, John's favourite way of relaxing at this time was reading detective novels.

When he went away on longer trips, or just for a day or so to give a lecture, she missed him terribly. "Nothing matters as long as there is John. I sometimes rely on God in this way but I am sorry to say not always. The tangible, the seen, is so real to me. 'Whom not having seen, we love.' *Sometimes* that has reality for me, but not always." Their feeling of closeness for one another was celebrated in her October 8, 1956 entry:

> This has been a radiant day. We celebrated our wedding day (40 years ago tomorrow) and every year happier than the year before. A life of highlights and shadows — but mostly all joy, thanks to J who has loved me with unswerving loyalty and devotion even when both of us were 'trying out' other relationships. We never really feared the loss of each other's love, though I confess J was much tried by me and I, too, a little by him.

The backward glance given by Betty in the midst of this paean to their love points to a major change in their lives. Once they left London for Edinburgh they clearly left behind the sexual explorations for which they had granted each other permission years before. Their married relationship, with all its "highlights and shadows," as Betty described it, became again the exclusive context for their intimacy. This diary entry reveals that more and more everything in their relationship is being integrated into the "friendship" between them that served as their lighthouse in all the storms they lived through over the years. Their married love was increasingly growing in the direction of what John had always believed was the deepest form of relating between two persons. How much the voluntary — as well as culturally enforced — sexual exclusiveness of their Edinburgh years conspired with aging to contribute to this gentle deepening of their feeling for one another is not determinable, nor is it the heart of the matter. What counts immensely is that both of them, as they moved into old age, were growing in a friendship with one another that was at once more peaceful and more spiritually passionate.

At the same time, and certainly not unconnected with aging, they were both feeling the onset of significant physical ailments. John had lumbago that could act up suddenly and sometimes leave him almost unable to move. Betty suffered, sometimes quite suddenly, from attacks of shingles that incapacitated her. She was also beginning to feel chest pains of such strength that sometimes she could not even bend over. They were harbingers of the major heart attack that she would suffer in 1959. Meanwhile, John worked at a torrid pace at the university, running his department, teaching his classes, correcting hundreds of papers as well as doing the increased administration he had taken on more than a year before. Betty was doing a significant amount of work herself, on her painting and with the University Women's Club which included her dear friends June Bedford and Marjorie Pilley.

In December 1954 Macmurray had been named Dean of the Faculty of Arts at Edinburgh, a position he held from January 1, 1955 to December 31, 1957. It was a time when the university was growing and major decisions were being made in curriculum (especially for a proposed Honours Degree in Architecture), extra-mural education, faculty development and the construction of new buildings, including Hume Tower which currently houses the Department of Philosophy. Despite his reputation among some of his graduate students for a certain monk-like detachment, Macmurray was judged by his colleagues to be a well-organized administrator with an unusual capacity to evoke creative discussion and exchange in the Faculty of Arts Committee meetings. Here, as in his own department, he was not an initiator or a particularly creative person; the creative ideas came mainly from others. But he fostered and encouraged creativity by asking good questions, stating needs clearly, and finding gentle ways to build consensus in a meeting. He also cared deeply, communicated openly, and he was fair. But it cost him in time and energy. On January 14, 1955, he told Sandy Duncan:

> I have just taken over the job of Dean of Faculty. I had hoped to resign from the Court but the Principal is very pressing that I shouldn't; so I have agreed to cut a few time-consuming committees — PhD, School of Scottish Studies, Provincial Council — and see how things go. It will be a heavy lot, but I hope manageable. I've not done anything to speak of to prepare the Giffords for publication. I must do it in summer.

Close to his heart as Dean was the new Department of Nursing which he strove to keep associated with the Arts rather than the Science faculty on the grounds that it is primarily *persons* that nurses attend to, not diseases. He was convinced, partly from his own experience for two years in the Medical Corps in World War I, that healing requires a felt knowledge of the needs of the whole person. His success, at least temporary, in achieving that goal in March 1956 was perhaps his most obvious accomplishment in his efforts to maintain the humanistic focus in the University. Certainly it was much appreciated by the nurses who invited him back five years after his retirement to give a major lecture entitled "Nurses in an Expanded Health Service." The Dean's work grew significantly over those three years. In June 1957, six months before leaving his post, Macmurray wrote a long letter to the authorities in the University describing the change that had taken place and urging that the Deanship be reconceived as a full-time position.

Around 1954, John and Betty began working with Giles Cooper, the architect-brother of Jocelyn Campbell, on plans for their new house in Jordans where they had decided to go when they retired. They were returning to the Quaker village where they lived during the war, partly for a softer climate and partly for the bucolic tranquillity which both of them were looking forward to so much during their retirement. Their new property in Jordans was not in the centre of the village where their old "Home Base" stood, but down on Wilton Lane, close to walking paths and Downfield Dell which continued to be a nesting place for birds. The house was going to be an L-shaped bungalow with the wing on the back to include, among other things, a studio for Betty. Cost estimates rose appreciably when they decided to install central heating, and the wing had to be forgotten. Betty's studio would be a small out-building just behind the house. When it was completed, they named it "Hatherly Brake" after the country home of Betty's godmother Hyde in Cheltenham where Betty had spent delightful times as a child.

Getting there, and getting out of the rat race, was something John longed for. His correspondence with very close friends from the early 1950s on gives hints of what he stated plainly on January 20, 1956, to his dear friends Irene and Donald Grant who were still living in London:

> I wish we saw you oftener. It is isolated and cold here: and I keep wishing for the end of it. We are getting on with the plans of the new house, and will be down to see about it on the spot at Easter time. When it is ready — I hope in the summer of next year — we shall move in and I'll do my last session from a hotel. Then I hope we can knit up the old friendships again and get back to important things. The running of a faculty — indeed all administration — is no doubt necessary, but it is so trivial, a mountainous collection of trivialities.

The retirement of the Moral Philosophy Professor, as the initial contract indicated, would normally have come with his seventieth birthday. After much thought and financial calculation, John and Betty decided that John would request early retirement despite the cut in pension it would entail. They had both had enough of the pressured life, and John's work as Dean had been especially intense. Those years had definitively revealed to him

the more pragmatic directions the University was taking at every level —
including in his own Department of Philosophy where the assistants were
beginning to push for the ending of the traditional division between Moral
Philosophy and Logic and Metaphysics so they could get more variety in
their teaching. That preference pointed to a future for which John had little enthusiasm. He was more than content to move towards complete
retirement within a reasonable time after he left the Deanship in December
1957. Arrangements were finally made for him to retire formally on
September 30, 1958, with the understanding that he would be freed from
all duties and responsibilities at the University by the summer of that year.
His temporary successor in the department would be Professor Emeritus
Alexander Macbeath, a former Gifford Lecturer who had just finished as
Professor at Queen's University, Belfast. The Moral Chair would be occupied only on October 1, 1959 by Winston Herbert Frederick Barnes, until
then Professor of Philosophy at the University of Durham. It was the day
after A.D. Ritchie, the last true polymath in the Scottish system, resigned
the Logic and Metaphysics Chair.

Macmurray's departure — accompanied so soon after by that of Ritchie
— was recognized by many as the end of an era as well as the ending of
a personal career. And that was indeed so. The primary place of the
Humanities had been lost in the passing of a culture. In his heart John
knew there was little anyone could have done to prevent the loss, though
this never stopped him from fighting the good fight. There were farewell
parties and accolades that summer that testified to how much he was loved
and respected. Some months later, on November 12, 1958, the Senate formally acknowledged his retirement. The formal statement read by Charles
Stewart, the secretary to the university, at that Senate meeting recognized
Macmurray's Scottish roots and war service, his huge popularity as a
teacher, his effectiveness as dean, and his many academic and popular
writings. It also characterized him as a philosopher, and in the elucidation
of what that had meant, the secretary revealed that Macmurray did not
entirely lack recognition for his philosophical approach:

> There are those who say that philosophers nowadays may be
> divided into antiquarians and linguists. It is true that the urgency of
> our present problems has daunted some, and the success of
> scientific method as compared with reflective analysis has
> discouraged others, leaving few to survey widely and interpret
> boldly. Macmurray has always been one of these few. Yet he is not
> to be thought of as a doomed but determined metaphysician
> fighting a rearguard action against advancing science. On the
> contrary he is in favour of science. Indeed for a moral philosopher
> his support of social science has been quite remarkable. Nor is he

ever on the defensive. His cast of thought is essentially probing and forward-looking. If he does criticise some prevalent modes of thought it is scientism he is dealing with, a very different thing from science. Thus we must think of Macmurray as an originator not a conservative, one who makes new claims for philosophical thinking and is quite content to let some of the old ones lapse.

Macmurray was not there to hear it. Late that summer, he and Betty had moved to their new home in Jordans and he had immediately departed on a major lecture tour in the USA that would keep him away from Betty and their new home for a full fourteen weeks. Before leaving Edinburgh, Betty had done the *de rigueur* stripping down of their possessions, including the burning in their backyard incinerator of the many letters they had received over those fourteen years. She also burned many of her paintings at the same time since space in their new home was so limited and there was no thought that any of the works were worthy of public storage, She notes in her diary, that it was only when her portrait of John was being swallowed up by the flames that she was overcome with the awareness that there was a deep masochism at work in this act of destroying these letters and canvases, precious bearers of the affection of friends and of their personal history and her creativity. Ruefully, she acknowledged that no one could accuse John and her of clinging nostalgically to the past, of not living in the present with their eyes fixed on the future. And it was true. But as the smoke curled up around her silent meditation on what she was doing, that was very cold comfort.

Chapter 16

Retirement in Jordans (1958–70)

More than a year before he retired Macmurray had received an invitation from the Danforth Foundation in the United States to come to the United States for a lecture tour of American colleges and universities, with the accent on smaller colleges that were rarely able to hear from foreign scholars. It was an invitation he could not accept while he was still Dean of Faculty, but with the end of his university career on the horizon he could entertain the idea more seriously. He did so with some financial calculations in mind as well. When he and Betty began contemplating an early retirement they had to contend with the prospect of a lower pension, not a small consideration since John was still supporting his mother. The remuneration from the Danforth Visiting Lectureship would make the reduction in pension less burdensome and had the advantage of being over and done with in four months, so Macmurray accepted the invitation for the autumn of 1958.

He was away ninety-nine days and during that time visited thirty different cities and towns across the USA. The first part of the tour took him to Chicago and included talks at campuses in the Midwest, across the northern States to Washington and Oregon, and then to various centres in California. The return section brought him through Wyoming, Colorado, Texas and Louisiana, back into the Midwest, and finally to Colby College in Maine and to Sarah Lawrence College in New York State. It was an exhausting trip during which he gave two and sometimes three talks at each school. His topics ranged widely and included many of his familiar religious, social and philosophical themes.[1]

It is more than a bad pun to suggest it was a *tour de force*. His lecturing style as well as his thoughts captivated the American students as much as they had the British. In addition to his official talks he visited classes and gave interviews to students and scholars alike. Although break-days were structured into the tour it was an intense fourteen weeks for him and his main respite came from writing letters to Betty. His letters all contain something about the events of the day and his observations on the people and how the talks are being received, but they concentrate mostly on his longing to be with her in their new home and settling into their new life together. One in particular stands out as the communication of a long-time companion. On October 9, their wedding anniversary, he wrote to her from Spokane, Washington and for the only time recorded in written words expresses his feeling about the choices they made along their forty-two-year journey in marriage. He addresses her as "Darling wife," and after thanking her for her lovely letters to him (two of which arrived that same day), turns to their anniversary:

> This is to say 'Many happy returns' and how wholly and utterly glad I am that we met and fell in love and married. Such a rich and wonderful marriage it has been; perhaps because it has had to rise above our failure to have children. It was that, of course, that made us turn to outsiders for sexual satisfaction for a while. But neither you nor I ever really thought that this sort of thing could break the bond between us. I often wish, and you do too, that these things had never happened, and that there was no one at all, when we look back, but you and me together. But I am sure that this natural wish is a natural foolishness. There is something better than innocence, and that is the choice that is based on knowledge. I prize — in my deepest heart — far more the choice to do without sex for love of you, and it has stood the test for more than a dozen years. No one can say that it is based on ignorance and fear. No one can say that my conviction about love and its meaning are the result of a life-long sex-suppression and frustration. So our unity, my darling, is richer and stronger for these "aberrations" (shall we call them?) than it could ever have been without them. It is a love that has "looked on tempests": and never been shaken.

He refers to his favourite Shakespearean sonnet ("Let me not to the marriage of true minds ...") writes the first few verses for her, then continues:

> So you and I stand together in perpetual and unshaken love that has triumphed over childlessness and "faithlessness" so that these have only served to demonstrate the absolute eternity of our union. Think this, my darling, with me, and it will make your eyes sparkle and make a youthful current run in your blood. I think your love for me is wonderful, and that mine for you can match it ... God bless you, and keep you whole and happy for me till I get back from this short absence. And rapidly the time is going![2]

He was back with Betty on December 21 and joined her in the final preparations for celebrating their first Christmas in their new home.

In 1959, John Macmurray and his wife applied for and were accepted as members of the Quaker Community. It was an acceptance for which John was always grateful. This ended his long self-exile from membership in any organized Christian body. With his professional career ended, he no longer felt he needed to preserve himself from official associations that might have made it difficult for him to speak frankly about what he was thinking and what he actually believed. And he did feel the need for community in the expression of his faith. The Quakers fulfilled another requirement: they offered the fullest welcome with the fewest demands. Kenneth Barnes quotes John as telling him that he turned to the Quakers because there was no "need to sign on the bottom line to a statement of which there is no meaning"; that is, there was no need to declare his stance on dogmas. Being able to be completely honest in religious matters was, at least since 1917, a conviction for Macmurray that he held to fiercely. For him it was as necessary as breathing. In 1963, he had occasion to assert in writing once again, "a rule that I made for myself years ago: 'Under no conditions will I say that I believe anything that I cannot believe effectively'."[3] With the Quakers he could live that conviction as comfortably as anywhere. And the Society of Friends, having applied their own wise forms of "testing," received John and Betty warmly. Betty was a reluctant convert. As an artist she yearned for more expression of feeling and ritual in religion and for that reason she openly admitted that she was drawn to the Catholic Church. She became a Quaker because it was the preferred religious home for John rather than for herself.

Later that year Betty was struck down by a life-threatening heart attack which laid her up for months. John became her nurse and it was a job for which he had competence. Their nephew Duncan, who was living in Lebanon with his family and running the Quaker school there, flew home to be with them for a short time when Betty was released from hospital. While Betty spent a lot time in bed recovering, John began designing, preparing and planting his garden. The limey soil they inherited was hard to break up and he wanted to grow acid-loving plants so he brought in some burned peat-blocks and crushed them into the soil to neutralize it a bit. He then built the garden up in steps so no plants would be shadowed by others from the sun. When it came to selecting plants he calculated the blooming seasons of each so when he wrote to his mother in June the next year he was able to praise the performance of the lilacs, broom and azaleas which were just finished their displays, and tell her that the weigela and deutzia were on schedule to bloom next. He noted that their sole rhododendron was just coming into flower along with the pinks and first roses, and proudly announced a big crop of strawberries from his small patch, along with the news that his peach tree already had fruit the size of walnuts, and he was just about to get his tomato plants in. For autumn blooming he had already planted gladioli, purple michaelmas daisies, roses, marigolds and nasturtiums. He spent hours with his hands in the soil, and that gardening in silence, filled with the immediacy of the earth

and growing things, became his preferred form of prayer and contemplation — though he never called it that. Betty's period of convalescence
was also a time for him to revise his second set of Gifford lectures for
publication. By the time he wrote that June letter to his mother, *Persons in
Relation* was almost ready to go to the publishers.

By 1962 the Campbell family had left Lebanon and returned to Jordans
where they stayed for two years just down the road from Hatherly Brake.
They saw the Macmurrays most days. Ross, their son, used to cycle home
from school past Hatherly Brake and would stop every day for tea and a
chat and the warm scones that Betty had baked. Later, when the
Campbells moved back to Edinburgh, Ross remained at his boarding
school in Hertfordshire, and would occasionally spend weekends with
John and Betty. He kept up a correspondence with them at that time, sending poems and adolescent thoughts. Typically, they took these seriously
and discussed literature and "life" with him in a respectful way. As
Jocelyn recalled, those first two years in Jordans after 1962 were very
happy ones. They had two wonderful Christmases when Betty cooked the
goose and brought it to the Campbell house in a basket to lay alongside all
the other delicacies. They were joined by the all the members of both sides
of the Campbell family. And they recalled with affection John and Betty
at the piano singing Scots songs in quavering voices, especially one about
a childless, young couple that had a particularly poignant refrain: "And
they never nocht [needed] the cradle." It was a song into which Betty and
John could pour real feeling.

Betty regularly wrote John a special note each Christmas. It was to
pause and say just a few words to her husband about what he meant to her.
Her 1959 message dwelled on the key events of that fateful year of her
heart attack:

> Darling John,
>   How can I thank you enough for all your love & care for me this
> very difficult year. What untiring devotion, even to the detriment of
> your own health.
>   And now we both go Quakering into the future together. May
> you find an outlet for your genius this year.
>   Yours,
>   Betty

Despite retirement, John complained to his mother that there was always
too much to do. The "too much to do" arose because he continued to serve
on doctoral committees and, at that moment, had two dissertations sitting
on his desk waiting for reading and reporting. He was also getting known
by the Quaker community outside Jordans and that led to invitations to

speak and to write for their publications. It is clear that he had other projects of his own in mind, some that never got done. In a letter to Sandy
Duncan in 1955 he had mentioned wanting to do a book of his own on
ethics. Some time after that, he spoke to his mother about writing a book
on politics. In March 1958, having received congratulations in a letter
from Irene Grant on the publication of *The Self as Agent*, he replied to her
from Hatherly Brake where they were spending the Easter holidays of his
last term: "After I get the second volume to the printer ... I have the notion
to sit down and write up parts of the two sets of lectures in a more popular form, working out the concrete implications."[4] In fact, none of these
proposed books got written, except for one possible exception.

Around the same time in1960 Macmurray accepted the invitation of
Kenneth Muir, his 1930s Christian Left associate and now a celebrated
Shakespearean scholar, to deliver the Forwood Lectures at Liverpool
University in 1961. The Forwoods were a theological series, and John's
presentations were published as a book that same year under the title
Religion, Art and Science (RAS). In the four lectures Macmurray visited
many of his earlier themes. As the last major expression of his thought it
is fair to say *RAS* is more a distillation and refinement than an advance on
his earlier work. Kenneth Muir recalled years later that these lectures were
not particularly well-received by the audience; they were supposed to be
theological lectures and Muir got some criticism from his colleagues
because they were not more theological.[5]

Betty's health was improving so much by mid-1960 that they felt able
to accept an invitation for John to come to the University of the West
Indies to give some lectures over the winter. Due to complications, they
had to wait until February to leave for Jamaica where they stayed six
weeks and John gave six major lectures as well as participating in many
other meetings, classes and consultations.

During the summer of 1963, John was stricken with a severe bronchial
affliction that laid him low for weeks. It was Betty's turn to nurse him, which
she did with as much care as he lavished on her during her convalescence a
few years earlier. In early September, although still a bit weak, he and Betty
decided with enthusiasm to accept the invitation of Donald and Irene Grant
to come to London for a holiday and take over the Grants' apartment in Great
Ormond Street during their own three-week absence in Scotland. John and
Betty spent two weeks in London and had the best and longest holiday they
had had since their 1950 visit with Edwin and Willa Muir touring in Rome
and Florence. John's response to their first few days of "Londoning" in a letter to Irene and Donald captures him — and Betty — beautifully:

> Yesterday we shopped in Regent Street, and after lunch at Dickins
> & Jones we dropped down to the Criterion Cinema and saw *Tom*

Jones. Lovely colour photography and the ruin of a good story. They picked out all the bawdy bits and crammed them together to make a stupidity. But one gets used to that! We are just going to have lunch at home and then off to Drury Lane to see *My Fair Lady*. We don't expect very much but it will be nice to have seen it.

... My throat is completely healed and I feel fighting fit. The magic of London, perhaps? Betty says: No! It was she who prayed for a miracle and got it. In scientific moments I imagine it was that my doctor took a chance with streptomycin! Perhaps all three! ... Betty sends her love with mine. She is writing a book called *A Fortnight in London*, and she sits of an evening gazing out at the people and pigeons and shops and houses, and so absorbing inspiration.

The letter reveals the light-heartedness of those days away and also the tender relationship between them where, when things are going well, it really doesn't matter if the cause of the healing is magic, miracles or antibiotics, or all three. And Betty, gazing out the window at London life was sketching out images for a book, yes, but almost surely, as well, being filled with memories of her times with Roy de Maistre and her many friends and night-time walks through the city in her glorious 1930s in London.

But there is more going on in the letter than that. It also signals the growing depression about the state of the culture that John had been feeling for years. This will not be the last time he uses the word "stupid" to describe not only Richardson's *Tom Jones* (in contrast to Fielding's *Tom Jones*) but what he saw as the desensitizing and thoroughly undirected quality of the new society that was taking shape around them. He now tries simply to avoid being buffeted by it as far as he can manage. At the end of his March 1958 letter to Irene Grant anticipating in his imagination the goodness of retirement he wrote: "What I am *really* looking forward to is being finished for good and all with Universities!" There is no doubt that the falling off he found happening in universities pervaded all aspects of their culture. It constantly confirmed for him the intimate bond that exists between educational institutions and their surrounding culture. They needed each other and yet neither one could be significantly good if the other was significantly inferior.

That cultural critique didn't stop them from having fun in London! They saw *The Sleeping Beauty* at Covent Garden, went to *The Mousetrap* the next day, *The Severed Head* the day after. And on the weekend, he reported, they were going to Festival Hall for a Beethoven Concert by a French pianist. The only thing they wanted to go to but had to miss was a concert by the Russian violinists, the Oistrakhs. And they took Willa Muir — a widow now since Edwin's death in 1959 — to lunch in Chelsea where she lived and was writing her memoirs that would be published within a few years of this meeting. The only thing that slowed John and Betty down was an attack of lumbago that made John "waste a lot of time lying on a hot water bottle." But that came only on the second last day of a holiday that may have, in retrospect, been the honeymoon they missed in 1916 when, the day after they were married, John had to rush back to lead his men on the Somme battlefield.

Adding to the involvements that took him away from his cherished garden, John did the four BBC talks entitled "To Save from Fear", the ones that earned for him from his ninety-seven-year-old mother the trenchant query: "That's all very well, John, but where is God in all this?" It seems she and the Liverpool theologians, along with the ghost of A.D. Lindsay, had a similar problem with him! In fact, these Lenten talks were profound explorations by Macmurray of God's way with human beings as revealed in Jesus. They also conveyed what John felt the world needed if members of the human family were to undertake a "common life" together. In those talks he reflected on fear as the major barrier to full living, a conviction he had held for three decades:

> For Jesus, the mortal sickness from which men suffer is fear. It is from fear that we need to be saved. 'Indeed!' you may say, 'don't you mean *from sin?*' No; I think not. Sin doesn't seem to trouble Jesus so much. He dealt with sin by forgiving it. His judgment of fear was far more drastic. Do you remember the man in the parable of the talents — the one who had one talent only? You remember, when he came to give his account to his master he said: 'I was afraid, and hid my talent in the earth.' And for that he was cast into the outer darkness.[6]

If love was the root of all good and the deepest truth of our nature then fear was the root of all evil. And the implication for Macmurray was that our human mission to eliminate as far as possible the need for fear was simply the other side of serving the cause of celebrating genuine love.

Early in 1964, Macmurray was invited by his fellow Quakers to give their prestigious Swarthmore Lecture. It was an occasion for him to speak not primarily as a philosopher but as a man of faith to men and women of faith in his own Quaker family. Because of that intimate context, for the first time in his life he wrote an opening piece of "autobiography" that described his religious development through childhood and young adulthood up until he left Oxford for his first lectureship in Manchester. It stands as a powerful example of narrative theology. His full text was published in 1965 as a small book entitled *Search for Reality in Religion*. It remains a highly readable work presented in four "Movements": his personal faith journey as a youth, followed by his view of the nature of religion, of Christianity, and of the Christian mission in the world. Much to the disappointment of many of his listeners, he was able to cover only the first "movement" of his text in the actual lecture. It is his last book. And, despite many short references to aspects of his life in other writings, it is the most autobiographical he ever became.

In April they went to Edinburgh where Macmurray delivered the annual Nursing lecture. Between the Nursing Department and Macmurray there was a mutual love affair. When Macmurray set it up, the Nursing Studies Unit was the first university course for nurses in the country. He had also "pleaded for the University to go further and institute the first degree in nursing in Great Britain."[7] It was, as he said, his effort to help with the reform of the so-called "Health Service." Because of his own experience as a medic he was able to speak to the nurses from the inside in a way they deeply appreciated.

A month after they returned from Scotland, John and Betty heard from Irene Grant that Karl Polanyi had died. John wrote a note to Ilona and their daughter Kari expressing their sadness at his passing. He noted simply to Irene: "He was a great soul and has done a work in the world which counts — and altogether for good. I wish I had seen more of him."[8] This succinct statement holds within it many questions, starting with: Why did they not see one another and keep an active communication going after their very active collaboration in the 1930s? There may be no one reason. But, by 1964, there had been more than twenty years of silence between John and Karl precisely when their interests continued to show huge overlaps — in their global perspective and their socialism, in their conviction that economics finds its proper place embedded in culture, not vice versa, and in their clear understanding that Fascism can be victorious without any Fascist movement, a view that was becoming increasing relevant in the face of the military-industrial domination of politics throughout the West and especially in the United States. Their views of the dangers, and the directions to be taken for cures, were very similar throughout their lives. However, there is no indication they ever visited one another when John was in North America or when Karl came to England. Shortly before he died, Karl Polanyi launched an international journal called *Co-Existence* in which he hoped to stimulate cross-disciplinary communication on behalf of the new world order that was so much needed. It sounds like the sort of thing Macmurray himself just a few years later announced himself interested in getting going. But there is no indication that when he sought out like-minded sponsors in various countries of the world Polanyi approached Macmurray for his personal support. There is no sign that Macmurray even knew the journal was being launched. Perhaps only Irene Grant, who knew both men well, could have cast some light on this silence.

Towards the end of 1964, John began having abdominal pains that the doctors examined and found to be caused by colon cancer. Happily, the affected area was small and the cancer was confined within the colon. The operation, and his recovery, went very well. Betty wrote loving letters to him almost every day even though she was also visiting him regularly. Within a few days he was reading books, and recommending that Betty read Geoffrey Smith's *The Business of Loving* partly because it gave him some understanding of the new generation, and partly — remembering his own youth — it triggered feelings of how he himself might have fit into the young hero's shoes were he that age now. It was a feeling for the good- ness of the "new" — of something lying beyond his own experience, sim- ilar to the way he felt after reading D.H. Lawrence years earlier. It was a feeling that would be strengthened for him later in his relationship with Duncan and Jocelyn's children as they grew up and brought their joys and concerns to Betty. The children thrust him into relating to them personally, and their personalities and development revealed to him the goodness alive in the present, despite the cultural decline which tended to play a large part in his perceptions.

The good encounters and lovely moments were plentiful and it would be wrong to think of Macmurray as other than a basically peaceful person at this time of his life. Even when he sounded disgruntled about the direc- tions society was taking — which was often — he continued to believe passionately in two things that gave him hope: first, the world was in God's hands, and that was the very ground of his peace; second, the "world revolution" that was sweeping up everyone whether they liked it or not was as much an invitation to a new positive unity among peoples as a sign of deep civilizational breakdown. There are many indications he looked for these signs of new life even in the cultural fragmentation he deplored.

Disgruntlement and sadness continued to sweep over Macmurray not because he was aging or because of what he called his "presbyterian incubus" but because he was so aware that so many choices and actions being taken in society made cooperation with this invitation to a new world order less achievable. The failures were historical and objective! He was never a fan of the United States as a nation for this reason, though he enjoyed most of the individual Americans he met on his three visits there. He found the Americans' innocence and naiveté combined with their power and complacency both alarming and dangerous. On balance he found them, as he told Reg Sayers a few years later, a bigger threat than the Russians to world peace. It was in light of this general situation, as well as the war in Vietnam and the violent actions of the state police to the civil rights marchers in Alabama and Mississippi, that he wrote mordantly to Donald and Irene on April 7, 1967:

... any chance of seeing you before Donald returns to darkest America? I had hoped he had finished these peregrinations, and especially now when it seems that it may not be pleasant, or even a safe place to go to. But perhaps it is necessary for him. I feel happier refusing invitations nowadays — especially to America. I have nothing new to say anyhow; and it is a mistake to repeat oneself. And I don't understand this new world we have blundered into. The only thing I feel sure of is that it is a very *stupid* world; and I find myself meditating on a book that is not likely to be written, called 'Education for a Stupid Society.'

However, he couldn't resist the temptation. Just over a year later, at the height of the social turbulence in France, Germany, Czechoslovakia, the United States and other countries, he sat down and penned the first few pages of an essay entitled precisely: "Education for a Stupid Society."[9] What might be surprising, in terms of his negative attitude to current culture expressed earlier, is that Macmurray lines up in total support of the students pitted against the dominant culture which he sees them battling. It casts fresh light on his wider, and longer, cultural viewpoint.

At the outset of the essay, Macmurray notes the turmoil in education at the end of the 1960s, then quickly revisits his own experience and reflections of fifty years earlier in order to situate his current convictions: When the First World War ended, the youth who fought that war realized that their elders, who "had first made that war possible, then probable, and finally inevitable" and then sent their children to fight it, did not in fact believe what they mouthed about justice and the good society. Their essential success with their youth in education, therefore, was not in the schools where the same platitudes ruled the airwaves but in the example given by their actions. And the real message came to this: "We have nothing to hand on to you by way of vision and values for a life worth living — despite what we say." As he saw it, what the adults in power actually handed on across three generations was two world wars, innumerable smaller ones, and now the frantic effort to prevent a third — also of their own preparing! Conversely, students over the same three successive generations had grown, on the one hand, in scepticism about the merits of their own culture and, on the other, in conviction and frankness in condemning it.

The students are condemned by the elders for complaining, but not knowing what they want to replace what they say is wrong. This is used an argument by the elders to disregard the student "revolution" as trivial and to disparage it as merely hormonal. Macmurray is convinced this is a particularly perverse and self-interested mistake. It is natural not to know ahead of time what shape the future should have. You only find your way

to appropriate social structures by living and experimenting with them, not
by applying a preconceived idea, like the Nazis, for example. Only an idealist rather than a realist could condemn this state of natural ignorance on
the part of the students. The fact that the students become the elders leads
people to say cynically: "It was always thus." But that is not so! It evades
the particular and specific irrationalities that pervade the west in the twentieth century and these are quite different from the eternal struggle
between older and younger generations in any society. He observes
poignantly and even poetically:

> The present group of students and of teenagers will soon grow up
> and cease to trouble the world as they are doing now. They will
> marry and they will find responsible positions to fill in the work of
> the world. The revolutionary fervour will be tamed, and largely
> forgotten in the pressure of the necessities of adult life. Their place
> will be taken by others, of course. But more important than this is a
> fact that we are very apt to overlook. Their attitude and outlook in
> adult life will still be shaped by the education that they have
> undergone. The scepticism, the sense of failure and frustration will
> remain; and when they come to educate their own children, they
> will realize that they cannot give them any clear guidance. This
> indeed is the generation of the permissive society. "Let the children
> find out for themselves, and do as they please. We can't help them.
> Let's hope that they will do better than us." So the depth of the
> spirit of rejection and scepticism will increase with each generation
> as it feeds upon itself. The only way out lies through the solution
> of the major problems that plague us, beginning with the problem
> of war.

What Macmurray notes here is that as life moves on and real problems are
not faced honestly and solved effectively, fewer and fewer people find
anything offered by their society, culture and educational experience that
leads them to a sense of personal dignity or to generosity of spirit and willingness to give themselves to a common life that is worthy of them. They
know the goals and methods of their elders are not able to handle the fresh
problems.

There is a great consistency between the cultural condemnations
Macmurray offered in this late sixties essay and those he raised during the
First World War and in 1919. They are not directed first at the student
rejection of the status quo but at the blind and fearful clinging of the elders to a bankrupt status quo which they know, but refuse to admit, has no
moral vision or energy in it. It is not resistance in him to a new way of
doing things that is at issue but precisely a refusal on the part of those in

power and leadership to embrace a new way of doing things. The "stupidity" he scorns is — now, as after World War I — essentially on the part of the elders, and only derivatively in the youth. In fact, he finds the students in each generation have been progressing in their capacity to sniff out mendacity and comment on it honestly and forthrightly.

In June 1968, at the time he was writing his essay, he noted that the new feature of the "student revolution" that gave him added hope was its international character. It gave him hope that the fixed pattern of the white, western (and twenty years later he might have added "patriarchal") way of running things might finally be seriously challenged and even broken. In 1968, through the media the students knew — what he and his fellow soldiers did not and could not know in those early years after World War One — how many of their peers in other countries had identical feelings about the education they were being given and the culture they were being taught to support.

Despite his knowledge of the seriously limited perspective of these students and why they deserved the label of "new barbarians" that was pinned on them, Macmurray believed that their voice in the demoralized and decadent West, even if they did not remain faithful to it themselves, was a voice of prophecy. He was sad but not surprised when concessions — and, in some cases, repression — rather than honest change in the direction of deeper justice marked the end of that phase of resistance to the mechanisms driving western governments and institutions. Just a year earlier, commenting on these heavy issues and the technological fixations controlling policy and decisions in world affairs, he ended a letter to the Grants with a sigh:

> ... We were thrilled to hear that young Donald was going with a
> grant to study in the States. I do hope he enjoys it, though I'm not
> too sure about this hobnobbing with computers. Did you know that
> they have set up in Edinburgh University, of all places, a
> department of machine intelligence! They seem to be proud to be
> the victims of a metaphor.

As much as he felt the burden of these illusions holding sway, he was not impervious to delight when Faber & Faber announced to him in 1968 that they were printing his Gifford Lectures in paperback form. He felt they must be among the first Giffords to be put into this popular form, and Betty reported to the Grants on his enthusiasm for the project and the prospect of his ideas reaching more people, especially young people in whom he placed his hope.

In fact, during these years — and a bit earlier — John's philosophy began making an impact in certain corners of psychology and psychiatry in Britain. There is no firm indication that he was kept informed about it or ever got actively involved with the people engaged in it. One of the earliest works that acknowledge him is the 1961 book *Personality Structure and Human Interaction* by the psychiatrist Harry Guntrip. In the Thirties, Guntrip had studied under J.C. Flugel, a friend and colleague of Macmurray's at University College, London, and also with R.D. Fairbairn at Edinburgh. Guntrip claimed to have "been thoroughly trained in a personal relations school of thought ... in the philosophy of John Macmurray."[10] He had attended Macmurray's lectures at UCL and read most of Macmurray's books up to the date of his own book.

In the late 1950s and the 1960s, more psychiatrists were questioning the approach to psychological pathology that viewed illness as an internal condition of the individual alone. They were getting interested in exploring a psychiatry that, in both diagnosis and therapy, took into account the patient as a person and included the person's relationships and social situation. It was an exploration launched with enthusiasm by a group of psychologists and psychiatrists in Aberdeen who were labelled the Abenheimer/Schorstein Group after the two men who brought the participants together. Its members included R. Gregor Smith, R.D. Laing, John MacQuarrie and others. Macmurray's works were read by the group because of his view of personal reality as constituted by relationships. His works were the only philosophical ones they felt they could include. By then the analytic tradition had spread so widely that their psychological concerns were of no interest to mainline academic philosophers in Britain whom they studiously avoided. Younger psychologists coming along at the time, such as John Shotter at Nottingham and Colwyn Trevarthan at Edinburgh, leaned heavily on Macmurray's philosophy in their research on the interaction of mothers and infants and found Macmurray's views of creative participation by infants in these relationships confirmed; in fact this active relating in the infant was found to occur even earlier in the child's life than Macmurray had suggested in his famous chapter on the subject in *Persons in Relation*.

For similar reasons, but at the other end of life, Macmurray's ideas on personal relationship were being fervently embraced by Dame Cicely Saunders in her efforts, through her St Christopher's Hospice begun in 1967, to formulate reasons for the type of palliative care she envisioned for the dying. In Britain, Saunders was credited with "putting a human face on death." She saw the dying person not as an organism that was fading away but as *a person* who, in the midst of suffering and diminishment, was making a *life* passage and was able to be accompanied and consoled by other persons, by touch, by listening and conversation, by laughter, prayer and even shared silence. Cicely Saunders understood that the dying have much to give to others as well as to receive from them. She was attempting to "de-medicalize" palliative care by challenging the view that every person dying of an unstoppable disease was somehow a sign of "failure" on the part of members of the medical establishment. The passage towards and through death was unavoidable, and Saunders taught that it could be made with trust and acceptance. Much of the language and many of the concepts she needed to express this "revolutionary" view for palliative care she gratefully admitted finding in the writings of John Macmurray.

In 1966, John began an exchange of letters with Walter Jeffko, an American doctoral student who was writing a dissertation on Macmurray's view of morality. On August 13, 1966, Macmurray wrote a long answer to a series of questions on fundamental issues put to him by Jeffko. When the student noted a certain incompleteness in Macmurray's moral philosophy, Macmurray made it clear that he although he always viewed his accomplishments in philosophy as incomplete he thought he had done a fairly efficient job of dealing with morals — within the scope of his purposes at the time — in the middle chapters of *Persons in Relation.* However he acknowledges that:

> I have not written a treatise on morals, though I have often thought of it. The reason is that I have never set out to expound a philosophy. In a sense, I haven't 'a philosophy.' I have been concerned with one thing only, to shift the centre of all philosophising from thought to action. Beyond this I think of all that I have written which is not *ad hoc* lecturing on this and that, as providing illustrations, chosen not very systematically, of the kind of difference the shifting of the centre makes on the traditional treatment of recognized philosophical problems. I am inclined to think, moreover, that the 'philosophies' of many philosophers have been the work of their commentators. I can only hope that some future thinkers will see how fundamental and how important my suggestions are, and develop them. Perhaps I might say that I have been concerned not to write a philosophy but to define a new 'type' of philosophy within which others might write *their* philosophies.[11]

When Jeffko asked him about whether "action" or "the personal" takes priority in his philosophy, Macmurray offers a rare reflection on the genesis of his foundational thinking:

> These aspects developed separately in my mind, and I spent many years trying to find the way to unite them. I am doubtful how well I succeeded in doing this; but I have always held to the conviction that the philosophy of the personal is the final goal; and that the

primacy of the practical over the theoretical (for thought) is a
necessary prelude to any satisfactory theory of the personal.

This is, of course, the heart of his work. He states for Jeffko the basis of
any moral philosophy for which he "could take responsibility." It would,
he says:

> ... rest on the conviction that the rightness of action depends upon a
> reference to the creation of universal community; and that a totally
> moral activity would be totally heterocentric, totally concerned
> with "the other" and with myself only as necessarily involved with
> the other. 'The creation of community is the end of action' might
> be a formulation I should accept.

This repeats almost word for word — as he well knows — the substance
of his position in *Persons and Relation* written twelve years earlier.
Perhaps somewhat more surprising, it is the viewpoint he articulated first
in his 1913 journal reflections in London and then again in his first known
article on this topic written in 1925. It suggests that his apparently con-
genital "cultural dismay" may well be related to the fact that at no time in
the post World War I decades has there been, as far as he could see, any
sign that the distinctively "personal" form of relating and his view of
world community had made any significant headway in penetrating the
imaginations and desires of people in the West.

In relation to a question about the viability of "metaphysics"
Macmurray tells Jeffko: "For me philosophy, like history, is all-inclusive.
Nothing falls outside it; in no sense is it a 'specialism.' Or, as I have sometimes put it: 'As a philosopher, I consider myself a specialist in anti-spe-
cialism'." His answer to Jeffko's question about his views on immortality
repeats his long-held view:

> ... I would never *deny* it. It is a possibility; and the evidence, so far
> as it goes, seems to me to be in favour of such a belief. But I have
> always been anxious to avoid speculation in philosophy and to
> stand by the evidence. I am not convinced that my philosophical
> standpoint *demands* immortality, at least in the ordinary sense. But
> I have committed myself to the view that only the past exists. I
> have a belief, which I cannot fully substantiate, that there are other
> dimensions of time than the one we are conscious of in acting. So
> the possibility of the world *of men* coming to an end doesn't bother
> me; and my whole standpoint does demand that there must be a
> God. If I were to speculate, I should suggest that perhaps in this
> life we sketch a base-line from birth to death, and that after death

this whole line moves upwards in a second dimension of time. So, after death I should not *live* further in the basic time line, but yet would have the whole of my life as the basis of a richer, more timeful action. But for myself, I prefer to leave it to God and not to be too curious.

Again, apart from adding this interesting dip into speculation on different dimensions of "time," Macmurray takes the same somewhat detached approach to the question we can detect in his essay on "Conservation of Personality" published in *Reason and Emotion* thirty years earlier. The consistent reason for this attitude to the question of immortality over the course of forty years was precisely that he found it a question arising from an idealist perspective which in turn arises from a perverted sensibility about where we seek "reality" — elsewhere, rather than here. He had already stated this for another correspondent in March 1948:

> What I object to is the *desire* for immortality as a substitute for the claims of the present world and the reality of action. The traditional conception of immortality in our civilisation comes from Plato and is bound up with his radical pessimism and aristocratic dislike of the practical life. I prefer the original Christian doctrine of a resurrection of the body myself. And ... it [the concern for immortality] is bound up with the idea of the *isolated* self, i.e., the self as *mind*, withdrawn from community into the private world of its own images and ideas.[12]

This goes a distance towards explaining why the energy he invested in exposing all forms of idealism made him impatient, even curt, at times about questions defined by what he called the "Greek" or the "Roman" viewpoint. He told Jeffko at the end of the letter:

> In general, I should point out that your objections rest upon the adoption of the type of philosophy which I reject. So far as you accept Aquinas you accept, in principle, Aristotle. To me, the Greek mode of thought, and Aristotle's in particular, is incompatible with the Hebrew mode, and so with any properly Christian one. The kind of problems you are raising, and the kind of criticisms you are formulating belong to a kind of philosophising which I have been struggling to put behind me.

At first blush, that may not be totally convincing. Why "Aristotle in particular" — to speak first of an incidental point here? It is Greek philosophy as grounded in idealism that has exercised his basic distaste, and this should apply as much to Plato as to Aristotle. In Aristotle specifically, it was the organic viewpoint with its application of a notion of natural tele-ology to human action that Macmurray rejected. But in his empirical turn, even in the midst of his idealism, Aristotle was more "this-worldly" than Plato.

At the risk of psychoanalysing Macmurray, one might wonder if in that rejection of Aristotle Macmurray wasn't partly attempting to cast out his own demons. His rejection of idealism assumed the status of a visceral revulsion. He saw that it systematically caused evil and avoided bringing about good for people in the world, while it took very good care of the power élite. So his was a passionate, not just an intellectual, rejection of idealism. It was, to use a more Hebrew category, a "holy anger" in him. However he was also revolted, we can surmise, because it had damaged him personally. It is fair to say, because he said it himself on more than one occasion, that he was wounded emotionally and prevented from becoming emotionally free, especially in the area of sexuality, by the "incubus" of Presbyterianism in himself. Unlike his wife, he was never consciously able or willing to attribute this wound to his parents' own lack of freedom, although he was quite willing to lay his unfreedom at the feet of his childhood religious culture.

But there is another way in which Macmurray seems to remain an ideal-ist, though not in the sense in which he condemned it. The British Idealism he inherited was not unrelated to the Hebrew-Christian notion of the heav-enly Kingdom, God's mountain, the *parousia*, where, to quote from both Scriptures, the "wolf will lie down with the lamb", "every tear would be wiped away" and "death will be no more." This expressed itself in his con-viction that the goal of universal community in justice and love based on common humanity was grounded in a recognition that this was God's pur-pose for the world. It could be said that he himself was a philosopher of action, but one who was never, and could never be, fully purged of idealism in the sense of having a "vision of the whole" which guides his analysis and judgments. But, he could also be charged in such statements with what he himself readily admitted: remaining an Aristotelian idealist himself at least to some degree — and especially after he read Marx. Two examples suffice. His almost wilful affirmation, for the longest time, of the Russian social experi-ment to the point of turning a blind eye to the evils being perpetrated by its leaders could be interpreted as an ideological shadow hanging over some of his writings in the 1930s and certain talks at Jordans during the war, as well as in aspects of his work for the Anglo-Soviet Public Relations Committee at the same time. Conversely, his own rejection of capitalism and his belief in a strong place for Marxian dialectical process in history tended to give him a determinist's view of the "inevitable" decline of capitalism. Hope sometimes led him into the kind of speculation beyond what the facts permitted. When he whispered to Kenneth Barnes that the bombing of London which they were witnessing from the Chiltern foothills spelled the "death of capitalism," he was being as speculative as any idealist. In his last years he acknowledged that his affirmation of Marxist theory got the better of him in some judgments. He saw it as a failing and implicitly, but never explicitly, judged it to have been a sign of the residual idealism in both Marx and himself.

Along this line of idealist projections, a final question might be asked: Why does specifically Christian theology have to follow *only* the Hebrew mode of thought with what Macmurray called its healthy avoidance of dualisms? The freedom from dualism along with its assertion of monotheism were the foundations of Hebrew religion as Macmurray saw it, and these were its essential advantage for him. But are there no significant limitations in ancient Hebrew categories? And is *all* thought based on Greek premises unable to add *anything* worthwhile to knowledge despite its idealist foundations? Macmurray's fixed attitude on this point manifested itself often over the years. It revealed itself in a social setting around this time when he and Betty were visiting their friends Gordon and Esther Muirhead who lived just down Wilton Lane from them. In the course of their conversation Esther expressed her enthusiasm for the Prologue to the Gospel of John. Macmurray responded rather abruptly, even dismissively: "Yes, but that's Greek, and Jesus was a Semite."[13] For all Macmurray's brilliance and wisdom, this may not have been the last word on the Johannine Prologue!

These objections should not deflect us from recognizing and acknowledging both the wisdom in his answers and the generosity and care with which Macmurray engaged Jeffko's questions. The young man's inquiry went on — into areas of valuation, Situation Ethics, American Pragmatism, why Macmurray joined the Quakers, and so on, and to every question Macmurray responded with respect and with thanks for being drawn into clarifying his positions. One of the most unusual of Macmurray's positions — the final one he was asked by Jeffko to clarify — was his conviction that love is exclusively for the other, not for oneself. The disjunction seems severe, as well as being puzzling. His doctrine here seems not only to rupture something in the unity he is aiming for but to leave the individual in a strangely suspended condition with regard to himself, even out of touch with the Gospel where believers are enjoined to "love your neighbour as yourself." Jeffko asked why Macmurray so disparaged any form of "self-love." Macmurray gave him the fullest statement on this point — satisfying or unsatisfying — that we have anywhere in his writings:

It is the term 'love' in this context which I object to. To use it is at least to seem to approve of narcissism, or a fixation upon the self. I

agree that one *cares for* oneself, and it is right to do so — provided
it is for the sake of the others. Love delights in its object; but to
delight in oneself is to be unconscious of one's imperfections and
wickedness. A man's attitude to himself cannot be the same as his
attitude to anyone or anything else. Or [to put it] otherwise — love,
as a positive motive, is self-transcending; it contains the possibility
of complete self-sacrifice for the other. The capacity for self-
transcendence *is* one's rationality. So though I don't deny the
possibility of 'self-love' I can only interpret it as a failure to be
human, to be rational in the extended sense that I give to the term
when I talk, for instance, of emotional rationality. Love is, for me,
by definition 'for the other.' To love oneself would then mean to
make oneself the *object* of one's love and so of one's intention.
This is contrary to my conception of the reality of oneself and so I
must reject it. One cannot be one's own 'other.'[14]

The paragraph contains the sublime along with what may be a touch of the
ridiculous. That we are made for self-transcendence which manifests itself
most truly in love for another is profoundly true. That we cannot be
"other" to ourselves, and so cannot delight in ourselves as we can in others, follows from the first statement — though not without complexity due
to all that is implied in the human capacity for self-awareness. But to
switch to a moral basis for argument and say we cannot delight in ourselves because we know our own imperfections and wickedness sounds
more like his mother than himself. Do we not know a fair amount about
the imperfections and wickedness of the others whom we love — and
delight in? And do we not still love them? The focus on imperfection and
evil is, even by his own best insights — starting with the breakthrough
insights in his youthful journal — really beside the point in this matter.
Love of the other *as other* is his main focus and it is only confused by
appealing to my knowledge of *my* evil as a reason for not accepting that I
can rejoice in my goodness — especially since my goodness is not self-
generated, it is not to *my* credit. Having said that, it remains true that our
attitude to ourselves cannot be the same as our attitude to others; his position, in its essential point, is profoundly true.

In 1967, at the same time as he was writing these letters to Walter
Jeffko, John wrote to Frances Barnes, who was confined to bed attempt-
ing to recover from a stroke, saying she probably has much to think about.
However, he adds that:

... ["thinking"] can be a weariness and even a disease. I've taken to
meditation instead — first to find out things about myself that I
didn't know. But that didn't work; indeed it began to produce ill

effects; and I decided that I was the kind of person who shouldn't think about himself at all and that the less I knew about myself [the better]. So instead I took to meditating on my friends; being glad of them and giving thanks for them and thinking about them to discover *why* they were so worth knowing and loving. These were good meditations, and you, of course, came into them; and I still keep them going. Nothing but good comes from them; indeed I have remembered friends that I had forgotten. Recently I have combined this with meditations on philosophy ... I have recovered ideas that once held my attention but which had been forgotten. And a few I still find important.

I am really recommending meditation to you. Probably you are an adept and know all about it, while I am a tyro. It is so different from thinking, which is so much something one *does*, a drive of the will. Meditation is a kind of creative passivity in which your mind presents you with things, and puts them through their paces, develops them, while you sit or be still and listen, watch and so discover. Inspiration must come this way, I suppose; but I am not inspired![15]

This is a significant statement because it shows what Macmurray meant by meditation and how he felt about himself in doing it. There is a humanness to this account that leaves a reader with a sense that something "normal" going on in meditation, something that in one form or another each of us has experienced, even if not according to some conscious discipline. But the text leaves us with questions as much as it gives answers about Macmurray's attitude to what he calls contemplation — a necessary and good activity in art for him and yet a suspect and even rejected activity in the area of religion. Why this huge split between art and religion in relation to contemplation? His fear of idealism in religion remains so strong he cannot bring himself to accept a positive functioning of contemplation in religion. He continues to be suspicious of mysticism, while maintaining a naive view of mysticism as somehow being "stuck in one's own head" rather than as a way of relating to the world in faith-filled — not fantasy-filled — imagination. Perhaps with his intensely sensitive view of the dangers of being caught in one's ideas he was emotionally incapable of viewing religious contemplation as a subordinate but necessary form of engaging the world. It at least explains why he was deeply suspicious of religious contemplation.

Somewhat related to this theme of contemplation he had answered a question from Jeffko concerning "being" in his philosophy by saying there was no place for a category of "being" over and beyond "reflection" and "action" in his philosophy. Once he had designated "action" as the form of "be-ing" for persons, a category such as "being" became redundant in his view. This perspective may have made it somewhat harder for him to entertain a positive view of religious contemplation. Finally, it is a bit surprising that the Quaker form of silent prayer joined with his own very positive position on emotional rationality did not stimulate a more positive view of religious contemplation in Macmurray.

In the end, Macmurray's view of mysticism or even simple contemplation seems to be an idealist one that is not entirely consistent with the rest of his philosophy. It cries out for a modification at the theoretical level that would give contemplation in religion the same positive status it has in his view of art and somewhat less so in science. The greatest irony of all was that in his garden, beyond all efforts at theory or explanation, he enjoyed the simple contemplation (at heart "religious") that frequently escaped him in the more formal exercises he called meditation, and seemed to escape him almost entirely when he formulated his notion of religious reflection.[16] The time spent among his plants was also passed, if testimonials can be trusted, in outrageously charming his neighbours who remembered him with great fondness. As Geoffrey Wright, ninety-two years old in 1995, observed:

> When we talked it was usually when he was working in his garden and always about simple things; he didn't tax me at all. They were both delightful people. He was really a lovely man. He had done nothing in his life except become lovely.[17]

In the Quaker community John was well accepted, and in 1966 was asked, at least on a temporary basis, to serve as an elder. He accepted, but only on that basis. Although gentle, John had a temper that could flare up, and he sometimes got quite angry about the proclivity of some Friends, as he put it to Gordon Muirhead, "to talk openly about everything on any occasion."[18] This offended his sense of restraint, especially around deeply personal things. He would not speak often at the prayer meetings, and when he did it was simple, clear and short. He spoke of Jesus in a very natural and very ordinary way. Once, after a prolonged silence during one Sunday morning prayer meeting, he stood up and said: "Other people matter." Then he sat down.[19] Sometimes, especially in the 1970s after they had moved back to Edinburgh, he would sometimes seem to doze off and nod during meetings. But then he would suddenly stand up and speak in utterly clear and coherent sentences, just as he had done in his finest years as a teacher.

It was in the late 1960s that the signs of increasing old age showed themselves beyond any doubt. John was experiencing health problems. He was prone to bronchitis, and got frequent colds that seemed to fell him when they hit. In 1967 he resigned his position on the board of Kenneth and Frances Barnes' Wennington School (see p.196) which, the year before, had transferred from Lancashire to Wetherby in Yorkshire. Also, because his neck had grown too stiff for him to be able to look back when he was driving in reverse he had a small accident with his car that contributed to him conscientiously giving up on driving entirely. And the greatest sign of all — because he could no longer manage his garden by himself — he hired a gardener to come for five hours a week to help keep things in the condition he wanted.

Betty's heart was not giving her trouble but she was ordered to give up on all entertaining and anything that could create a strain. She also could be laid low by sciatica and she had arthritis in her shoulder, arm and knees that often incapacitated her. Despite her physical limitations at the time she continued to paint at a furious pace and sold some of her works to interested friends. She tells Irene and Donald Grant that she has got John going on some writing again "but he only seems to persist at it for about an hour and a half. I spend *hours* blubbering in paint." [20] John admires her art, but from a distance. He complains about himself to Kenneth Barnes:

> I'm so glad that you and others find Betty's pictures good to be with. I wish I was more naturally responsive to pictures than I am, although I have learned a lot. I am a philosopher, and so tend to want 'explanations.'[21]

They were also losing many of their dear friends. In 1966, after forty-three years in Jordans, the Coopers — Jocelyn's parents — left for retirement at Muker in Swalesdale. Roy de Maistre, after suffering a serious stroke, died in London in early 1968 and Betty took it as a great loss, as though a part of her own life had broken off and sunk under the waves with the passing of her painting instructor and dear friend. A Quaker neighbour, Betty Jenkins, died in Jordans and John gave the eulogy at her funeral, a talk that was filled with serenity. A short time later, Anna Friedlander died in University College Hospital in London. She and her husband had come in 1939 as the first refugees the Macmurrays had taken in at Home Base, their first Jordans house, and she had become one of their oldest and dearest friends. And then, after suffering two strokes and lingering on for months in a state of "second childhood," Frances Barnes died in late Spring 1969. John wrote an obituary for her in the Quaker magazine *The Friend*. In a letter just before her death, John wrote to console Kenneth who was depressed and even blaming himself for Frances' condition. John was a paragon of gentleness and encouragement — until his last paragraph:

Still, I understand very well the feeling of despair at night, when
one feels that all that one has done is meaningless. I am quite used
to it myself; so much so that I have learned to laugh at myself and
say: 'Who can say, least of all you!' We have probably done better
than we think and a lot better than we know.[22]

On October 1, 1968, a bigger blow had struck. John's younger brother
Joseph, the real gardener in the family, quietly committed suicide. He had
lived in a great and abiding melancholy for much of his sixty-eight years.
He was a man of faith but, along with others of his family, had been possessed by a sense of his imperfections and lack of personal worth combined with a deep emotional restraint. He ended his life simply, with an
overdose of sleeping pills, sitting in his chair at home with the bible
opened on his lap. Joseph's daughter Morag remembers John's "frozen"
voice on the phone when the news was given to him. He had little to say
at the moment to Morag or Edith, her mother — which was unlike him in
situations outside his family. He told them he would try to come to the
funeral, but Betty's intense arthritis during those days kept him at home
and made him her nurse for over a week longer. Knowing that the circumstances of Joseph's death might seriously threaten Mrs Macmurray's
health, the family simply told her that Joseph had died and left it at that.
John wrote a letter of condolence to Edith and Morag and, sixteen days
after Joseph's death, spent just two sentences on his death in a belated letter to his mother. There is no record that John, in conversation or by letter, ever mentioned Joseph again. In writing to his mother in May 1969,
after talking about his garden — which was always the first item discussed
in his letters to her — he tells her:

I have been meditating a lot upon the faithfulness of God, in all its
many aspects ... What moves me most is the way His faithfulness
to us takes no regard to our lack of faithfulness to Him — just as
he sends his rain upon the evil and the good alike.[23]

He often spoke to her of religious things since, despite her judgmental
nature, she was a faith-filled person, a fact he had always recognized.
Three years earlier he had commented to her on the ups and downs in
the Quaker meeting, and then observed to her: "The only thing that I
never doubt is my discipleship of Jesus. Perhaps that's enough."[24] In his
birthday greetings to her in September 1969 on her 102nd birthday, he
sent her a yellow Maréchall Niel rose and recalled how his father,
James, had told them of his pleasure in a Maréchall Niel rose in his own
father's garden many years before. He tells her tenderly: "I hope it will
reach you in good shape and that you will remember how father loved

it, and love it now for his sake as well as for mine." He ended that letter with a reminder of what he considered his greatest gift from her:

> What I owe you most of all is that I have always been a Christian,
> and always shall be. For this my gratitude to you is very deep and
> very constant. I am not sure how *religious* I am, but I am sure that
> my first loyalty is and has always been to the Lord Jesus. What I
> mean by a Christian has changed as I have studied Him, and now I
> mean simply that I am one of his disciples. And because I am a
> philosopher by trade I cannot take that discipleship for granted, nor
> can I accept any interpretation of its meaning because it is ancient
> or familiar. I must search and go on searching for the truth of it
> and, of course, with His help. So pray for me that I shall be guided
> aright and kept free of self-assertion or self-will.[25]

What clearer sign can there be of the unity of his life focus, from the
years of his journal to his old age? It was shortly before this that he
formed the idea of writing a little book about Jesus, a desire that took
shape, after much meditation and labour, five years later in a simple
pamphlet entitled *The Philosophy of Jesus* which was presented as a talk
in 1972 to the Quaker communities in Amersham and London. In
October 1968 he had given a talk on "The Rediscovery of Christianity"
to the Quaker General Meeting in Amersham and told Barnes it had
wiped him completely. "I was terrified of it when I was preparing it, and
prostrated after it for a couple of days. Psychosomatic, I fear."[26] In
another letter a month earlier he commiserated with Barnes and said
"much of our fatigue is emotional exhaustion." This perception of himself as moved by unnamed fears deeper than his conscious knowledge
has, by this time, become a conviction based on experience in him,
though he does his best, as he shows in the letter to Barnes, not to allow
them to control him.

By the early summer of 1969, John and Betty came to the decision to
move back to Edinburgh. Making this decision was not a long or difficult
process for them since by some kind of serendipity they each, apart from any
conversation with each other, had been struck by the idea while they were
sleeping. And they liked it. The reasons for moving were the obvious ones:
John was already seventy-eight years old and Betty was just a few months
shy of it. Taking care of the house was getting too much for them, most of
the gardening since 1967 was already in the hands of the Irishman whom
John called "a real gardener," they needed to be closer to good medical care,
and they wanted to be closer to family and long-time friends at a time when
travelling was becoming less and less possible. Betty told Mrs Macmurray in
an August letter that, in addition being closer to his mother, "John wants very

much to be nearer to ... libraries. He wants, or thinks he wants, to write another book."[27] The voice of practicality, and longtime experience of his history with writing, rings out to the end.

They had come to an agreement with Duncan and Jocelyn Campbell that the two families would buy a house together. They needed a place large enough for the Campbell family (which now had four children in it), that also gave the Macmurrays sufficient space without Betty needing to use any stairs. Cost was also a consideration. The Macmurrays had hoped to move by September but the search for a suitable house was a rather protracted one that ran right into the winter.

On October 9, their wedding anniversary, John wrote his usual anniversary letter to Betty in which he grasped the quality of that moment in their lives and shared it with her:

> My darling wife,
> This is the 53rd anniversary of our marriage and the last one in Jordans. I can say truly that today I love you better and with more understanding than ever before. Indeed, you are now everything to me.
> Thank you for these twelve wonderful years with you in Jordans. We shall never forget them. And as we go back to Edinburgh let it be to plumb the depths of friendship completely. After that we shall be ready to depart.
> Your friend and lover,
> John

By mid-January, after a few false alarms, Duncan and Jocelyn finally found an ideal place on Mansionhouse Road and the purchase arrangements were put in order. John wrote to Donald and Irene Grant about it a few days before the deal was closed:

> The house is in Mansion House Rd. [*sic*], in the Grange district; stands on its own grounds, with a nice garden, walled. We shall have most of the ground floor — three good rooms and a smallish kitchen ... We shall be pretty well self-contained; with our drawing-room a large squarish room (23 x 21 + large bow window) and two fair-sized rooms on the other side of the house with the kitchen sandwiched between them. We shall know whether we've got it on Tuesday. So keep your fingers crossed for us.[28]

In March, just a few weeks after John's seventy-ninth birthday, the Macmurrays said their goodbyes to their friends in Jordans — far fewer now than formerly — and to the simple bungalow they had built for themselves. They left the name "Hatherly Brake," written in large script, imbedded in the outside wall near the front door where it remains to this day. Turning away from the place (after undoubtedly burning all the correspondence they had received over the previous twelve years!) they set out on the road back to their home country.

Chapter 17

Edinburgh: The Final Years (1970–76)

After their arrival in Edinburgh in March 1970, John and Betty slowly turned their section of No. 8 Mansionhouse Road into home. Despite the separate spaces assigned to each family, the house effectively became one home for the Campbells and Macmurrays. They often had their meals together and each day after school the children would pop into Betty's kitchen or John's study to say hello and report on their day. The children's friends always met the Macmurrays. In turn, John and Betty made sure the Campbells met their visitors, and spent time with them when circumstances allowed. And there was the beloved garden which quickly became a community adventure for the whole family.

It was the first time that John was able to live day by day something like the version of community he had envisaged in the early thirties. Months after their arrangement was in place he asked Jocelyn if she felt the living together was a success for their family. When she said she thought it was working wonderfully he was visibly pleased and told her about his long-time desire to live in a community. He felt their closeness, yet with separate areas in the house, was ideal. Getting acclimatized to the new situation took time but by mid-August of 1970, surrounded by their familiar objects and enjoying their close contact with the Campbell family, Betty wrote to their old neighbourhood friend in Jordans, Esther Muirhead, that they felt ready to look outwards again.

Before leaving Jordans, John had graciously agreed to give Esther Muirhead whatever help he could towards getting published a small book on mysticism that was edited by Esther and written by Edith Cooper, a friend of hers. The book was purportedly a series of "messages" from people who had died which were the product of "unconscious automatic writing" over a period of years by the author. This was definitely not Macmurray's preferred field of operations! Nevertheless John had undertaken to help Esther find a publisher for *From the Silence*, and had even, with huge reluctance, agreed to do a Foreword for it. The commitment to a Foreword was actually made not to Esther but to his friend, Malcolm Barnes, an editor for George Allen & Unwin, the publisher John was asking to consider the book. He promised Barnes that he would "write a Foreword to guarantee its integrity."[1] In May, just a couple of months after arriving in

Edinburgh, John sent Esther a handwritten "only-copy" of his Foreword and asked her to sent him back a typed copy of it, which she did. In those few paragraphs he states clearly: With regard to the author's claim that the messages came to her from people who "once lived upon the earth, I myself have neither the faith to share such a belief nor the temerity to reject it." He acknowledges that this Foreword is simply and exclusively a testimony to the "integrity and good sense" of the editor and, on the editor's assurance, of the author. Has a Foreword ever been so guarded in its endorsement?!

Despite his best efforts the book was refused by George Allen & Unwin. John was genuinely disappointed for Esther. As for trying Gollancz, he writes her, "I don't think I'm *persona grata* in the new ownership." He was referring to Victor's daughter whom he had criticized with regard to a manuscript not long before. He encourages Esther to seek out a publisher who might consider the book *because of* its origin rather than *despite* its origin.[2] After telling Esther he would not expect American publishers to show any great enthusiasm, he offers to write Prebendary E.F. Carpenter of Westminster Abbey, a long-time friend in "the Society of Jews and Christians of which we are both members." By this time he is clear: what she needs is a hardheaded businessman. And by December he is obviously anxious to back away from the whole project. He wonders to her if it wouldn't be better to get a Foreword from Dom Bede Griffiths who might be able to say, "This is a marvellous book" rather than John's own, " I see no overt problem with this book." In the end, the book, renamed *Beyond the Silence* at some point, was never published. But the effort he put into it over the course of a year, including the exchange of letters with Esther, remains a testimony to how solicitous John was in caring for other people, even when there was nothing in it for himself, and possibly something for him to lose. This generosity was shown to Gordon and Esther again the next year when John helped their brilliant and engaging son, Andrew, receive the consideration he deserved when he applied for medical school.

Because Mansionhouse Road was not a throughway to any main artery in the city, John found No. 8 the quietest house they had ever lived in. (How it could have been quieter than Hatherly Brake in Jordans is beyond imagination!) It was also centrally located so it was an easy walk through the Meadows to the University library where, as he told Kenneth Barnes in November, he spent as much time as he could.

> I've been reading more serious philosophy and more examples of
> "advanced" literature than I have looked at ever. The latter,
> however, bore me quickly and usually I fail to get through them.[3]

Betty confirmed John's torpid reaction to contemporary literature. In fact, his interests simply lay elsewhere and he pursued them with all the vigour that remained in him. She reveals with pride that he was asked to be a member of the Theological Club which he had belonged to in the fifties, an invitation he accepted and one which led to some fine conversations and exchange. He also joined the University Club which gave some promise to both of them for some social life in familiar surroundings. The main theme of those first months back in Edinburgh was summed up in an earlier letter to Esther Muirhead: "We are both working hard and thriving on it."[4]

Early in June they visited John's mother along with his sisters Lilias and Helen who were all together in Lilias' house in Auchtermuchty, though Helen's tenure was temporary. This visit occasioned one of the wry observations Betty made to Esther about John's mother:

> He visited his old mum a few weeks ago — 102 3/4 plus. She told him he walked & spoke much better after he'd been a night in her house! & advised him to remember that he was an old man and mustn't overdo things!
>
> She is having quaint little hallucinations: such as an imaginary doctor being told off by his wife for paying so much attention to her! & the D. Replying: "Oh no! Mrs Macmurray is a lady & would never allow that!!!" Does one detect an erotic frustration? And three days ago she received ten pounds of grapes from the S. African government. (This is a usual practice it has with centenarians). She immediately asked her young daughters (both over 70 & nearer to the eighties) to pick out a choice bunch & to send it to a certain man friend of hers. When they made further enquiries they discovered — as she didn't know where he lived or who he was — that it was another of her 'boy friend' hallucinations. Poor old mother! — the strictest Puritan who ever lived! — being beaten at the finish by her subconscious repressions.[5]

When Mrs Macmurray turned 103 that September, Betty reflected to Esther:

> Sometimes think she will see us all out. You never saw such a well cared for old lady — every care and comfort under the sun. I sometimes feel that her two young daughters (77 & 75) are losing their lives to prolong hers.[6]

That last remark was quite pointed. Helen had suffered a thrombosis that summer and was in Auchtermuchty mainly for a period of recovery. Lilias, who was only two years younger, had to care at that point for her older sister along with her mother. A few months later, Helen — who had also broken her ankle — was taken by her daughter Diana to live with her in Newcastle. That took some pressure off Lilias, and worry off John and Betty. But Mrs Macmurray kept perking along, and when she celebrated her 104th birthday the next September Betty demurely asked Esther: "Is it seemly to live so long?"

John responded differently to his mother. Her approach to the end of her life drew out of him a deeper solicitude and thanksgiving for her. In the spring before that 104th birthday she had been quite sick for weeks and John wrote to console her saying he had been praying for her the evening before and again that morning. "What was my prayer for you? It was just that you should be kept quiet in spirit and free of all secret fears."[7] It was a perfect prayer, and one he was, perhaps inadvertently, saying for himself, as well.

A letter from Betty to Esther towards the end of their first year in Edinburgh strikes an entirely different note. She observes that although John's philosophy is still not being accepted at the University ...

> ... there are a few even now who are trying to job off some of his ideas as their own creation. John seems indifferent but I doubt he's being quite as much indifferent as he seems. I am sure he must feel lonely — the price of greatness perhaps.[8]

This information could only have come to her from their friends at the University or through John himself. There were, in fact, suspicions at the time among people who knew Macmurray's work that some material in the writings of one well-known British philosopher looked very much like it had been lifted almost directly, and without attribution, from one of John's volumes of Gifford Lectures. The fact that Macmurray made nothing of it gives something of the measure of the man.

Their reinsertion into Edinburgh society is filtered to us through Betty's eyes: "We seem to be quite popular! But the philosophers here are scared of John's work. Not *one* of them has called. Bastards!"[9] This was strong language, and only partly reflected the situation. Certainly, on their return to Edinburgh, the members of the Philosophy faculty, apart from Errol Bedford, paid no attention to John. Socially, however, they had been warmly welcomed back by many friends including Professors Jackson and Hayes, William Stuart Murie, the Montgomerys, Kemers and many others. Their faculty friends were entertaining regularly and they accepted these invitations with pleasure. Some, such as Victorine Schilsky, Frances Gordon and Mary Sturrock came by almost weekly. An attractive young woman named Moira McLean called regularly to discuss philosophy and religion with John. These were meetings he enjoyed and which gave him some encouragement for the future of his work. This feeling was confirmed by occasional calls from

students in Britain and overseas who were studying his work. However, even
with these very positive contacts, the outlook for John's philosophy among
professional philosophers, as Betty noted, remained bleak.

They also got to know some of their new neighbours, especially
Douglas and Margaret Falconer, living at No. 21, whom they had met but
got to know only slightly during the fifties. Douglas was a professor of
genetics and Margaret had done classics at Oxford, so although their conversations were always social there was background from both universities they could share. The Falconers had a handicapped son, Andy, and
Betty was a marvel of naturalness with him, always knowing what to say
to him and how to be comfortable just sitting with him. Andy's mother
claimed that he spoke coherently for the first time through his contact with
Betty. On one occasion when John and Betty were going over to visit,
John decided to give Andy a rose from his garden. He paused and pondered in his garden in order to choose the best looking one — even down
to the colour and shade. Betty was driven to distraction by the delay, but
for John, in terms of what he wanted to convey in giving the flower, the
delay didn't matter. Their respective relationships with the lad captured
both of them perfectly. It was simply another testimony to a fact recognized by everyone who met them that John and Betty both, in their very
different ways, had an immense gift for friendship.

In September they took a trip with their nephew Alastair and his wife
Wynne, this time to Skye. They went through Glencoe, as Betty reports,
"where my ancestors massacred nearly all of John's ancestors ..." She was
referring to the battle where the Campbells (aided by the English) massacred the Macdonalds. In that same letter, on a totally different subject, she
confesses to Esther:

> By nature I am not really a very happy person, lacking the faith and
> serenity John has. I sometimes should like to pick a quarrel with
> him, just for the childish fun of the thing. He is busy in his mind
> and quite solitary in many ways. If I ask him: 'What are you
> thinking of?', expecting perhaps some worry or near decision
> waiting to be made, it is never so. Even at three in the morning
> he'll reply: 'philosophy, Jesus, America, China,' or such-like. Why
> should this make me mad? Because, I suppose, it's nobody's
> business to be nosey at this hour.[10]

Another possible explanation for her small fit of pique, of course, is that
in these reflective moments he did not seem to be consumed by intro-
spection or self-doubt as she felt herself to be. The fact that in his silence
he could be thinking of something totally other than himself, and this was
regularly the case, was too much distance between their temperaments for

her to handle comfortably. But she was always honest enough to say so whenever she noticed it.

In 1969, after his wife Frances died, Kenneth Barnes re-married after just a few months and celebrated this new turn in his life by taking an international tour with his wife, Eleanor, that brought them eventually to the Quaker centre at Pendle Hill, Pennsylvania, where Kenneth studied and also gave some talks on Quakerism in England and Wennington School (see p.196) in particular. Macmurray had answered Kenneth's letters from there with one of his own on August 17, 1970:

> Your account of the 'American scene' was both distressing and amusing. Such complete idealism in religion is so long out of date here that one can only laugh at its continued existence. I expect a lot of it is because they were never properly in either of the two wars, or there wouldn't have been enough idealism left to take them into Vietnam. What a mess they are making of their enforced world 'leadership'!

This theme of world leadership, always a major concern for him, became a special feature in John's thinking and his communications with Barnes over the next two years. John's vision since the First World War had been resolutely set on world unity. However, everywhere he looked he found those who were in the position to effect change in that direction thwarting it, deliberately, or by ignorance and negligence. In 1967, he had written a review of Arnold Toynbee's *Change and Habit: The Challenge of Our Time.* In it he noted Toynbee's unique gifts, as a wide-ranging historian with a sociological background, for commenting on the need for the people around the world to confront rather than evade the issues of nuclear armaments and world population. He supported Toynbee's call for an imaginative and life-serving way to put a genuine world-authority in place over all nuclear matters that might serve to evade a disaster. In terms of world population, he also supported Toynbee's focus on the need to put in place a similar authority that could control the production and distribution of food.[11] It is not surprising that he found himself of "one mind" with Toynbee on these matters. They had known one another since Balliol days and had long ago found their views of society and religion intersected in fundamental ways. Toynbee came to visit them in Edinburgh, and after his conversation with John, Duncan and Jocelyn joined them for dinner together.

The need for world structures beyond national and corporate ones constantly preoccupied John. As he wrote to Barnes and to the Grants, the United States was nowhere near able or willing to transcend its self-interest enough to play such a role that would be, at once, one of leadership and service. So Macmurray became occupied in his mind again with how to deal with the massive transformation in images and in ways of living that he knew the world needed. The solution, he proposed to Barnes, was at once local and global. First, he tells Barnes of his work on the philosophy of Jesus in which he came to a clear understanding that Jesus chose for pacifism, not for open and violent confrontation, as he faced what a free life might mean in the Roman Empire. Jesus decided that an advance towards "the freedom of the children of God" might be achieved not by attacking the Roman Empire violently but by transforming it from within. But how? By choosing a nucleus of disciples who would declare the end of kingdoms based on fear and proclaim a "kingdom" based on trust and justice. This proclamation of a new kind of kingdom would be supported by action — a life together in community, lived according to these values. Strategies would, of course vary according to different social situations.

The resonances of this analysis with his 1930s thinking on a "new society" are immediately apparent. Now, in the 1970s, this struggle was to be waged against *but within* the heart of what he, along with many others, called "the consumer society." His imagination turned at once to the Quaker form of community and to the first generation of Christians as described in the Acts of the Apostles. He wondered if the Quakers, and other people willing to live that way, might not be able to play a role in society today similar to that of the first and second generation of Christians in the Roman Empire. In this dreaming, he was returning to his ideas about setting up small communities; ideas he had shared with Betty and the Grants almost forty years earlier. For Quakers, the hope would be:

> ... finding a solution to the consumer society, by being in it but not
> of it. Why wouldn't we all — or perhaps it would have to be the
> young ones and any other friends who will join them — pool all
> their incomes (and capital?) and fix a plain but sufficient income
> for each person — and dependents, etc. allowing for special
> responsibilities — it would take a lot of working out; but it is
> possible: and all that is left over should go straight to relieving
> distress in the world outside. I don't believe anything less
> spectacular — and, in a new sense, 'other-worldly' — is of any use.
> We would really be a society of friends. Friends for the new world!
>   It would be fun working out the difficulties, and how they could
> be overcome.[12]

Some of this thinking was presented in his talk and subsequent pamphlet called *The Philosophy of Jesus*. The other side of his strategy took form that summer as a dream:

> ... [for] the creation of a world friendship society to prepare in time
> against the coming need to have a basis for the international

machinery to meet the desperate problems that are coming, and that can only be met by the world acting as one. That goes round and round in my mind and changes shape continually.[13]

Both Macmurray and Barnes were tremendously excited by a radio interview with the enthusiastic Ivan Illich that they had heard on the BBC. Duncan Campbell had given a number of lectures on Illich at the university and had already introduced John to Illich's writings. Illich had come to Edinburgh and lectured on fresh approaches in education to a sold-out hall. During the radio interview on his philosophy of education Illich had made a distinction between "expectation" (worldly and controlling) and "hope" (spiritual and humble) which touched Macmurray so much he used it at his Quaker Meeting for Worship the following Sunday. It is at least interesting that he was so touched by the distinction. In fact he used it himself, at least implicitly, in his teaching to the Christian Left group thirty-five years earlier when he was addressing the essentially religious nature of their involvement with political issues and urging the young people to find a spiritual freedom from *needing* "success" in their projects. Illich's approach to education fired up Macmurray's imagination once again around education and its relationship to society. It also evoked his frustration about the current state of education and the world, all of which he shared with Barnes:

I am prepared to admit what you say so well — that our leaders (!) *cannot* do anything sensible: the situation forbids it. That is why I have been thinking so much about founding a Society for world friendship. To aim at a world community is to aim *past* all the governments, and in a way that they can hardly object to without realising that they are making fools of themselves too clearly.[14]

Macmurray had already discussed this idea with Margaret Gibbins, a leading Quaker, and proposed to do so with Douglas and Dorothy Steere with whom he and Betty were soon to have lunch. He had tried to describe the idea to Sir William Stuart Murie, one of his students at Balliol in the 1920s who had recently retired from his post as the top civil servant in Scotland. Murie was a totally charming man who admired John greatly, but in the conversation it quickly became clear to John that Murie had no idea what John was talking about. That encounter, or rather non-encounter, with a man he believed would immediately grasp his concerns chastened Macmurray and made him decide that it was better not to *write* about it. "There ought to be a wise secrecy about it until its nucleus is established ..."[15] He refined his idea in a variety of ways but it was too late in life for him to actually undertake any action to see the dream into reality.

By 1972, John was completing several years as an intellectual and spiritual guide for Kenneth Barnes in addition to having served, from its beginning, in the role of Chairman of the Board at Kenneth's Wennington School (see p.196). That year, despite his status as an emeritus board member, was to be the most intense one of his association, and the last. Just before Barnes left for his world travels he turned the school over to a new headmaster, a good and scholarly man, who proceeded to prove himself misplaced in the job. As things grew worse for Wennington, both financially and relationally, John quietly urged every possible positive course of action for Kenneth who was by then simply a member of the Board — but clearly an influential one. John finally concluded that, for the sake of the school, the new man must leave the post. In two letters to Barnes he masterfully analysed the situation with the new headmaster, explained why he declined to take an active role despite — and also because of — the new master's huge respect for him, and advised a course of action that would, on the Board's part, be at once firm and clear as well as respecting and generous in its termination procedures with the incumbent. The painful process was carried out pretty well as Macmurray had advised. However, the school, which had operated on a shoestring and "contributed services" for so long, was not able to find its way financially. As the normal demands of life in the seventies impinged upon the utopian simplicity of Wennington's operating structures and relationships it was decided, out of a concern for justice, that staff members could no longer be expected to serve while receiving only the very low wages that Wennington could afford. With no financial reserves, and a declining enrolment that was caused by the uncertainties of its past few years, the school was forced to close its doors. Wennington, as an experiment in progressive education, ceased to exist in 1975, almost thirty-five years after it began. It had been founded on the philosophical vision of John Macmurray and, throughout its entire existence, had profited from his care and guidance as well as his financial contributions. It was a clear instance of that rather rare event: putting one's energy and money where one's mouth was — for a lifetime.

In addition to Barnes, there was another planet that orbited around John Macmurray — though a more distant one — who is worthy of mention since he claimed so much of Macmurray's energy during those final years of his life and, in fact, gave him, among other things, much encouragement and affection. Back in 1948, a young Canadian named Reg Sayers living in Toronto had written Macmurray two letters attesting to the influence of Macmurray's writings on him. He had also put several questions to Macmurray, hoping for responses from the "master." Graciously, Macmurray answered Sayers' letters at some length. In the course of doing so he found himself driven to point out, similar to the way he did with

Jeffko, that Sayers' viewpoint was firmly locked into an idealist perspective. He noted sharply, after Sayers asserted as his own John's hope concerning a new logic of the personal: "Yes, we need a new logic of the personal. [But] Logic doesn't control anything except thinking and language." He also pointed out Sayers' strong acceptance of an organic viewpoint in his many remarks, obviously thinking them to be reflections of Macmurray's views: "All this paragraph is an expression, sentence by sentence, of the Hegelian philosophy — which I am seeking to overcome." The last part of this first letter to Sayers states firmly, in the face of many large generalizations made by his admirer:

> It is easy to *think* a community of mankind: it is even easy, in moments of exaltation, to *feel* at one with all this world. But it is a very different thing to achieve a material cooperation in friendship of all the people and races of mankind. The men who have really tried it have always had a bad time. Jesus was crucified for it; Socrates was executed for it, and Gandhi was shot for it only the other day. The problem is to change the motives by which 200 million people live their daily lives.[16]

Not so amazingly, this set the young man on his heels a bit, and apart from a short questionnaire in 1952, Macmurray did not hear from him again until 1970, when he showed up on the horizon, all sails raised, to stay in John's life till the end — and in Betty's for sometime after that. What is somewhat amazing is that despite Reg Sayers' persistence in not grasping Macmurray's philosophy accurately, John chose to entrust the fate of his works, even in one corner of the world, to the hands of this fervent but somewhat misdirected disciple. Nevertheless, because Macmurray was not dismissive of Sayers at this precarious beginning, great good flowed from the relationship that could not have been anticipated. In the course of their correspondence which from John's side still exists, Macmurray left a series of statements that, somewhat like his letters to Jeffko, add his own interpretations of his work and his feeling about its contribution.

In a long letter on November 18, 1970, he answers a question about his position on pacifism — a matter broached earlier in the encounter with Max Plowman in 1937 — and he commented forthrightly:

> ... I am not absolute over this. For me it must be an issue of personal conscience; and I object to its being used in political propaganda. If I claim rights of conscience for myself, I must grant them to others who take the opposite view: and, as you suggest, they are the majority — even on conscience grounds. My argument could be simply that what we want *cannot* be war by violence; and

those who realise this should abstain. But if I had been a Quaker
when the second world war broke out I should still have judged, as
I did in fact, that 'Hitler had to be stopped,' and if I had been
young enough I should have felt obliged to stop him. But I was
alway glad that there were pacifists. They have a real calling, and
must stand by it, and I feel committed to it now.

With regard to the fate of his own philosophy which was getting little public recognition, he stated plainly:

> ... I shall be satisfied if I have pointed the way to the possibility of
> a philosophy of the personal. I always thought that my work would
> be ignored by the professional philosophers, so I am not upset by
> the correctness of my forecast. On the other hand, I have had many
> personal letters, from [people in] all parts of the world, to say that
> my writings had meant much to them. But there is no one that I
> know whom I could count upon to carry on my own philosophy,
> though I have read a few accounts of it which have seemed to me
> excellent ... So things are moving slowly; and I have no doubt that
> the question of a successor will solve itself in due course.

The more notable of the works he was referring to was the dissertation of
Frank Kirkpatrick which he believed "does attempt to carry some aspects
of my writings farther than I have done; and it is very able work." [17] At the
end of this letter, Macmurray expresses no sadness over the slow acceptance of his philosophy. On the contrary, his sadness is directed at himself.
He notes, as he surveys his work at this point, "I have often deep feelings
of disappointment with a lot of it."

In April 1971 Sayers made a personal visit to Macmurray during which
he declared his intention to create a John Macmurray Society in Toronto,
dedicated to the study and discussion of Macmurray's thought and for the
purpose of making John's work better known in Canada. Macmurray, at
Sayers' request, sent a "Message" on May 14 to be conveyed to those present at the founding meeting. In it, he promised a fuller letter to follow. In
the three paragraphs of this message, he conveyed his gratitude to the
members and his hope that they would feel their efforts were worthwhile.
Concerning his writings, he reminded them that:

> ... there is no such thing as a complete and systematic philosophy
> to be found in them. Anyone who digs out of my writings a "John
> Macmurray philosophy" must have read it into them himself. Mine
> is a pioneering work ... It aims to lift philosophy from the organic
> plane to the personal.

He closed the short message hoping that "you will find your study and your effort successful and rewarding. The qualities it especially demands are patience and humility."[18] The promised "letter to follow" was written three days later on May 17, addressed to Sayers himself, and it was blistering:

> It was good to meet you and to talk with you. You will appreciate that I was a little alarmed when I first heard that you were proposing to form a 'John Macmurray Society'. You did not even ask my permission, and if you had I should probably have tried to persuade you not to. As a professional philosopher I feel strongly opposed to self advertisement. In philosophical circles, in Europe at least, it tends to produce the opposite result from the one intended. ... But what really troubled me was that I had no way of judging your competence to carry out properly such a delicate proposal. I have discovered that my writings deceive people, by their literary clarity, into thinking that they understand my philosophy; whereas it is a very difficult business. It is very easy to think that they understand my position when they are completely at sea ...
>
> Now that we have talked together I am more satisfied, though not entirely. I am entirely convinced of your sincerity and devotedness to the cause you have taken up. I am less satisfied on the score of your understanding — I mean *philosophical* understanding — of my work. You talked a great deal. But you didn't want to listen very much. Some of what you said helped me to judge how well you understood me; but not very much of it ... I have perhaps become too suspicious because I have suffered most from people who thought they understood me but didn't. From a few things that pleased them they took it for granted that I agreed with them on all points. With you I found it rather difficult to find anything that I either disagreed or agreed with. It would have had to be made much more exact for either ...
>
> No more now. All good wishes. It is nice to know you.
>   Yours sincerely,
>   John Macmurray

Reg was apparently unperturbed by this letter. He had met the master. He had his Society — and John's "acceptance" of it. And he was in regular correspondence with the most important person in his life. Within days, he responded to the letter at length and sent the Macmurrays a gift of Canadian maple syrup. He also, if Betty's interpretation is sound, suggested in the letter that, owing to his age, John's mental faculties are not so good as they were![19] If that is so, this is indeed a rare form of *chutzpah*. In replying, Macmurray made no reference to that observation. He returned to his view that his philosophy "can't be made 'popular.' To do so would be to caricature it. It is itself very serious and very difficult." He goes on to note the pivotal issue in the "transformation" of philosophy he is talking about:

> *The Self as Agent* is the thing that must be studied; and especially the attempt to relate what I have to say to the modern philosophical tradition, especially through Kant. I don't have a philosophy; but a background of philosophical scholarship, both ancient and modern, which brings me to the collapse of the organic philosophies of the last century. My question is then: Where do we go from here? And my Gifford Lectures are an attempt to answer this question — to outline the direction of advance that the historical situation demands. It hardly goes farther.

Macmurray ends this June 25 letter noting that Sayers does not understand his view of "action" in relation to the classical problem of determinism, which Sayers had raised with him once again. Macmurray states that his approach through action dismisses the question at its foundations because, although everything that is must be determined, action focuses on determining the future.

> What we can determine is, of course, *conditioned* and so *limited* ... What makes action possible is knowledge — objective knowledge, and in revealing what is possible, it of course also reveals what is not possible ... So in discovering the limits of our freedom we discover how and in what respect we are free. The essential point however is to realise that to deny freedom is to deny the possibility of action; and this is ridiculous, because we act and we know we act. For me, at least, freedom is simply the capacity to act — no more no less.[20]

Whether or not the assertion of personal action as real was enough for Sayers is not known. But Macmurray's essential position on interpersonal action and relationships as having metaphysical significance was slowly becoming recognized. Through the University's Theological Club, Macmurray came to meet Thomas Torrance, a member of the theological faculty who had been one of Karl Barth's students. After a period of resistance to what he felt was Macmurray's Humanistic Christianity, Torrance had been quite taken by Macmurray's philosophy of personal relations, and leaned on it significantly in his systematic theology book entitled *Theological Science*. That gave John much encouragement that he did not hold back from sharing with Sayers.

Late in 1971, Sayers sent Macmurray a copy of a letter he had received from Eugene Forsey, Macmurray's Balliol student from Canada who had attended John's 1936 conference in Belleville, suggesting that Macmurray had at one time been a communist. John felt it was important to reply to that:

> It amazed me because Eugene was far more of a communist after his early visit to Russia than I ever was. In case there are other similar enquiries I had better let you have my own answer. I have never been a communist, nor ever thought of being one. I studied Marx and decided that his major mistake was about the social meaning of religion ... Jewish religion is not idealist ... [I]t destroys completely the Marxist notion that the belief in another world is the core of religion. After that I turned to Christianity as revolutionary Judaism.[21]

When Reg, a short time later, sent John a clipping from a newspaper about Communists and Christians talking together, it occasioned a reflection that seems important almost forty years after those heady days when he was most involved in these issues himself:

> It is interesting to think back to the time when I thought that a reciprocity was possible. And now that we have dialogues going between this country and Russia ... I am no longer very interested. It seems too forced, from both sides. I am not invited from our side — carefully not invited, I think; and know of communists whom I should like to talk with and would believe in as people but they are, equally carefully, not invited by the other side. The dialogues are not between people but between points of view. If a new communism were to arise, without being strangled at birth by the old communists who have already accounted for most of the original communists who made the Russian Revolution, there might be hope. I believe it will come — but not in my time ...[22]

Sayers' letter, leading into this response, had included birthday greetings from himself, followed by birthday congratulations from Sayers' WEA group in Toronto, as well. John was touched, even though he knew perfectly well it was Sayers who initiated and perhaps even carried out the WEA gesture. With Sayers, it was as though John came to appreciate that the heart of the matter was not that Sayers understood his philosophy — he didn't, really — but that Reg was drawn to elements of his philosophy that had touched his life, and then he simply admired John, and in a certain sense loved him. For the rest he felt compelled to be a missionary of John's teaching. Because of the warmth and care flowing from the elfin and dogged little man in Toronto, John's heart opened up, and his correspondence with Sayers reflects a forthright gratitude. He reveals a genuine affection for Reg, in return. It was a unique relationship for John, based on something quite other than a long personal history together or a genuine philosophical solidarity, neither of which existed with Reg.

In April 1972, Sayers proposed to arrange for a Canadian reprinting of *Conditions of Freedom,* which was no longer available, and Macmurray agreed as long as Queen's University Press gave their permission. He added prudently: "No changes or new introduction would be desirable." In this same letter, Macmurray notes with interest that Sayers revealed he was brought up Roman Catholic then left the Church. John says he did the same as a Protestant but is convinced that the most promising thing is critical engagement with one's tradition. With regard to the situation in the world: "In some ways I think the movement in Catholicism is the most promising. I used to say to students — if you are in, stay in. If you are out, stay out. But get together and talk about it."[23]

This remark is interesting for more reasons than because it is an instance of Macmurray respecting the full freedom of his students in the area of religion. Because of his love for freedom in thought and action and his respect for diversity of cultural expression Macmurray saw himself as essentially within the Protestant tradition, and he admitted this freely in his Christian Left days. Protestantism was not only his heritage but also the wide tradition where he felt he could most be himself. However, because of his passion for an urgent and energetic building of world community, Macmurray showed here his growing sympathy for positive elements in Roman Catholicism, especially after the Second Vatican Council. He saw its vast outreach, the centrality of the communal Eucharistic ritual in its sacramental system, its diversity of cultures, and its respect for the role of reason in its theological tradition as huge pluses for advancing an effective form of world-wide community.[24] On June 24, 1973, perhaps after having read of the initiatives being taken in parts of the Church in Latin America and hearing of the first written expressions of Liberation Theology, he told Kenneth Barnes:

> ... I am coming to think that it is likely to be the Roman Church which bears the main burden of the religious revolution in our time! ... there are signs already of the break-through ... 'The last shall be first' is still good doctrine. If the main bearers of the change were to be those who are farthest advanced I should of course choose the Quakers. Perhaps a combination of the two — which we have in you and Eleanor — is the most likely of all.

He was referring to Kenneth's wife being a Catholic. As a lover of freedom himself and a rejector of authoritarianism under any guise, he was well aware how this positive judgment about movements in the Catholic Church might, for many people, simply not be credible. What he was seeing was what he hoped would be an ongoing conversion in the Catholic Church in the direction of putting its emphasis on Gospel-action in the world, not on the self-protective criterion of fidelity to articulated dogma which had ruled for so many centuries. But this business of a more authentic form of Christianity excited him, in the main, because of the world context at that very time. His perspective on the Catholic Church related to his more urgent concern: his efforts to form a world friendship society. Both of them are tied in for him with how the ideals of the Gospel, as an impetus to world community, can be realized.

How the world was able to be "changed for the better" was his major interest during these years, even to the last major public address he prepared in 1972, called "The Philosophy of Jesus," which he presented first in the University Theology Club on May 9. John acknowledged that he was "not very satisfied with the result" despite putting a great deal of time and reflection into the project.[25] The lecture probably tries to do too much in a short space; and it is good to recall that in earlier references in his letters to this subject he spoke of writing a "small book." This larger work he had in mind was, by this time, simply more than he could manage.

The lecture outlines his version of the pacifist view of Jesus noted earlier. He analyses the mission of Jesus as an open method for the formation of community, the living of a love that brings justice, the overcoming of fear by trust, and the cure of the deeds of evil by forgiveness based in truth and in love. This is the only method by which the establishment of the Kingdom of God on earth can be realized, and there is no recipe for it. It is a mission to form true community, and the church of Christ is meant to be the vanguard of that community. As he writes to another correspondent, "I believe that a rediscovery of Christianity is due—even overdue."[26] This helps to explain the potential synthesis he envisages between constructing the world friendship society he imagines and the current positive changes in the Catholic Church, the largest and most cohesive Christian institution in the world.

Two things seem notable in his approach to this burning issue of forming world community, both of them significant. First, his vision never sacrifices the local to the global, or vice versa, as is shown in his notion of a world friendship society made up of small Quaker or Quaker-like communities living simply and giving their excess to the world's poor. It includes, as well, both the gift of leadership that arises only in personal contact, and the need for an institution that offers the structure, beyond inspiration and face-to-face relations, to see actions through to completion at the widest level. Second, it is clear once again, that despite his membership in Christian-Jewish dialogue for over forty years, Macmurray did not think in inter-faith terms (apart from Judaism) when he conceived of the religious revolution the world needs. He put his own hope firmly on a re-discovered Christianity. His 1928 letter to the Jerusalem Missionary Council Executive Committee, mentioned earlier, showed his personal conviction about the primacy and normative nature of the Incarnation of Christ and of the Christian community, not as dogma-driven ghetto but as way of life open to all things human. It was from that viewpoint that he answered a letter of Stanley Peck in 1972 who was asking John for his impression of the Divine Light Mission, a Hindu-related group. John was clearly not impressed and gave Peck his reasons. He ended:

> None of them are [*sic*] a patch on Christianity in religious
> understanding. Indian religion is very idealist, and since you now
> have my pamphlet 'Idealism against Religion,' you will guess what
> that means to me.[27]

A careful reading of his position on the primacy of Christianity suggests that it escapes being open to charges of totalitarianism, on the one hand, while extending a challenge of its own to a "politically correct" relativizing of *all* religions — and religion itself — on the other.

A final note on Macmurray's "take" on Roman Catholicism in 1973 might be added. Since the mid-1960s, John discovered that a significant number of the dissertations focusing on his work were being undertaken by American students enrolled at Catholic universities in the United States. Among these, Jesuit-run schools were prominent. The impression this gave him was strengthened when Philip Mooney, a New York Jesuit doing a dissertation on Macmurray at Fordham University, "came to Jordans and adopted us," as John described it to Barnes. Mooney continued to visit the Macmurrays even after his doctoral work was completed and on these trips he would fill John in on changes taking place in the post-Vatican II Catholic Church. He may also have told John about his former professor Robert Johann SJ who taught Macmurray's works in his classes at Fordham and whose book, *Building the Human,* incorporated much of Macmurray's thought. The net result was that the eighty-year-old Macmurray was informed about current Catholic realities far beyond what one might expect for a retired Protestant professor living on the edge of the Edinburgh academic culture with which he had only occasional contact. When Sayers asked him early in 1973 if there was any one group that gave him encouragement with regard to his own work being read and studied, he answered simply, on the basis of his knowledge from Mooney and from Reg himself, "I believe quite a number of American Jesuits are interested."[28]

The most public Jesuit-related activity taking place was left unmentioned by him. For several months in the early 1970s he worked on an essay on "Objectivity and Science" for a *Festschrift* in his honour that was being edited by Professor Thomas Wren of Loyola University, a Jesuit school in Chicago. The *Festschrift* was published first in 1975 in the Dominican-sponsored journal called *Listening: A Journal of Religion and Culture,* and later that same year as a book, entitled *The Personal Universe.* Macmurray's article was completely recognizable in terms of his earlier work. He presented science as a mode of human self-transcendence, but one which was subordinate to art and religion which were portrayed as progressively fuller modes of human self-transcendence and, therefore, fuller modes of achieving an *objective* relationship with reality.

Much of the time, John felt these efforts to widen the scope of humanistic imagination were almost in vain. He found it was a losing battle in the new technological culture trying to have scientists as well as members of society recognize the strict limits of science and the equally limited possibilities of technology to provide the good life. To accept these limits, he felt, would accomplish two important goods: Science would no longer be idolized and could then carry on its work as simply one of several forms of human reflection on reality. With the limits of science recognized, named and accepted, people could then consciously direct their non-scientific yearnings and hopes to goals appropriate to them, goals that lay beyond the blandishments of consumer-capitalism to satisfy.

Even after John had become an "octogeranium," as Norman Kemp Smith had playfully described himself at their front door years earlier, he felt driven to hammer at Barnes and Sayers for their uncritically positive views of science and its capacities.[29] He found their glorification of science, and its accompanying disparagement of all forms of institutional religion (especially Roman Catholicism), outdated and unhelpful in the 1970s. He believed announcing *the limits* of science was a more urgent concern. Just a few weeks before his eighty-third birthday he illustrated this conviction referring to a very specific point with Barnes, revealing in his letter an intellectual vibrancy and focus surprising in a man his age:

> In particular, I am worried by physicists' attempt to go farther than they are justified by offering physical explanations of sense experience. With sight, for instance, they start with light reflected from the object to the retina and carried to the brain (somehow, perhaps as electric currents?) *where they produce sensations of colour.* This last statement is quite out of place. He [the scientist] should stick to the *physical*, i.e., return from the brain to movement

of hands or feet via the efferent nerves. There is no place in the
physical world (in the scientist's sense) for anything mental, such
as sensation. If the brain produced the image in the mind, the
image would *be* the object — as the subjective idealists try to make
it: so you are landed in the difficulty of accounting for the
existence of the object which started the process by reflecting the
light.[30]

It is clear that although the growing complicity between science and capitalism troubled him greatly, he saw the intellectual error in scientism as
part and parcel of the same cultural degeneration. In addressing the problem he was at once philosopher and cultural critic. Some might wish to
add: religious prophet.

During this time Betty was working almost every day on her memoirs.
Since 1971 she had been putting together great quantities of material from
across the decades and writing up her account of events as she recalled
them, sometimes with great literary flair and poignancy. John's letters to
his friends during this period suggest that she is making great progress;
one actually speaks of her "putting the finishing touches" on the memoirs.
In fact, these memoirs, very extensive and touching on all periods of her
life, remained in a disjointed state to the end. As she wrote to the Grants:

> I'm closer to the beginning than the end. I am torn between literacy
> and illiteracy, so to speak! The tendency is for me to prefer the
> former. But it isn't nearly as racy & down to earth as the latter.[31]

That ambivalence seems to have created a paralysis she couldn't get over.
Perhaps the greatest barrier of all — and this is addressed openly by her
on more than one occasion — was finding a viewpoint for the memoirs
that would give her a sense that the elusive unity in her life had somehow
revealed itself. In the end, the unity she often felt was entirely missing in
her own life, compared to the continuous thread binding up what she saw
as the noble life and purposes of her husband, was simply not able to be
identified, let alone captured in words. When she died in May 1982, the
multiple pages lay loose or in binders at the bottom of her trunk, so many
petals not able to be formed into a rose.

On April 23, 1973 — Easter morning — a phone call came from Lilias
in the early hours saying John's mother had just died in her sleep that
night. She was five months from her 106th birthday. John was driven to
the funeral ceremony by Duncan and Jocelyn. Betty stayed home since her
arthritis was acting up and her pain was being exacerbated by a serious
bronchial condition. Mrs Macmurray's body was taken to Glasgow where,
with John, his sisters, Duncan and Jocelyn and other relatives present, she

was laid to rest beside her husband who had died forty years earlier and her daughter Mary who died the year after her father.

His mother's death affected John deeply, far more than he might have expected given her advanced age. He went into a depression that left him feeling utterly isolated. He was often listless, unable to write even letters for weeks on end. Some members of the family felt that John never recovered from his mother's death despite his best efforts to get back into things. Betty wrote to the Grants a month after the funeral telling them about the fatigue that often overcomes both of them, saying: "John gets depressed over it even more than I do." She went on to comment on his writing. Unconscious of it, she may have been speaking of symptoms of the medical condition, a constriction of blood-flow to the brain, that would eventually prove fatal for him:

> John takes such infinite care and so much time in writing it tires him very much. He hasn't got the ready pen, and every word is studied. He complains of himself a lot — his loss of memory and his desire not to meet many people and to do nothing much at all except rest and read. Why not? He has used his brain too logically all his life — to the exclusion of many delights, of other forms of literature and life. He read T.S. Eliot's *Four Quartets* for the first time the other night![32]

While Macmurray was preparing his ill-fated essays on education for a publication that didn't happen, Ivan Illich appeared on British television with his enthusiastic vision of an education that was truly free and person-centred. Macmurray and Barnes exchanged energetic reflections on the state of educating and teaching in Britain, with Macmurray, as usual, having the last say:

> Have we reached a point where our method of educating children is now fixed for good, and cannot be altered except by a general social revolution? I find myself tracking this back to the need for universal education and the lack of real teachers. If you need more and more teachers, you soon reach the point at which you have to use a large majority of teachers who are incompetent: and so have to be taught how to have a go at teaching in a way that will mitigate the worst effects of their natural incapacity.
>
> I am all for Illich. He is a born teacher: but if you were to try to reorganize your schools on his lines, you would fail because you could only find a few people capable of it. So again you would have to systematise the thing and train your teachers in the system ... You and I are natural teachers, and we make the worst sort of situation

efficient; and we consider the majority of our colleagues to be incompetent at their job. Isn't this natural incompetence what makes them think of themselves not as teachers but as researchers? They don't teach well because they can't do it, and never will be able to. So when I ask myself how do *I* do it, I don't know the answer. Do you think there is any way in which we can teach teachers to teach? Up to a point perhaps; but we are soon back into training them not to make the worst mistakes according to some system we have thought out for the purpose.[33]

Germane to this tale of woe about teachers is the funny-sad account he gave Barnes of his recent exposure to the teaching of A.J. Ayer, his successor as Grote Professor in London, who had so pilloried his predecessor Macmurray in his autobiography. Macmurray had gone to the talk with Duncan Campbell who reports that, throughout Ayer's presentation, John simply shook his head in disbelief. He was in a feisty mood when he wrote this letter, adding spice to his narrative:

The last philosophical lecture I heard was by Ayer. I went to it because the friend who runs the John Macmurray Society in Toronto — where Ayer has been holding forth — asked him about me; and he replied that he thought I was dead long ago. So I thought a confrontation was desirable, and sat in the front seat under his nose. And I tried to follow him. But after half an hour of effort, I had to give up. He does not talk to his audience but for subsequent publication, I expect. But nothing came of it. I thought that what he was saying was pointless; and I suspect that he thinks the same of what I have to say, if he ever attends to it.[34]

The experience with Ayer was not so much a personal encounter as a symbolic one. It confirmed Macmurray's distance from what passed as academic philosophy in the university world with which he had been familiar. It also perhaps puts an edge on the reflection that Dorothy Emmet, who had Macmurray in mind, offered to Philip Hunt in 1994: "There is a constant need for the philosopher to submit himself to continuous criticism if he is to influence people."[35] Macmurray had effectively made his choice years earlier to "go to the public" rather than to try to engage his academic colleagues. But it had not been a perverse or self-indulgent choice. In fact, there are historical reasons to believe it was his only real choice if he was not to spend his days and nights in ineffective squabbling. The issue was not about the refinement or correction of ideas, the context implied in Professor Emmet's understandable observation. It was all about the atmosphere and standpoint in which ideas are generated, the mode of thinking in which questions are pursued, the motives for the inquiry in the first place, and, throughout, the meaning of what one took for "reality." Macmurray knew that. He knew he represented not only a minority but a counter-cultural position. He was a voice from another cultural planet; and he knew, finally, that he couldn't change that fact by more conversation or dialectic. That knowledge, along with his faith that God was still at work in the world (a point he cited on more than one occasion), were probably the basis for his peace. He knew his ideas and his overall view of things could not to be taken seriously unless his *viewpoint* and *approach* were taken seriously. That was a pre-philosophical issue; it was a cultural one, and that's why so much of his sense of the break-up of things was analysed and measured in cultural terms. He spent his last years noting the positive signs and looking forward to a time that he himself would not see when his ideas, and especially his perspective on the primacy of personal relations, would appear not only plausible but necessary. Even in this, he did not long for the past; he longed for the future.

However this disposition which fluctuated emotionally between sad resignation and genuine peace depending on the day did not remove his interior loneliness. In the same 1973 letter to Barnes in which he gave his account of the non-meeting with Ayer, he pointed to another distance he felt closer to home:

> I hold on to my little group of Quakers here ... but ... if I am moved to say something from my own centre, I feel that this is not what they respond to.
>
> The fault is no doubt mine. I am tired; and have days very often when ... my attempts at thinking are ineffective.[36]

He felt this interior loneliness at the same time in his life that he enjoyed the new community in family and with close friends. He remained convivial, gracious and often full of fun, giving love — with generous hugs and his unforgettable smile — and receiving this warmth from others with equal pleasure. There was no question about the joy that reigned in their home with the Campbell family and the basic peace and affection that characterized his relationship with Betty. Part of John's increasing sense of isolation was undoubtedly the result of aging, and feeling himself to be part of the passing generation. But that alone does not explain the loneliness, sometimes leading to deep depression, that he had signalled at different times since the early 1940s.

At least two factors apart from aging must be included in any effort to understand his sense of isolation. Historically, the rapid drift of western civilization after the Second World War away from humanistic perspectives on world problems was a deep pain for him. For him, it was not just

an isolated event. Everything negative that the First World War represented about western civilization was not relieved but confirmed for him
by the end of the Second World War. No lessons had been learned from
that horror, just as no healing revolution in attitude, viewpoint or action
had been achieved earlier after the economic Crash in 1929. The failure to
respond appropriately to the Nazi genocide inflicted on the Jews or to contain the evils of nuclear weapons were massive failures simply to *care* for
humanity. Grasping for prosperity and power, not conversion to world community, was what the nations, the new ones as well as the old ones, seemed
to want. He was absolutely sure it was a wrong-headed choice. His years at
Edinburgh confirmed how deep the rot had penetrated, in fact, right to the
heart of the finest universities. He was not condemning young people! In
fact, he probably had more hope and joy in young people than many in his
generation with a much more sanguine view of recent historical developments. His major negative judgments in his lifetime were, in fact, directed
against his forefathers and his peers, and the drive to technological control
to which they had subscribed at such cost. And, it was not the passing of
his own culturally-familiar world that he mourned, but rather the passing of
the opportunity to choose and build a world based on the humane values
that were being lived in the community of his own home. He did not just
regret, he *grieved and mourned* this lost opportunity to begin forming a
world society worthy of his grandnieces and nephews, worthy of their children, and their children's children. He "hated" the technologically-driven
'substitute for a humane culture that was being chosen and that would be
their heritage. And it must be said again: he had dedicated his lifework to
what was clearly the losing side in this battle for a better world. After a lifetime given to serving the ways of peace, he simply recognized that the
chances of an even more deadly and absurd war were, by the early 1970s,
as near as ever. For him, this was not mere historical fact; it was the truth
about the wounds in his civilization which he had, for his entire adult life,
been trying to heal. His profound sadness, looked at from this world-ori-
ented perspective, was at once intimate and historical. Intimate, because his
own life's work could, at times, appear to him to have been totally ineffective. Historical, because it was a sickness caused by the West, and affecting
the world at large. No individual or family relationship, no matter how positive, could displace entirely this larger sadness.

There is a further set of more personal signals concerning his tendency
to depression that he has been giving over his adult lifetime. He was
hounded, in his weaker moments, by the "demons" in his own psychic
make-up. It could be said that this is true of everyone. However, as Betty
noted in her memoirs, John's sensitive nature combined with his insight
into what "a full human being is meant to be" made him passionate for his
own human growth and susceptible to depression when the obstacles to it

felt intractable. His angel was also his demon. And the form of his demon was his deep sense of personal unworthiness, a sentiment he more than once attributed to the "incubus" of Presbyterianism, the negative sense about self, and the rigidity and control of feeling and behaviour, that had shaped his early upbringing. It had formed the grain in the wood of his very being. It was an emotional constraint he simply had to live with; it was not something he could "overcome" by some kind of muscular decision or regimen, despite his many efforts to do so. He recognized it in the frequent disjunction he saw in himself between his fine intellectual grasp of a truer and freer way of living and his emotional incapacity to simply live it spontaneously. In this connection, although he never spoke of it, John must have known, as well as Betty did, that his fingers simply could not reproduce on the piano the music he heard in his head. He certainly recognized a similar rupture in himself in his letter to Irene Grant forty years earlier when he confessed to her that he trusted Betty and Donald more than himself in sexual matters because as a child he had suffered in that part of himself through his upbringing. This wound may have crept silently into his philosophy, perhaps more unconsciously this time, in his firm conviction that, in the "business" of loving, others matter entirely; I matter very little.

The fact that his feelings of unworthiness were culturally induced did not make them less personal. And the fact that these feelings were so seldom manifested — as they were, to some degree, in his irritated outburst with Betty (about sometimes "wanting to be dead") in their after-dinner conversation at Bright's Crescent years earlier — did not remove their power to depress his soul. This feeling was not a passing shadow; it was an enduring one that was simply a dimension of his character, part of what he always had to live with. That he was so unrelentingly gracious, compassionate and solicitous with others, especially those in real need, only shows the depth of his capacity to transform that wound into an energy of healing for others.

Towards the end, as the sun was setting on his life, it may be that the death of his mother, his reduced energy, and diminished activity, allowed more space for the shadows to play. This does not suggest that his joy in his family and his love for Betty were facades over what some might label his "real" feelings. This joy in his marriage and in the Campbell family *was* real, absolutely real; and salvific for him. It is evident that he saw his family and close friends in this light. They were a blessing beyond compare, and everything about his presence to them in these years suggests he lived in an abiding gratitude for their love.

Macmurray continues his correspondence after his mother's death to the degree, as he himself notes, that he can get over his "fits of detesting pen and paper." He reveals openly to Sayers, Barnes and the Muirheads that "motherlessness" has left him bereft, without energy and even without motivation.[37] But that was hardly the full picture. In his letters after mid-1973 he still combines a wry sense of humour with comments on world affairs, with reminiscences on the old days in Scotland when Christmas was a workday (a Presbyterian resistance to pagan festivals) and New Year's was *the* holiday. He shows a wonderful concern for each of his friends, including an extraordinarily tender and energetic support for the aspirations of young Andrew Muirhead who was pursuing his medical education at Manchester. Betty wrote to Esther about Andrew saying that he is just the kind of boy she would so much love to have as a grandson, and how she would love to be a grandmother. And it is likely that, even while John enjoyed his grandnieces and nephews so much at precisely this level, Andrew touched similar chords in his heart as he did in Betty's.

Macmurray kept up a sharp interest in the kind of philosophy he recognized as the real thing. Sayers had sent him a copy of *Building the Human* by Robert Johann, the Jesuit professor at Fordham University, and his reaction was opposite to the one he had with Ayer's lecture:

> I am thrilled by it. It is a book that I might of [*sic*] written myself, if I could have overcome the effects of being an academic philosopher; and which I should have written. I have never come across any book that was so close to my own think [*sic*]. It makes point after point which I have made; and so far I haven't come across anything in it that I didn't gladly accept. In fact it makes me hoot with pleasure.

Macmurray goes on to say the only point of disagreement he has is with Johann's strong support of Teilhard de Chardin:

> I disliked him when I read him, mainly because he claims he was doing science, and not philosophy, which I find it difficult to believe is not being dishonest. Perhaps I should try him again. He possibly, like so many competent scientists, doesn't know what science is about and how it works ... But I expect that a lot of the things de Chardin is trying to say I *should* agree with. It is most his wrong way of expressing them that I find making me annoyed.[38]

In letters answering specific questions about his philosophy put to him by Barnes and Sayers he finds an occasion, to restate something of his place in philosophy as he sees it. In October 1973 he had done a critical reading of a manuscript of Barnes's and sent him his appraisal. In the course of it, he was led by a statement of Barnes on Macmurray's philosophy to review Descartes' unique contribution to western thinking and our scientific culture but this only led him into a review of what came afterwards, and how he fit into the pattern:

There followed the shift of interest to the biological field; and gave us the dialectical philosophy of becoming and the idea of evolution, and the philosophies of idealistic and realistic evolutionism — -the philosophies of process, supporting the development of biological science.

This is where I came in. Seeing this — the historical correlation of science and philosophy — and seeing also the collapsing of the biological philosophies, I asked: "What next?" And the answer was clear: the sciences of the personal — psychology and sociology. And that must mean a philosophy of the personal to run parallel with them.

This is why I claim that I almost alone amongst philosophers in this country have stayed in the true line of philosophical development. Some scientists — like Michael Polanyi and Alistair [sic] Hardy — have done something like it within Gifford lectures. But the professional philosophies have, in a bunch, gone whoring after strange Gods (or no Gods!).[39]

He concludes this reflection with a final and important observation. Attempts to produce a psychology failed, he believes, because:

... they were conceived in terms of the matter-mind dualism, as sciences (or philosophies) of mind. And the breakthrough came only when it [sic] was conceived as a science of human behaviour. And I then judged — from this, and for other reasons also — that any philosophy which would run parallel to psychology and sociology would have to start from the person as agent.

I hope this screed may help you to follow my development in its relation to the science-philosophy controversy;

On February 26, 1974, Macmurray responds to several questions put to him by Mr Sayers, including one about Whitehead whom he says:

... is a thinker I admire very much: I think of him as the last of the Evolutionary or Zoological Philosophers; and a great man, and of course I think of my own work as an effort — and even a successful effort — to go farther.

In this context of his own "successful effort," he asks concerning the meetings of the fledgling John Macmurray Society: "Is there anyone who can come and give a good, critical approach to it [my thought]?"[40] It was a next-level engagement he knew was absolutely necessary. This was certainly on his mind again, just as it was when Walter Jeffko had challenged him some years earlier. In the early 1970s, John was helping A.R.C. (Sandy) Duncan get his book on Macmurray's philosophy ready for publication. Clear and accurate as the book was it remained mainly a work of exposition. Despite his gratitude, Macmurray expressed some disappointment that Duncan had not taken a more critical stance towards his work, and wished he had at least raised some critical questions about John's approach and conclusions in a final chapter.

This appeal for criticism was something of a two-edged sword so soon after the re-orienting of philosophy he laid claim to having articulated. On the one hand, the critics who did arise were almost uniformly judged by Macmurray to have misunderstood his project because they approached his work from the old, dualistic perspective. On the other hand, those who were grasping the weight and tenor of his accomplishment were, for the most part, still in a pre-critical mode of appropriating it. They were looking for other authors who took that viewpoint, or they were just beginning to read other authors from that viewpoint. The time for criticism had not yet become ripe for them. He probably knew that, and yet it was both a natural humility and a shrewd effort to avoid ending up in the garbage heap, on the one hand, or on a chaste and fruitless pedestal for some of his followers (and Sayers might have been at the front of the class on that one) that made him push the "constructive criticism" button so firmly and frequently. And, to be far less psychoanalytic about it, he knew criticism meant serious engagement with his thought, and that counted as a fond hope for him.

He appreciated the role of sound criticism, and it was clear he was able to offer it himself, to Sayers, Barnes, his students, and even to an old friend from Jordans who asked for his judgment on an important point. On January 2, 1973, Macmurray wrote to Geoffrey Wright, who had described John as a "lovely" man, in the clearest of terms:

> Dear Mr Wright,
>   I am sorry to have taken so long in replying to your letter of December 8 about the possibility of a book examining the psychology of Jesus Christ. You are very right to realize that there is little enough material in which such an examination could be made. I should say that there is so little that the result would be completely subjective, and indeed would need to be a work of imaginative fiction. So I can't agree that there is the germ of a good idea in this. The idea seems to me to be ridiculous and irresponsible; which should be avoided in the interest of religion, science and common sense.
>   Yours truly,
>   John Macmurray[41]

Even as Macmurray was recovering from the loss of his mother, arranging her affairs, and helping his sister Lilias get located in the new Abbeyfield Home quite close to Mansionhouse Road, he could not avoid being very interested in the outside world and in how his friends were faring, including what they were doing, reading and thinking. His belief in "counter cultural" communities and gatherings of new energy took a new twist in terms of seeing certain nations as potentially this kind of community. He expressed this while answering Sayers on a point he had made with Macmurray:

> I have a hunch that the important things in our own time are likely to come from the fringe cultures — I mean from societies which belong in a broad sense to one of the major cultures, but not to its central embodiment. Canada, it might be, since its culture is broadly British, but modified in various ways — by the French element, by its nearness to the USA, and so on. And now that I can no longer wander about the world and see for myself, I feel that I want to be told by people I can trust. Here in Scotland I am so near the central break-up of the capitalist culture that it is really difficult to think and behave constructively. In Canada you are at a distance: so how does what is happening in Europe — especially the build up of the enlarged community — look to a Canadian with a wide outlook on social development? And perhaps what happens in Europe is no longer of central importance. Where would you look for the decisive events and ideas?[42]

This is an interesting viewpoint for Macmurray after a full fifty years of struggle for a social transformation in the West. In the 1920s he had refused the invitation to a faculty position offered by Princeton and again by a university in Canada on the grounds that his philosophy had to be written in the very crucible of the cultural crisis, and not on the periphery where its full force was not felt and full responsibility for past and current failures might legitimately not be acknowledged. Now, after his best efforts had come to nought, he feels that it is precisely on the periphery that some creative imagination and freedom to act for the future might be hoped for.

As the winter of 1973–74 closed in on them, both he and Betty were hit with greater force by physical ailments. John suffered from a viral infection that he says stayed with him until after his eighty-third birthday in February. It forced him to cancel a talk at the Student Philosophical Society, which distressed him since it was to be his first occasion to be with students in a long time, and the last time he expected to present his philosophical thoughts in public. It was actually the beginning of a succession of small, but hardly incapacitating, illnesses, as John described them, that never left him entirely. One morning Betty found him on the floor. He said he was asleep and fell off his chair. Somewhat depressed, he complained to her that he has come to a dead-end, and she observes to Esther: "I believe he feels guilty if he isn't trying to write."[43] Frequently, Betty, too, complained about the strangeness of modern society:

> What to do about the new culture?!! It seems so two-dimensional to me. Cheap and uncomforting to the soul, but I suppose the soul is 'old hat' these days, too. No depth charges. It makes us both feel old and pretty lonely. We miss Jordans as it used to be. A sense of real values.

But there were many streaks of sunlight cutting through these occasionally dense clouds. Their life in the family, especially the growing and changing of the children, was a great joy for them. The 200-year old grandfather clock that had come through his mother's family and had rung the quarter-hours in his childhood home was now in their home, needing work, but still giving John a gentle reminder of his childhood and his mother. John also got word that a Spanish edition of his Gifford lectures was out, upon which he exclaimed to Barnes: "My clientèle is broadening!" Meanwhile, people were approaching him to put pressure on Faber for reprints of his books, and that gave him consolation that he shared with Barnes: "I begin to think that I stand well with all the people in this country except the professionals." He followed the election campaign and because the Labour Party leader Harold Wilson seemed to improve considerably after his rather boring start he overcame his temptation to vote Liberal: "I shall stick to Labour, even if I have to stand shoulder to shoulder with [Enoch] Powell!"[44] He was finding it impossible to write so he spent his time reading, and finally got through the volumes of Walter Scott which he had never read before.

   Despite his conviction that "there is no possible proof for or against" an afterlife, at Sayers' request he took another stab at explaining his image of what immortality might look like when one took it as certain that biological existence was impossible after death:

> ... what bothers me is not the future but the past. Suppose I say — as I have said — that only the past exists, for the future is not yet existent and the present is the only point of action, the point of transition to the future. Suppose then that I consider my life in relation to time: running from the date of my birth to the date of my death. Now I cannot go on to any date subsequent to my death. But my completed life exists after I am dead. Why should it not form the base-line of a movement in *another dimension of time*? If I seek to

think another life, this is now I should think it, and none of it ever goes beyond the time of my death; it just goes in a different time altogether, at right angles, one might say to my present life. This view is therefore untouched by any biological argument. It rests of course on the assumption that time has more than one dimension, just as space has. And then all the arguments for an 'afterlife' remain unaffected by the impossibility of the biological functions carrying on after death.

He encourages Sayers to think this over and see what he makes of it. He concludes:

some philosophers have argued for multiple dimensions of time, without any religious conclusion because, I believe, of this difficulty of giving meaning to the existence of the past.[45]

When John was asked about the development of his philosophy by Harold Stafford, a Quaker writing an article on John for *The Friend*, he replied simply: "My essential attitude has not changed since I began; and this finds its fullest expression in my Gifford Lectures"[46] This recalls a much longer letter John wrote on August 19, 1971, to Daniel Wako, a director of personnel for an institution in East Africa who had likely met John and heard him speak when he travelled for the Inter-University Committee in the early 1950s. In a long, valedictory-like reflection he faces a slightly different question than the one Stafford put to him:

Now there is your latest letter with questions — mainly whether and how the passage of time and growth of experience have changed my views and convictions. I think that I can truly say that I have not changed them basically at all. But I should add to this that if I were writing these books now, I should write them cautiously to make as sure as possible that I should not be misunderstood. I know that I have the gift of clarity in expressing what I mean, but I have found that it can easily be a deceptive clarity. The clarity of my writing is the result of hard thinking carried through to the end with continual reference to experience. I have found that without this, people can misunderstand me because what I say seems very clear and easy to follow. But of course they think it is the light of their own inadequate understanding. And there are others who are concerned to believe that I mean what *they* believe. So if I were writing it now, I should make this less possible. I would make it more difficult to understand easily and I should write in a way that insisted on the reader thinking hard for himself and should provide more of the background that belongs to what I am saying. For instance, in the essay on The Virtue of Chastity, I made a point of saying that I was not making chastity easier to achieve but more difficult. Now I should develop & explain this; and repeat and underline it. The thing I have learned from interesting experience is the extent to which people deceive themselves about their own feelings and so confuse the basic issues.

But that said, I would repeat fundamentally I have not had to change my mind about anything really important. And when you ask in closing: 'What would you say, now at age eighty, that life has taught you?' I must reply: 'The main thing is that it is always people who matter, everything else matters comparatively little. For myself it is the other people who matter. I matter little or nothing except for their sake.'[47]

By the end of 1974, John's really good days have become less frequent than his bad ones, although he is still quite fit. He wrote to Gordon and Esther Muirhead on December 8:

I have been wanting to write to you, and finding letter-writing very difficult. I haven't been able to write and feel foolish. So this evening I have decided to have a try and see what happens.

The letter stopped there; he apparently could write no more. After he died, Betty found the unnfinished letter among his papers and sent it to the Muirheads as it was. This was his last written communication with them. He caught "a nasty flu bug" in December that levelled him for weeks; and it was only in May that he felt himself more or less back to normal.

Early in 1975 an effort was made by Kenneth Barnes to get Macmurray's name on Prime Minister Wilson's Honours List. He lined up a considerable number of supporters among whom were: Lord Soper, Dr John Robinson (formerly Bishop of Woolwich), Very Reverend Ronald Selby Wright, Moderator of the Church of Scotland and Chaplain to the Queen; Edward Carpenter, Dean of Westminster; Professor H. D. Lewis, Anthony Storr, John Mackintosh MP, Professor Thomas Torrance, Norman Porteous, Nathaniel Meckem, Dr Kathleen Bliss and several others. The letters of support were uniformly strong, with some even fervent in their affirmation of his worthiness for public honour. The best of them is surely the one from Professor Thomas Torrance who described John Macmurray "as the quiet giant of modern philosophy, the most original and creative of savants and social thinkers in the English speaking world." He took two pages to show why he thought so (see Appendix for the full text). For some reason never communicated to Barnes, the initiative failed.

Through the final months of 1975 John was steadily weakening. He was delighted to hear from Reg Sayers that fourteen of his early letters to Richard Roberts had been located in the archives of the United Church of Canada, and copies would be coming. The letters were important to see again, and they confirmed John in his memories and his gratitude. In December he wrote to a Bishop Hunter on the death of his wife Grace:

> Christmas is only a few days ahead of us, and I am glad indeed that I am comforted myself in sending good wishes to a friend whom I am sure knows how to celebrate Christmas as it should be celebrated, in the spirit of the resurrection; I have found that this spirit and belief does not do away at all with the grief and sadness of human loss. I discovered this when my mother died a few years ago at the age of one hundred and five, because the loss and the grief that goes with it has nothing to do with time but has everything to do with faith.[48]

His last letter, written on June 1, 1976, was to "My dear Reg" — that little black sheep with no status in any flock, that least likely of all the disciples, whose love for John and belief in his work had completely won Macmurray over. His trust in Sayers was for years now of a different order than professional communication; it was peaceful, fraternal, and without a hint of self-protection.

> I have reread all of these letters, and so has Betty, and we have both come to the conclusion that you should feel yourself free to use any and all of these letters for whatever purpose you think best.

And his last words, so fittingly, were words of gratitude; to be delivered by Reg to the daughter of Richard Roberts "for making these old letters available to you for the use of the John Macmurray Society."

Throughout the late days of spring and up to early June Macmurray held his own, but he was not getting any stronger. Betty had an extremely hard time watching her John lose his memory and his physical control. The pillar of her own strength was crumbling before her eyes and she could not prevent it from happening. In her efforts to make things normal again she corrected him constantly and became quite impatient with him. Although John had frequently asserted that after World War I he had lost his fear of death, anxious feelings did sweep over him on occasion towards the end, and one of the family sat with him, day and night, during those days. Alastair and his wife Wynne were called two days before he died.

They came, and Wynne, who was a nurse, kept him as comfortable as possible. From time to time he seemed to hallucinate. He would clutch the hand of the person closest to him, or pluck at the bed covers as though removing something. Despite all that, the evening before he died he asked for a glass of sherry and bacon and eggs, which he enjoyed!

The doctor had come by regularly all that week, but at the end there was little she could do. John had a diseased and enlarged heart and the flow of blood to the brain was seriously curtailed. His chest was filled with fluid and his breathing on his last afternoon was not so much laboured as erratic, and getting worse with each passing hour. The end came more suddenly than anyone expected. Just before he died, he clutched at his sister Lilias' hand and exclaimed: "Mother!" — not surprising in his confused condition since she looked so much like their mother.

John Macmurray died at home at 9:30 pm on June 21, 1976, with the members of his family around him. After the others went to bed, Betty "slipped into the room to be near him till they took him away the next day."[49] Their sixtieth wedding anniversary was a mere four months away. Macmurray's funeral service and cremation were at Morton Hall Crematorium in Edinburgh on June 25. As his wife noted in her diary: There was no music. The chaplain introduced the ceremony, however since he did not know John Macmurray he gave a formal but not a personal statement about the deceased. The ceremony took the form of a Quaker service. Moira McLean gave a reading and others spoke. Kenneth Barnes and many of Macmurray's staff from the fifties were there to recognize his passing.

The interment of Macmurray's ashes took place in Jordans at 11:00 am on July 31 in the little cemetery adjoining the Friends Meeting House where William Penn, his wife and nine of their sixteen children were laid to rest. John was laid to rest in the same row as their sister-in-law and dear friend Mary, the mother of Duncan and Alastair. As Betty told Donald and Irene Grant, "It feels as if he will be going home again there in that beautiful graveyard, where the birds sing all day, beside the cherry meadow and Penn's grave."[50] For the memorial service in the Meeting House which follows the interment, Betty chose readings from the fourth chapter of the First Letter of John ("If you do not love your neighbour whom you do see, how can you love God whom you do not see?") and from Chapter 15 of the Gospel of John ("God is love, and he who abides in love abides in God, and God in him."). They were the same readings selected by their Jesuit friend Philip Mooney for a Eucharistic liturgy he celebrated with John and Betty in their living room on that very day, the Feast of St Ignatius, a year earlier. As well, an excerpt was read from a 1961 article on friendship that John had written for *The Seeker.*

In the days after John's death, obituaries appeared in many of the major newspapers and some journals in Britain. Many of them were somewhat *pro forma*, but many others weren't. The one by Professor D.N. MacKinnon, Professor of Divinity at Cambridge, published in *The Tablet* penetrated to the heart of Macmurray's philosophic achievement and his public service — as a Christian and, at once, a critic of the churches. *The University of Edinburgh Journal* obituary by James Mitchell Ph.D., a former student of Macmurray's, concentrated on the man in all his particularity as unforgettable academic guide and as a distinctive thinker who "sounded" like an idealist, yet was grounded in concrete action.

When the grey, round-topped gravestone, identical to all the others in the cemetery, was put in place a few months later, John's family name appeared on it as "Mac Murray." Betty quietly had it taken away and redone because she knew how particular John was "about his name being one word." She wrote to Esther thanking her for receiving her in their home after the memorial service in Jordans. She reminded her of the letter John had received years earlier from Ann Morrow Lindbergh thanking him for the strength his writing gave her at the time of her child's kidnapping and murder. Betty now tells Esther, and the Grants, that she just received a note from a lady who said that, as a young woman, she was given *Reason and Emotion* by Mrs Lindbergh — in fact, her own copy of the book — with the inscription in the fly-leaf: "You see, there are two of us."

These were consolations that Betty very much needed. Not only was she missing John more than words could express; she was still reeling under the shock and hurt of seemingly having been ignored or even forgotten by him in his last hours. In the midst of thanking the Grants for their kindness and intimate friendship for years, she confessed: "It has been a bitter, bitter pill to swallow that John gave no sign at the end, no wave of the hand in acknowledgment of the past, or of the future possibility of reunion." She ended the letter to her friends: "O please, please, live forever!"[51] But this almost violent feeling of yearning and desperation was not the last word for her. Just a few days later she had an experience that situated in a much more positive light the anguish in her heart. She mentioned it to Esther as a great consolation:

> When I stood at the side of the bed [?] which at present represents John's grave, I felt stripped, as if all that had ever been was not & had only been a dream world. Reduced to nothingness. But budding [?] love seemed to flow through me again, love of him, & even love of life, as if he was still there, a living presence! *Real,* not an image of reality.[52]

Betty Macmurray lived for six more years, pouring her attention as far as her health permitted on her grandnieces and nephews, especially Anne who came to her with her joys and concerns. She continued to work spasmodically on her memoirs which she may have known by then would never come to completion; it was a way of being at home for her. She died in May 1982, and her remains lie alongside her husband's in the tiny, tranquil Quaker graveyard at Jordans. Despite the more traditional Quaker practice of having no music during the funeral ceremony, there was music at hers; it was how she wanted it.

Endnotes

SRR: Macmurray, *Search for Reality in Religion*
RE: Macmurray, *Reason and Emotion*

Introduction

1. Introduction to "History of Greek Philosophy" lecture notes. Manchester University, 1919–20.
2. *Ibid.,* p.94.
3. *The Self as Agent,* John Macmurray, New Jersey and London: Humanities Press International Inc., 1991.
4. *Persons in Relation,* John Macmurray, "Introductory," Amherst NY: Humanity Books, 1999, p.12.
5. *Ibid.,* p.13.
6. Lord George MacLeod, as quoted in *Gather the Fragments,* edited by Allan Ecclestone, Sheffield: Cairns, 1993, p.54.

Chapter 1

1. Story recounted in *The Times Educational Supplement*, "Scottish Diary," June 25, 1976, p.3.
2. Unpublished essay "Reflections on the Notion of an Educated Man," delivered on November 17, 1965 at the University of Bristol. Original typescript belonging to JM is in John Macmurray Collection, Regis College, Toronto.
3. See *Search for Reality in Religion* (henceforth *SRR)*, London: Quaker Home Service and Toronto: John Macmurray Society, 3rd impression, 1984, p.6. The "First Movement" (pp.5–28) is autobiographical and serves as the major public source for Macmurray's view of his religious development.
4. The Covenanters were Scots who held firmly to the Presbyterian faith and traditions, and resisted the English effort to replace Presbyterianism with Anglicanism in Scotland.
5. *SRR,* p.6. See also no. 9 below.
6. *SRR*, p.7.
7. *Reason and Emotion* (henceforth *RE*), Humanities Press: 1992, p.15.
8. *SRR*, p.10.
9. In 1859, an evangelical prayer movement broke into mainline Presbyterian life with a call to personal conversion and forgiveness, and the invitation to embrace Jesus as one's personal saviour. The public meetings included the invitation to declare this salvation in open prayers and public declarations of repentance. The joy engendered in this release was expressed in tears and especially in vibrant hymns. This evangelical revival reached a fever pitch with the tours of the Americans, Dwight Lyman Moody (1837–1899) and Ira D. Sankey which took place in the mid-1870's in England and Scotland. The two men swept Britain into a religious fervour. Moody's simple, passionate and completely sincere homespun form of preaching and Sankey's enthusiastic and heartfelt hymns touched the hearts of aristocrats, leaders and ordinary people alike who agreed with Sankey's frank appraisal that "the Church is dying of "respectability." These evangelists injected feeling and joy — and even humour — into religious expression, which opened the floodgates on a hunger in the people that was held in check for too long by a morose, rigid and overly formalized mode of public religion. In London, Moody and Sankey literally became the 'rage.'

The effects of the tour were felt for decades in worship groups, social reform movements and new forms of bible study. Torrie and Alexander were part of the next generation of evangelical preachers, building on this evangelical movement that had begun fifty years before (cf. *Moody without Sankey*, by J.C. Pollock, Hodder & Stoughton, 1952.)

10. These three men represented the finest expression at Glasgow University of nineteenth century British Idealism (see Chapter 4). Briefly, it was a philosophical movement that united several aspects of nineteenth century intellectual and religious life: (a) it was idealist in so far as it embraced in the philosophical imagination a vision of what the world, taken as a natural and human unity, was meant to be; (b) it was Christian in so far as it proposed that this vision was really a human articulation of the divine goal of human self-realization working already in the mind of God and in the Spirit of God alive in the world and in human minds and hearts; (c) it was also Christian in so far as this vision was to be put into practice in projects of education, social reform, care for the poor and the proclamation of the dignity of all. That is, it was to be expressed in the hands and in other-centred concern. A last point but hardly the last word: (d) it was nineteenth century in so far as it embraced the view of an evolutionary, progressive movement towards this ultimate personal and societal self-realization. British Idealism was, therefore, a powerfully optimistic and missionary philosophy that embraced the advance of society as a dimension, if not the equivalent, of the advance of the Kingdom of God on earth. It is not difficult to see how this Weltanschauung became a congenial environment for the young Macmurray.

Chapter 2

1. There are two novels written by friends of Macmurray in which he serves as the model for the main male character. Both are by women. Nan Shepherd used John as her model for the character "Luke" in her book *The Quarry Wood published in 1928. John's wife Betty wrote a strongly autobiographical novel entitled* Out of the Earth in the early 1930's in which the character "David" is the heroine's husband.

   Nan Shepherd and Betty Macmurray — along with May Anderson — were best friends in Aberdeen. Both Nan and Betty graduated in 1915 together. They all knew John during his university years when the highly intellectual and moral quality of his character — to say nothing of his articulateness — featured with such sharpness in him. They were friends with John through Betty for years afterwards, as well. The sense given by the books is that each woman was at once drawn to him and distanced from him by these elements in his character.

2. "Cultivation of the Personal I." 1949. Unpublished essay in John Macmurray Collection, Regis College, University of Toronto, Canada.

3. Glasgow University: Student records, University Calendars and Prize lists (1909–13) and *Search for Reality in Religion*, p.11.

Chapter 3

1. This paragraph seems so explicit, though modest in its expression, that one might conclude that the meaning of what passed between them on that occasion is clear. In fact, in her memoir notes, Betty Macmurray asserts that she and John did not make love until after

they were married. This was John's wish, she intimates, rather than her own.

Chapter 4

1. *A History of Balliol College,* H.W. Careless Davis. Revised by R.H.C. Davis and Richard Hunt, and supplemented by Harold Hartley and others. Oxford: Basil Blackwell, 1963. pp.223f.
2. *Search for Reality in Religion,* p.20.
3. *The Army and Religion: An Enquiry and Its Bearing on the Religious Life of the Nation,* London: Macmillan & Co., 1919, p.162.
4. *Ibid.,* p.162.
5. *SRR,* pp.20f.
6. *Ibid.,* p.21.
7. *Ibid.,* p.21.
8. *Biographical Dictionary of World War I,* entry on "Ludendorff, Erich," by Holger H. Erwig and Neil M. Heyman, London: Greenwood Press, 1982, pp.232f.
9. "John Macmurray: Personal Reflections by Kenneth Barnes," an unpublished manuscript.
10. Macmurray describes making this choice to read both sides of the Realist/ Idealist fight during his student years. This autobiographical anecdote occurs in the unpublished paper entitled "Logic and Psychology."
11. *SRR,* pp.22f.
12. *Ibid.,* pp.23.
13. *Ibid.,* p.22.
14. *Ibid.,* p.22.

Chapter 5

1. The records of the University of Manchester show that the Philosophy Department offered courses that year which may have been given by Macmurray as Lecturer in Political Philosophy, but no listing is given. There is also no mention here of the Pre-Socratics course that will be referred to further on.

2. "Professor Macmurray's Departure," *Rand Daily Mail,* Johannesburg, November, 1922.
3. Letter of John Macmurray to Irene Grant, September 22, 1926.
4. "To Save From Fear,"*Quaker Monthly,* Vol. 43, Nos.5–8, May-August, 1964.
5. These lecture notes are in the Special Collection in the University of Edinburgh.
6. Letter to Samuel Alexander, June 4, 1921. Samuel Alexander Archive, John Rylands Library, University of Manchester, Manchester, UK.
7. David Nicholls, *Deity and Domination: Images of God and the State in the 19th and 20th Centuries,* London: Routledge, 1989, p.33.
8. Reference to talk by this title made in a Letter to the Editor of the Johannesburg *Star.* 1922. Date unknown.
9. The lecture, given to the WEA, was reported at some length in the Johannesburg *Star,* 1922. Date unknown.
10. A more detailed version of this event can be found in Alan Paton's biography on Hofmeyr. Paton knew the Macmurrays, and on a visit to Britain in 1951 while he was preparing the biography, he consulted John and Betty on that sad event of almost thirty years earlier. In a June 10, 1951 letter to John and Betty he wrote: "... thanks for helping me put the story of a very strange, imperfect and noble man against the background of his times."
11. Balliol College Minutes, November 23, 1922.
12. Macmurray's biographical listing in the Balliol College Register for 1913–14 notes that he was also given the job of Junior Dean. This is not likely since, in the list of Fellows throughout the 1920s, this title is held by K.N. Bell who had become a Fellow in 1919.

Chapter 6

1. Taken from the August 9, 1991 letter of Sylvia Brown, who served as secretary to Professor Gilbert Murray, to her friend, Professor Dorothy Emmet.

2. Quoted from the interview of Philip Hunt, president of the John Macmurray Fellowship, with Prof. Dorothy Emmet in Cambridge, April 14, 1994.

3. The full term 'mode of apperception' obviously has borrowings from Kant's language, but the portion 'mode of' reveals something Macmurray gained from Kant's romantic contemporaries. The recognition that the truth we hold is historically, psychologically and culturally conditioned was articulated by the German Romantics — whom Macmurray was reading seriously in the mid-1920s.

4. With the new science, the rejection of authority in truth matters took as its pivot the certainty of "outer" experience (that is, observation and verification), as well — as Galileo testified. This aspect of experience would gain the focus of the British philosophers.

5. Quoted from Lady Drusilla Scott's *A.D. Lindsay*, a biography of her father, p.105.

6. *A.D. Lindsay*, Scott, pp.105f.

7. Professor Emmet was referring to Macmurray's understanding of what mov ed Kant — after he read the romantic philosophers Hamann, Lessing and Herder — to say in his Introduction to the Second Edition of the *Critique of Pure Reason* that: "he [Kant] found it necessary to deny knowledge in order to make room for faith." The Kantian philosophy which began by assuming the primacy of theory had concluded to the primacy of the practical — expressing Kant's dualistic split. Macmurray believed that Kant's option to see Reason as primarily practical indicated a major advance that philosophy needed to take seriously.

It must be said that Macmurray brought some of this jocular opprobrium upon himself (cf. earlier in this chapter). In fact, there are no reading notes left by Macmurray showing a reading of the second and third Critiques. His 60 pages of lecture notes entitled 'The Life and Writings of Immanuel Kant' (1925) are based on the early writings of Kant and the first Critique. His extensive reading notes under the title 'Kantians and Anti-Kantians' are notes on the positions of other authors, not Kant himself. It is only in Chapter 2 of The Self as Agent that we find 'indications' of a fuller range to his reading of Kant than may have been granted by the Balliol students mentioned by Professor Emmet. But, it must be said, indications are not proof.

8. Scott, *A.D. Lindsay*, p.106.

9. A hint of their philosophical differences comes out in their very different readings of Bosanquet's philosophy of the state. Lindsay seems to have endorsed Bosanquet almost entirely. For Macmurray (as was pointed out in the last chapter), despite the hugely positive gains Bosanquet made in the direction of concreteness in his philosophy of the state, he fails to get beyond Idealism — especially in the form of nationalism viewed as the only viable basis for the state. On the other hand, both Lindsay and Macmurray, in their mature view of the philosophy of knowledge, used action in the world, not the rearrangement of ideas in the mind, as the pivot for knowing reality. As noted earlier, Macmurray read Kant through a lens that emphasized 'the primacy of the practical' in Kant's notion of Reason after the first Critique. Macmurray arrived at a view of the primacy of human activity

(action) in knowledge in the mid-1920s. Lindsay may have come to that view later.

10. Excerpt from the letter of Professor David Cairns to Louis Roy OP, September 1, 1981.

Perhaps unknown to Professor David Cairns the younger, his father David S. Cairns had, at the end of that academic year, written to John Macmurray as his son's tutor, asking Macmurray for an honest appraisal of his son's capacities in philosophy. On October 4, 1927, Macmurray responded by first noting how well the young man was doing. He gets more particular:

... I know what you mean when you say that his mind is intuitive and imaginative rather than speculative or logical. On the whole I prefer that kind of mind — for philosophical purposes — to the other. It counteracts the paralysing tendency to abstractness. What has worried me about him always is a want of selective ability. He runs to side issues. Every problem that arises in the course of a general inquiry carries him off, ...

After further comment on David's intellectual style, both in strengths and weaknesses, Macmurray continues with advice that David take a course in Kant, and finally — since he is in Greats — to include some Modern philosophy, as well. The letter clearly reveals not just a 'feeling' for how his student is, but an understanding of how the young man's mind works. It shows a high level of personal knowledge, along with personal care. It seems Macmurray gave this kind of attention to all his students.

11. From a conversation between Sir William Stuart Murie and the author, April 13, 1988.

12. From the memoirs of Eugene Forsey, *A Life on the Fringe*, Toronto: Oxford University Press, 1990, p.36.

13. Remark made by Prof. George Davie during a conversation with the author in May 1995.

14. In the September 22, 1926, letter to Irene Grant referred to in the previous chapter, Macmurray sends Betty's best wishes to Irene along with his own, and ends: "We envy you your two babes — having remained persistently unfruitful ourselves, to our great sorrow." There is some indication from family conversation that Betty may have had a miscarriage during these Balliol years.

15. Richard Roberts saved five or six letters from Macmurray between 1925 and 1936 in which Macmurray's feelings as well as thoughts are expressed concerning his developing philosophy of "the personal" (see next chapter). The originals are in The United Church Archives, Emmanuel College, Victoria University, University of Toronto.

16. Letter of JM to Richard Roberts: January 29, 1928.

17. Letter to Helen, January 22, 1924.

Chapter 7

1. These authors reserved the word "reason" for the scientific mode of knowledge they were disparaging, and used "faith" or "art" to speak of the kind of knowing that included feeling which they were promoting. However, when we get to Kant, the term "Understanding" describes what Hamann refers to as "reason." And Kant speaks of "Reason" for what, as I just noted, they call "Faith" or "Art."

2. The focus on action (at that time Macmurray was still calling it simply "human activity") received significant attention during his remaining courses at Balliol, especially in his courses on ethics. In a particularly important fifty-page set of lecture notes on "the nature of agency and ethical action," he begins by proposing the very

Kantian-sounding problem: Can we define the conditions of the possibility of apprehending agency? It serves an occasion for him to explore what he is learning from the Romantics: the relationship of feeling to objects and the generation of the idea of value as an expression of a necessary relation between a feeling and an object. This leads him into a detailed study of agency and the relationship of action to idea since, he concludes, it is only in free and creative action that the synthesis of feeling and object in value is thinkable.

Macmurray observes for his students that his movement through the course is very similar to Kant's in the Grundlegung, with this qualification: "... for Kant the distinction between 'ought' and 'is' is a de facto distinction, while I have tried to show that the 'is' is unthinkable except in terms of the 'ought'." His conclusion is that the absolute status of Kant's "good will" is — now that he has made action the more inclusive and conceptually prior reality — what he means by free and spontaneous activity. From this perspective, he brings his deduction to its final conclusion that "the ultimate presupposition of all possible experience is the free agent," and the ultimate free agent, without whom the world would make no sense, is God.

In the final section of the course, where he explores the more concrete elements in his view of the primacy of activity, he states that the common world of activity (religion, in its widest meaning) implies both a common world of objects (science) and a common world of feelings (art/morality) and a de facto unity of these two. But this unity, taken alone — for example in the generation of Kant's "impulse" —

would render only an organic world view, not a distinctively human one. It would, as yet, be only the ethically "given," not the ethically "determined" which arises only through the exercise of freedom. Consequently, free activity — the concern of ethics — is the domain in which object and feeling not only come together in initial impulse but are raised to a higher power by knowledge and freedom. Impulse is transformed into intention, that is, into deliberate moral agency which "can only be conceived as an actualization in terms of deliberate purpose, of what is potentially given, i.e., as the transformation of the actual common world."

3. Notes entitled *Schopenhauer: The World as Will and Representation*, John Macmurray Special Collection, University of Edinburgh, p.63.

4. Macmurray's first attempt at building this reflection of action and the distinctively "personal" mode of being into his courses appears in the 1924–25 set of lecture notes entitled "The Place of Ethical Studies in Philosophy." He notes there that the question: "What am I to do?" only makes sense once I know the answer to a prior question: "What am I?" He spends much of the first part of the course giving a thorough review of the major answers given in western philosophy to the question: "What am I?"

a. A complicated mechanism for the transformation of energy. (materialism)

b. A member of society. 'My station and its duties'

c. An intrusive element of reason. (Stoicism and Kant)

d. An immortal soul

e. An organic being driven by unconscious motives.

He then proposes that the truest answer must be one based on the question: "What is the nature of personality?" With this perspective guiding him, he then frames the rest of the course in terms of a philosophy of action expressed within the overarching context of personal relationship.

In this orientation he reveals a great deal. First of all, he is not convinced the world can be comprehended even though, as he suggested to his students, he believes firmly in seeking the degree of coherence that is achievable. He also states that the world is intelligible only through the category of personality. That is, the impersonal mechanical and organic elements of the world are not denied, they are to be understood as dimensions of a fuller conception of unity called "the personal". In terms of bald logic he is saying: The impersonal cannot explain the personal; the personal can explain the impersonal for it contains it within itself. Working out the full implications of this judgment is the natural next and necessary step in western philosophy, and what he believes is desperately needed. The project entails overcoming modern dualism by thinking the unity of the world in a way that does full justice to all its content, and yet does so within fully rational terms.

5. See *Adventure: The Faith of Science and the Science of Faith,* by Burnett Streeter, Catherine M. Chilcott, John Macmurray, Alexander S. Russell, London: Macmillan and Co. 1927, as well as his 1926 article in The Hibbert Journal entitled "Christianity: Pagan or Scientific?" and the 1926 article "The Function of Experiment in Knowledge," published in the Proceedings of the Aristotelian Society.

6. *Adventure*, B. Streeter, Macmillan & Co. London: 1927, p.25.

7. *Ibid.* pp.23f.

8. Two clarifications should be offered. First, "personality" as used here means a "fuller" mode of being than a merely material object or an organism. Secondly, the term 'personality' can be applied to God only analogously. As Macmurray suggested in a footnote much later in his life: It is simply the best category we have available for exploring the meaning of God. But at this point, he states that we should be quite comfortable using it in relation to God since the elements of simultaneous immanence and self-transcendence are peculiar not to God alone but to any personal being.

9. *Adventure*, p.178.

10. *Ibid.,* p.179.

11. *Ibid.,* p.180.

12. Unfortunately, no copy of this sermon can be found.

13. He goes on to quote Lotze in a conviction he comes to hold himself. "In actual life the varying judgments of science *'have never been able to break the belief that in its feeling for the value of things and their relations, our reason possesses as genuine a revelation as in the principle of logical investigation, it has an indisputable instrument of experience'.*"

14. Letter of JM to Roberts, January 29, 1928.

15. "What I Live By," *The Student Movement,* Vol. XXX, No. 9, July 1928, pp.199–200.

16. *Ibid.* pp.199–200.

17. The BBC lectures were published by Faber & Faber as *Freedom in the Modern World.* (1932). Many of Macmurray's clarifications and further development of earlier themes appeared in *Reason and Emotion* (1935). The expanded meaning he gives to 'reason' and 'rational' are addressed specifically in chapters 1 and 3, but they characterize, by his own definition, all the other chapters, as well.

18. Letter of John Macmurray to David S. Cairns, August 10, 1928.

Chapter 8

1. Letter to his mother, Sept. 14, 1928. John's family was living in Moffatt at the time.
2. The address was 25 The Bolton Studios, Redcliffe Road, London SW 10. It was just off the Fulham Road, on the north side — about 15 minutes walk from the South Kensington underground station.
3. The Minutes of College Committee show that John Macmurray was appointed on August 1, 1928 with the title of "Grote Professor of Philosophy of Mind and Logic" with the status and designation of Appointed Teacher. With this status, he was thereby admitted to the Faculty of Arts and to membership on the Board of Philosophical Studies. Until 1928, philosophy and psychology at University College had been one department. With Macmurray's arrival, they were divided into two departments, with Prof. C. Spearman taking charge of psychology and Macmurray heading philosophy from Room 3 on the mezzanine level of Crabb Robinson Hall.
4. Cf. "London University Celebrates Its Centenary," *The Listener,* by Sir Edwin Deller, July 1, 1936. Vol. xvi, No. 390, pp.1–4, 26. Deller was named Principal of the University in 1929.
5. "Unity of Modern Problems," *Journal of Philosophical Studies*, 4, 1929. p.179.
6. *Ibid.* p.179.
7. *Ibid.* p.179.
8. "Ye Are My Friends," Pamphlet. London: Quaker Home Service, 1979.
9. *Ibid.*
10. One student who became a novelist saw Macmurray as exemplifying precisely this kind of wisdom, and found similarities in the Indian tradition. Leo H. Myers wrote some novels based in India, and in one he included as one of his characters a guru whose character and statements Myers admitted were derived from his acquaintance with Macmurray and his writings. Cf. *The Pool of Vishnu,* L.H. Myers, London: Jonathan Cape, 1940. In his acknowledgments, Myers especially thanks John Macmurray.
11. Letter to Roberts, February 19, 1929.
12. *Leaders of the Church of England 1828–1978*, David L. Edwards, London: Hodder & Stoughton, 1978, pp.346f.
13. Letter to Roberts, February 19, 1929.
14. Letter to Roberts, March 24, 1929.
15. "Symposium: The Principle of Personality in Experience," *Proceedings of the Aristotelian Society,* XXIX, (1928–29), pp.316–30.
16. A UCL official, Mrs C. Budden, confirmed in a July 31, 1985 letter to Rev. Stanley Sharples that no copy of the lectures exists in UCL files. The lectures were announced in the UCL calendar, and given during the course of the 1929–30 academic year. In an October 10, 1930 letter to Roberts, Macmurray writes: "I've been trying — without much speed so far — to get my lectures on "The Personal" into book form." So, it is clear the lectures were not only given but likely in a fairly complete form as written texts.
17. *Freedom in the Modern World* (1932), Humanities Press, New Jersey, 1992.
18. At which point he will turn on the individualism at the heart of the Protestant inspiration and challenge it to think relationally, that is, communally.
19. Quoted by Macmurray in his November 13, 1930 letter to R. Roberts.
20. Given the wording of this last paragraph to Roberts, Sandy Lindsay's 1928 appraisal of his

younger colleague's faith: that Macmurray reduced religion exclusively to the relations of human persons — thereby dismissing God — might threaten to raise its gory locks once again. This is hardly warranted. Macmurray is here opposing personal relations to impersonal ones, not to God. He consistently, though often only implicitly, means by God: the distinct, personal being who grounds all personal relations.

21. This information comes from A.R.C. Duncan in a conversation with the author.

22. This judgment on the 1930s for him is one he shared with his wife some twenty years later when they were living in Edinburgh. It is recorded in the diaries of Betty Macmurray from the 1950s.

Chapter 9

1. For much of the history of the BBC throughout the 1930's, I lean heavily on the excellent unpublished paper entitled "John Macmurray and the BBC: 1930 to 1941" by Philip Hunt, President of the John Macmurray Fellowship in Britain.

2. "Foreword" by Charles Siepmann to *Freedom in the Modern World*, John Macmurray, Atlantic Highlands NJ: Humanities Press, 1992, pp.xxxv-xxxvi.

3. Letter to Helen, April 13, 1930.

4. Letter to Donald Grant who lived in Vienna at the time. June 1, 1930.

5. *Freedom in the Modern World*, "Preface to the First Edition," pp.xli-xlii.

6. *Ibid.*

7. "Professor Macmurray and his Critics," *The Listener*, September 3, 1930, p.372. Letters to the Editor of Vincent McNabb OP and Martin D'Arcy SJ.

8. Letter to Richard Roberts, October 10, 1930.

9. Letter to Richard Roberts, November 13, 1930.

10. A Landmark in Broadcasting," *The Listener*, by John Macmurray. April 13, 1932, p.538.

11. "Education for Change," *The Listener*, April 13, 1932. p.524.

12. Reith wrote a memo making these points on November 5, 1936. On June 7, 1934, Oswald Mosley had led his two-year old British Union of Fascists (BUF) in a major rally at Olympia, London. In 1936, Mosley led an explicitly anti-Jewish demonstration in Whitechapel where violence broke out and many people were injured. The Government, disturbed by the increasing paramilitary style of the BUF, passed the Public Order Act that year banning the wearing of political uniforms. It had a partial limiting effect, but the BUF continued to become strongly anti-semitic. It was well-known that, in this stand, they reflected the views of many prominent British people at the time. This was the tinder-like context in which Reith made his decision.

13. A lively and contentious correspondence at the BBC over Macmurray's proposed talks was softened and communicated to Macmurray by Rev. Eric Fenn who worked on the series. Fenn was the former Assistant to Archbishop Temple and served as a planner and coordinator of the Liverpool SCM Conference in January, 1929 where Macmurray gave a major talk. Temple was surely responsible for Fenn getting this BBC position.

14. "John Macmurray and the BBC" by Philip Hunt. Unpublished paper, p.11.

Chapter 10

1. Letter of Betty Macmurray to Irene Grant. February 18, 1933. The book was not accepted by Gollancz. It was published in 1935 in

London by Peter Davies with the author's name listed as E. Hyde.

2. Letter to Helen, February 15, 1930.

3. Earlier that year he had been asked by Yale to become their professor of ethics, but he had refused, knowing it was not the solution to the social problems he felt so acutely.

4. Letter to Helen, February 9, 1931.

5. Letter to Samuel Alexander, September 20, 1931. Papers of Samuel Alexander, John Rylands University Library, University of Manchester.

6. The text of *The Western Tradition* remained in a trunk at home with several of Macmurray's other papers.

7. This thesis can be seen most clearly in his books *Freedom in Modern World*, *Reason and Emotion*, and *Clue to History*.

8. Letter to Irene Grant, August 18, 1932.

9. A.D. Lindsay, had written a book entitled *Karl Marx's Capital*. On p.6 of *The Western Tradition* Macmurray shows a knowledge of both the content of Marx's views and Marx's replacing of a theoretical by a practical starting point in his social analysis.

10. "Foreword" to *Moscow Dialogues*, p.x.

11. Certainly, the fact that Hecker, among thousands of other intellectuals and social leaders — to say nothing of millions of Ukrainians — was put to death within a few years by those very leaders suggests that a different kind of "definite and consistent philosophical theory" than Macmurray had in mind was at play in the intentions and actions of those leaders. Macmurray, along with many others, had to deal with these facts. How satisfactorily Macmurray and his friend Karl Polanyi dealt with it remains a question.

12. *Search for Reality in Religion*, p.25.

13. *Ibid.* All the quotations that follow immediately below are from *SRR*, pp.26f.

14. The story of this venture is told in Esther Simpson's own words in the book *Refugee Scholars*: *Conversations with Tess Simpson*, Edited by R.M. Cooper, Lees: Moorland Books, 1992.

15. Letter of Karl Polanyi to Donald Grant. December 7, 1929. Archives of the Karl Polanyi Institute, Concordia University, Montreal. File 76 (b).

16. Letter to Donald Grant. January 8, 1933.

17. Letter of Betty to Donald and Irene "from the train" *(im Zug)* within hours of leaving Vienna. Circa January 5, 1933.

18. There are several books on Orage and The New Age. See bibliography.

19. Guild Socialism was based on the premise that "men could not be really free as citizens unless they were also free and self-governing in their daily lives as producers." G.D.H. Cole, *The Second International*, London: Macmillan, 1963, p.244.

20. A thorough treatment of this experiment is given by Derek Edgell in *The Order of Woodcraft Chivalry 1916–1949 as a 'New Age' Alternative to Boy Scouts*, Edwin Mullen Press, Lewiston: 1992. John's only active participation for the group was the lecture he gave (cf. Report on pp.493–95). It was published in a somewhat modified form along with four other short essays in a pamphlet entitled *The Grith Fyrd Idea*.

21. The conference was reported in the *Times* for Tuesday, February 21, 1933.

22. See Andrew Rigby's *Initiation and Initiative: An Exploration of the Life and Ideas of Dmitriji Mitrinovic.*.

23. Letter to the Editor, *New Britain Quarterly*, Vol.1, No.2, January-March, 1933, p.69.

24. "Invitation," *New Britain Weekly (NBW)* Vol.1, No.1, May 24, 1933, p.5.

25. "What to Do?", *NBW*, Vol.1, No.2, May 31, 1933, p.37.

26. "Fascism?", NBW, Vol.1, No.3, June 7, 1933, p.70. This distinction clearly went unheeded or was denied not only by Oswald Mosley and his British Fascist Union founded the year before, but also by many people of influence in the country.

27. He spoke in his February 20 letter to Irene Grant of three lectures. *The Philosophy of Communism* contains four lectures — ending the three expository and critical chapters with a final one called "Practical Issues." It appears that all four were delivered as lectures.

28. *PC*, p.53. This is probably the first time Macmurray uses the expression "persons in relation," one which remains with him and serves as the title of volume two of his Gifford Lectures.

29. *PC,* p.72.

30. *PC,* p.91.

31. *PC,* p.92.

32. "Equality," *NBW*, Vol.1, No. 5. June 21, 1933, p.135.

33. "The Social Unit," *NBW,* Vol.1, No. 8. July 12, 1933, p.235.

34. Letter of JM to Donald Grant, July 9, 1933. John's respect for the local groups was well founded, but they were able to make very little headway against the central committee when a plenary conference was held the following year. The details of the rise and demise of the New Britain Movement — and Dimitrije Mitrinovic's role in it — can be found in Andrew Rigby's book *Initiation and Initiative.* The movement and its journal withered, essentially through mishandling by the leadership after Macmurray's resignation — within three years of its birth.

35. *NBW*, Vol.1, No.26. 15th November 1933.

36. Letter of JM to Donald Grant, July 9, 1933.

37. Betty, May and Nan had known one another for years. It was while the three of them were students at the University of Aberdeen (from which they graduated together in 1915) that John got to know the other two young women and they got to know him. As mentioned in Chapter 2, a little known fact is that John Macmurray served as Nan Shepherd's model for the character Luke in her first novel entitled *The Quarry Wood* (1928).

38. Conversation with Alastair Campbell. April 14, 1988.

39. Conversations with Alastair Campbell. April 14, 1988 and May 9, 1993.

40. This distinction is the major theme explored in his 1932 article "What Is Philosophy?", as well.

41. Letter of JM to IG. July 27, 1933.

42. Letter of Betty to IG from Aberdeen. Undated. Written in mid-September, 1933.

43. Letter of JM to Irene Grant. April 16, 1933.

44. Letter of Donald Grant to author. May 3 & 7, 1996.

45. Letter of JM to Irene Grant. September 14, 1933.

46. *Some Makers of the Modern Spirit*, edited by J. Macmurray, p.44.

Chapter 11

1. Gaitskell's review of Freedom in the Modern World was published as "Professor Macmurray and the Modern World" in the University College Magazine, Vol.9, No. 3, June 1932, pp.129–34.

2. Conversations with A.R.C. Duncan in Summer of 1987. Also, *National Dictionary of Biography* and *Twentieth Century Britain: An Encyclopedia.* 1995.

3. Description offered by June Bedford who studied philosophy with JM at UCL. Conversation with author on June 3, 1995.

4. Conversation of author with Mrs

Diana Hurman, Tunbridge Wells, April 25, 1988.

5. Taken from the column: "A Scotsman's Log," and an article entitled "Up Baker Street and into the Park" by Wilfrid Taylor, *The Scotsman*, February 5, 1971. Testimony to Macmurray's superb teaching, both in content and manner of presentation, comes from many sources throughout his career. Among them at UCL, cf. Marjorie Reeves, *Christian Thinking and the Social Order: Conviction Politics from the 1930s to the present Day,* p.11. Also, personal interviews of author with Dr Vincent Hope, October 17, 1986 (Edinburgh), Ruth Isbister, April 8, 1996 (UCL), Marjorie Reid January 31 and February 8, 1996, and October 25, 1997 (UCL and Christian Left meetings), Lewis Miller, April 12, 1996 (Edinburgh), Dr William Gibson, May 7, 1996 (Christian Left), Dr James Gibson, April 25, 1996 (Christian Left). Interviews with students from Balliol were noted in Chapter 8.

6. See Macmurray's response entitled "The Challenge of Communism" to the talk by Prof. H.G. Wood, Director of Studies at the Woodbrooke Centre, in the pamphlet entitled *Christianity and Communism*. March 1934.

7. John Middleton Murry, the founder of the Adelphi Institute and *The Adelphi* publication, will be noted in the next chapter.

8. "The Nature of Philosophy," *Marxism*, p.37.

9. "The New Materialism," *Marxism*, p.51.

10. *Ibid.* p.62.

11. The information contained in this section is to be found in the Archives of the Karl Polanyi Institute, Concordia University, Montreal, Quebec, Canada. The 1934 file, Box 5.

12. Letter of Karl Polanyi to Joseph Needham. June 8, 1934. Apart from this letter, there is no record of these papers Macmurray read at High Leigh.

13. "Christianity and Communism: Towards a Synthesis," *Christianity and the Social Revolution*, p.523.

14. *Ibid.* p.524.

15. "The Maturity of Religion II," *Reason and Emotion*, p.156.

16. *Ibid.* p.524.

17. Letter of K. Polanyi to J. Needham. October 11, 1934.

18. *Christianity and the Social Revolution*, p.526.

19. "Christianity and the Social Revolution," R.H. Tawney in *The New Statesman and Nation*, Literary Supplement. November 9, 1935. pp.682 & 684.

20. "Christianity and Society," *New York Herald Tribune*, Sunday, June 14, 1936. p.18.

21. Reports circulated in Macmurray's family well after the book came out that he actually dictated *Creative Society* to his assistant Ephro Sideropoulo and came to edit it himself only after it had been put into galleys.

22. Only *The Clue to History*, still being revised at this time, could challenge it at this level. In fact, *The Clue to History* supplements it.

23. "The Essence of Fascism," *Christianity and the Social Revolution*, Gollancz, p.365.

Chapter 12

1. Memoir notes of Betty Macmurray.

2. Rayner Heppenstall, *Four Absentees*, p.133.

3. The history of this remarkable organization can be found in the 1992 book *Refugee Scholars: Conversations with Tess Simpson*, edited by R.M. Cooper. I am indebted to Ms. Evelyn Wilcock for some particulars concerning Macmurray's relationship with Theodor Adorno and Alfred Sohn Rethel which she discovered

through her own research in AAC files. (Personal letter to author 31 March 1996).

4. Dr Andreas Kramer of Goldsmith's College believes Macmurray was an influence on Adorno's thought.

5. This comes from the transcript of a conversation between JM and R. Sayers prepared by Mr Sayers.

6. *Reason and Emotion*, p.7.

7. *Reason and Emotion*, p.7.

8. Cf. Letter of John Macmurray to Irene Grant, September 14, 1933.

9. Douglas McClelland, a young communist associate of The Christian Left in the 1930s testified to the impact the book had on him and his friend in the Christian Left, Alfred Cannon. They would take days off in the country precisely to hike and discuss different chapters of the book with one another. (Interview of Douglas McClelland with author, May 12, 1995).

10. Quoted by John Macmurray in letter to Irene Grant. December 6, 1935.

11. Letter of John Macmurray to Irene Grant. December 6, 1935.

12. *Life of John Middleton Murry*, F.A. Lea, p.233.

13. Letter to Mary Marr from Max Plowman. February 29, 1932. In *Bridge into the Future: Letters of Max Plowman*, edited by D.L. P., London: Andrew Dakers Ltd., 1944, p.424.

14. Letter to John Middleton Murry (JMM) from Max Plowman (MP). February 10, 1932. *Bridge,* p.421.

15. Letter to JMM from MP, June 13, 1933.

16. Letter to JMM from MP. June 15, 1933. *Bridge*, p.466.

17. Letter to Mrs Mary Marr from MP. October 20, 1933. p.477.

18. Letter to Jack Common from MP. December 1, 1935. *Bridge*, p.547.

19. Letter to Geoffrey West from MP. January 4, 1936. *Bridge*, p.552.

20. Cf. *Pacifism in Britain 1914–45:* *The Defining of a Faith*, by Martin Ceadel, p.314.

21. Letter to Irene Grant from JM. December 6, 1935.

22. "The Meaning of Peace," by Karl Polanyi. (File: 1935–36) Archives of the Karl Polanyi Institute, Concordia University, Montreal, Quebec, Canada.

23. Letter of MP to Maud Petre. February 6, 1939.

24. Letter of MP to Leslie Stubbings. March 23, 1939.

25. *The Life of John Middleton Murry,* by F.E. Lea, pp.223f.

26. Letter of JM to Reg Sayers, April 14, 1970.

27. Letter of JM to Reg Sayers, November 18, 1970.

28. Letter of JM to Reg Sayers, March 19, 1972. Macmurray presents his 1972 reflections on Jesus in his lecture and publication entitled "The Philosophy of Jesus."

Chapter 13

1. Letter of J. Macmurray to Irene Grant. September 14, 1933. See also Chapter 10, note 45.

2. The details here come from the Memoirs of Barbara Cass-Beggs, wife of David Cass-Beggs. Both of them were members of the Christian Left from its earliest meetings at the Grants house at 25 Pyecombe Corner and the summer Q Camp conference s held annually from 1935 to 1938.

3. *News Sheet of the Auxiliary Christian Left.* July 1, 1936, p.3. The signatories of The Christian Task were: Helen Cam, Barbara Cass-Beggs, David Cass-Beggs, Mary Ewen, Donald Grant, Irene Grant Winifred Jacobi, Hush Lister, Kenneth Muir, Gladys Painter, Karl Polanyi, Margaret Ridley, Norman Ridyard, Betty Russell, Kathleen Saw, Leonard Schiff, Grace Stephen, Fanny Street, Ray South, Roy Tregenza, Mary Whitehead, Avrille Williams,

Alice Wrigley, Mrs Young, Elsa Young, Marjorie Young *(Ibid.*, p.2).

4. Conversation of author with Dr William Gibson, Victoria, British Columbia, May 7, 1996. Also: Conversation of author with Kenneth Muir. May 12, 1995.

5. A statement by Macmurray quoted in the Summary of Proceedings of Jan. 18, 1936 meeting. Given to Michael Fielding by Irene Grant.

6. Letter from JM to Irene Grant. June 2, 1936.

7. Taken from the deed of the Terry Foundation describing the endowment fund for the delivery and subsequent publication of "Lectures on Religion in the Light of Science and Philosophy."

8. Letter of Richard Roberts to his daughter Gwen. June 25, 1936. United Church of Canada Archives, Emmanuel College, University of Toronto.

9. "A Week with John Macmurray," *The New Outlook*, by Ernest Thomas, July 15, 1936. p.668.

10. Notes by Harriet Forsey on talks of John Macmurray at the "Religion in the Modern World" conference, Belleville Ontario, June 1936. Published and distributed by The Associated Literature Service, Montreal, p.14.

11. Letter of JM to Richard Roberts. December 30, 1936.

12. *Ibid.*

13. Letter of JM to Irene Grant. Undated but probably October, 1936 (this judgment made by Irene Grant and conveyed to Michael Fielding).

14. Letter of JM to Richard Roberts. December 30, 1936.

15. *Ibid.*

16. Letter of JM to Irene Grant, February 13, 1938.

17. *Ibid.*

18. "The Rediscovery of Christianity" is the title of a lecture he gave in a 1938 series at St Clement's Church, London. It was also the title for a talk he gave to a Quaker community in Amersham, near London, in 1968.

19. Letter of JM to Richard Roberts. December 30, 1936. In this remark, Macmurray is referring to the early writings of Karl Barth, not his later ones. So this is not the last word. A bit farther on, I note that Macmurray refers to Karl Barth's positive efforts to confront the Nazis when he spoke in Britain in 1937 — a clear instance of Barth as a Christian theologian interpreting the meaning of history and confronting the forces of history.

20. All information and quotations from this trip are taken from the 32pp pamphlet entitled *Report of a Recent Delegation to Spain. April 1937,* London: Victor Gollancz Ltd. 1937. This reference is to p.6.

21. Letter of JM to Irene Grant. May 19, 1937.

22. Letter of JM to Rev Eric Fenn. November 26, 1937.

23. Letter of JM to Irene Grant. February 13, 1938.

24. See the 48pp pamphlet "The Christian Answer to Fascism," The Christian Left, 172 Russell Court, London WC1. It is also worth noting that the Canadian connection in the Christian Left was at its strongest at this time. There was Gregory Vlastos of Queen's University, Kingston, Ontario, David Cass-Beggs (with his wife Barbara), Joe Reid, who was soon to marry Marjorie Young, a stalwart founding member of the CL, Ruth Isbister, and Bill and Jim Gibson (with Caroline who was soon to become Jim's wife).

25. The Christian Left and the Beginnings of Christian-Marxist Dialogue: 1935–45," by David Ormrod, in *Disciplines of Faith: Studies in Religion, Politics and Patriarchy*, London: Routledge & Kegan Paul, 1987, p.447.

Chapter 14

1. Soon after getting back from the North American trip he had an occasion to meet Carl Jung. Jung, who was just returning to Europe from the United States himself, asked Macmurray what he thought of the Americans. Searching for words, John said he found them warm and hospitable, but emotionally somewhat one-dimensional. Jung exclaimed "Yes! I put it differently. I say they have no shadow."

2. University College, London, *Annual Report (1937–38)*, p.63.

3. "Creative Morality," Swedish radio broadcast. August 9, 1939. John Macmurray Collection, Edinburgh University and Regis College, University of Toronto.

4. See University College, London, Archives. Philosophy Department "Aberystwyth Transfer" file, p.1.

5. Letter of JM to Kenneth Barnes. November 3, 1939.

6. Letter of JM to Kenneth Barnes. November 25, 1939.

7. Letter of John Macmurray to Irene Grant. May 26, 1940.

8. Taken from "The Moot and Polanyi: Notes from MSS of Bill Scott — Polanyi Biography, XVIII–56–70, H".

9. It may be that the Oldham Archives will reveal correspondence on this question of Macmurray's total absence from The Moot.

10. See the University College, London *Annual Report (1940–41)* pp.23ff. See also *The World of UCL 1828–1990,* Negley Harte and John North, Revised edition 1991. London: UCL, 1990, pp.180f where the authors note: "The Library suffered most drastically from the air-raids. The manuscripts and rare books were evacuated to the solid rock cellars of the National Library of Wales at Aberystwyth, but some 100,000 books and pamphlets were destroyed as a result of the 1940 attack."

11. *Challenge to the Churches: Religion and Democracy*, John Macmurray, London: Kegan Paul, Trench, Trubner & Co., The Democratic Order series, edited by Francis Williams, p.61.

12. "The New Community," *New Phineas: The Magazine of University College London*, Summer 1941. pp.14–19.

13. Conversation of author with Alastair Campbell. May 9, 1993. It had been expressed even earlier by Alastair in a November 10, 1991 letter to the author.

14. "Freedom in the Personal Nexus," *Freedom: Its Meaning* edited by Ruth Nanda Anshen. New York: Harcourt, 1940, and London: George Allen and Unwin 1942. p.176–93.

15. *The Left News*, No. 59.May, 1941.

16. In his opening statement in "The Liberal Tradition and Negative Democracy," Macmurray wrote:
    We are under the necessity of passing from an era of negative government to an era of positive government ... So far the transition from negative government has resulted invariably in the loss of democracy and the substitution of some form of totalitarian or fascist government. The problem of positive government is still unsolved. (See Constructive Democracy, p.7).

17. Letter of John Macmurray to Stanstead Bury, Secretary of University College. September 25, 1942.

18. Letter of the college secretary to John Macmurray. October 1, 1942.

19. Letter of JM to his mother. September 16, 1942.

20. *Britain & Russia: The Future*, Peace Aims Pamphlet, No.12. London: National Peace Council. July 1942. Reprinted 1943, p.11.

21. Letter of John Macmurray to the

provost of University College, London. April 26, 1944.

22. Letter of John Macmurray to the Provost of UCL, May 15, 1944.

Chapter 15

1. Review of *Education for a World Adrift,* by Sir Richard Livingstone, in *Political Quarterly*, vol. 14, 1943, pp.290f.

2. "The Contemporary Function of Moral Philosophy," Inaugural address, October, 1944. University of Edinburgh Special Collection.

3. *Ibid.*

4. This was stated in a letter to his mother from Jordans, September 15, 1944.

5. A quotation from a talk he gave in 1948 at the 6th Congress of Universities of the Commonwealth held at Oxford on July 24 on the decline of Arts faculties in British universities. He noted that "they were succumbing to the technological outlook and becoming a set of departments providing professional training and encouraging specialized and often pointless research." Reported in the *Times* on Monday, July 26.

6. Ayer's actions were reported to the author by George Davie. Ayer's attitude was only confirmed by the negative and ridiculing view he gave in his autobiography to the condition of the philosophy department that Macmurray handed over to him.

7. Quoted from "Reminiscences of John Macmurray," by Peter Heath who served first as Assistant and then as Lecturer in Macmurray's department until 1958 when Macmurray retired and Heath went to St Andrew's before going to the University of Virginia.

Macmurray's voice was really too soft to penetrate to all corners of Minto Hall. When he was asked by Lewis Miller, one of his students between 1950–54, if he had ever considered using a micro-phone, he said: "No, I did not want anything to come between me and the students." When Miller inquired if Macmurray ever had stage fright before a lecture, the master replied "I always do." The commitment he had to communication with his students and all his listeners was clearly not a technique, it was the spiritual character of the man.

8. Dr Vincent Hope, a student of Macmurray in the 1950s, observed about Macmurray's manner in class that: "As a listener, you knew he was addressing you now, he was speaking from the heart, and he seemed so wise and sure and strong. Everyone loved to listen to him. Everyone felt they were listening to Moses reading the truth as dictated by God! In the end, I felt in a way I was conned; he was so magical and captivating!" (Interview with author, October 17, 1986).

9. Heath, "Reminiscences."

10. Heath, "Reminiscences."

11. From interview of author with Dr Richard Hamilton, October 17, 1986.

12. Referred to in a letter of Dr Vincent Hope to Rev. Stanley Sharples, September 22, 1969. Macmurray's absent-mindedness was sometimes extreme — as his wife attests.

13. A statement made by Prof. George Davie in conversation with author on May 16, 1995 in the University Staff Club at the University of Edinburgh.On this theme of being "individualists," Davie enjoyed Edward Caird's joke about Scottish philosophers and their concern for objectivity: "They are all objectivity-oriented; only some put objectivity in the wrong place."

14. *Ibid.*

15. Cf. Tom Nairn's "Obituary of Ernest Gellner 1925–1995" in *The University of Edinburgh Bulletin*, 6 December, 1995, p.8. Nairn, a

member of the Edinburgh Department of Sociology, studied with Macmurray.

16. Viewpoint stated by Betty Macmurray in her 1950s personal journal. This was also the view of Thomas Torrance who had just arrived at Edinburgh in the mid-1950s. (Interview with author on May 16, 1995).

17. Taken from a "Memoir on John Macmurray" written by Kenneth Barnes.

18. The quotation comes from an August 19, 1971 letter he wrote to Daniel Wako in East Africa, and it reflects almost word for word his stated position in *Persons in Relation*.

19. An example of both these themes and Macmurray's willingness to address them with a variety of audiences was his 1958 talk "Towards World Unity" delivered to students at Colby College in Waterville, Maine.

20. Letter of JM to Stanley Peck, January 21, 1951. In this same letter Macmurray comments in a self-deprecating way on his writings on Communism in the 1930s.

21. Letter of JM to Willa Muir, August 18, 1966.

22. Newbattle Abbey College carried on in modified form and continues to be Scotland's only adult residential college, offering programmes especially for those who have missed opportunities in earlier life to obtain qualifications, knowledge or skills.

23. This is the view of Duncan Campbell, Macmurray's nephew with whom John and Betty were living at the time. The manuscript was also refused when it was sent, after Macmurray's death, by Duncan Campbell to the University of Edinburgh Press.

24. View of June Bedford in conversation with author, June 3, 1995.

25. Max Born and Macmurray had great affection for one another. Macmurray loved to hear from Born of his advanced work in science and how his views differed from those of Einstein. They also chatted warmly about the universe in its essential meaning — Macmurray from the viewpoint of a Christian believer, Born from that of a gently resigned agnostic. Both found community-in-spirit pivotal for the 'faith' that kept them going.

26. This is reported from conversations with Macmurray by several people including Duncan Campbell, Reg Sayers and A.R.C. Duncan. A less colourful version is stated by JM in a letter with a slightly different wording. Referring to Buber he wrote: " I met him once and was wholly at one with him." Letter of JM to Stanley Peck, July 21, 1972. Copy in the John Macmurray Collection, Regis College, University of Toronto.

27. From December 6, 1957 letter of Martin Buber to John Macmurray. Quoted in Betty Macmurray's 1950s diary.

28. Lord Gifford was a Scottish judge who bequeathed in his will funds to each of the four founding Scottish universities to endow lectures on "natural theology, in the widest sense of the term." By the time Macmurray gave his lectures, the series had been going for more than seventy years.

29. Neil Spurway, *100 Years (and More) of Natural Theology: A History of the Gifford Lectures*, Oxford: Blackwell.

30. On August 20, 1953 he wrote to Irene Grant: "I'm trying to get my second set of Giffords written now, but they move slowly. I'm hoping they will get under way soon, so that I shan't have to write them as I deliver them as happened this last session."

31. *The Self as Agent*, p.15.

32. *The Self as Agent*, pp.100–102.

33. Since these terms are most com-

monly used in electricity, and the application of them to personal action is — at best an analogical one — they are terms that some of his graduate students, as we have seen, perhaps fairly described as "unsatisfactory."

34. *Persons in Relation*, p.224.

35. *Persons in Relation*, p.224.

36. Taken from summary of Philip Hunt of his personal interview with Dorothy Emmet on April 14, 1994. Her view of Macmurray, her former teacher, was that "as a lecturer, he was fascinating; as a tutor, he left something to be desired. But he had a real gift for inspiring the young. That very gift ... might have led him astray." It was in that interview that she described Macmurray as a "maverick" philosopher who might have served his cause better if he had stayed more in touch with his professional colleagues.

37. One of the few times in the 1950s that Macmurray expressed disappointment that his work had not being acknowledged arose when his friend Donald Grant came to visit them on May 9 1956. In the conversation, Donald was speaking of the Christian Left days in London and referred to John as a "prophet." John observed to his friend that he was "chosen to come to Edinburgh because Calder [Sir William Calder, the Principal] and the others on the Committee felt a prophet was needed. But alas, a prophet isn't acknowledged in his own hometown, so to speak." (Quoted in Betty's diary). It should be noted that at this time neither of his two volumes of Gifford Lectures was yet published.

Chapter 16

1. All that remain by way of written record of these American Lectures are ninety pages of extremely sparse and ragged notes on subjects such as The Defence of Freedom (we can only save freedom by extending it), World Society (the meaning of the "world" revolution we are living in), mother and child (the original form of personal development), Time and Scientists (how to understand time philosophically), You and I (the structure of personal relationship), Morality and Moral Problems, The Ethics of Friendship, The Ghost in the Machine, Doing and Thinking, The Idea of the State, Reason and Emotion, The Place of History in Knowledge, Philosophy and the Psychological Sciences, Apperception and Ethics, and The Celebration of Communion. Macmurray continued to speak in "publishable prose" with the props of those sketchy, almost unintelligible notes.

2. Letter of JM to his wife, October 9, 1958.

3. Quoted from Macmurray's "Postscript," to *Green Pastures,* a 1929 play by Marc Connelly (London: Delisle Ltd. 1963, p.107). This Delisle edition of the Connelly play was produced in supportive response to the appearance of *Honest to God* by Rev. J.A.T. Robinson. Macmurray was one of three people asked to comment on a 'Conclusion' to the play written by Vincent Long.

4. Letter of JM to Irene Grant, March 24, 1958.

5. Taken from telephone conversation between Kenneth Muir and the author, May 12, 1995.

6. *To Save from Fear,* Quaker Home Service: London, 1979. p.7.

7. Letter of JM to Irene Grant, May 10, 1964.

8. *Ibid.*

9. "Education for a Stupid Society," Essay in Regis College Collection, University of Toronto.

10. *Personality Structure and Human Interaction*, by Harry Guntrip, 1961, pp.18f.

11. Letter of JM to Walter Jeffko, 13th August, 1966.

12. Letter of JM to Reg Sayers, March 6, 1948.

13. Recounted by Esther Muirhead in a conversation in Jordans on May 5, 1995.

14. Letter of JM to Walter Jeffko, 22nd August, 1967.

15. Letter of JM to Frances Barnes, October 27, 1967.

16. When Kenneth Barnes asked him late in 1968 to write something on meditation, John wrote back: "As to my thoughts on meditation, I don't believe that I went far enough with the practice to warrant me in writing about it. I may go back and try again. I've been reading about mysticism, on the assumption that my life-long antipathy to it is just mistaken, but so far I am not convinced. But I'll keep the possibility of an article in mind." (Letter of JM to K. Barnes, December 1968 — undated).

17. From conversation of author with Geoffrey Wright on May 6, 1995.

18. From conversation of author with Gordon Muirhead, May 6, 1995.

19. Noted by Esther Muirhead in conversation with author, May 5, 1995.

20. Letter of Betty Macmurray to Donald and Irene Grant, June 23, 1968.

21. Letter of JM to Kenneth Barnes, July 8, 1968.

22. Letter of JM to Kenneth Barnes, (first part missing). April 1969(?).

23. Letter of JM to his mother, May 4, 1969.

24. Letter of JM to his mother, April 24, 1966.

25. Letter of JM to his mother, September 16, 1969.

26. Letter of JM to Kenneth Barnes, October 27, 1968.

27. Letter of Betty Macmurray to Mary Anna Macmurray, August 5, 1969.

28. Letter of JM to Donald and Irene Grant, January 15, 1970.

Chapter 17

1. Letter of John Macmurray (JM) to Esther Muirhead (EM), April 1, 1970.

2. Letter of JM to Esther Muirhead, July 16, 1970.

3. Letter of JM to Kenneth Barnes, October 20/November 5, 1970.

4. Letter of JM to Esther Muirhead, April 7, 1970.

5. Letter of Betty Macmurray to Esther Muirhead, June 16, 1970.

6. Letter of Betty Macmurray to Esther Muirhead, September 12, 1970.

7. Letter of JM to his mother, April 6, 1971.

8. Letter of Betty Macmurray to Esther Muirhead, November 9, 1970.

9. Letter of Betty Macmurray to Esther Muirhead, January 6, 1972.

10. Letter of Betty Macmurray to Esther Muirhead, September 27, 1971.

11. Review of *Change and Habit* in *The Friend*, May 24, 1967, pp.355f.

12. Letter of JM to Kenneth Barnes, January 31, 1972.

13. Letter of JM to Kenneth Barnes, July 23, 1972.

14. Letter of JM to Kenneth Barnes, August 20, 1972.

15. *Ibid.*

16. Letter of JM to Reg Sayers, March 6, 1948.

17. Letter of JM to Reg Sayers, November 18, 1970.

18. Letter of JM to Reg Sayers containing only his Message "to those present at the founding meeting on May 20th." May 14, 1971.

19. Letter of Betty Macmurray to Esther Muirhead, June 26, 1971.

20. Letter of JM to Reg Sayers, June 25, 1971.

21. Letter of JM to Reg Sayers, November 20, 1971. There may have been other reasons why Macmurray could have profited from making this statement more public. In a book that came out on the life of

Geoffrey Shaw not long after this exchange, the author Ron Ferguson noted that Shaw was much taken by Macmurray's thought and believed it had a message for the future. Ferguson then summed up this philosopher by saying: "In his early days Macmurray was a political radical and was for a spell a member of the Communist Party. Macmurray's intellectually pilgrimage eventually led him to embrace Christianity" (p.31). Two major errors in one paragraph!

22. Letter of JM to Reg Sayers, February 21, 1972.

23. Letter of JM to Reg Sayers, April 24, 1972.

24. In a May 12, 1966 letter to Kenneth Barnes he shows that his openness to these aspects of the Roman Church did not remove his strong rejection of its practical authoritarianism and the primacy it placed on dogma in religion.

25. Letter of JM to Reg Sayers, April 24, 1972.

26. Letter of JM to Reg Sayers, February 26, 1974.

27. Letter of JM to Stanley Peck, July 21, 1972.

28. Letter of JM to Reg Sayers, January 30, 1973.

29. In a letter of July 16, 1972, Macmurray criticises Sayers on this point: "... I do think you were inclined to take *science* too seriously; almost as a kind of modern 'Holy Writ.' It isn't. I have a great respect for science and a considerable deal of scientific knowledge. It is *the limitations* of science that make it dangerous. And your anxiety about 'resurrection' seems to me rather exaggerated."

30. Letter of JM to Kenneth Barnes, January 23, 1973.

31. Letter of Betty Macmurray to Donald and Irene Grant, May 30, 1973.

32. *Ibid.*

33. Letter of JM to Kenneth Barnes, June 24, 1973.

34. Letter of JM to Kenneth Barnes, August 29, 1973.

35. Taken from Philip Hunt's summary of his interview on John Macmurray with Dorothy Emmet, April 14, 1994. Files of the John Macmurray Fellowship in Britain. C/o Mr Philip Hunt, 8 Prospect Place, Camden Road, Bath, UK.

36. Letter of JM to Kenneth Barnes, August 29, 1973.

37. Letter of JM to Reg Sayers, May 30, 1973, just a month or so after his mother's death. He wrote concerning her passing:

... [when] I got back to Edinburgh, the relief gave place to a deepening sense of loss. I remembered how much she had meant to me and how heavily I had leaned on her and avoided anything that she would have been hurt by or disapproved of, even when it was all right by me. I thought I can get over this long ago [sic]. I found I hadn't; and the last fortnight, when I have been adjusting to motherlessness, I have been unwell and quite incapable of normal work and though [*sic*].

38. *Ibid.*

39. Letter of JM to Kenneth Barnes, October 18, 1973. The very next month Macmurray wrote to Barnes again. He commented on Karl Popper's *The Open Society* which he appreciated. He goes on to say about Popper: "I never met him but once, when I helped to interview him, and joined with A.D. Lindsay in sending him to the job in New Zealand." He continued:

... As for my own work, I claim it carries on the traditional development of western philosophy directly whereas Wittgenstein and the linguistic lot deserted it and found something else to put in its place. Wittgenstein was a big man; Ayer, of course, is a little one, but he happened to introduce the logical positive line to this country. He knows more about Soccer football than about philosophy.

40. Letter of JM to Reg Sayers, September 4, 1974.

41. Letter of JM to Geoffrey Wright quoted in full in Betty Macmurray's Memoir notes.

42. Letter of JM to Reg Sayers, August 25, 1973.

43. Letter of Betty Macmurray to Esther Muirhead, September 10, 1974.

44. Letter of JM to Kenneth Barnes, February 26, 1974.

45. Letter of JM to Reg Sayers, February 26, 1974.

46. Cf. "The Importance of John Mac-murray for Friends," by Harold Stafford, *The Friend*, July 16, 1976.

47. Letter quoted in Betty Macmurray's Memoir notes.

48. Excerpted from Memoir notes of Betty Macmurray.

49. Letter of Betty Macmurray to Esther Muirhead, July 10, 1976.

50. Undated (late June or early July 1976) letter of Betty Macmurray to Donald and Irene Grant.

51. Letter of Betty Macmurray to Donald and Irene Grant, August 24, 1976.

52. Letter of Betty Macmurray to Esther Muirhead, August 26, 1976.

Appendix

Letter of March 6, 1975, from Professor T.F. Torrance, Faculty of Divinity, University of Edinburgh, to Kenneth Barnes.

Dear Mr Barnes,

I am in entire agreement with the idea that John Macmurray's name ought to appear in an Honours List and respond very willingly to your invitation to write a letter in support of any move to promote this.

John Macmurray is the quiet giant of modern philosophy, the most original and creative of savants and social thinkers in the English speaking world. If his thought is revolutionary, as it certainly is, the kind of revolution he has in view is not revolt but the reconstruction of the foundations of life and knowledge with a view to a genuinely open and creative society of the future. His impact has not been as spectacular as that of Ayer or Popper, but it is incomparably greater for it soaks into philosophical, social and religious thought like sunlight upon the earth, with a similar result in living fruit. In what he has done through his teaching and writing there is a longer period between germination and harvest, for his thought penetrates deeply and pervasively into the foundations of human existence; if, then, he has not yet been appreciated as he ought to be, it is because he is something like fifty years ahead of the rest of us.

Let me indicate briefly three ways in which he has made an incomparable contribution to modern thought.

First of all, arising out of his early study of Marxism, Communism, Christianity and Science in the development of European philosophy, he has destroyed the old dichotomy between reason and experience, theory and practice, throwing greater light than anyone else on what we mean by reason and rationality, and the search of the truth for the truth's sake. In all this it is the practical relation between reason and empirical reality that has been predominant, which Macmurray has explored and developed in such a way as so reveal the deep intrinsic coherences which hold together science and religion within the structure of human thought and society in man's continuing exploration of the universe.

In the second place, Macmurray has opened up for us modes of rational behaviour in the unity of the physical and the spiritual in which we transcend the cultural split between arts and science. He has brought to light the destructive tendencies in European thought at work in its hitherto predominantly analytical methods and sought to replace them by essentially integrative methods in which art and emotion and the great virtues of personal and social being are free to develop in such a way that far from being reactionary, so far as science is concerned, they contribute essentially to the scientific spirit of western civilisation. He has shown that science is possible only within a larger framework of non-scientific issues and concerns, for the activity of science is necessarily embedded in a much deeper realm of human experience. Science itself must have a non-scientific basis in a fullness of human and social experience; but this also means that the non-scientific modes of thinking have a validity greater than we have been able to accord them in the eras of positivism and reductionist analytical thought. In other words, Macmurray has made, in my view, one of the greatest possible contributions to the development of human culture and civilization.

In the third place, Macmurray has not only exposed the damaging dualisms that have fragmented our western ways of life and thought, but has thrown all his weight into getting behind and overturning the essentially individualistic and atomistic ways of regarding the human person which stem from Descartes and Locke and which have been built into the foundations of modern psychology and social science. While therefore he has appreciated to the fullest the whole development of socialist thought, he has shown that genuinely social ends cannot reach fulfilment without a restructuring in our basic notion of personal existence. This means a renouncing of the Lockean notion of society in which persons are organised through their external relations (ideas that are as deeply embedded in American as in Marxist political philosophies), and the finding of a new way of transmuting society into community through an essentially relational rather than an atomistic or particulate notion of the human person. The implications of this were early evident in his attack upon the ruinous individualistic notions embedded in Freudian psychology and his attempts to restructure psychology in terms of mother love; but he has developed this way of thinking, above all in his great Gifford Lectures, in such a way that, in my view, it makes the most distinguished contribution yet given in our times to the philosophy of society. The way in which Macmurray has shown the profound integration between science and social existence will prove, I am sure, the most creative ingredient in future change in our social existence. One other great thinker in our time can be compared to him in this respect, Michael Polanyi.

Yours sincerely
Thomas F. Torrance

Bibliography

A: Books by John Macmurray

The Boundaries of Science: A Study in the Philosophy of Psychology. [BS] London: Faber & Faber, 1939.

A Challenge to the Churches: Religion and Democracy. [CC] London: Kegan Paul, Trench, Trubner & Co., Ltd., 1941. No. 9 in the series "The Democratic Order," ed. by Francis Williams.

Clue to History. [CH] London: SCM Press, 1938.

The Conditions of Freedom. [CF] Toronto: Ryerson Press, 1949. Reprinted with Introduction by Walter Jeffko, Atlantic Highlands: Humanities Press International Inc., 1993.

Constructive Democracy. [CD] London: Faber & Faber, 1943. Two lectures delivered at University College, London, in December 1942. Contains "The Liberal Tradition and Negative Democracy"; and "The Problem of Positive Government."

Creative Society: A Study of the Relation of Christianity to Communism. [CS] London: SCM Press, 1935.

Freedom in the Modern World. [FMW] London: Faber & Faber, 1932. Reprinted with Introduction by Harry Carson, Atlantic Highlands: Humanities Press International Inc., 1992.

Interpreting the Universe. [IU] London: Faber & Faber, 1933. Reprinted with Introduction by A.R. C. Duncan, Atlantic Highlands: Humanities Press Inc. 1996.

Persons in Relation. [PR] London: Faber & Faber, 1961. Reprinted with Introduction by Frank G. Kirkpatrick, Atlantic Highlands: Humanities Press International Inc., 1991, and by Humanity Books, Prometheus, Amherst NY, 1999.

The Philosophy of Communism. [PC] London: Faber & Faber, 1933.

Reason and Emotion. [RE] London: Faber & Faber, 1935. Reprinted with Introduction by John E. Costello SJ, Atlantic Highlands: Humanities Press International Inc., 1992, and by Humanity Books, Prometheus, Amherst NY, 1999.

Religion, Art, and Science: A Study of the Reflective Activities in Man. [RAS] The Forwood Lectures 1960. Liverpool: Liverpool University Press, 1961; reprinted by The John Macmurray Society, Toronto, 1986.

Search for Reality in Religion. [SRR] The Swarthmore Lecture 1965. London: George Allen & Unwin Ltd., 1965; reprinted London: Quaker Home Service, and Toronto: John Macmurray Society, 1984 & 1995.

The Self as Agent. [SA] London: Faber & Faber, 1957. Reprinted with Introduction by Stanley M. Harrison, Atlantic Highlands: Humanities Press International Inc., 1991.

The Structure of Religious Experience. [SRE] London: Faber & Faber, 1936, and New Haven: Yale University Press, 1936.

B: Books in which Macmurray Contributed Chapters

"Beyond Knowledge," in *Adventure: The Faith of Science and the Science of Faith*, edited by Burnett H. Streeter *et al.* London: Macmillan and Co. Ltd., 1927, pp.21–45.

"The Challenge of Communism," in *Christianity and Communism*, by Wood, H. G. and John Macmurray, London: The Industrial Christian Fellowship, 1934, pp.14–32.

"Changes in Philosophy," in *This Changing World*, edited by J.R.M. Brumwell, London: George Routledge & Sons, 1944, pp.236–47.

"The Christian Movement in Education," in *Modern Problems in Education*, edited by E.D. Laborde, Cambridge: University Press, 1939, pp.39–48.

"Christianity and Communism: Towards a Synthesis," in *Christianity and the Social Revolution*, edited by John Lewis and others, London: Victor Gollancz, 1935, pp.505–26. Also published by Scribner's, New York, 1936.

"Dialectical Materialism as a Philosophy," in *Aspects of Dialectical Materialism*, edited by H. Levy and others, London: Watts & Co., 1934, pp.31–53.

"The Early Development of Marx's Thought," in *Christianity and the Social Revolution*, edited by John Lewis and others London: Victor Gollancz, 1935, pp.209–36. Also published in 1936, NY: Scribner's.

"Freedom in the Personal Nexus," in *Freedom: Its Meaning*, edited by Ruth Nanda Anshen, NY: Harcourt, 1940, pp.176–93. Also George Allen & Unwin, London: 1942.

"From Aquinas to Newton," in *Some Makers of the Modern Spirit*, edited by John Macmurray, London: Methuen, 1933, pp.90–97.

"Gandhi's Faith and Influence," in *Mahatma Gandhi: Essays and Reflections on His Life and Work*, edited by Radhakrishnan, S., London: Allen & Unwin, 1939, Also Jaico Publishing House, Bombay, 1956.

"The Grith Fyrd Idea," in *The Grith Fyrd Idea*, edited by John Macmurray and others, Godshill, Salisbury: The Order of Woodcraft Chivalry, 1933, pp.5–10. "The Woodcraft Way" Series: No.19.

"Introductory," in *Some Makers of the Modern Spirit*, edited by John Macmurray, London: Methuen, 1933, pp.37–44.

"The Modern Spirit: An Essay," in *Some Makers of the Modern Spirit*, edited by John Macmurray, London: Methuen, 1933, pp.1–36.

"The Nature and Function of Ideologies," in *Marxism*, edited by John Middleton Murry, London: Chapman & Hall, 1935, pp.59–75.

"The Nature of Philosophy," in *Marxism*, edited by John Middleton Murry, London: Chapman & Hall, 1935, pp.27–42.

"The New Materialism," in *Marxism*, edited by John Middleton Murry. London: Watts, 1935, pp.43–58.

"Objectivity in Religion," in *Adventure: The Faith of Science and the Science of Faith*, edited by Burnett H. Streeter *et al*, London: Macmillan and Co. Ltd., 1927, pp.177–215.

"Religion in Transformation," in *This Changing World*, ed. J.R.M. Brumwell, London: George Routledge & Sons, 1944, pp.248–262.

"Science and Objectivity," in *The Personal Universe: Essays in Honor of John Macmurray*, edited by Thomas E. Wren. Humanities Press, Atlantic Highlands, NJ, 1975, pp.7–23.

"Summary," in *Some Makers of the Modern Spirit*, edited by John Macmurray, London: Methuen, 1933, pp.179–188.

"Towards World Unity." *The Student Seeks an Answer*, edited by John Clark (Waterville) Maine: Colby College Press 1960), pp.307–27.

"Trench Religion," in *The Army and Religion*, edited David S. Cairns, Macmillan & Co., London: 1919. pp.162f. (Unattributed sections).

"Valuations in Fascist and Communist States," in *Class Conflict and Social Stratification*, edited by T.J. Marshall, London: Le Play House Press, 1938, pp.180–91.

"What Makes an Experience Religious?," in *Quakers Talk to Sixth Formers*, by Kenneth Barnes, Kathleen Lonsdale and John Macmurray, London: Friends Home Service Committee, 1970, pp.53–58.

"What Religion Is About," *in Quakers Talk to Sixth Formers*, by Kenneth Barnes, Kathleen Lonsdale, and John Macmurray, London: Friends Home Service Committee, 1970, pp.47–52.

"Ye Are My Friends," in *The Purpose of God in the Life of the World*. London: SCM Press, 1929, pp.165ff.

C: Articles, Essays, Pamphlets and Talks by Macmurray

"Address by Professor John Macmurray," *Philosophy*, Vol. IX, #36 (Oct. 1934), pp.510f.

"Address of the Special Visitor," *University College/University of London*, London: H.K. Lewis & Co.,1948, pp.1–5. (Address to Assembly of Faculties).

"The Basis of Religious Life Today," *The Seeker* (Apr. 1961), pp.3–14.

"Beyond Nationality," *The Listener* (Apr. 3, 1941), pp.471f.

"Britain and Russia: The Future," *Peace Aims Pamphlet* 12 (1942), pp.6–14.

"Can Science See Us Through?," *New Britain Quarterly* 1/1 (Oct. 1932), pp.6–12.

"Can We Trust the Experts?," *The Listener* (Nov.25, 1931), pp.911f.

"The Celebration of Communion," *The Listener* 56 (Dec.20, 1956), pp.1027–28. (3rd of 4 talks in series entitled "What Is Religion About?")

"The Christian Apologetic in the Modern World," Conference on the Preparation for Ministry, York. (April 2–6, 1929), 20 pp. (Printed privately by Wm. Temple & E. Fenn)

"Christianity and the Churches," *News Sheet of the Auxiliary Christian Left*, No.3 (Oct.5, 1936), pp.3–4.

"Christianity: Pagan or Scientific?," *The Hibbert Journal* 24 (1926), pp.421–33.

"Church and State," Part II, The Church and the Roman Empire, pp.309–11, and Part III, Church and State in the Middle Ages, pp.360–62, published in unidentified periodical.

"The Coming Election," *British Weekly* (Oct.24, 1931), pp.1686f.

"Coming to Grips With Democracy," *The Listener* (Dec.2, 1931), pp.963f.

"The Community of Mankind," *The Listener* (Dec. 24, 1941), 4th talk in a BBC series entitled "Persons and Functions," p.856.

"The Conception of Society," *Proceedings of the Aristotelian Society* 31 (1930 –31), pp.127–42. Delivered at the Aristotelian Society Meeting, Monday, March 16, 1931.

"Concerning the History of Philosophy," *Proceedings of the Aristotelian Society*,

Suppl.25 (1951), pp.1–24. Published in: *Freedom, Language and Reality*, London: Harrison & Sons Ltd. 1951.

"Conditions of Marriage Today," *Marriage Guidance*, ed. by Charles F. Davey, Vol.9, No.12, Dec.2, 1965, pp.379-385.

"The Conflict in Our Emotional Life," *The Listener* (Jan.20, 1932), p.105. A talk in a four-part BBC series entitled "The Modern Dilemma." Part of *Freedom in the Modern World* (qv).

"A Crisis of Culture: The USSR and the West," London: National Peace Council, *Peace Aims Pamphlet* No.42, (1948). 15 pp. This is 2nd ed. The 1st ed. was published in 1947 under title "East-West Relations and the World's Peace." Comment by Christopher Dawson and rejoinder by John Macmurray in 2nd edition.

"Danger of Solving Our Work Problems," *The Scotsman*, Wednesday, April 24, 1957. Article in a series entitled: "Towards an Industrial Philosophy."

"Democracy in the Balance," *The Listener* (Oct.24, 1934), pp.692f. Second of two talks given by JM under theme of "Personality, Freedom and Authority," in a BBC series under the general title: "Freedom and Authority in the Modern World." See "Freedom Is Power" below.

"Developing Emotions," *Saturday Review* 41 (Sept.13, 1958), pp.22 & 52.

"Do We Run Away from Our Problems?," *The Listener* 7 (Jan. 13, 1932), pp.56f. A talk in a four-part series entitled "The Modern Dilemma."

"Do You Believe in Moral Progress?," *The Listener* (Feb.23, 1938), pp.418f.

"The Dualism of Mind and Matter," *Philosophy* 10 (1935), pp.264–78.

"Economic Laws and Social Progress (I)," *The Auxiliary Movement* 29, n.5 (Feb.1927), pp.117f.

"Economic Laws and Social Progress (II)," *The Auxiliary Movement* 29, n.6 (Mar. 1927), pp.141f.

"The Effort to Understand Ourselves," *The Listener* (Apr. 30, 1930), pp.764f.

"Equality," *New Britain Weekly* 1:5 (June 21, 1933), p.135.

"Evangelical Reality," *British Weekly* 86: 2228 (July 11, 1929), p.315.

"A Faith for the Modern World," *The Listener* (Feb.3, 1932), pp.182f. Fourth talk in a four-part series entitled "The Modern Dilemma."

"Fascism?" *New Britain Weekly* 1:3 (June 7, 1933), p.70.

"Fellowship in a Common Life," *The Listener* (Dec.11, 1941), p.787. The second of four talks in BBC Series entitled: "Persons and Functions."

"The Foundation of Economic Reconstruction," London: National Peace Council, *Peace Aims Pamphlet* No.15 (1942), pp.3–11. Introductory to conference held Sept 25–28, 1942.

"Freedom Is Power," *The Listener*, (Oct.17, 1934), pp.650f. One of two talks. First talk of two under theme of "Personality, Freedom and Authority." See "Democracy in the Balance."

"Freedom of Intellect and Feeling," *The Listener* (Jan.27, 1932), pp.137f.

Third talk in a four-part series entitled "The Modern Dilemma."

"The Function of Experiment in Knowledge," *Proceedings of the Aristotelian Society* 27 (1926), pp.193–212. Delivered on March 7, 1926.

"The Functions of a University," *The Political Quarterly* 15, No.4 (1944), pp.277–85.

"Government by the People," *Journal of Philosophical Studies* 2 (1927), pp.532–543.

"Has Religion a Message for Today?," *Reynolds Illustrated News* (Nov.24, 1935), p.2.

"How It Strikes a Contemporary: What Are the Real Issues?", *British Weekly* 91:2345 (Oct.8, 1931), p.23.

"The Idea of a University," *The Times Literary Supplement* (Dec.4, 1970), p.2.

"Idealism against Religion," (booklet), London: The Lindsey Press, 1944. pp.5–22.

"The Influence of British Philosophy During 'Those Forty Years'," *British Weekly* 81:2089 (Nov.11, 1926), pp.164f.

"An Invitation to the Young Men and Women of Britain," *New Britain Weekly* 1:1 (May 24, 1933), p.5.

"Is Art a Form of Apprehension or a Form of Expression?", *Proceedings of the Aristotelian Society,* Suppl.5 (1925), pp.173–89.

"Is a Democratic Culture Possible?," *The Listener* (Dec.16, 1931), pp.1064f.

"Is Education Necessary?," *The Listener* (Oct 7, 1931), p.581.

"Isn't Christianity 'Played Out'?," *Asking Them Questions*, ed. Ronald Selby Wright, Oxford: Oxford University Press, Vol.3, 1950, 2nd impression, pp.204–11.

"The Kingdom of Heaven," Sermon preached in Balliol College, Oxford on Sunday, May 29, 1929. The Oxonian Press, 1929.

"Knowledge for Use," *The New Phineas: The Magazine of University College London,* Spring 1942, pp.15f.

"A Landmark in Broadcasting," *The Listener* (Apr. 13, 1932), pp.538.

"Learning to Live," Pamphlet #5 of BBC Series *The Changing World*, London: BBC Publications Department (1931).

"Liberties in a Planned State," *The Friend*, May 21, 1943, pp.345–47.

"The Limits of Interference Between Sovereign States," *British Weekly* 87:2252 (Dec.26, 1929), p.283.

"Living in Freedom," vol.6, *The Listener* (Dec.30, 1931), pp.1149f.

"The May Reviews" (includes 'Our Relations with Russia'), *British Weekly*, Vol. LXXXVI, No. 2219, May 9, 1929, p.127.

"Mechanical Morality," *The Listener* (June 25, 1930), p.1132.

"Mental Health and Personal Relationship," (pamphlet) Scottish Association for Mental Health, (March 1956), pp.1–11.

"The Nature of Reason," *Proceedings of the Aristotelian Society* (1934/5), pp.137–48. Delivered at the March 25, 1935 Meeting.

"The New Community." *The New Phineas: The Magazine of University College, London*, Summer 1941, pp.14–19. Foundation Address given in March 1941 at Bangor when University College London moved to Aberystwyth and Bangor, Wales for the war years.

"Nurses in an Expanded Health Service," *The Nursing Mirror* (1964), pp.113–15 and pp.135–37.

"Obituary for Frances Barnes," *The Friend*, June 27, 1969, p.796.

"On Discoveries in Political Philosophy: A Conversation with John Macmurray," *Northwest Review*, vol.2, (Fall/Winter 1958), pp.5–20.

"The Pattern of Our Time: A Philosophical Analysis," *British Export Industrial Magazine for the Future*, vol.2, No.3, December, 1947, pp.85–93.

"People and Their Jobs," *The Listener* (Dec.4, 1941), p.759. First of four talks in BBC Series entitled: "Persons and Functions."

"Personality," *Vox Studentium*, Vol. 3., No. 2, pp.3–6. December, 1925 .

"A Philosopher Looks at Psychotherapy," *Individual Psychology Medical Pamphlets* No.20, The C.W. Daniel Co., London (1938), pp.9–22.

"The Philosopher's Business," *University of Edinburgh Quarterly* 15:2 (Summer 1952), pp.86–92.

"The Philosophy of Jesus," (Pamphlet) London: Friends Home Service Committee, 1973. reprinted in 1977. First published in four parts in consecutive issues of *Quaker Monthly*: Nov. 1972 Vol.51 #11, pp.201–4; Dec. 1972 Vol.51 #12, pp.222–25; Jan. 1973 Vol.52 #1. pp.9–11; Feb. 1973 Vol.52 #2, pp.29–32.

"The Principle of Personality in Experience," *Proceedings of the Aristotelian Society* 29 (1928/9), pp.316–30.

"Prolegomena to a Christian Ethic," *Scottish Journal of Theology* 9:1 (Mar. 1956), pp.1–13.

"The Provisional Basis of the Christian Left," *Christian Left* no.10 (Feb. 1938), pp.3–6. (Joint commentary on above by John Macmurray and Irene Grant.)

"Reality in Thinking," *The Listener* (May 21, 1930), pp.912–13. From a talk given on May 19.

"Reason in Action," *The Philosopher* 12 (1934), pp.5–10.

"The Relation of the University to Its Local Community," *University of Edinburgh Journal* 19:3 (Spring 1959), pp.159–168.

"Religion in the Modern World," *Plan,* 6:1 (Jan.1939), pp.3–11.

"Religion in Russia," *The Left News*, No.65 (November, 1941), pp.1903–4.

"Religion in Russia," *Anglo-Soviet Public Relations* Leaflet 1 (1942).

"The Religious Task of the Christian Left," *Christian Left*, no.7 (March 20, 1937), pp.3–5.

"Reply", (see "Russia and Finland ..." below).

"Report of a Recent Religious Delegation to Spain," London: Gollancz, April 1937, pp.1–32. Joint Report by Dean of Canterbury, D.R. Davies and others.

"Rudolph Euken," *British Weekly* 80:2082 (Sept.23,1926), p.518.

"Russia and Finland: Should Soviet Action Be Condemned?," *Christian Left* no.18 (Mar.1940), pp.5–8. Includes a 'Reply' by Macmurray (p.12) to a letter.

"Science in Religious Education," *The School Science Review* 32:116 (Oct.1950), pp.2–5.

"Self-Realization," *The Expository Times* 8 (1930), pp.24–26.

"The Significance of Religion," *New Britain Weekly* 1:10 (Aug.2, 1933), p.329.

"Social Morality," *The Listener* (July 2, 1930), pp.33f. (From a talk on June 30.)

"The Social Unit," *New Britain Weekly* 1:8 (July 12, 1933), p.235.

"Socialism and Democracy," *Christian Left* no.18 (Mar.1940), pp.1–5.

"Socialism and Ethics," *The Left News*, No. 59 (May, 1941), pp.1725–31.

"Some Reflections on the Analysis of Language," *Philosophical Quarterly*, 1 (1951), pp.319–37.

"The Sources of Unreality," *The Listener* (May 14, 1930), p.860.)

"Teachers and Pupils," publication unidentified, (Nov.1964), pp.17–24.

"Three Kinds of Freedom," *The Listener* (June 18, 1930), p.1073. (From a talk on June 11.)

Through Chaos to Community, London: National Peace Council, *Peace Aims*

Pamphlet no.24 (1944), pp.3–20. Contains two lectures: "Reconstruction and World Revolution," and "The Religious Issue in Reconstruction."

"Time and Change," *Proceedings of the Aristotelian Society*, Suppl.8 (1928), pp.143–61.

"To Save From Fear," *Quaker Monthly,* Vol.43, No.5–8, May-August 1964, pp.3–11. (Four Lenten talks on BBC: Fear & Faith, Feb. 26; Faith & Love, Mar. 4; The New Society, Mar. 12; The World Today, Mar 11.) (Pamphlet) London: Friends Home Service Committee, 1979.

"Today and Tomorrow: A Philosophy of Freedom," *BBC Talks Pamphlet* no.57, pp.3–28.

"Training the Child to Live," *The Listener* (Dec.9, 1931), pp.990–92.

"The True Morality," *The Listener* (July 9, 1930).

"Two Lives in One," *The Listener* (Dec.18, 1941), p.822. Third of four talks in BBC Series entitled "Persons and Functions."

"The Unity of Modern Problems," *Journal of Philosophical Studies* 4 (1929), pp.162–79.

"The Universal Family," *The Listener* 56 (Dec.27, 1956), pp.1073–74. Fourth of four talks in BBC Series entitled "What Is Religion About?"

"Unreal People," *The Listener* (June 4, 1930), pp.988f. (From a talk on June 2.)

"Viewpoint: John Macmurray," *Quaker Monthly* 45:4 (1966), pp.49–53. (Interview with Malcolm Muggeridge, Kenneth Barnes, and Lord Soper.)

"The Vital Importance of True Feeling," *The Listener* (May 28, 1930), pp.937f.

"Vox Collegii," *University College Magazine*, Vol.10, No.3, March 1933, pp.74–77.

"Vox Collegii," *University College Magazine*, Vol. 15, No. 1, Autumn 1937, pp.10–12. [On the importance of tradition.]

"War to Peace," *Industrial Welfare and Personnel Management*, Sept./Oct., 1943. pp.146–50.

"The Way of Freedom," *The Listener* (July 16, 1930), p.106.

"What About Communism?," *New Britain Weekly* 1, 4 (June 14, 1933), p.102.

"What I Live By ," *Student Movement* 30:9 (July 1928), pp.199–200.

"What is Action?," *Proceedings of the Aristotelian Society*, Suppl.17 (1938), pp.69–85. Delivered July 9, 1938 in Symposium with A.C. Ewing and O.S. Francks in joint session with the Mind Association.

"What is Freedom?," *The Listener* (June 11, 1930), p.1042.

"What is Philosophy?," *Proceedings of the Aristotelian Society,* suppl.11 (1932), pp.48–67.

"What is Religion About? (I)," *The Listener* 56 (Dec.6,1956), pp.916f. First of four talks in a BBC Series entitled "What Is Religion About?"

"What is Religion About? (II)," *The Listener* 56 (Dec.13, 1956), pp.984f. Second of four talks in BBC Series entitled "What Is Religion About?"

"What is Unreality?," *The Listener* (May 7, 1930), pp.808f.

"What to Do," *New Britain Weekly*, Vol.1, No.2, (May 31,1933), p.37.

"Ye Are My Friends," (Given on the evening of Jan. 3rd at a conference in Liverpool, Jan.2–7, 1929). Published as a pamphlet in 1943 & 1972, and again in 1979 along with "To Save from Fear", London: Quaker Home Service Committee.)

D: Forewords, Introductions, Letters to Editors, Postscripts and Prefaces

"Foreword," in *Credo! A Faith for Today*, by M.R. Bennet, London: Frederick Muller Ltd., 1944.

"Foreword," in *Common Faith or Synthesis*, by J.B. Coates, London: George Allen & Unwin Ltd., 1942, pp.5–9.

"Foreword," in *Moscow Dialogues: Discussions on Red Philosophy*, by Julius F. Hecker, London: Chapman and Hall, 1933, pp.*ix-x*.

"Introduction," in *The Claim of Morality*, by N.H.G. Robinson, London: Gollanz, 1952, pp.9–13.

"Introduction," in *Jordans: The Making of a Community*, London: Friends Home Service Committee, 1969, pp.1–15.

"Introduction," in *Lectures on Ethics*, by Immanuel Kant, trans. by Louis Enfield, London: Methuen, 1930, pp.*ix-xiii*.

"Introduction," in *Rebel Religion: Christ, Community and Church*, by B.C. Plowright, New York: Round Table Press, 1937, pp.11–13.

"Letter to the Editor," *New Britain Weekly*, Jan. 9, 1933, Vol.1, No.2. p.69.

"Mysticism and Religion," *Theoria to Theory*, vol.3, No. 2, January 1969, p.74. (Letter to the editor.)

"Postscript," in *Green Pastures*, by Mark Connelly, (London: Delisle, 1963), pp.106–12.

"Preface," in *How Do You Do, Tovarish?*, by Ralph Parker (London: George G. Harrap & Co., Ltd., 1947), pp.5f. Vol. III of *The Soviets and Ourselves*.

"Preface," in *Landsmen and Seafarers*, by Maurice Lovell (London: George G. Harrap & Co., Ltd., 1945), pp.5–6. (This is Vol I. of *The Soviets and Ourselves* by Maurice Lovell, K.E. Holme, and Ralph Parker.)

"Preface" in *Some Makers of the Modern Spirit*, edited by J. Macmurray, London: Methuen, 1933.

"Preface," in *Two Commonwealths*, by K.E. Holme, (London: George G. Harrap & Co., Ltd., 1945), p.5. Vol. II of *The Soviets and Ourselves*.

"Professor Macmurray and His Critics," *The Listener*, (Sept.10, 1930), p.412.

"Was Jesus Excommunicated?," *Student Movement* 37:3 (Dec. 1934), p.58.

E: Book Reviews by John Macmurray

Barker, Ernest, *National Character*, in *British Weekly*, 82:2134 (Sept. 22, 1927), p.53.

Barton, William, *The Moral Challenge of Communism* (The Swarthmore Lecture for 1966) in *The Friend*, (June 3, 1966), pp.637–39.

Blanchard, B., *Reason and Analysis*, in *Expository Times*, 74 (1962–63), pp.229f.

Cadoux, C.J., *Christian Pacifism Re-examined*, in *The New Statesman and Nation*, (Dec.7, 1940), p.572.

Eddington, A.S., *The Nature of the Physical World*, in *British Weekly*, 85:2204 (Jan.24, 1929), p.386.

Harris, Errol, *Revelation Through Reason*, in *The Expository Times*, 71:3 (Dec. 1959), pp.72f.

Heard, Gerald, *The Third Morality*, in *The New Statesman and Nation*, (Mar. 20, 1937), p.486.

Lee, Atkinson, *Sociality: The Art of Living Together*, in *Journal of Philosophical Studies*, 4 (1929), p.147.

Lindsay, Erica, *Losing Religion to Find it*, in *Philosophy*, 11 (1936), pp.209f.

Livingstone, Sir Richard, *Education for a World Adrift*, in *Political Quarterly*, vol.14, 1943, pp.290f.

Mackinnon, D.M., *A Study in Ethical Theory*, in *The Expository Times*, 69 (1957–58), pp.203f.

Milne, A.J.M., *The Social Philosophy of English Idealism*, in *The Expository Times*, 73 (1961–62), pp.297f.

Niebuhr, Reinhold, *Human Destiny*, in *The New Statesmen and Nation*, 26 (Oct.2, 1943), p.220.

—, *The Children of Light and the Children of Darkness*, in *The New Statesmen and Nation*, 29 (Jan. 9, 1945), pp.375f.

Peters, Richard S., *Reason, Morality and Religion,* The Swarthmore Lecture for 1972, in *Quaker Monthly*, 51:9 (Sept.1972), pp.161–66.

Ramsay, Ian, *Freedom and Immortality*, in *The Expository Times*, 72 (Oct. 1960), p.136.

Reckitt, Maurice, ed., *Prospect for Christendom*, in *The New Statesman and Nation*, Vol.30, (Oct.20, 1945), p.269.

Reid, L. A., *Ways of Knowledge and Experience*, in *The Expository Times*, 72:11 (1960–61), pp.331f.

Robinson, John A. T., *The Human Face of God*, in *The Friend*, (May 4, 1973), pp.523–24.

Samuel, Sir Herbert, *Philosophy and the Ordinary Man*, in *Philosophy*, 7 (1932), pp.334f.

Schmidt, Prof., *The Origin and Growth of Religion*, in *The Listener*, (April 15, 1931), p.649.

Singer, Charles, *The Christian Failure*, in *The Political Quarterly,* (July 1944), pp.85f.

Smuts, J.C., *Holism and Evolution*, in *British Weekly*, 81:2099 (Jan.20, 1927), p.418.

Sturzo, Dom Luigi, *Church and State for Democracy*, in *The New Statesman*, 18 (1939), p.933.

Toynbee, Arnold, *Change and Habit*, in *The Friend*, (May 24, 1967), pp.355f.

Selver, Paul, *Orage and 'The New Age' Circle: Reminiscences and Reflections,* London: George Allen & Unwin Ltd. 1959.

Smout T.C. & Wood, Sydney, *Scottish Voices 1745–1960,* London: Fontana Press, 1991.

Strachey, John, *The Theory and Practice of Socialism,* London: Victor Gollancz, 1936.

Taylor, A.E. *The Faith of a Moralist.* 2 vols. London: Macmillan & Co. Ltd., 1930

Torrance, Thomas F., *Theological Science,* UK: Oxford University Press, 1969.

Trethowan Illtyd, *Absolute Value: A Study in Christian Theism,* London: George Allen & Unwin Ltd. 1970.

Vlastos, Gregory, *Christian Faith and Democracy,* New York: Edward W. Hazen Foundation, 1938.

Walker, Andrew Lochhart, *The Revival of the Democratic Intellect: Scotland's University Tradition and the Crisis in Modern Thought,* Edinburgh: Polygon Press, 1994.

Webb, Clement C.J., *God and Personality*, London: George Allen & Unwin, 1919.

Index

The Personal World

John Macmurray on self and society

Selected and introduced by Philip Conford

For philosophy to be at all relevant, it must either increase an understanding of the world or our ability to change it. At best it can do both. This is a test John Macmurray passes with flying colours. I hope more people discover him.

From the foreword by the Rt Hon. Tony Blair MP

This selection from his writings, with an introduction and commentary, reveals the work of this great thinker in all its clarity, depth and inspirational quality.

Philip Conford PhD took degrees in philosophy and literature at the University of East Anglia, and obtained his doctorate with research into the history of the organic movement. He is author of *The Origins of the Organic Movement,* also published by Floris Books, and editor of *The Organic Tradition* and *A Future for the Land.*

Floris Books